MANAGING OPENNESS

MANAGING OPENNESS

TRADE AND OUTWARD-ORIENTED GROWTH AFTER THE CRISIS

Mona Haddad and Ben Shepherd, Editors

THE WORLD BANK
Washington, D.C.

1818 H Street NW
Washington DC 20433
Telephone: 202-473-1000
Internet: www.worldbank.org

1 2 3 4 14 13 12 11

ISBN: 978-0-8213-8631-6
eISBN: 978-0-8213-8632-3
DOI: 10.1596/978-0-8213-8631-6

Library of Congress Cataloging-in-Publication Data

Managing openness : trade and outward-oriented growth after the crisis / edited by Mona Haddad and Ben Shepherd.
p. cm.
Includes bibliographical references and index.
ISBN 978-0-8213-8631-6—ISBN 978-0-8213-8632-3 (electronic)
1. International trade. 2. Balance of trade. 3. International economic relations. 4. Global economy. I. Haddad, Mona. II. Shepherd, Ben. III. World Bank.
HF1379.M3555 2011
382'.3—dc22

2011001903

Cover photo: Corbis
Cover design: Tomoko Hirata, World Bank

CONTENTS

Figures

Tables

ABOUT THE EDITORS AND CONTRIBUTORS

Mona Haddad is Sector Manager of the World Bank's International Trade Department. In this capacity, she manages the group responsible for supporting the development and implementation of trade-related activities at both country and regional levels. These include trade policy analysis, competitiveness, and trade facilitation. Prior to joining the Trade Department, she was the Regional Trade Coordinator for the East Asia Region, where she worked on trade issues in various countries, including China, Indonesia, the Lao People's Democratic Republic, and Vietnam.

Ben Shepherd is the Principal of Developing Trade Consultants Ltd. He is a trade economist and international development consultant, having worked on a wide range of trade and development issues with organizations such as the World Bank, the Organisation for Economic Co-operation and Development, the Asian Development Bank, the United Nations, and the Food and Agriculture Organization. He specializes in providing policy-relevant research, as well as capacity-building seminars for researchers working in trade and development.

About the Contributors

Mahani Zainal Abidin, Chief Executive, Institute of Strategic and International Studies, Malaysia

Enrique Aldaz-Carroll, Senior Economist, World Bank, Indonesia

Ulrich Bartsch, Senior Economist, World Bank, India

Muhammad Chatib Basri, Senior Lecturer, Department of Economics, University of Indonesia

Chad P. Bown, Senior Economist, Development Research Group, World Bank

Vittorio Corbo, Centro de Estudios Públicos, Chile

Jaime de Melo, Professor, Department of Economics, University of Geneva; Center for Economic Policy Research; Foundation for International Development Study and Research

Barry Eichengreen, George C. Pardee and Helen N. Pardee Professor of Economics and Political Science, University of California, Berkeley

Gustavo H. B. Franco, Chairman, Rio Bravo Investimentos

Caroline Freund, Lead Economist, Development Research Group, World Bank

Abhijit Sen Gupta, Associate Professor, Jawaharlal Nehru University, India, and Consultant, World Bank, India

Mona Haddad, Sector Manager, International Trade Department, World Bank

Gordon Hanson, Professor of Economics and Director, Center on Pacific Economies, School of International Relations and Pacific Studies, and Department of Economics, University of California, San Diego

Ann Harrison, Director of Development Policy, Development Research Group, World Bank

Catherine Hausman, Ph.D. Student, Department of Agricultural and Resource Economics, University of California, Berkeley

Hiau Looi Kee, Senior Economist, Development Research Group, World Bank

Jamus Lim, Economist, Development Prospects Group, World Bank

Alyson Ma, Associate Professor of Economics, School of Business Administration, University of San Diego

Philip Martin, Professor and Chair, Comparative Immigration and Integration Program, Department of Agricultural and Resource Economics, University of California, Davis

Nicole A. Mathys, Swiss Federal Office of Energy and University of Neuchatel, Switzerland

Donald Mitchell, Consultant, World Bank, Tanzania

Laura Munro, Graduate Student, Columbia University and the London School of Economics

Ha Nguyen, Economist, Development Research Group, World Bank

Sjamsu Rahardja, Senior Economist, East Asia Financial and Private Sector Unit, World Bank

Jaime Ros, Professor of Economics, Universidad Nacional Autónoma de México and University of Notre Dame

Christian Saborowski, Consultant, World Bank

Klaus Schmidt-Hebbel, Professor of Economics, Catholic University of Chile

Luis Servén, Senior Adviser, Development Research Group, World Bank

Ben Shepherd, Principal, Developing Trade Consultants Ltd.

Vera Songwe, Lead Economist and Adviser, Office of the Managing Director Africa, South Asia, Eastern and Central Europe, and Human Resources, World Bank

Ari Van Assche, Associate Professor, Department of International Business, HEC Montréal

Fausto J. A. Vieira, Chief Economist, Rio Bravo Investimentos

Jing Wang, Postdoctoral Fellow, University of Western Ontario; Associate Researcher, Chinese Academy of Social Science

John Whalley, Professor of Economics, University of Western Ontario, and Distinguished Fellow, Center for International Governance Innovation, Waterloo, Ontario

Deborah Winkler, Consultant, International Trade Department, World Bank

Roberto Zahler, President, Zahler & Co.

Albert Zeufack, Director, Khazanah Research and Investment Strategy, Malaysia

ACKNOWLEDGMENTS

First versions of a number of chapters in this volume were presented at the "Managing Openness: Outward-Oriented Growth Strategies after the Crisis" conference held at the World Bank in Washington, D.C., on May 10, 2010. The editors are grateful to Ann Harrison, who co-organized the conference, as well as to Chad Bown, Barry Eichengreen, Gustavo Franco, Klaus Schmidt-Hebbel, and John Whalley, who presented their work. Otaviano Canuto, Luis Ernesto Derbez, Homi Kharas, and Justin Lin also participated as panelists, and we are grateful for their many questions and insights. The conference brought together academics, researchers, and policy makers from around the world, and participants' contributions were very helpful in shaping the final product.

Many people provided assistance during the manuscript's preparation. We are grateful to Homi Kharas for providing overall guidance. Laura Munro contributed outstanding editorial assistance. Sebastian Saez also reviewed key chapters and provided important inputs. Stacey Chow played a key role in organizing the May 2010 conference, and she provided constant program support during the book's preparation, as did Cynthia Abidin. The World Bank's Office of the Publisher managed the publication process very efficiently, and we are grateful in particular to Mary Fisk and Stephen McGroarty for their help and guidance.

ABBREVIATIONS

ASEAN	Association of Southeast Asian Nations
ASI	Annual Survey of Industry
BRICs	Brazil, the Russian Federation, India, and China
BTA	border tax adjustment
CDS	credit default swaps
CEPAL	United Nations Economic Commission for Latin America
CPO	crude palm oil
EAP	economically active population
ETS	emission-trading system
EU	European Union
FTA	free trade agreement
GATS	General Agreement on Trade in Services
GATT	General Agreement on Tariffs and Trade
GDP	gross domestic product
GEM	growing emerging market
GMM	generalized method of moments
GHG	greenhouse gas
GNI	gross national income
GPN	global production network
GTI	global trade imbalance
H1N1	a type of influenza virus
HHI	Herfindahl-Hirschman Index
HS	harmonized system
IMF	International Monetary Fund
KP1	first Kyoto Protocol
LDC	least-developed country
LNG	liquefied natural gas
LP	labor productivity
M2	the total amount of money available in a given economy at a particular time
MA-OTRI	market access overall trade restrictiveness index
MIER	Malaysian Institute of Economic Research
MERCOSUR	Southern Common Market
MFN	most-favored nation
MP	Montreal Protocol
MSS	market stabilization scheme
NAFTA	North American Free Trade Agreement
NBER	National Bureau of Economic Research
n.e.s.	not elsewhere specified
OECD	Organisation for Economic Co-operation and Development
OPEC	Organization of the Petroleum Exporting Countries
OTRI	overall trade restrictiveness index

PDBC bonds	Pagarés Descontables del Banco Central
PEMEX	Mexico's state oil monopoly
R&D	research and development
RBI	Reserve Bank of India
Re	Indian rupee
repo	repurchase
SACU	Southern Africa Customs Union
SAR	special administrative region
SITC	Standard International Trade Classification
SRR	statutory reserve requirement
TFP	total factor productivity
ToT	terms of trade
TTB	temporary trade barrier
TWP	temporary worker program
UNCTAD	United Nations Conference on Trade and Development
UNFCC	United Nations Framework Convention on Climate Change
WTO	World Trade Organization
yoy	year on year

1

MANAGING OPENNESS: FROM CRISIS TO EXPORT-LED GROWTH, VERSION 2.0

Mona Haddad and Ben Shepherd

The global financial crisis is stimulating a broad reassessment of economic integration policies in developed and developing countries alike. The crisis was associated with a great trade collapse—the sharpest in recorded history and the deepest since World War II (Baldwin 2009). The trade collapse affected all countries and products, although to different extents. While signs of recovery are starting to solidify, deeper questioning of the causes of the crisis and the merits of globalization has surfaced. The emergence of China and the imbalances of its trade with the United States are shaking the stability of the global system. Are these imbalances sustainable, or do they need to be adjusted to avoid another global crisis? What impact would these adjustments have on the trade of developing countries if they mean that China consumes more and the United States saves more? Openness has helped support growth in many countries—to unprecedented levels in Brazil, China, Indonesia, Malaysia, and others. Yet today many are concerned that openness is creating vulnerability, and vulnerability can hurt growth. No one believes that inward orientation is the solution or that domestic consumption alone can boost growth, even in large countries. The longer-term benefits of openness more than compensate for the short-term negative impacts of trade shocks. The question is not whether to remain open but rather what kind of safety and insurance systems—at the micro- and macrolevels—to put in place to better hedge against shocks from globalization.

As developing countries try to find answers to these questions, they also face a drastically changed trade environment. The crisis proved that protectionism is no longer the name of the game; it remained largely under control, thanks to a solid multilateral regime as well as to a new system of production sharing across countries, which does not lend itself naturally to broad-based protectionism. Moreover, the role of South-South trade is growing, giving developing countries new opportunities to export and new opportunities to import cheaper capital goods—now produced in countries like China or India—that allow them to industrialize faster. Thus, while outward-oriented growth is here to stay, it needs to be put in a different perspective and packaged with additional policies. As the world emerges from the crisis, we expect to see the development of an "export-led growth version 2.0" model that reflects these new dynamics.

Roots of the Crisis and Global Imbalances

The crisis started in the industrial world but spread rapidly to developing countries through financial and trade channels. Its financial origins are embedded in the flawed regulation and perverse incentives that governed financial markets at least from the 1999 repeal of provisions in U.S. law that controlled speculation and separated investment banks from depository banks. The crisis manifested itself in developing countries through shocks related to the balance of payments—a sudden stop in capital flows; the collapse of export demand and prices; and the disappearance of trade credit lines, repatriations, and dividend remittances.

Despite its financial origins, the crisis had enormous effects on the real economy. As credit conditions tightened, employment and consumer confidence fell, and U.S. economic activity slumped, while the voracious appetite of the

United States for imports started to flag. Global trade values plummeted in the second half of 2008, before starting to recover in 2009. Besides a sudden stop in capital flows, the crisis was "the first *modern* sudden stop in trade flows" (Eichengreen, chap. 2, this volume).

During the crisis and recovery period, there have been renewed calls, particularly in the United States but also among the Group of 20 (G-20), for a comprehensive process of global rebalancing. Although global imbalances may not have caused the crisis, they certainly played a supporting role in its genesis. The prospect that some degree of global rebalancing could take place in the aftermath of the crisis has important implications for developing countries, since it would imply a major realignment of global trade flows. The question of whether global imbalances are sustainable in the medium to long term is thus not only an important financial question, but also an emerging issue for trade policy.

Only in the past few years have global imbalances become a bilateral story of the U.S. deficit and China's surplus (Servén and Nguyen, chap. 3, this volume). China's surplus only recently displaced the surplus of countries like Japan and the rest of Asia, and the surplus of the European Union (EU) disappeared only around 2005 (figure 1.1).

Some believe that global imbalances are unsustainable (*disequilibrium approach*). They argue that the United States has been recklessly increasing public and private expenditure, prompted respectively by fiscal expansions and financial innovations. As the world's largest debtor—at 25 percent of gross domestic product (GDP) in 2009—the United States must necessarily undergo a depreciation of the dollar larger than the 30 percent drop since its 2002 peak. This depreciation will lead to an improved trade balance and a slowdown of capital inflows into the United States.

Others believe that imbalances are the result of structural factors in other countries, which if unchanged will cause the imbalances to persist mainly because of international asymmetries in the supply and demand for financial assets (*equilibrium approach*). Underdeveloped financial markets in emerging economies cause capital to flow to rich countries—driven by volatility, risk perception, and a savings glut in developing countries. This process can continue as long as financial markets in emerging economies remain underdeveloped and U.S. assets remain readily available. On the demand side, the absence of social safety nets encourages emerging markets to have high levels of private savings, thus constantly putting them in a net creditor position. Moreover, imbalances can be maintained at equilibrium if emerging markets hoard foreign assets as a policy choice in pursuit of export-led growth by depressing consumption or accumulating foreign assets as a precaution against external shocks such as a sudden stop of foreign capital inflows.

Clearly, the sudden stop of capital inflows into the United States implied by more extreme versions of the

Figure 1.1. Current Account Imbalances for Selected Countries as a Percentage of World GDP, 1980–2009

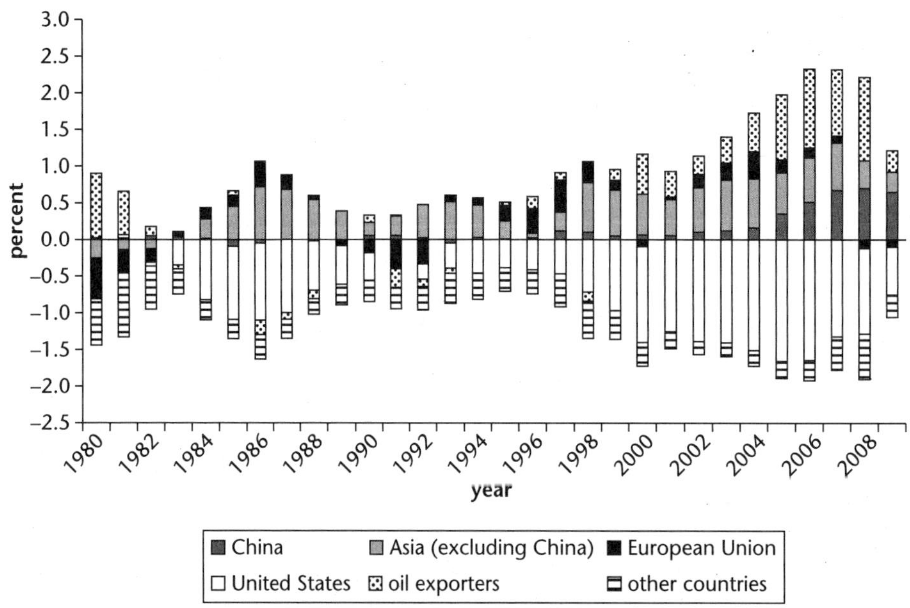

Source: Servén and Nguyen, chap. 3, this volume.
Note: GDP = gross domestic product.

disequilibrium approach did not actually happen. In fact, quite the reverse occurred. Capital fled to the safety of low-risk U.S. Treasuries during the crisis, with U.S. residents repatriating capital and with inflows from foreign investors picking up after 2008 in the large-scale acquisition of Treasuries (figure 1.2). With the continued absence of mature financial markets in emerging economies and the cushion provided by reserves in the immediate aftermath of the crisis, capital could plausibly continue to flow to developed countries, and global imbalances could persist for some time yet in the postcrisis economy. Indeed, the crisis has highlighted the intrinsic instability of financial markets and may even encourage some emerging economies to go slow on financial development.

One path toward reducing global imbalances is an increased emphasis on domestic markets by developing economies. This process is evident in China's stated intention to ease dependence on exports, for example. Amid the clamor for renminbi appreciation, Eichengreen (chap. 2, this volume) argues that the current level of the renminbi reflects, rather than determines, the current structural policy followed by China: depressing consumption, holding down the real exchange rate, and plowing savings into investment of tradable manufactures, with a view to encouraging growth of the manufacturing sector. It is therefore the surrounding policies that would have to change for the renminbi to appreciate. Nascent financial development in China—allowing firms to issue bonds and borrow from banks rather than rely solely on retained earnings—and the increasing development of supply chains and production networks with their accompanying positive externalities are both positive signs. Further changes that would facilitate adjustment could include the development of social safety nets, the liberalizing of financial markets, and the reform of corporate governance to encourage payment of dividends. These changes, however, would lead only to a *gradual* appreciation of the exchange rate and not a sudden adjustment of global imbalances.

The Impact of the Global Financial Crisis on Trade and Protectionism

The financial crisis led to the largest drop in global trade volumes since World War II, with a simultaneous drop in global trade flows in the fourth quarter of 2008 for all major regions of the world. Real trade fell 12 percent in 2009, with World Trade Organization (WTO) estimates of a year-on-year decline of 30 percent in the first quarter of 2009 (figure 1.3). For some countries, the drop was enormous: Japanese exports fell by 50 percent between February 2008 and February 2009. However, while imports collapsed in most countries, four growing emerging markets recorded positive import growth from 2007 to 2009: Brazil, China, India, and Indonesia (Freund, chap. 4, this volume). This outcome could herald the beginnings of a "new world trade order," with these countries showing resilient growth in global import demand in the face of the crisis, despite a depreciation of the exchange rate in the case of Brazil and Indonesia.

The extent of the drop in trade has puzzled economists. They have attributed the magnitude of the collapse

Figure 1.2. Gross Capital Inflows to the United States from Emerging Markets, 2000–09

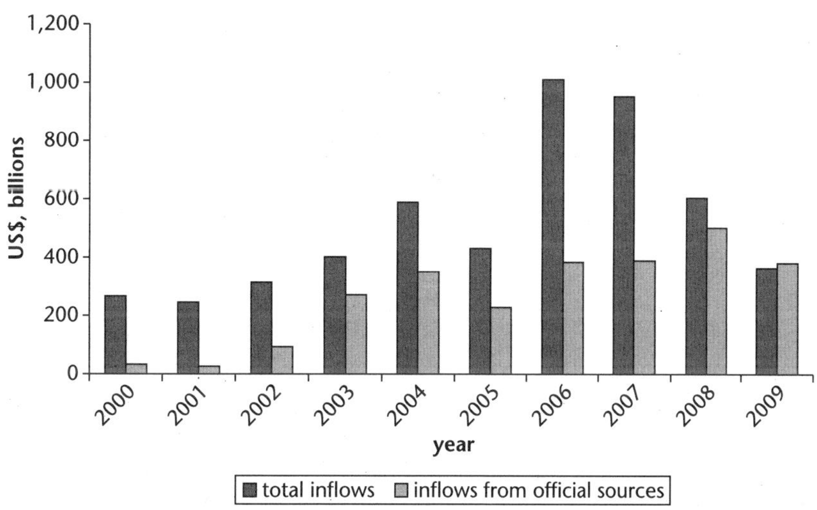

Source: Servén and Nguyen, chap. 3, this volume.

Figure 1.3. Monthly Import Growth by Region, January 2008–November 2009

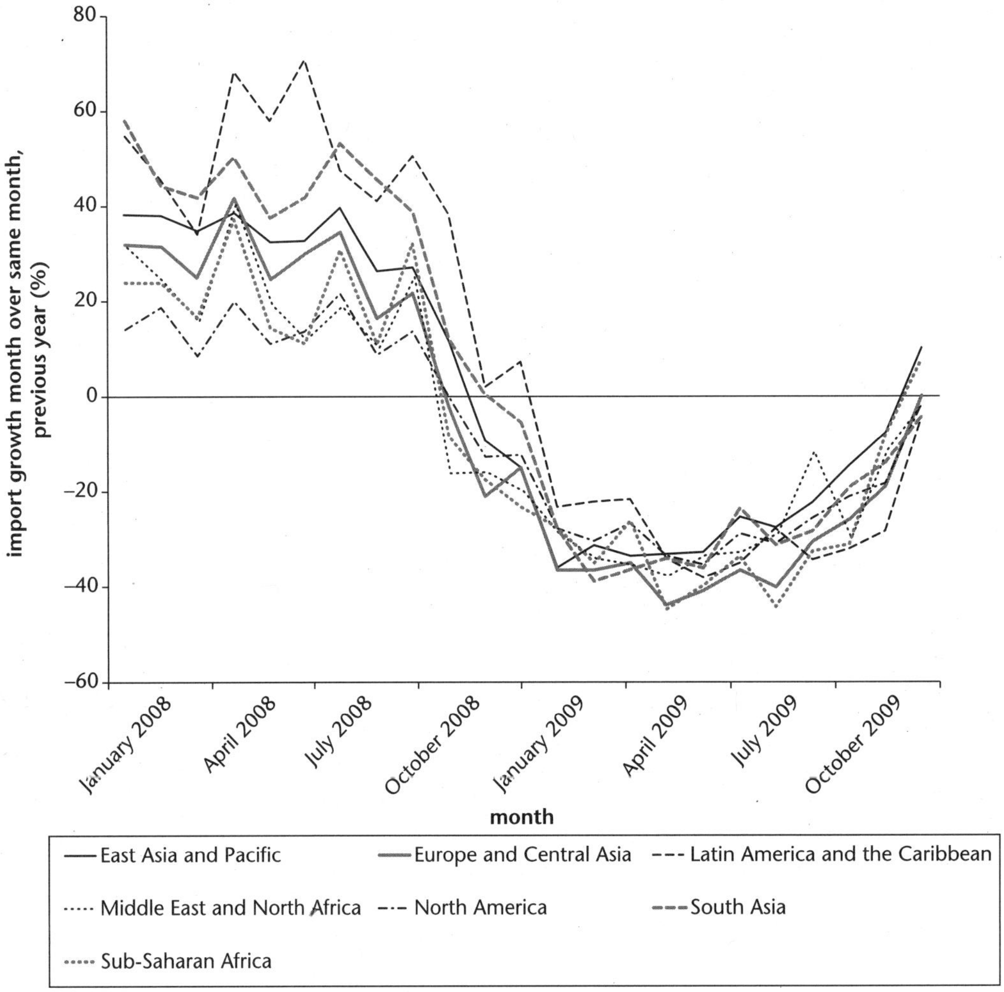

Source: Bown and Kee, chap. 6, this volume.

to protectionist measures, disruptions to the supply of trade credit, and the development of global supply chains, among other possible causes. Trade finance was certainly disrupted when the crisis first started and credit markets froze, but the joint response of official export credit agencies, intergovernmental organizations, and governments quickly limited its effect. Because trade credit is collateralized, it was possible to keep credit flowing. For longer-term policy, however, central banks and national export credit agencies need to devise stronger crisis responses and move away from reliance on multilaterals. In addition, the need for trade finance highlights the importance of holding reserves: where parts, components, and other inputs going into the manufacture of exports are themselves imported, central banks and export credit agencies have to provide trade finance in foreign exchange (Eichengreen, chap. 2, this volume).

Global supply chain production has become increasingly prevalent in recent years. Households put off the purchase of "big-ticket" items such as consumer durables—vehicles and electronics, for example—when the economy is down. These are exactly the types of goods that now tend to be produced through global supply chains. A significant drop in demand for these goods thus contributed to the magnitude of the trade collapse. Furthermore, in practical terms, this form of production is more sensitive to disruptions in trade credit: if component exporters cannot get credit, then assemblers cannot get parts, and even a limited financial disruption can break all the links in the chain. International production networks can be particularly sensitive to these types of changes in trade costs (Ma and Van Assche, chap. 21, this volume).

As the financial crisis unfolded over 2008–09, some feared that countries would resort to "beggar-thy-neighbor" trade policies similar to those in place during the Great Depression. However, despite a significant drop in international trade, "the world did not witness a 'disintegration'. of globalization in the sense of a policy-reinforced rush to disconnect from the global economy as seen in the 1930s" (Franco and Vieira, chap. 7, this volume). Protectionism, while "murky"—Evenett (2010) identifies 300 trade-restricting measures of some sort between the fourth quarter of 2008 and the fourth quarter of 2009—was neither as intense nor as broadly based as the tariffs and quantitative restrictions seen in the 1930s.

The good news is that the protectionist measures that come up are now mainly WTO-consistent temporary trade barriers (TTBs): antidumping, countervailing duties, and safeguard measures (Bown and Kee, chap. 6, this volume). The trade impacts of these measures have been extremely limited, affecting on average 0.5 percent to 1.0 percent of total imports, with overall increases in protectionism of roughly the same order of magnitude.

This outcome is a positive affirmation of the global multilateral trading system under the WTO, owing perhaps to the design of WTO rules that allow for a relatively small incidence of new protectionism through permissible TTBs. Countries have committed to the rules of the global trading system and the WTO, and they now have an interest in upholding them. The muted protectionism was also possibly a result of the increasing globalization of supply chains.

Although the overall resort to protectionism has been limited, the pattern of trade protection that has emerged has some important implications for South-South trade. The biggest imposers of TTBs were not the large, developed markets, but Argentina, India, Indonesia, and Turkey. China's exporters bore the brunt of the new protectionist measures. Eighty percent of the total value of trade on which the G-20 imposed new TTBs in 2008–09 was on imports from China. The new TTBs in 2008–09 affected more than US$20 billion worth of China's exports, or about 2 percent of its precrisis, 2007 volume. The emerging pattern of protectionist trade policies thus has a strong South-South flavor: South-North trade was largely unaffected in this way, with developing countries continuing to have access to rich-country markets.

All in all, the multilateral trading system, with the WTO at its center, has weathered the storm relatively well. The global trade environment is likely to remain conducive to outward-oriented growth strategies over the medium term, although the emerging pattern of South-South protectionism gives some cause for concern in light of the increasing importance of that type of trade.

Should Countries Reassess Export Orientation?

Such a huge shock to world trade, combined with severe macroeconomic instability, made it natural for policy makers and commentators to call into question some of the basic assumptions underlying the system. Trade and economic integration policies are no exception. Outward-oriented or export-led growth strategies are being reassessed for a variety of reasons. First, the trading system quickly transmitted simultaneous negative shocks in major markets to the rest of the world. Second, global rebalancing over the medium term might limit the capacity of newly developing countries to rely on overseas demand in the same way that China has or that the Asian Tigers and Japan did before it. Some claim that "the era of export-led growth is over in its current form" (Klein and Cukier 2009, 11).

A broad policy implication that has grown from a reassessment of export-led growth is that developing countries should focus more on building internal markets and supplying domestic demand. They will thus be relatively less exposed to negative demand shocks from abroad. Recent statements by China suggest that it may indeed be moving toward greater reliance on domestic consumption.

In addition, Rodrik (2009) suggests that a particular type of industrial policy should be used to promote development of the domestic tradables sector, but without the currency devaluations that many countries have relied on in the past. Developing countries could then reap many of the gains associated with export-led growth and not have to rely on large external surpluses. However, the efficacy of industrial policy is hotly debated, and the quantitative evidence in favor of its effects on trade and growth is scarce and inconclusive (Harrison and Rodríguez-Clare 2009). Moreover, the type of industrial policy envisaged by Rodrik (2009) relies heavily on relatively efficient and transparent governance institutions, the lack of which is a major development constraint in many countries.

An important lesson to emerge from Eichengreen and from Haddad et al. in this volume (chaps. 2 and 11, respectively) is that outward-oriented growth is indeed not a risk-free strategy. In fact, openness brings a number of economic risks with it, most notably the potential for increased volatility of the national economy due to its openness to shocks abroad. This factor has important implications for the policy instruments needed to manage the risks that come with outward orientation—policy instruments that should be an integral part of the export-led growth version 2.0 model.

Export diversification should remain a key policy objective for developing countries, because it can help manage the risks that come with the benefits of openness. Countries with more diversified export bundles exhibit a weaker link between openness and increased volatility of output. To some extent, the process of market diversification is already well under way with the rise of South-South trade. Developing countries still have considerable scope, however, for intensifying the process, in particular for further diversifying the range of products they export. Despite recent gains, low-income countries remain relatively dependent on a concentrated bundle of export goods, many of which are resource dependent; that dependence, in turn, makes them more susceptible to international shocks in those markets (Hanson, chap. 8, this volume).

A threshold effect influences the relationship between diversification and the trade-off between openness and volatility (Haddad et al., chap. 11, this volume). However, because most countries are already at a sufficiently high level of export diversification, an increase in openness is not likely to be associated with increased economic volatility. Many other countries are heading in the right direction (figure 1.4). Of course, countries with highly concentrated export bundles—such as some commodity exporters—are not yet in that situation, and measures to promote diversification could be beneficial.

Among the available policy instruments for promoting export diversification, trade facilitation and lowering of barriers to market entry stand out. Moreover, they have the important advantage of keeping incentives neutral across firms within sectors and across sectors in the economy. Trade facilitation and lower entry barriers intensify competitive pressures and speed export innovation. They help create a situation in which winners can pick themselves.

Figure 1.4. Diversification Trends among Selected Countries, 1981–2005

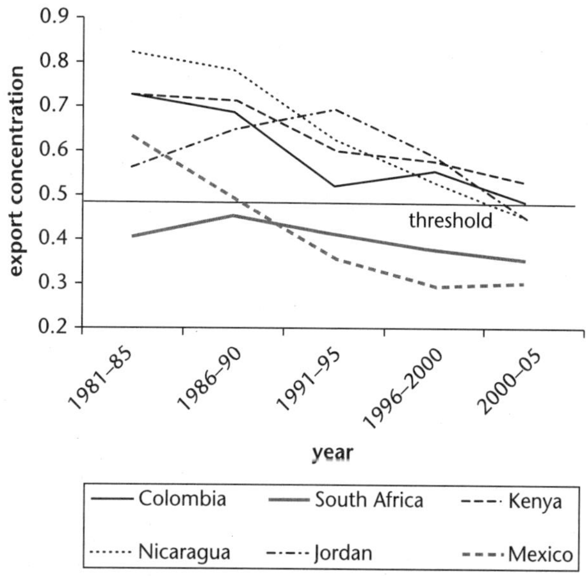

Source: Haddad et al., chap. 11, this volume.

The ongoing emergence of an export-led growth version 2.0 model suggests that most countries have not lost sight of the important dynamic benefits that openness can bring. Examples include technology transfer, learning-by-exporting, increased competitive pressure that reduces markups and improves efficiency, and economies of scale—particularly for small countries. Although the macrolevel "openness and growth" literature of the 1990s ground to a stalemate of result and counterresult in the early 2000s (Rodriguez and Rodrik 2001), the new firm-level evidence provides consistent and highly convincing evidence that more open sectors experience faster productivity growth (Bernard et al. 2007).

Outward-oriented growth strategies have brought considerable economic benefits to a range of countries over recent decades. The examples of Malaysia (Haddad, Winkler, and Zeufack, chap. 12, this volume) and even Africa (Songwe and Winkler, chap. 19, this volume) confirm that those benefits remain important for developing countries, because exports tend to increase firm productivity, which is the engine of long-term economic growth. These mechanisms are more important than ever following the trade and financial crises. As economies around the world emerge from the crisis, they will naturally look to engagement with world markets as a source of growth and development. This impetus behind outward-oriented growth is therefore likely to remain firmly in place.

Besides the role of export diversification in helping a country mitigate the impact of external and internal shocks, sound macroeconomic fundamentals are vital too—especially for smaller and more open economies that are subject to greater income volatility risk. Such measures include holding high reserves, especially to fill the trade-credit gap, and establishing and funding specialized credit agencies for trade finance. Reducing the budget deficit and maintaining policies for greater regulation of financial markets, particularly for dealing with the capital inflows of the carry trade, are also important. Those economies that rely heavily on durable manufactures produced through global supply chains should focus especially on export diversification.

A number of countries were able to move proactively to support their economies through the crisis, thanks to foresight and prudent macroeconomic management. Chile is an important example (Zahler, chap. 15, this volume).

Despite having a more open and outward-oriented economy than many other countries in Latin America, Chile recovered quickly from the crisis, helped along by healthy international copper prices. Its "sound fundamentals and strong macroeconomic management provided a buffer against the global economic recession" (Zahler, chap. 15, this volume). Prudent fiscal policy during times of strong growth—with a fiscal surplus reaching nearly 9 percent of GDP in 2007 compared with an average fiscal deficit of 0.2 percent of GDP in other Latin American countries—gave the government room for significant macroeconomic stimulus in the face of the recent crisis.

Another important feature of the crisis is that although the major developing countries were hit hard by the trade effects of the crisis, they have rebounded strongly. Haddad et al. (chap. 11) highlight the fact that the medium-term benefits of outward-oriented policies outweigh the short-term costs associated with the negative impact of the shocks from the crisis. This point is true not only for major developing countries, but also for many small, open, developing countries, thanks in part to the growing strength of trade links between China and the South (Wang and Whalley, chap. 10, this volume). On the one hand, this dynamic underscores the importance of promoting South-South trade in the future. On the other hand, it also shows the stabilizing effect of the greater integration of a number of developing countries with large internal markets—primarily Brazil, the Russian Federation, India, and China (BRICs)—into the world economy. As development continues in those countries and purchasing power increases, their role as demand stabilizers will also become more important.

Changing Dynamics in Global Trade

In the future, the likely drivers of export growth and diversification in developing countries are the developing countries themselves; these countries will play a vital role through South-South trade (Hanson, chaps. 8 and 9, this volume). GDP growth in low-to-middle-income developing countries has led to increased import demand, which has played an important role in boosting exports and promoting export diversification in low-income countries. Low- and middle-income countries accounted for 31 percent of world imports in 2008.

Concerns that weak consumption growth in the United States might undermine the viability of export-led development may be exaggerated. Dependence on U.S. demand for imports has generally lessened, although the United States is still a key source of demand for exports from the Western Hemisphere, for oil products, and for apparel from low-income countries. Low-income countries remain specialized in resource-intensive exports, but they are taking small steps up the value chain through expansion in apparel production. Although the export baskets of middle-income countries are more diversified than those of low-income countries, low-income countries are steadily closing the gap.

How sustainable is this new trade pattern? The recent diversification is based primarily on strong fundamentals, namely, economic growth in importing countries and greater competitiveness in exporting countries. If middle-income countries continue along the recent upward trend, import demand will continue to grow in the next decade. Developing countries experienced strong improvements in relative competitiveness in most sectors. And this phenomenon is not limited to "acronym" countries such as the BRICs and GEMs (growing emerging markets, including Brazil, China, India, and Indonesia): other middle-income nations have enjoyed improvements in export competitiveness similar to those the BRICs experienced. The role of South-South trade is therefore likely to be greatly enhanced in the export-led growth version 2.0 model.

Among potential developing-country import markets, China is obviously a major player. Wang and Whalley (chap. 10, this volume) examine China's South-South trade relations before and after the crisis. By 2007, China's exports to and imports from the South accounted for 21 percent and 35 percent of total trade, respectively. India and Brazil are the most rapidly growing trade partners, having experienced thirty-two- and fifteenfold increases, respectively, in their bilateral trade with China since 1995. Latin America and Africa are the largest regional sources of trade growth, with more dispersion across countries in Asia. In contrast to its total trade, China runs a significant trade deficit with the South because of its imports of resource products. Assuming unchanged growth rates, by 2015 Southern trade will account for over 50 percent of China's total, and by 2025, India will account for over 50 percent of China's trade. Finally, China's trade with the South was relatively less affected than average by the great trade collapse, in part because of a successful stimulus package.

The overall improvements in South-South trade notwithstanding, the temporary trade barriers imposed during the crisis were South-South in nature (figure 1.5). Of the stock of TTBs that developing-country users had in place in 2009, 68 percent were imposed on imports from other developing economies. Because TTBs fell less heavily on developing-country exports trying to reach high-income markets, it is clear that improving the security of access for developing countries to Southern markets should remain a priority. Enhanced South-South regional engagement—through

Figure 1.5. Combined G-20 Use of Selected Temporary Trade Barriers by Import Source, 1997–2009

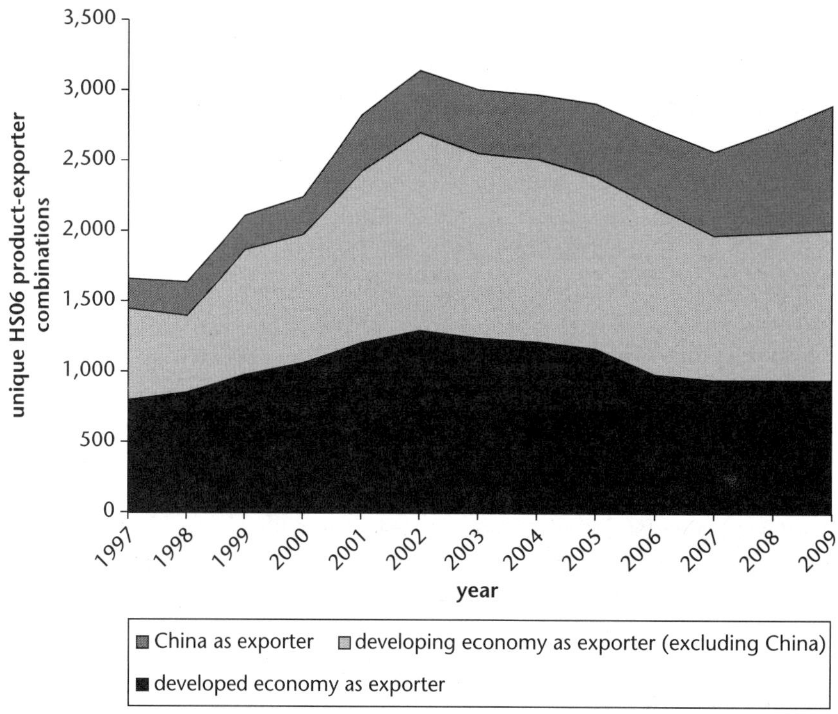

Source: Bown and Kee, chap. 6, this volume.
Note: HS06 refers to the six-digit level of the Harmonized System.

WTO-consistent agreements—would be one step in this direction. Another possible line of action would be to ensure better access to the WTO dispute settlement system for Southern countries, so that they can continue to open desired markets in other developing economies.

The New Trade Policy Agenda

The emerging postcrisis environment poses a number of challenges and presents important opportunities for developing countries. Commodities trade is booming, largely to the benefit of developing countries. Demand for temporary workers is also rising because of shortages in labor markets in developed countries and increasingly in middle-income countries. The nature of production and trade is changing, with much of it taking place through production-sharing networks. This evolution opens new opportunities for countries that can latch onto these networks, but it will leave out less competitive countries. Finally, we can no longer ignore the impact of production and trade on the environment.

While trade policy specialists are no strangers to commodity markets, a number of new dynamics will prove particularly important in the postcrisis environment (Mitchell and Aldaz-Carroll, chap. 20, this volume). First, commodities have had a relatively less severe crisis: thanks to strong demand from developing countries—especially China—the drop in commodities trade was less than in other sectors, and the rebound has been stronger. Second, commodity markets are now more closely than ever linked to energy markets because of the increasingly important role played by biofuels. As a result, price prospects are strong in oil and agriculture markets alike (figure 1.6). Of course, all is not unmitigated good news for commodity exporters: stronger governance and efficient regulation will be necessary to manage commodity wealth and to avoid some of the negative impacts that have accompanied previous instances of high prices, such as the "Dutch disease."

A much newer issue on the trade policy agenda relates to the increasing importance of global production networks (GPNs). Their prevalence may have been one vector by which the global trade collapse was propagated, as final demand shocks were transferred to suppliers of intermediate inputs. Evidence based on Chinese processing trade shows that intranetwork trade suffered a disproportionately large fall during the crisis: it appears to be more sensitive to cyclical fluctuations than regular trade (Ma and Van Assche, chap. 21, this volume). Evidence of a "bullwhip" effect is

Figure 1.6. Real Commodity Price Indexes, History, and Projection, 1960–2020

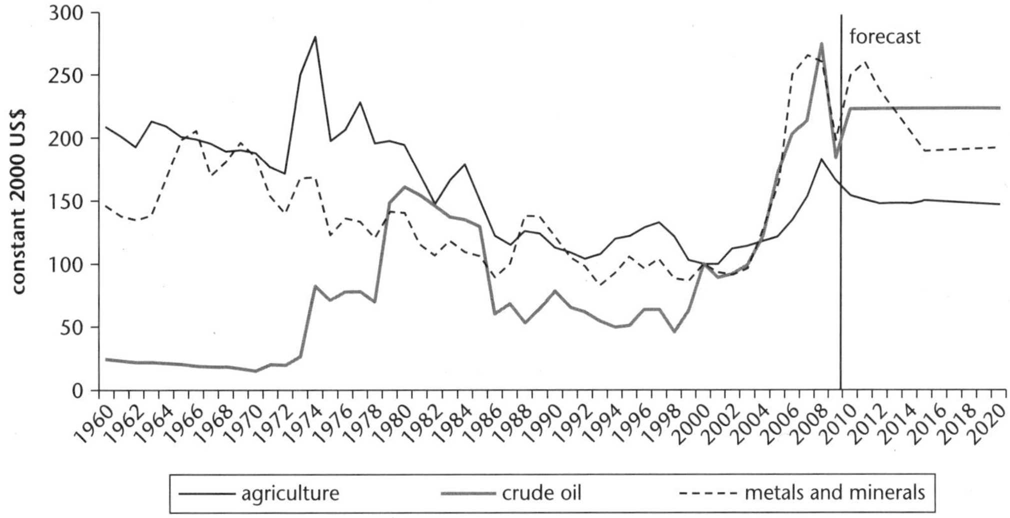

Source: Mitchell and Aldaz-Carroll, chap. 20, this volume.

also clear: the drop in Northern demand for Chinese goods caused local manufacturers to run down inventories of imported intermediates, which magnified the overall trade drop. Following the crisis, GPNs are being geographically consolidated (Milberg and Winkler 2010). With the crisis over, the challenges are rising for developing countries seeking to enter or upgrade within a GPN. The consolidation has contributed to fiercer competition and allowed only those with specific capabilities to remain in the game. Business as usual will not work: developing countries need to design new strategies to benefit from opportunities from the growing presence, and importance, of GPNs (Cattaneo, Gereffi, and Staritz 2010).

Shifting from trade in goods to movements of people through international migration, we see more opportunities for developing countries (Martin, chap. 22, this volume). The economic gains from freeing up migration could potentially be larger than those stemming from a feasible Doha Round of trade liberalization. The demand for migrant labor is expected to continue to expand in the coming decades: the decline in labor migration associated with the global financial crisis is likely a temporary hiccup in an otherwise upward trend. Most of this demand for migrants will be in the industrial countries, but some of the sharpest increases in the demand for migrant labor are expected to be in middle-income developing countries such as Brazil, Costa Rica, Libya, Malaysia, South Africa, and Thailand. This trend parallels the role of South-South relations in the trade area and raises the question of the capacity of nontraditional destinations to absorb new migrant flows.

Finally, perhaps the most crucial part of the "new" trade agenda is the emerging links between trade policy and the environment, particularly climate change. The December 2009 Copenhagen meeting marked a fundamental change in direction, which potentially puts the global climate change and trade regimes on a collision course (de Melo and Mathys, chap. 23, this volume). Alternative architectures for the next climate change agreement lend themselves to four areas in which trade will play a role: as a purveyor of technological transfer; as a mechanism for separating where abatement takes place from who bears the costs of abatement; as a participation mechanism; and as a way to address the pressures for border adjustments. Perhaps an umbrella agreement with leeway—where much initial mitigation would take place unilaterally, as under the early days of the General Agreement on Tariffs and Trade—might be the most promising way ahead for preserving an open world trading system.

Conclusion

According to the work brought together in this volume, we argue that reports of the death of export-led growth are greatly exaggerated. Although the nature of outward-oriented growth strategies is likely to change over the medium term to give greater prominence to South-South trade, the fundamental mechanisms are likely to remain in place. Similarly, there is a good chance that some degree of global imbalance will persist over the medium term, which means that any realignment of trade flows that takes place is unlikely to be so sharp that it becomes impossible for developing countries to continue leveraging international markets as part of their growth strategy. It is significant that from the broad range of country experiences discussed in part V of this volume, the overall impression that emerges is one of a continuing policy-level commitment to outward-oriented growth. There is very little evidence that major economies are seriously reconsidering their degree of engagement with the global trading system. Nevertheless, we should continue to monitor trade policies for signs of retreat from this position should economic hard times continue longer than expected. The weight of evidence suggests, however, that the trade and trade policy implications of the global crises should not be overstated.

Going forward, policy makers can do much to ensure that the global trading environment remains as receptive as possible to outward-oriented growth strategies. On the one hand, concluding the WTO's Doha Round would provide business with additional certainty about the future shape of trade policy and would encourage investment in export-oriented industries. One important benefit the Round could deliver would be to establish binding trade policy ceilings that are closer to the current levels of applied tariffs (Messerlin, forthcoming). The crisis experience shows that countries are reluctant to increase tariffs other than at the margin, for good economic reasons. They can enhance certainty and promote trade over the longer term by locking in that position through tariff bindings.

Policy makers will also need to address the increasing importance of South-South trade. They should pay greater attention to the reduction of South-South trade barriers, particularly nontariff barriers that can hold back the emergence of the "export-led growth version 2.0" model we referred to earlier. Enhancing the engagement of some developing countries in the Doha Round could be one useful way of moving forward in this area. Another possibility is for the emerging body of South-South regional agreements to focus on the implementation of deep and broad-based liberalization commitments. Indeed, given the rise of production networks, particularly in Asia, regional agreements are likely to move more and more in this direction, thereby facilitating the emergence of cross-border supply chains.

If the global economic crises highlight anything about policies of outward-oriented growth, it is that they are obviously not a panacea for development. No set of policies is. Rather, outward-oriented growth brings both opportunities and risks for developing countries. The key is in finding the appropriate set of policies to manage openness, one that maximizes its benefits and minimizes its costs. The evidence presented in this volume suggests that many developing countries are now engaged in that process and will continue along that course for the foreseeable future.

Bibliography

Baldwin, R. E., ed. 2009. *The Great Trade Collapse: Causes, Consequences, and Prospects*. London: Centre for Economic Policy Research.

Bernard, A. B., J. B. Jensen, S. J. Redding, and P. K. Schott. 2007. "Firms in International Trade." *Journal of Economic Perspectives* 21 (3): 105–30.

Cattaneo, O., G. Gereffi, and C. Staritz. 2010. *Global Value Chains in a Postcrisis World: A Development Perspective*. Washington, DC: World Bank.

Evenett, S. J., ed. 2010. *Tensions Contained . . . for Now: The 8th GTA Report*. London: Centre for Economic Policy Research.

Harrison, A., and A. Rodríguez-Clare. 2009. "Trade, Foreign Investment, and Industrial Policy for Developing Countries." Working Paper 15261, National Bureau of Economic Research, Cambridge, MA.

Klein, B. P., and K. N. Cukier. 2009. "Tamed Tigers, Distressed Dragon." *Foreign Affairs* 88 (4): 8–16.

Messerlin, P. A. Forthcoming. "The Doha Round." In *Handbook of Trade Policy for Development*, ed. A. Lukauskas, R. M. Stern, and G. Zanini. Oxford: Oxford University Press.

Milberg, H., and Winkler, D. 2010. "Trade, Crisis, and Recovery: Restructuring Global Value Chains." In *Global Value Chains in a Postcrisis World: A Development Perspective*, ed. O. Cattaneo, G. Gereffi, and C. Staritz, 23–72. Washington, DC: World Bank.

Rodriguez, F., and D. Rodrik. 2001. "Trade Policy and Economic Growth: A Skeptic's Guide to the Cross-National Evidence." *NBER Macroeconomics Annual* 15: 261–338.

Rodrik, D. 2009. "Growth after the Crisis." Working Paper, Commission on Growth and Development, Washington, DC.

PART I

THE CRISIS, GLOBAL IMBALANCES, AND REBALANCING

2

MANAGING OPENNESS: LESSONS FROM THE CRISIS FOR EMERGING MARKETS

Barry Eichengreen

Another discussion of the global financial crisis requires some justification.[1] The justification for this one is that the lessons of the crisis for emerging markets and their management of openness are still not adequately understood. Important questions remain unanswered. This chapter focuses on three.

First, who was hit, and why? And, in a related question, what policies should emerging markets follow to minimize the effects of global volatility? While more than a little has been written on this subject, it is not clear that a consensus has yet formed.

Second, what explains the outsize response of trade that was one of the principal transmission belts for the crisis? This crisis may have been just another "sudden stop" of capital flows, not unlike the sudden stops of the past, but it was the first *modern* sudden stop in trade flows—something that deserves further analysis.

Third, and finally, what was the role of global imbalances in the crisis? The answer to this last question again has implications for what kind of policy adjustments emerging markets should make going forward.

Who Was Hit, and Why?

The impact of the crisis varied enormously. Comparing demeaned real gross domestic product (GDP) growth in the third quarter of 2008 to the first quarter of 2009 at seasonally adjusted annual rates, growth fell by an astounding 35 percentage points in Latvia, 30 in Lithuania, and 25 in Estonia, compared to less than 5 percentage points in Argentina, India, and Poland. This handful of outliers, both positive and negative, already points to hypotheses. More open economies were hit harder. Countries with large current account deficits were hit harder (see figures 2.1 and 2.2.) Countries that had restrained the rate of growth of credit and had more flexible exchange rates did better. In contrast, the role of the government budget deficit is not clear; it is not obvious that countries with larger fiscal surpluses did better, in other words (see figure 2.3).[2]

The question is whether these and other regularities stand up to scrutiny when analyzed using data for a larger sample of emerging markets. Rose and Spiegel (2009) are skeptical. They link the severity of the growth decline, along with some ancillary measures of financial distress, to a set of indicator variables in 2006, the eve of the crisis, and find few robust regularities. One interpretation of this finding is as confirming the weak predictive power of so-called early-warning indicators, something to which some have pointed previously.[3] Crises differ. Market behavior and policy responses change, not least in response to the development of early-warning indicators themselves. In this view, there is no telling when a country will be hit or how hard. The appropriate policy response is therefore to invest in insurance. This view, for example, has some appeal to those who live on active earthquake faults and have learned to keep flashlights and bottled water on hand.

Another interpretation is that it is not so much crises that differ as countries. The impact of the same shocks and policies may be different in low-income, low-to-middle-income, and middle-income countries, given differences in market structure and development. Mody (2010) finds, for example, that the positive correlation that one might

Figure 2.1. Ratio of Current Account to GDP, 2007, versus Change in Growth, 2007–09, All Emerging/Developing Countries

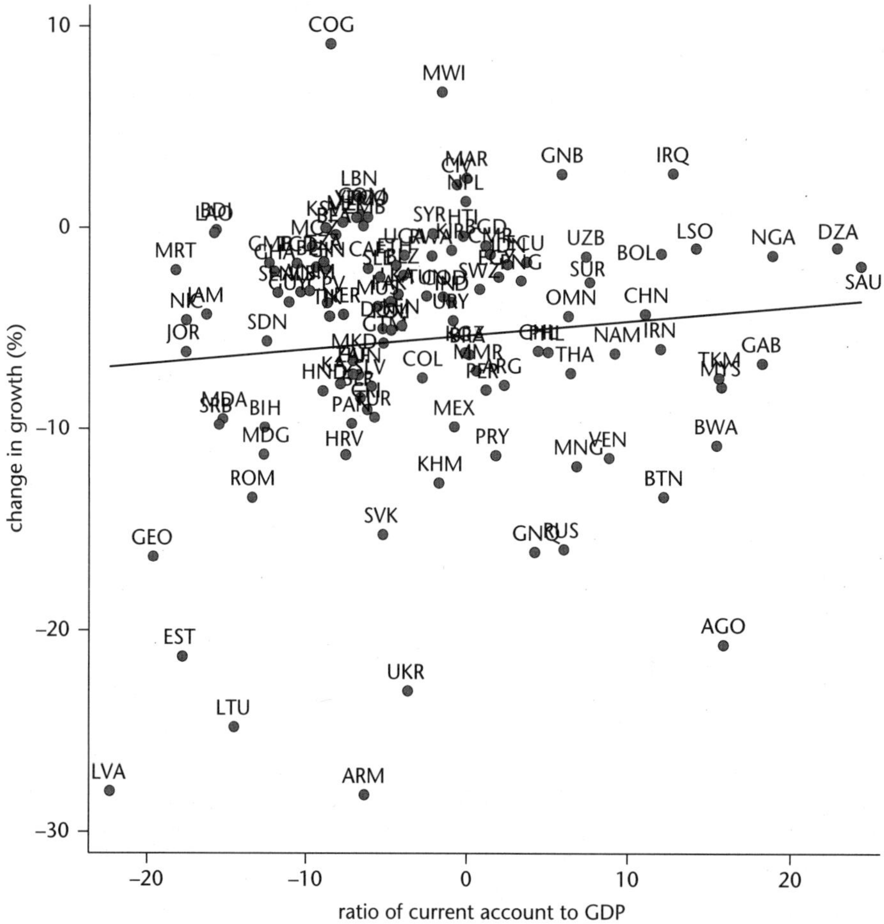

Source: World Economic Outlook (database), International Monetary Fund (IMF), http://www.imf.org/external/pubs/ft/weo/2010/01/weodata/index.aspx.

expect between large current account deficits and the fall in output (as countries with large deficits found them increasingly difficult to finance) is evident only in lower-middle-income countries (the middle tier of developing countries), not in upper-middle or low-income economies. Berkmen et al. (2009) find that the financial channel was more important than the trade channel for emerging markets (defined as developing countries with reasonably open capital markets) but that the trade channel was more important for a broader sample of developing countries (trade mattered more for the financially less connected low-income countries).

Alternatively, the difficulty of identifying sources of vulnerability may reflect neither that crises differ nor that countries differ but rather that the link between a country's characteristics and its susceptibility to disturbances is nonlinear. An example is the role of reserve accumulation in providing insulation from shocks. Berkmen et al. (2009) find no evidence that countries with more reserves had better crises. Blanchard, Faruqee, and Das (2010) report the same negative conclusion: when they include both reserves and short-term liabilities as shares of GDP, the latter matters but the former does not. Others like Obstfeld, Shambaugh, and Taylor (2009), in contrast, find a link between reserves and financial stability. Policy makers like Brazilian central bank governor Henrique Meirelles have similarly argued that they played an important stabilizing role in the crisis (see MercoPress 2010). The postcrisis behavior of emerging markets, which has been to accumulate more, is certainly consistent with this view.

The obvious reconciliation is that of Moghadam (2010). Reserves play a stabilizing role but only to a point. In a liquidity crisis in which investors are deleveraging, foreign borrowings must be repaid, and the scarcity of foreign exchange puts severe downward pressure on the local currency. Having the reserves needed to repay most or all of

Figure 2.2. Exports as a Percentage of GDP, 2007, versus Change in Growth, 2008–09, All Emerging/Developing Countries

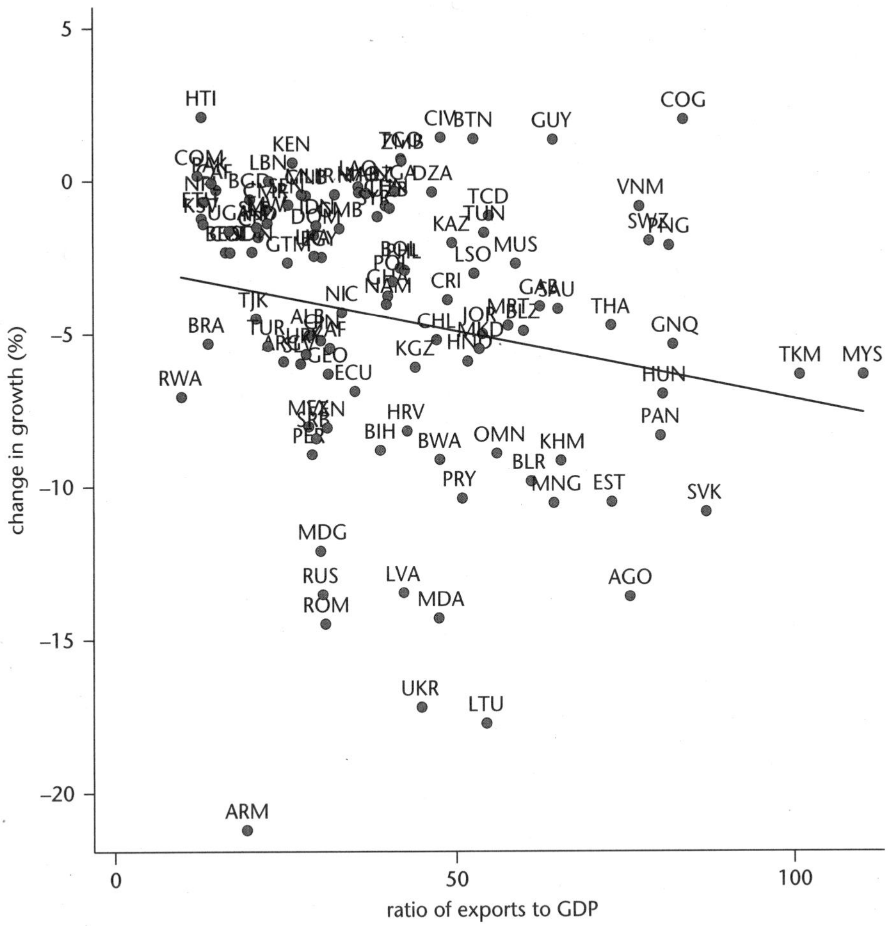

Source: World Economic Outlook (database), IMF, http://www.imf.org/external/pubs/ft/weo/2010/01/weodata/index.aspx; World Development Indicators (database), World Bank, http://data.worldbank.org.

those short-term foreign obligations, provide banks and firms with scarce foreign exchange, and support the exchange rate is of considerable value—as anyone who was in the Republic of Korea in November 2008 would know. At some point, however, perhaps when reserves match the value of short-term obligations coming due, the marginal benefit of having more reserves begins to diminish. Whether, beyond that point, they do anything to enhance stability further is questionable. In other words, the relationship between reserves and stability is nonlinear. The least squares parabola in figure 2.4 is consistent with this view.[4]

This much is intuitive. The problem is that there is less than full agreement on the point at which diminishing returns set in. Moghadam's data suggest that this happens around the point at which reserves match a country's external financing requirement (the sum of the current account deficit, short-term debt, and medium- and long-term amortizations of the public and private sectors) (see figure 2.5.) Others like Wyplosz (2007) argue that reserves continue to yield significant stability benefits beyond that point. It can be the stock rather than simply the maturing portion of the foreign debt that matters if investors, in a panic, scramble to sell it off. It may be M2 that matters if the liabilities of the banking system are in foreign currency or the country is committed to pegging the exchange rate.

The exchange rate is another variable that appears to bear a nonlinear relationship to the impact of the crisis. The evidence is quite strong that countries pegging their currencies had worse crises, other things equal. Flexibility helps when confronted by an unprecedented shock. Berkmen et al. (2009) and Blanchard, Faruqee, and Das (2010) both report that countries with pegged rates suffered deeper output collapses even after controlling for a range of other economic and financial variables.[5] But both also suggest that more flexibility was not always better. What significantly enhanced stability was moving from a peg to a managed float, not moving from managed flexibility to a free float.

Figure 2.3. Government Budget as a Percentage of GDP, 2007, versus Change in Growth, 2008–09, All Emerging/Developing Countries

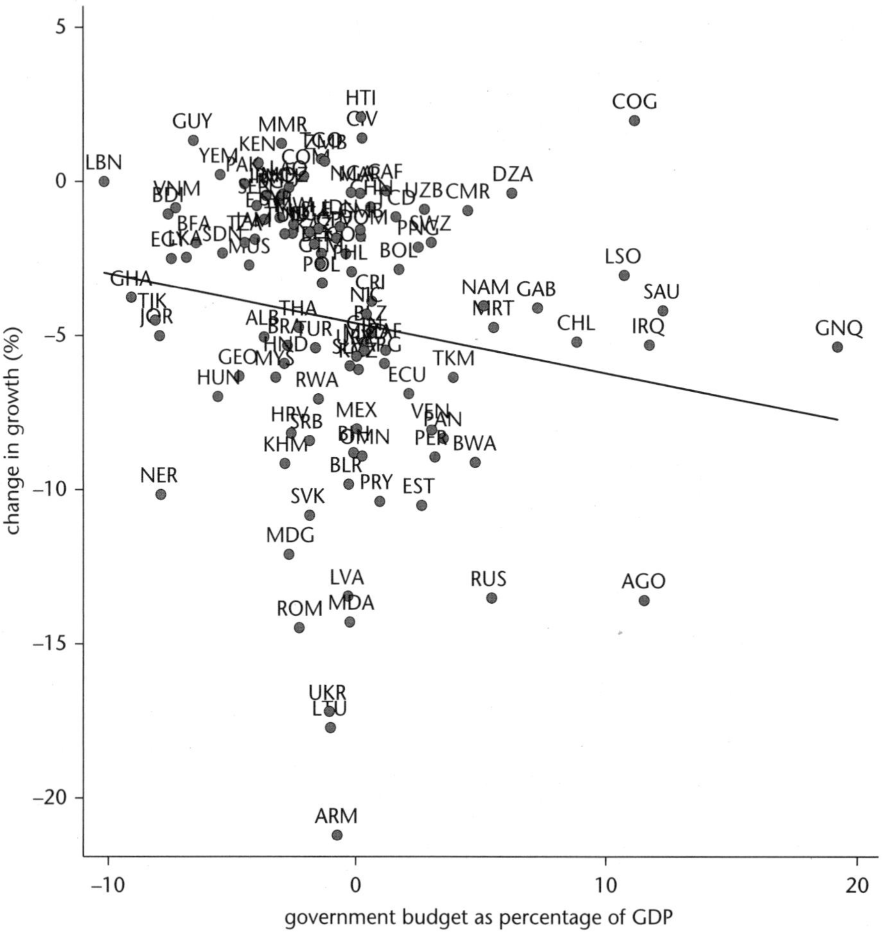

Source: World Economic Outlook (database), IMF, http://www.imf.org/external/pubs/ft/weo/2010/01/weodata/index.aspx; Economist Intelligence Unit (database), *Economist*, http://www.eiu.com.

Perhaps the most striking correlation is that countries with larger, better-developed, and more open financial systems did worse in the crisis.[6] This observation again makes sense intuitively. The shock originated in financial markets. Financial links were an important transmission belt. Hence, countries with relatively large financial systems and whose markets were open to foreign investors felt the crisis first and most acutely. The Republic of Korea, for example, suffered because half its stock market capitalization was in the hands of foreign investors, who held a fire sale in response to their own financial distress. Countries with better-developed financial systems had tended to have more short-term external debt, which made for a more serious crisis (figure 2.5).[7] Figure 2.6 shows that countries with repressed financial systems had their own problems in the crisis, but it confirms that countries with highly open financial systems, shown at the right of graph, did worse than countries with some restrictions, shown in the middle. (Note that the index of restrictions on inflows and outflows is from Schindler 2009, where a higher value means more restrictive.)

The question is what to do about it. If the crisis just past is a once in a 100-year firestorm, then the correct answer, presumably, is nothing. But if it was a salutary if expensive reminder of the intrinsic instability of financial markets, then the lesson must be "go slow on financial liberalization and opening." The Indian approach of going slow on domestic deregulation and opening is the right one. The Brazilian approach of using taxes to discourage short-term foreign capital is the right one. The implication, like it or not (and some in the World Bank will not like it), is that financial development in emerging markets will be slower than otherwise.

The problem, again, is that the information needed to know how far to go in this direction is not available. There

Figure 2.4. International Reserves as a Percentage of Short-term External Debt, 2007, versus Change in Growth, 2008–09, All Emerging/Developing Countries

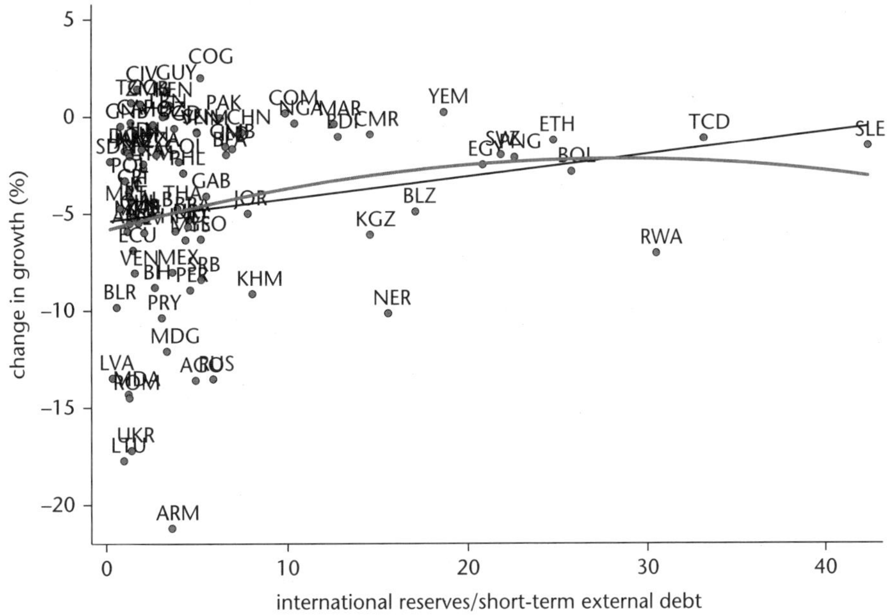

Source: World Economic Outlook (database), IMF, http://www.imf.org/external/pubs/ft/weo/2010/01/weodata/index.aspx; World Development Indicators (database), World Bank, http://data.worldbank.org.

is ample and convincing evidence that financial development and openness have a positive impact on growth and inclusiveness.[8] The evidence is ample and convincing, that is, when one draws it from good times. But it is equally clear that financial development and openness expose countries to additional problems in bad times, when financial markets fail. Two studies establishing that point are Vlachos and Waldenstrom (2005) and Eichengreen, Gullapalli, and Panizza (2009). The problem is that there are no good estimates with which to balance the marginal benefits of the first effect against the marginal costs of the second. Again, the relationship may be nonlinear: the early stages of financial development and integration may have significant net benefits, but those benefits diminish subsequently.

It is, of course, possible to give more nuanced advice. That is, rather than slowing financial development, perhaps developing countries should slow only certain forms of financial development. Countries whose banks funded themselves on the wholesale market, especially abroad, were vulnerable when liquidity evaporated. Those in which the ratio of deposits to domestic private sector loans was high did relatively well.[9] Highly leveraged as opposed to highly developed financial markets can be especially dangerous, in other words. Countries in which a relatively high share of foreign capital inflows were in the form of portfolio capital (short-term portfolio flows in particular) did poorly. This is an old finding from statistical post mortems on the 1997 Asian crisis; Tong and Wei (2009) and World Bank (2010a) show that it continues to hold. Markets that were permissively regulated, resulting in the strongly procyclical behavior of credit, and not simply markets were the problem.[10]

Why Was the Collapse of Trade So Dramatic?

The magnitude of the collapse of trade is a second important mystery to be unraveled before moving to policy recommendations. The suspects are clear: protectionist measures, disruptions to the supply of trade credit, and the development of global supply chains. It is unclear, though, how much weight to attach to them.

Protectionism was likely averted largely as a result of lessons learned from historical experience. Comparisons of the Great Recession with the Great Depression, which were rife in 2008–09, pointed to the importance of avoiding the kind of protectionism that compounded the earlier slump. World Trade Organization disciplines helped, as did cooperation among the Group of 20 and monitoring of countries' compliance by organizations like the World Bank and Global Trade Alert. But there was still a good deal of murky protectionism. Evenett (2010) identifies more than 300 trade-restricting measures of one sort or another between the fourth quarter of 2008 and the fourth quarter of 2009.

Eichengreen and Irwin (2009) exploited the Great Depression parallel to suggest where the danger was greatest.

Figure 2.5. Short-term External Debt as a Percentage of GDP, 2007, versus Change in Growth, 2008–09, All Emerging/Developing Countries

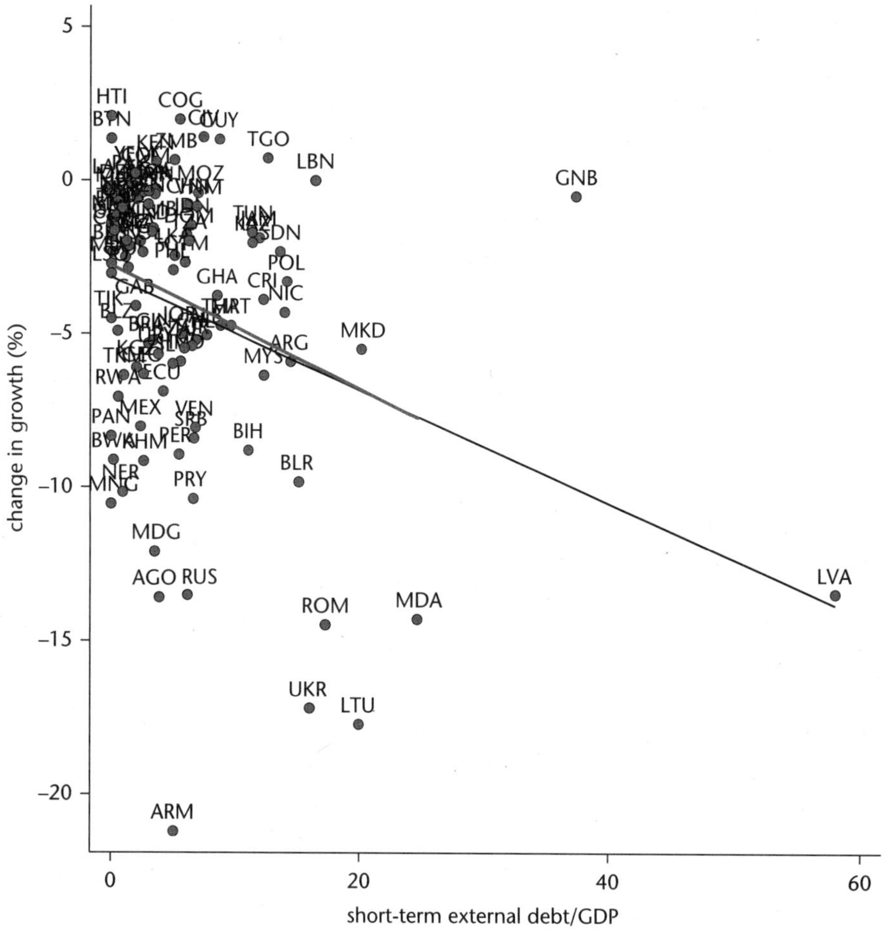

Source: World Economic Outlook (database), IMF, http://www.imf.org/external/pubs/ft/weo/2010/01/weodata/index.aspx; World Development Indicators (database), World Bank, http://data.worldbank.org.

In the 1930s, recovery policy meant monetary policy. To promote recovery, countries abandoned defense of their exchange-rate pegs, cut interest rates, and allowed their currencies to decline. Unlike during the recent crisis, reductions in interest rates in the 1930s were not accompanied by aggressive quantitative easing.[11] Other countries felt the effects through two channels. To the extent that they saw their currencies appreciate as a result of their neighbors' policies, their competitiveness worsened and their problems deepened. They lost reserves, and, to maintain their pegs to gold, their central banks were forced to tighten. But to the extent that their neighbors began to recover and, as a result, consumed more foreign as well as domestic goods, they also felt a positive locomotive effect. The evidence for the 1930s is that the first channel dominated: depreciation was beggar thy neighbor.[12] Countries that felt themselves beggared responded with restrictive trade policies that distorted their economies and further transmitted the contraction internationally. Protectionism was a byproduct of their failure to act and, more generally, of the inadequate coordination of stimulus policies.

This time, recovery policy meant not only sharp reductions in interest rates, often to zero, but also aggressive quantitative easing and fiscal stimulus. With quantitative easing, the locomotive effect as opposed to the beggar-thy-neighbor effect of expansionary monetary policy was stronger. The cross-border spillovers of expansionary fiscal policy were positive as well.[13] Whereas in the Depression, it had been the passive countries—those that did not take a policy response to the crisis—that had the strongest incentive to protect, this time it was the active countries that saw other countries as free riding on their efforts. This explanation, in a nutshell, is the genesis of "buy America" policies: some U.S. policy makers saw an expensive but necessary US$787 billion fiscal stimulus as also benefiting other countries insofar as the associated spending fell on

Figure 2.6. Average Financial Credit Restrictions, 2005, versus Change in Growth, 2008–09, All Emerging/Developing Countries

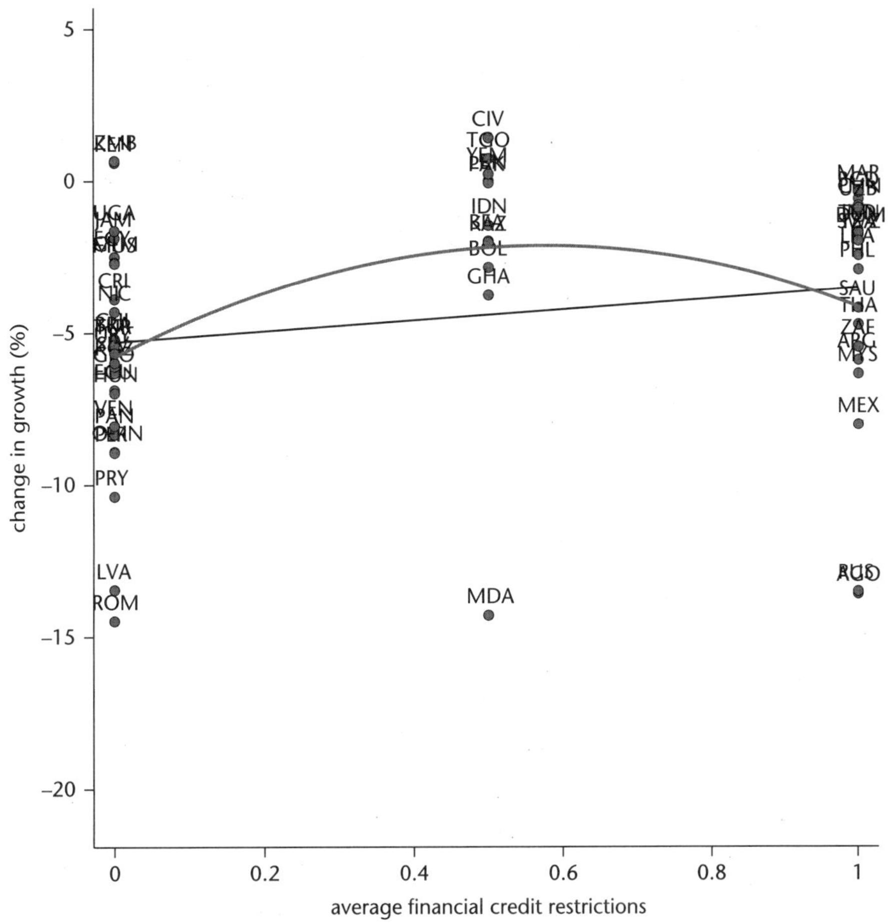

Source: World Economic Outlook (database), IMF, http://www.imf.org/external/pubs/ft/weo/2010/01/weodata/index.aspx; Schindler 2009.

imports as well as U.S. goods, and unfairly so insofar as other countries did not respond with stimulus programs of their own. The evidence of protectionism in the past three years is broadly consistent with this pattern.

To be sure, countries were much more successful now than 80 years ago in coordinating their policy responses to the crisis, which appears to be more evidence of their having learned from history. That increased coordination limited complaints about free riding and contained the protectionist impulse. Kee, Neagu, and Nicita (2010) conclude that only 2 percent of the decline in world trade in 2008 was attributable to increased protectionism. That number may be an underestimate, however; unlike other authors (Evenett 2010, for example) who consider trade restrictions broadly defined, Kee, Neagu, and Nicita (2010) look only at tariffs. A more encompassing measure would yield a somewhat higher number. Still, the conclusion that trade policy was not a major factor in the collapse of trade would probably still stand.

It is plausible that disruptions to the supply of trade finance might have been important in the collapse of trade. Trade, by virtue of its time-intensive nature, depends on finance, and this was, after all, a financial crisis. Iacovone and Zavacka (2009) show that the exports of firms more dependent on external finance fall by more in banking crises than those of firms that self-finance and that have more tangible assets and hence better collateral.

On the other hand, Mora and Powers (2009) argue that this effect was quantitatively small because the disruption to flows of trade credit was limited in duration and extent. Although other credit markets froze up, trade finance declined to only a limited extent, a few exceptional cases notwithstanding. Because trade credit is collateralized, it was possible to keep credit flowing. Official export credit agencies, for their part, stepped in to help. Developing countries, then, need to put their central banks and national export credit agencies in a position where they can also help, rather than relying just on the multilaterals. To the extent that parts, components, and other inputs going into the manufacture of exports are themselves imported, the central banks and export credit agencies in question have to provide trade finance in foreign exchange—another reason, above and beyond those discussed earlier, to hold reserves.

These last observations lead to a word on the role of trade in parts and components. This trend is relatively new in developing countries but one in which Asian countries in particular have become deeply implicated. It is widely cited as a factor in the strong reaction of trade in 2008–09. The explanation appears to be especially popular among Japanese economists (for example, Tanaka 2009), who must account for the fact that Japanese trade fell so dramatically in the crisis (export volumes fell by an astounding 50 percent between February 2008 and February 2009). Japan's extensive involvement in trade in parts and components is an alluring explanation.

The evidence is not convincing, however. If the difference now is that the parts and components in laptops are produced in Taiwan, China, but the machine is assembled in China, causing the components to cross national borders and be counted twice in the trade statistics, it is true that the same decline in the demand for laptops can result in a larger recorded drop in trade, since it causes the volume of global trade to fall by approximately the value of two laptops (ignoring the value added in assembly). But while this factor can explain why the absolute value of the fall in trade was large, it cannot by itself explain why the percentage fall in trade was so large or why the elasticity of trade with respect to income has been rising.[14] With assembly through global supply chains, there is twice as much trade in laptop parts and components. A fall in demand by one laptop causes recorded trade to fall by twice as much. But with both the numerator and denominator multiplied by two, elasticities are unchanged.[15]

For production fragmentation to be implicated in the collapse of trade, it is necessary to argue two things: first, that only some goods are produced using global supply chains and, second, that goods so produced were affected most strongly by the negative demand shock. It is possible to defend both arguments. In periods of high uncertainty, firms and households will put off spending on big-ticket items. (Baldwin 2009 refers to these items as "postponables.") These postponements occur especially in the uncertain conditions associated with financial disruptions, since big-ticket purchases have to be financed. Romer (1990) showed that it was demand for consumer durables that fell off so significantly in the early stages of the Great Depression. And a number of those products—motor vehicles, consumer electronics—are now heavily involved in global supply chains.

One wonders also about the interaction of production fragmentation with the two earlier explanations for the collapse of trade. It could be that the articulation of supply chains renders trade more sensitive to disruptions in the provision of trade credit. If component exporters cannot get credit, then assemblers cannot get parts, and even a limited financial disruption can break all the links in the chain.[16] This explanation is the trade equivalent of the O-ring theory of economic development.[17]

In this case, it is of course in the interest of the assemblers to provide the component exporters the credit they need. But it is not obvious that the assemblers will be able to obtain credit in a truly global credit crisis or that they will have the earnings with which to fund such credit themselves, absent an ability to get the parts they need to assemble and export. Perhaps, then, disruptions to the supply of trade credit and production fragmentation interact.

Similarly, protectionism and supply chains may interact. Freund (2009) observes that firms using global supply chains tend to alter the location of production in a slump. She gives the example of Porsche, which decided to cut the assembly of its cars in Finland in 2009 while maintaining its operations in Germany, one presumes for political economy reasons, given that Porsche is a German-owned company. In this case, it is precisely the exports assembled through international supply chains that disappear, despite the fact that those products are identical down to the finest detail to those that the German plant assembles for export.

The Role of Global Imbalances

As for the role of global imbalances in the crisis, some might expect them to have a place of prominence in this discussion, since I have written in the past of the dangers of their disorderly correction.[18] Of course, the crisis about which I worried then was not exactly the same as the crisis the world went on to experience. With benefit of hindsight, most of the blame for the crisis appears to belong elsewhere, although global imbalances probably played a role.

Fundamentally, I see the crisis as the result of flawed regulation and perverse incentives in financial markets. Regulators bought into the arguments of those regulated that financial institutions could safely operate with a thinner capital cushion. They accepted the premise that capital adequacy could be gauged on the basis of banks' internal models and, where these were absent, ratings of securities provided by commercial credit rating agencies—notwithstanding the incentives for the proprietors of the banks to tweak their models to minimize estimated risks and capital requirements and the tendency for the credit rating agencies, as investment advisers as well as issuers of ratings, to fall prey to conflicts of interest. The regime that resulted was capital poor and dangerously procyclical. Regulators neglected liquidity, assuming away problems in wholesale money markets. Banks were allowed to hide risks in conduits and structured investment vehicles and window dress their balance sheets. Agency problems flourished at each stage of the originate-and-distribute process. Mortgage brokers had no fiduciary responsibility to homeowners. Banks not keeping a participation in the complex derivative securities they originated felt no responsibility to investors. The structure of compensation encouraged bank executives to roll the dice, disregarding the implications of their actions for the survival of the firm. And the regulators averted their eyes. That is my summary of the crisis, in one paragraph.

Of course, this summary goes only an inch below the surface. The deeper question is how these extraordinary circumstances were allowed to arise. Here, I would cite a powerful ideology of deregulation stretching back to at least the Reagan-Thatcher years. I would cite excessive confidence in quantitative methods of risk management, Value at Risk, and of asset pricing. The academy, too, fell prey to a powerful collective psychology.[19] In addition, the intensification of competition, with the Glass-Steagall restrictions starting to crumble even before passage of the Gramm-Bliley-Leach Act in 1999, encouraged banks to take on additional leverage in their desperation to maintain normal returns. Finally, a conscious policy in the United States of starving the regulators of human and financial resources had a role in the crisis. It is hard to understand the precrisis behavior of the Securities and Exchange Commission any other way. That is my summary of the deeper causes of the crisis, again in one paragraph.

But if the match that ignited the fire lay elsewhere, in lax regulation and perverse incentives in financial markets, global imbalances poured fuel on the flames. With significant amounts of foreign capital, official capital in particular, flowing toward the United States, long-term interest rates were lower than they otherwise would have been. This influx of capital fed the housing boom. Reinhart and Rogoff (2009) show that the connection between capital inflows and housing booms is a historical regularity. My own ongoing work with Kevin O'Rourke and Augustin Benetrix on housing booms and busts, using data for a panel of countries in the Organisation for Economic Co-operation and Development (OECD) in recent years, again suggests that developments in house prices are strongly correlated with capital flows. Foreign capital inflows into U.S. housing markets made it easier for financial institutions to finance the teaser rates on option-ARMs (adjustable-rate mortgages) that sucked more households into the market. Again, although global imbalances might not have been at the center of the housing boom in the United States, they played a supporting role.

Beyond the housing market, the downward pressure on U.S. interest rates resulting from foreign official and private purchases of U.S. Treasury and agency securities could have contributed to the crisis through a number of channels. First, lower nominal interest rates encouraged institutions to take on more risk to match previous nominal returns.[20] Investors use nominal returns as a gauge of manager performance. If nominal returns go down, they may take this decline as the manager's fault and withdraw their funds. To retain their clients, managers are then forced to move into riskier assets and employ more leverage.

Second, some investors, such as pension funds and insurance companies, have fixed contractual liabilities. They are required to pay out fixed nominal amounts to their investors. If market interest rates go down more than the company expected when signing the contract, the yield on safe securities may not be enough for it to meet its obligations. Again, survival will require portfolio managers to move into riskier investments or take on more leverage. Banks that have issued certificates of deposit to their customers and whose other liabilities bear fixed interest rates may likewise find themselves squeezed.

Third, lower interest rates cheapen wholesale funding. Lower wholesale money market rates encourage financial intermediaries to expand their balance sheets. The impact will be most visible among broker-dealers relying on the wholesale money market for much of their funding and among conduits and special-purpose vehicles that issue commercial paper to fund their investments in speculative assets.[21]

Finally, if lower interest rates and more ample liquidity boost equity prices, including the equity prices of financial institutions themselves, those institutions will want to increase their lending to restore previous levels of leverage. Higher share prices for banks mean that they have more capital but also that they are not fully "loaned up." Some of their capital is effectively sitting idle. If the firm's lending capacity is not being fully used, it will seek to correct that situation. Low interest rates that translate into higher equity prices will thus trigger a lending boom.

The question is how much difference capital inflows made for U.S. rates. Craine and Martin (2009) estimate that 10-year bond yields were at least 50 basis points lower in 2005 than they would have been had there been no additional foreign purchases from the beginning of 2004. Bandholz, Clostermann, and Seitz (2009) suggest that 10-year bond yields were 70 basis points lower as a result of foreign capital inflows. Warnock and Warnock (2009) suggest that the increase in U.S. Treasuries held by foreigners depressed Treasury yields by 90 basis points. These views show a reasonably high degree of consensus on magnitudes, at least by the standards of the economics profession.

In the end, one must ask how different the course of the crisis would have been had 10-year bond yields been 50, 70, or even 90 basis points higher. One answer is, not very different. The problems of lax regulation and skewed incentives in financial markets would still have been there. The problems implicit in the originate-and-distribute model would still have been there. Problems in the mortgage-broking industry would still have been there. The conflicts of interest of the rating agencies would still have been there. The incentives for risk taking created by the structure of executive compensation and too-big-to-fail would still have been there. With wholesale funding modestly more expensive, leverage modestly less, and investors stretching less for yield, outcomes would have been less extreme. When the boom unwound, it would have unwound less violently. But, qualitatively, outcomes would have been the same.

Another answer to the "how different" question is, very different. Economic dynamics are nonlinear. Crises are nonlinear. It is just conceivable that a difference of 70 basis points would have meant an entirely different outcome. We will never know.

How Should Emerging Markets Respond?

The financial crisis was born and bred in the United States. To the extent that global imbalances played a role, low U.S. saving rates were, in turn, central to the development of those imbalances. But it takes two to tango. The story would be incomplete without also acknowledging the contribution of the surplus countries: China, emerging East Asia, the Middle East oil exporters, and surplus OECD countries like Germany and Japan.

The roles of these different countries and regions of course varied over time. Early on, surpluses were relatively evenly balanced, while more recently China in particular has dominated the surplus side of the equation. Emerging markets, as exemplified by China, now face a dilemma. Should they stick with their tried-and-true development strategy, which has entailed restraining domestic consumption, keeping the real exchange rate low, and plowing savings into investment in tradable manufactures, and thereby risk the reemergence of global imbalances and the associated crisis risks as demand again picks up in the United States? Or should they abandon that strategy for another?

In thinking about this problem, economists should not become fixated on the nominal exchange rate (the politicians can argue over that). The exchange rate is an outcome or a relative price that results from the elements constituting the development strategy, not a policy variable in and of itself.[22] In China, to pick an example not entirely at random, the strategy has been to restrain domestic consumption to mobilize large amounts of domestic savings for investment in capacity to produce tradable manufactures. Limited financial development, a limited social safety net, and limited pressure on enterprise managers to pay out dividends are all mechanisms that help maintain this balance of consumption and investment. With domestic consumption low, the relative price of nontraded goods is low. The prices of exportables are relatively high. To observers ignorant of the policy mix, the renminbi looks undervalued. But given the policy mix, the prevailing real rate is the market equilibrium. Were it not, China would experience faster inflation, and the real exchange rate would adjust through this mechanism.

Should China now change its policy mix (more rapidly)? The answer, logically, should flow from an analysis of the conditions that made the original policy mix desirable. The policy mix has been beneficial for some years now as a way of promoting the flow of resources into a manufacturing sector that would have been suboptimally small, owing to other distortions, in its absence. A policy mix that depresses the real exchange rate may be a second-best way of overcoming distortions (financial market underdevelopment that limits the availability of start-up capital, for example) that would otherwise discourage the growth of high-value-added manufacturing.[23] Or it may be a way of encouraging activities that throw off positive externalities (learning effects external to the manufacturing firm, for example) that would otherwise be undersupplied by even a well-developed market. Both kinds of distortions have probably been present in China, which is why this particular development strategy has been so successful.

The question is whether those distortions have now become less pronounced, so that the authorities can begin modifying the policy mix. This is properly a question for specialists on Chinese capital markets and Chinese manufacturing, not for me. For what it is worth, I think China has made good progress in terms of financial development. Enterprises are increasingly able to float bonds and borrow from banks, permitting them to rely less on the retained earnings they amass as a result of the prevailing policy mix. (To be clear, *increasingly able* does not mean *freely able.*) Through integration, collaboration, and the development of supply chains and production networks, manufacturing firms are better able to appropriate some of the positive externalities thrown off by their activity. (In this case, *better appropriate* is different from *fully appropriate.*) If this assumption is correct, then the policy response should be to begin to move gradually away from the prevailing policy mix. Policy makers can encourage consumption (by developing the social safety net and liberalizing financial markets). They can encourage enterprises to pay out dividends (by reforming corporate governance). As consumption of nontraded goods, among other things, rises in response, the real exchange rate will adjust. China can take the adjustment either through inflation (which will raise the relative price of nontraded goods) or renminbi appreciation (which has the same effect). My own preference would be for the latter.

How quickly should it move? The answer depends on how quickly the distortions just described diminish; that much is obvious. But it also follows that, since the diminution of financial market constraints, the development of collaborative relationships among firms are gradual rather than discontinuous processes, the change in the policy mix, and therefore the level of the real exchange rate, should also adjust gradually rather than discontinuously. A sudden sharp appreciation of the renminbi, in other words, does not seem the best approach. This logic calls for gradual appreciation over time.

But if one believes that global imbalances contributed to the crisis and that China's large surpluses, emanating from its policy mix, contributed to those imbalances, then this argues for rather faster appreciation. If one believes that China's policies (of course, not only China's), operating through the channel of global imbalances, have implications for global financial stability (and, thus, implications external to the country), then it should optimally step up the pace of renminbi appreciation. And what is logically true of China is true, to a greater or lesser extent, of other emerging economies in East Asia and other parts of the world.

In Sum

Openness has been tremendously beneficial for emerging markets. Over the past 30 years, the shift toward a more market-led system, stable macroeconomic and financial policies, and greater openness in international transactions have yielded enormous benefits in economic development and growth. Notably, greater openness is only one of a constellation of related policies: it is not openness per se that matters but its combination with other policies. While this makes it difficult to isolate the contribution of openness among other factors to the improvement in economic performance, most would share a strong intuitive sense that openness has played an important role.

But openness also has a downside in that it exposes countries to external shocks. It heightens the need for policies to shield relatively fragile developing economies. For developing countries where trade remains the principal channel through which shocks are transmitted, recent events underscore the importance of making contingency plans for the possibility that trade credit might dry up and exports may collapse. Central banks should hold reserves to fill the trade-credit gap. They should establish and fund specialized export credit agencies. They should prearrange support with multilaterals and other extranational agencies in a position to help. Given the special sensitivity to such disruptions of durable manufactures produced through global supply chains, countries heavily dependent on these products should redouble their efforts at export diversification.

For emerging markets where financial links are now the principal channel through which foreign shocks are transmitted, the regulatory framework for domestic financial markets needs to be strengthened. Such strengthening means tightening supervision and regulation along the obvious dimensions and, given the crisis, worrying more about leverage, liquidity. and transparency. It means using a portfolio of policies to deal with capital inflows associated with the carry trade: first, fiscal tightening; second, tightening limits on lending by domestic banks; third, additional exchange-rate flexibility to introduce two-way bets into financial markets; fourth, sterilized intervention; and fifth (and finally, if the preceding measures do not work), taxes on capital inflows. It means holding reserves adequate for dealing with the consequences of sudden stops and, indeed, with the wholesale liquidation of foreign holdings. Achieving this last goal means two things: one, identifying more precisely what constitutes an adequate level of reserves under these circumstances; and, two, negotiating reserve-pooling and emergency-swap facilities to minimize the cost of reserves, whether at the regional level—such as the Chiang Mai Initiative Multilateralization, CMIM, or the Latin American Reserve Fund, FLAR—or through bilateral swaps with the Federal Reserve and the European Central Bank, or at the International Monetary Fund.

Finally, emerging markets must think about gradually transitioning away from a tried-and-true growth model that has emphasized saving at the expense of consumption, slowed financial development, and successfully promoted export-led growth but at the same time contributed to global imbalances. China and others are already committed to this transition. But to complete it successfully, they need a clearer understanding of the underlying distortions that made for the success of the earlier strategy. Without this insight, it is hard to know how quickly to move away from it. And they need to bear in mind that policies that had unquestionable benefits domestically also added fuel to the fire that resulted in the financial crisis.

Notes

1. This chapter was first presented as a paper at the World Bank Conference on Managing Openness, May 10, 2010. I thank Gisela Rua for helpful research assistance.

2. Berkmen et al. (2009) find some support for the hypothesis that countries with stronger fiscal positions were hit less severely but caution that this evidence is weak. Budget data here are from the Economist Intelligence Unit.

3. As in Eichengreen, Rose, and Wyplosz (1995).

4. Data for five outliers—Algeria, Botswana, Benin, Cape Verde, and Uganda—were dropped for clarity. Including them deforms the parabola a bit but does not change the story.

5. IMF (2010) dissents from this emerging consensus, concluding that there was no difference in the depth of the recession between countries with pegs and floats.

6. Alexander et al. (2008) is an example of a study showing that the severity of the crisis was increasing in the size of the financial sector.

7. Note that I show the least squares regression line both with and without the outlier, Latvia.

8. See, for example, World Bank (2010b), chapter 2, for a summary of the evidentiary base.

9. Latvia and Korea were among the countries with the lowest ratios of deposits to private sector loans; neither did well during the crisis. More generally, Berkmen et al. (2009) and World Bank (2010a) show that countries with more leveraged domestic financial systems (higher ratio of domestic credit to domestic deposits) did poorly in the crisis.

10. Thus, Mody (2010) finds that economies that had overheated in 2008 saw larger decelerations in 2009. Berkmen et al. (2009) and World Bank (2010a) similarly find that countries with more rapid credit growth tended to suffer larger growth decelerations. Of course, any Polish policy maker could have told you this.

11. A few dramatic counterexamples like Japan notwithstanding.

12. This was the influential view of Nurkse (1944). Evidence for it is in Eichengreen and Sachs (1985).

13. Normally one would think them ambiguous: the direct spending effect on other countries is positive, but the positive impact on interest rates of fiscal expansion is negative, since it crowds out investment in neighboring countries. In a little trap, of course, the second channel is rendered inoperative.

14. As documented by Freund (2009).

15. A nice exposition of this is O'Rourke (2009).

16. One is reminded of some of the incipient disruptions to trade and production in Europe with the Icelandic volcano eruptions of April 2010.

17. See Kremer (1993).

18. In Eichengreen (2007).

19. A longer reflection on the role of economists in the crisis is Eichengreen (2009).

20. This is the mechanism discussed by Gambacorta (2009).

21. The effect will be less, though by no means absent, among commercial banks relying on retail deposits for most of their funding. That the expansion of balance sheets should be proportionately greater among broker-dealers than commercial banks is emphasized by Adrian and Shin (2009).

22. As I argue at more length in Eichengreen (2008). A similar argument is Song, Storensletten, and Zilibotti (2010).

23. High-value-added relative, specifically, to agriculture and traditional manufacturing.

Bibliography

Adrian, T., and H. Shin. 2009. "Financial Intermediaries and Monetary Economics." Staff Report 398, Federal Reserve Bank of New York. New York.

Alexander, L., et al. 2008. "Global Recession and Response." *Citigroup Economic and Market Analysis.* December 3. http://www.realclearmarkets.com/articles/econ1.pdf.

Baldwin, R. 2009. "The Great Trade Collapse: What Caused It and What Does it Mean?" VoxEU. November 27. http://voxeu.org.

Bandholz, H., J. Clostermann, and F. Seitz. 2009. "Explaining the US Bond Yield Conundrum." *Applied Financial Economics* 19: 539–50.

Berkmen, P., G. Gelos, R. Rennhack, and J. Walsh. 2009. "The Global Financial Crisis: Explaining Cross-country Differences in the Output Impact." IMF Working Paper WP/09/280, International Monetary Fund, Washington, DC.

Blanchard, O., H. Faruqee, and M. Das. 2010. "The Initial Impact of the Crisis on Emerging Market Countries." Brookings Papers on Economic Activity. Brookings Institution, Washington, DC.

Craine, R., and V. Martin. 2009. "Interest Rate Conundrum." *B. E. Journal of Macroeconomics* 9: 1–27.

Eichengreen, B. 2007. *Global Imbalances and the Lessons of Bretton Woods.* Cambridge, MA: MIT Press.

———. 2008. "The Real Exchange Rate and Economic Growth." Growth Commission Working Paper 4, World Bank, Washington, DC.

———. 2009. "The Last Temptation of Risk." *National Interest.* May–June. http://www.nationalinterest.org.

Eichengreen, B., R. Gullapalli, and U. Panizza. 2009. "Capital Account Liberalization, Financial Development and Industry Growth: A Synthetic View." UNCTAD Polis Working Paper 144, United Nations Conference on Trade and Development, Geneva, Switzerland.

Eichengreen, B., and D. Irwin. 2009. "The Slide to Protectionism in the Great Depression: Who Succumbed and Why." NBER Working Paper 15142, National Bureau of Economic Research, Cambridge, MA.

Eichengreen, B., A. Rose, and C. Wyplosz. 1995. "Exchange Market Mayhem: The Antecedents and Aftermath of Speculative Attacks." *Economic Policy* 21: 249–313.

Eichengreen, B., and J. Sachs. 1985. "Exchange Rates and Economic Recovery in the 1930s." *Journal of Economic History* 49: 341–59.

Evenett, S., ed. 2010. *Will Stabilization Limit Protectionism? The Fourth Global Trade Alert.* London: Centre for Economic Policy Research.

Freund, C. 2009. "Demystifying the Collapse in Trade." VoxEU. July 3. http://voxeu.org.

Gambacorta, L. 2009. "Monetary Policy and the Risk-Taking Channel." *BIS Quarterly Review* (December): 43–53.

Iacovone, L., and V. Zavacka. 2009. "Banking Crises and Exports: Lessons from the Past." Policy Research Paper 5016, World Bank, Washington, DC.

IMF (International Monetary Fund). 2010. World Economic Outlook. Washington, D.C.: IMF.

Kee, H. L., C. Neagu, and A. Nicita. 2010. "Is Protectionism on the Rise? Assessing National Trade Policies during the Crisis of 2008." Policy Research Working Paper 5274, World Bank, Washington, DC.

Kremer, M. 1993. "The O-Ring Theory of Economic Development." *Quarterly Journal of Economics* 108: 551–75.

MercoPress. 2010. "Crisis Lesson: Better to Rely on International Reserves than IMF Credit says Brazil." http://www.en.mercopress.com. April 24.

Mody, A. 2010. "Who Fell in 2009." VoxEU. January 21. http://voxeu.org.

Moghadam, R. 2010. "Emerging Market Countries and the Crisis: How Have They Coped?" April 19. http://www.imf.org.

Mora, J., and W. Powers. 2009. "Decline and Gradual Recovery of Global Trade Financing: U.S. and Global Perspectives." *VoxEU.* November 27. http://voxeu.org.

Nurkse, R. 1944. *International Currency Experience.* Geneva: League of Nations.

Obstfeld, M., J. Shambaugh, and A. Taylor. 2009. "Financial Instability, Reserves and Central Bank Swap Lines in the Panic of 2008." NBER Working Paper 14826, National Bureau of Economic Research, Cambridge, MA.

O'Rourke, K. 2009. "Collapsing Trade in a Barbie World." http://www.irisheconomy.ie/index.php/2009/06/18/collapsing-trade-in-a-barbie-world/.

Reinhart, C., and K. Rogoff. 2009. *This Time is Different: Eight Centuries of Financial Folly.* Princeton, NJ: Princeton University Press.

Romer, C. 1990. "The Great Crash and the Onset of the Great Depression." *Quarterly Journal of Economics* 98: 85–106.

Rose, A., and M. Spiegel. 2009. "Cross-country Causes and Consequences of the 2008 Crisis: International Linkages and American Exposure." NBER Working Paper 15358, National Bureau of Economic Research, Cambridge, MA.

Schindler, M. 2009. "Managing Financial Integration: A New Data Set." IMF Staff Papers 56, International Monetary Fund, Washington, DC.

Song, Z., K. Storesletten, and F. Zilibotti. 2010. "The 'Real' Causes of China's Trade Surplus." VoxEU. May 3. http://voxeu.org.

Tanaka, K. 2009. "Trade Collapse and Vertical Foreign Direct Investment." VoxEU. May 7. http://voxeu.org.

Tong, H., and S.-J. Wei. 2009. "Composition Matters: Capital Inflows and Liquidity Crunch during a Global Economic Crisis." NBER Working Paper 15207, National Bureau of Economic Research, Cambridge, MA.

Vlachos, J., and D. Waldenstrom. 2005. "International Financial Liberalization and Industry Growth." *Journal of International Finance and Economics* 10: 264–84.

Warnock, F., and V. Warnock. 2009. "International Capital Flows and U.S. Interest Rates." *Journal of International Money and Finance* 28: 903–19.

World Bank. 2010a. "From Global Collapse to Recovery." Office of the Chief Economist for Latin America and the Caribbean, World Bank, Washington, DC.

———. 2010b. *Global Economic Prospects.* Washington, DC: World Bank.

Wyplosz, C. 2007. "The Fuss over Foreign Exchange Reserve Accumulation." VoxEU. May 28. http://voxeu.org.

3

GLOBAL IMBALANCES: PAST AND FUTURE

Luis Servén and Ha Nguyen

Global imbalances—that is, large current account deficits and surpluses in the global economy—have taken center stage in the debate on the international economic outlook. Academic and policy scholars have offered contrasting views about their role in precipitating the global crisis, the potential threat of the imbalances to economic stability around the world, and the policy measures that should be taken to "rebalance" the global economy. This chapter discusses the nature of global imbalances and their implications for economic stability and for developing-country growth strategies.

The U.S. current account deficit grew virtually without interruption from 1995 to 2005 (figure 3.1). It peaked in 2005 and 2006 at over 1.5 percent of world gross domestic product (GDP). Thereafter, it declined to about 1.2 percent of world GDP in 2008, and preliminary estimates suggest that it fell under 1 percent in 2009. During the late 1990s, the counterparts to the U.S. deficits were large surpluses from Japan and emerging Asian countries, excluding China, as well as the surplus of the European Union (EU) during the years of the Asian crisis (1996–97). After 2001, however, the situation changed radically. As the U.S. deficit grew, the surpluses of China and the oil-exporting countries accounted for an increasing share of the U.S. overall current account deficit (figure 3.2). Moreover, since 2005, the surplus of the EU has almost completely disappeared, and China's surplus has grown to exceed the combined surpluses of Japan and the rest of emerging Asia. During 2007–08, the bilateral deficit with China accounted for around 40 percent of the overall U.S. deficit. Hence, the popular (but inaccurate) view of global imbalances as a problem of the United States versus China has started making some sense only in the past two or three years.

Since the current account surplus is identically equal to the difference between saving and investment, the trends in these two variables in different countries and regions provide some information about the sources of changes in their respective external imbalances. Figure 3.3 shows that rising saving has led to widening current account surpluses in emerging economies (namely, oil-exporting countries and Asia). In oil-exporting countries, this was driven by the persistent rise in world oil prices, while in Asia this reflected rising saving in the region's emerging markets. In particular, extremely high levels of saving are observed in China (over half of GDP). Saving and investment rates have both risen in China since 2000, but savings grew at a faster rate. A disaggregate analysis reveals that the increase in total saving reflects primarily the rise of corporate saving, which in recent years has hovered around 20 percent of GDP, although household saving has also been on the rise (Kujis 2005, 2006; Prasad 2009). Many observers attribute China's high levels of corporate saving to the weak corporate governance of large enterprises.[1] In any event, the result has been a major increase in China's current account surplus, which peaked at 10 percent of GDP in 2007.

China's high level of saving stands in sharp contrast with low saving in the United States. Indeed, falling saving was the principal source of the increasing external deficits of the United States from the end of the 1990s to 2003. After 2003, the trends in the current account were driven primarily by changes in investment—increasing until 2006 and then decreasing. In particular, the reduction of the external imbalance of the United States in 2007–08 reflects the fact that, although saving rates remained on a declining trend, investment rates fell even more quickly. Aside from the United States, other industrial countries have undergone relatively modest changes in saving and investment rates. In the EU, the slightly decreasing trend in saving over the past decade led to a gradual reduction, and eventually a

Figure 3.1. Current Account Imbalances for Selected Countries as a Percentage of World GDP, 1980–2009

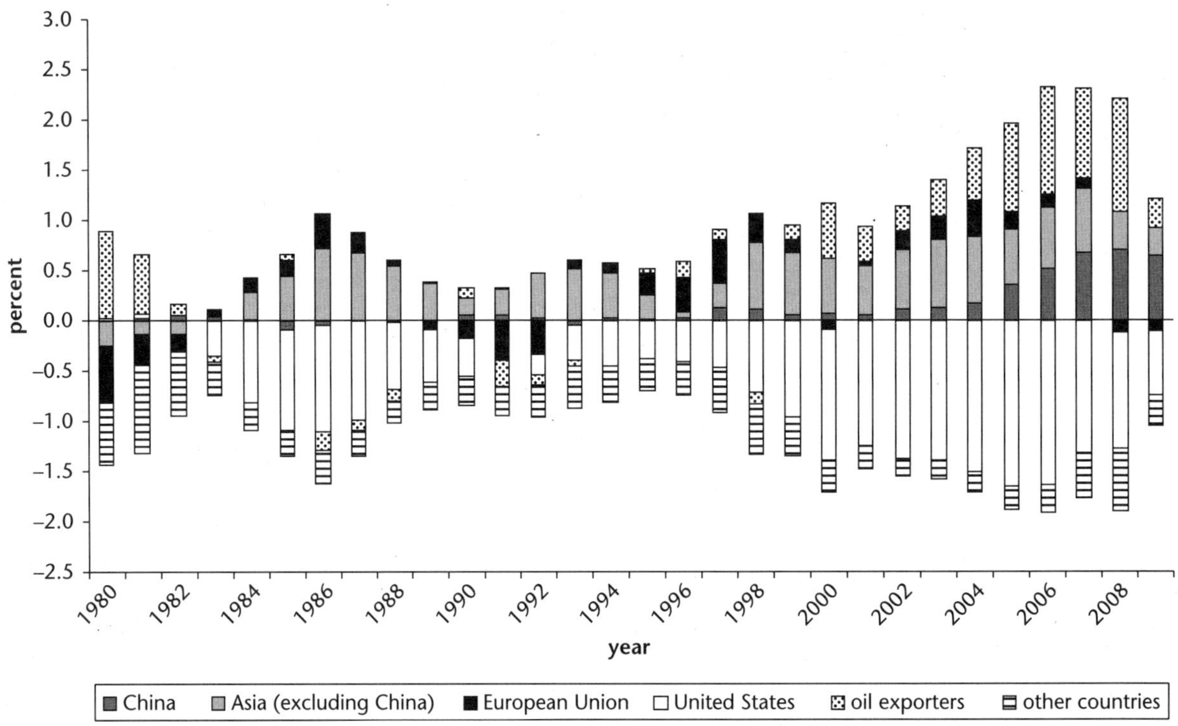

Source: World Economic Outlook (database). International Monetary Fund (IMF), http://www.imf.org/external/ns/cs.aspx?id=28.
Note: GDP = gross domestic product. The 2009 data are the International Monetary Fund's estimates.

Figure 3.2. U.S. Bilateral Current Accounts with Other Countries, 1999–2009

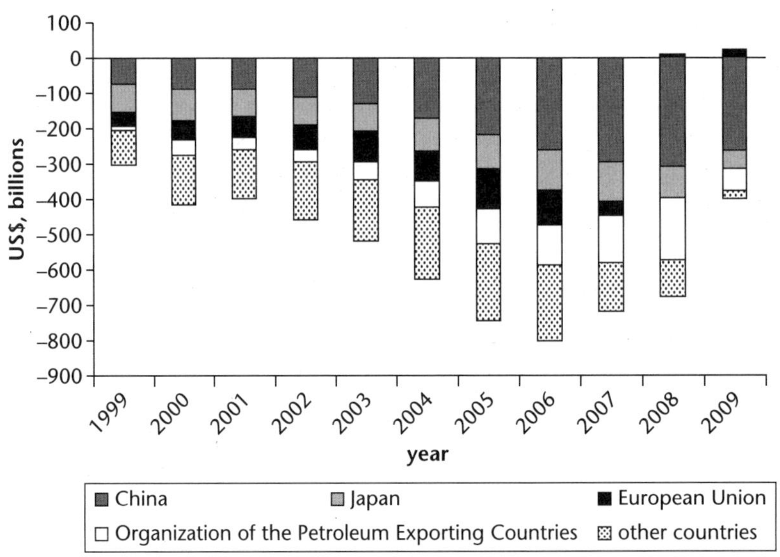

Source: International Economic Accounts (database), Bureau of Economic Analysis, http://www.bea.gov/international.

reversal, of the area's current account surplus. In Japan, saving and investment rates both followed a downward trend over the 1990s. However, in the past decade, both rates remained fairly stable, and the current account maintained a modest surplus.

In spite of their recent rise to prominence in the debate over the roots of the crisis, global imbalances are not a new phenomenon. In fact, the 1980s witnessed a situation qualitatively similar to that observed in recent years, characterized by large U.S. current account deficits funded by other

Figure 3.3. Saving and Investment Rates as a Percentage of GDP in Selected Countries, 1990–2008

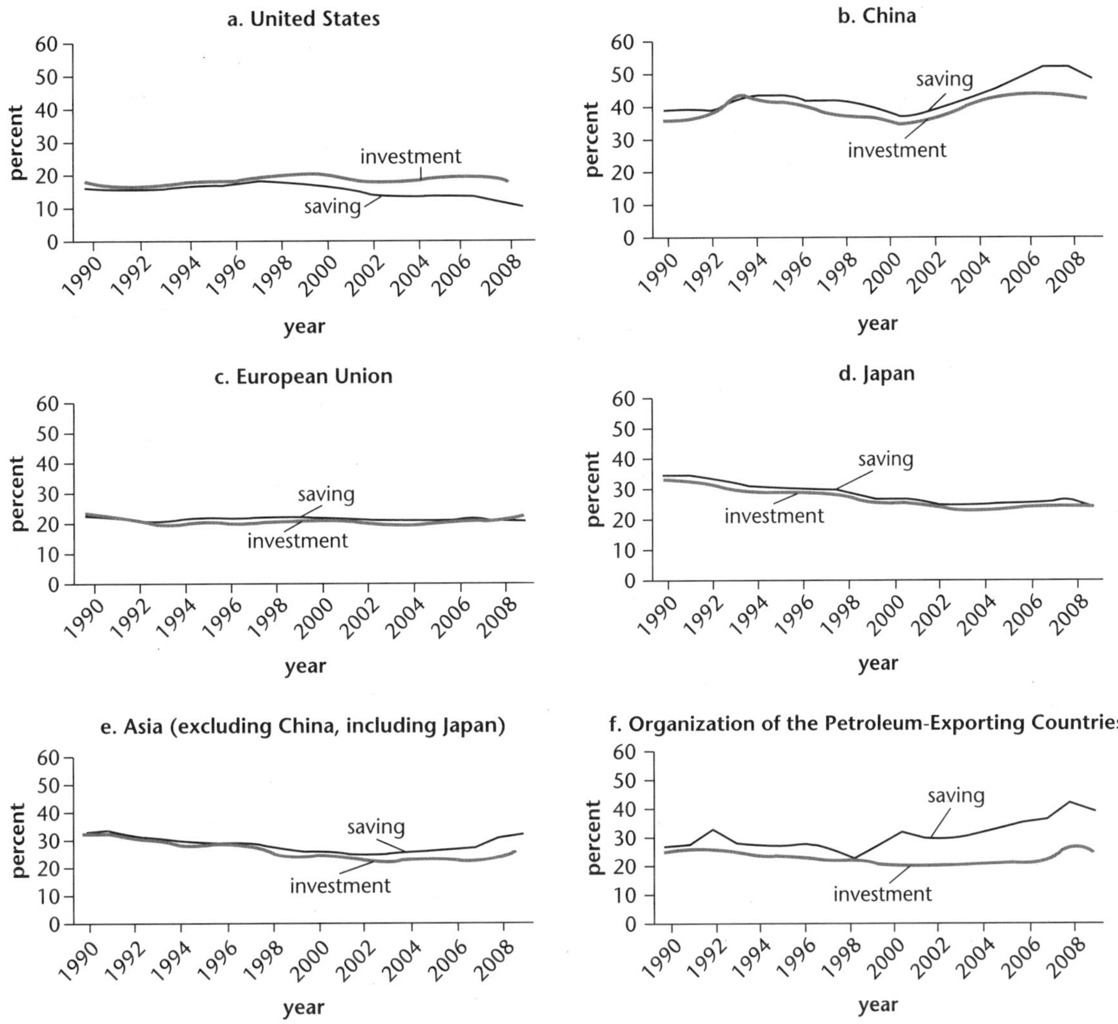

Source: World Development Indicators (database), World Bank, http://data.worldbank.org. World Economic Outlook (database), IMF, http://www.imf.org/external/ns/cs.aspx?id=28.

countries (figure 3.1). Two important differences, however, distinguish these episodes. First, both the duration and the magnitude of the U.S. deficits of the 1980s were substantially lower than those in recent years. In particular, in the 1980s U.S. deficits exceeded 1 percent of world GDP in only 3 years, as opposed to 10 years in the present circumstance. Second, in recent years emerging economies have been primarily responsible for funding the U.S. external deficit (as well as the deficits of other advanced countries), unlike in the 1980s when such funding came mostly from other rich countries, primarily Japan. In other words, the recent global imbalances involve a flow of capital from poor countries to rich countries, against the prediction of conventional economic theory that developing countries should be net capital importers.[2]

These distinguishing features of the global imbalances of recent years suggest that the factors behind them may be different from those at play in the 1980s. Understanding such factors is important to assessing how global imbalances may evolve after the world crisis and to gauging the potential risks that their continued presence could pose to the world economy.

The rest of this chapter is organized as follows. The next section summarizes various views in the academic literature on the nature of global imbalances. The following section reviews recent trends in global imbalances and discusses alternative scenarios for their future evolution, their impact on developing countries, and the appropriate policy responses. The final section concludes.

The Nature of Global Imbalances

At the risk of over-simplifying, we can distinguish two basic views among academics and policy analysts on the nature of global imbalances. What we shall label for want of a better term as the *disequilibrium approach* considers global imbalances an unsustainable phenomenon, requiring adjustment of the U.S. current account and a major depreciation of the dollar. This correction could come in the form of a sudden stoppage of capital flows into the United States and collapse of the exchange rate (Roubini 2009, for example). The second view, or *equilibrium approach,* asserts that global imbalances represent a situation that, absent changes in its deep determinants, can be self-sustaining. We next review the main lines of both approaches.

The Disequilibrium Approach

The view that current global imbalances are unsustainable starts from the intertemporal budget constraint dictating that a country's net liability position against the rest of the world at any given time cannot exceed the present value of its future current account surpluses.[3] This requirement makes it entirely possible for a country to run current account deficits for a long time, as long as it is capable of running sufficiently large surpluses in the future. Such could be the case of developing countries that borrow from developed countries to invest and accumulate capital and repay their debts once they reach a higher stage of development (Kraay et al. 2005). Alternatively, a developed country could also run current account deficits if in the future it is expected to grow faster than the rest of the world. In effect, the country finances its consumption by borrowing against its future income. In this vein, Engel and Rogers (2006) argue that the U.S. current account deficit might be an outcome of such intertemporally optimizing behavior.

Many observers are concerned, however, that the large U.S. external deficits are the result of an unsustainable increase in public or private expenditure, prompted respectively by fiscal expansions and financial innovations. Whether the deficits reflect intertemporally optimizing behavior or excessive spending, the net foreign asset position of the United States has clearly undergone a steep decline. From a creditor position amounting to 10 percent of its GDP at the beginning of the 1980s, the United States had shifted into a debtor position approaching 25 percent of GDP in 2009. In absolute terms, this debtor position is the biggest in the world. Thus, according to the disequilibrium approach, this trend is unsustainable, and the country needs to change the sign of its trade balance at some point. Such a shift, in turn, would entail a depreciation of the dollar to increase U.S. net exports.

According to this view, the adjustment process might not be very different from the one that led to elimination of the U.S. external deficits of the 1980s. Figure 3.4 compares

Figure 3.4. U.S. Multilateral Real Exchange Rate Index, 1980–2009
quarter 1, 2002 = 100

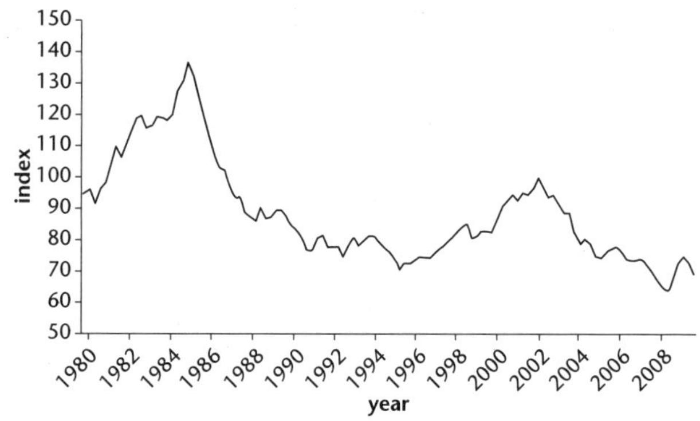

Source: International Financial Statistics (database), IMF, Washington, DC. http://www.imfstatistics.org.

the trends in the real effective exchange rate of the dollar during that episode (1981–92) with those observed in the past decade (1998–2009). From its peak at the beginning of 1985, the dollar had depreciated over 40 percent by the end of 1991. The virtual elimination of the current account deficit accompanied the depreciation. In contrast, over the past decade the dollar has followed a pattern of depreciation similar to that observed in the 1980s, although the magnitude of the depreciation since the peak in early 2002 to date has been smaller—around 30 percent. Moreover, external deficits have remained quite large, at least until 2008. Under the disequilibrium view, these deficits suggest that further real depreciation of the dollar is still to come. In fact, numerous studies have subjected the magnitude of the trade balance correction, and of the depreciation necessary to achieve it, to detailed analysis (Obstfeld and Rogoff 2005, 2009, for example).

Correcting these external imbalances, according to the disequilibrium view, demands a *real* adjustment—a reversal of the trade balance. But recent literature has underscored the potentially important role that *financial* adjustment can also play. Changes in the prices of a country's foreign assets and liabilities also affect its net foreign asset position. In particular, changes in asset prices—that is, capital gains and losses on foreign assets and liabilities—imply that the current account balance no longer determines the change in net foreign assets.

Although financial adjustment has received little attention, it is especially important in the U.S. case owing to return differentials: assets held by U.S. investors abroad yield higher returns than U.S. assets held by foreign investors (Hausmann and Sturzenegger 2004; Gourinchas and Rey 2007a; Forbes 2010). Hausmann and Sturzenegger

(2004) note that, despite holding a negative net foreign asset position of nearly 20 percent of GDP in 2004, the United States still earned a US$30 billion positive net return that year.[4]

In turn, depreciation of the dollar also favors the United States because its external liabilities are denominated mostly in dollars, while its assets are denominated in other currencies. Therefore, a depreciation of the dollar generates a wealth transfer in favor of the United States: the value of its liabilities falls relative to the value of its assets. This process is exactly the reverse of what usually happens in emerging markets when their exchange rate undergoes a real depreciation because they are typically indebted in foreign currency.

Hence, depreciation of the dollar has a dual effect on the external asset position of the United States. On the one hand, it generates a real adjustment through an improving trade balance. On the other hand, it generates a financial adjustment through capital gains for the United States (losses for the rest of the world). Simplistic assessments of the depreciation of the dollar—and the trade surplus—required to put the external position of the United States on a sustainable trajectory can lead to exaggerated conclusions unless they take into consideration this second effect, which is becoming increasingly important given the sharp rise in cross-country asset holdings in the past two decades.

How big is the financial adjustment effect? The topic has been debated extensively (for example, Blanchard, Giavazzi, and Sa 2005; Gourinchas and Rey 2007b). It is hard to give a precise answer because of the lack of sufficiently detailed information on the composition of U.S. external assets and liabilities (Curcuru, Thomas, and Warnock 2008). Observers, however, generally agree that financial adjustment does play a significant role and that ensuring sustainability of the U.S. external position will require a much more modest depreciation of the dollar than what would be necessary if external adjustment had to take place only from the trade balance.

As an illustration, figure 3.5 (from Nguyen 2010) offers an assessment of the financial adjustment that occurred during the period 1994–2007 through changes in stock and bond prices. After 2002, it generated large gains for the United States, which peaked at 4 percent of U.S. GDP in 2006 and 2007—an order of magnitude similar to that of the current account deficits of those years. Two main factors were at play. First was the relative decline in U.S. stock market prices since 2000, which generated capital losses for foreign investors (see Kraay and Ventura 2005 for a detailed discussion). Second was the depreciation of the dollar after 2002.

The Equilibrium Approach

In contrast to the disequilibrium view, the equilibrium approach explains global imbalances as the result of structural factors or policies in other countries that have led to a steady accumulation of assets in the United States by the rest of world. Absent changes in such structural factors and policy choices, global imbalances could persist. Although details vary in different versions of the equilibrium approach, one

Figure 3.5. U.S. Valuation Effects and Current Account as a Percentage of GDP, 1994–2007

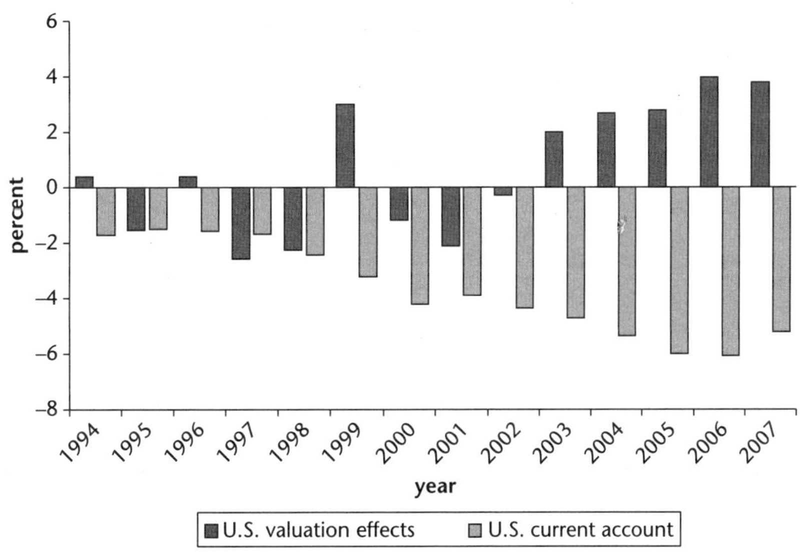

Source: Nguyen 2010.

common feature is an emphasis on the capital account. This emphasis contrasts with that of the disequilibrium approach on the current account.

We can further distinguish two main versions of the equilibrium approach. The first one underscores international asymmetries in the supply of or demand for financial assets. Caballero, Fahri, and Gourinchas (2008a, 2008b) suggest that international savers prefer assets of countries with more advanced financial markets—the United States in particular—because local assets in emerging countries are plagued by volatile yields or risk of expropriation. A growth acceleration in emerging countries (or an oil price boom) that increases their wealth and saving—the ultimate causes of the so-called global saving glut (Bernanke 2005)—leads them to expand their holdings of U.S. assets. Such an expansion, however, can occur only by raising the volume of U.S. assets available to international investors and thus increasing the U.S. current account deficit. This process can persist as long as its driving force—the underdevelopment of financial markets in emerging countries—remains unchanged. As a result, capital flows "uphill," from poor to rich countries.

On the demand side, international asymmetries may arise from the limited appropriability of returns on emerging-market assets (Mendoza, Quadrini, and Rios-Rull 2009). Asymmetries may also arise from the shortcomings of the social protection system in emerging economies (Carroll and Jeanne 2009), which force individuals to save more for retirement or to protect themselves from the risk of unemployment. In either case, the result is that savers in emerging countries tend to save more than those in industrial countries. In a context of international financial integration, this tendency leads to a global equilibrium in which emerging countries acquire a creditor position, whereas advanced countries are net debtors. If the ultimate determinants of this equilibrium remain unaltered, global imbalances and uphill capital flows can persist indefinitely.

The second version of the equilibrium approach emphasizes policy makers' choices as the main cause of the accumulation of external assets by emerging markets. Again, the argument has two variants. The first variant asserts that hoarding foreign assets results from the so-called new mercantilist development strategy: the attempt of a number of emerging markets—particularly in East Asia—to pursue export-led growth. The mercantilist strategy calls for an undervalued real exchange rate to preserve export competitiveness.[5] The best way to achieve this outcome is by compressing domestic spending, particularly consumption, which inevitably leads to persistent current account surpluses and accumulation of foreign reserves.

Under appropriate circumstances, the mercantilist strategy may succeed in accelerating economic growth. However, its merits from the welfare standpoint are questionable, because large-scale accumulation of external (and typically low-yield) assets involves major opportunity costs in forgone consumption and investment (Korinek and Servén 2010). Nevertheless, as long as Asian emerging markets stick to the export-led strategy, global imbalances can remain in operation indefinitely.

Alternatively, emerging-market authorities may choose to accumulate foreign assets for precautionary reasons.[6] In the absence of mechanisms for international diversification of aggregate risk, emerging countries integrated into the global financial system need to self-insure against external shocks such as disruptions of international capital flows (for instance, like what occurred in the crises of Asia and the Russian Federation in the 1990s). Emerging countries accumulate external assets, preferably short-term instruments, from which they can draw in the event of a "sudden stop." Unless the global financial system generates new international diversification mechanisms, this precautionary accumulation of foreign assets is unlikely to end.

What does the empirical evidence say about the validity of these arguments? To begin with, the massive accumulation of international reserves by emerging economies during the past decade seems to confirm that deliberate hoarding has played an important role. Between 1998 and 2008, international reserve holdings of emerging countries (figure 3.6, panel a) increased fourfold, while those of industrial countries rose only 50 percent (figure 3.6, panel b). As a result, the volume of international reserves held by emerging markets at present greatly exceeds that of industrial countries. For example, at the end of 2008, China's foreign reserve stock was almost as large as that of all industrial countries combined. Reserve holdings in the rest of emerging Asia have also increased dramatically. But the phenomenon is not confined to Asia; Latin American economies (with Chile at the top) and oil-exporting countries have also accumulated large volumes of international reserves over the past decade.

Even if the accumulation of international reserves, or external assets more broadly, was a deliberate policy choice of emerging economies, the question remains whether caution in the face of volatile international capital flows or the pursuit of competitive exchange rates was the driver. Aizenman and Lee (2007) examine the question empirically using data from 49 countries in the 1980–2000 period; they conclude that both motives were at work but that the precautionary saving motive was more important. Jeanne and Ranciere (2009), in turn, conclude that the accumulation of external assets since 2000 has been too

Figure 3.6. Foreign Reserve Stock of Industrial and Emerging Countries, 1991–2008
constant 2000 US$, billions

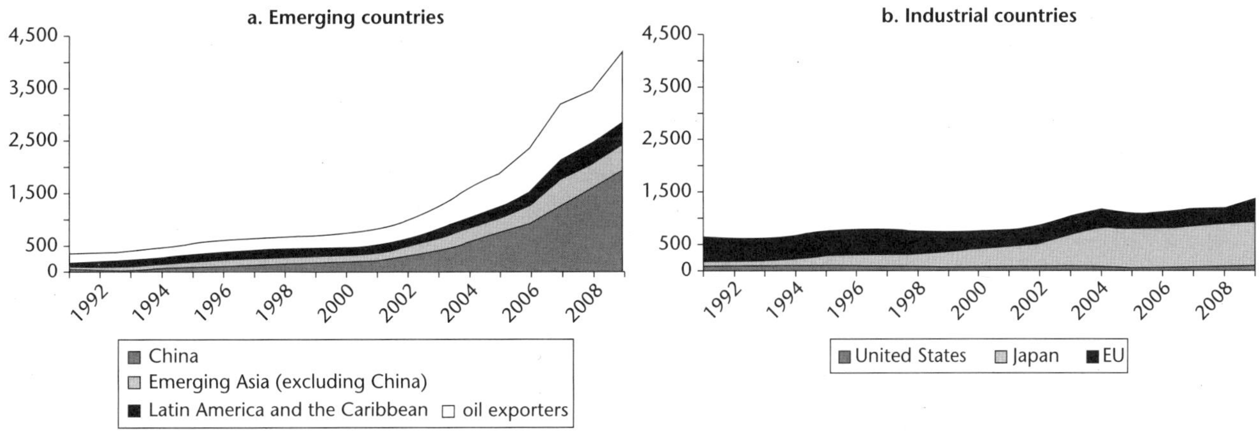

Source: World Development Indicators (database), World Bank, http://data.worldbank.org.

large, particularly in Asia, to be justified by the precaution motive alone.

If deliberate policy choices were the main force behind the accumulation of U.S. assets, however, official capital inflows to the United States should predominate over private flows. Figure 3.7, though, shows that the picture is more mixed. Net purchases of U.S. assets by central banks and other government bodies from emerging markets in Latin America, Asia, and the Middle East have grown increasingly large in the 2000s. After the onset of the crisis in 2007, they became the sole source of inflows from these countries. But in the years up to 2007, non-official investors accounted for the majority of emerging-market inflows to the U.S. economy.

The predominance of private capital in the total flows from emerging markets in the run-up to the crisis lends some support to the first version of the equilibrium approach: that global imbalances are primarily caused by asymmetries in the supply of or demand for international assets. Forbes (2010) offers some corroborating evidence, based on an analysis of the geographical origin of private capital flows to the United States. She finds that investors from countries with less-developed financial markets tend to hold greater shares of their investment portfolios in the United States, which is in accordance with the equilibrium approach espoused by Caballero, Farhi, and Gourinchas (2008a, 2008b) and Mendoza, Quadrini, and Rios-Bull (2009) discussed above.

The Future of Global Imbalances and Implications for Developing Countries

The world crisis has led to a reduction, or at least a temporary one, in global imbalances. Indeed, the current account deficit of the United States, measured as a proportion of GDP, has fallen to less than half of its peak—from 6.1 percent of GDP in the second quarter of 2006 to 2.8 percent in the second quarter of 2009 (figure 3.8). Moreover, the decline accelerated during 2009, undoubtedly helped by the recession.[7] The contraction of the external imbalance of the United States reflects, on the one hand, the decline of private investment, especially in construction, and, on the other hand, an increase in private saving.

Thus, are global imbalances going to disappear? It is difficult to give a conclusive answer about their future. It depends on a constellation of real and financial forces whose evolution is difficult to predict. Nevertheless, it may be useful to think in terms of two broad scenarios—the return of global imbalances versus the narrowing of global imbalances—and their consequences for developing countries' growth strategies.

The Return of Global Imbalances

To the extent that the deep determinants of the imbalances remain largely unchanged, global imbalances may well be restored after the crisis. Several indicators seem to point to their likely return.

First of all, the crisis did not lead to a "sudden stop" of capital flows to the United States, which could have given rise to a disorderly adjustment of global imbalances and an abrupt depreciation of the dollar. Instead of the depreciation that many had predicted, the dollar experienced an initial appreciation (see again figure 3.4). International investors "flew to safety" in low-risk U.S. Treasury debt, at the expense of all risky assets—from corporate debt to emerging-market assets. The dollar became the reserve

Figure 3.7. Gross Capital Inflows to the United States from Emerging Markets, 2000–09

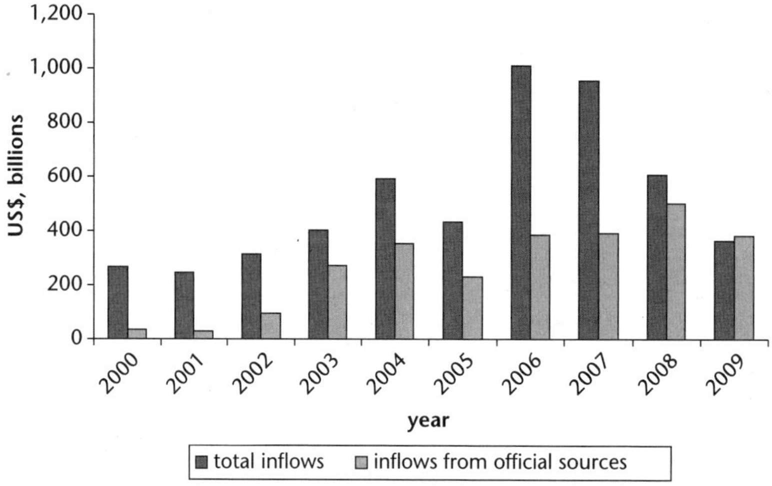

Source: International Economics Accounts (database), Bureau of Economic Analysis, http://www.bea.gov/international.

Figure 3.8. U.S. Current Account as a Percentage of GDP, Quarters 2 and 4, 1990–2010

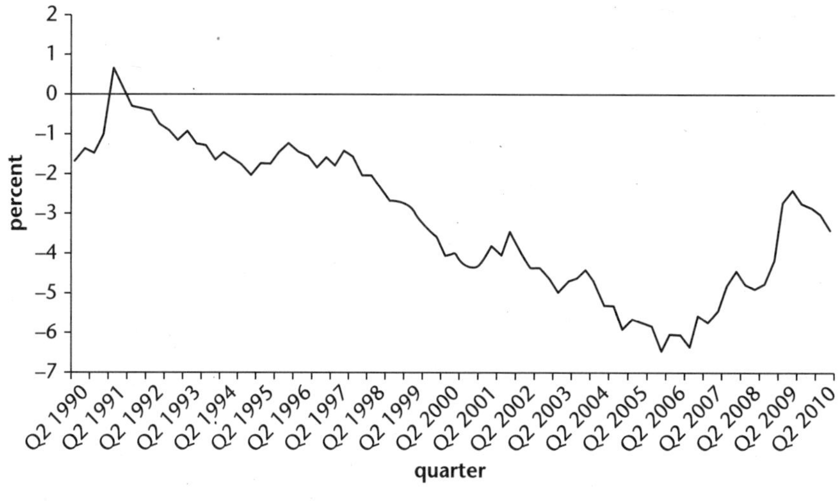

Source: International Economics Accounts (database), Bureau of Economic Analysis, http://www.bea.gov/international.

currency of last resort, and the government of the United States, the borrower of last resort. Paradoxically, the United States, undeniably the source of the crisis, also turned out to be the last refuge of international investors.

Throughout the global turmoil, the United States has had no difficulty financing its (narrowed) external imbalance. However, capital flows to the United States have undergone important changes (see figure 3.9). Capital flows from nonresident investors were positive and followed an upward trend from the late 1970s until late 2006. Capital flows from resident investors in recent decades were mostly negative, indicating capital outflows from the United States. However, at the onset of the subprime turmoil in mid-2007, these patterns changed abruptly: capital inflows from nonresidents collapsed, and outflows of residents reversed, reflecting capital repatriation by residents to stem losses in domestic markets or to seek safe haven from the global turbulence. In 2009, however, the data reveal a return to precrisis trends: capital inflows of foreign investors and outflows of resident investors.

Figure 3.10 offers an additional look at the capital flow pattern. Foreign investors steadily accumulated all types of U.S. assets until 2008. As the crisis hit in 2008, investors withdrew from U.S. assets for a short time, selling off agency bonds in particular. Thereafter, investors returned

Figure 3.9. U.S. Gross Capital Inflows in Long-term Securities from Residents and Nonresidents, 1989–2010

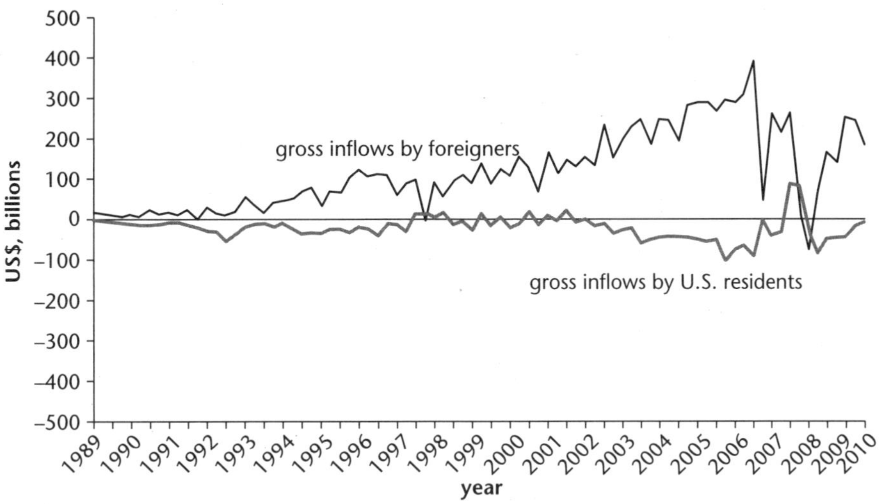

Source: U.S. Department of the Treasury, updated from De la Torre, Schmukler, and Servén 2009.

Figure 3.10. Net Foreign Purchases of U.S. Long-term Securities and China's Net Foreign Asset Position, Quarters 1 and 3, 2000–10

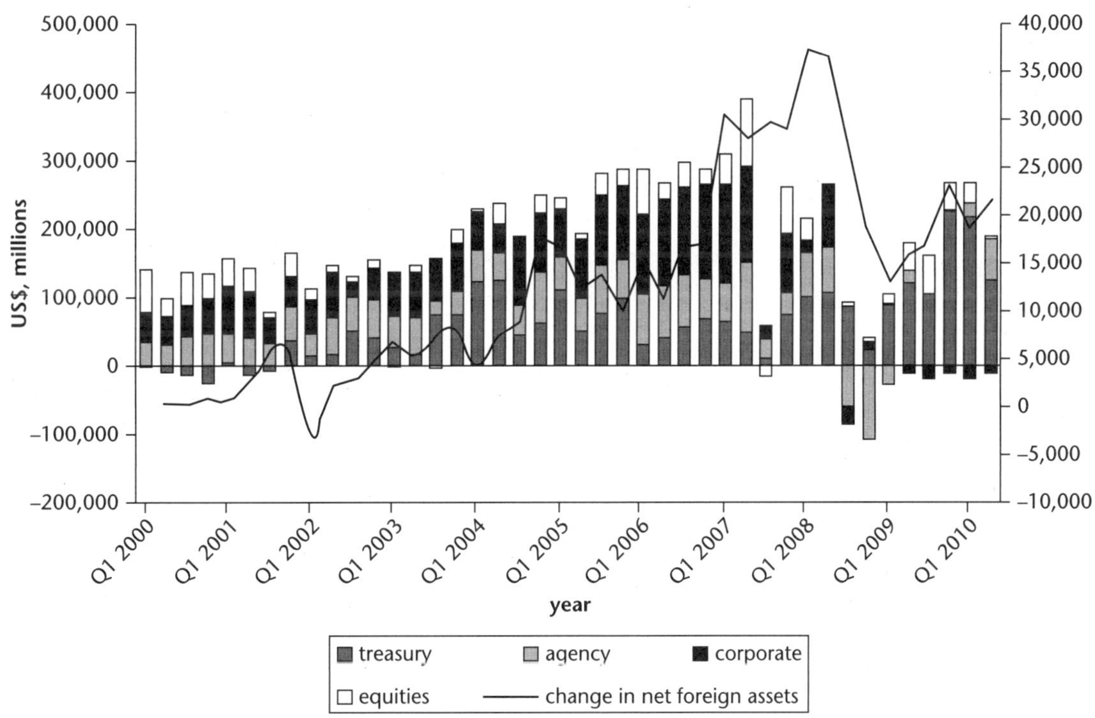

Source: Treasury International Capital System (database), U.S. Department of the Treasury, http://www.ustreas.gov/tic/ticsec.shtml; Statistics Database, People's Bank of China, http://www.pbc.gov.cn.

to large-scale acquisition of U.S. Treasuries and, to a more modest extent, equities. Interestingly, the capital inflow cycle of 2008–09 was closely matched by the timing of China's accumulation of foreign assets.

This pattern of capital inflows suggests that savers from developing countries will very likely continue to demand large volumes of financial assets from more developed markets, particularly in the absence of deep—and, to date, unforeseen—reforms to speed up the development of emerging countries' financial markets.

In addition, from a global perspective, the crisis has underscored the effectiveness of the self-insurance strategy pursued by emerging economies, as countries that had amassed large volumes of external assets managed to weather the global storm better than the rest. The crisis experience may encourage these and other countries to hold even bigger stocks of liquid foreign assets in the future, especially because even at the height of the turmoil some emerging economies feared weakening the confidence of international investors and were thus reluctant to use up their vast reserves (Aizenman and Sun 2009).

These global factors imply that the uphill pattern of capital flows is likely to persist. Indeed, recent forecasts of the International Monetary Fund (IMF) of China's gap between saving and investment suggest little decline in the external surplus from its high precrisis levels (figure 3.11, panel a). In turn, from the U.S. perspective, a quick rebound of the economy from the crisis could lead the way to the recovery of world trade and commodity prices and firm up the comeback of capital flows from emerging countries. Furthermore, the record U.S. public deficits could well prevail over the rise in private saving prompted by the fall in asset prices and household net worth, halting (although perhaps not reversing) the decline of the current account deficit (figure 3.11, panel b).

For small developing countries, this scenario would come close to business as usual, at least for some time. In a context of rapid recovery, Asian emerging countries could continue to pursue their export-led growth strategy based on currency undervaluation, further fueling the return of global imbalances. One potentially important difference, however, is that in the postcrisis world improved financial regulation, as well as enhanced investor awareness, will likely bring to an end the underpricing of risk that characterized the run-up to the global financial crisis. As a result, the cost of capital, especially for developing countries, is likely to be higher than it was in the precrisis world, so that the efficiency of investment will become a more pressing concern from the perspective of growth.

Vanishing Global Imbalances

Although less likely, a sustained narrowing of global imbalances could result from several causes. First, new mechanisms for diversifying international risk (such as the contingent credit facility recently established by the IMF) might begin to reduce the incentives for self-insurance. Governments in emerging economies could then diversify their portfolios away from low-yield short-term foreign assets and into more profitable investment opportunities. In turn, this decline in emerging countries' reserve holdings would help reduce systemic risk in the global financial system.

Second, a shift in portfolio diversification by international savers away from U.S. assets would also contribute to a narrowing of global imbalances. While savers have been diversifying since the late 1990s, the rate of diversification could accelerate in the face of renewed doubts about the future performance of the U.S. economy and the dollar, or if the recent turmoil in the U.S. financial system were to weaken the perceived appeal of U.S. assets.

Third, an early withdrawal of fiscal stimuli in the United States and other advanced countries would also reduce global imbalances. Such a course of action, however, could also delay the world recovery and put in jeopardy the export-led growth strategy pursued by a number of emerging markets. Although China and other major developing countries have weathered the crisis reasonably well thus far, they have done so in the context of aggressive fiscal stimuli in advanced countries. A reversal of the fiscal expansions in rich countries, and a longer-lasting global slump, would imply a further slowdown in global demand for developing-country exports.

From the perspective of low-income countries, the increase in import demand from middle-income economies could pick up some of the slack (see the chapters by Hanson in this volume). Low-income countries might then be able to offset, at least in part, the slowdown in demand from the

Figure 3.11. Saving and Investment Forecasts for China and the United States as a Percentage of GDP, 1991–2013

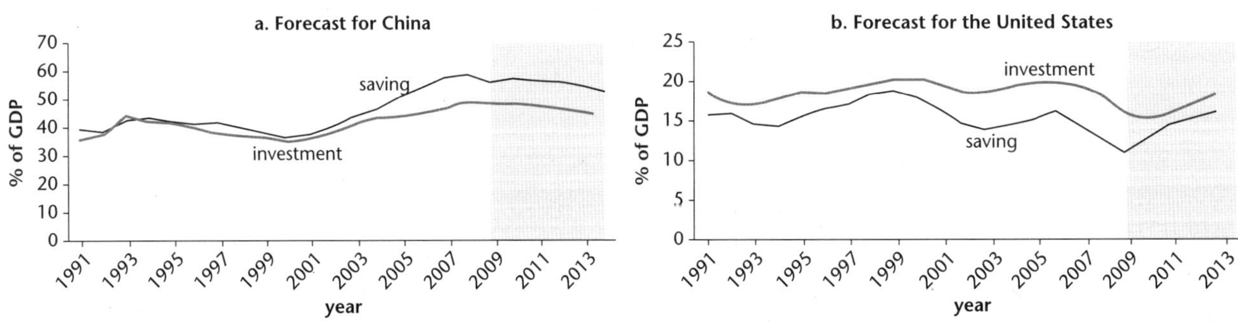

Source: World Economic Outlook (database), IMF, http://www.imf.org/external/ns/cs.aspx?id=28.
Note: The forecasts are shown in the shaded areas.

advanced economies. However, the export-led growth strategy pursued by a number of middle-income countries, notably in East Asia, would come under stress if global demand were to fall.

Promoting Growth in a Postcrisis World

Developing countries could encourage growth through several policy measures that take global imbalances into account. First, surplus emerging markets could rebalance their economies through an increased reliance on inward-looking growth. Such a shift may have already started, as suggested by China's massive fiscal stimulus implemented in 2009 with the stated objective of easing the economy's dependence on growth of world export markets.[8] In the short run, the stimulus helped China maintain its high growth rate, but concerns have arisen recently about the efficiency of the expenditures involved, as well as their possible contribution to asset bubbles.

In general, an orderly rebalancing of emerging economies with strong external positions and sound macroeconomic frameworks would also likely require an adjustment of exchange rates to reduce the accumulation of foreign assets and encourage domestic demand (Blanchard and Milesi-Ferreti 2009). Policy measures would also be needed to attack entrenched distortions, such as those causing excessively high saving rates (both in household and in corporate sectors) and those hampering development of the financial system. Indeed, while high saving rates in China and other emerging Asian countries reflect, in part, frugality and deep-rooted cultural values,[9] they are also partly attributable to weak social protection systems (Carroll and Jeanne 2009). As such, the strengthening of social safety nets underway in China and other emerging markets will likely reduce exorbitant household saving rates and promote consumption.[10] The process may take considerable time, but it should eventually allow a substantial increase in domestic demand.[11]

In China, and to a lesser extent in other surplus emerging markets, the distortions behind high corporate saving should also be addressed. Large state subsidies, monopolistic conditions, and fast growth have all generated massive profits for some Chinese sectors. Since the fiscal reform in 1994, however, most state-owned enterprises have not distributed dividends to shareholders or the state, choosing instead to retain their profits to finance potentially inefficient investment in the Chinese corporate sector (Kuijs 2005, 2006). A requirement for state-owned enterprises to distribute dividends could help channel saving into more productive uses through financial markets or would perhaps boost consumption.[12]

Another factor behind high corporate saving is the lack of financial options, such as a deep corporate bond market, which encourages firms to retain their earnings to finance future investments. In addition, repressed interest rates on alternative assets (bank deposits, for example) give firms an incentive to recycle their retained earnings into further investments, including those in marginally productive projects. Reforms to speed up the development of bond and equity markets would reduce firms' incentives to retain earnings and undertake possibly inefficient investments.

A different approach to speeding growth in developing countries in the postcrisis world is to actively promote the expansion of modern, high-value-added sectors through tax-cum-subsidy industrial policies (Rodrik 2009). In theory, these can be designed to replicate the effects of undervalued real exchange rates, that is, by encouraging the growth of tradable goods industries, without the dampening down of domestic demand and the accumulation of foreign assets that so far have characterized neomercantilist policies (and further increased global imbalances).

The risk of such a policy, however, is that the government, rather than the discipline of world markets, would dictate the sector composition of growth. Moreover, such a policy strategy would run counter to existing World Trade Organization agreements. More generally, it is subject to the same caveats and controversies that have long surrounded the use of industrial policy. While its theoretical justification is clear, its practical implementation often runs into insurmountable difficulties because governments might not have sufficient information to identify the "right" products or industries and because institutional weaknesses common in developing countries make such interventions prone to rent seeking and corruption[13]—and possibly even detrimental to the efficient allocation of resources, which is key to growth in developing economies.

Conclusion

The nature of global imbalances, their role in the world crisis, and their likely path in the postcrisis world have taken center stage in the debate over the international economic outlook. Although the crisis has temporarily reduced the magnitude of global imbalances, their future is far from certain. Absent radical national and global policy action, the structural distortions at the root of the imbalances are likely to remain in place, suggesting that global imbalances will return. In such a case, the global environment for developing economies could show little change relative to the precrisis situation, although stricter prudential regulation of the financial system postcrisis and a renewed perception of risk might lead to a persistent increase in the cost of capital and make its efficient use an even higher priority than before, particularly for deficit developing countries.

It is also possible, however, although less likely, that other forces triggered by the crisis would lead to a significant narrowing of global imbalances in the future. In that case, advanced countries' import demand growth could slow, and thereby pose a challenge for developing countries—particularly for surplus emerging markets that pursue export-led growth. Rising South-South trade might fill part of the global demand gap, but not all. The remedy would be for surplus developing countries to increase their reliance on inward-looking growth. Policy responses should emphasize reducing excessive savings and increasing domestic consumption and investment.

Notes

1. For instance, since the fiscal reform in 1994, large enterprises have the right to retain their profits.

2. This is the so-called "Lucas paradox"; see Lucas (1990).

3. Excluding the possibility of default and abstracting from capital gains and losses on external assets and liabilities.

4. They argue that if assets are valued according to the income they generate, the value of U.S. assets held abroad is much larger than officially measured. They term this discrepancy *dark matter* and attribute it to intangible assets such as superior technology and organizational knowledge embedded in foreign direct investment.

5. For example, for the case of China, Cline and Williamson (2008) survey existing estimates of the equilibrium value of the renminbi. Only 1 of the 18 studies in their survey concludes that the renminbi is overvalued. On average, the estimates indicate substantial renminbi undervaluation—on the order of 20 percent for the real effective exchange rate and 40 percent for the nominal bilateral renminbi-dollar exchange rate.

6. This of course is closely related to the explanations based on asset demand of Mendoza et al. (2009) and Carroll and Jeanne (2009) summarized earlier. In both cases, the underlying force is the lack of adequate insurance mechanisms. The main difference is that now the focus is on country-level insurance against external shocks rather than on individual insurance against idiosyncratic shocks.

7. Recent International Monetary Fund estimates, reflected in figure 3.1 above, suggest that the U.S. current account deficit fell to less than 1 percent of world GDP in 2009, as opposed to 1.2 percent in 2008.

8. However, recent signals from Chinese authorities do not offer much indication of an impending change in growth strategy, in spite of pressures from the IMF, the United States, and other advanced countries ("Wen Dismisses Currency Pressure" 2009).

9. For example, Wei and Zhang (2009) attribute the high household saving rates in China to a rising sex ratio imbalance and an increasingly competitive marriage market in the country.

10. The top stated priorities of the 2010 Chinese People's Congress included establishing a safety net of pension, health care, and unemployment benefits and providing free primary and secondary education ("China Wows to Improve Social Safety Net" 2010).

11. In China, this process may be already underway. For example, car sales recently exceeded those in the United States for the first time, partly as a result of tax incentives to buy cars with small engines ("China Auto Sale Surge" 2009).

12. The Chinese government announced some time ago its intention to require state-owned enterprises to pay dividends but did not specify when such policy would take place ("China Sets Dividend Scale for Its State-Owned Firms" 2007).

13. In fact, undervaluation through reserve hoarding can be viewed as a way to achieve the same objective, overcoming (at a cost) these obstacles; see Korinek and Servén (2010).

Bibliography

Acharya, V., and P. Schnabl. 2009. "Do Global Banks Spread Global Imbalances? The Case of Asset-Backed Commercial Paper during the Financial Crisis of 2007–09." NBER Working Paper 16079, National Bureau of Economic Research, Cambridge, MA.

Adrian, T., and M. Shin. 2009. "Money, Liquidity and Monetary Policy." *American Economic Review* 99: 600–605.

Aizenman, J., and J. Lee. 2007. "International Reserves: Precautionary vs Mercantilist Views." *Open Economies Review* 18: 191–214.

Aizenman, J., and Y. Sun. 2009. "The Financial Crisis and Sizable International Reserves Depletion: From 'Fear of Floating' to the 'Fear of Losing International Reserves'?" NBER Working Paper 15308, National Bureau of Economic Research, Cambridge, MA.

Bernanke, B. 2005. "The Global Saving Glut and the U.S. Current Account Deficit." Federal Reserve Board of Governors. http://www.federalreserve.gov/boarddocs/speeches/2005/200503102/default.htm.

Blanchard, O., F. Giavazzi, and F. Sa. 2005. "The U.S. Current Account and the Dollar." Brookings Papers on Economic Activity, Brookings Institution, Washington, DC.

Blanchard, O., and G. Milesi-Ferretti. 2009. "Global Imbalances: In Midstream." IMF Staff Position Note, International Monetary Fund, Washington, DC.

Caballero, R. 2010. "The Other Imbalance and the Financial Crisis." NBER Working Paper 15636, National Bureau of Economic Research, Cambridge, MA.

Caballero, R., E. Farhi, and P. Gourinchas. 2008a. "An Equilibrium Model of Global Imbalances and Low Interest Rates." *American Economic Review* 98 (1): 358–393.

———. 2008b. "Financial Crash, Commodity Prices, and Global Imbalances." *Brookings Papers on Economic Activity* 1–55.

Carroll, C., and O. Jeanne. 2009. "A Tractable Model of Precautionary Reserves, Net Foreign Assets, or Sovereign Wealth Funds." NBER Working Paper 15228, National Bureau of Economic Research, Cambridge, MA.

"China Auto Sale Surge." 2009. *Wall Street Journal.* September 9.

"China Sets Dividend Scale for Its State-Owned Firms." 2007. *Wall Street Journal.* December 12.

"China Wows to Improve Social Safety Net." 2010. Associated Press. March 8.

Cline, W., and J. Williamson. 2008. "Estimates of the Equilibrium Exchange Rate of the Renminbi: Is There a Consensus and If Not, Why Not?" In *Debating China's Exchange Rate Policy*, ed. M. Goldstein and N. Lardy, 131–54. Washington, DC: Peterson Institute of International Economics.

Curcuru, S., C. Thomas, and F. Warnock. 2008. "Current Account Sustainability and Relative Reliability." NBER Working Paper 14295, National Bureau of Economic Research, Cambridge, MA.

De la Torre, A., S. Schmukler, and L. Servén. 2009. "Back to Global Imbalances?" http://www.roubini.com/globalmacro-monitor/257276/back_to_global_imbalances.

Engel, C., and J. Rogers. 2006. "The U.S. Current Account Deficit and the Expected Value of World Output." *Journal of Monetary Economics* 53: 1063–93.

Forbes, K. 2010. "Why Do Foreigners Invest in the United States?" *Journal of International Economics* 80: 3–21.

Gourinchas, P., and H. Rey. 2007a. "From World Banker to World Venture Capitalist: The US External Adjustment and the Exorbitant Privilege."

In *G7 Current Account Imbalances: Sustainability and Adjustment,* ed. R. Clarida, 11-66. Chicago, IL: University of Chicago Press.

———. 2007b. "International Financial Adjustment." *Journal of Political Economy* 115 (4): 665–703.

Hausmann R., and F. Sturzenegger. 2004. "Global Imbalances or Bad Accounting? The Missing Dark Matter in the Wealth of Nations." Center for International Development Working Paper 124, Harvard University, Cambridge, MA.

Iossifov, P., M. Čihák, and A. ar Shanghavi. 2008. "Interest Rate Elasticity of Residential Housing Prices." IMF Working Paper WP/08/247, International Monetary Fund, Washington, DC.

Jeanne, O., and R. Ranciere. 2009. "The Optimal Level of International Reserves for Emerging Market Countries: A New Formula and Some Applications." http://www.econ.jhu.edu/People/Jeanne/JeanneRanciere_Feb09.pdf.

Kashyap, A. Forthcoming. "Comment on 'The Financial Crisis and Global Policy Reforms' by Barry Eichengreen." In *Asia and the Global Financial Crisis.* San Francisco: Federal Reserve Bank of San Francisco.

Korinek, A., and L. Servén. 2010 "Undervaluation through Foreign Reserve Accumulation: Static Losses, Dynamic Gains." Policy Research Working Paper 5250, Washington, DC, World Bank.

Kraay, A., N. Loayza, L. Servén, and J. Ventura. 2005. "Country Portfolios." *Journal of the European Economic Association* 3 (4): 914–45.

Kraay, A., and J. Ventura. 2005. "The Dot-Com Bubble, the Bush Deficits, and the US Current Account." NBER Working Paper 11543, National Bureau of Economic Research, Cambridge, MA.

Kuijs, L. 2005. "Investment and Savings in China." Policy Research Working Paper 3633, World Bank, Washington, DC.

———. L. 2006. "China in the Future: A Large Net Saver or Net Borrower?" Mimeo, World Bank.

Laibson, D., and J. Mollerstrom. 2010. "Capital Flows, Consumption Booms and Asset Bubbles: A Behavioural Alternative to the Savings Glut Hypothesis." NBER Working Paper 15759. National Bureau of Economic Research, Cambridge, MA.

Lucas, R. 1990. "Why Doesn't Capital Flow from Rich to Poor Countries?" *American Economic Review* 80: 92–96.

Mendoza, E., V. Quadrini and J. Rios-Rull. 2009. "Financial Integration, Financial Deepness and Global Imbalances." *Journal of Political Economy* 117: 371–416.

Nguyen, H. 2010. "Valuation Effects with Transitory and Trend Productivity Shocks." Research Working Paper 5174, World Bank, Washington, DC.

Obstfeld. M., and K. Rogoff. 2005. "The Unsustainable U.S. Current Account Position, Revisited." http://elsa.berkeley.edu/~obstfeld/NBER_ final.pdf.

———. 2009. "Global Imbalances and the Financial Crisis: Products of a Common Cause." Mimeo.

Portes, R. 2009. "Global Imbalances." In *Macroeconomic Stability and Financial Regulation: Key Issues for the G20,* ed. Mathias Dewatripont, Xavier Freixas, and Richard Portes, 19–26. London: Centre for Economic Policy Research.

Prasad, E. 2009. "Rebalancing Growth in Asia." Discussion Paper 4298, Institute for the Study of Labor (IZA), Bonn.

Rodrik, D. 2009. "Growth after the Crisis." Discussion Paper 7480, Centre for Economic Policy Research, London.

Roubini, N. 2009. "Will the Bretton Woods 2 (BW2) Regime Collapse Like the Original Bretton Woods Regime Did? The Coming End Game of BW2." http://www.rgemonitor.com/.

Wei, S.-J., and X. Zhang. 2009. "The Competitive Saving Motive: Evidence from Rising Sex Ratios and Savings Rates in China." NBER Working Paper 15093, National Bureau of Economic Research, Cambridge, MA.

"Wen Dismisses Currency Pressure." 2009. *Financial Times.* December 27.

4

REBALANCING TRADE AFTER THE CRISIS

Caroline Freund

Global trade imbalances have surged since the early 1990s. Figure 4.1 shows an index of global trade imbalances (GTIs)—the sum of the absolute values of trade balances across countries—in log levels. The average annual growth of global imbalances was 11 percent from 1990 to 2007, relative to only 1 percent in the previous 20 years. In contrast to global imbalances, global trade grew at a strong and steady pace of about 6 percent a year over the whole period.

The growth of global imbalances has been a cause for concern since the new millennium, when the GTI approached a level nearly twice the previous peak. As discussed in earlier chapters, some economists believe the surge in global imbalances contributed to the onset and severity of the financial crisis. For instance, Bernanke (2009) argues that imbalances were an important cause of the crisis because they depressed global interest rates, leading investors to search for higher yields and to underprice risk.

Obstfeld and Rogoff (2009) suggest that large global imbalances could also be a symptom of financial distress, without being a cause. They contend that policies pursued in Asian countries and the United States led to unstable financial conditions and global imbalances. As time passed, ever-growing imbalances magnified financial instabilities. Whether global imbalances are a cause or a symptom, however, they are malignant and are associated with an unstable financial system. A more stable financial system must therefore involve more balanced capital flows.

A world with more balanced capital flows has important implications for bilateral trade and global trade growth. As capital has migrated to the United States, so have imports. With more balanced capital flows, the United States could no longer be a rapidly growing market for the world's exports. And, with more balanced capital flows, China could not maintain export growth at precrisis levels. If capital flows do become more balanced, what will drive future trade growth is not clear.

The financial crisis has already shocked trade patterns, leading to a reduction in real trade of 12.2 percent in 2009,[1] a magnitude not seen since the Great Depression. The collapse of trade can be explained in part by the global imbalance view of the crisis. This view maintains that because of a global savings glut, global interest rates were severely depressed. The crisis caused interest rates to shoot up. Rising interest rates, in turn, led to a sharp drop in investment and consumption in borrower countries. The effects on industrial production and consumer goods, and therefore on trade, were especially strong. As both exports and imports fell dramatically, so too did the gap between them, immediately cutting imbalances to respectable levels.

The important question is whether the fall in trade and global imbalances is a short-run phenomenon or a structural change brought about by the crisis.[2] If it is a short-run change, many of the same issues that plagued the financial system in recent years are likely to reemerge. If it is a shift to more balanced flows, the world may be moving to a more stable financial system. In that case, however, trade patterns will look very different in the future.

In this chapter, we examine the extent to which the crisis is responsible for rebalancing trade and whether that shift is sustainable. Unlike other papers on current account adjustment, we approach the question from the real side.[3] First, we investigate how trade balances have adjusted following the financial crisis. Specifically, we calculate how much of the adjustment is a result of the drop in trade and how much is a result of rebalancing between export and import growth. We argue that a shift due to the drop in trade is likely to be reversed as global income expands but that rebalancing likely reflects shifts in attitudes toward saving and investment.

Figure 4.1. Global Imbalances and Global Trade, 1970–2007
logarithms normalized to 1970 = 0

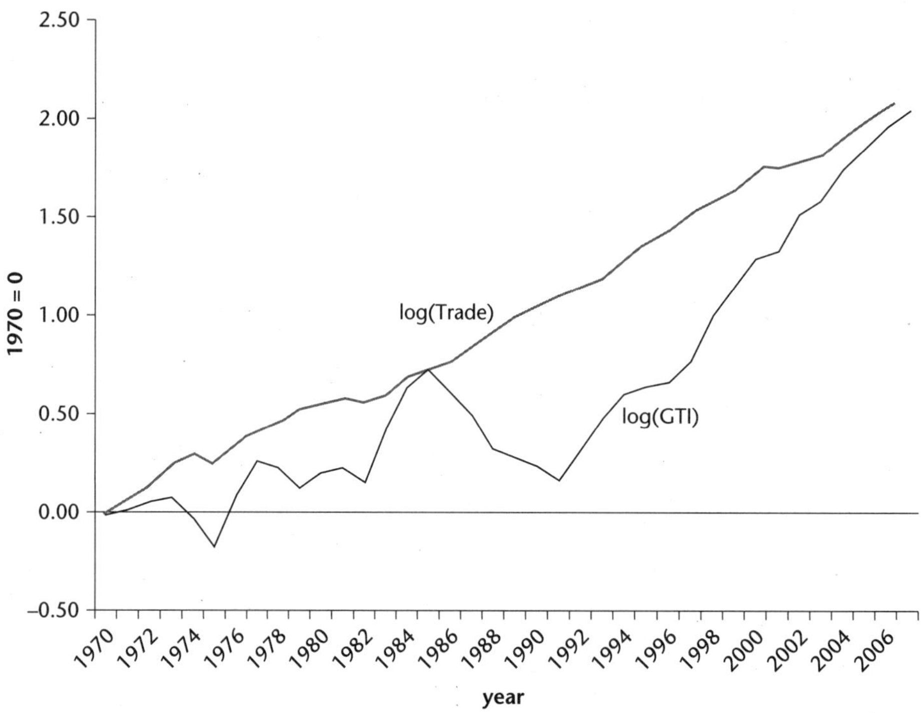

Source: Author's calculations and World Development Indicators (database), World Bank, http://data.worldbank.org.
Note: Data are in constant U.S. dollars, for a balanced sample of 73 countries that make up about 85 percent of global trade. Data are in logs and normalized to start from zero.

Second, we examine which countries are well positioned to drive trade growth and which countries are likely to benefit from changing demand patterns. Four large emerging-market countries have fared remarkably well in the crisis: Brazil, China, India, and Indonesia. In these countries, imports in 2009 increased above precrisis levels. Standard economic models imply that these rapidly growing emerging markets should be net importers of capital and goods; yet all but India have been running sizable trade surpluses in recent years. Conditions, however, may have now changed so that more typical patterns may emerge: that is, imports may grow rapidly in these large emerging markets as they become the future of trade growth.

The rest of this chapter is organized as follows. The next section examines how much of the decline in global imbalances can be explained by rebalancing and how much is due to the fall in trade. The following section discusses the changing patterns of global demand and the sustainability of those trends. The final section concludes with a discussion of the main risks that lie ahead. The presentation here focuses on results and policy implications and is nontechnical. For full details of data and methodology, readers are referred to the working paper version of this chapter.

The Decline in Global Imbalances: Rebalancing versus the Trade Collapse

Is an adjustment of global imbalances underway? And what would that imply for the pattern of trade and world trade growth? Using aggregate trade data, we find strong evidence that imbalances are adjusting: they fell by 26 percent from 2007 to 2009.[4] In this section, we analyze how much of the change in global imbalances during 2009 is due to rebalancing and how much is a result of the collapse in trade.

Average Change in Trade

Indeed, 69 percent of countries experienced a smaller surplus or smaller deficit following the crisis (table 4.1). In the typical country, more than two-thirds of the reduction was the result of rebalancing, whether the finding is based on a country's *average* change in trade or on the *global* average change in trade. Moreover, significant rebalancing in countries such as the United States and China appears to be underway. This change is a positive sign, because as trade expands after the crisis, major shifts will be required to maintain global balances.

Table 4.1. Change in Trade Imbalances due to Declines in Trade and Rebalancing Selected Economies, 2009

Economy	Economy average trade growth		Global trade growth		Change in net exports (US$, millions)	Change in net exports (%)	Net exports/ GDP (2007)
	Trade drop	Rebalancing	Trade drop	Rebalancing			
Algeria	−10.5	110.5	14.3	85.7	−26,600	−82	23.21
Australia	−7.2	107.2	16.6	83.4	11,600	−70	−2.01
Austria	1.4	98.6	1.1	98.9	−5,564	−1,044	0.14
Bolivia	−56.4	156.4	37.5	62.5	−403	−31	9.93
Bosnia and Herzegovina	58.1	41.9	90.0	10.0	724	−13	−37.12
Brazil	−0.7	100.7	30.6	69.4	−15,300	−38	3.08
Bulgaria	38.8	61.2	26.8	73.2	4,392	−44	−25.00
Canada	17.7	82.3	10.4	89.6	−44,600	−113	2.83
Cape Verde	−334.9	434.9	102.3	−2.3	82	−11	−51.29
Chile	36.8	63.2	28.1	71.9	−9,960	−42	14.94
China	−7.5	107.5	47.5	52.5	−64,600	−25	7.71
Colombia	−4.4	104.4	12.1	87.9	2,804	−97	−1.38
Croatia	81.8	18.2	57.4	42.6	2,746	−20	−22.88
Cyprus	98.1	1.9	119.4	−19.4	709	−10	−34.45
Dominican Republic	64.9	−64.9	129.0	−29.0	735	−9	−19.75
Ecuador	−0.6	100.6	2.9	97.1	−1,724	−403	0.93
El Salvador	39.8	60.2	43.6	56.4	1,270	−27	−23.64
Estonia	34.8	65.2	15.2	84.8	3,580	−77	−22.19
Faeroe Islands	11.3	88.7	12.7	87.3	248	−92	–
Finland	38.4	61.6	16.0	84.0	−6,105	−73	3.33
Germany	47.5	52.5	40.8	59.2	−76,800	−29	8.09
Honduras	−2.7	102.7	59.5	40.5	814	−20	−34.49
Hungary	0.4	99.6	0.3	99.7	5,758	−4,089	−0.10
Iceland	25.5	74.5	9.6	90.4	2,378	−122	−9.73
Indonesia	−31.9	131.9	23.3	76.7	−19,900	−50	9.21
Israel	26.3	73.7	24.1	75.9	4,951	−49	−6.00
Italy	37.5	62.5	22.5	77.5	6,024	−52	−0.55
Japan	21.3	78.7	17.0	83.0	−63,200	−69	2.09
Jordan	−18,149.9	18,249.9	26,152.3	−26,052.3	4	0	−53.21
Kazakhstan	807.7	−707.7	828.5	−728.5	−212	−1	15.00
Latvia	34.9	65.1	16.4	83.6	5,208	−71	−25.23
Lithuania	19.4	80.6	15.5	84.5	5,498	−76	−18.65
Luxembourg	379.4	−279.4	231.1	−131.1	310	−5	−12.24

(continued)

Table 4.1. *(continued)*

Economy	Economy average trade growth		Global trade growth		Change in net exports (US$, millions)	Change in net exports (%)	Net exports/ GDP (2007)
	Trade drop	Rebalancing	Trade drop	Rebalancing			
Malta	289.1	–189.1	143.1	–43.1	145	–8	–23.90
Mexico	30.2	69.8	21.9	78.1	5,396	–54	–1.01
Moldova	77.6	22.4	95.5	4.5	348	–12	–64.60
Netherlands	62.2	37.8	79.6	20.4	–8,130.3	–15	7.09
New Zealand	14.7	85.3	14.0	86.0	3,274.1	–83	–3.02
Norway	190.3	–90.3	166.7	–66.7	–3,925.9	–7	14.33
Pakistan	8.4	91.6	151.1	–51.1	1,189	–8	–11.00
Peru	–6.3	106.3	40.2	59.8	–2,413	–29	7.53
Philippines	297.4	–197.4	150.7	–50.7	392	–8	–3.61
Poland	14.1	85.9	22.2	77.8	13,500	–53	–5.98
Portugal	1,269.0	–1,169.0	1,115.6	–1,015.6	281	–1	–12.18
Romania	20.7	79.3	21.5	78.5	16,300	–54	–17.59
Russian Federation	96.7	3.3	79.3	20.7	–19,300	–15	10.08
Senegal	–71.9	171.9	61.8	38.2	630	–19	–30.23
Serbia	45.5	54.5	56.2	43.8	2,027	–21	–
Singapore	24.3	75.7	35.0	65.0	–12,100	–33	21.24
Slovak Republic	6.3	93.7	4.4	95.6	2,766	–263	–1.25
Slovenia	34.4	65.6	22.8	77.2	1,494	–51	–6.19
South Africa	18.4	81.6	14.6	85.4	7,796	–80	–3.47
Spain	36.8	63.2	24.1	75.9	66,000	–49	–9.71
Sweden	80.2	19.8	42.4	57.6	–4,280	–28	3.44
Tanzania	–302.7	402.7	114.1	–14.1	406	–10	–23.26
Turkey	28.7	71.3	30.6	69.4	24,000	–38	–9.66
United Kingdom	71.6	28.4	39.9	60.1	53,200	–29	–6.46
United States	40.0	60.0	31.9	68.1	290,000	–37	–5.65
Zambia	40.1	59.9	78.5	21.5	–91	–15	5.55
Median	28.7	71.3	31.9	68.1	629.6	–36.7	–3.6

Imbalance-widening economy	Economy average trade growth		Global trade growth		Change in net exports (US$, millions)	Change in net exports (%)	Net exports/ GDP (2007)
	Trade drop	Diverging growth	Trade drop	Diverging growth			
Albania	42.6	57.4	–106.9	206.9	–341	11	–28.35
Argentina	–13.9	113.9	–23.5	123.5	5,614	50	4.35
Armenia	–83.0	183.0	–78.5	178.5	–333	15	–24.30
Azerbaijan	3.1	96.9	–0.5	100.5	8,224	2,376	1.05
Belarus	–9.9	109.9	–18.1	118.1	–2,863	65	–9.82
Belgium	–352.7	452.7	–284.4	384.4	718	4	3.80
Czech Republic	–11.4	111.4	–13.5	113.5	3,716	86	2.53
Denmark	–9.8	109.8	–9.2	109.2	5,685	128	1.44
Egypt, Arab Rep.	53.4	46.6	–11.5	111.5	–11,000	101	–8.38
Ethiopia	83.3	16.7	–12.5	112.5	–4,238	94	–23.85
France	–350.4	450.4	–322.8	422.8	–2,116	4	–2.25
French Polynesia	–19.7	119.7	–121.6	221.6	–138	10	–
Hong Kong SAR, China	–28.3	128.3	–50.6	150.6	–5,426	23	–11.19
India	41.9	58.1	–81.5	181.5	–10,000	14	–5.81
Ireland	–33.0	133.0	–23.2	123.2	18,000	50	13.73
Korea, Rep.	–3.3	103.3	–6.6	106.6	25,800	176	1.46
Macao SAR, China	–299.3	399.3	–76.3	176.3	–565	15	–19.39
Macedonia, FYR	–45.5	145.5	–45.6	145.6	–480	26	–23.69
Malaysia	–100.0	200.0	–91.1	191.1	3,825	13	15.68
Mauritius	–154.8	254.8	–203.1	303.1	–96	6	–22.30
Mozambique	4.1	95.9	–7.6	107.6	–979	154	–7.97
Paraguay	78.2	21.8	–53.5	153.5	–677	22	–25.80
Switzerland	–2.3	102.3	–19.9	119.9	6,348	59	2.51
Taiwan, China	–246.5	346.5	–153.0	253.0	2,044	8	6.79
Thailand	–7.7	107.7	–33.9	133.9	4,796	34	5.56
Uruguay	44.7	55.3	–24.6	124.6	–369	48	–3.23
Zimbabwe	–3.4	103.4	–2.8	102.8	–1,092	425	–
Median	–9.9	109.9	–33.9	133.9	–333.3	34.5	–3.2
Median full sample	18.0	82.0	16.8	83.2	370.2	–14.8	–3.5

Source: Author's calculations based on the following databases: Datastream, Thomson Reuters, http://www.datastream.com; World Integrated Trade Solution (WITS), World Bank, http://wits.worldbank.org; World Development Indicators, World Bank, http://data.worldbank.org; National Statistics, Taiwan, China, http://eng.stat.gov.tw.

For the remaining 31 percent of countries, imbalances swelled. In the typical country, the trade drop caused imbalances to shrink by 10–34 percent, but this decline was more than offset by imbalance-expanding trade growth. The trade drop appears to have affected imbalances to a lesser extent when we employ country-specific trade growth rates. This is logical, however, because the methodology takes into account the fact that trade did not fall very much and even expanded in some of the countries with larger imbalances. Since the trade drop is smaller or absent, it has a smaller effect on imbalances.

What does this breakdown imply for the sustainability of the adjustment in global imbalances? The contraction in imbalances due to rebalancing is likely to be sustainable because it reflects changes in the underlying fundamentals, savings and investment. Rebalancing occurs when countries with large trade deficits have reduced their imports to a far greater extent than their exports and vice versa.

In contrast, the reduction of imbalances due to the sharp drop in trade is unlikely to be sustainable because a large drop in trade (such as the one that occurred in 2009) causes trade imbalances to retreat only if it affects exports and imports proportionately. If both imports and exports decline by a given percentage, the larger flow must decline by absolutely more and the difference will therefore also shrink. Thus, it follows that a reversal of the trade collapse would lead the proportion of the imbalance driven by trade to reemerge.

The Global Trade Imbalance

This section examines how the GTI was affected. Looking at the global trade balance, as opposed to the average change, puts more weight on large countries. It also better reflects the magnitude of the "global savings glut." Based on our sample, the GTI fell by 26 percent over the period 2007–09. Given that aggregate trade fell by about 11 percent, the trade drop contributed to about 42 percent of the decline in GTI. Moreover, rebalancing contributed 78 percent of the reduction in GTI (table 4.2).[5] Finally, we find that imbalance-augmenting trade growth contributed to expanding the GTI by 20 percent.[6]

Similar effects from rebalancing are also found using growth in country trade. In this case, however, the decline due to the trade drop is smaller (39.6 percent) because it takes into account that trade grew or fell by less than the global average in some countries. Expansion due to imbalance-augmenting growth is also smaller for this reason.

This phenomenon does not apply only to small countries. Three quarters of the decline in the global trade imbalance, which puts more weight on larger imbalances, stems from rebalancing. In sum, the trade drop was not the main reason behind the improvement in trade balances in 2009; instead, countries tended to rebalance trade flows.[7]

What Happened in the Asian Financial Crisis?

For a better understanding of whether the adjustment of global imbalances is sustainable over the medium to long term, we review the pattern of adjustment in the Asian crisis countries. The Asian financial crisis revealed a pattern similar to the recent crisis, with over 70 percent of countries showing greatly reduced imbalances immediately following the crisis (table 4.3). Four countries (the Republic of Korea, Malaysia, Singapore, and Thailand) show complete reversals, moving from a deficit to a large surplus. The adjustment in net exports was almost entirely due to rebalancing (92 percent), partly because the drop in trade was more moderate in the Asian crisis (9 percent on average) relative to the current event (15 percent).

What is especially striking is that the improvements in net exports tended to be sustained in the years following the crisis. Indeed, the Asian case shows that rebalancing as a result of major crises can be sustainable. In five out of the six economies with sizable deficits before the crisis (Hong Kong SAR, China; Korea; Singapore; Sri Lanka; and Thailand), the trade balance remained positive or continued improving over the next five years. Only the Philippines experienced a widening of the deficit after 1998, although it did not approach precrisis levels.

Table 4.2. Change in Global Trade Imbalance, 2007–09

Rebalancing	% Change in GTI	Trade drop	Rebalancing	Imbalance-augmenting growth
Global average % change in trade	26	39.6	78.1	–17.7
Country average % change in trade	26	42.5	78.2	–20.7

Source: Author's calculations based on the following databases: Datastream, Thomson Reuters, http://www.datastream.com; WITS, World Bank, http://wits.worldbank.org; World Development Indicators, World Bank, http://data.worldbank.org; National Statistics, Taiwan, China, http://eng.stat.gov.tw.

Table 4.3. Global Trade Balance Adjustment in Asian Crisis Economies, 1996–98

Economy	Economy average trade growth		Global trade growth		Change in net exports (US$, millions)	Change in net exports (%) 1996–98	Net exports/ GDP (1996)	Net exports/ GDP (1998)	Net exports/ GDP (2003)
	Trade drop	Rebalancing	Trade drop	Rebalancing					
Balancing									
Malaysia	0.2	99.8	0.0	100.0	14,800	–13,566	–0.11	20.42	18.18
Korea, Rep.	7.5	92.5	0.2	99.8	63,900	–282	–4.05	11.77	2.19
Singapore	10.8	89.2	0.3	99.7	12,400	–178	–7.51	6.63	17.1
Thailand	14.6	85.4	0.3	99.7	30,600	–171	–9.84	11.64	3.34
Philippines	–14.5	114.5	0.6	99.4	12,400	–95	–15.69	–1.03	–4.96
Taiwan, China	9.2	90.8	1.1	98.9	–8,250	–53	5.42	2.69	6.69
Hong Kong SAR, China	20.9	79.1	1.3	98.7	8,360	–43	–12.33	–6.59	–4.99
Sri Lanka	–50.5	150.5	3.8	96.2	211	–15	–10.36	–7.69	–7.58
Median balancing	8.3	91.7	0.5	99.5	12,400.0	–133.1	–8.7	4.7	2.8
Imbalance worsening									
India	4.4	95.6	–0.4	100.4	–6,040	152	–1.02	–2.38	–2.12
Indonesia	–11.8	111.8	–0.3	100.3	14,800	187	3.49	24.0	11.61
China	2.9	97.1	–0.2	100.2	32,500	244	1.55	4.58	1.49
Median imbalancing	–1.5	101.5	–0.3	100.3	13,753.3	194.3	1.3	8.7	3.7
Median full sample	4.4	95.6	0.3	99.7	12,400.0	–52.7	–4.1	4.6	2.2

Source: Author's calculations based on the following databases: Datastream, Thomson Reuters, http://www.datastream.com; WITS, World Bank, http://wits.worldbank.org; World Development Indicators, World Bank, http://data.worldbank.org; National Statistics, Taiwan, China, http://eng.stat.gov.tw.

Rebalancing across Countries and Future Trade Growth

Which countries are well positioned to drive trade growth in the future? While imports collapsed in most countries in 2009, four growing emerging markets (GEMs) bucked the trend. Indeed, Brazil, China, India, and Indonesia recorded positive import growth from 2007 to 2009. This section examines the recent emergence of the GEMs as drivers of trade growth and how this trend will affect exports from the rest of the world. First, the section discusses how rebalancing can occur and the role of these four countries in future trade growth. Then the focus shifts to a micro perspective and identifies the sectors and countries that will benefit from demand growth in the GEMs. And finally, the section discusses how much of import growth in these countries is at the intensive (old products) versus the extensive (new products) margin.

Rebalancing and Import Growth in the GEMs

Rebalancing can occur in three different ways: (a) both imports and exports decline, and the larger flow decreases by relatively more than the smaller flow; (b) the larger flow declines and the smaller flow increases; or (c) both flows expand, and the larger flow expands by relatively less than the smaller flow. These three modes have different impacts on global trade growth. The first way suggests that trade growth may stagnate in the near term as trade flows adjust, while the third way suggests positive trade growth and declining imbalances.

From 2007 to 2009, rebalancing occurred through the first mode in most countries: flows decreased and trade imbalances declined by relatively more because the bigger flow fell by a larger amount (table 4.4). However, in some countries, an *increase* in exports, imports, or both occurred following the crisis. For instance, imports increased in Brazil and China. Moreover, exports and imports both increased in India and Indonesia. These are four of the five largest countries in the world by population, making up over 40 percent of the total. Collectively, they accounted for 15 percent of the GTI in 2009. In theory, such fast-growing countries should be running external deficits and importing heavily for future growth.

To illustrate how these countries diverged from the rest of the world, figure 4.2 shows imports on a log scale and adjusted to begin at the same point in 2006. These four countries have seen a much stronger bounce back in imports than that observed in the rest of the world.

Moreover, while the surge in imports could be a temporary feature due to fiscal stimulus, this does not appear to be the case. China recorded a large fiscal stimulus in 2009, but Brazil, India, and Indonesia did not. Furthermore, a simple correlation between fiscal stimulus and import growth is small and insignificant, perhaps because most packages are geared toward domestic job expansion or because packages are slow to have an impact on import growth. Together with the rebalancing of imports and exports that has occurred, the continuation of import growth in these countries is a very positive sign. Indeed, these large emerging markets may be the future source of growth in trade.

Micro Effects

Import growth over the past 10 years has been robust, particularly for China and India. These two countries report nominal dollar export growth of over 500 percent. Figure 4.3 presents the sectors that are primarily responsible for the recent growth of imports in the GEMs. One of the most notable trends emerging in this figure is the sharp increase in imported fuels in all four countries.

Different patterns emerge among industrial goods, however. Overall, increases are recorded in machinery and transport and in miscellaneous manufactures, which include items such as prefabricated buildings, furniture, travel goods, clothing, footwear, and professional and scientific equipment. In particular, Brazil shows a jump in the imports of chemical products, China and Indonesia in miscellaneous manufactures, and India in machinery and transport.

When we examine exports to the GEMs as a share of total exports, interesting trends emerge among exporters at the regional and income group level. For regional trends, the share of exports to the GEMs has increased most in Sub-Saharan African countries, followed by South Asia (figure 4.4). With respect to income groupings, low-income countries, which have many of the natural resources needed for growth,[8] have seen an increasing share of their exports going to the GEMs, as have the high-income countries, which have capital goods. Middle-income countries, especially in Europe and Central Asia, have seen the smallest gains.

Intensive and Extensive Margins

Finally, consideration should be given to whether import growth in the GEMs is occurring at the intensive margin or at the extensive margin. Recent trade literature emphasizes the gains from trade as importing countries access new product varieties (that is, import growth at the extensive margin). For example, Broda and Weinstein (2006) find that 30 percent of U.S. import growth between 1972 and 2001 was in new varieties (the extensive margin). In addition, growth at the extensive margin would also suggest an additional welfare gain among the GEMs.

Table 4.4. Import and Export Growth in Deficit and Surplus Economies, 2007–09
percent

Deficit economy	Net exports/ GDP (2007)	Change in exports (%)	Change in imports (%)	Surplus economy	Net exports/ GDP (2007)	Change in exports (%)	Change in imports (%)
Iceland	−9.59	−15.78	−46.60	Ireland	13.67	−5.18	−28.11
Latvia	−25.43	−10.20	−39.49	Finland	3.39	−30.35	−25.96
Estonia	−21.73	−17.98	−35.49	Faeroe Islands	0.00	2.08	−22.88
Lithuania	−13.71	−4.01	−25.34	Sweden	3.42	−22.42	−21.89
Spain	−9.44	−11.32	−24.49	Taiwan, China	6.79	−17.34	−20.39
Romania	−17.69	0.40	−22.92	Denmark	1.44	−9.36	−15.64
Bulgaria	−25.40	−11.24	−22.65	Canada	2.77	−24.52	−15.31
United Kingdom	−5.47	−19.58	−22.43	Malaysia	15.94	−10.47	−15.23
Philippines	−3.50	−23.84	−22.38	Norway	14.39	−11.73	−15.01
United States	−5.76	−9.10	−20.26	Belgium	3.81	−14.13	−14.90
Malta	−23.74	−27.05	−20.25	Russian Federation	10.11	−14.39	−14.18
Italy	−0.55	−19.17	−19.92	Serbia	0.00	−5.44	−13.51
Slovenia	−6.17	−15.91	−19.41	Kazakhstan	14.30	−9.55	−13.27
South Africa	−3.42	−10.53	−19.04	Argentina	4.30	−0.56	−13.26
Slovak Republic	−1.25	−14.61	−18.57	Austria	0.14	−16.09	−12.58
Hungary	−0.10	−12.31	−18.36	Germany	8.07	−15.34	−11.94
Croatia	−23.00	−15.35	−17.98	Czech Republic	2.47	−8.16	−11.60
Turkey	−9.69	−4.79	−17.13	Japan	2.10	−18.42	−10.96
New Zealand	−2.92	−7.42	−17.08	Chile	14.61	−20.94	−9.71
Luxembourg	−12.28	−21.47	−16.97	Korea, Rep.	1.40	−2.14	−9.46
Mexico	−0.99	−15.51	−16.87	Netherlands	7.12	−9.49	−8.81
El Salvador	−23.21	−4.69	−16.72	Singapore	21.62	−9.75	−6.51
Israel	−6.10	−9.23	−16.38	Zambia	5.35	−6.61	−5.35
Macao SAR, China	−19.80	−77.88	−13.89	Thailand	5.63	−0.89	−4.40
Dominican Republic	−19.59	−17.41	−12.51	Switzerland	2.53	0.59	−3.32

(continued)

Table 4.4. *(continued)*

Deficit economy	Net exports/ GDP (2007)	Change in exports (%)	Change in imports (%)	Surplus economy	Net exports/ GDP (2007)	Change in exports (%)	Change in imports(%)
France	−2.25	−13.52	−11.89	Mayotte	0.00	−13.22	0.51
Moldova	−64.56	−7.78	−11.23	Zimbabwe	0.00	−31.60	2.47
Poland	−6.04	−3.61	−11.20	China	7.76	−1.34	5.05
Portugal	−11.98	−15.85	−10.78	Brazil	3.00	−5.22	5.75
Cyprus	−33.73	−9.48	−9.75	Azerbaijan	1.05	142.46	7.12
Bosnia and Herzegovina	−36.57	−5.36	−9.74	Peru	7.71	−3.58	7.23
Cape Verde	−52.87	85.62	−8.95	French Polynesia	0.00	−11.24	7.44
Honduras	−34.53	9.90	−8.83	Ecuador	0.93	−3.66	8.63
Hong Kong SAR, China	−11.34	−7.52	−5.57	Bolivia	9.84	10.06	25.19
Mauritius	−22.21	−12.93	−4.92	Indonesia	9.17	2.11	30.02
Macedonia, FYR	−23.61	−19.81	−3.53	Algeria	23.91	−24.88	42.08
Senegal	−29.37	30.47	−3.25	Median	4.06	−9.52	−10.34
Pakistan	−10.72	1.53	−2.84				
Belarus	−9.76	−12.33	−0.45				
Colombia	−1.40	8.94	−0.38				
Australia	−2.01	9.26	0.93				
Armenia	−24.29	−28.15	3.41				
Jordan	−53.20	12.23	4.02				
India	−5.92	4.42	7.62				
Albania	−28.79	0.95	8.38				
Tanzania	−23.50	51.78	10.34				
Paraguay	−25.33	15.37	18.81				
Uruguay	−3.19	19.21	23.37				
Mozambique	−7.93	−10.98	23.43				
Egypt, Arab Rep.	−8.33	42.35	66.07				
Ethiopia	−23.64	67.99	87.91				
Median	−11.98	−9.48	−11.89				

Source: Author's calculations based on the following databases: Datastream, Thomson Reuters, http://www.datastream.com; WITS, World Bank, http://wits.worldbank.org; World Development Indicators, World Bank, http://data.worldbank.org; National Statistics, Taiwan, China, http://eng.stat.gov.tw.

Note: Countries are sorted by import growth.

Figure 4.2. Growth of Imports in Brazil, China, India, and Indonesia and in the Rest of the World, 2006–10
logarithms, 2006 = 0

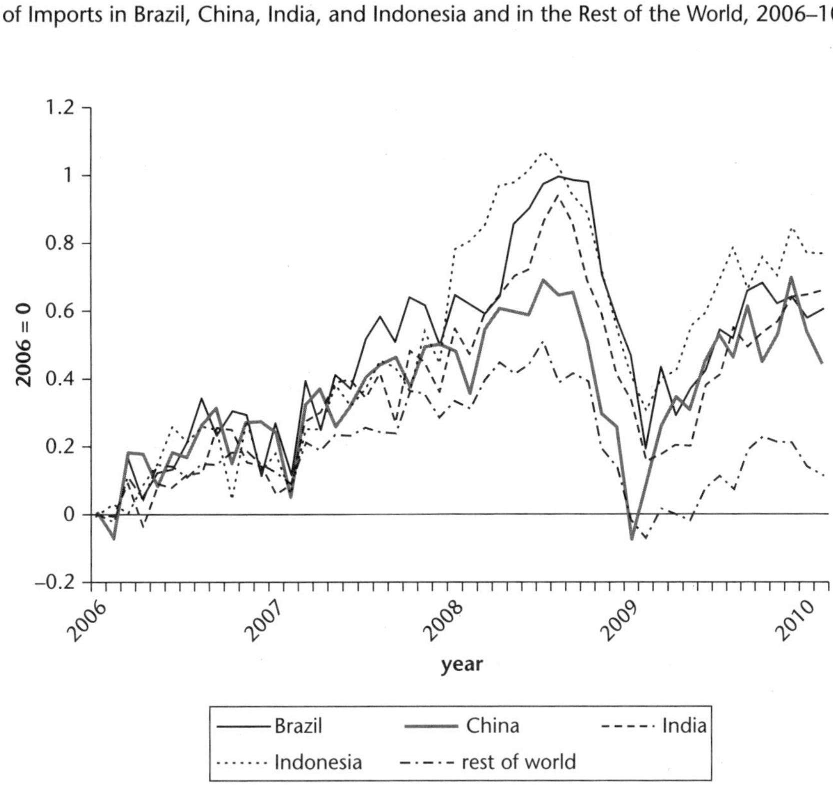

Source: Datastream, Thomson Reuters, http://www.datastream.com.

Figure 4.3. The Changing Nature of Imports in Brazil, China, India, and Indonesia, 1998 and 2008

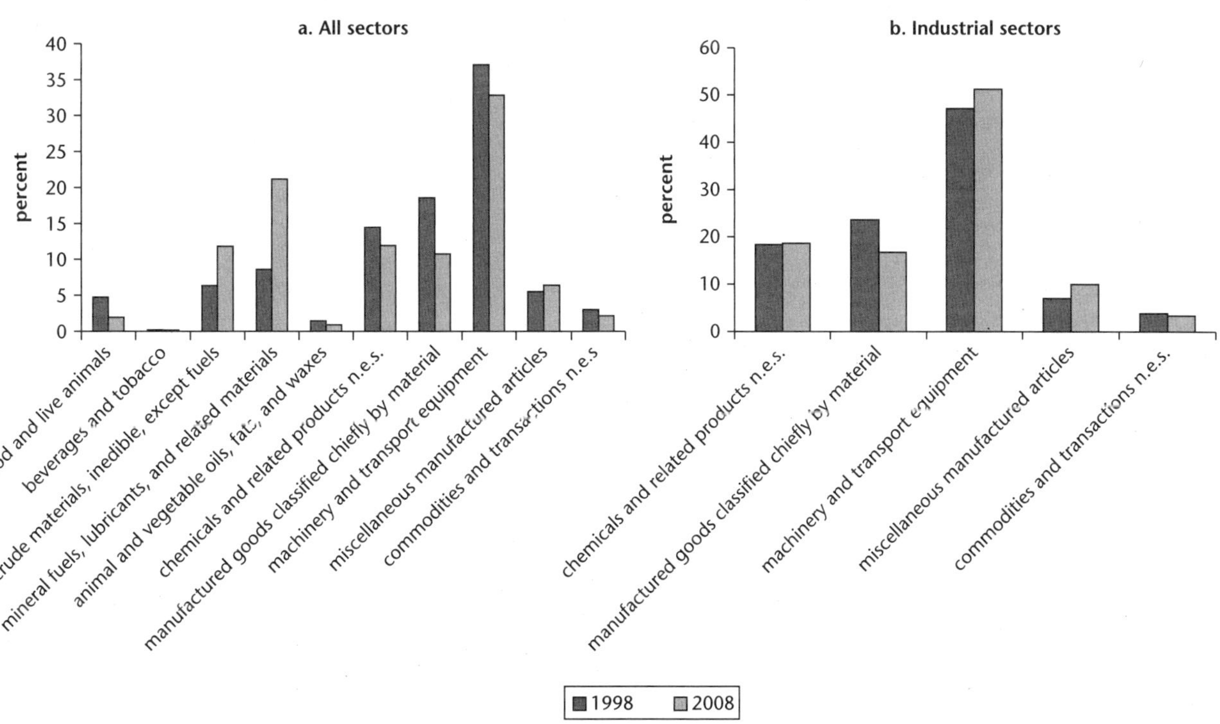

Source: World Integrated Trade Solution, World Bank, http://wits.worldbank.org.

Other authors highlight that export growth at the extensive margin may be an important indicator of successful growth. Indeed, a strong positive correlation has been found between the number of export varieties a country produces and its living standard (Funke and Ruhwedel 2001; Hummels and Klenow 2005). These findings suggest that future growth of exporting countries could look very different if import growth in GEMs is largely at the extensive margin.

Overall, import growth in the GEMs has been largely at the intensive margin (table 4.5). However, some growth has taken place at the extensive margin, especially in Indonesia. Thirty percent of Indonesia's imports in 2007–08 were from new exporters in that product.

For all the GEMs, low- and middle-income countries have the highest extensive share. High-income countries, especially countries in the Organisation for Economic Co-operation and Development, tend to have lower extensive

Figure 4.4. Share of Exports by Region and Income Group to Brazil, China, India, and Indonesia, 1997–98 and 2007–08

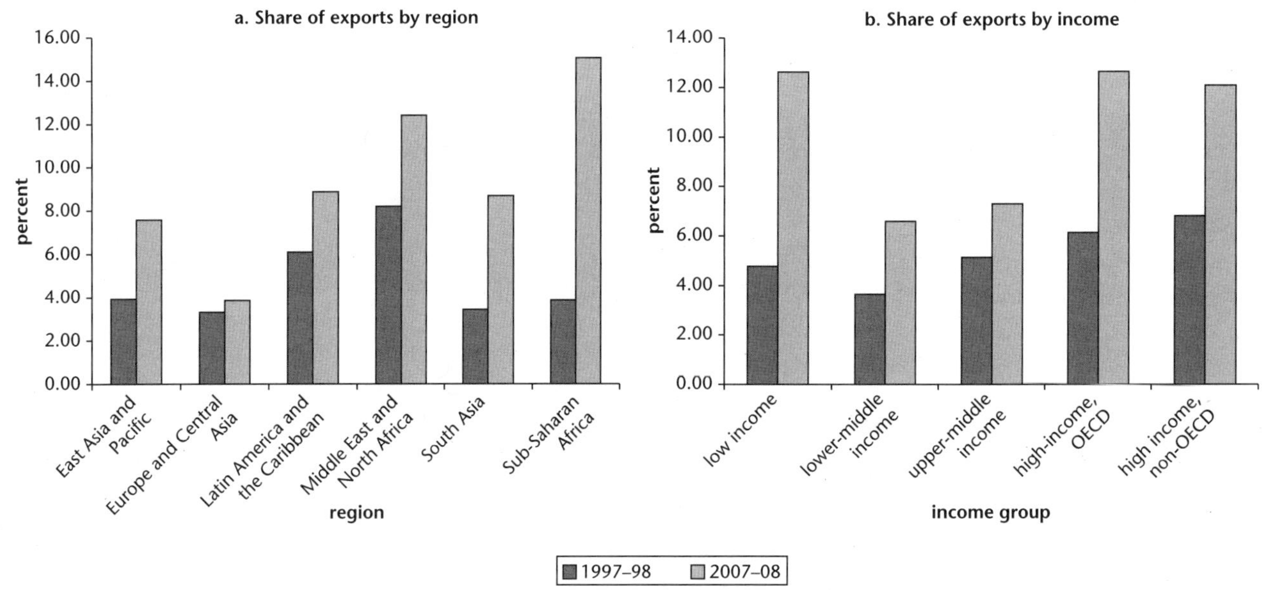

Source: WITS, World Bank, http://wits.worldbank.org; World Development Indicators, World Bank, http://data.worldbank.org.
Note: OECD = Organisation for Economic Co-operation and Development.

Table 4.5. Intensive and Extensive Margin of Total Imports for Brazil, China, India, and Indonesia by Income Group, 2007–09

	Brazil						
Income level	Import growth (US$, millions)	Extensive (%)	Intensive (%)	Region	Import growth (US$, millions)	Extensive (%)	Intensive (%)
All	141.03	17.91	81.91	East Asia and Pacific	709.61	12.35	87.86
High income, non-OECD	248.82	33.63	66.20	Europe and Central Asia	586.50	44.13	55.70
High income, OECD	70.27	6.25	93.65	Latin America and the Caribbean	100.00	21.27	78.70
Low income	601.83	24.02	75.79	Middle East and North Africa	905.39	83.76	15.98
Lower-middle income	873.21	30.68	69.32	South Asia	904.98	61.48	38.52
Upper-middle income	107.76	21.81	78.19	Sub-Saharan Africa	656.63	10.38	89.27

(continued)

Table 4.5. *(continued)*

China							
Income level	**Import growth (US$, millions)**	**Extensive (%)**	**Intensive (%)**	**Region**	**Import growth (US$, millions)**	**Extensive (%)**	**Intensive (%)**
All	592.31	8.41	91.53	East Asia and Pacific	1,058.54	9.47	90.53
High income, non-OECD	504.55	8.57	91.73	Europe and Central Asia	694.30	29.42	70.58
High income, OECD	477.69	4.19	95.87	Latin America and the Caribbean	1,786.41	18.76	81.40
Low income	1,189.67	28.21	71.66	Middle East and North Africa	1,289.81	11.19	88.84
Lower-middle income	1,410.49	13.10	86.57	South Asia	1,316.14	10.41	89.70
Upper-middle income	1,147.75	15.09	84.84	Sub-Saharan Africa	2,440.96	22.48	77.52

India							
Income level	**Import growth (US$, millions)**	**Extensive (%)**	**Intensive (%)**	**Region**	**Import growth (US$, millions)**	**Extensive (%)**	**Intensive (%)**
All	561.95	15.67	84.27	East Asia and Pacific	1,065.02	16.21	83.79
High income, non-OECD	803.70	7.22	92.62	Europe and Central Asia	705.04	46.17	53.51
High income, OECD	404.59	4.78	95.45	Latin America and the Caribbean	1,154.62	56.58	43.16
Low income	655.15	25.29	74.82	Middle East and North Africa	1,490.56	19.13	81.05
Lower-middle income	1,476.42	17.12	83.20	South Asia	470.20	47.21	52.79
Upper-middle income	612.71	38.62	61.19	Sub-Saharan Africa	607.96	22.18	77.78

Indonesia							
Income level	**Import growth (US$, millions)**	**Extensive (%)**	**Intensive (%)**	**Region**	**Import growth (US$, millions)**	**Extensive (%)**	**Intensive (%)**
All	210.45	30.30	69.85	East Asia and Pacific	721.80	26.17	74.02
High income, non-OECD	944.30	51.35	48.84	Europe and Central Asia	701.56	53.55	46.45
High income, OECD	77.27	11.33	88.64	Latin America and the Caribbean	191.37	34.94	65.06
Low income	247.78	43.51	56.49	Middle East and North Africa	160.71	36.55	63.45
Lower-middle income	637.74	16.76	83.24	South Asia	273.15	43.81	56.19
Upper-middle income	537.38	48.79	51.21	Sub-Saharan Africa	193.37	46.98	53.02

Source: Author's calculations based on data from WITS, World Bank, http://wits.worldbank.org; World Development Indicators, World Bank, http://data.worldbank.org.
Note: OECD = Organisation for Economic Co-operation and Development.

shares. In China, where the extensive margin was less than 10 percent of imports in 2007–08, nearly 30 percent of imports from low-income countries were goods that were not previously imported from those countries. Thus, for developing countries to take advantage of demand in the GEMs, they will need to continue finding new products to export.

Conclusion

In the coming years, global imbalances must be limited to ensure financial stability, with important implications for trade patterns and trade growth. More balanced capital flows imply that trade flows must also be more balanced and that the primary source of global demand can no longer be the U.S. market.

A new world trade order is already emerging, with large and growing emerging markets absorbing capital and goods from the rest of the world. In particular, Brazil, China, India, and Indonesia have demonstrated resilient global demand growth throughout the financial crisis, despite sizable exchange-rate depreciation in some countries when the crisis began (for instance, in Brazil and Indonesia), and without extensive fiscal support.

Financial stability and continued trade growth rely, in part, on the sustainability of this diversification of global demand. Fast-growing economies such as the GEMs need to continue pulling capital to higher yields and importing raw materials and machinery to ensure future growth. These requirements will tend to support the external sector in low-income countries, especially those rich in natural resources, and high-income countries with strong machinery sectors or natural resources.

While the adjustment process from a trade perspective appears to be moving in a positive direction, serious risks remain. Among these are a return to low savings in the United States and a reemergence of large imbalances. In addition, China's import strength may be temporary, as relatively cheap natural resources are purchased for future use and domestic consumption has tended not to expand in a sustainable way. Without the participation of these two countries, a more stable order cannot take hold. In Europe, continued financial problems, coupled with localized trade patterns, could lead to a much slower trade recovery. These countries will do well to look toward Asia over the coming years.

Notes

1. See World Trade Organization (2010).
2. Baldwin and Taglioni (2009) argue that a strong recovery has followed the sharp drop in trade and that it is likely to be accompanied by the same worrisome global imbalances that defined previous years.
3. For example, Blanchard and Milesi-Ferretti (2009) examine how imbalances have adjusted based on changes in savings and investment patterns across countries.
4. The sample in this chapter includes 86 countries through 2009, which together account for over 85 percent of world trade. Data are gathered from various sources and are measured in nominal U.S. dollars.
5. Change due to rebalancing is calculated as the change in the GTI due to rebalancing in countries where the imbalance shrank.
6. Change due to imbalance-augmenting trade growth is calculated as the change in GTI not due to the trade drop in the countries where imbalances expanded.
7. This is consistent with Blanchard and Milessi-Ferretti (2009). They examine global imbalances during the crisis from a macro perspective and find that significant adjustment in savings and investment patterns have occurred.
8. See the chapter by Mitchell and Aldaz-Carroll for further discussion of the future of commodity markets.

Bibliography

Baldwin, R., and D. Taglioni. 2009. "The Illusion of Improving Global Imbalances." VoxEU. November. http://www.voxeu.org/index.php?q=node/4209.

Bernanke, B. 2009. "Financial Reform to Address Systemic Risk." Speech at the Council on Foreign Relations, Washington, DC, March 10. http://www.federalreserve.gov/newsevents/speech/bernanke20090310a .htm.

Blanchard, O., and G. M. Milesi-Ferretti. 2009. "Global Imbalances: In Midstream?" IMF Staff Position Note SPN/09/29, International Monetary Fund, Washington, DC.

Broda, C., and D. Weinstein. 2006. "Globalization and the Gains from Variety." *Quarterly Journal of Economics* 121 (2): 541–85.

Colacelli, M. 2006. "Export Responses to Real Exchange Rate Fluctuations: An Empirical Analysis." Unpublished paper, Department of Economics, Columbia University, New York.

Evenett, S., and J. Francois. 2010. "Will Chinese Revaluation Create American Jobs." VoxEU. http://www.voxeu.org/index.php?q=node/4931.

Fang, W., Y. Lai, and S. Miller. 2006. "Export Promotion through Exchange Rate Changes: Exchange Rate Depreciation or Stabilization?" *Southern Economic Journal* 72 (3): 611–26.

Freund, C. 2009. "The Trade Response to Global Downturns: Historical Evidence." Working Paper 5015, World Bank, Washington, DC.

Funke, M., and R. Ruhwedel. 2001. "Product Variety and Economic Growth: Empirical Evidence for the OECD Countries." *IMF Staff Papers* 48 (2): 225–42.

Hummels, D., and P. Klenow. 2005. "The Variety and Quality of a Nation's Exports." *American Economic Review* 95: 704–23.

Obstfeld, M. 2002. "Exchange Rates and Adjustment: Perspectives from the New Open Economy Macroeconomics." NBER Working Paper 9118, National Bureau of Economic Research, Cambridge, MA.

Obstfeld, M., and K. Rogoff. 2009. "Global Imbalances and the Financial Crisis: Products of Common Causes." Paper prepared for the Federal Reserve Bank of San Francisco "Asia Economic Policy Conference," Santa Barbara, CA, October 18–20. http://elsa.berkeley.edu/~obstfeld/santabarbara.pdf.

Prasad, E., and I. Sorkin. 2009. "Understanding the G-20 Economic Stimulus Plans." Brookings Institution, Washington, DC. http://www.brookings.edu/articles/2009/03_g20_stimulus_prasad.aspx.

World Trade Organization. 2010. "Trade to Expand by 9.5% in 2010 after a Dismal 2009, WTO Reports." March 26. News release. http://www.wto.org/english/news_e/pres10_e/pr598_e.htm.

5

AN ANATOMY OF TRADE IN THE 2008–09 CRISIS

Mona Haddad, Ann Harrison, and Catherine Hausman

As discussed in the previous chapters, the global economic crisis of 2008–09 was accompanied by a severe fall in international trade. Baldwin (2009) characterizes the collapse as "sudden, severe, and synchronized . . . the sharpest in recorded history and deepest since WWII."

A number of hypotheses have attempted to explain what caused the collapse and why it became so widespread and deep.[1] While many highlight the fall in aggregate demand, some suggest that several supply-side factors may have played a role. Supporters of the demand shock hypothesis argue that the collapse in trade was the result of a synchronized postponement of purchases, especially of durable consumer and investment products. Eaton et al. (2010) and Levchenko, Lewis, and Tesar (2010) are among those arguing that the collapse in trade was primarily the result of demand-side shocks. By contrast, supporters of the supply shock hypothesis suggest that the collapse in trade was a consequence of the sudden financial arrest, which froze global credit markets and spilled over onto the specialized financial instruments that finance international trade. Others have noted that with the globalization of supply chains, a fall in manufactures could lead to an outsized fall in total trade, particularly if supply chains are disrupted. Finally, some highlight the role of rising protectionism.

In this chapter, we identify a new set of stylized facts on the 2008–09 trade collapse that can shed light on the importance of demand- and supply-side factors in explaining the fall in trade. In particular, we decompose the fall in international trade into product entry and exit, price changes, and quantity changes for imports to Brazil, the European Union (EU), Indonesia, and the United States. Our ability to separate price and quantity changes allows us to identify the upward trajectory of prices for manufacturing, which could be consistent with a role for credit constraints in explaining some—but obviously not the majority—of the collapse in world trade.

The rest of this chapter is organized as follows. The next section discusses recent changes in the extensive and intensive margin. The following section presents evidence of the role of demand and supply shocks in the onset of the trade collapse. The subsequent sections analyze how these trends vary by product type and income group. The following section discusses whether any of these trends were present before the crisis. The final section concludes. For full details of our methodology and data sources, readers are referred to the working paper version of this chapter.

Changes in the Intensive and the Extensive Margins

The speed and sustainability of recovery from the crisis depend partly on which margin, extensive or intensive, has been more affected by the crisis and by how fast it responds to fiscal stimulus. The intensive margin refers to changes in the value of exports due to changes in the quantities or prices of already exported goods. The extensive margin refers to changes in the value of exports due to changes in the number of goods exported or changes in the number of destinations to which a country exports old or new goods.

If significant fixed costs are associated with exporting or importing new products (that is, the extensive margin), then identifying the relative size of changes along the extensive and intensive margins is useful in predicting the speed of the recovery. For instance, we would expect a faster recovery if most of the changes in trade were on the intensive margin. Evidence from U.S. and French firms (Schott 2009; Bricongne et al. 2009, respectively) suggests that the intensive margin was more affected during this crisis than the extensive margin. These results are consistent with Bernard et al. (2009), who analyze past recessionary periods. Yet none of these studies has examined price changes. In this section, we discuss changes in the extensive and intensive margins in recent years.

In October 2008, the total number of bilaterally traded products began to fall in Brazil, Indonesia, and the United States (figure 5.1). The percentage fall in the total number of products was greatest for Brazil and Indonesia, reaching about 10 percent from peak to trough for both countries. By contrast, the percentage of products traded for the European Union did not decline, and the decline for the United States was half of that for Brazil and Indonesia, around 5 percent.

Brazil, the European Union,[2] Indonesia, and the United States all experienced a sharp drop in the total value of imports beginning in October 2008, with recovery beginning in early 2009 (figure 5.2). None managed to re-attain precrisis levels by the end of the period shown (September 2009). Developing countries experienced much greater volatility than the developed countries. Indeed, before beginning to recover, the total value of imports fell by nearly half for Brazil and Indonesia. At the end of the sample period, however, the total loss in trade was about the same for the developed and developing countries (around one-third of aggregate trade).[3]

Effects along the intensive margin dramatically outweighed the effects along the extensive margin, both in the U.S.-EU markets and in the Brazil-Indonesia markets (figure 5.3). Imports by the United States and the EU dropped from US$4 trillion in 2008 to US$3 trillion in 2009, a total fall of 25.2 percent from the first half of 2008 to the first half of 2009. The quantity effect accounted for over 15.9 percent out of the total 25.2 percent value drop, and the decline in prices accounted for only 5.5 percent. Net entry, the sum of exit and entry, was negative, but accounted for only a small portion of the change in total value. Imports by Brazil and Indonesia dropped from US$135 billion to US$109 billion, a fall of 18.9 percent from the first half of 2008 to the first half of 2009. For Brazil and Indonesia, changes in quantity accounted for 18.5 percent out of the total 18.9 percent drop in the value of trade, with product net exit accounting for 1 percent and a small price increase partially offsetting these effects. The results for the intensive and extensive margins match evidence by Schott (2009) and Bricongne et al. (2009), who find that for U.S. and French firms, changes in the intensive margin outweighed changes in the extensive margin.

Demand and Supply Shocks

Determining what happened to traded prices and quantities between 2008 and 2009 offers a new approach to determining the role of demand versus supply factors in the trade collapse. If the decline in trade was driven mostly by a negative demand shock, we would expect both prices and quantities to have been negatively affected. However, if supply-side shocks were important, we would expect an

Figure 5.1. Index of Total Number of Products Traded in Brazil, the European Union, Indonesia, and the United States, January 2007–September 2009

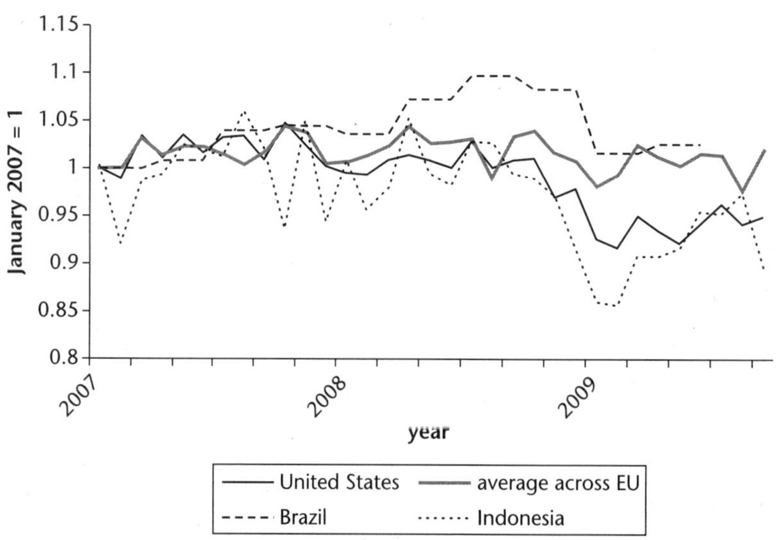

Source: Authors' calculations based on data from national statistics agencies.
Note: Products are tallied by partner country.

Figure 5.2. Index of Total Value of Imports for Brazil, the European Union, Indonesia, and the United States, January 2007–September 2009

Source: Authors' calculations based on data from national statistics agencies.

Figure 5.3. Change in Total Import Value of All Products in Brazil-Indonesia and United States–EU Trade, by Margin, 2008–09
percent

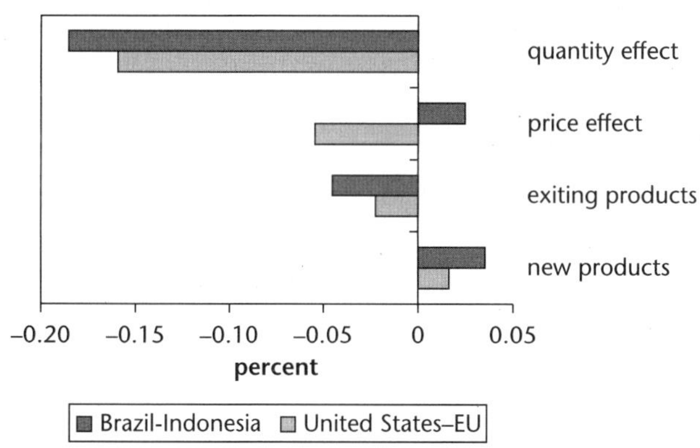

Source: Authors' calculations based on data from national statistics agencies.

upward pressure on prices because a reduction in trade credit would lead to a reduction in the supply of traded goods independently of the negative demand shock.

While the largest contributor to the crisis seems to be the demand shock, there is also systematic evidence of factors generating negative supply shocks in manufacturing. By extending work by Bernard et al. (2009) to decompose the intensive margin into price and quantity effects in an ordinary least squares linear regression, we find evidence of both demand and supply shocks. Indeed, at the aggregate level,[4] the evidence is consistent with a pure demand shock story: a fall in demand generated declines in prices and quantities. For the United States, 36 percent of the reduction in trade across all trading partners can be explained by a decline in prices, while 57 percent can be explained by a decline in quantity. The contribution of entry and exit accounted for less than 1 percent of the observed changes. In both the EU and Indonesia, the quantity declines dominated the price effect, while for Brazil the opposite is true. For all countries, the intensive margin again is substantially larger than the extensive margin. Exit again outweighs entry, leading to negative net entry in all regions.

However, if we restrict the sample to manufacturing, a different story emerges. We see that for manufactures, the fall in quantity continues to account for the major share of the observed trade collapse. However, for Brazil, Indonesia, and the United States there is also evidence of a supply shock: price increases offset the contribution of declining prices to the fall in trade. This finding is particularly striking for Indonesia. All in all, the evidence suggests that supply-side disruptions play a more important role in manufacturing.

Several outliers in these trends should be noted. For instance, members of the Organization of the Petroleum-Exporting Countries experienced larger price effects on their exports to the United States than did other countries. Oil-exporting countries, including Algeria, Angola, Iraq, the Russian Federation, Saudia Arabia, and República Bolivariana de Venezuela, show price effects that are larger (more negative) than the average. Their quantity effects are, correspondingly, smaller than the average. Other large trading partners—such as France; Germany; Italy; Japan; the Republic of Korea; Malaysia; Taiwan, China; and the United Kingdom—show larger quantity effects than the average across countries.

In an alternative decomposition of the total trade value[5] by trading partner, product, and average value,[6] we find that while the extensive margin experienced negative changes, the intensive margin mattered more. No country saw an increase in the number of trading partners from 2008 to 2009. In fact, Brazil lost almost 10 trading partners. All four regions also saw a fall in the number of products traded, although this was a very small percentage of the total loss. The largest changes were in average value, which fell by 10 to 28 percent across the various regions.

Variation by Product Type

Our research shows that these average effects mask enormous differences across different products. Figure 5.4 shows the difference between commodities and manufactures, where each margin is shown as a percentage of the change in total import value in 2008. The differences across product classes are striking. The negative price effect, apparent for the United States and EU when aggregating across all goods, is still evident for commodities but not for manufactures. With commodity prices falling during the crisis, it is not surprising that the price effect was large for commodities; it is, however, noteworthy that the price effect was generally limited to commodities; the price effect for manufactures was positive.

Since we know that demand for manufactures fell during the crisis, the effect on prices can tell us something about what happened to supply. Where prices rose or where they fell only slightly, it is plausible that supply shifted in. Thus, the evidence on manufactures, contrasted with commodities and particularly in the case of Brazil and Indonesia, points to a negative supply shock in manufactures in addition to the negative demand shock. This negative supply shock could be from fragmentation of the global supply chain or from reductions in trade finance.

The prevalence of supply shocks in the manufacturing sector is also confirmed when we analyze differences across product types. The largest total value change is in minerals, which fell by US$134 billion. Almost 90 percent of that decline was due to price falls. Machinery and electrical equipment and transportation equipment also experienced large falls in total volume, but almost all of the changes were due to a decline in quantity for these products.

Prices increased in the following product categories: chemicals, footwear, leather, miscellaneous, and transportation equipment (note that because the total value change is negative, a positive total price effect is represented by a negative percentage of the value change). Most of the large negative price effects were in product categories made up largely of commodities (animal products,

Figure 5.4. Variations in Price and Quantity in Commodities and Manufactures, 2008

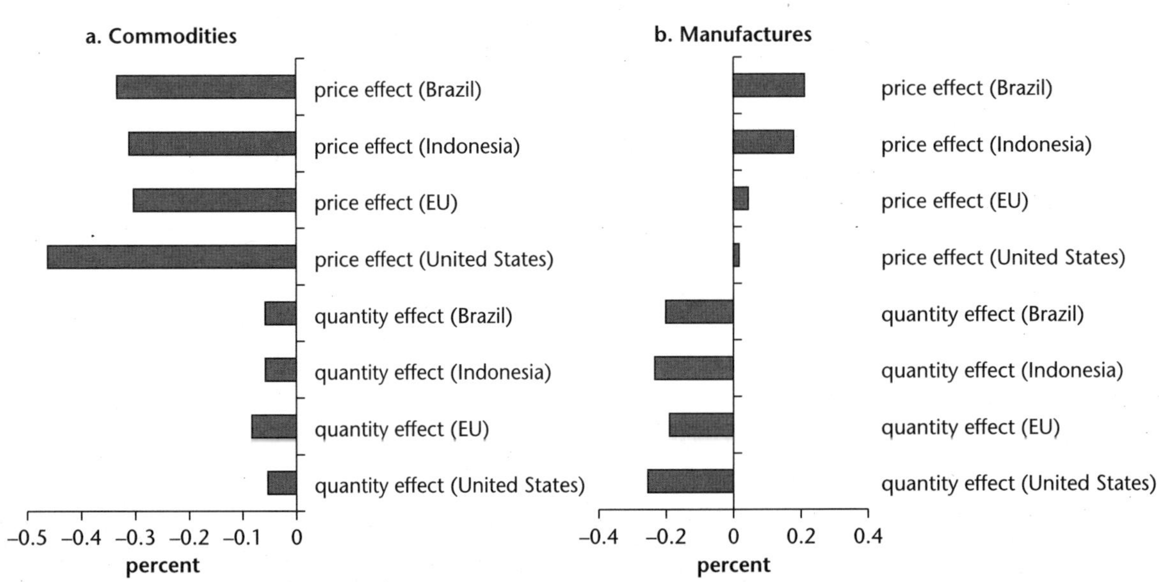

Source: Authors' calculations based on data from national statistics agencies.

minerals, and vegetable products). All products saw falls in quantity, with the quantity effect generally contributing to over half of the total effect. The quantity effect was relatively small for minerals, where the price effect was largest.

As figure 5.5 illustrates, differences in trade responses across modes of transport are not significant. However, a distinction can be made between manufactures and commodities. Commodities exhibited both price and quantity declines.[7] In contrast, manufactures showed quantity declines but mild price increases. The overall trends in figure 5.5 are consistent with an overall pattern of demand contraction, with some evidence of supply constraints in manufacturing. The largest price increases were in the leather and footwear sector, where credit constraints and trade frictions may have restricted supply. Finally, it is interesting to note that for many products, the quantity effect is larger for transport by air than for transport by sea.[8]

We also examine evidence on credit constraints by adopting the classification scheme of Bricongne et al. (2009) to separate products according to sectoral dependence on external finance. We restrict our analysis to manufactures. For the United States, price increases were most significant in sectors that are typically credit constrained, partially counteracting the large quantity effect. The EU does not show this effect. For Brazil, the overall import value for the finance-dependent sectors dropped (by 3 percent) but rose for the low-dependence sectors (by 9 percent). The overall import value also fell more for finance-dependent sectors (19 percent as opposed to 6 percent) in Indonesian imports.

Variation by Income Group

While the financial crisis originated in high-income countries, its effects on trade were rapidly transmitted to low-income countries. It has been hypothesized that the effects

Figure 5.5. Changes in Import Values across Product Types and Shipment Methods for U.S. Imports as a Percentage of Value by Margin, 2008

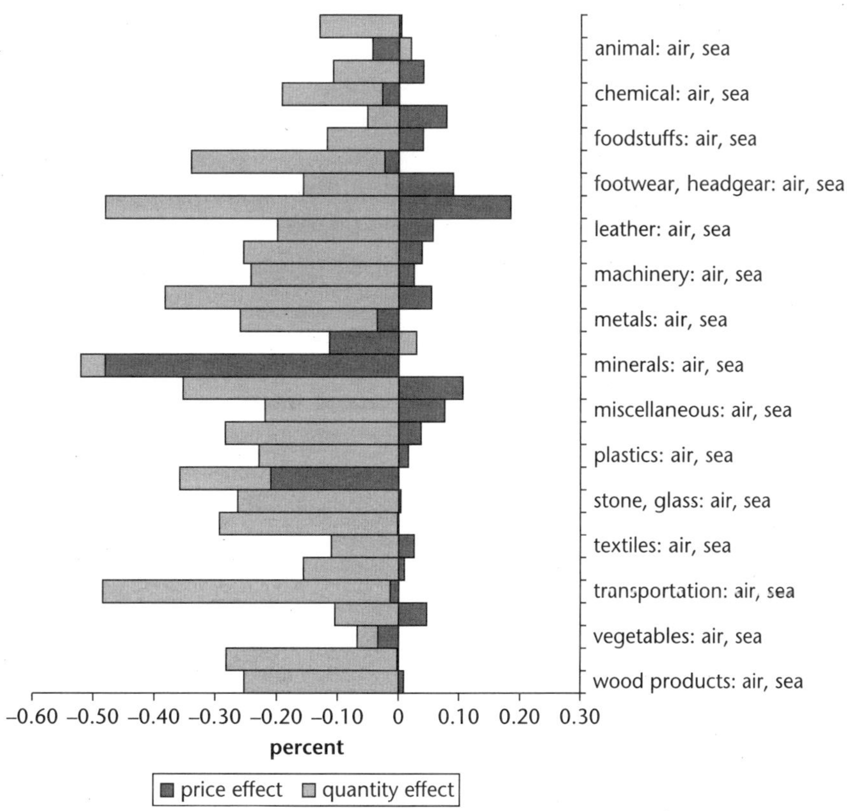

Source: Authors' calculations based on data from national statistics agencies.

Note: Within each product grouping (for example, animal products), the upper bar shows the effect on air shipments and the lower bar shows the effect on vessel shipments. The effects are percentage changes of the total effect within that shipment type. For instance, the price effect for animal products shipped by sea is divided by the total value in 2008 of animal products shipped by sea. Note that typically sea shipments were much larger in 2008, so the gross value changes for sea shipments are larger compared to those for air shipments than what is shown. Entry and exit are not shown and represent less than 5 percent of the change in any given category. Continuing products with unobserved price or quantity are also not shown.

of constrained trade finance could vary by exporter income (Malouche 2009; Berman and Martin 2010) and by geographic region (Berman and Martin 2010). On the one hand, high-income countries with well-developed markets were most affected in the financial crisis; on the other hand, low-income exporters with less-developed financial markets may be more reliant on trade finance originating in their trading partners. Countries with different levels of income export different baskets of goods, which embody different levels of quality and variety.

To analyze how the response in trade volumes changes with the income level of the exporting country, we classify trading partners in four categories: high, upper-middle, lower-middle, and low income, according to the World Bank's country classification. We also add China and Sub-Saharan Africa as separate categories, two regions where researchers have hypothesized that the trade fall was unique. As mentioned above, it has been theorized that the trade finance constraint could have been either much more severe or much less severe in Sub-Saharan Africa. China has been unique both because it recovered from the crisis more rapidly and because it has been a target for protectionism (Bown 2009). The story can be further elaborated by returning to the heterogeneity across trading partner income but restricting the sample to manufactures. The results are shown in figure 5.6.

Overall, upper- and upper-middle-income exports to developed countries were most affected by the crisis, with falls in the value of their exports reaching 25 percent to the United States and EU. Low-income countries were able to increase their exports to the United States and EU by 7 percent. The impact of the crisis on the exports of countries of various income groups to Brazil and Indonesia was very small. The most striking result is the large increase in exports of low-income countries to Brazil and Indonesia of nearly 30 percent between 2008 and 2009. This finding confirms that South-South trade is becoming increasingly important and was reinforced during the crisis. Sub-Saharan Africa, however, was not able to take advantage of these South-South trade opportunities as its exports to Brazil and Indonesia dropped 27 percent. China's exports to the United States and the EU dropped by only 8 percent, in line with other lower-middle-income countries; but China's exports to Brazil and Indonesia increased by 5 percent.

Figure 5.6. Percentage Change in Imports to Brazil and Indonesia and to the United States and the EU from Countries in Different Income Groups, 2008–09

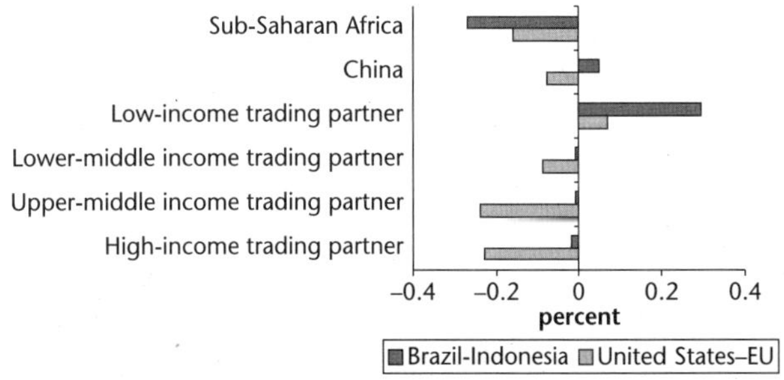

Source: Authors' calculations based on data from national statistics agencies.

Were Any of These Trends Present before the Crisis?

We examine whether these findings are unique to the crisis or whether they represent the continuation of historical trends. Figure 5.7 shows changes in each margin (in billions of U.S. dollars) for U.S. and Indonesian imports across quarters for 2007–09. Price and quantity changes are now defined relative to the previous quarter rather than to the same quarter of the previous year. Hence, the magnitudes of these changes do not match the magnitudes given in the other figures, but they do show the specific timing of the collapse in trade.

As expected, entry and exit do not play a large role in U.S. imports (before and after the crisis) but are more important in a developing country like Indonesia, where trade relations are thinner and less established. The quantity and price effects are not part of broader historical trends; rather, they match the timing of the global economic crisis. Manufacturing imports to the United States level off in the third quarter of 2008, as the crisis is beginning, and then plummet in the following two quarters. For this whole period, the negative quantity effect dominates, and there is a smaller positive price effect for the fourth quarter of 2008. Manufacturing imports to Indonesia follow a similar pattern, with a negative quantity effect beginning in the fourth quarter of 2008 and an initial positive price effect. Commodity imports to the United States also plummet in the fourth quarter of 2008, but here the negative price effect dominates. For commodity imports to Indonesia, both quantity and price effects are negative and begin around the fourth quarter of 2008.

Conclusion

In summary, the great trade collapse occurred along both intensive and extensive margins. The intensive margin had much greater impacts, with negative effects for both prices

Figure 5.7. Percentage Changes in Imports of Manufactures and Commodities to the United States and Indonesia, Second Quarter, 2007–Third Quarter, 2009

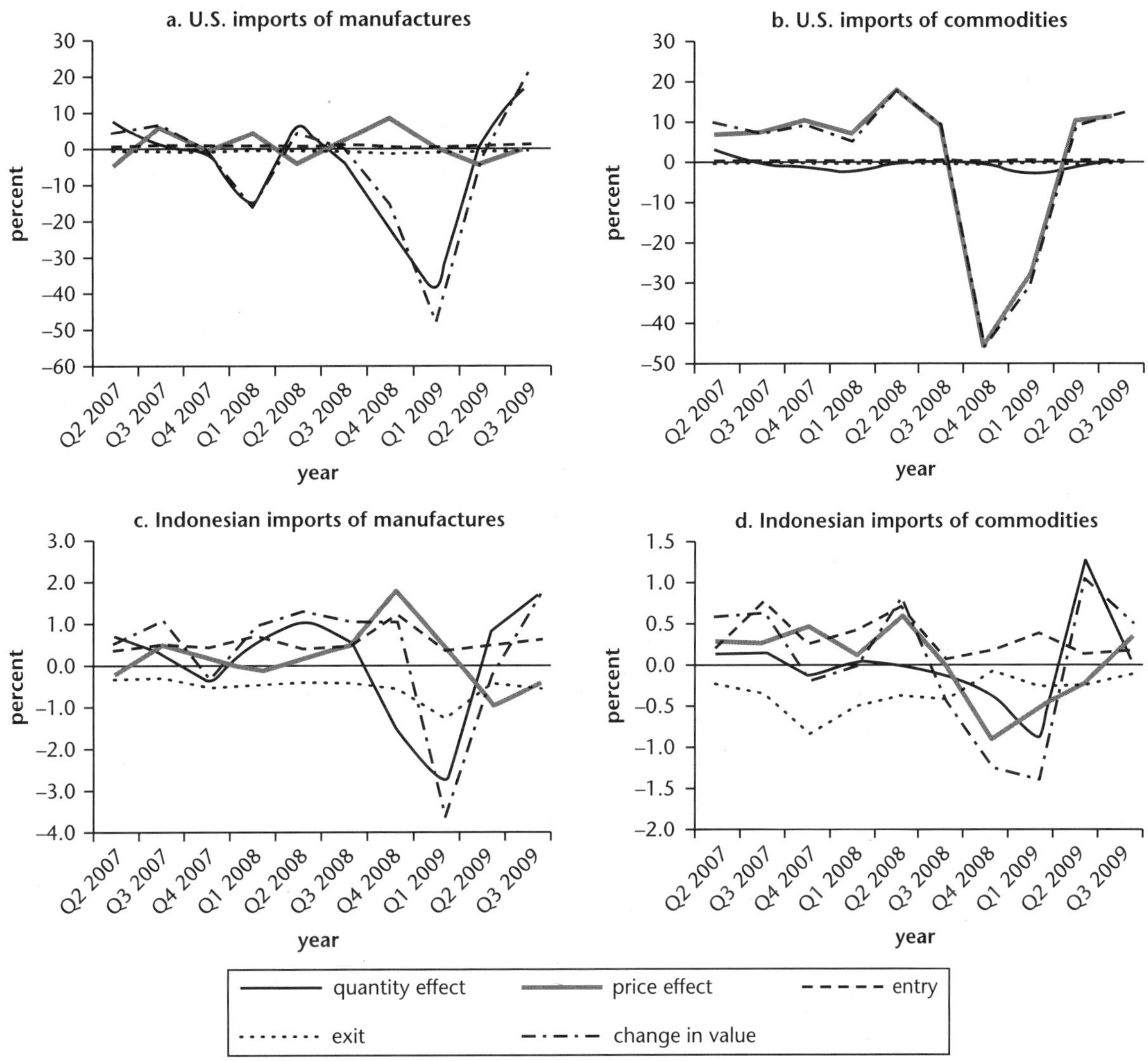

Source: Authors' calculations based on data from national statistics agencies.

and quantities. Across all products, most of the countries analyzed experienced a decline in new products, a rise in product exit, and reductions in quantity for product lines that continued to be traded. These effects are similar for high-income and middle-income partner countries, but trade with low-income partner countries was much less affected.

The evidence suggests that the intensive rather than the extensive margin mattered the most, consistent with studies of other countries and previous recessionary periods. On average, quantities declined and prices fell, which is consistent with a story in which the demand shock played a dominant role. Aggregating across all product categories, we find that the evidence is consistent with the conclusions reached by Eaton et al. (2010) and Levchenko, Lewis, and Tesar (2010), who argue that the collapse in trade was caused primarily by a synchronized demand-side shock.

However, these average effects mask enormous differences across different product types. Disaggregating the data into manufactures and nonmanufactures, we find that the price declines are driven primarily by commodities. Within manufacturing, however, while most quantity changes were negative, in many cases price changes moved in the opposite direction, particularly for products imported by developing-country trading partners. Consequently, within manufacturing, some evidence indicates that supply-side frictions did play a role.

Considerable differences emerge across product types and exporter incomes. Some have argued that South-South trade was less disrupted during the crisis. While this appears to be the case if one examines aggregate trade patterns across all goods, a large decline occurred in manufacturing trade with Sub-Saharan Africa. The most striking result is the large increase in exports of low-income countries to Brazil and Indonesia—nearly 30 percent between 2008 and 2009. We also find evidence consistent with the view that credit constraints could account for the price increases occurring in the manufacturing sector. For the United States, for example, price increases were most significant in sectors that are typically credit constrained.

Notes

1. For summaries, see Baldwin (2009) and Council of Economic Advisers (2010).
2. This is an average across the European Union.
3. Since the sample ends in September 2009, we do not capture the continued slow recovery since that period.
4. This level includes commodities.
5. The change in total trade value is included.
6. This follows Bernard et al. (2009).
7. Declines are indicated by both the dark and the light bars located on the left-hand side of the graph for minerals, stone and glass, animal products, and vegetables.
8. Products do not include chemicals, foodstuffs, and transportation equipment.

Bibliography

Baldwin, R, ed. 2009. *The Great Trade Collapse: Causes, Consequences and Prospects*, VoxEU.org Ebook, available at http://www.voxeu.org/index.php?q=node/4297.

Berman, N., and P. Martin. 2010. "The Vulnerability of Sub-Saharan Africa to the Financial Crisis: The Case of Trade." CEPR Discussion Paper 7765, Centre for Economic Policy Research, London, United Kingdom.

Bernard, A. B., J. B. Jensen, S. J. Redding, and P. K. Schott. 2009. "The Margins of U.S. Trade." *American Economic Review: Papers & Proceedings* 99 (2): 487–93.

Bown, C. 2009. "The Global Resort to Antidumping, Safeguards, and Other Trade Remedies amidst the Economic Crisis." Policy Research Working Paper 5051, World Bank, Washington, DC.

Bricongne, J.-C., L. Fontagne, G. Gauler, D. Taglioni, and V. Vicard. 2009. "Firms and the Global Crisis: French Exports in the Turmoil." Document de Travail 265, Banque de France, Paris.

Council of Economic Advisers. 2010. *Economic Report of the President*. U.S. Government Printing Office, Washington, DC.

Eaton, J., S. Kortum, B. Neiman, and J. Romalis. 2010. "Trade and the Global Recession." Working Paper 16, National Bank of Belgium, Brussels.

Levchenko, A. A., L. T. Lewis, and L. L. Tesar. 2010. "The Collapse of International Trade during the 2008-2009 Crisis: In Search of the Smoking Gun." Discussion Paper 592, Ford School of Public Policy, University of Michigan, Ann Arbor, MI.

Malouche, M. 2009. "Trade and Trade Finance Developments in 14 Developing Countries Post September 2008: A World Bank Survey." Policy Research Working Paper 5138, World Bank, Washington, DC.

Rauch, J. E. 1999. "Networks versus Markets in International Trade." *Journal of International Economics* 48 (1): 7–35.

Schott, P. 2009. "US Trade Margins during the 2008 Crisis." VoxEU. November 27. http://voxeu.org.

6

DEVELOPING COUNTRIES, NEW TRADE BARRIERS, AND THE GLOBAL ECONOMIC CRISIS

Chad P. Bown and Hiau Looi Kee

The financial crisis that began in mid-2008 quickly spread globally and resulted in a major shock to the international economy. The initial concern was whether the global economy would suffer as deep an economic decline as in the Great Depression of the 1930s. The onset of a coordinated recession across the world's major economies and a severe collapse in international trade flows further stoked fears of an impending protectionist backlash. Just as the 2008–09 recession led to injured industries and massive unemployment and drew comparisons to the Great Depression, the specter of the 1929 U.S. Smoot-Hawley tariffs and the subsequent international protectionist response of the 1930s created the worry that the recent crisis would result in a similar global imposition of new trade barriers and severely curtail the timely resumption of international trade (Eichengreen and Irwin 2009a, forthcoming; Irwin, forthcoming).

This chapter presents a set of stylized facts on the new protectionism that has emerged during the global economic crisis of 2008–09. We assess the magnitude and distribution of the policy changes that occurred by placing them into recent historical context. In line with the types of explicit trade barriers that countries have imposed during the crisis, we place special emphasis on the role of import restrictions resulting from national use of antidumping, countervailing duty, and safeguard policies.[1] Examination of the detailed evidence from the World Bank's *Temporary Trade Barriers Database* (Bown 2010c) on the evolving use of these policies also mandates that we pay particular attention to the interests of *developing* economies—both as imposers of new trade barriers and as exporters whose trade is most likely to be adversely affected by such barriers.[2]

To begin, figure 6.1 presents monthly data on the growth of imports from Freund and Horenstein (2010) for the period January 2008 through November 2009. The fourth quarter of 2008 saw a sudden and almost simultaneous drop in global trade flows for virtually all the major regions of the world. The trend continued through the first three quarters of 2009, which continued to register negative rates of import growth. The World Trade Organization (WTO) (2009, 3) estimates a year-on-year decline in world trade in the fourth quarter of 2008 alone as over 10 percent, with another year-on-year decline of 30 percent in the first quarter 2009. In our focus on protectionism during the crisis, we first clarify the limited role that trade barriers contributed to the trade collapse of 2008–09. The evidence we present on the timing and the scale of the new import protection under these barriers is consistent with the existing evidence that such protection likely contributed only slightly to the sharp decline in global trade flows.[3]

We examine the evolving changes in protectionism across countries resulting from the crisis to infer how such barriers may affect future patterns of trade, including the potential for a V-shaped postcrisis trade recovery. While the newly documented protectionism imposed during 2008–09 may have played a minuscule role in causing the global trade collapse, the emerging pattern of new trade

Thanks to Aksel Erbahar for outstanding research assistance.

Figure 6.1. Monthly Import Growth by Region, January 2008–November 2009

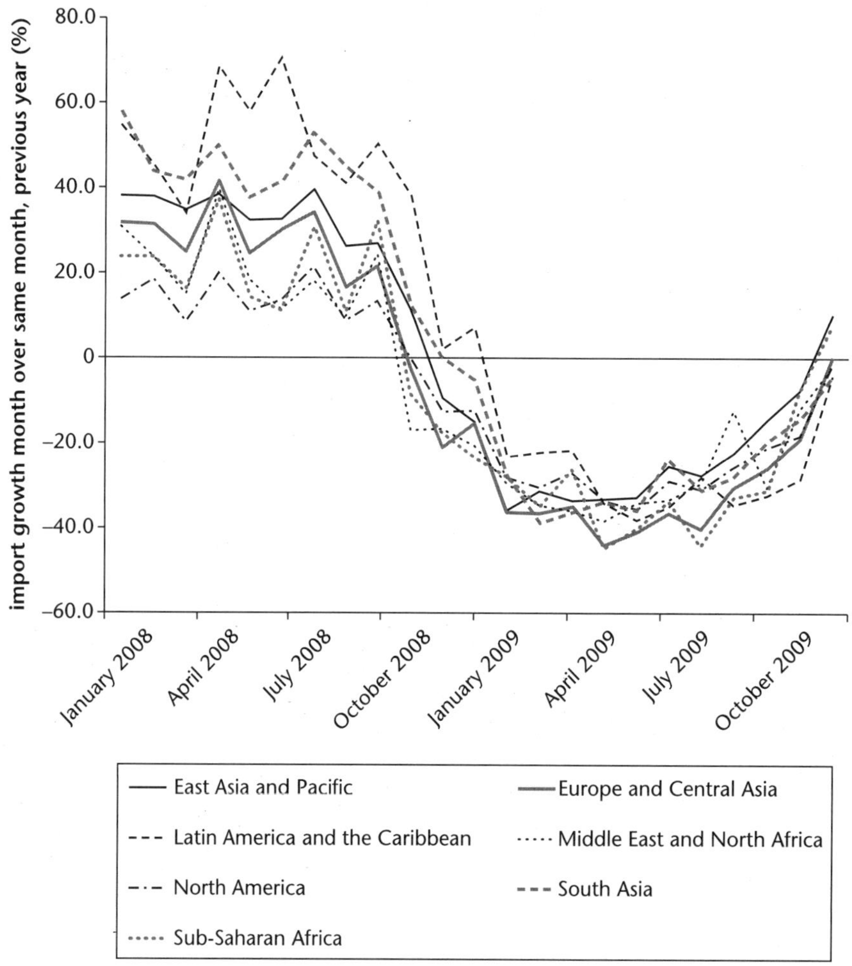

Source: Authors, based on data in Freund and Horenstein 2010.

barriers imposed across countries and exporters during the crisis is likely to have longer-term implications for the potential trade recovery in 2010 and beyond. Much of the evidence of new crisis-era protectionism is in the form of South-South trade barriers—policies such as antidumping that one developing economy imposes on the imports of other developing economies, including, but not limited to, imports from China. While this phenomenon is not new—that is, it had been trending in this direction long before 2008–09—it was certainly accentuated during the crisis period.

The chapter proceeds as follows. In the next section, we describe newly compiled, detailed data on the imposition of trade barriers from the perspective of the policy-imposing economies. The following section turns its attention to exporting countries and the impacts they have seen. We conclude the chapter with a final discussion of lingering issues and policy implications.

Protectionism from the Perspective of Domestic Industries and Importing Economies

We begin our analysis of protectionism during the crisis by examining it from the perspective of the policy-imposing economies and their imports that are likely affected by the imposition of new barriers to trade. We focus primarily on the Group of 20 (G-20) members as the policy-imposing economies.

Temporary Trade Barriers: Antidumping, Countervailing Duties, and Safeguards

Long before the onset of the 2008–09 crisis, most of the G-20 economies had a significant history of using at least one of the four policies that we refer to collectively as temporary trade barriers (TTBs): antidumping, countervailing duties, global safeguards, and the China-specific safeguard.[4]

For the purpose of tracking trends in *levels* of import protection over time, we group together these four TTBs because they are relatively substitutable forms of import protection. The WTO establishes a minimal set of conditions for each of the four different TTBs that national policy makers must follow in order to implement new import protection.

The Products Affected by TTBs and the Global Economic Crisis

In this section, we follow the methodology described in detail in Bown (2010b) and begin by assessing the "stock" of six-digit Harmonized Commodity Description and Coding System (HS) products on which an economy has imposed at least one of the four import-restricting TTB policies.[5] The basic argument for focusing first on the stock of products covered is that changes in the flow of new barriers imposed *and* removed can affect the level of TTB protection over time. The underlying stock of products that *could be* subject to a TTB is relatively fixed over time (at least at the six-digit HS level), and thus, our stock measure is a simple indicator of the scope of imported products affected by an economy's use of TTBs over time.

The first stylized fact is that the combined G-20 use of such temporary trade policies has resulted in a significantly higher stock of products covered by import protection in 2009 relative to precrisis levels.[6] The dark black line of figure 6.2 provides a summary from the World Bank's Temporary Trade Barriers Database of the combined major G-20 users of these four policies over the 1997–2009 period. While the database contains information for many of these economies that dates back further and even into the 1980s, 1997 is a useful starting point for the current analysis, because that is the first year in this sample in which each of the G-20 economies that we analyze started using these temporary trade barriers.

Figure 6.2. Combined G-20 Use of Temporary Trade Barriers, 1997–2009

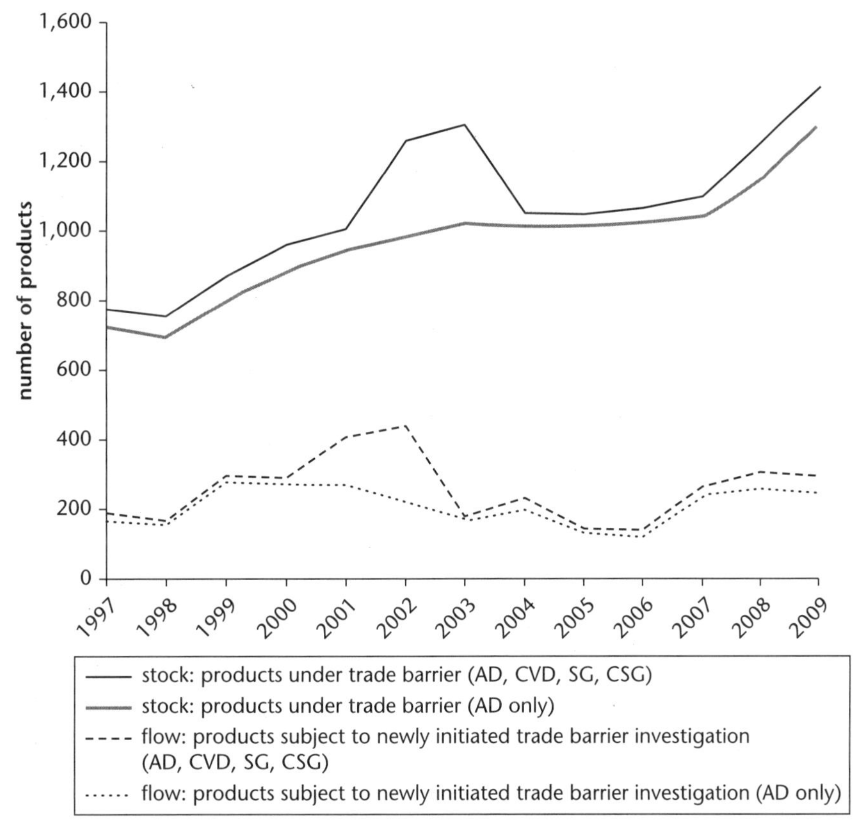

Source: Bown 2010b.

Note: Data on the stock of policies imposed and removed over 1988–2009 were compiled from the Temporary Trade Barriers Database. A "product" is defined at the six-digit HS level. Figure 6.2 illustrates the number of importing country–product combinations affected by policies such as antidumping, countervailing duties, global safeguards, and China-specific transitional safeguards. The data are aggregated over the following 12 G-20 economies: Argentina, Australia, Brazil, Canada, China, the European Union, India, Indonesia, the Republic of Korea, South Africa, Turkey, and the United States. The only major G-20 user of such policies not included in the figure is Mexico, for reasons described in the text. The "stock" includes both imposition and removal of import restrictions after terminations or sunset reviews. With roughly 5,000 six-digit HS product categories per importing economy and 12 policy-imposing countries, the maximum value that the vertical axis could possibly take is 60,000. AD = antidumping, CSG = China-specific transitional safeguards, CVD = countervailing duties, SG = global safeguards.

According to figure 6.2, by the end of 2009 the major G-20 users of TTBs together subjected 25 percent more import product lines to these trade barriers than they did in 2007. While the detailed information in the Temporary Trade Barriers Database does indicate that each of the four TTB policies was used during the crisis, the gray line in figure 6.2 shows that most of the products subject to the TTBs in place during 2007 through 2009 are covered by antidumping policies, which is still the primary TTB of choice for many governments. The dashed and dotted lines in figure 6.2 provide information on the potential "flow" of products that may be subject to new TTBs by illustrating the number of six-digit HS lines subject to newly initiated investigations each year.

As is also clear from figure 6.2, the increase in imported products subject to TTBs between 2007 and 2009 is part of a broader, longer-term upward trend in the use of these sorts of trade barriers. A number of these G-20 member economies undertook extensive tariff-cutting, trade liberalization episodes in the 1990s and early 2000s and subsequently promised to keep their *applied tariffs* low—either through WTO tariff "binding" commitments or through preferential trade agreements. Thus, a general increase in the stock of products subject to these *other*, more flexible TTB policies, which may be thought of as imperfect substitutes for tariffs, is perhaps not surprising. The broad sense from figure 6.2 is that this trend has been ongoing at least since 1997 and perhaps would have continued at some level irrespective of the crisis.

Figure 6.3 presents a second way to measure and examine the extent of imports covered by the TTBs imposed by the major G-20 economies in effect over time. The unit of measurement here goes beyond the product to include the number of distinct exporting-country targets that a new TTB over a given product affects. It therefore measures the combination of products and exporting countries affected by (only) antidumping, countervailing duty, and the China-specific safeguard policies: that is, omitting products subject only to global safeguard policies since such policies are applied on a most-favored nation basis against all foreign sources. The figure also breaks out the incidence of the exporters affected by these policies into three groups: developed-economy exporters, China, and other (non-China) developing economies.

Compared to 2007, figure 6.3 illustrates that the major users of these country-specific policies had a 12 percent higher stock of product-exporter combinations subject to TTBs by the end of 2009. Two main factors explain why the 12 percent increase from 2007 to 2009 of product-exporter combinations is lower than the 25 percent increase for products alone. First, the 2007 stock of products was less than the 2007 stock of product-exporter combinations, and starting from a lower baseline leads to higher growth rate. Second, as we describe in more detail below, the incidence of new barriers imposed between 2007 and 2009 was increasingly on a single foreign supplier (that is, products the G-20 imported from China). The stock of products the G-20 had covered with TTBs that was in effect by 2007 affected many more foreign suppliers on average than the new TTBs that added to that stock in 2008–09.[7]

Figure 6.3. Combined G-20 Use of Selected Temporary Trade Barriers by Import Source, 1997–2009

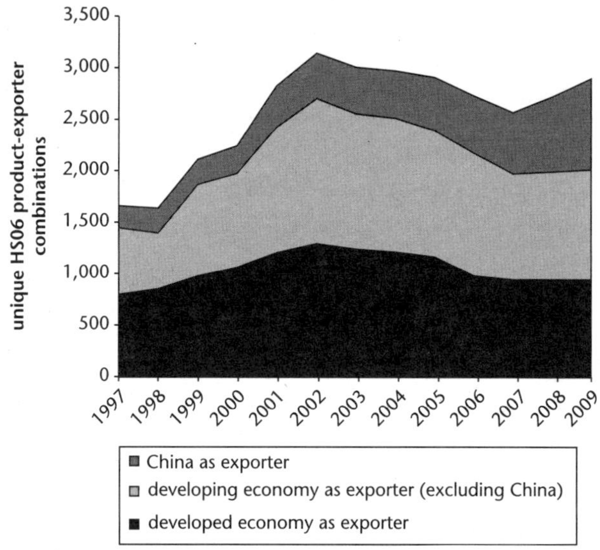

Source: Data on the stock of policies imposed and removed over 1988–2009 compiled from the Temporary Trade Barriers Database.
Note: A "product" is defined at the six-digit HS level. Figure 6.3 illustrates the number of importing country-product–exporting country target combinations affected by policies such as antidumping, countervailing duties, and China-specific transitional safeguards. The policies are aggregated over the following 12 G-20 economies: Argentina, Australia, Brazil, Canada, China, the European Union, India, Indonesia, the Republic of Korea, South Africa, Turkey, and the United States. Mexico is the only major G-20 user of such policies not included, and the reason for its exclusion in this figure is described in the text. The "stock" includes both imposition and removal of import restrictions after terminations or sunset reviews. Unlike figure 6.2, this figure does not reflect the economy's potential use of the global safeguards policy, which is not exporting-country specific.

Figure 6.3 illustrates this second point: how the incidence of the new TTBs added to the stock during 2008–09 was not uniform across export sources. China had 40 percent more exported product lines subject to these G-20 TTBs by the end of 2009 relative to the precrisis level of 2007. The combined increase for all other developing-economy exporters was 4 percent, while developed-economy exporters faced roughly the same number of products affected in 2009 as in 2007. We describe in substantially more detail these and other insights from the exporter's perspective below.

Table 6.1 summarizes the economy-by-economy differences across the major G-20 users of these TTBs. Column (1)

Table 6.1. Stocks of Temporary Trade Barriers Imposed by Individual G-20 Economies, 2009

G-20 economy imposer	Stock of products subject to such barriers in 2009 (1)	% change in (1) relative to precrisis 2007 level (2)	Stock of product–exporter combinations subject to such barriers in 2009 (3)	% change in (3) relative to precrisis 2007 level (4)	Share of (3) imposed against all developing economies (5)	Share of (3) imposed against China only (6)
Developing economies						
India	287	0.61	527	0.41	0.58	0.39
Turkey	256	0.46	276	0.19	0.88	0.55
Argentina	139	0.48	342	0.26	0.77	0.22
Brazil	82	0.22	113	0.06	0.70	0.42
Mexico	61	−2.84	80	−2.59	0.56	0.19
China	46	−0.10	132	−0.26	0.16	NA
South Africa	40	−0.18	59	−0.17	0.80	0.34
Indonesia	24	0.69	66	1.05	0.74	0.18
Total developing economies	935	0.41[a]	1,595	0.22[a]	0.68[b]	0.35[b]
High-income economies						
United States	260	0.10	781	0.05	0.63	0.22
European Union	137	−0.05	249	−0.07	0.86	0.41
Canada	69	0.16	238	0.08	0.70	0.26
Korea, Rep.	38	−0.44	72	−0.25	0.60	0.31
Australia	31	0.39	43	0.26	0.65	0.44
Total high-income economies	535	0.03	1,383	0.02	0.68	0.27

Source: Authors, based on data from the Temporary Trade Barriers Database (Bown 2010c).

a. Data on the stock of policies in place in 2009 compiled by the authors from the Temporary Trade Barriers Database (Bown 2010c). Column (1) includes products affected by the use of one or more of the following four policies: antidumping, countervailing duties, global safeguards, and China-specific transitional safeguards. Column (3) documents the number of exporting country–product combinations affected by the use of only three policies: antidumping, countervailing duties, and China-specific transitional safeguards. The "stock" includes both imposition and removal of import restrictions after terminations or sunset reviews. The maximum value that column (1) could take on for any one economy is roughly 5,000 six-digit HS products. In columns (2) and (4), the percent change from 2007 to 2009 aggregated for the developing economies does not include Mexico for reasons described in the text.

b. In columns (5) and (6), the developing-economy aggregated total does not include China's use.

lists the stock of six-digit HS products covered by at least one TTB in effect in 2009, defined consistently with the aggregated figure 6.2. Column (2) illustrates the percentage change in this stock for each economy when compared to the stock of products covered in 2007. Eight of the 13 G-20 economies listed in the table *increased* the number of products subject to these import restrictions in 2009 when compared to 2007—including Argentina (48 percent more products covered), Australia (39 percent), Brazil (22 percent), Canada (16 percent), India (61 percent), Indonesia (69 percent), Turkey (46 percent), and the United States (10 percent). Only China, the European Union, Mexico, the Republic of Korea, and South Africa reduced the number of products subject to such import barriers between 2007 and 2009.

Columns (3) and (4) of table 6.1 present economy-by-economy differences of the second approach of measuring the stock of imports covered by TTBs in 2009 (consistent with figure 6.3); that is, the product-exporter combinations affected by country-specific TTBs such as antidumping, countervailing duties and the China-specific safeguard. First, while the rank ordering of countries based on (3) is close to the ordering based on (1), it is not identical for two basic reasons. Most important, a larger economy may apply the same product-level TTB to more foreign sources simply because it imports a given product from more trading partners on average owing to its larger market. Furthermore, countries like India and Turkey were more likely to have global safeguard policies in effect in 2009. While any product covered by the global safeguard policy is captured in (1), we have chosen not to include product-exporter combinations subject to global safeguards in (3). Next, column (4) reports growth rates of TTB coverage of product–foreign source combinations in 2009 compared to 2007. Similar to the aggregated statistics described in reference to figure 6.3, on a country-by-country basis this statistic is generally lower than the percentage change for product coverage alone reported in column (2).

Columns (5) and (6) of table 6.1 report the incidence of the stock of temporary trade barriers in place in 2009 that were imposed on imports from *developing*-economy exporters overall and then specifically against China. Overall, 68 percent of the TTBs that G-20 developing economies had imposed by the end of 2009 were on the imports from *other* developing countries. They ranged from a low of 56 percent (Mexico) to a high of 88 percent (Turkey). Of this number, a large share of the TTBs were being imposed on imports from China—an average of 35 percent of all product-exporter combinations involved China, ranging from a low of 19 percent (Mexico) to a high of 55 percent (Turkey). The users of TTBs from high-income economies listed in table 6.1 were imposing roughly the same share of barriers on imports from developing economies *overall* (68 percent). However, and perhaps surprisingly, in 2009 high-income economies imposed a *smaller* share of their TTBs against China (27 percent) than did developing economies (35 percent).

More broadly, figures 6.4 and 6.5 illustrate the evolution of each policy-using economy's stock of imposed TTBs over time and across the three different trading partner categories; that is, the figures decompose figure 6.3 on the basis of policy-imposing countries.[8] Before turning to interesting differences in time trends across policy-using countries, we begin by noting substantial differences in the underlying *levels* of product coverage across the policy-using countries. Specifically, the cumulative levels in 2009 in each figure correspond to column (3) in table 6.1; for example, in figure 6.4, India had 527 product-exporter combinations covered by the TTBs imposed by 2009, which was almost 10 times as many as the 2009 number of only 66 for Indonesia.

Figure 6.4 illustrates the major *developing*-economy members of the G-20 that are users of the TTBs. As described above and summarized in table 6.1 column (4), the stock of product-exporter combinations targeted in 2009 increased in comparison to the precrisis 2007 levels for the following economies: Argentina (26 percent), Brazil (6 percent), India (41 percent), Indonesia (105 percent), and Turkey (19 percent). The only decrease in the stock of product-exporter combinations covered by TTBs during this period took place in China, Mexico, and South Africa.

The illustration for Mexico in figure 6.4 underscores why we have chosen to exclude it from the aggregated analysis pictured in figures 6.2 and 6.3.[9] In 1993, Mexico imposed new antidumping duties on China covering more than a *thousand* six-digit HS product lines (roughly 20 percent of all of its six-digit HS codes), and these duties stayed in place until October 2008 when an agreement was finally reached to remove them. Because this removal coincides with the timing of the 2008–09 global economic crisis (but is unrelated to the crisis) and is so extreme in scale, we have chosen to leave Mexico out of figures 6.2 and 6.3 to better capture the impact of the crisis on aggregate protectionist trends.

Figure 6.4 also reveals the prevalence of China and other developing economies as targets for developing-country use of these TTBs. Although there is some heterogeneity, this incidence of South-South protectionism through TTBs has been increasing over time. Some of the protectionism is certainly to be expected given the evolution of trade patterns and emerging-economy exports. Because a number of developing-economy exporters have become more successful at penetrating new markets for their products, including many developing-economy *import* markets, adjustment in national import-competing industries needs to occur. In some instances, domestic industries resist such adjustments and will request (and sometimes be granted) protection from the new import competition through additional TTBs.

Figure 6.5, which illustrates the time-varying stock of TTBs imposed by high-income economies broken out by the same three categories of exporters, shows several broad trends. First, the stock of TTBs in place by 2009 had declined relative to the post-1995 peak for all five of these economies. For Australia and the EU, the peak was around 1997; for Canada and the United States, it was during the recession of 2001–02.[10] Second, for Australia, Canada, the EU, and the United States, the stock of TTBs imposed on products from developed-economy exporters either remained unchanged or even decreased between 2005 and 2009. In contrast, for the products subject to the continuing TTBs, there is a compositional change toward using such barriers to confront imports from China and other developing economies.

The Potential Trade Impact of the New TTBs Imposed during the Crisis

The previous section provided one way to assess the changing nature of TTB protectionism: through examination of the stocks of products and product-exporter combinations affected by TTBs and of changes in those stocks during the 2008–09 crisis. Next, we provide estimates of the potential trade impact of the flow of TTBs newly imposed during 2008 and 2009.[11] We begin by matching the tariff line TTB policy data to 2007 (precrisis) bilateral, tariff line import data for the G-20 economies of interest. We hope to come up with a basic estimate of how much trade might be eliminated if the newly imposed TTBs were high enough to be prohibitive and with an estimate of the importance of the lost trade to total trade.

As an example, the value of 2007 Indian imports of products on which India would subsequently impose TTBs during 2008–09 was US$3.1 billion, which was 1.4 percent of its total 2007 imports (table 6.2). Of the US$3.1 billion of Indian imports subject to new TTBs in 2008–09, roughly 74 percent (US$2.3 billion) were new Indian TTBs

Figure 6.4. G-20 Developing Economies' Use of Selected Temporary Trade Barriers by Import Source, 1990–2009

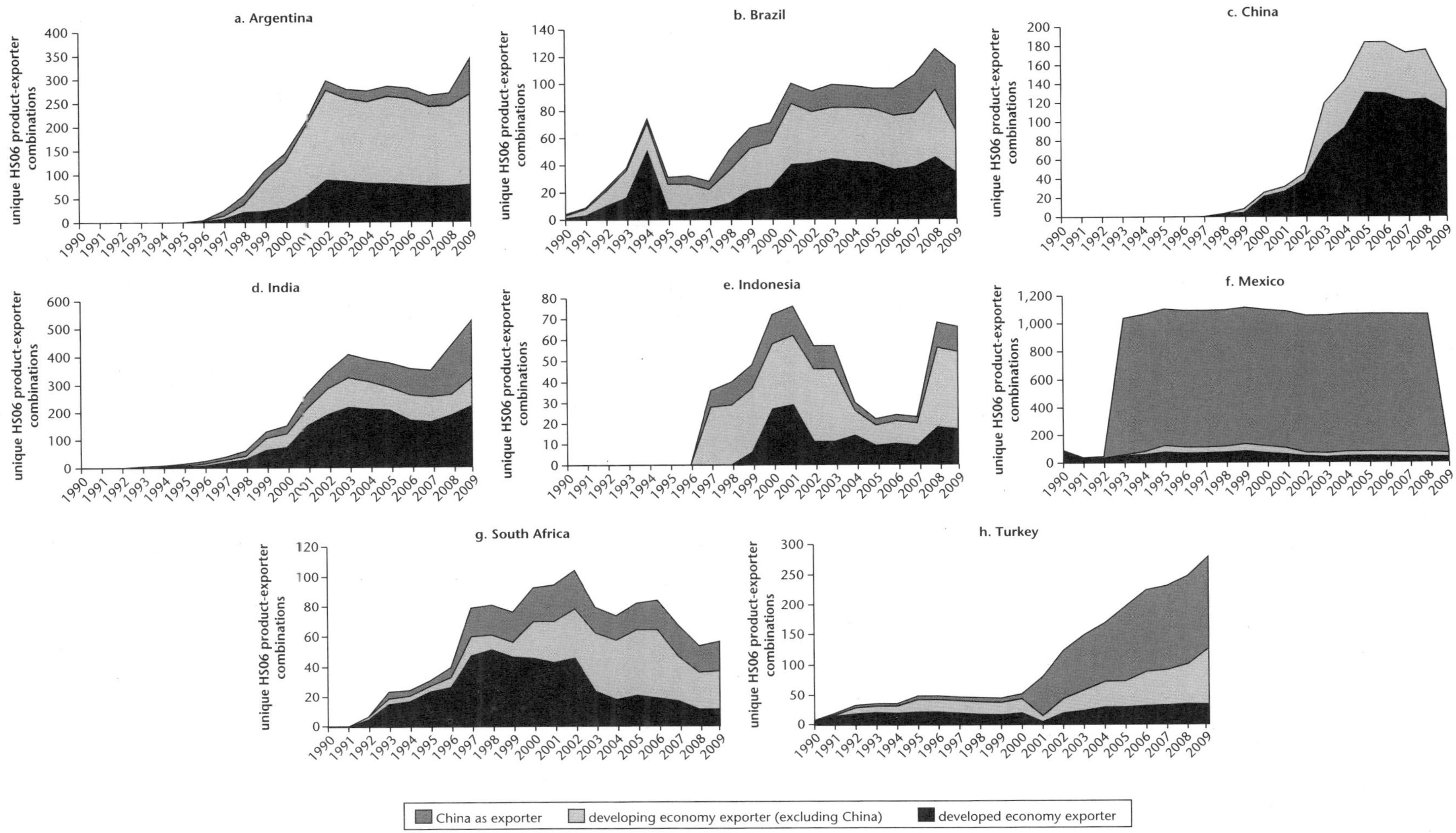

Source: Data on the stock of policies imposed and removed over 1988–2009 compiled from the Temporary Trade Barriers Database.
Note: A "product" is defined at the six-digit HS level. Each figure illustrates the number of importing country-product combinations affected because of the use of exporting-country-specific policies such as antidumping, countervailing duties, and China-specific transitional safeguards. The figures do not reflect the economy's potential use of the global safeguards policy which is not exporting-country specific.

Figure 6.5. G-20 High-Income Economies' Use of Selected Temporary Trade Barriers by Import Source, 1990–2009

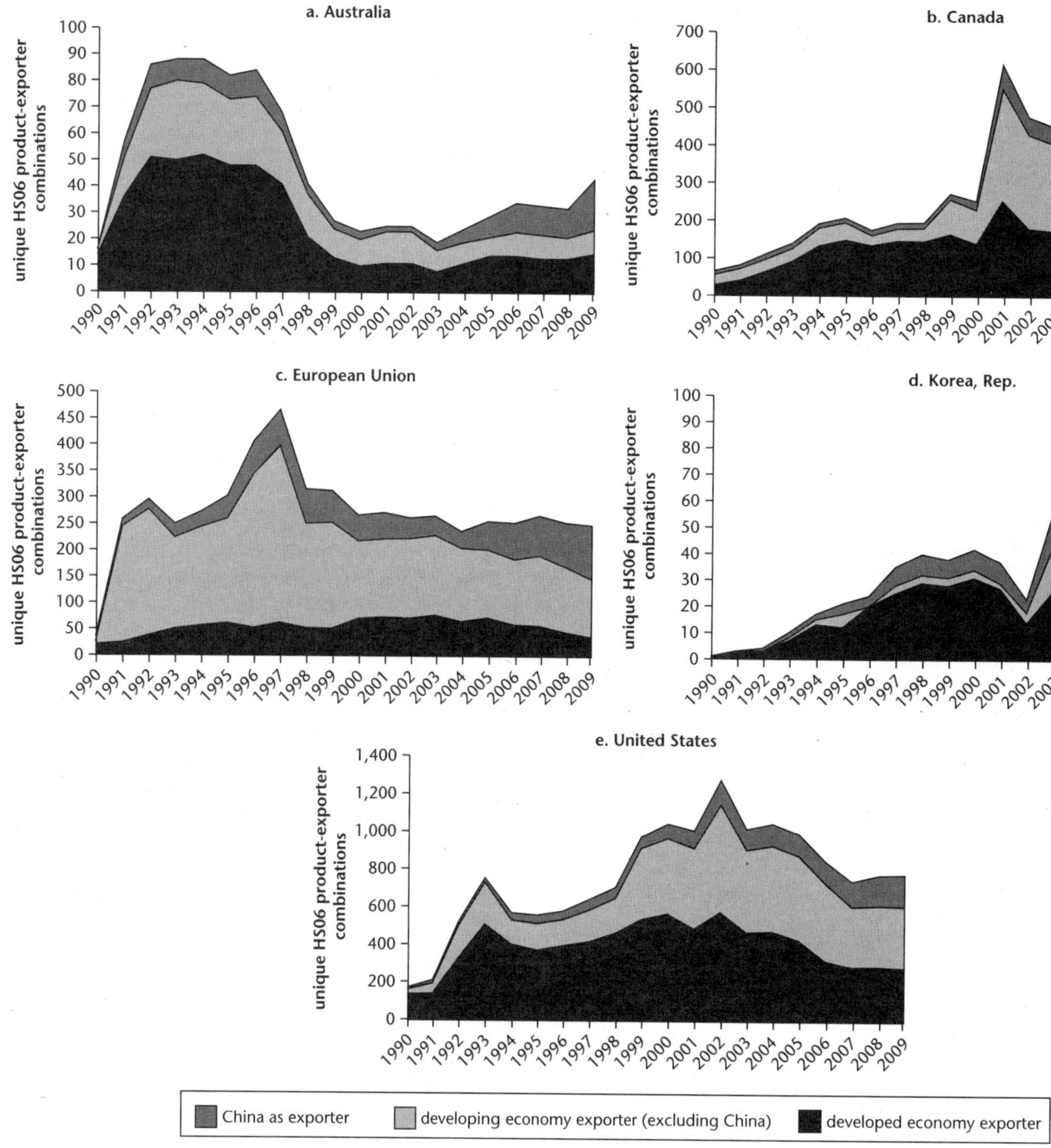

Source: Data on the stock of policies imposed and removed over 1988–2009 compiled from the Temporary Trade Barriers Database.

against imports deriving from China alone. Finally, US$2.3 billion in imports from China subject to new Indian import restrictions covered products that made up 9.5 percent of all Indian imports from China in 2007.

Country-by-country information provided in table 6.2 also indicates that the magnitude of trade potentially affected by India's new TTB policies was not typical of each of the major G-20 economies. Only Turkey (1.1 percent of 2007 total imports) imposed new TTBs in 2008–09 over a comparable share of its total imports. And while the United States (US$10 billion) and European Union (US$7.8 billion) imposed TTBs covering a greater *value* of imports than India, these new TTBs covered a much smaller fraction of each of these economies' overall 2007 imports (0.5 percent and 0.2 percent, respectively).

One common theme from the table is the extent to which China's exports have been subject to new TTBs imposed during the crisis. As we have described in the context of figure 6.3, the stock of Chinese exported product lines facing TTBs in 2009 was 40 percent higher than the measured stock before the crisis in 2007. Table 6.2 translates the new TTBs in 2008–09 imposed on China's exports as covering an estimated US$20.5 billion in trade in 2007. This number is roughly 80 percent of the entire amount of these economies' total 2007 imports covered by new TTBs imposed during 2008–09. Furthermore, the estimated

Table 6.2. G-20 Imports Subject to Newly Imposed Temporary Trade Barriers, 2008–09

G-20 economy imposer	2007 imports for products subject to new TTBs in 2008–09 (US$, thousands) (1)	Share of economy's total 2007 imports (2)	2007 imports from China subject to new TTBs in 2008–09 (US$, thousands) (3)	(3) as a share of (1) (4)	(3) as a share of all 2007 imports from China (5)
Developing economies					
India	3,140,000	0.014	2,332,000	0.743	0.095
China	2,447,700	0.003	n.a.	n.a.	n.a.
Turkey	1,940,000	0.011	640,000	0.323	0.048
Brazil	1,218,000	0.005	653,000	0.536	0.026
Argentina	303,800	0.007	167,400	0.551	0.033
Indonesia	289,026	0.004	123,533	0.427	0.014
Mexico	76,400	0.000	39,600	0.518	0.001
South Africa	7,803	0.000	5,631	0.722	0.001
High-income economies					
United States	9,990,000	0.005	9,080,000	0.909	0.027
European Union	7,750,000	0.002	6,540,000	0.844	0.010
Canada	673,000	0.002	622,000	0.924	0.017
Australia	281,600	0.002	272,200	0.967	0.012
Total	28,117,330	0.003	20,475,365	0.798[a]	0.018

Source: Temporary trade barriers imposed during 2008 or 2009 and 2007 import data on the economy's national tariff line level from Comtrade matched to tariff line policy data from the Temporary Trade Barriers Database (Bown 2010c).
Note: n.a. = not applicable.
a. The aggregated total subtracts out from the denominator the value of China's imports subject to its own new TTBs, since China does not impose TTBs on its own exports.

US$20.5 billion was 1.8 percent of the value of total Chinese exports to these particular G-20 markets in 2007.

Finally, table 6.2 presents data for the potential trade affected by the *aggregated* G-20 use of TTBs during 2008–09. While over US$28 billion in G-20 member economy imports from 2007 was subsequently subjected to new TTBs during 2008–09, that number was only 0.3 percent of these G-20 member economies' total imports.

Tariffs, Antidumping, and the Overall Trade Restrictiveness Index

Another way to study the potential crisis-era trade impact of policies such as tariffs and antidumping duties is to construct an overall trade restrictiveness index (OTRI) for each policy-imposing economy and compare their changes over time. The OTRI is a more sophisticated way to measure average tariffs, which takes into account the composition of import volume and import demand elasticities. A country's OTRI is higher than its import-weighted average tariff when it levies higher tariffs on the more elastic imported products: that is, when tariffs and import demand elasticities are positively correlated. Kee, Neagu, and Nicita (2010) constructed the OTRI for a wide range of countries over the crisis period using data on product-line tariff changes (International Trade Centre) and imposed antidumping duties (Bown 2010a).[12] Table 6.3 presents results for the G-20 policy-imposing economies broken into three categories: all sectors, manufacturing, and agriculture. The middle three columns present the estimates of the OTRI for 2008, the estimates of the OTRI for 2009, and the change from 2008 to 2009, respectively. The right-most column is the estimated *trade impact* in dollars of the changes in these economies' OTRI between these two years.

Among the G-20 economies, Argentina, the Russian Federation, and Turkey have the largest increases in their OTRIs, at 0.9, 1.2, and 0.8 percentage points, respectively. Since we do not have detailed data on antidumping use for Russia, its increase in OTRI is driven entirely by its increase in tariffs, mainly in the manufacturing sector. Similarly for Turkey, the increase in its agricultural tariff was the main culprit for its OTRI change, even outweighing the magnitude of its substantial resort to new antidumping duties during the crisis period.[13] For Argentina, roughly two-thirds of its OTRI increase and the resulting trade loss can be attributed to antidumping duties, while the remaining share is due to the tariff increases in its manufacturing sector.

For the EU and the United States, changes in antidumping duties had relatively more impact than tariff changes, particularly for manufactured products from China and other exporters.[14] These duties have resulted in a large loss in trade that overshadows the EU's tariff liberalization in the agricultural sector.

Table 6.3. Overall Trade Restrictiveness of G-20 Economies, 2008–09

Imposing economy	Sector	OTRI 2008	OTRI 2009	Change	Aggregate trade effects (US$, thousands)
Argentina	All	0.039	0.048	0.009	–914,534
Australia	All	0.044	0.031	–0.014	4,575,676
Brazil	All	0.080	0.083	0.003	–991,122
Canada	All	0.013	0.016	0.003	–1,857,762
China	All	0.064	0.068	0.003	–5,263,381
European Union	All	0.017	0.018	0.001	–1,935,871
Indonesia	All	0.033	0.027	–0.006	990,744
India	All	0.064	0.067	0.004	–1,833,246
Japan	All	0.044	0.044	0.000	–75,556
Korea, Rep.	All	0.093	0.093	0.000	–78,149
Mexico	All	0.017	0.015	–0.002	707,280
Russian Federation	All	0.096	0.108	0.012	–4,834,623
Saudi Arabia	All	0.040	0.040	0.000	–1,186
South Africa	All	0.033	0.031	–0.002	199,176
Turkey	All	0.020	0.028	0.008	–2,218,696
United States	All	0.011	0.017	0.005	–24,100,000
Argentina	MF	0.045	0.056	0.011	–926,261
Australia	MF	0.047	0.033	–0.014	4,447,388
Brazil	MF	0.089	0.093	0.004	-986,717
Canada	MF	0.009	0.010	0.001	–401,627
China	MF	0.055	0.055	0.000	646,881
European Union	MF	0.012	0.014	0.001	–3,648,412
Indonesia	MF	0.032	0.026	–0.006	902,396
India	MF	0.057	0.057	0.000	25,154
Japan	MF	0.011	0.011	0.000	130,473
Korea, Rep.	MF	0.042	0.042	0.000	–15,776
Mexico	MF	0.016	0.014	–0.002	745,403
Russian Federation	MF	0.076	0.088	0.012	–4,381,372
Saudi Arabia	MF	0.039	0.039	0.000	–304
South Africa	MF	0.030	0.029	–0.001	110,732
Turkey	MF	0.008	0.011	0.002	–628,322
United States	MF	0.011	0.017	0.006	–24,100,000
Argentina	AG	0.011	0.011	–0.001	11,728
Australia	AG	0.012	0.006	–0.005	128,288
Brazil	AG	0.033	0.033	0.000	–4,404
Canada	AG	0.058	0.087	0.029	–1,456,455
China	AG	0.161	0.203	0.042	–5,910,257
European Union	AG	0.081	0.073	–0.008	1,712,236
Indonesia	AG	0.044	0.038	–0.005	88,347
India	AG	0.248	0.352	0.104	–1,858,403
Japan	AG	0.316	0.317	0.001	–206,023
Korea, Rep.	AG	0.604	0.605	0.001	–62,371
Mexico	AG	0.021	0.022	0.001	–38,123
Russian Federation	AG	0.204	0.211	0.007	–453,253
Saudi Arabia	AG	0.043	0.043	0.000	–883
South Africa	AG	0.066	0.058	–0.008	88,444
Turkey	AG	0.212	0.314	0.102	–1,590,374
United States	AG	0.019	0.019	0.000	3,707

Source: Kee, Neagu, and Nicita 2010.
Note: All calculations are based on bilateral tariffs and antidumping duties, with the exception of India, Japan, and Korea when most-favored nation tariffs are used because of missing data. Changes reported in parentheses are estimated decreases in OTRI. AG = agriculture; MF = manufacturing.

Developing-Country Exporters and the Incidence of Crisis-Era Protectionism

In this section, we consider the impact of new, crisis-era G-20 protectionism from the perspective of the exporting economies subject to the trade barriers. We follow the same basic presentation approach as the previous section. Because so much of crisis-induced protection has come in the form of TTBs, we begin by examining changes in the pattern of the stock of exported products subject to TTBs over time. We then use the tariff-line import data matched to these TTBs imposed during the crisis to project the amount and distribution of exporters' trade possibly affected by the imposition of new TTBs in 2008–09. Finally, we turn to model-based estimates of the market access–OTRI.

Temporary Trade Barriers and the Incidence on Developing-Country Exports

While the stock of products subject to new temporary trade barriers in 2009 has increased 25 percent over the precrisis levels of 2007, the data also reveal a nonuniform impact of such barriers across exporters: both in the level and in the growth rate. As can be surmised from table 6.2, many of the new trade barriers during this period have affected China's exports.

Figures 6.6 and 6.7 provide evidence on how the imposed exporter-specific trade barriers are affecting a number of exporting economies over time, including during the crisis era. Both figures show data on the number of an economy's exported products subject to a G-20-imposed TTB each year, further broken down into two categories based on whether the policy-imposing country was a *developed* or a *developing* G-20 member economy.[15] In addition to the interesting trends in the data, there are also substantial differences in the level of TTB stocks imposed across exporting economies. For example in figure 6.6, European Union exporters had 223 (six-digit HS) products subject to foreign-imposed TTBs by the end of 2009, whereas exporters from the United States had only 91 products subject to foreign-imposed TTBs.

Figure 6.6 identifies and examines the main high-income exporting economies that have been subject to TTBs over time. As we have already mentioned (with respect to figure 6.3), in the aggregate exporters from high-income economies were subject to roughly the same stock of imposed TTBs in 2009 as before the onset of the crisis in 2007. The economy-specific panels in figure 6.6 also illustrate little heterogeneity during the crisis period across these different exporting economies. While the overall stock of TTBs imposed on these high-income exporting economies has remained relatively flat in recent years, even during the crisis, a longer time frame indicates some change in the *composition* of TTBs by policy-imposing economy. In each of the panels of figure 6.6, an increasing share of the products covered by TTBs imposed over time derives from policies imposed by *developing* economies.

Figure 6.7 presents the same breakdown of information for the TTBs affecting a number of *developing* economies whose exporters are subject to TTBs. As observed in the context of the aggregated figure 6.3, the stock of G-20 TTBs confronted 884 different Chinese exported product-import market combinations in 2009, a 40 percent increase over the stock of product-market combinations subject to G-20 TTBs in 2007. Brazil, India, Indonesia, Russia, South Africa, Thailand, and Ukraine are examples of other developing-economy exporters that confronted a relatively high number of their exported products subject to foreign-imposed TTBs in 2009. Nevertheless, as the economy-specific panels in figure 6.7 illustrate, there are differences across these economies in (a) the frequency with which they are subject to such TTBs, and (b) whether the importing-economy trading partner imposing the new TTBs is a developed or a developing economy. Finally, with the exception of Vietnam, it is also important to note that few countries classified as low income by the World Bank have a high stock of exported products subject to TTBs.

Table 6.4 summarizes key elements of information contained in figures 6.6 and 6.7. The first column provides data on which exporting countries face the greatest total quantity of imposed import restrictions on their traded products. By the end of 2009, China's exported products faced roughly four times as many G-20 TTBs as the second-most-affected exporting economy (European Union). Table 6.4 also provides estimates of the change in the 2009 stock relative to the precrisis year of 2007. The middle column of data again shows that, in the aggregate, exporters in developed economies face roughly the same number of such barriers in 2009 as they did in 2007. And while the stock of barriers facing all developing economies in the aggregate increased by 18 percent, those facing all developing countries aside from China increased by only 4 percent. Nevertheless, the increase in total combined product-import market coverage between 2007 and 2009 was particularly pronounced for developing-economy exporters such as India (17 percent), Indonesia (25 percent), Thailand (23 percent), and Vietnam (73 percent).

In addition to the exporter incidence associated with the crisis-era growth of such trade barriers, the last column of table 6.4 provides summary statistics on the extent to which the particular stock of exported products affected by TTBs in place by 2009 is South-South in

Figure 6.6. Exports of High-Income Economies Subject to Selected Temporary Trade Barriers, 1990–2009

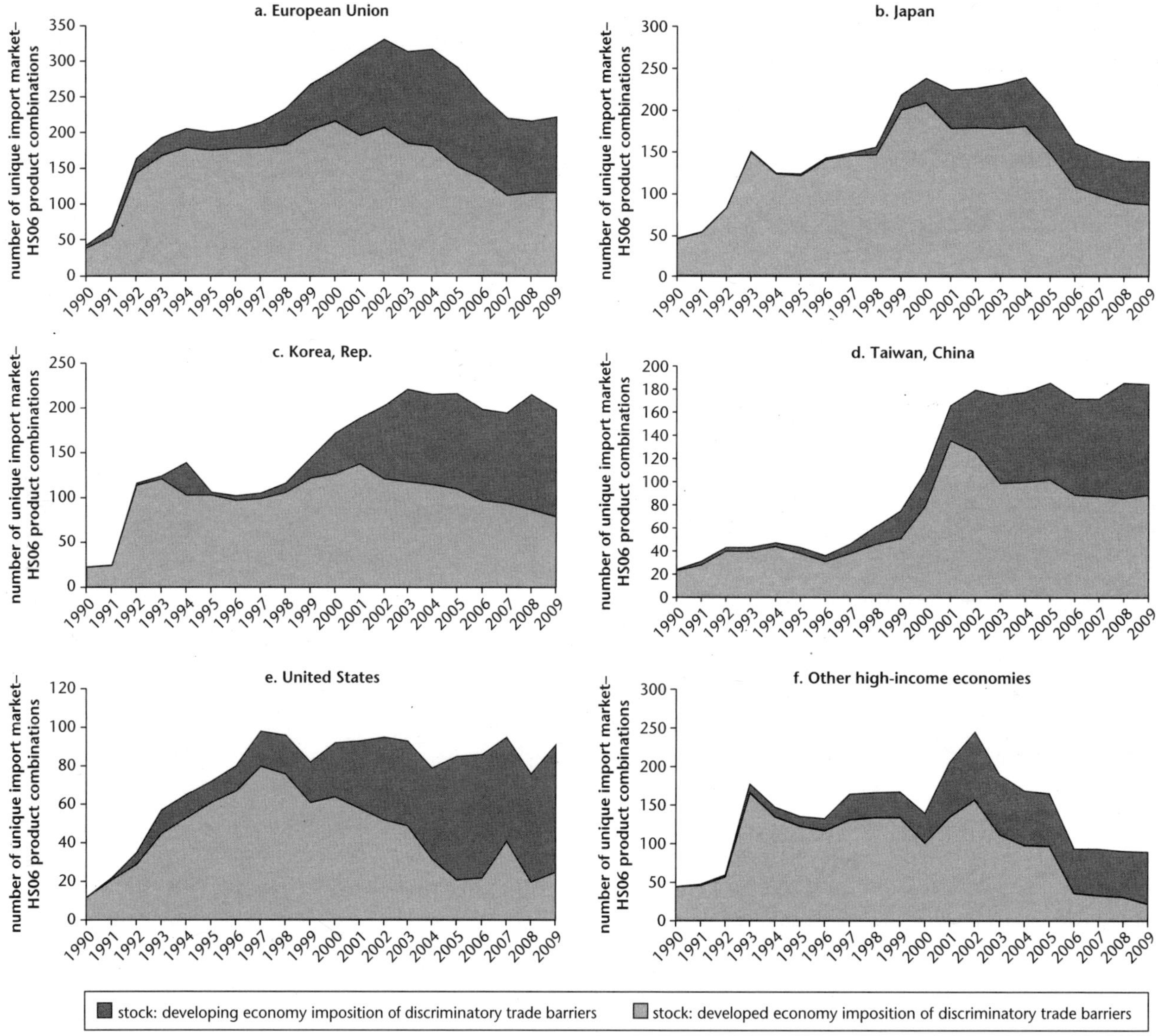

Source: Data on the stock of policies imposed and removed over 1988–2009 compiled by the authors from the Temporary Trade Barriers Database.
Note: The figures illustrate the number of importing country–product combinations affected by the use of policies such as antidumping, countervailing duties, and China-specific transitional safeguards aggregated over the following G-20 economies: seven developing (Argentina, Brazil, China, India, Indonesia, South Africa, and Turkey) and five developed (Australia, Canada, the European Union, the Republic of Korea, and the United States). The only major G-20 user of such policies not included in the figures is Mexico. The "stock" includes both imposition and removal of import restrictions after terminations or sunset reviews. With roughly 5,000 six-digit HS product categories per importing economy and 12 policy-imposing countries, the maximum value that the vertical axis could possibly take is 60,000. "Other" includes Australia; Canada; Croatia; Denmark; the Faeroe Islands; Hong Kong SAR, China; Israel; Kuwait; Liechtenstein; Macau SAR, China; Norway; Oman; Qatar; Saudi Arabia; Singapore; Trinidad and Tobago; and the United Arab Emirates.

nature. Overall, other developing economies imposed 52 percent of the TTBs facing developing-economy exporters in 2009. With a (somewhat arbitrary) threshold of 90 product-import market combinations as the cutoff defining which exporting economies were most severely affected by TTBs as of 2009, developing economies were responsible for more than 50 percent of the TTB-affected products for the following exporters above the cutoff: China (58 percent), Indonesia (53 percent), Malaysia (85 percent), South Africa (57 percent), and Thailand (60 percent). Only for major emerging-market exporters like Brazil (38 percent), India (37 percent), Russia (40 percent), and Ukraine (25 percent) did developing economies impose a minority of the TTBs they faced in 2009. And as figure 6.7 illustrates, even for these emerging economies, over time other developing economies are imposing an increasing share of the TTBs that confront their exporters.

Figure 6.7. Exports of Developing Economies Subject to Selected Temporary Trade Barriers, 1990–2009

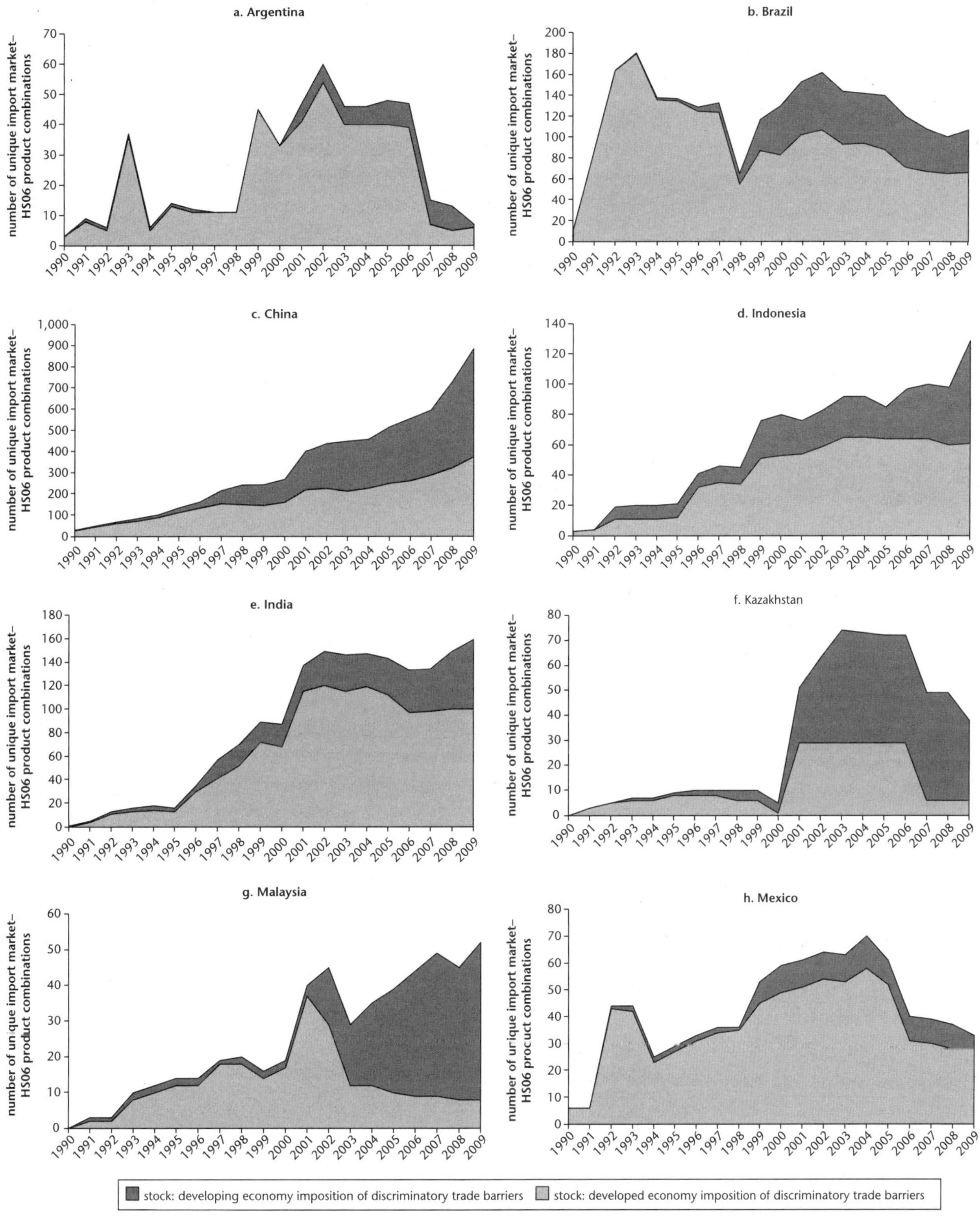

(continued)

Figure 6.7. *(continued)*

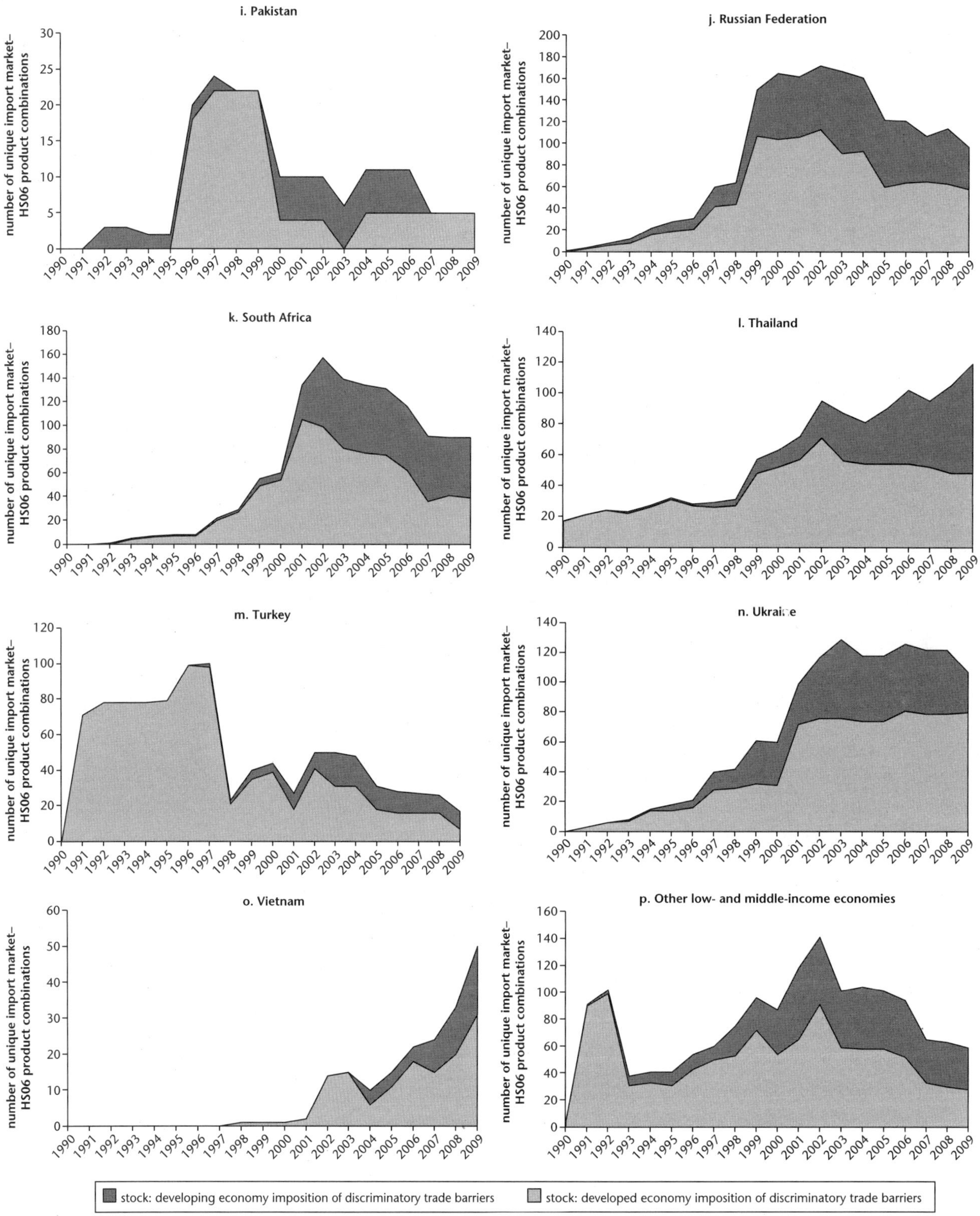

Source: See source notes to figure 6.6.

Note: "Other" includes Albania, Algeria, Armenia, Azerbaijan, Bangladesh, Belarus, Bosnia and Herzegovina, Chile, Colombia, Costa Rica, Côte d'Ivoire, Cuba, Dominican Republic, Ecuador, the Arab Republic of Egypt, Georgia, the Islamic Republic of Iran, Kyrgyz Republic, Lebanon, the Former Yugoslav Republic of Macedonia, Malawi, Moldova, Nepal, Nigeria, Paraguay, Peru, the Philippines, Sri Lanka, Uruguay, and República Bolivariana de Venezuela.

Table 6.4. Major Exporters Subject to Stock of Selected G-20 Temporary Trade Barriers, 2009

Exporting economy	Stock of product – import market combinations subject to such barriers in 2009 (1)	% change in (1) relative to precrisis 2007 level developing G-20 economies (2)	Share of (1) imposed on exporter by (3)
Developing-country exporters			
China	884	0.40	0.58
India	159	0.17	0.37
Indonesia	129	0.25	0.53
Thailand	119	0.23	0.60
Brazil	107	–0.01	0.38
Ukraine	107	–0.13	0.25
Russian Federation	97	–0.10	0.40
South Africa	90	–0.01	0.57
Malaysia	52	0.06	0.85
Vietnam	50	0.73	0.38
Kazakhstan	38	–0.25	0.84
Mexico	33	–0.17	0.15
Turkey	17	–0.46	0.59
Argentina	7	–0.76	0.14
Pakistan	5	0.00	0.00
Other developing countries	59	–0.10	0.53
Total developing-economy exporters	1,953	0.18	0.52
High-income exporting economies			
European Union	223	0.01	0.48
Korea, Rep.	199	0.02	0.60
Taiwan, China	185	0.07	0.52
Japan	138	–0.07	0.37
United States	91	–0.04	0.73
Other high-income countries	89	–0.04	0.75
Total high-income economy exporters	925	0.00	0.55

Source: Data on the stock of policies imposed and removed over 1988–2009 compiled by the authors from the Temporary Trade Barriers Database (Bown 2010a).
Note: The table illustrates the number of importing country–product combinations affected by the use of policies such as antidumping, countervailing duties, and China-specific transitional safeguards aggregated over the following twelve G-20 economies: Argentina, Australia, Brazil, Canada, China, the European Union, India, Indonesia, Korea, South Africa, Turkey, and the United States. Mexico is the only major G-20 user of such policies not included, and the reason for its exclusion in this table is described in the text. The "stock" includes both imposition and removal of import restrictions after terminations or sunset reviews. With roughly 5,000 six-digit HS product categories per importing economy and 12 policy-imposing countries, the maximum value that column (1) for any one exporting economy could possibly take is 60,000.

The Potential Trade Impact of New TTBs on Exports During the Crisis

Analogous to the approach adopted above, we move beyond examining stocks of six-digit HS exported products subject to TTBs and consider the *value* of exports potentially affected by the flow of the main G-20 users' imposition of new TTBs during 2008–09.

As an example, the value of China's 2007 exports that would subsequently be subject to new TTBs imposed by the other G-20 members during 2008–09 was US$20.5 billion, which was 1.8 percent of its total exports to those economies in 2007 (table 6.5). Of the US$20.5 billion in exports, US$4 billion was exported to developing economies, which was 3.5 percent of China's total exports to those economies. In contrast, US$16.5 billion was exported to developed economies, which was only 1.6 percent of China's total exports to those economies. As such, a much larger fraction of China's exports to other developing economies was subject to new TTBs in 2008–2009 than its exports to high-income economies.

A similar phenomenon holds for seven of the next most frequently targeted countries on the list of developing-economy exporters in table 6.5. India, Indonesia, Pakistan, Russia, Thailand, Turkmenistan, and Uzbekistan each had a larger share of its 2007 exports to other developing economies become subject to new TTBs in 2008–09 than the share of the 2007 exports sent to high-income economies. In the aggregate, 1.3 percent of the 2007 value of all developing-economy exports to G-20 developing economies would be subject to new TTBs in 2008–09,

Table 6.5. The Value of Exports Subject to G-20 Temporary Trade Barriers Newly Imposed in 2008–09

Exporting economy	2007 exports to G-20 subject to new TTBs in 2008–09 (US$, thousands)	% of total exports to to G-20 subject new TTB	2007 exports to G-20 developing economies subject to new TTBs in 2008–09 (US$, thousands)	% of total exports to G-20 developing economies subject to new TTB	2007 exports to G-20 developing economies subject to new TTBs in 2008–09 (US$, thousands)	% of total exports to G-20 developing economies subject to new TTB
Developing-economy exporters total	23,401,616	0.008	6,140,224	0.013	17,261,392	0.007
China	20,470,000	0.018	3,970,000	0.035	16,500,000	0.016
India	583,729	0.005	575,000	0.022	8,729	0.000
Indonesia	416,200	0.005	358,000	0.016	58,200	0.001
Russian Federation	389,500	0.001	343,000	0.007	46,500	0.000
Moldova	345,000	0.166	—	0.000	345,000	0.171
Thailand	278,000	0.002	278,000	0.008	—	0.000
Uzbekistan	186,000	0.038	186,000	0.182	—	0.000
Vietnam	128,861	0.003	7,861	0.001	121,000	0.003
Pakistan	128,000	0.008	128,000	0.054	—	0.000
Malaysia	99,000	0.001	99,000	0.002	—	0.000
Mexico	85,800	0.000	—	0.000	85,800	0.000
Turkmenistan	69,000	0.042	69,000	0.151	—	0.000
Brazil	62,400	0.000	45,200	0.001	17,200	0.000
Other developing countries	160,125	0.000	81,161	0.001	78,963	0.000
Total high-income exporting economies	4,720,216	0.001	3,287,316	0.002	1,432,900	0.000
European Union	1,308,000	0.002	1,130,000	0.003	178,000	0.000
United States	1,279,000	0.001	486,000	0.002	793,000	0.001
Taiwan, China	1,094,000	0.005	993,000	0.008	101,000	0.001
Korea, Rep.	552,000	0.002	408,000	0.003	144,000	0.001
Canada	136,032	0.000	32	0.000	136,000	0.000
Other high-income countries	351,184	0.000	270,284	0.001	80,900	0.000

Source: Temporary trade barriers imposed during 2008 or 2009, 2007 import data at the tariff line level from Comtrade matched to tariff line policy data from the Temporary Trade Barriers Database (Bown 2010a).
Note: Exports aggregated over the following twelve G-20 economies: Argentina, Australia, Brazil, Canada, China, the European Union, India, Indonesia, Mexico, South Africa, Turkey, and the United States. Korea is the only major G-20 user of such policies not included. The aggregated figures in this table may not match exactly those in table 6.2 due to rounding. — = not available.

whereas only 0.7 percent of their exports to G-20 high-income economies would be affected. These data provide additional evidence of the increasing prevalence of South-South protectionism in the crisis era.

MA-OTRI

A final approach used to identify which exporting countries are hardest hit by the G-20's changing trade policies during the crisis period is to use the market access overall trade restrictiveness index (MA-OTRI) (see table 6.6). Analogous to the OTRI described earlier, the MA-OTRI measures the average foreign tariff faced by a given country's exporters, taking into account export composition and the import demand elasticities of the importing economies. Kee, Neagu, and Nicita (2010) calculate the changes in the MA-OTRI for a wide range of countries over the crisis period due to trade policy changes of G-20 and non-G-20 countries.

Consistent with the impact described above that focused exclusively on TTBs and disregarded tariffs, the exporter most affected by G-20 changes in trade policy during the crisis was China. China's MA-OTRI increased by 1.5 percentage points, which translates to an estimated US$28 billion reduction in exports (if the model allows trade to fall more than the 2008 level) or US$5 billion (if the model restricts the value of the fall in trade to an amount no larger than the 2008 level). The biggest trade value impact facing China comes in the form of new G-20 antidumping duties imposed on manufacturing exports, particularly those imposed by developed economies such as the United States. This finding too is consistent with the results of table 6.5.

Nevertheless, the MA-OTRI results indicate that a number of other developing countries witnessed severe erosion of access to G-20 markets. Bosnia, Indonesia, Kazakhstan, and Panama each experienced an MA-OTRI increase in the range of 0.12 to 0.4 percentage points. Most of Indonesia's trade loss came from India's removal of a temporary tariff reduction on palm oil. Kazakhstan and Panama suffered mainly from additional tariff restrictions in the agricultural sector in China, India, and Turkey. Bosnia lost access to export markets in manufactured products to the EU. Bhutan, Botswana, Brazil, the Kyrgyz Republic, Lebanon, Russia, Sri Lanka, Tanzania, and Ukraine also experienced export reductions due to G-20 changes in trade policy, with a joint loss in access to export markets of roughly US$621 million.

Besides the developing countries, high-income economies such as the European Union; Hong Kong SAR, China; Israel; Korea; Norway; and the United States also faced an increasingly adverse impact of crisis-era restrictions on exports. In particular, China increased its tariff on salmon from Norway from 10 to 40 percent, which severely restricted Norway's access to the Chinese market, given the very elastic import demand for that product.

Other important insights arise from analysis of the MA-OTRI, given that we can also calculate the indexes at the sectoral level. Table 6.6 decomposes the overall changes into compositional changes for the agriculture and manufacturing sector MA-OTRIs during the crisis period. For agricultural products, increased tariff protection in Turkey on meslin and wheat spelt, as well as the European Union's on bananas, severely restricted the market access of Kazakhstan, Panama, and Russia. The agriculture MA-OTRI of these countries increased from 2 to 3.7 percentage points, resulting in a trade loss of US$738 million. The above-mentioned tariff reversal on palm oil by India explains a large part of Indonesia's MA-OTRI increase of 7.4 percentage points and the corresponding trade loss of $1.5 billion.

Argentina, Bosnia, Botswana, Brazil, Indonesia, Sri Lanka, and Ukraine are other countries aside from China whose manufacturing exports were adversely affected by increased barriers. Each of these countries saw its manufacturing MA-OTRI increase by 0.1 to 0.4 percentage points, and jointly their exports were decreased by US$550 million. For most countries, the main new G-20 trade barriers came in the form of increased tariffs, while the impact on Brazil and Indonesia was the result of additional antidumping duties imposed on manufactured goods.

Finally, while the intensity of G-20 imposed TTBs such as antidumping did increase during the crisis period, for a number of exporting economies the adverse impact on market access may be offset by simultaneous G-20 tariff reductions for other imported product lines. As such, we can reconcile some of the different magnitudes to the estimates presented in tables 6.5 (TTBs only) and 6.6 (tariffs and antidumping only). For example, table 6.5 indicates that India's exporters were subject to substantially more new TTBs and even that 2.2 percent (or US$575 million) of its 2007 exports to other G-20 developing economies would become subject to newly imposed TTBs during the crisis. Nevertheless, table 6.6 indicates that this adverse impact on market access due to TTBs was at least partially offset by new market access opportunities for Indian exporters of other products; one specific example turns out to be due to China's reducing its applied tariff on cotton imports from 40 percent to 6.4 percent. Furthermore, while Vietnam was also adversely affected by new TTBs, its MA-OTRI is positively affected by China's reducing its tariff from 378 percent to 25 percent for television imports

Table 6.6. Examples of Major Changes in MA-OTRI due to G-20 Trade Policy Changes, 2008–09

Exporting economy	Sector	2008	2009	Change	Aggregate trade effect (US$, thousands)
Norway	All	0.018	0.049	0.032	–8,307,226
China	All	0.045	0.060	0.015	–27,500,000
Indonesia	All	0.037	0.049	0.012	–1,676,246
Panama	All	0.024	0.031	0.007	–30,388
Kazakhstan	All	0.005	0.011	0.005	–338,276
Hong Kong SAR, China	All	0.026	0.030	0.004	–388,736
Bosnia And Herzegowina	All	0.005	0.009	0.004	–11,076
Botswana	All	0.002	0.005	0.003	–3,992
Tanzania	All	0.023	0.026	0.003	–6,707
United States	All	0.043	0.046	0.002	–3,688,027
Kyrgyz Republic	All	0.027	0.029	0.002	–1,605
Sri Lanka	All	0.052	0.053	0.002	–20,263
Israel	All	0.012	0.013	0.001	–101,276
Ukraine	All	0.030	0.031	0.001	–111,810
Korea, Rep.	All	0.045	0.047	0.001	–525,618
Brazil	All	0.041	0.041	0.001	–176,619
Russian Federation	All	0.009	0.010	0.001	–298,196
Lebanon	All	0.008	0.009	0.001	–1,185
Bhutan	All	0.000	0.001	0.001	–170
European Union	All	0.012	0.012	0.001	–4,134,099
China	MF	0.041	0.056	0.016	–27,500,000
Norway	MF	0.008	0.017	0.010	–2,092,733
Hong Kong SAR, China	MF	0.026	0.031	0.004	–390,103
Bosnia And Herzegovina	MF	0.003	0.007	0.004	–11,950
Botswana	MF	0.002	0.005	0.003	–3,992
Ukraine	MF	0.011	0.013	0.002	–131,633
Sri Lanka	MF	0.051	0.053	0.002	–19,061
Israel	MF	0.009	0.011	0.002	–107,292
United States	MF	0.017	0.019	0.001	–1,982,447
Brazil	MF	0.007	0.008	0.001	–217,877
Argentina	MF	0.007	0.008	0.001	–43,196
Korea, Rep.	MF	0.042	0.043	0.001	–532,827
Indonesia	MF	0.033	0.034	0.001	–122,079
Maldives	MF	0.007	0.007	0.001	–8
European Union	MF	0.010	0.011	0.001	–3,407,266
Norway	AG	0.070	0.218	0.148	–6,214,493
Indonesia	AG	0.062	0.136	0.074	–1,554,168
Russian Federation	AG	0.094	0.131	0.037	–380,338
Kazakhstan	AG	0.019	0.056	0.036	–325,425
Panama	AG	0.029	0.049	0.020	–32,022
United States	AG	0.239	0.248	0.009	–1,697,471
Malaysia	AG	0.059	0.068	0.008	–175,319
Tanzania	AG	0.030	0.037	0.007	–8,690
Bhutan	AG	0.002	0.008	0.005	–145
Bahrain	AG	0.087	0.092	0.004	–349
Kyrgyz Republic	AG	0.046	0.050	0.004	–1,620
Lebanon	AG	0.022	0.025	0.003	–1,038
Switzerland	AG	0.100	0.102	0.002	–14,096
European Union	AG	0.029	0.030	0.001	–726,839
Canada	AG	0.026	0.027	0.001	–221,993
China	AG	0.187	0.188	0.001	–39,327
Sri Lanka	AG	0.054	0.054	0.001	–1,202

Source: Kee, Neagu, and Nicita 2010.

and Russia's lowering of its tariff on imported rice. These are examples of countries whose overall market access opportunities did not deteriorate over the crisis period by as much as one might infer by relying solely on estimates of their realized loss of market access stemming from newly imposed TTBs. The overall impact of G-20 trade policy changes during the crisis era will ultimately be judged by the larger impact of two competing forces: whether exporters receiving new opportunities for market access were ultimately able to capitalize on them, or whether exporters that faced the imposition of new trade barriers were unable to identify ways to overcome them and had to reduce sales or exit the market.

Policy Implications and Conclusions

This chapter has identified a number of stylized facts regarding the evolving pattern of import protection associated with the global economic crisis. Overall, the major economies of the international trading system—in particular the G-20 members—largely refrained from using protectionist instruments that had been used during earlier crisis eras, such as across-the-board increases in applied tariffs and the imposition of new quantitative restrictions. Instead, most of the new protectionism came in the form of potentially WTO-consistent use of temporary trade barriers such as antidumping, countervailing duties, and safeguards.

Developing economies can take away important insights from the crisis-era implementation of new TTBs in particular. On one hand, the global economy could be heartened by the resilience of the world trading system under the WTO. Perhaps the resilience was due to the design of WTO rules allowing for a relatively small incidence of new protectionism through permissible TTBs. Perhaps other factors, such as the globalization of supply chains, have effectively reduced the threat of protectionism stemming from traditional political-economic forces. Whatever the cause, the new protectionism that emerged in 2008–09 was certainly not as bad as it might have been. Overall, by 2009 the stock of products affected by G-20 use of such TTBs had increased by 25 percent over those in place in 2007. Even this 25 percent increase in affected products in the aggregate is estimated to affect less than 0.3 percent of total trade.

On the other hand, it is also clear that the limited incidence of protectionism that did take place during the crisis was developing economy–centric in nature: it was disproportionately imposed by developing economies on developing economy exporters. Policy-imposing countries show substantial differences, with the largest increases in new TTBs being imposed by developing economies such as Argentina, India, Indonesia, and Turkey. In many instances, the new TTBs continue a precrisis trend of affecting South-South trade: in particular, 68 percent of the stock of 2009 TTBs that developing-economy users had in place were imposed on imports from other developing economies. In the aggregate, 1.3 percent of the 2007 value of developing-economy exports to G-20 developing economies would be subject to new TTBs in 2008–09. This percentage is almost twice as much as the only 0.7 percent of developing-economy exports to G-20 high-income economies that would subsequently be subjected to newly imposed TTBs during the crisis.

One interpretation of these data from the crisis era is that the world trading system somehow better shielded exports from developing economies to the higher-income markets from protectionism. The access of developing-country exporters to markets in high-income economies turned out to be more "secure" than their access to markets in other developing economies. Improving the security of market access associated with South-South trade is an important agenda item for the trading system. One policy implication is the possibility of providing developing-country exporters better access to the WTO dispute settlement system to continue to open up desired markets in other developing economies.[16]

Furthermore, China's exporters present a special case for consideration. Overall, imports sourced from China accounted for 80 percent of the total value of trade on which the G-20 imposed new TTBs in 2008–09. The stock of products exported from China subject to G-20 use of these TTBs in 2009 increased 40 percent relative to precrisis level of 2007. The new TTBs in 2008–09 affected more than US$20 billion worth of China's exports, or almost 2 percent of its (precrisis) 2007 level of exports. The fact that China's exports are subject to TTBs is not a new crisis-era phenomenon (Bown 2010c), but it is one that may have been heightened by the crisis. In part, the endogeneity of the G-20 policy response is likely affected by China's continued export successes even during the crisis.

Finally, it is worth noting that the final cross-country pattern as well as the depth of the new crisis-era protectionism is not yet completely known. Notwithstanding the possibility of a further deepening of the global economic recession begun in 2008 that may lead to a substantial increase in the flow of new government-conducted TTB investigations, the amount and distribution of G-20 import protection after the crisis will be the result of two yet-to-be-resolved policy questions. First, the postcrisis stock of TTBs will partly reflect dozens of forthcoming government policy-making decisions over whether to impose new TTBs that have yet to be concluded. Second, the postcrisis stock of TTBs that we have described throughout is only "temporary" if they are someday *removed*. Policy makers will ultimately be responsible for how the postcrisis trading system responds to the TTBs now imposed—whether they are removed through WTO dispute settlement or countries' adherence to sunset reviews and safeguards expirations—and this too will also substantially affect the legacy of crisis-era protectionism.[17]

Notes

1. In our discussion of separate estimates using the overall trade restrictiveness index (OTRI) and market access overall trade restrictiveness index (MA-OTRI) described later, we also examine the impact of the limited incidence of increases in applied tariffs. Nevertheless, aside from antidumping, countervailing duties, and safeguards, we do not examine the potential trade impact of other examples of "murky" nontariff barriers to trade taking place during the crisis (Baldwin and Evenett, 2009; Evenett, Hoekman, and Cattaneo, 2009). For example, we leave to future work the more difficult task of assessing the trade impact of subsidies or government bailouts during the crisis, many of which are captured in the Global Trade Alert (Evenett 2009) database.

2. This chapter draws heavily from two separate pieces of research to which the reader should refer for more detailed discussion, especially regarding methodology. See Bown (2010b) and Kee, Neagu, and Nicita (2010).

3. Baldwin (2009) presents a set of early research examining likely culprits behind the trade collapse of 2008–09, most of the evidence pointing toward an adverse demand shock. See also Freund (2009a, 2009b).

4. Antidumping has historically been the most prevalent of these four policy instruments (Prusa 2001; Zanardi 2004). As such, there is well-established theoretical and empirical literature examining determinants and impacts of the use of antidumping across countries. Recent empirical contributions, including examinations of developing economies, using detailed data provided in early versions of the Temporary Trade Barriers Database include Egger and Nelson (forthcoming), Moore and Zanardi (2009), Vandenbussche and Zanardi (2010), Bown (2008), Reynolds (2009), and Bown and Tovar (forthcoming). For a survey of the literature on antidumping, see Blonigen and Prusa (2003).

5. The yearly stock is computed through examination of all initiated investigations, the dates of imposition of the first trade barriers during (preliminary) or at the end of a (completed) investigation, and the date of removal for investigations. There are roughly 5,000 six-digit HS product categories per importing economy.

6. The twelve G-20 members included in figures 6.1 and 6.2 are Argentina, Australia, Brazil, Canada, China, European Union, India, Indonesia, the Republic of Korea, South Africa, Turkey, and the United States. G-20 economy member and TTB user Mexico is not included in the aggregated figures 6.2 and 6.3 for reasons described below. Japan, the Russian Federation, and Saudi Arabia are the only G-20 economies not represented in the analysis of the use of these temporary trade barriers since they did not actively use such policies during this time period. G-20 member countries France, Germany, Italy, and the United Kingdom are not included separately because their trade policy is determined by the European Union, the 20th member of the G-20. Even though many of these economies' use of TTBs started much earlier, we begin in 1997 because that is the time period in which each of the 12 G-20 economies in the sample were using at least one of their TTB policies, China being the last of the 12 as it adopted use of antidumping in 1997.

7. A third factor is that the set of underlying policies is also not identical, since figure 6.2 includes the products affected by the use of the global safeguards policy whereas figure 6.3 does not.

8. Just as in figure 6.3, figures 6.4 and 6.5 are again limited to capturing only these economies' use of the three exporting-country specific policies (antidumping, countervailing duties, and China-specific safeguards) and thus the figures omit any use of global safeguards.

9. Niels and Francois (2006) provide an empirical analysis of Mexico's earlier antidumping use. See also Finger and Nogués (2005).

10. Knetter and Prusa (2003) link macroeconomic determinants such as recessions and exchange rate fluctuations to the earlier use of antidumping by Australia, Canada, the EU, and the United States.

11. While comparable to the first estimates of this issue contained in table 7.4 of Bown (2009a), these figures are "improved" estimates of potential impacts for the following reasons. First, whereas the results in Bown (2009a) covered all newly initiated investigations between first quarter (1Q) 2008 through 1Q 2009, this table reports all temporary trade barriers imposed (preliminary and final) between 1Q 2008 and 4Q 2009. Second, the results in Bown (2009a) were estimated from 6-digit Harmonised System (HS) level data, whereas the results above are computed from actual tariff line import data (at the 8,9,10, or 12 digit level, depending on the reporting convention to UN Comtrade of the importing economy).

12. When comparing the magnitude and distribution of the estimated trade impacts of crisis-era policies, we should note that the exercises reported here drawing from Kee, Neagu, and Nicita (2010) and Bown (2010b) are not strictly comparable for a number of subtle, data-driven reasons. First, in constructing estimates for potential trade impact, Bown uses 2007 import data while Kee, Neagu and Nicita use 2008 import data. Second, Bown does not examine tariff changes but does examine antidumping, countervailing duties, global safeguards, and China-specific safeguards, while Kee, Neagu, and Nicita examine tariff changes and antidumping (but not countervailing duties, global safeguards, and China-specific safeguards). Third, Bown relies on policies imposed in all of 2008 and 2009, whereas Kee, Neagu, and Nicita examine tariff and antidumping duties imposed between June 2008 and September 2009 only. Despite these slight differences in approach, the results are broadly consistent in magnitude of effects across policy-imposing economies and the distribution of the incidence across exporting countries.

13. Turkey is one of the few economies for which newly imposed global safeguards may have also had a large trade impact during the crisis, and these are not captured in the OTRI estimates of table 6.3. While such policies are captured in table 6.2, the table 6.2 estimates would not capture the impact of Turkey's new tariff impositions in the agricultural sector that are captured in table 6.3.

14. These results would be reinforced by inclusion of estimates of the September 2009 U.S. imposition of the China-specific safeguard on imports of Chinese tires.

15. To be consistent with the analysis presented above, again we exclude Mexico and thus focus on the other 12 major TTB-using G-20 economies.

16. Bown (2009b) presents a set of proposals describing how developing-country exporters might use WTO dispute settlement to better secure their access to other developing-country markets.

17. While safeguards have typically been removed as scheduled, the evidence on timely removals for antidumping is much less convincing (Moore 2006; Cadot, de Melo, and Tumurchudur 2007).

Bibliography

Baldwin, R., ed. 2009. *The Great Trade Collapse: Causes, Consequences and Prospects*. VoxEU.org. E-book.

Baldwin, R., and S. J. Evenett, eds. 2009. *The Collapse of Global Trade, Murky Protectionism, and the Crisis: Recommendations for the G20*. VoxEU.org. E-book.

Blonigen, B. A., and T. J. Prusa. 2003. "Antidumping." In *Handbook of International Trade*, ed. E. K. Choi and J. Harrigan, 251–84. Oxford: Blackwell Publishers.

Bown, C. P. 2008. "The WTO and Antidumping in Developing Countries." *Economics and Politics* 20 (2): 255–88.

———. 2009a. "The Global Resort to Antidumping, Safeguards, and other Trade Remedies amidst the Economic Crisis." In *Effective Crisis Response and Openness: Implications for the Trading System*, ed. Simon J. Evenett, Bernard M. Hoekman, and Olivier Cattaneo, 91–118. London: Centre for Economic Policy Research and World Bank.

———. 2009b. *Self-enforcing Trade: Developing Countries and WTO Dispute Settlement.* Washington, DC: Brookings Institution Press.

———.2010a. "China's WTO Entry: Antidumping, Safeguards, and Dispute Settlement." In *Handbook of International Trade*, ed. Robert C. Feenstra and Shang-Jin Wei. Chicago: University of Chicago Press for the NBER.

———. 2010b. "Taking Stock of Antidumping, Safeguards, and Countervailing Duties, 1990–2009." Policy Research Working Paper 5436, World Bank, Washington, DC.

———. 2010c. "Temporary Trade Barriers Database." World Bank, Washington, DC. http://econ.worldbank.org/ttbd.

Bown, C. P., and P. Tovar. Forthcoming. "Trade Liberalization, Antidumping and Safeguards: Evidence from India's Tariff Reform." *Journal of Development Economics.*

Cadot, O., J. de Melo, and B. Tumurchudur. 2007. "Anti-dumping Sunset Reviews: The Uneven Reach of WTO Disciplines." Working Paper 6502, Centre for Economic Policy Research, London.

Egger, P., and D. Nelson. Forthcoming. "How Bad Is Antidumping? Evidence from Panel Data." *Review of Economics and Statistics.*

Eichengreen, B., and D. A. Irwin. Forthcoming. "The Great Depression and the Protectionist Temptation: Who Succumbed and Why?" *Journal of Economic History.*

———. 2009a. "The Protectionist Temptation: Lessons from the Great Depression for Today." VoxEU. March 17. http://voxeu.org.

Evenett, S. J. 2009. "Global Trade Alert: Motivation and Launch." *World Trade Review* 8 (4): 607–09.

Evenett, S. J., B. M. Hoekman, and O. Cattaneo, eds. 2009. *Effective Crisis Response and Openness: Implications for the Trading System.* London: World Bank and Centre for Economic Policy Research.

Finger, J. M., and J. J. Nogués, eds. 2005. *Safeguards and Antidumping in Latin American Trade Liberalization: Fighting Fire with Fire.* New York: World Bank and Palgrave.

Freund, C. 2009a. "The Trade Response to Global Crises: Historical Evidence." Policy Research Working Paper 5015, World Bank, Washington, DC.

———. 2009b. "The Trade Response to Global Downturns." In *The Great Trade Collapse: Causes, Consequences and Prospects.* VoxEU.org. E-book.

Freund, C., and M. D. Horenstein. 2010. "Trade Watch Data." World Bank, Washington, DC. http://go.worldbank.org/EWEDUHSI50.

Irwin, D. A. Forthcoming. *Peddling Protectionism: Smoot-Hawley and the Great Depression.* Princeton, NJ: Princeton University Press.

Kee, H. L., I. C. Neagu, and A. Nicita. 2010. "Is Protectionism on the Rise? Assessing National Trade Policies during the Crisis of 2008." Policy Research Working Paper 5274, World Bank, Washington, DC.

Knetter, M. M., and T. J. Prusa. 2003. "Macroeconomic Factors and Antidumping Filings: Evidence from Four Countries." *Journal of International Economics* 61 (1): 1–17

Moore, M. O. 2006. "An Econometric Analysis of U.S. Antidumping Sunset Review Decisions." *Weltwirtschaftliches Archiv* 142 (1): 122–50.

Moore, M. O., and M. Zanardi. 2009. "Does Antidumping Use Contribute to Trade Liberalization in Developing Countries?" *Canadian Journal of Economics* 42 (2): 469–95.

Niels, G., and J. Francois. 2006. "Business Cycles, the Exchange Rate, and Demand for Antidumping Protection in Mexico." *Review of Development Economics* 10 (3): 388–99.

Prusa, T. J. 2001. "On the Spread and Impact of Antidumping." *Canadian Journal of Economics* 34 (3): 591–611.

Reynolds, K. M. 2009. "From Agreement to Application: An Analysis of Determinations under the WTO Antidumping Agreement." *Review of International Economics* 17 (5): 969–85.

Vandenbussche, H., and M. Zanardi. 2010. "The Chilling Trade Effects of Antidumping Proliferation." *European Economic Review* 54 (6): 760–77.

WTO (World Trade Organization). 2009. *International Trade Statistics 2009.* Geneva: WTO.

Zanardi, M. 2004. "Antidumping: What Are the Numbers to Discuss at Doha?" *World Economy* 27 (3): 403–33.

7

TURNING TOWARD CHINA? THE 2008 CRISIS AND ITS INFLUENCE ON BRAZIL'S DEVELOPMENT MODEL

Gustavo H. B. Franco and Fausto J. A. Vieira

This chapter addresses issues pertaining to the advancement and style of Brazilian economic development in the years to come in the aftermath of the 2008 crises and the lessons it entails. Globalization, the distinguishably superior performance of export promotion over import substitution policies, and especially the rise of China are factors that overwhelmed the debates on openness and on trade and industrial policies to support economic development. Against the background of the consequences of the first systemic crisis of the globalized economy, policy makers in Brazil are facing hard choices on the next steps in economic development.

The analysis proceeds as follows. The next section briefly reviews the reform record and some of the singular features affecting Brazilian openness during the crucial years of stabilization and redefinition of the Brazilian development model. The next section chronicles events and policy responses after the global panic produced by the demise of Lehman Brothers. We start from a discussion of the reasons why, for Brazil, some external shocks turn into severe crises while others go almost unnoticed. The section then provides a detailed analysis of the transmission mechanisms functioning in this crisis, some quite novel, on which we will focus. In the last section, we discuss the way ahead, beyond "exit strategies" from the exceptional measures deployed during the more acute moments of the crisis. In fact, in some cases atypical measures were reversed during the crisis, while other policy measures advanced and even accelerated. Finally, we draw conclusions about the future of Brazilian development.

Trends in Brazilian Trade Orientation before the 2008 Crisis

An outward-oriented policy stance could have been a natural casualty of a worldwide financial crisis originating in the world's core economy, and with a variety of aggravating circumstances coming mostly from the developed world. This possibility was all the stronger for a country like Brazil, which has a long tradition of inward-oriented economic growth. "Turning inward" would not be in dissonance with what happened from 1929 onward in a similar situation of global crisis. Carlos Diaz Alejandro has said of that period that developing nations will never forgive developed economies for the massive betrayal of the Ricardian theories they always preached. Yet, despite the precipitous fall in international trade in 2008, the world did not witness a "disintegration" of globalization in the sense of a policy-reinforced rush to disconnect from the global economy as was seen in the 1930s. Much to the surprise of some observers, that kind of de-globalization has gained little or no traction in Brazil.

It is true that there are isolated signs of protectionist practices and mercantilistic leanings and some complaints about "asymmetries" or anticompetitive practices, with regard to China in particular. But the magnitude of exchange-rate fluctuations overshadows the importance of the discussion on competitiveness differentials and, for that reason as well, of the discussion of more structural ways to develop innovation and comparative advantage. It is as if the capital account, or short-term financial factors, at least in times of turmoil, have become a dominant influence over the "factory level" elements traditionally associated with trade and industrial policies. As turmoil appears to be all the more frequent, one wonders what is left to discuss in the field of trade and industrial policies in this brave new world.

For all the talk of globalization, Brazil remains one of the least-open economies on the planet, at least as far as ratios of trade to gross domestic product (GDP) are concerned (Figure 7.1). It has a contentious track record on trade liberalization and an extended history of inward-oriented industrialization strategies. Yet, the crisis was relatively mild in Brazil, thanks to its domestic market.

The crisis brought the usual plethora of shocks related to the balance of payments—collapsing export demand and prices, disappearance of trade credit lines, sudden stop of capital flows, repatriations, and dividend remittances. The response was a major exchange-rate depreciation, some deployment of international reserves to sustain trade flows, and some action in the field of derivatives to prevent excesses that could further destabilize the currency. An additional impact on Brazilian banks, to be examined in more detail below—although not directly related to the banking stress going on in the Northern Hemisphere—was perhaps the key element in explaining the unusually sharp drop in industrial production and GDP in the last quarter of 2008. If it were not for this accident, the picture of economic growth in Brazil in 2009, where it was near zero, could look much more like the stronger outcomes in India and China.

Although there is no sign of a crisis-related backlash in favor of import substitution, protectionism, and other practices of the past, that is not to say that there have been no changes in development thinking. In fact, the crisis could be a decisive element in swinging the balance of ideas toward more "Chinese-inspired" policies that are in sympathy with past practices and institutions in Brazil and whose suitability is very much contested.

Before extending the argument, let us take a step back and understand first how firmly Brazil had come to embrace globalization in the past two decades. Several good arguments explain these new attitudes, nearly all related to the hyperinflation experience ending in 1994, which many saw as a clear indication of the exhaustion of the old development model. Starting from the late 1980s, when defenders of an import substitution strategy could still be found, hyperinflation and stabilization policies had an overwhelming influence in all spheres of thought. Ultimately, this attitude helped establish the concept that extreme inflation was but a clear expression of the collapse of the old inward-oriented development model based on "heterodox" (so-called Keynesian) notions of public finance and heavy protectionism. This approach proved to be so powerful that the design of policies to end hyperinflation and stabilize the economy turned into a broad program of reforms affecting every aspect of the old model.

The strength of this revisionist thinking was proportional to the size and resilience of inflation. According to the Fischer, Sahay, and Végh (2002) redefinition of "high

Figure 7.1. Trade to GDP for Selected Economies, 1995–2000

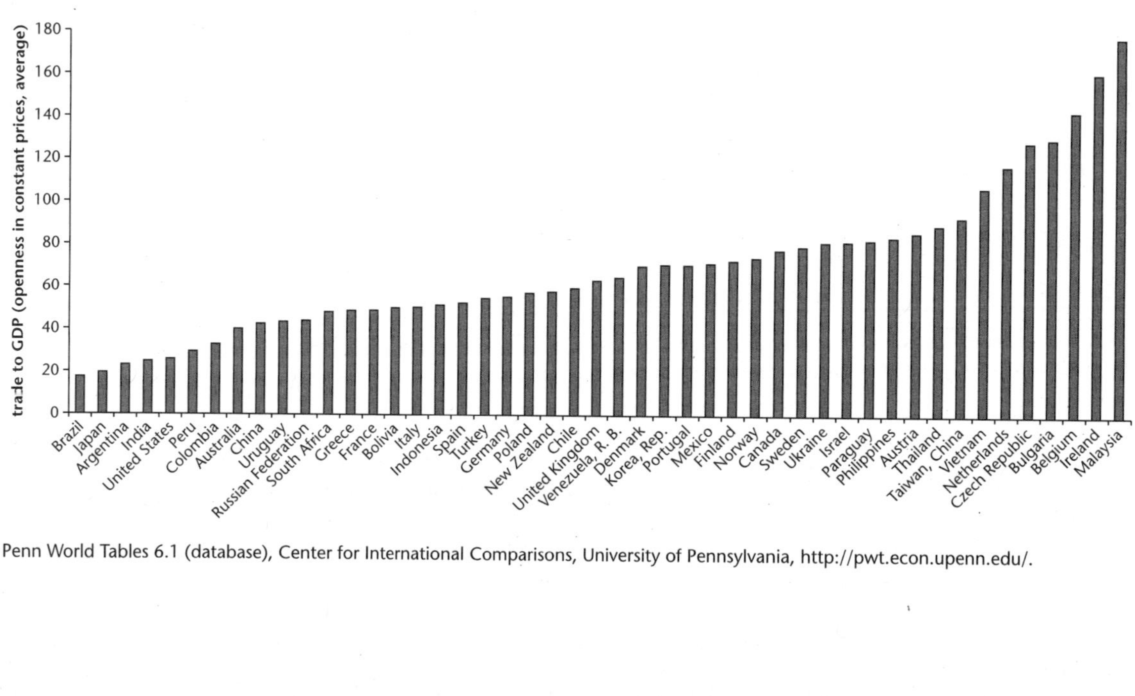

Source: Penn World Tables 6.1 (database), Center for International Comparisons, University of Pennsylvania, http://pwt.econ.upenn.edu/.

inflation" as 100 percent or more on a 12-month rolling basis, Brazil started its high inflation episode in April 1980 and finished it 182 months later in June 1995. In this period, accumulated inflation reached the extraordinary number of 20,759,903,275,651 percent—equivalent to an average *monthly* inflation rate during these 15 years of nearly 16 percent. It is hard to argue that intelligent economic life can exist in such conditions, let alone healthy economic growth. The 1994 monetary reform leading to a successful stabilization—the Real Plan—marked a major turn toward market-driven mechanisms in trade and industrial policies as opposed to anything Brazil had experienced in the past.

A major wave of liberalizing measures followed stabilization, along with ambitious deregulation and privatization programs. To many, this process was a kind of "fall of the Wall": reforms seemed as profound and far reaching as those seen in Eastern Europe. Yet, macroeconomic instability, most notably affecting exchange rates, prevented price signals produced by the milder structure of protection from having their full impact on productivity and competitiveness. Openness improved, though not in a very striking way, as seen in figure 7.2. Despite this progress, Brazil remained stuck with dismal levels of openness as compared to other countries, as seen in figure 7.1.

The magnitude of real exchange-rate variations may have been one explanation for the good yet unimpressive record of productivity and GDP growth, particularly the indications on the correlation between total factor productivity (TFP) and openness suggested in table 7.1.

Figure 7.2. Openness Indicators, Brazil, 1960–2009

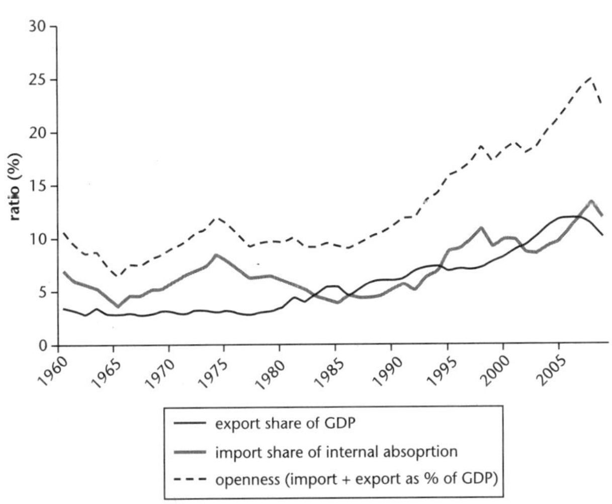

Source: Penn World Tables 6.1 (database), Center for International Comparisons, University of Pennsylvania, http://pwt.econ.upenn.edu/; Bloomberg, www.bloomberg.com.

No doubt crises in 1994, 1997, 1998, 1999, 2001, and 2002—some of which were made more serious by incidents linked to the stabilization process—may have prevented more substantial gains from reforms and from the new policy stance. Promises related to growth and competitiveness, all crucial to opening the political gates to large-scale reforms, seemed unfulfilled. It appeared that the reform program had stopped short of full implementation or, alternatively, that its allegiance to the canons of the so-called Washington Consensus was misdirected. Ultimately, good results in growth and productivity are the elements around which one builds the constituencies supportive of reforms. Otherwise, reformers are bound to political weakness, as was indeed the case in Brazil.

Extensive soul-searching inquiries were conducted while the leftist administration of President Luis Inacio Lula da Silva came to power in 2003. Its policies, however, did little to settle the issue. There was no sign of a move away from conventional macroeconomic policies. But neither was there any sign of a backlash against the most contentious reform processes associated with the Washington Consensus, foremost among which were privatization and trade liberalization. No further advancements, however, were considered. Reforms came to a halt altogether, as if the country needed to heal from the political wounds of the aggressive reforms conducted during the Cardoso years. The maintenance of the policy stance, most notably a primary surplus amounting to 4 percent of GDP, especially in the absence of external shocks, led to an extended period of good macroeconomic performance produced mostly by increased credit and personal consumption. Many welcome signs of a "crowding-in" phenomenon were visible and pointed to promising new directions for the composition of growth.

Growth was significantly higher than observed during the Cardoso years: 4.4 percent on average in 2002–09, against 1.8 percent on average for 1995–2001. This difference obviously reflects the fact that Cardoso carried the load of fighting hyperinflation and was hit by three external crises—worse results, nevertheless. Little change could actually be seen in the rates of aggregate investment in the two presidencies: gross fixed capital formation remained under 20 percent of GDP, as seen in figure 7.3, throughout the 1990s and 2000s.

Insufficient aggregate investment has been constantly highlighted as the most important obstacle to sustained high growth, and the contrast to China highlighted in figure 7.3 is anything but accidental. During the years of military rule, public savings were at a historical high, adding to private savings to sustain investment rates over 25 percent of GDP. With additional help from "external

Table 7.1. GDP Growth and Various Estimates of Labor and Total Factor Productivity Growth in Brazil, 1985–2007
average annual growth rates, %

Source	1985–92	1993–97	1998–2002	2003–07	Measurement
GDP growth	2.3	4.0	1.7	3.6	
Rossi and Ferreira (1999)	–2.49[a]	2.15[a]	n.a.	n.a.	TFP
	1.1[b]	6.21/7.97[c]		n.a.	LP
Ferreira (2001)	–0.48	7.45	n.a.	n.a.	LP
	–1.03	2.0/4.3	n.a.	n.a.	TFP
Pinheiro et al. (2001)	–0.7–0.65[d]	2.1–2.6[d]	n.a.	n.a.	TFP
Bonelli (2002)	–0.68[e]	7.19/8.31[e]	n.a.	n.a.	LP
Authors' estimate	–2.3	1.6	–0.7	0.9	TFP
Gomes, Pessoa, and Veloso (2003)	–2.0/–2.9[f]	1.0/0.1[f]	n.a.	n.a.	TFP[f]
Souza (2007)	—	1.35/1.69[g]	–0.45/–0.16[g]	0.94/1.67[g]	TFP

Sources: Rossi and Ferreira 1999; Ferreira 2001; Pinheiro, I. Gill, L. Severn, and Thomas 2001; Bonelli 2002; Gomes, Pessoa, and Veloso 2003; Souza 2007.
Note: LP = labor productivity; TFP = total factor productivity; n.a. = not applicable; — = not available.
a. 1985–90 and 1991–97.
b. 1985–89,
c. 1990–93 and 1994–97.
d. Extreme values on sectoral estimates, 1981–93 and 1994–2000.
e. 1985–90, 1990–95, and 1995–2000.
f. 1976–1992 and 1992–2000, estimates for TFP and "discounted" TPF, capturing shifts at the technological frontier.
g. Estimates with reference to the national accounts of 1985 and 2000 for quarter 1, 1992–quarter 4, 1997; quarter 1, 1998–quarter 3, 2003; and quarter 4, 2003–quarter 4, 2006.

Figure 7.3. Investment and Growth of GDP in China and Brazil, 1967–2009

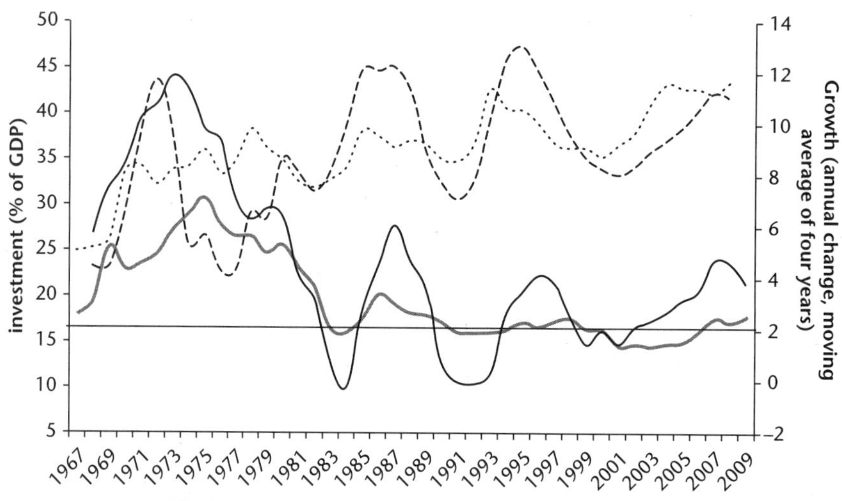

Sources: Penn World Tables 6.1 (database), Center for International Comparisons, University of Pennsylvania, http://pwt.econ.upenn.edu/; Bloomberg, www.bloomberg.com.

savings"—that is, current account deficits—Brazil lived its "economic miracle" during these years. The similarities of the growth model, mechanisms, and discourse with contemporary China are remarkable and at the same time puzzling. The average annual GDP growth rate for Brazil in 1967–78 was 9.5 percent, the very same rate observed in China for 1990–2000. The Brazilian economic miracle did not last long, though. The transition to democracy started in the first half of the 1980s and was expedited by the deteriorating performance of the economy, especially after the hit taken in 1982 with the Mexican and Brazilian moratoria. The first civilian government was inaugurated in 1985, with inflation running at 215 percent for the calendar year 1984. When President Sarney's administration left office in

March 1990, inflation reached an all-time high of 83 percent in that month. During these incredible five years of the so-called New Republic, an explosion of social demands all converged on the budget. They found expression in the 1988 Constitution, which led to a fiscal crisis and hyperinflation. This episode was a rare case of peacetime hyperinflation, of which the most visible cause was the inconsistency between social demands expressed in sharply increased government consumption (mostly related to social security, health care, education, and social overheads, all summarized by the expression *social debt*), ambitious public investment programs, and society's stiff resistance to raising the tax burden. These mechanisms have been extensively discussed elsewhere (see, for instance, Franco 1999) and the issue to note for our purposes is that, after the Real Plan, a new "growth equation" would have naturally evolved if private savings and investment made up for the eroded savings and investment capability of the public sector. Budgetary, fiscal, social security, and tax reforms, along with extensive internal debt and restructuring of public banks, addressed the fiscal crisis and set the stage for a crowding-in process. Privatization was crucial in transferring investment responsibilities to the private sector in important sectors: petrochemicals, steel, mining, telecommunications, and electricity, among others. To judge from the huge magnitude of investment programs of privatized enterprises, this was by far the most important contribution privatization has made to the long-term development of the country, much beyond the debt cancelations derived from direct privatization revenues.

The years following the success in stabilization saw developments in all these fields, but they were not broad enough to produce any significant increase in private savings and investment, as seen in figure 7.3. In fact, the continuous difficulty in improving the fiscal situation maintained the economy in a chronic crowding-out situation, whereby the continuous growth of the private economy was not matched by budgetary improvements to allow a changed aggregate demand composition. Unusually high interest rates—as a matter of fact, the highest in the world—offered a clear expression of the problem and represented, unquestionably, a leftover from the hyperinflation years. It was as if Brazil had succeeded in ending the infection producing hyperinflation, but the antibiotics did not completely eradicate fiscal malpractices that remained in the system. Although the remaining malpractices were on a much smaller scale, they were large enough to produce a classic crowding-out situation, maintaining interest rates at levels that were and remain exceedingly high. No wonder investment ratios are so small in the country with the highest real interest rate in the world; this is the challenge to address so that private investment can approach levels observed in emerging Asia. Much progress was made, however, in reducing the size of the problem through the years, and many would explain the flamboyant behavior of Brazilian capital markets up to late 2008 as an indication of the beginning of a crowding-in process. Yet, resistance to further improvements in fiscal policies drove the economy toward overheating and toward renewed inflationary pressures. The central bank was indeed initiating a tightening cycle when the Lehman Brothers event changed everything.

The 2008 Crisis: Impacts and Responses

At first glance, the 2008 crisis was an external shock and, in this regard, was very similar to others that had taken place on several occasions in the past. Some of these external shocks turned into crises, understood as financial distress always accompanied by significant adverse changes in GDP growth. Other shocks did not, and an interesting issue is to investigate factors that leverage the impacts of such events.

It light of the myriad external shocks experienced through the years—1974, 1979, 1982, 1987, 1989, 1991, 1994, 1997, 1998, 1999, 2001, 2002 and 2008—it is interesting to ask when and why they "cause" a recession. As a prelude to the discussion of the 2008 shock and ensuing recession, we ran two equations to offer a summary of past experience, as shown in table 7.2. They are probit and logit equations assessing the factors affecting the probability of a recession for the reference period.

The coefficients reveal a curious "counter-Keynesian" result, whereby higher fiscal deficits *increase* the likelihood of a recession, although we cannot rule out reverse causality here. An important point is that an increase in the deficit of one percentage point does not make a huge difference in the range between a fiscal surplus and a deficit of 3 percent. But a one percentage point increase above the threshold of a 3 percent deficit increases the probability of a new recession by 22 percent. More important, the strongest element reducing the probability of a recession is the ratio of international reserves to external debt. It works like an insurance policy: when the international reserves ratio is low (0–20 percent), increasing it by one percentage point reduces the probability of a recession by 2 percent. As in the 1980s, the mix of low reserves and a high current account deficit is conducive to frequent recessions (at the time designated as "stop and go" policies). Nevertheless, when the international reserves ratio is higher than 20 percent, increasing it by one percentage point reduces by 0.5 percent the probability of a recession, instead of 2 percent when the ratio is lower. Another point is that when the

Table 7.2. Estimation Results, Model of Recession, and GDP Growth in Brazil

	Recession dummy		GDP growth
	Probit	Logit	OLS
Global growth	–0.82	–1.49	0.48
	(0.02)	(0.05)	(0.04)
Reserves to external debt	–0.05	–0.09	0.04
	(0.09)	(0.10)	(0.03)
Fiscal deficit	0.38	0.64	0.00
	(0.03)	(0.05)	(0.98)
d (saving ratio)	–0.25	–0.44	0.40
	(0.03)	(0.05)	(0.03)
d (terms of trade)	0.00	–0.01	0.22
	(0.98)	(0.91)	(0.00)
Constant	1.63	3.03	–0.25
	(0.24)	(0.22)	(0.89)
Number of observations	29	29	29
R-square	0.49	0.49	0.52

Source: Authors' calculations.
Note: t-statistics are in parentheses. Recession dummy is a variable for Brazilian recessions as indicated by Fundacao Getulio Vargas.
OLS = ordinary least squares.

world is in a recession or growing below trend, an increase of one percentage point in global growth reduces by 18 percent the probability of a new Brazilian recession. When the world is growing above trend (higher than 2.5 percent), the impact is much lower: an increase of one percentage point in global growth reduces the probability of a Brazilian recession by just 1.3 percent instead of 18 percent.

The third equation is an ordinary least squares version of the first two but with economic growth as the dependent variable. The importance of international reserves in this equation can be explained only if one accepts that instability produced by external shocks has had such an overwhelming effect on growth that its antidote, reserves, seems to be more important at first glance than any other long-run structural elements. In a less shock-prone economy, this result would appear surprising, but in a shattered emerging economy with a long history of macroeconomic instability, it makes perfect sense.

External shocks are usually thematic, often related to geographies (Asia, the Russian Federation, Mexico, and so forth) or to specific issues (oil, commodities, or hedge funds in trouble). This time, the theme was broad and far reaching: banks. The worldwide deleveraging and risk-reduction movements produced sudden stops in almost all types of capital inflows, sharp terms-of-trade losses, falling external demand, repatriations of portfolio investments, and even some disruption in foreign trade mechanisms because of the disappearance of trade lines and sharply increased country risk premium. The direct impact on the exchange rate was brutal: from September onward, in 45 days the real lost approximately 45 percent of its value.

Some very unusual influences were behind such a big depreciation of the currency, and the problem was, unfortunately, connected to foreign-exchange derivatives. The surprisingly wide dissemination of "toxic" derivatives products affecting balance sheets of nonfinancial corporations of all sizes multiplied the impacts of the real depreciation on Brazilian companies in novel and dangerous ways. Some interesting parallels are found here with what happened in the United States related to asymmetry of information: some banks sold highly dangerous products to their clients with little explanation of implicit risks, or with outright misrepresentation, and buyers lacked the skills to discuss the products or the capability to manage the risk, or they simply acted on trust. The template is very much the same for the structured products based on subprime mortgages in the United States and for the derivatives based on exchange rates in Brazil.

The scant available evidence indicates that a few hundred companies were offered to launch far out-of-the-money put options, which they sold to the banks from which they drew their working capital financing. Thanks to the premium of these options, companies could *reduce the costs of bank financing* in exchange for the puts they sold, albeit with a very clear underestimation of the risks involved. Notional amounts were huge and potential losses unlimited, if the exchange rate were to depreciate enough to reach the strike prices. If not, it appeared to be only a sophisticated mechanism to reduce the cost of capital.

With the unusually large devaluation taking place from September 2008 onward, and at a very rapid pace, the disaster materialized, and these options reached their strike points. Many prime companies entered acute distress, especially in the case of listed companies, where the size of the exposure had to be made public, with truly devastating effects for those involved: Aracruz, Sadia, and Votarantim were the outstanding examples of massive value destruction, while a few hundred other nonpublic companies in the same situation were able to negotiate quietly with their creditors. There was no precise account of how many companies and how much was involved in such operations. Some of the largest banks reported some features of their exposures, with numbers varying from US$500 million to US$1.5 billion in the three banks reporting on these deals. These disclosures unquestionably represented only a fraction of the size of the problem. The Aracruz situation alone (the equity value of the company was around US$9.6 billion in June 2008) involved losses of approximately

US$8 billion and presumed notional amounts between 5 and 10 times this. How exposures of this order of magnitude could be entered without appearing on any regulator's radar screen is a very relevant and difficult question to address, but it is outside the scope of this chapter. Yet, this was one of the key features of the crisis transmission into Brazil.

The rush to stop or to hedge these exposures in futures markets for the real at the derivatives exchange in Brazil (BM&F Bovespa) put enormous pressure against the real and forced the central bank to act very swiftly on the sale of foreign exchange swaps to feed those willing to endure the losses and close these exposures. In parallel, the Brazilian Development Bank (BNDES) provided direct support to some of the companies in distress. The central bank reported some US$33 billion in sales of such swaps, which, given their nondeliverable characteristic, did not affect international reserves. A comparable amount in hard reserves was deployed in a number of ways (outright sales, funding of trade-related credit lines, purchase of Brazilian paper, and the like) less to lean against the wind than to reinstate markets for trade financing. BNDES resources deployed in bailouts cannot be precisely ascertained; yet figures for overall credit provided by BNDES in January 2009 increased to some 9 percent of GDP from less than 6 percent in August 2008!

It is quite remarkable that all such actions and direct bailouts were directed to help companies remedy the losses produced by an undetected and yet incredibly dangerous dissemination of toxic products with a huge potential for destruction. Nothing like this had been seen in other crises. Yet, by far the strongest and most worrisome aspect of the crisis was felt in some Brazilian banks that were in no way involved with toxic derivatives, except perhaps indirectly through the heightened public concern about banks and the presumption that they could be affected by toxic derivatives. Brazilian banks at large had little or no direct connection to events going on in the United States and Europe. Nevertheless, the transmission of a "risk aversion shock" to Brazil was very concrete, and in many respects its impact seemed like what had happened a few years previous when Banco Santos failed. This episode involved a small-to-midsize bank specializing in wholesale funding from institutional investors on the liability side and in the corporate middle market on the asset side. When the central bank intervened in Banco Santos in 2004, many concerns spread through the wholesale time deposit market, producing a major increase in standards and risk aversion on the part of the major players in this market, mostly pension funds. Other middle-market banks with funding needs similar to Banco Santos suffered significant losses in their funding, producing considerable stress, although for a short time only. No other casualties occurred in this episode.

During the second half of 2008, and very clearly after the Lehman failure, Brazilian banks found themselves in a situation that resembled the aftermath of the Banco Santos intervention. It appeared more serious than the direct impact of the crisis on banks through reductions in trade lines and in all other forms of external funding. Indications are that medium-sized banks as a group lost nearly half their deposits in the two months following the Lehman Brothers event. The central bank deployed offsetting measures on a massive scale, and again no casualties resulted from what was a genuine bank run. One of these measures was the creation of specially insured deposits up to R$20 million for every individual investor, although with a limit for the receiving bank of up to either twice the value of its capital or the level of deposits in June of 2008, whichever was larger, but limited to R$5 billion per institution. This very exceptional guarantee has not been removed so far, raising real concerns about moral hazard.

One important factor that helps explain the system's resilience is that Basel ratios have been significantly higher in Brazil than in most other countries: Basel ratios are 13 percent of risk-weighted capital, and the average for the system is 18 percent. These higher ratios are due not just to regulatory requirements, but also to the absence of limited liability protection for controlling shareholders and directors in the event of intervention and liquidation. This latter factor results in overly conservative banks, with chronic excess capital, little maturity mismatching (transformation), and asset concentration of very short-term operations. This feature of Brazilian banking legislation may surely be a new twist in the regulatory issues under discussion in the United States. (This point is extensively discussed in Franco and Rosman 2010.) In addition, 11 middle-sized banks among the ones most pressured listed their shares in the two years before the crises, each one raising its capital by R$1.5 billion on average.

The tradition of heavy regulation—combined with the weight of state-owned banks, notably Banco do Brasil, BNDES and Caixa Economica Federal, and the novel function of the FGC (Fundo Garantidor de Créditos, the local equivalent of the U.S. Federal Deposit Insurance Corporation)—increased the "arms-length" intervention capacity of the authorities very considerably. In this particular episode, both federal banks were extremely active in the secondary market of credit portfolios. They decisively helped banks in distress sell their less liquid assets in order to honor redemptions.

Another important prudential resource was the fact that reserve requirements in Brazil are very high compared to other countries. This requirement is not justifiable from a monetary policy viewpoint, since these reserves serve to provide funding for government credit programs, mostly related to agriculture and housing. These excess reserve requirements should rightly be considered a distortion. However, it is no less true that they may have an important "precautionary" function as the requirements can be adjusted to effectuate sharp changes in bank liquidity. Significant reductions in such requirements undertaken during the critical days of the crisis represented some additional R$100 billion in cash to banks (total time deposits were R$1.25 trillion in June 2008). Figure 7.4 shows how state-owned banks maintained the level of new credit, avoiding a worse deterioration in consumption, when private banks were decreasing their new loans.

The monetary authorities, state banks included, played their part and avoided any accidents in the banking system, which would have been disastrous to the economy. Yet, the acute bank distress had very considerable repercussions. The credit contraction produced by the banks in distress was particularly strong in the sales cycle of durable goods, most notably vehicles (30 percent year on year). The paralysis in credit was sharp: credit came to a standstill, surely causing the rarely seen contraction of industrial production observed in the fourth quarter. As seen in figure 7.5, industrial production indexes displayed volatility typical of financial data, and the most impressive decreases were associated with durable goods, thus less affected by contraction of external demand than by paralysis of domestic credit stemming from financial distress.

The return to normality in the financial system was quick, despite the huge depreciation of the real and its impact on the corporate sector. It is true that there was little foreign-denominated public debt and thus no balance sheet losses to the public sector. Yet, the most important of all differences with respect to previous external shock-induced crises was related to the inflationary consequences of external adjustment. Previously, big devaluations were needed to restore external balance, and working out the adjustments for the inflationary consequences was always painful. This time, however, the terms of trade loss was so severe that it more than offset the impact of the real's depreciation on prices. Wholesale prices fell, bringing down consumer price indexes just when the central bank was at the beginning of a tightening cycle. In this respect, the crisis provided a free ride for monetary policy, because the central bank could reverse course and pursue aggressive *reductions* in interest rates where just the opposite was expected before the Lehman Brothers event. This uncommon circumstance allowed monetary policy to help banks and the real sector without departing from inflation targeting and without the central bank openly admitting any other influence in fixing the interest rate other than the normal course of business in pursuit of the inflation target.

With the rapid normalization of the credit channels affecting automakers and durable manufacturers, the effects of historically low interest rates started to be strongly felt in the ensuing recovery. In this particular issue, the crisis may have advanced the clock, as the economy reacted

Figure 7.4. Ratio of Outstanding Credit to Total Assets in Brazil's Medium-Size and State-Owned Banks, 2008–09

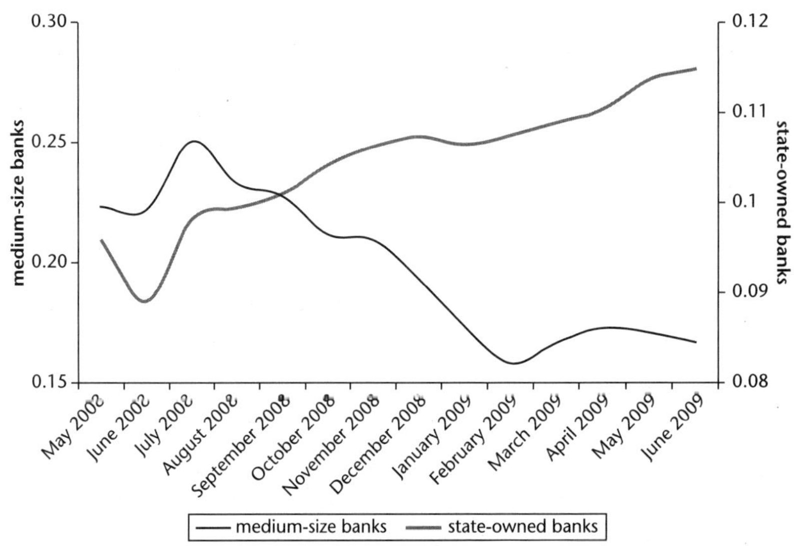

Source: Brazilian Central Bank databases, http://www.bcb.gov.br.

Figure 7.5. Industrial Production in Brazil, 2000–10

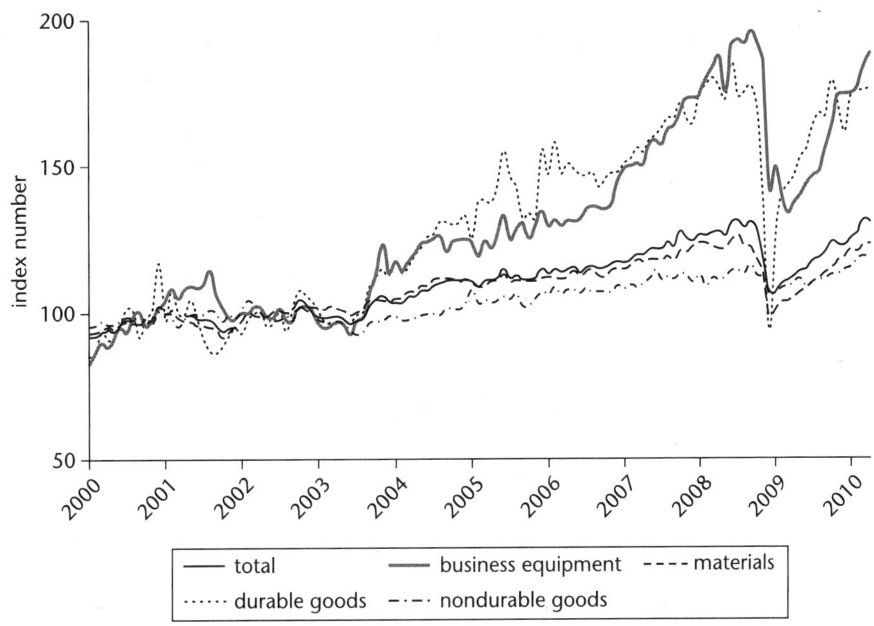

Sources: IBGE (Brazilian Institute of Geography and Statistics) databases, http://www.ibge.gov.br.

beautifully to interest rates closer to civilized levels. Yet, as a byproduct of the crisis, the government increased fiscal spending and openly alluded to "countercyclical policies." Soon Brazil was again facing crowding-out symptoms and overheating just as before the Lehman event, and possibly in a stronger way.

For completion of the picture, a few words are necessary on what happened to foreign trade. The fall in export volumes helped deepen the contraction in activity, but as shown by the growth decomposition methodology (figure 7.6), the fall in import volumes was bigger, and, consequently, net exports were positive for three quarters after the beginning of the crisis. Indeed, the domestic market was much more relevant both to the contraction in the fourth quarter of 2008 and most especially to the recovery in the second quarter of 2009. In the first quarter of 2009, a huge fiscal stimulus reduced the decrease in GDP. After that, the restoration of new loans by state-owned banks (figure 7.4) encouraged personal consumption and private investment. The massive depreciation of the currency had a strong impact on the trade balance and the current account, and for this particular reason the authorities, especially in the Finance Ministry, seemed not entirely unhappy with developments in the foreign exchange market. Complaints about continued currency overvaluation had been frequent in the years before the crisis and had prompted policy makers to implement restrictions on capital inflows of certain types through taxation at the moment of entry. These restrictions were instantly removed as the crisis set in.

The "Exit" and New Directions in Development

The crisis and recovery in Brazil, to judge from the description in the last section, had a somewhat more complex relation with the global financial crisis than one would infer from the usual transmission channels. Moreover, and in contrast with other countries, it is not exactly right to argue that Brazil deployed very exceptional policy measures unlikely to remain or to be sustainable in normal circumstances. Whereas interest rates in developed countries were set close to zero in quantitative easing schemes to be reversed at some point in the future, in Brazil, they remained at a solid 8.75 percent throughout the crisis. This nominal interest rate is, unfortunately, the *lowest* at least since the 1950s. Reserve requirements, even after being substantially reduced, still represented a remarkably high percentage of all deposits (31 percent), hardly justifiable on monetary policy grounds. Fiscal policy was already on an expansionary footing before the crisis, but the chance was not missed to ratchet up a few more notches, given the alleged need for "countercyclical" stimuli. The impact of this display of naive Keynesianism is very much a matter

Figure 7.6. GDP Growth in Brazil, 2008–10

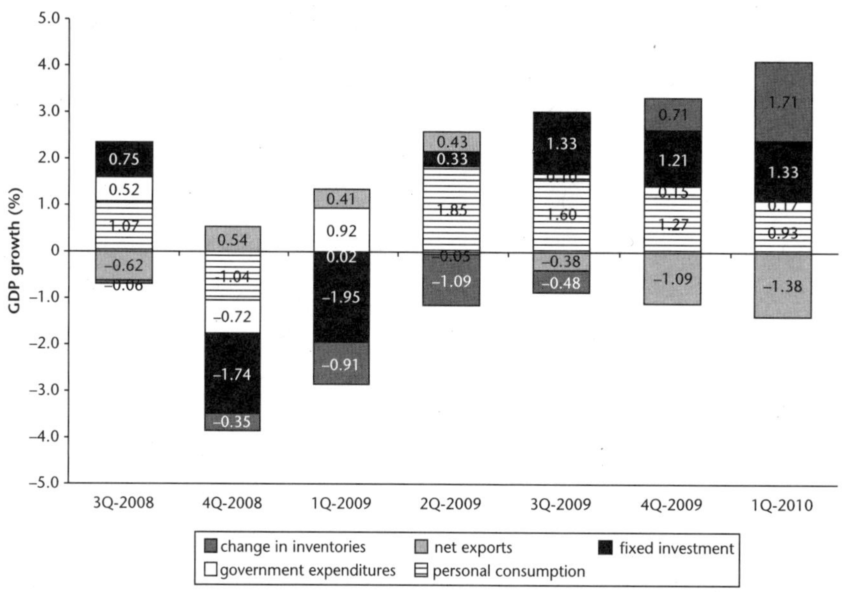

Source: IBGE National Accounts (database), http://www.ibge.gov.br.

for discussion; it was not very prudent, especially in light of Brazil's delicate track record of broken promises in the fiscal domain, and one can legitimately question whether it was really necessary.

In the first quarter of 2010, thanks to sharply increased private consumption, the economy was overheating again; inflation was displaying worrying signs, capacity utilization and the labor market were stretched, and the central bank started a new tightening cycle. The return of a crowding-out configuration on the back of a heightened fiscal and credit impulse loaded with rhetorical overtones somewhat deviant from orthodox thinking could be explained, as a first approximation, by the political cycle. Election-motivated spending sprees can be seen all over the planet, and Brazil is no exception. Yet, there seemed to be more to it, as the nature and extent of government activism during the crisis and recovery may well be indicative of new directions in economic policy in the coming years. The challenge of increasing investment rates and thus attaining sustainable high growth looms large and open, and in emerging markets in general, and in Brazil in particular, one can say that policy paradigms have been significantly affected. In the decade of reforms, emerging markets looked to Washington for recipes, most notably from the multilaterals from which emerged the much vilified "consensus." Now, all curiosity is directed toward China.

China's continued flamboyant success in economic growth invites speculation on how replicable the "Chinese model" might be in other emerging economies. For Brazil, dealing with China as a trading and investment partner has been a rewarding experience, given the complementarities between the two economies, although with the usual commercial tensions. Emulating China is an entirely different proposition. It is an idea that seduces the emerging world partly in view of the legacy of the Bush administration and of the banking crisis, which could do little else but eliminate what was left of the Washington Consensus. But it also has something to do with the Chinese policy mix. Perhaps the first thing to catch the attention of a Brazilian observer is the importance of the accumulation of reserves. There was a time when one would diminish the importance of reserves, evoking the New Zealand example of a country in which a pure float made it unnecessary to hold expensive international reserves (and the more expensive, the higher the interest differential). Emerging markets hardly ever adopted this wisdom; "fear of floating" is by far the rule with very few exceptions, as is well known. The crisis has only reinforced in a dramatic way the mercantilistic view that current account surpluses and reserve accumulation are the shortest way to prevent external shocks from hurting domestic growth, as indeed suggested by the empirical exercise in table 7.2. Yet, the lure of the Chinese examples goes well beyond that.

In Brazil, the debate over the next steps in economic development can be said to refer particularly to China, or more specifically to some key features of the Chinese policy mix that seem somewhat similar to the realities of the Brazilian economy. It was noted above, in connection to figure 7.3, that there are similarities between China today and Brazil during the "economic miracle" years of the military regime. It is interesting to push this analogy a bit further. On the demand side, one can argue that not only was government investment the key driver of growth, but also that "financial repression" was essential for mobilizing "forced savings" out of the private sector, which, in itself, biases demand toward investment to the detriment of consumption and thus biases relative prices toward tradables or toward a "competitive" exchange rate. Up to this point, Brazil in the 1970s and China today look very much alike.

On the supply side, however, the distinguishing feature of China is the demography, or the excess supply of labor, combined with the deficit of democracy. This latter feature is also important for the demand side of the model to the extent that it reduced pressures toward public spending on social security and overheads, which further biases relative prices toward tradables. This was less clearly the case of Brazil in the 1970s.

The effect of these demand and supply elements is the unusual combination of low interest rates and high savings (and public investment) and a very "competitive," or undervalued, exchange rate, which is, as put by Eichengreen in this volume, "an outcome, or a relative price that results from the elements comprising the development strategy, not a policy variable in and of itself."

In fact, the Chinese "model" outlined above is not at all distant from Arthur Lewis's (1954) classic analysis of growth under "unlimited supply of labor," an analogy that was common in Brazil in the 1970s. In this model, wages are permanently at a "subsistence level," and growth results in a number of paradoxes: capital accumulation does not increase wages but profits, which means increasing inequality (share of profits in GDP) and a rising investment rate (gross fixed capital formation), because capital accumulation does not affect wages so long as surplus labor prevails. Since savings result exclusively from profits, the rising share of profits in GDP implies a rising savings rate, or increased "forced savings," consistent with a current account surplus.

The Lewis analysis as applied to China is intriguing and not at all inconsistent with Easterly's (2005) finding of a negative correlation between real exchange-rate overvaluation and per capita growth rates. It may be incompatible with Rodrik's (2008) contention that undervaluation *promotes* economic growth to the extent that it provides a second-best policy that offsets shortcomings in competitiveness and infrastructure deficiencies, precluding export performance. The issue is at the very core of the current Brazilian debates, because the currency has been, since the monetary reform in 1994 and absent crises, under a constant appreciation trend. In the early years of stabilization, given its exchange-rate–based character, the problem appeared to be temporary. But the currency experience years later, under Lula, was similar and all the more revealing: the policy mix in Brazil biases the economy toward a stronger currency, which is by no means "Chinese" and, for this particular reason, detrimental to growth. Again, it should be argued that the mix might be a low-growth one, *having appreciation as a consequence*, which is entirely different from arguing that the fixing of the exchange rate at overvalued levels was in itself a drag on growth.

If one looks at Brazil having in mind the demand side of the Chinese model, many common features can be found. Mechanisms of "financial repression" producing "forced savings," many of them created in the 1970s, are still in place, though with much less weight than they once had. Several important mechanisms are worth mentioning, given the present administration's declared or revealed intentions of using them more intensively: public commercial and development banks (sometimes public commercial banks behaving as development banks) growing in importance, thanks to acquisitions, heavy capitalizations, and expansionary credit policies; public enterprise–sponsored pension funds engaged in government programs; tax-fed budget funds with "organic" connections with development banks (like FAT/BNDES and FGTS/CEF); and reserve requirements and credit "directions" imposed on private banks. All these mechanisms are contentious, because they involve conflicts of interest between private shareholders or participants and public endeavors and also because they are ultimately "para-fiscal" activity somehow affecting the public deficit. To that extent, these mechanisms only aggravate a crowding-out situation that is typical of Brazil and not at all Chinese. The root of Brazil's difficult fiscal situation, as mentioned in the first section of this chapter, is spending related to social security, health, and education to an extent unthinkable in China, yet normal for any industrialized Western democracy. Hyperinflation was indeed a demonstration that Brazil could not have public investment at levels comparable to the ones seen in China and have government consumption at the levels of southern Europe.

On the supply side of the Chinese model, Brazil no longer possesses the demography and the (lack of) democracy that maintain China under the regime of "unlimited supply of labor," with all its implications for wages and the exchange rate. Absent these conditions, the movement of public investment toward a "Chinese model" is bound to produce a marked deterioration in the fiscal accounts and the necessity of crowding out private spending, most likely investment demand, to accommodate government programs and credit on an increased scale. Following the recovery from the 2008 crisis, the "Chinese" trends in Brazil are visible in the authorities' articulations of economic policy. The proximity of elections seems to produce spending sprees and rhetoric hostile to U.S.-style neoliberalism, a combination that seems to point to the East as paradigm. Yet, the social and economic realities of Brazil do not seem to allow much replication of the Chinese policy mix. In fact, the fiscal limitations would seem to point quite otherwise.

The question of what the competing model should be is not that difficult. Its basic assumption is simple enough: further fiscal restraint would succeed in lowering the cost of capital, whether because it would soften the "loose fiscal and tight money" deadlock or because it would inevitably improve sovereign risk ratings a couple of notches above the "investment grade" status. These are, in essence, the fundamental explanations for the one economic pathology that singles out Brazil as a low-investment country: the interest rate. The brief period of time in which Brazil had nominal interest rates below 10 percent, for the first time in the past 40 years, offered a glimpse of a new reality regarding borrowing, leveraging, capital markets, and equity valuations that captured people's imagination. In many respects, the sensation was as far reaching as the one caused by the end of high inflation, and there is no coincidence in this analogy, given that these pathologies shared the same origin. Historically, Brazilian companies are extremely averse to any form of indebtedness—exceptions are prime corporations with access to international capital markets—which emphasizes as one forceful implication the fact that capital expenditures are made mostly out of retained earnings. This is actually a microexpression of a low rate of gross fixed capital formation in the aggregate and a convenient way to look at the reason why interest rates are indeed the one important obstacle preventing private investment and saving from reaching levels consistent with high economic growth on a sustainable basis. There is nothing simple about it; in fact, it is as complex as saying that inflation can be stopped if only the central bank would stop printing money. Fiscal restraint is counterintuitive in an economy with substandard growth, especially in politicians' minds. In fact, politicians tend to behave in just the opposite way, expanding public spending along Keynesian lines and ultimately making things worse.

Bibliography

Bonelli. R. 2002. "Labor Productivity in Brazil during the 1990s." Texto para Discussão 906, IPEA, Rio de Janeiro.

Easterly, W. 2005. "National Policies and Economic Growth." In *Handbook of Economic Growth*, ed. P. Aghion and S. Durlauf. Amsterdam: Elsevier.

Ferreira, P.C. 2001. "Grupos de interesse, determinantes da política comercial e produtividade industrial." Artigo preparado para o Instituto Futuro Brasin, São Paolo.

Fischer, S., R. Sahay, and C. Végh. 2002. "Modern Hyper- and High Inflations." *Journal of Economic Literature* 40 (3): 837–80.

Franco, G. H. B. 1999. *O Desafio Brasileiro: ensaios sobre desenvolvimento, globalização e moeda*. São Paulo: Editora 34.

———. 2000. "The Real Plan and the Exchange Rate."*Essays in International Finance.* Department of Economics, International Finance Section. Princeton University, Princeton, NJ.

Franco, G. H. B. and L. A. C. Rosman. 2010. "A crise bancária norte-americana: algumas lições da experiência brasileira." In *Risco e Regulação*, orgs. M. Garcia and F. Giambiagi. Rio de Janeiro: Campus & Elsevier.

Gomes, V., S. Pessoa and F. Veloso. 2003. "Evolução da produtividade total de fatores na economia brasileira: uma análise comparativa." *Pesquisa e Planejamento Econômico* 33 (3): 389–434.

Lewis, W.A. 1954. "Economic Growth under Unlimited Supplies of Labor." *The Manchester School* 22 (2): 139–91.

Moreira, M. M. 2004. "Brazil's Trade Liberalization and Growth: Has It Failed?" Occasional Paper 24, INTAL, Buenos Aires.

Pinheiro, A. C., I. Gill, L. Severn, and M. Thomas. 2001. "Brazilian Economic Growth in 1900–2000: Lessons and Policy Implications." Paper presented at the Third Annual Conference on Global Development Network, Rio de Janeiro, December 9–12.

Rodrik, D. 2008. "The Real Exchange Rate and Economic Growth." *Brookings Papers on Economic Activity* 2: 365–412.

Rossi, J. L. Jr., and P. C. Ferreira. 1999. "Evolução da produtividade industrial brasileira e a abertura comercial." *Pesquisa e Planejamento Econômico* 29 (1): 365–412.

Souza, J. R. C. 2007. "Estimativa do produto potencial para a economia brasileira: atualização utilizando o sistema de contas nacionais referência 2000." Nota Técnica, IPEA, Brasilia.

PART II

OPEN BUT NOT DEPENDENT: SOUTH-SOUTH TRADE AND EXPORT DIVERSIFICATION

8

CHANGING DYNAMICS IN GLOBAL TRADE

Gordon Hanson

The economic crisis of 2007–09 has led to a severe decline in world trade. Between the fourth quarter of 2007 and the second quarter of 2009, world merchandise imports dropped by a staggering 36 percent. Trade levels began a modest recovery in the third quarter of 2009, but they are still far below precrisis highs.

Will the Great Recession encourage developing countries to adopt more inward-oriented development strategies? Although U.S. import demand helped sustain export growth in developing countries over the past two decades, it may not fully recover from the crisis of 2007–09. Countries following an export-led development strategy may find themselves producing goods for which there are insufficient foreign buyers to sustain steady increases in per capita income (Rodrik 2009). Conceivably, the response of some countries could be a shift away from trade and investment openness. Developing countries may start to reverse reforms that have reduced barriers to foreign trade and investment and eased regulations on industries and labor markets in recent decades.

It is easy to overstate the potential for de-globalization. No prominent international economists are advocating a wholesale rejection of openness as a foundation for economic development. The countries that have adopted more inward-oriented development strategies recently, such as Argentina, Bolivia, and República Bolivariana de Venezuela, began doing so before the crisis hit. However, many developing-country policy makers have a sense that emerging markets are too reliant on the world economy and on the United States, in particular.[1]

In considering the future of globalization in the developing world, we must first assess the nature of global trade today. How dependent are developing countries on particular markets or particular goods for their exports? On the demand side, how important is the United States for the growth of developing-country exports? On the product side, has trade expanded more for countries that export manufactures than for those that produce primary products?

One of the main findings of this chapter is that developing countries are the new drivers of global trade. Middle-income countries (including, but not limited to the BRICs, or Brazil, the Russian Federation, India, and China) have become an important source of demand for exports from low- and middle-income countries. Gravity model estimates suggest that growth of gross domestic product (GDP) in developing countries has led to increased demand for imports, which has played an important role in boosting exports of low-income countries. Concerns that weak consumption growth in the United States might undermine the viability of export-led development would appear to be exaggerated. Dependence on U.S. demand for imports has generally lessened, although the United States is still a key source of demand for exports from the Western Hemisphere, for oil products, and for apparel from low-income countries.

This chapter also focuses on the new supply patterns that have emerged since the mid-1990s. Developing countries have captured a larger share of world exports in the past decade. Low-income countries remain specialized in resource-intensive exports, but they are making small steps up the value chain through expansion in apparel production. Middle-income countries' export baskets are more diversified than those of low-income countries, but low-income countries are steadily closing the gap.

The next section discusses the relative role of developing countries and the United States in driving trade demand. The following section examines changing dynamics on the supply side. The final section concludes.

The New Drivers of Global Trade

In the past decade, the destination markets for developing-country exports have shifted. Although these exports used to be directed largely at high-income countries, they are now moving increasingly toward other developing economies instead. As a result, the share of low- and middle-income countries in total world imports has nearly tripled, from 12 percent in 1996 to 31 percent in 2008 (figure 8.1). Within this group, the BRICs' share of world imports more than tripled, from 4 percent to 12 percent. Consequently, high-income countries now account for less than 70 percent of world imports, compared with nearly 90 percent a little over a decade ago.

This shift in demand has had varying impacts on specific exporter groups. Imports of *low- and middle-income countries* from all other income groups (that is, low-, middle-, and high-income nations) increased since 2000. In particular, low- and middle-income countries absorbed half of the export growth of low-income and lower-middle-income nations (table 8.1). Significantly, the shift in demand away from high-income markets is not driven only by the BRICs. Other low- and middle-income countries are also driving new demand: of the 13 percent increase in market share for low- and middle-income nations, the BRICs account for 5 percent and other countries account for 8 percent. Demand from the BRICs is generally growing at a faster rate, but other low- and middle-income countries still import a bigger share of exports from all income groups, apart from upper-middle-income countries.

Figure 8.1. Share of World Imports by Importer Income Group, 1996–2008

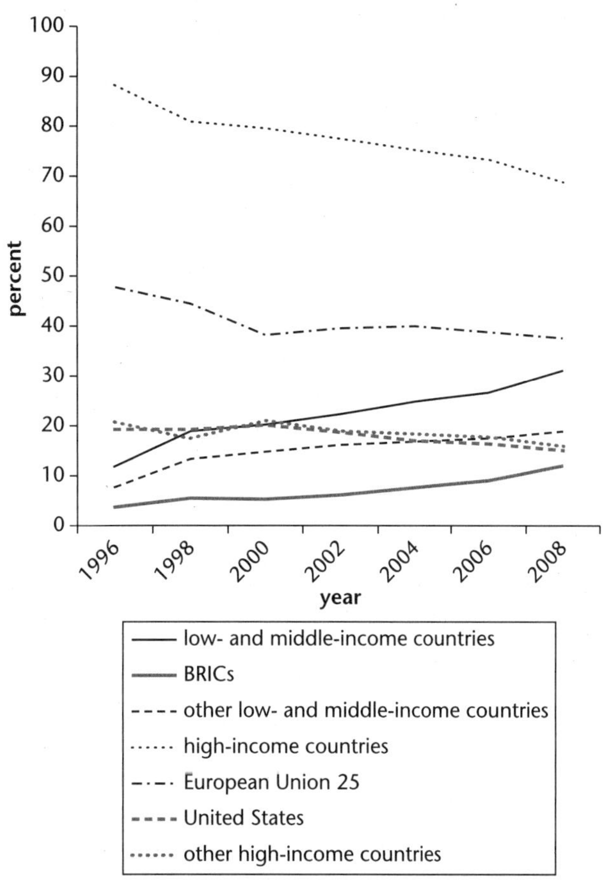

Source: Author's calculations, based on data from UN Comtrade (database), United Nations, http://comtrade.un.org.

In general, the rising share of exports to developing countries has meant a natural fall in the share of exports to high-income nations. The share of imports to the European Union (EU) has shrunk since 2000: its import share from the BRICs and other high-income countries has increased, but the share has fallen significantly for imports from low- and lower-middle-income countries. The share of exports of developing countries to the United States fell for all income groups except for low-income countries. However, low-income country exports to the United States still account for only 18 percent of total exports from these countries.

The varied changes in bilateral absorption patterns suggest that the story is not just about differential rates of income growth across high-income countries. Were this the case, then the logic of the gravity model of trade (Feenstra 2004) would suggest that countries increase or decrease their consumption of goods across exporters in constant proportions. Other factors—for instance, bilateral trade or investment agreements, the strategies of multinational firms, and the effect of income levels and income distribution on patterns of import demand—clearly account for why the share of goods going to the United States or the EU rises for some groups but falls for others.

Effects of a Drop in U.S. Consumption

Despite these changing trends, the United States continues to remain a major export destination for Latin America and the Caribbean, for oil exporters worldwide, and for low-income countries in East and South Asia. With respect to Latin America and the Caribbean, Mexico and Central America are particularly dependent on U.S. demand. The United States also absorbs large amounts of oil from the Middle East and other petroleum exporters, but the oil import demand of middle-income countries such as the BRICs is steadily increasing. For low income countries in Asia, the importance of the U.S. market is predominantly in apparel exports. The United States and the EU absorbed over three quarters of the growth in recent (2000–08) apparel exports from low-income nations, with East and South Asian nations being the main producers.

Table 8.1. Share of Exports by Country Income Groups and Destination Market, 2000 and 2008
percent

Importing region	Low (%)			Lower middle (%)			Upper middle (%)			BRICs (%)			High (%)		
	2000	2008	Δ	2000	2008	Δ	2000	2008	Δ	2000	2008	Δ	2000	2008	Δ
Low- and middle-income countries	28	41	↑	23	41	↑	18	31	↑	17	30	↑	21	30	↑
BRICs	11	16	↑	9	23	↑	6	13	↑	3	8	↑	5	12	↑
Others	17	25	↑	14	18	↑	12	19	↑	14	22	↑	15	18	↑
High-income countries	72	59	↓	77	59	↓	82	69	↓	83	70	↓	79	70	↓
EU25	36	25	↓	26	21	↓	26	31	↑	25	28	↑	43	43	↑
United States	15	18	↑	25	19	↓	40	27	↓	24	20	↓	17	12	↓
Others	21	16	↓	27	19	↓	15	11	↓	35	22	↓	20	15	↓

Income group of exporting country

Source: Author's calculations, based on data from UN Comtrade (database), United Nations, http://comtrade.un.org.

But these findings suggest that concerns that a consumption bust in the United States might threaten global economic cooperation are exaggerated. The most adverse impacts of a slowdown in growth of U.S. import demand would likely be felt by Latin America, the Caribbean area, and China. With the potential for growth in domestic consumption in China, however, the displacement of Chinese goods from the U.S. market may not be a grave concern.

Distinct changes in import demand have also occurred at the regional level. In Europe and Central Asia, export destinations have diversified, moving away from the EU and the United States and toward low- and middle-income countries, including the BRICs (at least for Bulgaria and Poland). In countries from the Middle East and North Africa, South Asia, and Sub-Saharan Africa, there is a shift in exports toward the BRICs and low- and middle-income countries in general. East Asian exports are shifting strongly toward the BRICs and other low- and middle-income economies in all countries except Cambodia. Latin American exports too are shifting toward other low- and middle-income countries but more modestly than in the other regions. The United States remains the dominant destination for nearby Guatemala and Mexico.

Low-income countries in Latin America and South Asia are the most dependent on import demand from high-income nations. The United States absorbed more than 15 percent of recent (2000–08) export growth in just 7 of the 22 regional income-group exporters: 3 are in Latin America and the Caribbean, and the others are low-income countries in East Asia and the Pacific (because of apparel exporters in the region), lower-middle-income countries in Sub-Saharan Africa (primarily because of Nigeria's oil exports), the upper-middle-income countries in the Middle East and North Africa (primarily because of oil exports from the Persian Gulf), and China.

Continued U.S. Demand for Oil and Apparel Exports

From 2000 to 2008, the United States absorbed 20 percent of export growth from low-income countries, but 14 percent came from just two sectors: petroleum and apparel. Similarly, the United States absorbed 15 percent of export growth in lower-middle-income countries, with 13 percent of that growth in petroleum. U.S. absorption of export growth is spread across more than two sectors only for upper-middle-income countries and the BRICs, reflecting the diversification in the exports from these countries.

Absorption by the EU, though also concentrated, is not as extreme as the United States. The EU absorbs 20 percent of exports from low-income countries, with about half coming from apparel and one-quarter from food products. The EU and the United States together absorbed 79 percent of low-income countries' export growth in apparel and footwear over the 2000–08 period, making these destination markets overwhelmingly important for exporters of low-end manufactures.

Although the United States captures a significant share of oil and apparel exports, producers of these goods are not necessarily at risk from U.S. belt-tightening. Given the relatively inelastic demand for oil and semidurable apparel, a major reduction in U.S. consumption growth in these products seems unlikely. More likely candidates for import reductions would be durable goods in the machinery, electronics, and transportation equipment sectors, which are major exports for upper-middle-income countries.

The United States clearly remains an important market for developing countries, but developing countries, as a group, have greatly increased in importance. Low- and middle-income countries, including the BRICs, absorb 63 percent of low-income-country exports of petroleum, 70 percent of their exports of iron and steel, and 52 percent of their exports of food products. The only sectors with minimal absorption are electronics and other products (which include capital-intensive instruments and arms). Low- and middle-income countries thus appear to have done more to help low-income exporters diversify their exports than has the United States or the EU.

The Role of GDP Growth in Developing Countries' Demand for Imports

The expanding role of low- and middle-income countries as a source of import demand can be partially explained by the rapid growth in their GDP. As these economies grow relative to rich countries, their expanding import demand absorbs an ever-larger share of global exports. Over the period 2000 to 2008, average annual growth in real GDP was 9.7 percent in China, 7.3 percent in India, 6.5 percent in Russia, and 3.5 percent in Brazil. In other low- and middle-income countries, it was 4.3 percent. By contrast, GDP growth averaged approximately 2 percent in United States and the EU. The much stronger growth performance of low- and middle-income nations in the past decade is associated with export growth in their developing-country trading partners. A gravity model provides quantitative confirmation of this relationship by decomposing sources of growth in developing-country exports into portions associated with their own GDP growth and the GDP growth of their trade partners.[2]

Higher GDP growth rates in low- and middle-income economies explain a significant portion of the growth of exports from low-income countries: 51 percent of export growth in low-income Middle East and North Africa, 42 percent of export growth in low-income Europe and Central Asia, and 21 percent of export growth in low-income Sub-Saharan Africa. All of these figures exceed the contribution of the United States and EU combined. In middle-income countries, the contribution of GDP growth in low and middle-income countries to export growth is smaller.

Despite similar growth performances, the gravity model suggests that the United States and the EU make very different contributions to export growth in particular developing regions, owing to differences in the strength of their trade ties. In Europe, Central Asia, and the Middle East and North Africa, the contribution of U.S. GDP growth to regional export growth is less than 3 percent. U.S. GDP makes a larger contribution to export growth in lower-middle-income countries in Sub-Saharan Africa (in part because of strong trade ties between the United States and Nigeria), low-income South Asia, and upper-middle-income East Asia and the Pacific, with contributions above 5 percent in each case. Not surprisingly, the most important U.S. contribution is in Latin America and the Caribbean, where it accounts for 13 percent of export growth.

Relative to the United States, GDP growth in the EU makes a larger contribution to export growth in Europe and Central Asia, the Middle East and North Africa, and South Asia. It makes a smaller contribution to export growth in East Asia and the Pacific and in Latin America and the Caribbean. These results are as expected, given that Europe has relatively stronger trade ties with nearby North Africa, Central and Eastern Europe, and Central and South Asia.

The gravity model captures only partial equilibrium relationships between growth in importer GDP and growth in developing-country exports. GDP growth may have indirect effects on trade that the model does not pick up. That is, the model analyzes the direct impact of GDP growth in an importing country on growth in bilateral imports from one of its trading partners, disregarding the potential indirect effects of off-shoring or global production networks. Income growth in the United States, for instance, may increase demand for apparel imports from Vietnam, which may in turn increase Vietnam's demand for textile imports from Malaysia.[3]

The conceptually correct way to measure exports would be as in-country value added, excluding the value of imported intermediates. However, no nation follows this convention in measuring trade flows. As a result, observed trade overstates the shipment of value added between nations. Although it is a valid concern, the amount of double counting would have to be immense to explain away the observed increase in absorption of exports by low- and middle-income countries.

In summary, middle-income countries are emerging as powerful drivers of growth in global import demand. However, a drop in U.S. import demand could still have an adverse impact on the Western Hemisphere, oil producers, and apparel-exporting nations. Meanwhile, GDP growth in developing countries will continue to play a stronger role in growing global import demand in the future.

The Effects of Changes in Demand on Supply Patterns

From 1996 to 2008, low-income countries' share of world exports rose from 0.7 percent to 1.1 percent (figure 8.2). Low-income countries are expanding trade, but overall

Figure 8.2. Share of World Exports by Exporter Income Group, 1996–2008

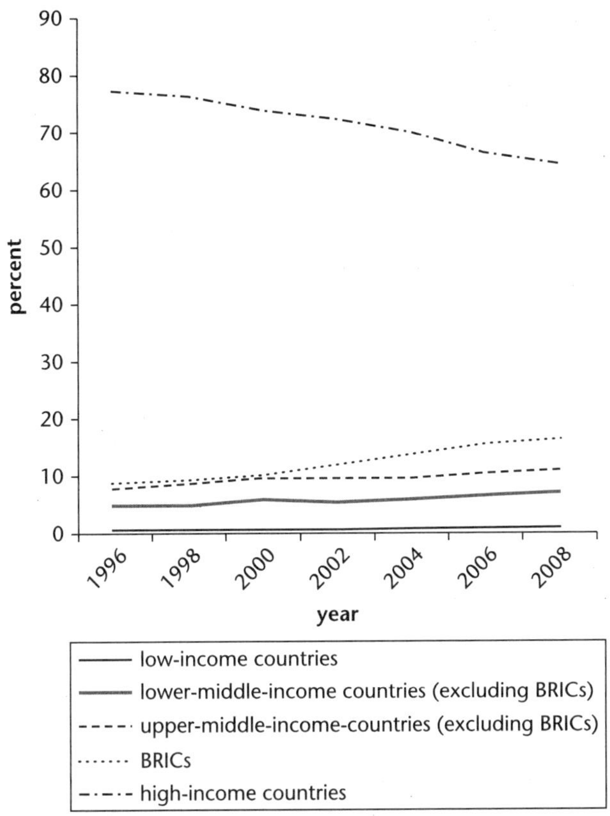

Source: Author's calculations, based on data from UN Comtrade (database), United Nations, http://comtrade.un.org.

they still remain small players in global commerce. Lower-middle- and upper-middle-income countries (excluding the BRICs) saw their combined export share rise from 13 percent to 18 percent. The BRICs' global share of exports shows an impressive rise from 9 percent to 17 percent. They now export nearly as much as all other low- and middle-income countries combined.[4] As the export share of low- and middle-income groups grew, the global export share for high-income countries correspondingly fell from 77 percent to 65 percent. For the first time since the early 20th century, high-income countries accounted for less than two-thirds of world exports, with their share likely to continue shrinking in the years to come.

Specialization in Low-Income Countries

From 1998 to 2006, just two products,[5] apparel and petroleum, accounted for 51 percent of the growth in exports of low-income countries. The next two, food products and iron and steel, bring the total to 76 percent. For low-income countries, export growth appears to be almost entirely resource dependent, relying on raw labor (apparel), mineral resources (petroleum, iron ore), or agricultural land (food products). Low-income countries export little in the way of chemicals, electronics, machinery, or transportation equipment, all of which are intensive in human or physical capital.

One way in which low-income countries are moving up the value chain is by expanding apparel production. In 1996, 86 percent of exports from low-income countries was concentrated in two major product categories (food products, apparel and footwear) and three minor products (textiles, petroleum, iron and steel). In 2008, these five products continued to account for nearly 80 percent of low-income country exports, but their relative importance had changed. Apparel, petroleum, and iron and steel became even more important, while textiles and food products became less important. The growing export share of apparel products relative to textiles marks a step up the value chain for low-income countries. The changing product mix of exports from low-income countries can also be seen as a response to the declining relative demand from the EU (a main importer of food products from low-income countries) and increasing relative demand from middle-income countries such as the BRICs (key importers of oil, iron, and steel).

As low-income countries have increased apparel exports, middle-income countries' share of apparel exports has declined. In 1996, for example, apparel accounted for 23 percent of BRIC exports, due almost entirely to the contribution of China. Yet, by 2008 the share of apparel exports had fallen to 11 percent, as China experienced more rapid export growth in other sectors. China, as well, is moving away from apparel and footwear (at least in a relative sense), opening the way for lower-income nations to fill global demand for these goods. One possible explanation for this shift is that productivity growth in middle-income countries is putting upward pressure on wages, thereby pricing them out of the labor-intensive apparel sector. This phenomenon has been occurring in high-income countries for several decades, although import barriers in these countries have prevented them from losing their apparel edge entirely. This factor could also account for the entry of low-wage nations into markets that were earlier the bastions of middle- or high-income nations.

The Increasing Diversity of Exports from Middle-Income Countries

Reliance on a dominant export product is lower for richer countries in all regions except South Asia (because middle-income Pakistan is more specialized than low-income

Bangladesh) and Sub-Saharan Africa (because of the presence of oil-exporting Nigeria among middle-income countries in the region).[6] The average export share of the dominant export exceeds 20 percent in all lower-middle-income regions but exceeds only 13 percent in all upper-middle-income regions. The export share of the dominant export for low-income countries equals or exceeds 25 percent in all regions except South Asia. Thus, not until countries exceed a gross national income per capita of around US$4,000 does their most important export account for less than a fifth of total shipments abroad.

Of course, diversification at the income group level may hide specialization among individual countries. However, these results are roughly consistent with recent literature that finds that from the 1970s to the mid-1990s, countries became more diversified in the allocation of employment across sectors as their incomes rose from low levels to higher levels. Imbs and Wacziarg (2003) document that the relationship between the sector concentration of employment and per capita GDP is U-shaped. Countries become more diversified during initial phases of development and less diversified in later stages. An estimation of export diversification levels with the Herfindahl-Hirschman Index (HHI) also confirms that low-income countries are the most specialized, while high-income countries are the least. Interestingly, the difference between low-income countries and all other countries is much larger than the difference between middle- and high-income countries. Distinct from Imbs and Wacziarg (2003), much of the diversification in exports appears to occur in the early stages of economic development. Little apparent increase in specialization occurs as a country moves from the middle-income to the high-income group.

Although middle-income countries have diversified exports more than low-income countries, some specialization still exists. Given the prevalence of middle-income countries in the Middle East and North Africa, petroleum is the most common product specialization among middle-income countries. In 2007, the dominant export of middle-income countries in the Middle East and North Africa accounted for 60 percent of shipments abroad, versus 92 percent for low-income countries in the region.[7]

In contrast, the BRICs are more diversified across products, exhibiting a pattern of sector growth that looks similar to high-income countries. That said, the BRICs do have relatively high shares in exports of apparel and electronics and relatively low shares in chemicals and transportation equipment. The first two sectors are intensive in lower-skilled labor (China specializes in electronics product assembly, which is not skill intensive), whereas the second two sectors are relatively intensive in physical capital. The BRIC countries have little in common in their export patterns except for scale. Export growth in Brazil is concentrated in food products and iron and steel. Export growth in Russia is concentrated in oil. India's export growth is concentrated in chemicals, nonmetallic minerals, and iron and steel.[8] Export growth in China is concentrated in machinery and electronics. Thus, while the BRICs as a group resemble other middle-income countries, individually they are heterogeneous.

Changing Patterns of Export Diversification

As seen in the HHI in figure 8.3, specialization levels have notably declined for low-income countries, from an HHI value of 0.25 to 0.16 over the 10-year period.[9] For these countries, this change is equivalent to going from an equal export spread across just four products to an equal export spread across about seven products (out of the over 1,200 products they could export). While either case represents a high degree of specialization, the movement toward greater diversification among low-income countries is pronounced.

This increasing diversification among low-income countries is significant, given that all other country-income groups have become somewhat *more* specialized in their exports over the period. In 2007, the average HHI for lower-middle-income countries was 0.12 and 0.07 for upper-middle-income countries. It should be emphasized that the changes in the HHI distributions for middle- and high-income countries are slight and therefore unlikely to be statistically significant. Still, the pronounced increase in export diversification of low-income countries stands in stark contrast to changes for middle- and high-income countries.

The HHI results can be partially explained by the decline in food exports, which fell from nearly one-third of low-income country exports to 17 percent in 2008. The movement out of food products and into other goods, especially petroleum, apparel, and iron and steel, appears to have helped make low-income countries more diversified, although they are still more specialized than higher-income countries.

One might imagine that the distribution of HHIs would depend on whether oil exporters are included in the data. These countries tend to be highly specialized in crude petroleum and petroleum refining. Yet, even when the 20 major oil exporters are dropped from the sample, the plots look highly similar.[10] The phenomenon of increasing diversification among low-income countries and modestly decreasing diversification among middle- and high-income countries thus holds for non-oil exporters.

In summary, middle-income countries are much more diversified in their export mix than low-income countries

Figure 8.3. Average Export HHIs of Non-oil-Exporting Countries Weighted by Exports, 1997 and 2007

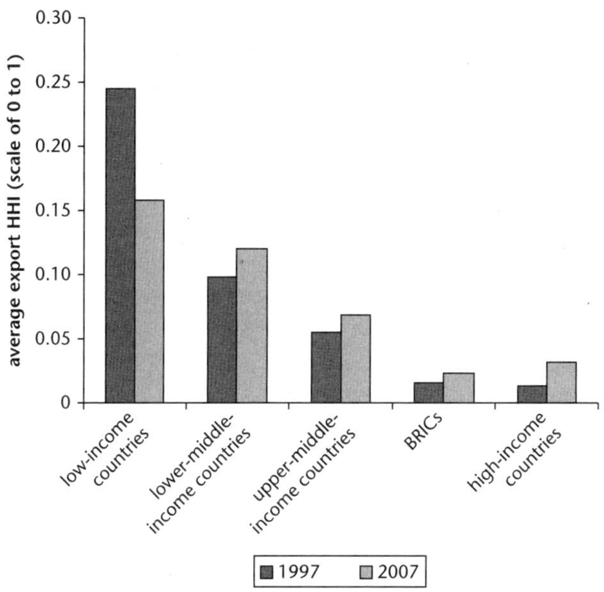

Source: Author's calculations, based on data from UN Comtrade (database), United Nations, http://comtrade.un.org.

and are approaching diversification levels comparable to some high-income countries. However, low-income countries are now closing part of the export diversification gap. Furthermore, middle- and high-income countries have actually become slightly less diversified in their exports in recent years. The proximate cause of rising absolute and relative export diversification in low-income countries is a movement away from heavy reliance on food products toward other sectors.

Conclusion

Trade levels have fallen since the crisis, but the growing demand for exports in developing countries suggests that falling consumption in the United States is not as harmful to global trade as some have claimed. Middle-income countries (including, but not limited to, the BRICs) have become an important source of demand for exports from low-income and lower-middle-income countries. A simple gravity model suggests that GDP growth in developing countries plays a role in their growing demand for imports. And as demand from middle-income countries has risen, dependence on the United States as a destination market for developing-country products has lessened. However, the United States is still a key driver of demand for exports from the Western Hemisphere, for oil products, and for apparel from low-income countries.

In response to changing dynamics on the demand side, new supply patterns have emerged. Developing countries have captured a larger share of world exports in the past decade. Low-income countries remain specialized in resource-intensive exports, but they have diversified to a certain extent, both in the regions they supply and in the types of goods they produce. Low-income countries are also making small steps up the value chain through expansion into apparel production.

The degree of export diversification in middle-income countries is quite similar to that in high-income countries, with richer nations being only somewhat more diversified. Yet, despite the greater export diversification in middle- and high-income countries, it is low-income countries that have experienced the greatest increase in diversification, closing a significant part of the gap that exists between them and richer nations. The recent phase of globalization therefore appears to have helped low-income nations expand the range of goods they produce for foreign markets.

Notes

1. Interestingly, dependence on the United States does not appear to have been a predictor for which countries suffered most from the economic crisis (Rose and Spiegel 2009).

2. For full details of data, methodology, and estimation results, see the working paper version of this chapter.

3. It should be noted that the gravity model does not focus on where GDP growth in importers and exporters comes from. Nothing in the analysis is informative about whether rapid GDP growth in low- and middle-income countries is sustainable. We can only interpret from the model that if growth continues, it is likely to generate further increases in demand for exports from other developing countries.

4. Among the BRICs, China and India are classified as lower-middle-income countries and Brazil and Russia are upper-middle-income countries.

5. Products are grouped according to factor intensity. Using four-digit 1996 Harmonized System (HS) product classification codes, we construct 12 aggregates: raw and processed food products (HS 1–24); petroleum products (HS 27); chemicals (HS 28–40); textiles (HS 41, 50–60); wood and paper products (HS 44–49); apparel and footwear (HS 42–43, 61–67); nonmetallic minerals (HS 25, 68–71); iron and steel (HS 26, 72–83); machinery (HS 84); electronics (HS 85); transportation equipment (HS 86–89); and other manufactures (HS 90–97). Other manufactures include optical instruments, clocks, musical instruments, arms, furniture, toys and games, miscellaneous goods, and works of art. These product aggregates are similar to those in Leamer (1984), who examines industry factor intensity more formally.

6. The dominant export is defined as the product with the highest export levels according to four-digit 1996 HS product classification codes. The dominant export varies across countries, regions, and income levels. The most common dominant export good is crude petroleum (HS 2709), which meets the criterion for 6 low-income countries, 18 middle-income countries, and 8 high-income countries, followed by refined petroleum (HS 2710), for 3 low-income, 9 middle-income, and 13 high-income countries. Other (less) common dominant exports include frozen fish, petroleum gases, passenger and transport ships, and rough lumber. Most of these goods are intensive in the use of natural resources of some kind. Export specialization frequently follows from resource abundance, especially for low-income countries.

7. This figure is calculated as a centered moving average for 2006–08. We average the maximum shares across years rather than show shares for

individual years to account for the impact of temporary global price shocks on export values. The data are weighted by country shares of global exports.

8. Service exports associated with the off-shoring of call centers and other backbone services are important in India's total exports but are not included in the data we use.

9. To examine export specialization patterns more systematically, we calculate the export Herfindahl-Hirschman Index for each country, which measures the concentration of exports in individual products. This provides a scalar measure for each country's export specialization.

10. Major oil exporters are defined as countries for which petroleum or petroleum-related products were the dominant export in both 1997 and 2007 and for which the share of the dominant export in a country's total export exceeded 25 percent.

Bibliography

Feenstra, R. C. 2004. *Advanced International Trade.* Princeton, NJ: Princeton University Press.

Imbs, J., and R. Wacziarg. 2003. "Stages of Diversification." *American Economic Review* 93 (1): 63–86.

Leamer, E. E. 1984. *Sources of Comparative Advantage.* Cambridge, MA: MIT Press.

Rodrik, D. 2009. "Growth after the Crisis." Discussion Paper 7480, Centre for Economic Policy Research, London.

Rose, A. K., and M. M. Spiegel. 2009. "Cross-Country Causes and Consequences of the 2008 Crisis: International Linkages and American Exposure." Working Paper 15358, National Bureau of Economic Research, Cambridge, MA.

9

SOURCES OF EXPORT GROWTH IN DEVELOPING COUNTRIES

Gordon Hanson

The world economy is beginning to recover from the Great Recession of 2007–09. Industrial production in emerging economies, after falling sharply in the second half of 2008, began to grow in early 2009. World trade also began to rebound at this time. The financial crisis, though crippling in its effects on rich countries, did not infect developing economies outside of Eastern Europe (de la Torre 2010). Indeed, the exposure of emerging economies to the recession has been limited largely to a contraction in the global demand for their exports. With that contraction easing, world trade is likely to continue to expand in 2010.

As discussed in the previous chapter, trade patterns have changed dramatically over the past decade. Most notably, developing countries have become a prime source of growth in demand for exports from other developing countries. And while developing countries have increased their share of global imports, high-income countries have become relatively less important destinations for developing-country goods. So what has driven this change in trade flows? The primary reason is that the locus of economic growth has shifted from high-income to middle-income nations. Middle-income countries account for an ever-larger source of global demand because they are now growing much more rapidly than high-income economies.

In this chapter, we explore whether recent changes in global trade patterns are likely to be sustained as the global economy recovers. Naturally, a prolonged collapse in economic growth in the BRICs (Brazil, the Russian Federation, India, and China) or other middle-income economies would profoundly affect global trade. But without such an interruption, are trends in global trade expected to continue? The answer depends on two factors. First, has recent growth in middle-income economies been robust; that is, does it represent long-run growth based on growth in total factor productivity, capital investment, and skill upgrading, or is it simply a temporary deviation from a more modest trend? Second, is export growth in developing nations being matched by improvements in their export capacity, allowing the expansion of exports to be sustained?

To address these questions, we examine the contribution of changes in export competitiveness and importer growth in gross domestic product (GDP) to growth in exports by developing countries over the period 2000–2007. The rest of the chapter is organized as follows. The next section discusses changes in global trade patterns and GDP growth over the past decade. The following section explores the sustainability of these trends based on the findings of a gravity model. The final section concludes.

Recent Trends in Global Trade and GDP

To understand the relationship between economic growth and global trade patterns, we must examine basic trends in trade flows and GDP growth.

Changing Trade Patterns

A growing trend of export diversification has emerged in the past decade. In particular, exports from low-income countries have become more diversified (table 9.1). While low-income countries are still specialized in agriculture; extractive industries; and apparel, footwear, and textiles, they have also begun shifting into sectors in which they had relatively low export participation in the past, including iron and steel (metals) and machinery; electronics; and transport equipment.

Relative to low-income countries, lower-middle-income countries are more diversified. In 2007, the most important

Table 9.1. Export Shares by Sector and Developing-Country Income Group, 2000 and 2007
percent

	Income group					
	Low		Lower middle		Upper middle	
Sector	2000	2007	2000	2007	2000	2007
Agriculture	16.4	12.8	5.0	2.8	6.2	6.0
Food, beverage, tobacco, wood	6.7	6.3	5.4	4.1	7.5	7.1
Extractive	26.3	24.0	16.8	17.9	27.3	36.2
Chemicals	2.6	3.9	6.3	7.1	5.9	6.3
Apparel, textiles, footwear, leather	38.1	34.2	22.0	14.4	7.8	4.3
Metals	3.1	7.7	4.6	7.6	8.9	10.8
Machinery, electronics, transport	4.8	7.2	28.5	37.0	32.6	25.9
Other	2.0	3.9	11.4	9.1	3.7	3.4

Source: Author's calculations based on UN Comtrade (database), United Nations, http://comtrade.un.org.

sector was machinery, electronics, and transportation equipment (37 percent of exports); and extractive industries was the second most important (18 percent of exports in 2007) for lower-middle-income countries. One notable shift for lower-middle-income countries is the decreasing importance of apparel and textiles, whose share of exports fell from 22 percent in 2000 to 14 percent in 2007. Of course, this change can be attributed largely to the decreasing relative importance of apparel in China's exports.

Upper-middle-income countries exhibit similar diversification patterns as lower-middle-income countries, with the primary difference being that extractive industries (36 percent of exports in 2007) are more important than machinery and electronics (26 percent of exports in 2007). This finding is not surprising, given the preponderance of oil exporters in the Middle East and North Africa in this income group.

Over the past decade, export patterns have also varied within income groups across regions. While apparel is important for low-income countries overall, much of this significance is due to East Asia and the Pacific and South Asia, where in 2007 apparel accounted for 37 percent and 89 percent of exports, respectively. In the Middle East and North Africa and Sub-Saharan Africa, in contrast, the primary export sectors were agriculture, extractive industries, and metals.

Among lower-middle-income countries, the shift into machinery and electronics was strongest in East Asia and the Pacific, where the sector accounted for 46 percent of exports in 2007. Extractive industries are important for Sub-Saharan Africa, the Middle East and North Africa, Europe and Central Asia, and Latin America and the Caribbean. Finally, for upper-middle-income countries, machinery and electronics are a major export industry for East Asia and the Pacific and for Latin America and the Caribbean, while extractive industries are the major source of exports for the Middle East and North Africa, Europe and Central Asia, and Sub-Saharan Africa.

New trends have also emerged with respect to destination markets. Developing countries are an increasingly important source of export growth for low- and middle-income economies (table 9.2). The share of exports destined for low- and middle-income countries has risen significantly, with the most pronounced growth occurring in lower-middle-income exporters.[1] The BRICs have attracted much attention owing to their large size and rapid rates of recent economic growth, but they are by no means the only drivers of export growth in developing countries.

Trends in GDP Growth

To understand whether the above-mentioned patterns in global trade are sustainable, we first take a closer look at the decomposition of GDP. Figure 9.1 presents the trend and cyclical components of GDP for several groups of countries. Each plot shows log GDP (left-hand scale), the trend component of log GDP (left-hand scale), and the cyclical deviation from trend (right-hand scale).

Among the BRICs, GDP growth seems to be generally associated with trend GDP rather than cyclical variations (figure 9.1a). China and India have clearly experienced trend growth over the past three decades. Moreover, after a recession in the early 1990s, China's GDP has shown little cyclical variation. The cyclical component of India's GDP is similarly modest. In Brazil, trend growth has accelerated and cyclical variation has dampened over time. Russia shows a sharp break in its trend growth in the late 1990s, after which point cyclical variation declined.

For the most part, other middle-income countries experienced more cyclical variation in GDP and sharper differences in trend GDP growth than the BRICs (figure 9.1b). The Republic of Korea has had a strong positive GDP trend that weakened somewhat after 2000. Trend growth in Mexico, Poland, and Turkey accelerated after 2000. Trend growth was modest in Argentina and South Africa, with the former showing large cyclical variation and the latter showing relatively little. Indonesia and Thailand experienced large cyclical variation in GDP around the Asian

Table 9.2. Export Shares by Destination and Developing-Country Income Group, 2000 and 2007
percent

	Income level					
	Low		Lower middle		Upper middle	
Destination	2000	2007	2000	2007	2000	2007
Low and middle income						
East Asia and Pacific	12.4	15.5	6.7	10.1	4.7	9.8
Europe and Central Asia	4.3	5.3	2.1	4.4	3.2	5.9
Latin America and the Caribbean	1.0	1.1	2.1	3.8	6.8	6.5
Middle East and North Africa	0.1	0.1	0.1	0.2	0.2	0.2
South Asia	2.6	3.8	0.8	2.5	0.7	1.3
Sub-Saharan Africa	0.9	1.9	0.5	1.2	0.3	0.6
Subtotal	21.3	27.7	12.3	22.2	15.9	24.3
High income						
Americas	17.2	22.3	28.6	24.7	40.0	28.4
Asia	17.8	13.9	35.0	26.7	12.3	9.6
Europe	40.0	32.5	22.3	24.4	31.2	37.1
Pacific	3.8	3.6	1.7	2.0	0.7	0.7
Subtotal	78.8	72.3	87.6	77.8	84.2	75.8

Source: Author's calculations based on Comtrade (database), United Nations, http://comtrade.un.org.

Figure 9.1. Log GDP with Trend and Cyclical Components in Selected Countries, 1978–2008
a. BRICs

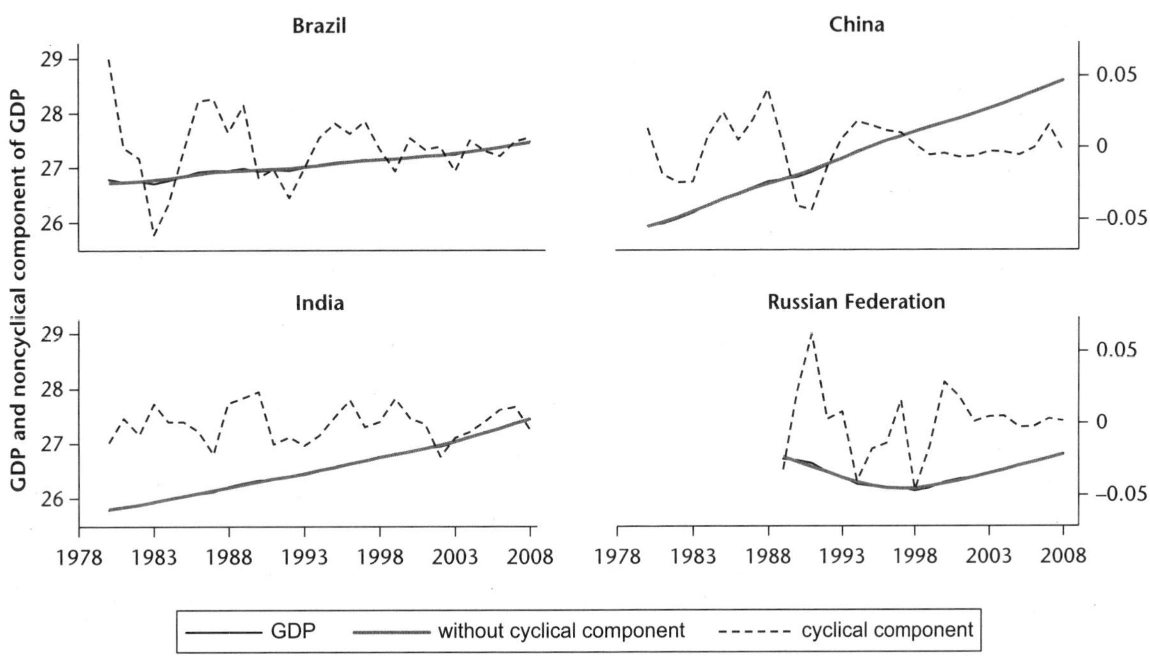

(continued)

Figure 9.1. *(continued)*
b. Selected other middle-income countries

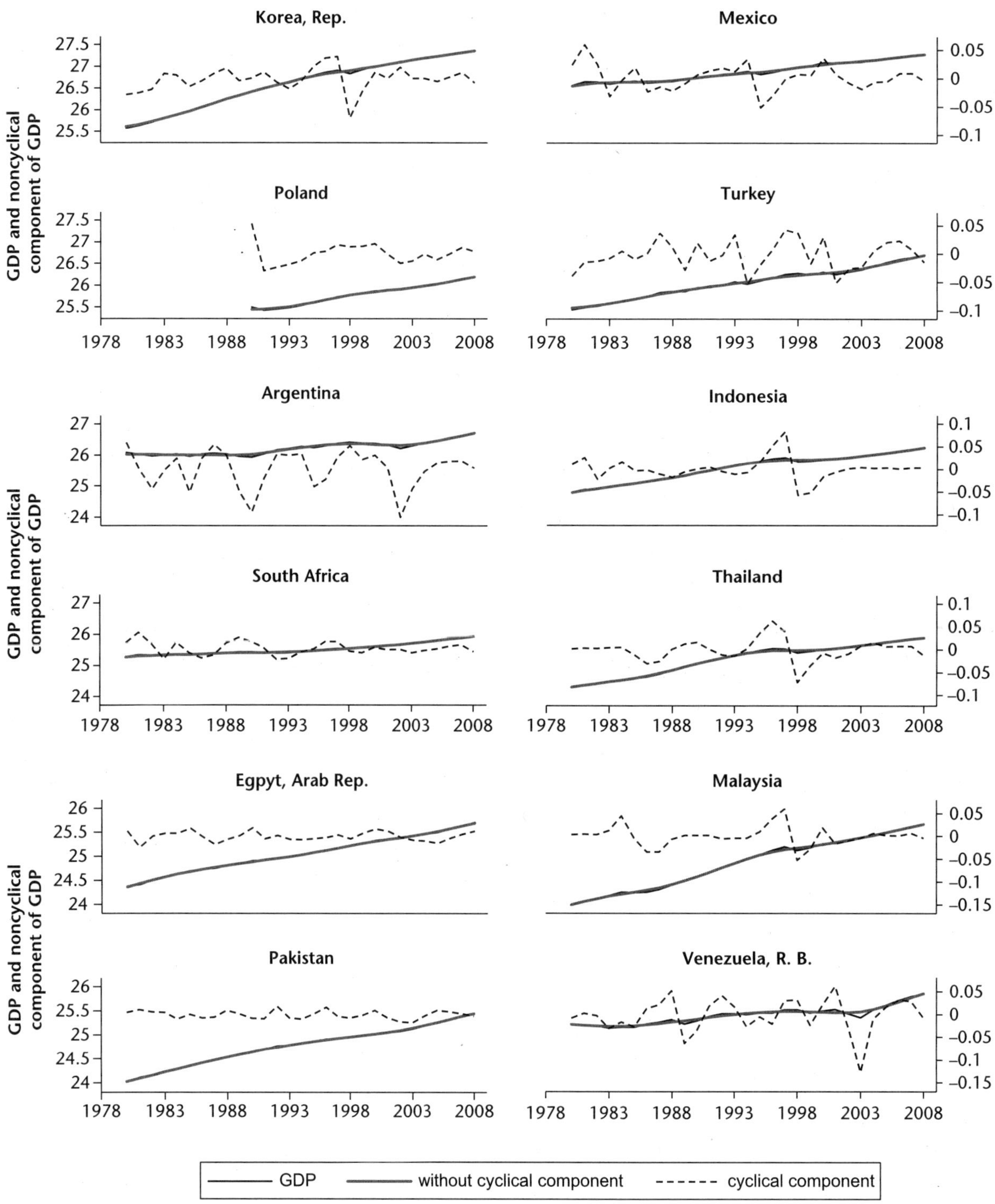

(continued)

Figure 9.1. *(continued)*
c. Selected high-income countries

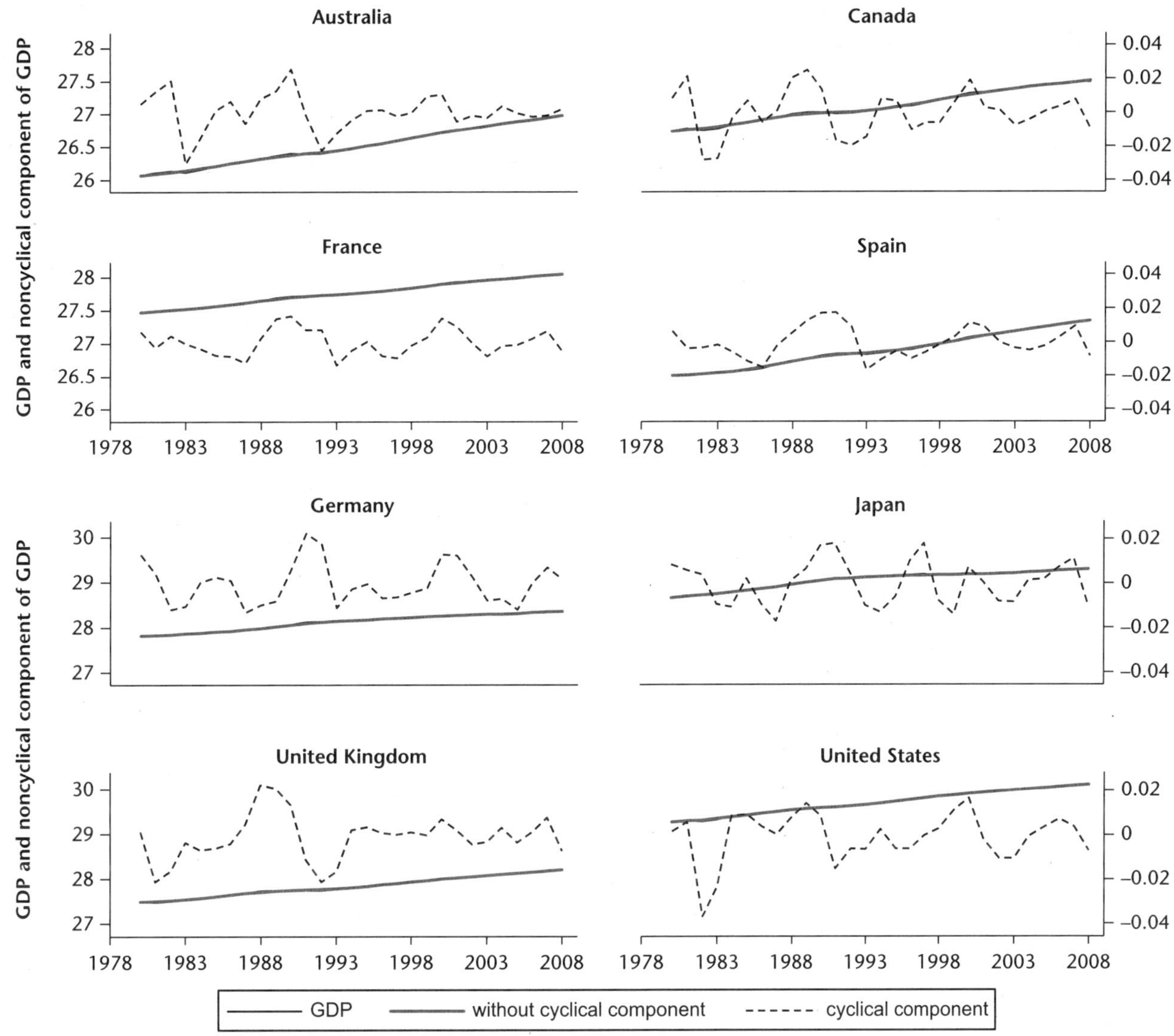

Source: Author's calculations.

financial crisis in 1997–98. The crisis was accompanied by a dampening of trend growth, which later accelerated in the early 2000s. Malaysia resembles other Asian countries with volatility in the late 1990s and an uptick in trend growth in the 2000s. The Arab Republic of Egypt and Pakistan exhibit stable trend growth, with only modest cyclical variation. The República Bolivariana de Venezuela follows the Latin American pattern of strong cyclical variability and several breaks in trend growth.

The magnitude of variations in the business cycle is relatively similar across high-income countries (figure 9.1c). Australia, Canada, and Spain exhibit more rapid trend growth in GDP than France, Germany, the United Kingdom, and the United States. Japan shows a marked slowing in its trend growth in the early 1990s, consistent with the beginning of the country's economic stagnation.

All in all, middle- and high-income countries show considerable variation in the pace and stability of trend growth in GDP and in the contribution of the cyclical component to GDP changes. From these figures, it is not immediately apparent which component of GDP growth, the trend or the cycle, is most important for growth in import demand.

Are Global Trade Patterns Sustainable in the Future?

To shed light on the question of the sustainability of trade flows, we employ a gravity model of trade. There are two steps to this analysis. First, we apply the Eaton and Kortum (2002) gravity model to determine the contribution of changes in supply conditions to export growth and how these conditions vary across exporting countries. Second, we use the Hodrick-Prescott (1997) filter to examine how trend growth and cyclical growth are related to changes in import demand. The rest of this section discusses the findings of these models. Full technical details are available in the working paper version of this chapter.

Changes in Export Competitiveness and Implications for Export Growth

Is export growth in developing nations being matched by improvements in their export capacity, allowing the expansion to be sustained? To address this question, we specify a gravity model based on the Eaton and Kortum (2002) model of trade. Our sample is composed of 49 countries, which collectively accounted for 98 percent of global GDP in 2000.[2] The sample covers more than 36,000 changes in bilateral trade flows at the sector level from 2000 to 2007.

Product-level data from the Comtrade database are aggregated into eight sectors: (1) agriculture, meat and dairy, seafood; (2) food, beverages, tobacco, wood, paper; (3) extractive industries; (4) chemicals, plastics, rubber; (5) textiles, apparel, leather, footwear; (6) iron, steel, and other metals; (7) machinery, electronics, transportation equipment; and (8) other industries. Each sector is a collection of industries that share similar factor intensities and are likely to rely on similar technological or institutional foundations as a basis for production.[3] Based on this model, the following findings emerge.

First, developing countries experienced pronounced improvements in export competitiveness relative to developed economies in the 2000s (table 9.3). Low-income countries increased competitiveness in agriculture, apparel and textiles, metals, and other industries and lost competitiveness in food processing and extractive industries.[4] Lower-middle-income countries improved competitiveness in all sectors except extractive industries. Lower-middle-income countries also show the strongest relative improvement among all income groups in five of the eight sectors (food processing; apparel and textiles; chemicals; metals; and machinery and electronics). Upper-middle-income countries increased competitiveness in agriculture, food processing, extractive industries, apparel and textiles, and other industries. Because developing nations saw improvements (or no change) in their competitiveness in most sectors, it is not surprising that high-income countries saw a decline: high-income countries of the Organisation for Economic Co-operation and Development (OECD) lost competitiveness in all sectors, and high-income non-OECD countries lost competitiveness in all sectors but one (chemicals). Moreover, the results are largely unchanged when the BRICs are excluded from their respective income categories. This finding indicates that other middle-income nations have enjoyed improvements in export competitiveness similar to those experienced by the BRICs.

Second, changes in export competitiveness, whether associated with changes in technology or with changes in

Table 9.3. Mean Change in Export Competitiveness by Exporter Income Group, 2000–07

Income group	(1)	(2)	(3)	(4)	(5)	(6)	(7)	(8)
Including BRICs								
Low income	0.023	–0.030	–0.013	0.001	0.055	0.046	–0.003	0.064
Lower-middle income	0.014	0.032	–0.014	0.062	0.090	0.081	0.093	0.034
Upper-middle income	0.033	0.008	0.041	–0.003	0.055	–0.018	0.007	0.038
High income								
OECD	–0.022	–0.051	–0.014	–0.029	–0.019	–0.032	–0.061	–0.058
Non-OECD	–0.059	–0.014	–0.010	0.014	–0.036	–0.011	–0.077	–0.063
Excluding BRICs								
Low income	0.023	–0.021	–0.010	–0.011	0.069	0.024	—	0.064
Lower-middle income	0.012	0.035	–0.012	0.064	0.091	0.088	0.095	0.034
Upper-middle income	0.028	0.007	0.040	–0.003	0.056	–0.016	0.008	0.038
High income								
OECD	–0.021	–0.050	–0.014	–0.028	0.015	–0.031	–0.061	–0.058
Non-OECD	–0.058	–0.011	–0.015	0.016	–0.034	–0.006	–0.076	–0.059

Source: Author's calculations.

Note: The mean change in exporter competitiveness is the mean exporter fixed effect from gravity regressions reported in the working paper version of this chapter. Means are weighted by 2000 country export levels. Columns indicate broad sectors: (1) agriculture; (2) food, beverages, tobacco, wood products; (3) extractive industries; (4) chemicals; (5) apparel, textiles, footwear, leather; (6) iron, steel, other metals; (7) machinery, electronics, transportation equipment; (8) other industries. — = not available.

production costs, account for approximately 11 percent of the variation in bilateral export growth from 2000 to 2007. GDP growth in exporting countries explains a small fraction of changes in export competitiveness, suggesting that changes in export capabilities are not simply a byproduct of overall economic expansion.

Third, trends in changes in export competitiveness emerge at the regional level (table 9.4). East Asia and the Pacific showed improvements in export competitiveness across all sectors (with or without China included). Europe and Central Asia, Latin America and the Caribbean, and South Asia increased competitiveness in all sectors but one (metals, chemicals, and agriculture, respectively). The Middle East and North Africa increased export competitiveness in three sectors: agriculture, apparel and textiles, and machinery and electronics. Sub-Saharan Africa, in contrast to other developing regions, did not improve export competitiveness in any sector. Overall, East Asia showed the largest or second-largest improvement in export competitiveness (competitiveness increased in six of the eight sectors) and Sub-Saharan Africa showed the largest decline (competitiveness decreased in six of the eight sectors).

While BRICS are not the only drivers of the rising competitiveness, their performance is still remarkably impressive relative to other large economies (figure 9.2). China is one of the top five countries in improvement of export competitiveness in all eight sectors, India is in the top five in seven sectors, Brazil is in the top five in two sectors, and Russia is in the top five in one sector. However, other middle-income nations have also shown strong growth in export competitiveness, with Turkey in the top five in six sectors, Poland in the top five in six sectors, and Argentina in the top five in four sectors.[5] High-income nations, in contrast, show weak improvements in export competitiveness. Japan and the United Kingdom are among the bottom five performers in six of the eight sectors, and the United States is among the bottom five performers in four sectors. The República Bolivariana de Venezuela is the sole middle-income nation with consistent poor performance, showing up in the bottom five countries in seven of the eight sectors.

Finally, several secondary trends can be seen in the results of the gravity model. First, for apparel and other industries (primarily instruments and specialized equipment), distance became a less important impediment to trade in the 2000s. Second, in agriculture, metals, and machinery and electronics, lack of a common language became a more important impediment to trade over the period. Third, colonial heritage became a more important factor for trade in the agriculture, chemicals, apparel, and metal sectors over the period. Finally, having an existing regional trade agreement or a new agreement post-2000 is uncorrelated with trade growth.

Table 9.4. Mean Change in Export Competitiveness by Exporter Region, 2000–07

Region	(1)	(2)	(3)	(4)	(5)	(6)	(7)	(8)
Low- and middle-income countries[a]								
East Asia and Pacific	0.037	0.035	0.027	0.052	0.096	0.107	0.054	0.033
Europe and Central Asia	0.038	0.029	0.075	0.041	0.087	–0.041	0.092	0.161
Latin America and the Caribbean	0.028	0.011	0.029	–0.025	0.042	0.007	0.034	0.011
Middle East and North Africa	0.025	–0.006	–0.006	0.000	0.073	–0.014	0.031	–0.021
South Asia	–0.010	0.036	0.103	0.065	0.060	0.086	0.078	0.018
Sub-Saharan Africa	–0.036	–0.076	–0.061	–0.037	–0.062	–0.018	–0.037	–0.038
High income all regions	–0.022	–0.050	–0.013	–0.027	–0.021	–0.031	–0.062	–0.059
Low- and middle-income countries[b]								
East Asia and Pacific	0.037	0.042	0.027	0.055	0.097	0.109	0.056	0.033
Europe and Central Asia	0.026	0.027	0.070	0.044	0.096	–0.041	0.096	0.166
Latin America and the Caribbean	0.022	0.009	0.028	–0.026	0.042	0.009	0.034	0.011
Middle East and North Africa	0.026	–0.006	–0.003	0.001	0.074	–0.013	0.032	–0.020
South Asia	–0.010	0.038	0.102	0.069	0.060	0.088	0.078	0.018
Sub-Saharan Africa	–0.034	–0.070	–0.059	–0.043	–0.054	–0.019	–0.039	–0.038
High income all regions	–0.022	–0.050	–0.014	–0.027	–0.017	–0.031	–0.062	–0.058

Source: Author's calculations.

Note: The mean change in exporter competitiveness is the mean exporter fixed effect from gravity regressions reported in the working paper version of this chapter. Means are weighted by 2000 country export levels. Columns indicate broad sectors: (1) agriculture; (2) food, beverages, tobacco, wood products; (3) extractive industries; (4) chemicals; (5) apparel, textiles, footwear, leather; (6) iron, steel, other metals; (7) machinery, electronics, transportation equipment; (8) other industries.

a. Including BRICs.

b. Excluding BRICs.

Figure 9.2. Change in Relative Export Competitiveness of Selected Countries by Industry, 2000–07

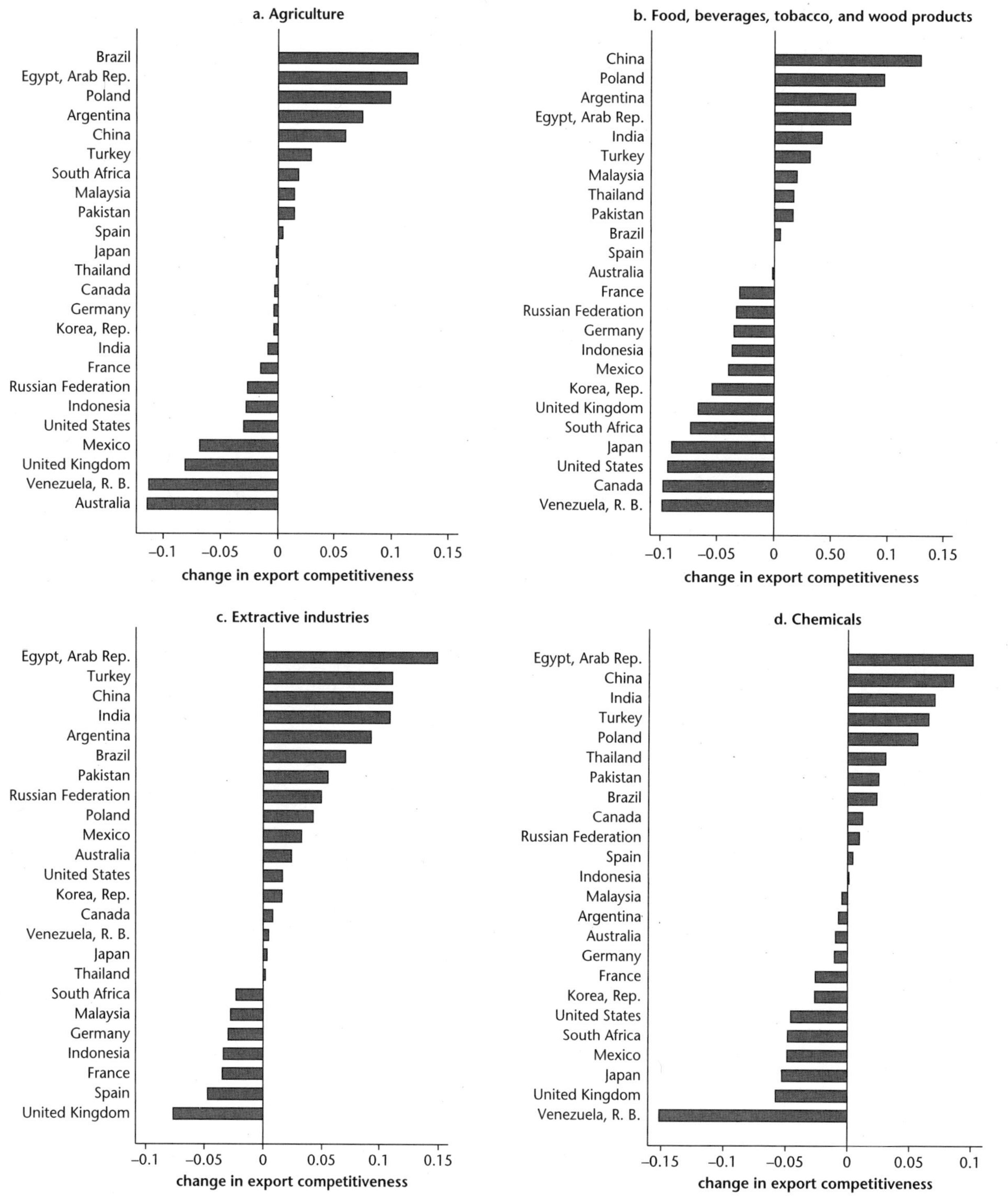

(continued)

Figure 9.2. *(continued)*

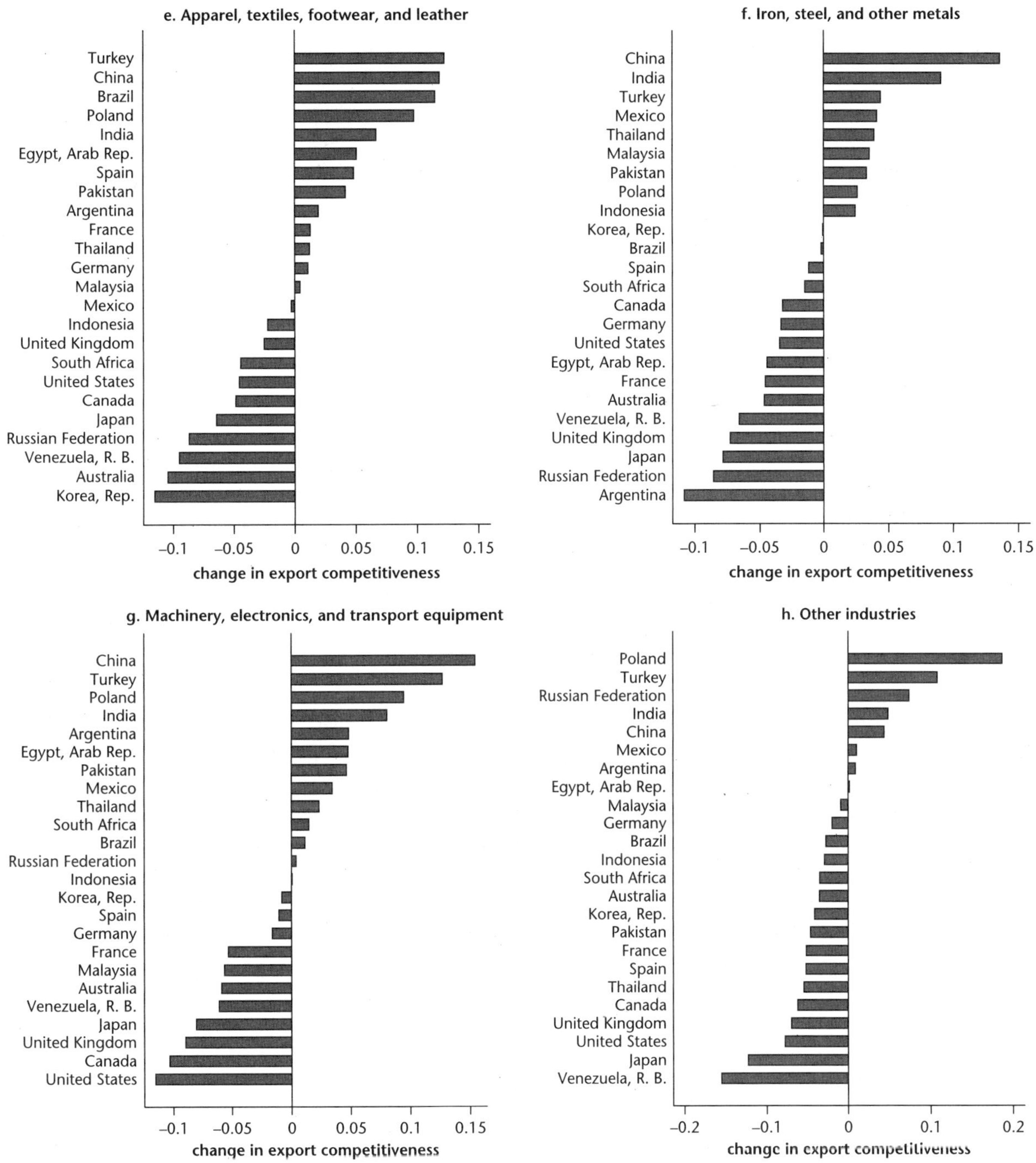

What Is Driving the Demand for Imports—Trend Growth or Cyclical Growth?

Are middle-income economies experiencing long-run growth based on growth in total factor productivity, capital investment, and skill upgrading, or are they experiencing simply cyclical growth? In a second exercise, we estimate a modified version of the gravity model to evaluate the contribution of different components of GDP growth to growth in demand for imports. We replace importer fixed effects in the gravity model with importer GDP broken down into two components: change in the trend component captures long-run economic growth, and change in the cyclical component captures changes in business cycle conditions. We use the Hodrick-Prescott filter to decompose

GDP based on annual data from the World Development Indicators database over the period 1960–2008.[6]

Overall, the primary source of variation in import demand seems to be variation in trend GDP, rather than variation in business cycle fluctuations. While growth in bilateral trade is strongly positively correlated with changes in trend GDP, it is weakly correlated with changes in the cyclical component of GDP, suggesting that the recent growth in trade derives from structural economic growth in importing nations.

At the country level, more specific trends emerge in the 2000s. Income growth was associated almost entirely with the GDP trend in the BRICs and many Asian nations[7] (for example, Indonesia, Malaysia, and Thailand), but other middle-income countries had a more varied experience: in Latin American nations (for example, Argentina, Mexico, and the República Bolivariana de Venezuela) the cyclical variation seemed to be a more important component of growth. Moreover, the GDP trend in large high-income nations is considerably smaller in comparison to middle-income countries (and to smaller high-income nations, such as Australia, Canada, and Spain).

Finally, the gravity estimation reveals that changes in trend GDP are strongly positively associated with trade growth, while cyclical variation in GDP positively affects trade in just one industry, metals. These results are silent on whether the flexible trend GDP growth estimated over the 1960–2008 period will continue. What they do show is that the trend component of GDP is what matters for trade growth. To the extent that GDP trends in middle-income nations continue, there is every reason to believe they will continue to be an important source of demand for growth in imports.

Conclusion

In this chapter, we examine the contribution of changes in export competitiveness and importer GDP growth to growth in exports by developing countries over the 2000–07 period. One of the main findings is that developing countries have enjoyed significant improvements in their export competitiveness since 2000. East Asia and the Pacific exhibited the strongest performance, with improvement in export competitiveness in all sectors (with or without China); Europe and Central Asia, Latin America and the Caribbean, and South Asia show improvements in export competitiveness in most sectors; the Middle East and North Africa shows improvements in export competitiveness in a few sectors; and Sub-Saharan Africa shows improvements in export competitiveness in no sectors.

We also find that changes in relative exporter capabilities can account for approximately 11 percent of the variation in bilateral export growth over 2000–07. Thus, important sources of trade growth are improvements in exporter technology and reductions in exporter production costs (part of which may be related to global production networks).

Moreover, it seems that GDP growth plays only a modest role in changes in countries' export competitiveness. That countries vary in their sectoral rankings of improvements in export competitiveness is initial evidence this is not the case. Thus, other factors must also be at work, presumably related to technological advancement in exporter technology and reductions in exporter production costs. Eaton and Kortum (2002) demonstrate that countries that are more integrated into global production networks may have lower production costs, which would show up in a higher exporter fixed effect (or in time differences in larger increases in exporter fixed effects). However, given the concentration of these networks in just two of the eight sectors (apparel and textiles; machinery, electronics, and transportation), cross-border trade in inputs is unlikely to be an important factor in changes in export competitiveness in the other sectors (agriculture, food processing, extractive industries, chemicals, and metals).

Finally, we find that the recent growth in trade was driven by trend growth, as opposed to cyclical growth, in importing nations. What does this mean for future growth in trade among developing countries? If GDP trends in middle-income countries persist, we have a strong basis for predicting that developing nations will be a significant source of growth in demand for imports in the coming decade. This possibility is especially important for growth in trade, given the likelihood that the European Union, Japan, and the United States may have anemic growth in the medium run.

Notes

1. It should be emphasized that these figures understate the importance of low- and middle-income destinations, owing to the sample restrictions placed on the data. See the working paper version of this chapter for further details.

2. The list of importers is presented in the working paper version of this chapter. To remove zero trade associated with small samples, the sample excludes very small exporters (countries with a population in 2000 of less than 1 million inhabitants) and small importers (countries with less than 0.1 percent share of world GDP in 2000). Due to missing GDP data in the World Development Indicators our sample also excludes Taiwan, China; several Gulf States (Bahrain, Kuwait, Oman, Qatar, and the United Arab Emirates); war-torn countries (Afghanistan, Iraq, and Somalia, and

the Palestinian territories); and tightly controlled economies (Cuba, the Democratic People's Republic of Korea, Myanmar, and Zimbabwe).

3. This aggregation scheme is similar to that used by Harrigan (1997) and Romalis (2004) for Standard Industrial Classification industries. See the working paper version of this chapter for further details.

4. There was little relative change in the other industries.

5. Changes in export competitiveness could in part reflect unmeasured changes in trade barriers in destination countries (for example, for Poland and Turkey) or the effects of currency devaluation during the 2000 to 2007 period (for example, in Argentina).

6. We use the same sample of 49 countries as in the first exercise. See the working paper version of this chapter for further details on the construction of this model.

7. This occurred outside of the Asian financial crisis period in 1997–98.

Bibliography

de la Torre, A. 2010. "Update on LAC and the Global Crisis: The Worst Is Over but What Lies Behind?" Mimeo, World Bank, Washington, DC.

Eaton, J., and S. Kortum. 2002. "Technology, Geography, and Trade." *Econometrica* 70: 1741–79.

Harrigan, J. 1997. "Technology, Factor Supplies, and International Specialization: Estimating the Neoclassical Model." *American Economic Review* 87 (4): 475–94.

Hodrick, R. J., and E. C. Prescott. 1997. "Postwar U.S. Business Cycles: An Empirical Investigation." *Journal of Money, Credit and Banking* 29 (1): 1–16.

Romalis, J. 2004. "Factor Proportions and the Structure of Commodity Trade." *American Economic Review* 94 (1): 67–97.

10

CHINA'S TRADE AND INVESTMENT WITH THE SOUTH PRE- AND POSTCRISIS

Jing Wang and John Whalley

China has seen a remarkable eightfold increase in real per capita gross domestic product (GDP) since the mid-1970s. That growth has been accompanied by a large increase in trade and, since the early 1990s, inward foreign investment. More recently, it is China's expanding engagement with the South—Africa, developing Asia, and Latin America—which has been changing rapidly and growing at higher rates than total trade and investment, albeit from a small base. China's growing engagement with other developing countries is the focus of this chapter, and we summarize data both pre- and postcrisis, as well as making forward projections. To our knowledge, no others have attempted this analysis. We draw heavily on Chinese source material.

The picture that emerges is one of rapid change. The share of Southern trade in China's total trade shows little change in the 1990s but then begins to increase at an accelerating rate. Southern trade is now over 25 percent of China's total trade—35 percent of imports by value and in the 20s for exports. Trade with developing countries—both imports and exports—relative to trade with developed countries, after some relative slippage in the 1990s, began to pick up speed following China's entry into the World Trade Organization (WTO), and its share increased consistently though the 2000s until 2007. On the import side, imports of oil and materials, especially from Africa, are key. On the export side, exports to countries elsewhere in Asia show the largest growth.

By country, some notable changes occur in China's trade. Especially prominent is trade between India and China, which increased by a factor of 33 between 1995 and 2007, or at a little less than four times faster than the growth rate of China's total trade (in this chapter, growth rates always mean the rate compared with the same period of the previous year). From small levels of trade in 1995, China had become India's largest export market and India had become China's fourth-largest market by 2007. Trade with Brazil also showed rapid growth, at a factor of 18 between 1995 and 2007.

Given this pace of change, we make some forward projections assuming that average 2005–07 growth rates of trade remain unchanged (which in the current crisis is a strong assumption). Our findings show an even greater acceleration in these trends as the levels of fast-growing Southern trade rise. Our projections indicate that China's Southern trade will grow to 50 percent of its total trade by 2020 and to 60 percent of its total trade by 2027. The compounding effects of the extremely high growth rates of China's trade with India and Brazil are such that in a surprisingly short period these bilateral trade flows will come to dominate China's trade. China, in turn, will even more quickly become the world's largest trading entity.

We then turn to China's foreign direct investment (FDI) involvement with the South. Data show China's FDI inflows from the South as small and only slowly changing, with a small dip in the early 2000s and a rise in 2006–07. Shares are steady in the 10 percent range of total FDI inflows. On the FDI outflow side, the picture is different, with sharp growth in recent years. This increase is reflected in even higher growth rates of FDI from China to Africa, Brazil, India, and elsewhere than occurs with trade. FDI flows to India increased by over ninetyfold during the 1995–2007 period.

We also discuss how the financial crisis has seemingly affected the rapid growth of China's involvement with the

South. We present data on trade for 2008 and early 2009 that show a fall in China's Southern trade but at a much smaller rate than the drop in China's total trade. The share of Southern in total trade thus continues to rise. According to data on FDI flows in 2008, China's inflows and outflows both kept growing, but Southern growth rates were a little below those of total growth. FDI outflows doubled in 2008, and inflows increased by over 20 percent.

Finally, we place this discussion in a broader policy context, noting China's growing ties with India and China's regional trade arrangements, which are heavily Southern in focus. Combined with the emergence of an assertive South on climate change policy, given the data we present, Southern countries appear likely to increase their focus on China both diplomatically and strategically.

China's Trade with the South, 1995–2007

Although, as we show, China's trade shares with the South have been increasing, we need to give a careful definition of *South* in this context. The issue is particularly important in the cases of Hong Kong SAR, China, and Taiwan, China, which are not members of the Organisation for Economic Co-operation and Development (OECD), have substantial trade with China, and have high GDP per capita. Here we define the *South* as Africa, Latin America, and Asia, excluding Hong Kong SAR, China; Japan; the Republic of Korea; Singapore; and Taiwan, China. Trade with Hong Kong SAR, China, and Taiwan, China, grows at about the same rate as China's total trade, and we emphasize that including those trade flows in Southern trade produces considerably lower growth rates in China-South trade flows than we report later. This grouping of Asian countries that we denote as Asia* in this chapter includes India, Indonesia, Malaysia, Thailand, and Vietnam. The *South* here is thus Africa, Asia*, and Latin America. Because we exclude other countries, a small downward bias may therefore exist in our calculations of Southern trade shares for China.

We begin with the precrisis period (1995–2007). The size of China's trade (imports and exports) with major Southern countries and regions for 1995, 2001, and 2007 is set out in table 10.1. The absolute value of exports to Southern regions and major countries almost doubled (except Mexico with a ninefold increase) between 1995 and 2001, and exports in 2007 increased by a factor over 6 to every region compared to 2001. China's exports to India increased by a factor of 13 between 2001 and 2007. China's 2007 exports to and imports from the South are 21 percent and 35 percent of total trade, respectively. Over 70 percent of China's Southern trade is with developing countries in Asia. Thus, trade has increased steadily over time, with a dramatic change between 2001 and 2007 (figure 10.1).

Table 10.1. China's Total Trade (Imports and Exports) with the South, 1995, 2001, and 2007
US$, billions

	Exports			Imports		
Region or country	**1995**	**2001**	**2007**	**1995**	**2001**	**2007**
Africa	2.5	6.0	37.3	1.4	4.8	36.4
Asia[*a]*	14.3	26.1	172.3	12.0	39.1	250.9
Latin America	3.1	8.2	51.5	3.0	6.7	51.1
Total South	19.9	40.4	261.1	16.4	50.6	338.3
East and South Asia						
India	0.8	1.9	24.0	0.4	1.7	14.6
Indonesia	1.4	2.8	12.6	2.1	3.9	12.4
Malaysia	1.3	3.2	17.7	2.1	6.2	28.7
Thailand	1.8	2.3	12.0	1.6	4.7	22.7
Vietnam	0.7	1.8	11.9	0.3	1.0	3.2
Latin America						
Argentina	0.3	0.6	3.6	0.4	1.3	6.3
Brazil	0.8	1.4	11.4	1.2	2.3	18.3
Mexico	0.2	1.8	11.7	0.2	0.8	3.3
Other countries						
Egypt, Arab Rep.	0.4	0.8	4.4	0.03	0.08	0.2
South Africa	0.6	1.0	7.4	0.7	1.2	6.6

Source: China Statistical Yearbook 1996, 2002, 2008, National Bureau of Statistics, http://www.stats.gov.cn/english/statisticaldata/yearlydata/.

a. Asia* excludes Japan; Hong Kong SAR, China; Korea; Singapore; and Taiwan, China.

Figure 10.1. China's Exports and Imports with the South, 1994–2008

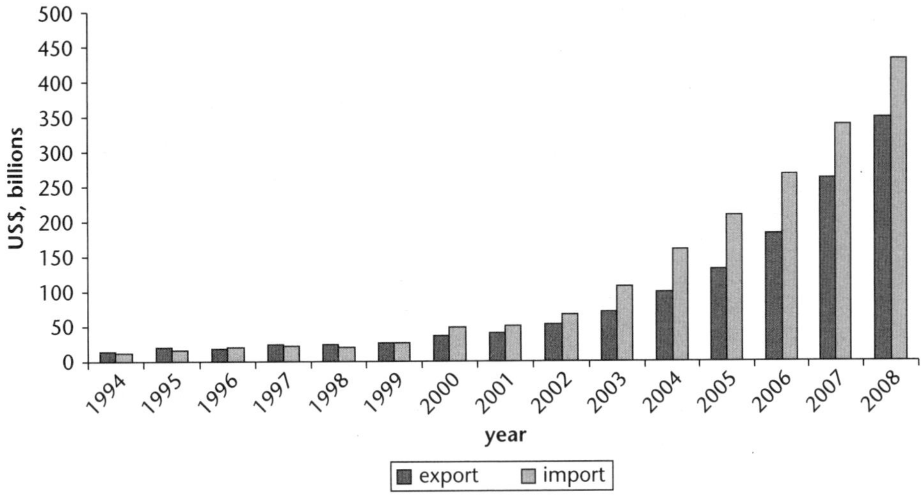

Source: Authors' calculations based on data from *China Statistical Yearbook*, 1996–2009, National Bureau of Statistics, http://www.stats.gov.cn/ english/statisticaldata/yearlydata/.

The growth of China's trade with Southern regions and major countries is remarkably high, with the highest, Indian-Chinese trade, running at 35 percent per year over the whole period and accelerating to 64 percent on the export side in 2007. The growth rates of China's Southern trade in all time periods are much higher than those of Northern trade, as would be expected in light of figure 10.1. On the export side, China's exports to India are the highest; growth rates of exports to Brazil are also high. On the import side, China's imports from Africa increased most during 1995 to 2007, but these growth rates have been slowing in recent years. The same is true for Asia* and for total trade with the South. Growth rates of imports from Latin America and South Africa, however, continue to increase.

China's entry into the WTO has also apparently had significant impacts on China's Southern trade. Kowalski and Shepherd (2006) observe that trade barriers affecting South-South trade are much higher than those affecting North-North or North-South trade, according to 1985–2002 data. Their econometric analysis suggests that South-South trade is more sensitive to tariff reductions, and their simulations also suggest that China would gain more than twice as much from liberalization of trade with Latin America, the Middle East and North Africa, and Sub-Saharan African countries as from liberalization with other Asian countries.

China's Southern trade performance after entry into the WTO supports this position. Table 10.2 reports changes in average growth rates for subperiods before and after 2001. Export growth rates after 2001 were at least 40 percent beyond those before 2001 (Indonesia) and increased by three times in the highest case (India). Import growth rates increased by at least 10 percent (Africa before 2001 had high growth of 39 percent) and at most 1.8 times (South Africa). For total Southern trade, growth rates of exports and imports both doubled after 2001. These differences in the growth rates of China's Southern and Northern trade are large, reflecting the more rapid growth trend of China's Southern trade after 2001.

We can also compare the growth rates of China's Southern trade to those of worldwide South-South trade. These data show China's share of South-South trade growing by a little over 3 percent to 9 percent on the export side and 12 percent on the import side by 2006. China's Southern trade growth was more rapid than world South-South trade growth, and this activity is reflected in China's share of world South-South trade, which increased consistently between 1995 and 2002. For 2007, the ratio is likely higher again, given the growth of China's trade.

Table 10.3 reports the shares of China's trade with Southern countries in major product groups in 2007. On the export side, China exported 22 percent of its total exports to the South. Among major product groups, 36.4 percent of China's exports of chemicals and 29.3 percent of its exports of transport equipment went to the South. Also, the South bought about 30 percent of textiles, clothing, and base metal and related products. The rapid growth of China's exports to the South, especially after its entry into the WTO, implies growing Southern demand for Chinese products.

Table 10.2. Average Annual Growth Rates in China's Trade with the South, Pre- and Post-2001
percent

	Export			Import		
Region or country	1995–2001	2002–07	Change[a]	1995–2001	2002–07	Change[a]
Africa	20.0	35.9	1.8	38.8	42.0	1.1
Asia*	15.6	37.0	2.4	25.3	36.8	1.5
Latin America	20.1	36.5	1.8	20.3	41.6	2.0
South (above)	16.8	36.6	2.2	25.2	37.8	1.5
North (rest of world)	11.7	27.3	2.3	9.6	21.2	2.2
South						
Brazil	25.9	44.1	1.7	15.8	42.9	2.7
India	19.7	53.7	2.7	30.1	46.0	1.5
Indonesia	20.7	28.5	1.4	15.2	21.5	1.4
South Africa	18.5	39.1	2.1	12.7	35.2	2.8

Source: Authors' calculations based on data from *China Statistical Yearbook 1996–2008,* National Bureau of Statistics, http://www.stats.gov.cn/english/statisticaldata/yearlydata/.
a. Change = growth rate after 2001/growth rate before 2001.

Table 10.3. China's Southern Trade Shares in Major Product Groups, 2007
percent

Exports to the South	Share	Imports from the South	Share
Nonmanufactured	24.5	Nonmanufactured	70.5
Manufactures	21.3	Manufactures	26.4
Chemicals	36.4	Oil	78.9
Textiles, yarn, and clothing	28.8	Minerals (excluding oil)	63.8
Base metals and related products	28.7	Jewelry, precious metals and products	36.9
Transport equipment	29.3	Electronics	32.5

Source: Authors' calculations based on Development Research Center of the State Council of China database, www.drcnet.com.cn.

On the import side, the South dominated China's imports of nonmanufactured products in 2007. And the South is an extremely important supplier of strategic materials for China, accounting for 78.9 percent of China's imports of oil and 63.8 percent of its imports of other minerals. These data reinforce the impression of increasing trade links between China and the South.

All these data thus seem to point in one direction: China's trade involvement with the South is growing rapidly and is accelerating. The fastest-growing patterns of this trade appear to be with other large and rapidly growing Southern economies: Brazil and India.

China's Future Trade with the South

Next we turn to some projections of China's future Southern trade based on the annual rates of trade growth that applied in 2005–07. These projections inevitably imply growing Southern trade for China, but the speed and potential implications for the trading system are striking. The simulation considers what could happen if China's Southern trade were to keep growing at these rates out to different dates. We also assume China's trade with the world grows at rates applying in 2005–07. For these projections, the sum of China's Southern and Northern trade in the year yields China's total trade, and we project trade levels with the South in the future.

According to these projections, China's trade with the South will grow rapidly. Although at present China's Southern trade is substantially less than half of its total trade, its more rapid growth implies that China's Southern export and import shares will keep rising relentlessly. Also, as China's exports grow more rapidly than imports, China's trade surplus will keep growing. If China's trade with India were to continue on the same track as during 2005–07, India would become China's largest market in about 10 years, and China's trade with the South would be about twice that with the North. Even though China's productivity growth, the absorptive capacities of Brazilian and Indian markets, and countries' economic growth in the medium and long term are uncertain, these projections indicate what could happen if China's Southern trade were to keep growing at 2005–07 rates.

Using the same assumptions, we can also project when China's Southern trade will dominate China's foreign trade. These projections are shown in figures 10.2 and 10.3. China's exports to the South will exceed 50 percent and 60 percent of its total exports by 2023 and 2030, respectively, and imports from the South will exceed 50 percent and 60 percent of China's total imports by 2013 and 2017,

Figure 10.2. Projections of China's Southern Export Share, 2008–30

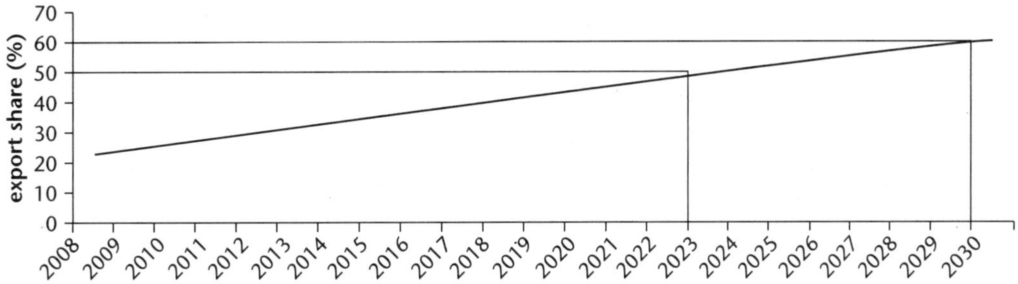

Source: Authors' calculations.

Figure 10.3. Projections of China's Southern Import Share, 2008–30

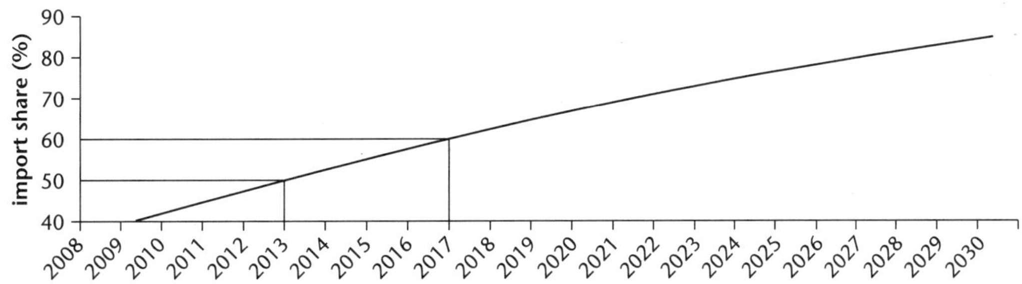

Source: Authors' calculations.

respectively. South-South trade will exceed 50 percent of China's total trade by 2020 and will exceed 60 percent by 2027. The South will be China's major trade partner surprisingly soon if these growth rates are maintained.

China's FDI Flows with the South

In addition to its trade relationships, China has also experienced growing interactions with Southern economies through FDI flows, especially through outflows from China. FDI inflows and outflows both began from very small bases in the 1990s, but on the outflow side they have experienced rapid growth over the past few years. As with trade, we can evaluate whether China's Southern investment (both inflows and outflows) grew more quickly than China's total foreign investment flows. In passing, we note that the South here is the South as above, and in the process we exclude the Cayman Islands and the British Virgin Islands as tax haven–based conduits. Both of them rank in the top five country destinations for Chinese outward FDI.

Before China's entry into the WTO, its outward investment was very small. Data on China's Southern investment activity is reported in tables 10.4 and 10.5. Table 10.4 reports the levels involved for various subregions, and table 10.5 gives the country breakdown for 2007. Total Chinese outward foreign investment over the whole period 1978–2001 was only US$8.4 billion, in contrast to annual flows today of over US$2 billion. Although statistics before 2003 are lacking, using the limited information available we can still calculate growth rates for China's foreign investment.

China's annual FDI inflows increased from an average of US$45 billion between 1997 and 2002 to US$74 billion in 2007, and the Southern share increased from 3.2 percent to 6.2 percent. Outflows grew from US$2.8 billion in 2003 to US$26 billion in 2007, and the Southern share doubled from 8 percent to 16.5 percent. Much more rapid growth therefore occurs for the Southern share than for the Northern share, and the change (from a small base) is larger than for trade. In addition, by region and country the geographical composition of FDI flows are more balanced than those for trade.

Table 10.6 reports the annual average growth rates of China's FDI flows by region and country. The contrast between Northern and Southern flows is striking. Inflows from the South grew substantially but declined in 2007,

Table 10.4. China's Average FDI Inflows and Outflows to the South and the World, 1997–2007

	Inflows from			Outflows to		
Time period	South (US$, millions)	World (US$, millions)	South share (%)	South (US$, millions)	World (US$, millions)	South share (%)
1997–2002 (average)	1,690.3	45,229.0	3.7	—	—	—
2003–06 (average)	3,064.5	59,369.9	5.2	760.9	9561.9	8.0
2007	4,669.1	74,767.9	6.2	4,366.4	26,506.1	16.5

Source: Authors' calculations. Inflow data based on China Statistical Yearbook 2008, National Bureau of Statistics, China, http://www.stats.gov.cn/english/statisticaldata/yearlydata/. Outflows data are from 2007 Statistical Bulletin of China's Outward Foreign Direct Investment, Ministry of Commerce of the People's Republic of China, http://hzs.mofcom.gov.cn/accessory/200909/1253868856016.pdf.
Note: The inflow data use China's foreign direct investment flows and are smaller than data from the UNCTAD database. The outflow data are nonfinancial outward FDI flows. — = not available.

Table 10.5. China's FDI Inflows from and Outflows to the South, 2003 and 2007
US$, millions

	Inflows			Outflows		
Region, country, or group	2003 (US$, millions)	2007 (US$, millions)	2007/2003	2003 (US$, millions)	2007 (US$, millions)	2007/2003
Africa	617.8	1,486.8	2.4	74.8	1,574.3	21.0
Asia*[a]	1,423.2	2,187.5	1.5	198.0	2,367.4	12.0
Latin America*[b]	263.6	994.8	3.8	21.9	424.7	19.4
Total	2,304.6	4,669.1	2.0	294.6	4,366.4	14.8
Southern regions, countries, or groups						
ASEAN*[c]	867.0	1,206.7	1.4	122.5	570.4	4.7
ASEAN	2,925.4	4,391.2	1.5	119.3	968.1	8.1
Brazil	16.7	31.6	1.9	6.7	51.1	7.7
India	15.9	34.0	2.1	0.2	22.0	146.8
South Africa	32.5	69.2	2.1	8.9	454.4	51.3

Source: Authors' calculations based on *China Statistical Yearbook 2008, 2007,* National Bureau of Statistics, http://www.stats.gov.cn/english/statisticaldata/yearlydata/; *Statistical Bulletin of China's Outward Foreign Direct Investment,* Ministry of Commerce of the People's Republic of China, http://hzs.mofcom.gov.cn/accessory/200909/1253868856016.pdf.
Note: ASEAN = Association of Southeast Asian Nations.
a. Asia* excludes Japan; Hong Kong SAR, China; Korea; Singapore; and Taiwan, China.
b. Latin America* denotes Latin America except the Cayman Islands and the British Virgin Islands.
c. ASEAN* denotes the ASEAN except Singapore (Brunei Darussalam, Cambodia, Indonesia, Lao People's Democratic Republic, Malaysia, Myanmar, the Philippines, Thailand, and Vietnam).

with sharp declines for Brazil, India, and South Africa. The growth rates on outflows from China are dramatically different, with a growth rate in 2007 of many hundreds of percent. According to the *World Investment Report 2008* (UNCTAD 2008), FDI inflows into developing countries increased 21 percent over 2006, which is almost the same as the growth rates of African and Latin American FDI into China but a slower growth rate for FDI of Asian developing countries into China. China's Southern FDI inflow increased only 16.7 percent. In 2007, FDI outflows from South, East, and Southeast Asia reached a new high, with growth of 46 percent.

Table 10.7 reports growth rates of China's Southern FDI and total FDI. Here, the striking feature on the inflow side is the persistently higher growth rate of Southern-origin FDI. On the outflow side, the relative North-South outflows are volatile: both grew, but in 2007 the outflow to the South was sharply higher, which produces a higher average growth rate over the period 2004–07. As with trade, the picture conveyed by FDI data is one of relatively accelerating integration with the South through FDI flows, especially on the outflow side.

Similar to the earlier trade projections, we can project China's FDI with regions and major countries assuming that growth rates between 2005 and 2007 remain unchanged into the future. Again, the sum of Southern and Northern projected FDI yields China's total FDI.

According to these calculations, China's FDI inflows and outflows will grow very quickly if growth rates between 2005 and 2007 are sustained. More striking growth would occur on the outflow side. China's outward investment boomed in recent years, and its growth rates between 2005

Table 10.6. Average Annual Growth of China's Southern and Northern FDI Flows, 1998–2007
percent

Region or country	Inflows 1998–2007	Inflows 2005–07	Inflows 2007	Outflows 2004–07	Outflows 2005–07	Outflows 2007
Africa	35.8	24.6	22.1	145.8	86.3	202.8
Asia*	6.5	7.1	11.4	115.9	140.3	343.9
Latin America*	32.4	64.7	21.4	165.5	115.1	333.7
South (above)	13.2	18.2	16.7	118.0	112.5	279.3
North (rest of the world)	5.5	7.6	19.7	75.9	120.1	157.7
Southern countries, regions, or groups						
ASEAN*	5.0	4.9	10.6	60.5	73.8	180.1
ASEAN	3.6	13.2	31.0	86.4	94.0	181.1
Brazil	202.4	21.0	−43.1	126.2	169.4	406.7
India	356.9	39.9	−35.0	866.2	1110.5	292.5
South Africa	100.4	−13.6	−27.1	368.2	457.3	1015.4

Source: Authors' calculations based on national sources. *China Statistical Yearbook 2008, 2007,* National Bureau of Statistics, http://www.stats.gov.cn/english/statisticaldata/yearlydata/; *Statistical Bulletin of China's Outward Foreign Direct Investment*, Ministry of Commerce of the People's Republic of China, http://hzs.mofcom.gov.cn/accessory/200909/1253868856016.pdf.
Note: ASEAN = Association of Southeast Asian Nations.
a. Asia* excludes Japan; Hong Kong SAR, China; Korea; Singapore; and Taiwan, China.
b. Latin America* denotes Latin America except the Cayman Islands and the British Virgin Islands.
c. ASEAN* denotes the ASEAN except Singapore (Brunei Darussalam, Cambodia, Indonesia, Lao People's Democratic Republic, Malaysia, Myanmar, the Philippines, Thailand, and Vietnam).

Table 10.7. Growth of China's Southern FDI and Total FDI, 1998–2007
percent

Year	Inflow from South	Inflow from World	Inflow Difference	Outflow to South	Outflow to World	Outflow Difference
1998	13.5	0.5	13.0	—	—	—
1999	−19.3	−11.3	−8.0	—	—	—
2000	15.7	1.0	14.8	—	—	—
2001	15.8	15.1	0.7	—	—	—
2002	28.1	12.5	15.6	—	—	—
2003	−0.1	1.4	−1.6	—	—	—
2004	23.4	13.3	10.0	134.4	92.6	41.8
2005	9.4	−0.5	9.9	31.4	123.0	−91.7
2006	28.6	4.5	24.1	26.9	43.8	−16.9
2007	16.7	18.6	−1.9	279.3	50.3	229.0
Average	13.2	5.5	7.7	118.0	77.4	40.6

Source: Authors' calculations based on national sources: *China Statistical Yearbook 2008, 2007,* National Bureau of Statistics, http://www.stats.gov.cn/english/statisticaldata/yearlydata/; *Statistical Bulletin of China's Outward Foreign Direct Investment*, Ministry of Commerce of the People's Republic of China, http://hzs.mofcom.gov.cn/accessory/200909/ 1253868856016.pdf.
Note: — = not available.

and 2007 were very large. China's investments in India, for instance, increased by 11 times in these years. These projections thus paint a dramatic picture, but China would remain a large source of FDI even if these growth rates were only half as high.

Since developed-country markets are the main destination for China's outward investments and have had higher growth rates in recent years than the South, these projections suggest that the Southern share of China's total outward investments will decline in the future. The picture on the inflow side, however, is the opposite. China's FDI inflows from the South grew more rapidly in recent years than those from the North, with the result that China's FDI inflows from the South will exceed 50 percent and 60 percent of China's total FDI inflow by 2022 and 2024, respectively. These projections are displayed in figure 10.4.

Figure 10.4. Projections of Southern FDI Inflow Share for China, 2008–30

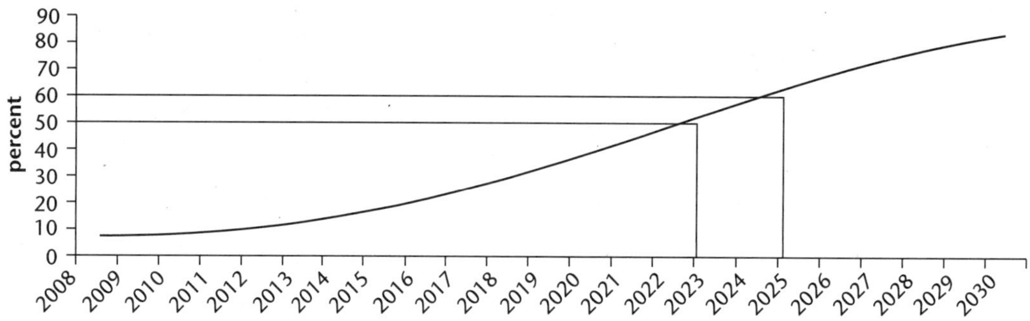

Source: Authors' calculations.

Table 10.8. China's Southern Trade Pre– and Post–financial Crisis, 2008 and 2009
US$, billions

	Exports							Imports						
	2008				2009			2008				2009		
Region or country	**Q1**	**Q2**	**Q3**	**Q4**	**Q1**	**Q2**	**Q3**	**Q1**	**Q2**	**Q3**	**Q4**	**Q1**	**Q2**	**Q3**
Region														
Africa	10.1	12.9	14.6	13.2	10.1	11.7	12.8	13.9	16.2	15.6	10.2	5.7	9.5	13.3
Asia*	46.4	57.4	64.7	55.8	39.5	47.8	54.3	71.3	79.6	88.5	64.3	46.8	60.3	71.7
Latin America	13.9	18.1	22.5	17.0	10.5	12.6	16.2	14.6	19.3	22.8	14.8	9.4	16.5	20.6
South	70	89	102	86	60	72	83	100	115	127	89	62	86	106
Country														
India	6.9	8.7	8.8	7.1	6.0	7.0	*8.1*	6.3	7.1	4.3	2.7	3.3	3.3	3.2
Indonesia	3.6	4.4	5.2	4.0	2.6	3.5	*3.9*	3.7	4.1	3.9	2.6	2.3	3.3	3.7
Malaysia	4.7	5.3	5.8	5.5	3.6	4.7	*5.3*	7.4	8.5	9.5	6.7	5.5	7.0	9.2
Thailand	3.5	4.2	4.4	3.4	2.6	3.0	*3.7*	6.2	6.4	7.0	5.9	4.4	6.0	7.0
Vietnam	4.1	4.4	3.3	3.3	2.8	3.6	4.5	1.1	1.0	1.3	1.0	0.9	1.2	1.2
Argentina	1.1	1.5	1.6	0.9	0.6	0.8	1.1	1.7	1.8	3.4	2.5	0.9	1.2	1.3
Brazil	3.6	4.8	6.4	3.9	2.3	2.7	4.3	4.9	8.1	10.5	6.1	3.4	8.1	9.7
Mexico	2.8	3.6	4.0	3.4	2.3	2.8	3.4	0.9	1.0	1.0	0.8	0.8	0.9	1.0
Egypt, Arab Rep.	1.3	1.5	1.7	1.4	1.1	1.3	1.3	0.1	0.2	0.1	0.1	0.0	0.1	0.3
South Africa	1.9	2.2	2.4	2.1	1.6	1.6	2.0	2.0	2.6	2.4	2.2	1.5	2.2	2.5

Source: Authors' calculations based on monthly data of *China Customs Statistics,* China Customs Information Center, http://www.haiguan.info.

The Financial Crisis and China's Southern Trade

China's export-oriented economy has been severely affected by the financial crisis, and so we report only preliminary data for 2008 and 2009 on Southern trade and shares (table 10.8). For trade data, the absolute values of China's Southern trade are considerably higher in 2008 than 2007 but decline substantially in the spring of 2009 and increase again in the summer of 2009. Trading levels in the second and third quarters of 2009 are still far less than the levels in 2008. On both the export and the import side, China's trade with major Southern countries and regions presents the same trend between the first quarter of 2008 and the third quarter of 2009. Trading volumes increased steadily before the third quarter of 2008; then they decreased for two quarters with a trough in the first quarter of 2009, rebounding slowly from the second quarter of 2009.

Table 10.9 reports the commodity composition of China's total imports between 2008 and 2009 (bilateral data by commodity are unavailable). These largely remain as they were precrisis, with declines in mineral fuels and growth in industrial products. These data suggest that China's trade structure has not changed during the crisis

Table 10.9. Commodity Composition of China's Imports in the Financial Crisis, 2008 and 2009
percent

	2008						2009				
Item	Jan.	Mar.	May	Jul.	Sept.	Nov.	Jan.	Mar.	May	Jul.	Sept.
Primary products	30.7	31.9	34.0	33.5	32.4	29.1	27.0	27.0	28.6	30.4	28.5
Food and live animals	1.3	1.2	1.3	1.1	1.2	1.2	1.7	1.7	1.6	1.5	1.4
Beverages and tobacco category	0.2	0.1	0.2	0.1	0.1	0.4	0.2	0.1	0.2	0.1	0.2
Non-food raw materials (excluding fuel)	15.3	14.3	15.0	14.8	15.4	14.8	14.2	14.5	14.2	14.2	14.1
Oil	12.9	14.9	16.3	16.2	14.3	11.1	9.9	9.1	10.9	12.5	10.8
Mineral fuels, lubricants and related materials	13.2	15.2	16.6	16.5	14.8	11.5	10.4	9.9	11.9	13.8	11.9
Animal and vegetable oils, grease, wax	0.7	1.0	1.0	1.0	0.8	1.2	0.4	0.8	0.8	0.9	0.9
Industrial products	69.3	68.1	66.0	66.5	67.6	70.9	73.0	73.0	71.4	69.6	71.5
Chemical products and related products	11.1	10.7	10.4	11.4	10.3	9.7	11.4	11.7	11.5	11.1	11.0
Manufactured goods classified by raw materials	9.9	9.8	9.6	9.3	8.9	9.7	9.9	10.9	12.1	11.1	10.6
Steel	2.4	2.5	2.2	2.3	2.4	2.6	3.0	3.1	3.0	2.6	2.6
Base Metals and Related Products	6.6	6.6	6.2	6.0	5.9	6.1	6.7	7.5	8.5	7.7	7.5
Machinery and transport equipment	38.7	38.4	36.8	37.3	39.8	42.2	43.1	41.7	39.3	38.7	40.9
Miscellaneous manufactured articles	9.3	8.9	8.8	8.2	8.2	8.6	8.1	8.4	8.2	8.3	8.7
Unclassified goods	0.2	0.3	0.4	0.2	0.4	0.7	0.5	0.3	0.3	0.3	0.3

Source: Authors' calculations based on China Customs Statistics, China Customs Information Center, http://www.haiguan.info.

but that China's manufacturing industries may have declined because of the financial crisis.

As table 10.3 shows in part, the South is the major source of China's oil and mineral imports, with the oil share increasing from 54 percent to 79 percent during 2004 and 2007 and the mineral shares constant around 60 percent between 1999 and 2007. Also China's import shares of other product groups from the South have increased in recent years. Table 10.9 shows that China's import share of oil deceased significantly after November 2008 and that it began to rebound slowly after May 2009, while the level of September 2009 is still lower than that of 2008. The level of September 2009 imports partly reflects the fall in oil prices and partly the compression of China's domestic industries, findings supported by data on industrial consumption of power.

Figure 10.5 reports growth rates of China's Southern trade postcrisis, which plays a more important role during this time. It grew by more than 30 percent in 2008; in contrast, the rate of China's Northern trade growth was only 13 percent. (China's total trade grew 18 percent in 2008.) Compared with the same period in 2008, China's trade with almost every market contracted during the spring and summer of 2009. The exceptions are exports to Africa, which increased by 0.7 percent in the first quarter of 2009, and imports from Vietnam, which increased by 22 percent in the second quarter of 2009. On the export side, China's Southern trade fell less than Northern trade during the first half of 2009, but Latin American trade fell the most. On the import side, China's Northern trade performed better than Southern trade. Imports from India were only half those of the spring and summer of 2008.

Figures 10.6 and 10.7 suggest that China's imports from the South in summer 2009 increased over the same period for the previous year at a slower rate. They grew more rapidly compared to spring 2009, raising the share of Southern trade in the summer of 2009. China's exports to and imports from the South in the second quarter of 2009 were 26 percent and 36 percent of total trade, respectively, increasing by 1.6 points and 3 points, respectively, compared to shares in the first quarter of 2009. This share of exports is higher than that of 2008, but the share of imports is still lower by 2.3 percentage points than that of 2008. These numbers suggest that China's Southern trade has played a more prominent role in its trade recovery on the export side. The relative fall on the import side reflects lower oil prices and large oil imports from Africa.

China's Trade Performance and That of Other Asian Countries during the Financial Crisis

We next draw a comparison between the trade performance of other Asian countries and China during the financial crisis. Monthly growth rates of major Asian economies' total exports and imports (compared with the same month of the previous year) are reported in figures 10.8 and 10.9. Asian trade fell rapidly amid the global financial crisis.

Figure 10.5. Growth Rates of China's Southern Trade Pre– and Post–financial Crisis Compared to Same Period of Previous Year

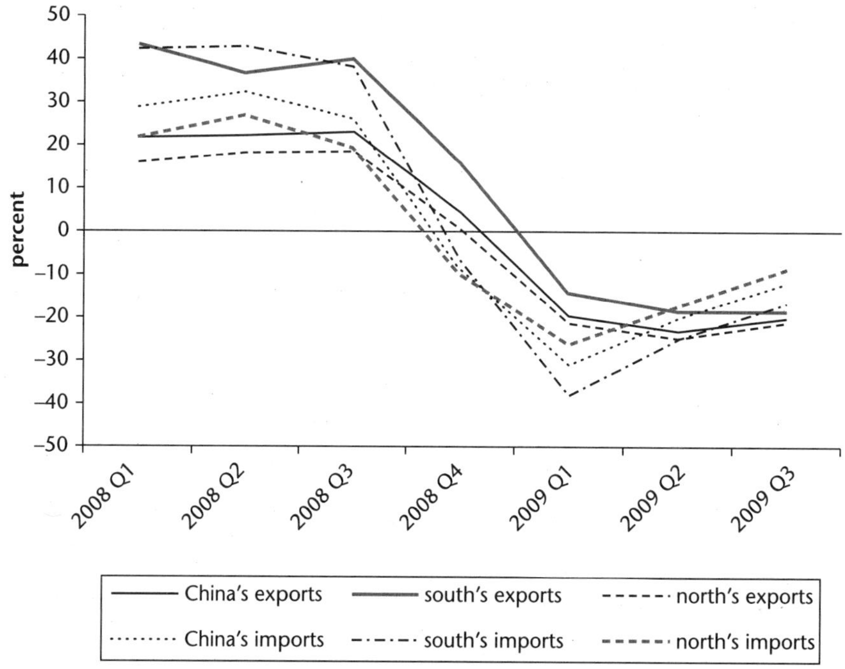

Source: Authors' calculations based on data from China Customs Statistics, China Customs Information Center, http://www.haiguan.info.

Figure 10.6. China's Regional Export Shares Pre– and Post–financial Crisis, 2007–09

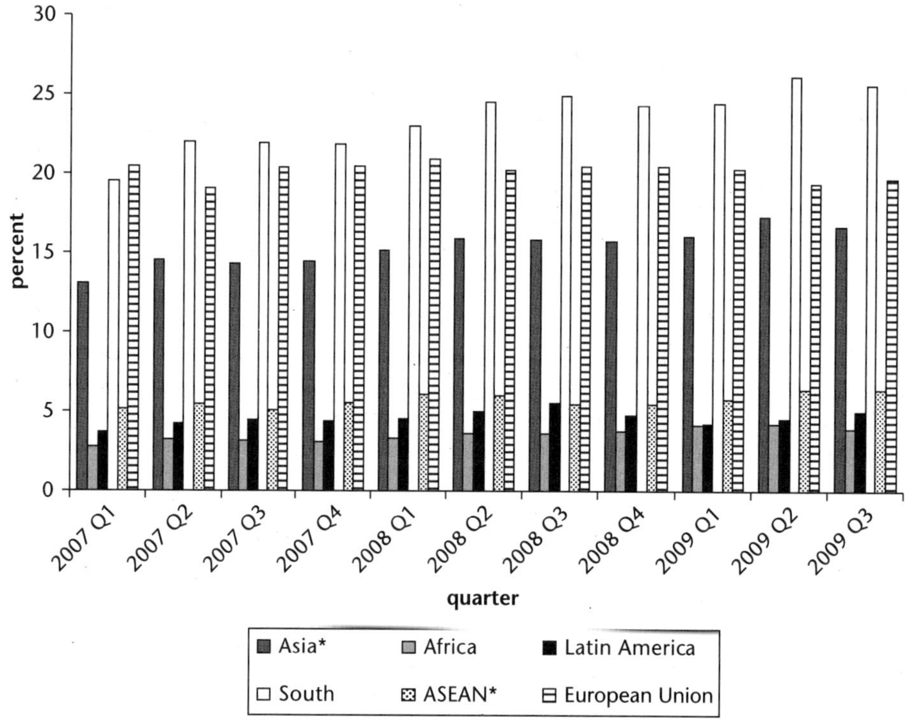

Source: Authors' calculations based on the data from China Customs Statistics, China Customs Information Center, http://www.haiguan.info.
Note: ASEAN = Association of Southeast Asian Nations; ASEAN* = ASEAN excluding Singapore.

Figure 10.7. China's Regional Import Shares Pre– and Post–financial Crisis, 2007–09

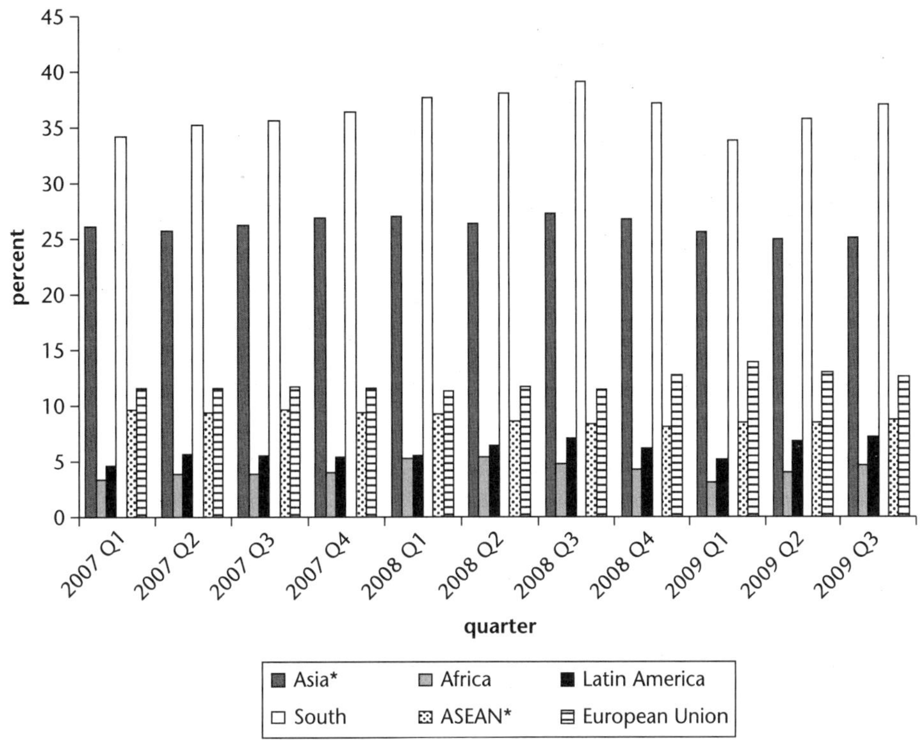

Source: Authors' calculations based on the data from China Customs Statistics, China Customs Information Center, http://www.haiguan.info.
Note: ASEAN = Association of Southeast Asian Nations; ASEAN* = ASEAN excluding Singapore.

Figure 10.8. Export Growth Rates of Key Asian Economies during the Financial Crisis Compared with Same Month of Previous Year, 2008–10

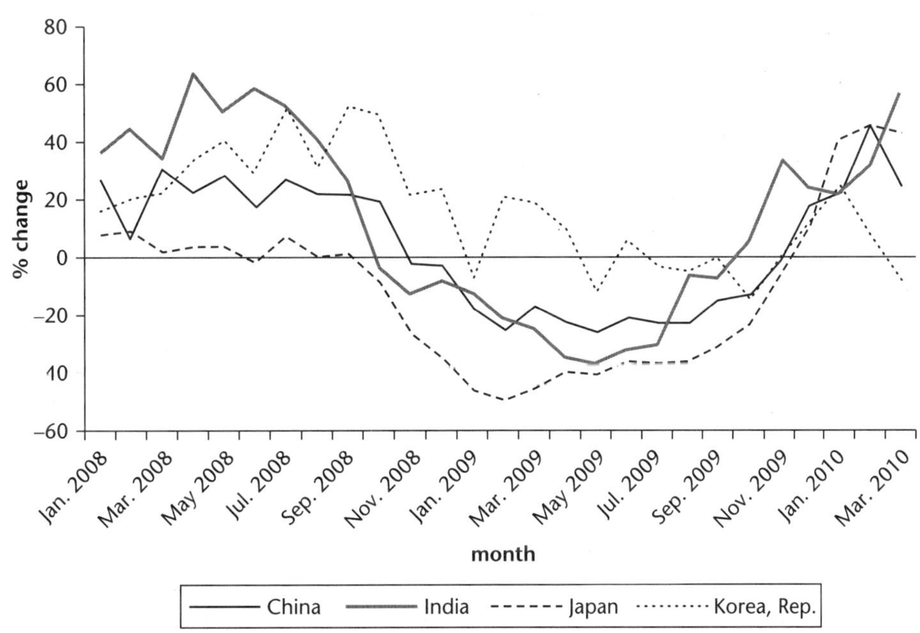

Source: Authors' calculations based on national sources: China Customs Statistics, China Customs Information Center, http://www.haiguan.info; Indian DGCIS (Kolkata) Database, Ministry of Commerce and Industry of India, http://www.dgciskol.nic.in/; Trade Statistics of Japan, Ministry of Finance of Japan, http://www.customs.go.jp/toukei/info/tsdl_e.htm; Korean Customs Statistics, Korea Customs Service, http://english.customs.go.kr.

Figure 10.9. Import Growth Rates of Key Asian Economies during the Financial Crisis Compared with Same Month of Previous Year, 2008–10

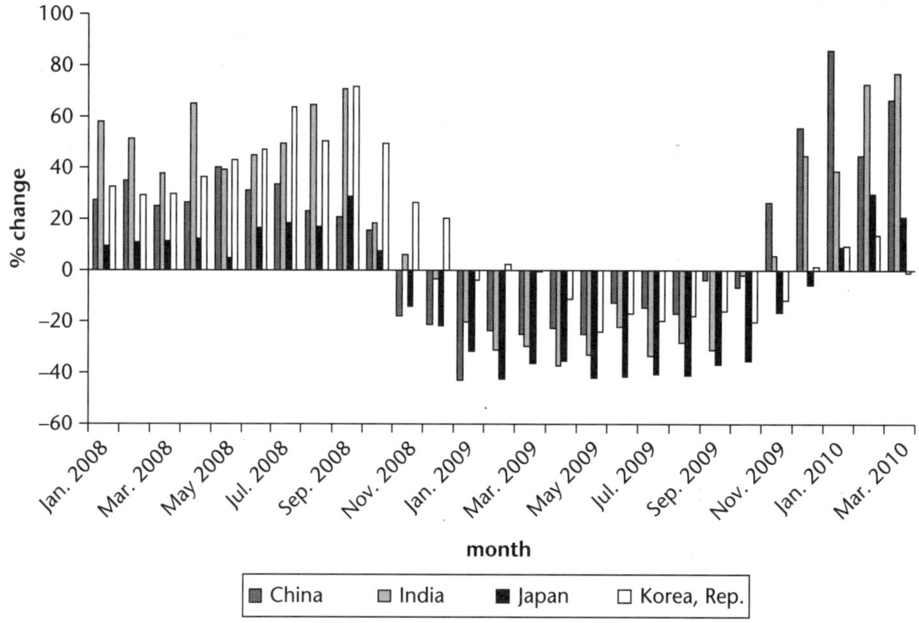

Source: Authors' calculations based on national sources: China Customs Statistics, China Customs Information Center, http://www.haiguan.info; Indian DGCIS (Kolkata) Database, Ministry of Commerce and Industry of India, http://www.dgciskol.nic.in/; Trade Statistics of Japan, Ministry of Finance of Japan, http://www.customs.go.jp/toukei/info/tsdl_e.htm; Korean Customs Statistics, Korea Customs Service, http://english.customs.go.kr.

Among these countries, Korea has performed much better than the others, with strong positive growth in the whole of 2008 on both the export and the import sides, and has experienced a smaller decline than the others in 2009. On the export side, the worst performer was Japan. With sluggish growth precrisis, Japan's exports shrank over 30 percent for 10 months, and they were almost half those of the previous year in the first quarter of 2009. On the import side, in addition to the strong performance by Korea, data on the other countries' imports seemed to follow a pattern that the faster the growth rate had been precrisis, the larger the decline was during the crisis. The trade of all countries started to rebound at the end of 2009, with a solid rebound in 2010.

Next we compare the situation of Asian countries' imports during the crisis. Demand for these materials reflected the situation of the real economies. For imports of oil, these countries' demand grew rapidly before October 2008 and then fell sharply (except for Korea). Because the fluctuations in global oil prices influenced every country equally, the less significant decline in Korean demand for oil indicates that the crisis had a weaker impact on the Korean economy. For other minerals, India experienced the most rapid growth precrisis and the sharpest decline during the crisis. For base metals and related products, Korean imports grew the most rapidly in 2008 and fell sharply in 2009, while Japan's grew the most slowly precrisis and dropped most postcrisis. China's demand for base metals dropped considerably during the crisis and started to rebound in May 2009, following China's stimulus package, almost two quarters ahead of the rebounds in other countries' imports of base metals.

Next we compare two major partners and assess their trade performance with individual Asian countries. One is the United States, the largest developed country and the source of the global financial crisis, and the other is China, the largest developing country and neighbor of these Asian countries. Growth rates of trade between the United States and Asian countries are reported in figures 10.10 and 10.11. Japan's exports to the United States started to decline in February 2008 and fell the most in the first quarter of 2009, with less than half the exports of the same period in 2008. Asian countries' exports to the United States all fell sharply from January 2009 to August 2009, with a monthly decline of 23.9 percent for China, 58.4 percent for Japan, 28.2 percent for Korea, and over 30 percent for other countries. Thailand's and China's exports to the United States rebounded at the end of 2009 and followed other countries with a significant rebound in 2010.

Figure 10.10. Growth Rates of Asian Economies' Exports to the United States during the Financial Crisis, 2008–10

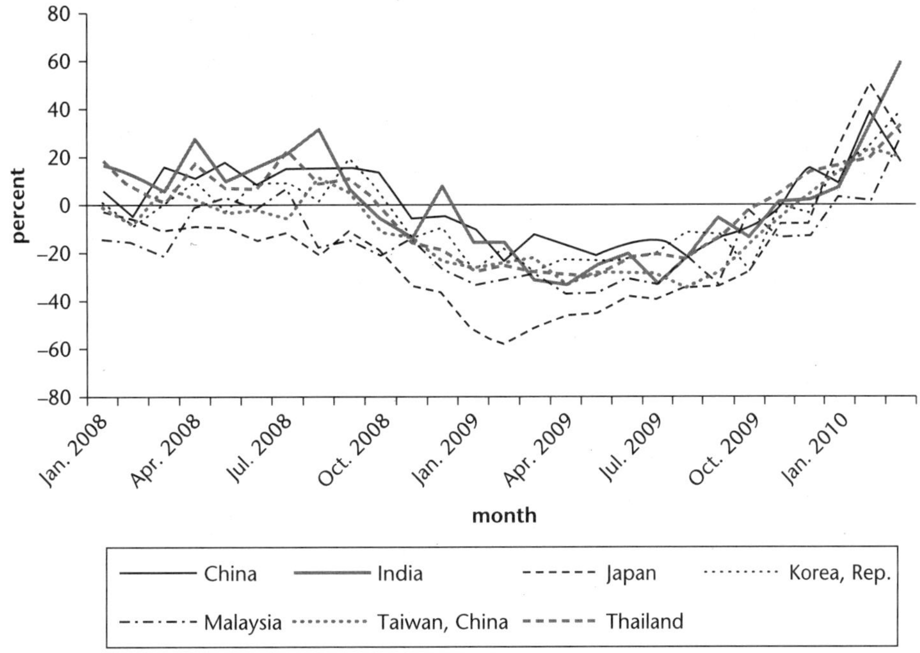

Source: Authors' calculations.

Figure 10.11. Growth Rates of Asian Economies' Imports from the United States during the Financial Crisis, 2008–10

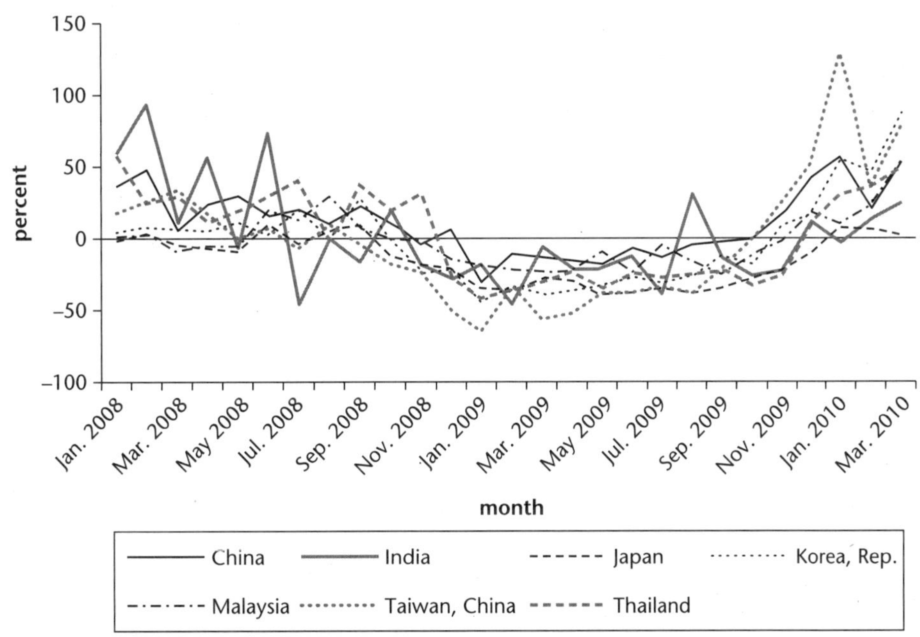

Source: Authors' calculations.

On the import side, the demand of India; Korea; Taiwan, China; and Thailand for U.S. products declined more than their exports to the United States, with monthly declines of 46.3 percent, 44.4 percent, 65.2 percent, and 41.7 percent, respectively. China's exports to and imports from the United States are similar in trend, but imports show a stronger rebound than exports in 2010, which contributed to China's trade deficit in March 2010. Similar to exports, the most severe decline in imports also occurred in first quarter of 2009.

The growth rates of other Asian countries' trade with China are reported in figures 10.12 and 10.13. Exports by India; Korea; Taiwan, China; and Thailand fell sharply from the last quarter of 2008 and declined more than exports to the United States in percentage terms. Japan's exports to China declined less than those to the United States during the crisis, and this result is slightly better than Japan's total export performance. All countries' exports to China rebounded strongly from the end of 2009. These countries' imports from China fell sharply from the first quarter of 2009, lagging a couple of months behind exports to China, and started to rebound from the end of 2009, almost at the same time as exports. The rebound speed of imports is significantly lower than that of exports, which suggests that China's large market for foreign goods is contributing to the recovery of its neighbors' trade.

Institutional Dimensions of China's Growing Southern Links

China's growing trade and investment links are matched by growing institutional connections with the South, based on the recognition by China and other developing countries of common interests. As a result, China is likely to emphasize cooperation with other developing countries as the starting point for its Southern diplomacy. As Wen Jiabao indicated in 2004, China has good political relationships with other developing countries, and economic cooperation should mutually empower them. China thus seeks to combine trade, investment, and foreign aid to deepen multilateral and regional cooperation with developing countries and safeguard the interests of developing countries in international trade organizations and multilateral mechanisms.

China's diplomatic initiatives toward the South thus reflect the growing economic interest in those countries. After its entry into the WTO, China focused on two major directions in foreign trade policy. One was to support the WTO system, and the other was to try to play a more important role in negotiations. China first tried to strengthen cooperation, especially with developing countries, and emphasize links to least-developed countries and small economies. Another approach was to deepen bilateral and

Figure 10.12. Growth Rates of Asian Economies' Exports to China in the Financial Crisis, 2008–10

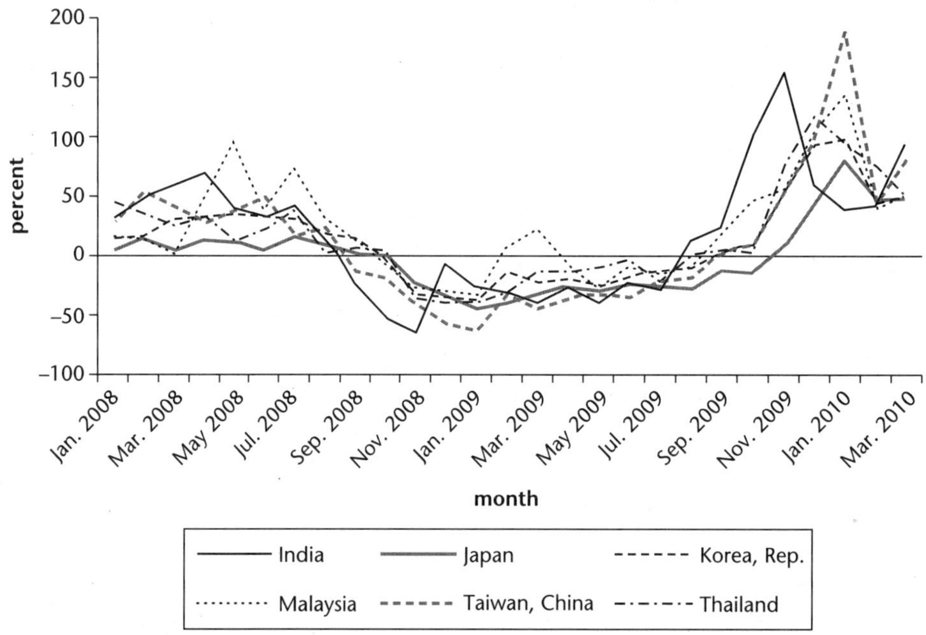

Source: Authors' calculations.

Figure 10.13. Growth Rates of Asian Economies' Imports from China in the Financial Crisis, 2008–10

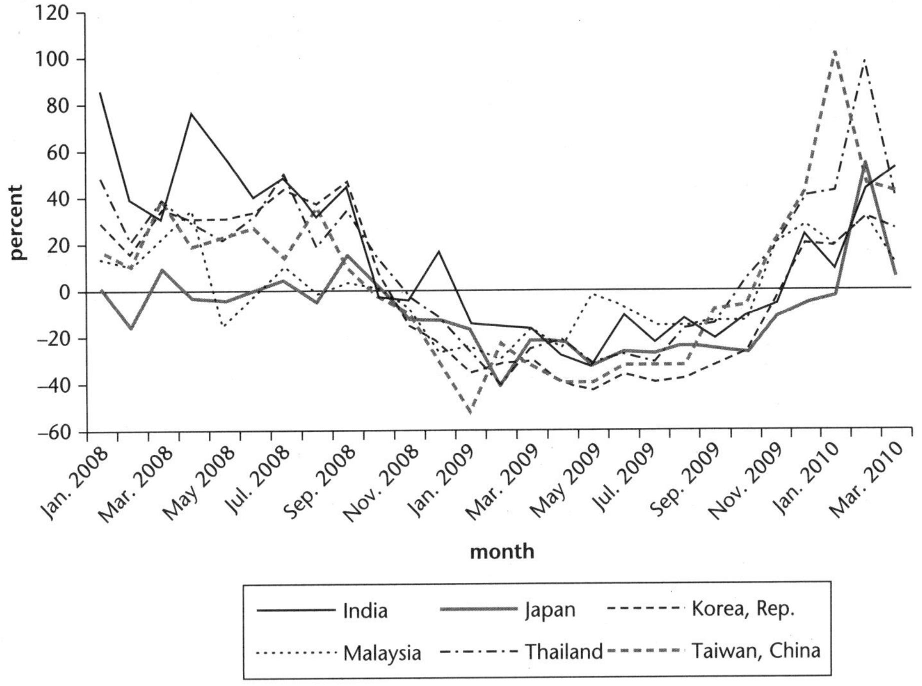

Source: Authors' calculations.

regional trade cooperation, and especially building free-trade agreements (FTAs). This effort began with adjacent countries and then extended to a wider area, especially emerging economies in Africa and Latin America. At the same time, China sought closer cooperation with energy and strategic material suppliers, especially Arab countries.

China's regional free-trade arrangements with developing countries began when it joined the Bangkok Agreement in 2001. The Bangkok Agreement settled the origin of products eligible for preferential concessions among members. China then concluded a framework agreement on comprehensive economic cooperation with the Association of Southeast Asian Nations (ASEAN) in 2002, a starting point for China's FTAs. China and ASEAN then agreed on tariff concessions from 2005 and will now build a China and ASEAN Free Trade Area (CAFTA) by 2015.

With FTAs in place with ASEAN and Pakistan, China already has closer trade relationships with most major developing countries in Asia except India, although here there is the prospect of an agreement. In April 2005, during Wen Jiabao's visit to India, the two governments announced a joint feasibility study on a China-India regional trade arrangement. The study was completed in October 2007 and reached consensus on trade in goods, trade in services, investment, trade facilitation, and economic cooperation. Formal negotiations on a China-India FTA are still not underway, and the progress of bilateral FTA negotiations between China and India is slower than that between India and Japan and Korea.

China has also reached agreements with Africa. Based on good political relations since 1949, and the simultaneous liberalization of China and Africa since the 1970s, economic cooperation between China and Africa is growing rapidly (Zhang Qingmin 2007). Evidence of these closer ties is the Forum on China-Africa Cooperation jointly set up by China and Africa in October 2000. China made major commitments including debt relief of 10 billion yuan for African countries. China also gave some of Africa's least-developed countries tariff-free treatment for 190 tariff headings of goods. This tariff preference was later extended to nearly 500 tariff headings. Negotiations on an FTA between China and the Southern Africa Customs Union (SACU), including Botswana, Lesotho, Namibia, South Africa, and Swaziland, started in 2004; and South Africa recognized China's market economy status at the same time. Both sides are now pushing the negotiations forward to a substantive stage.

China's relationship with Latin America has also developed rapidly following the improved openness of developing countries in Latin America from the end of the

1980s. A China-Chile FTA was signed in 2005 and covers trade issues such as market access, rules of origin, sanitary and phytosanitary measures, technical trade barriers, trade remedies, and dispute settlement mechanisms. A China-Chile investment agreement is now under negotiation. In addition, a China–Costa Rica FTA is now under negotiation. A feasibility study was completed in 2008, and three negotiations have been carried out thus far, with some progress on trade in goods and services.

A China-Peru FTA was signed in 2009. On trade in goods, over 90 percent of Chinese and Peruvian goods will receive zero tariff treatment in stages. On services, both countries will open further their service markets to each other, based on WTO commitments. On the investment side, both countries will grant investors national treatment and most-favored nation treatment. China and Peru also reached consensus in other fields such as intellectual property rights, trade remedies, rules of origin, customs procedures, technical barriers to trade, and sanitary and phytosanitary measures.

The China-Peru FTA has become a symbol for new bilateral relations between China and other developing countries in Latin America. For instance, Brazil is a founding member of the Rio Group, a member of MERCOSUR (Southern Cone Common Market), a leading member of the Group of 77 and the Group of 15, and an observer of the Non-Aligned Movement and is rich in minerals and oil. Chinese and Brazilian governments have proposed in-depth consultations on issues of common interest such as an FTA.[1] Economic cooperation between China and Brazil has become closer in recent years, and China became Brazil's largest trading partner in 2009. President Luiz Inácio Lula da Silva sought to strengthen cooperation between these two countries and to play a greater role in dealing with the global financial crisis when he visited China in April 2009. During this visit, Brazil and China signed cooperation protocols involving fields such as agriculture, science and technology, space, energy, ports cooperation, mining, and renewable energy. With these, a "loans-for-oil" deal over 10 years involving US$10 billion between the China Development Bank and the Brazilian national oil company (Petrobras) was signed. In addition, the two governments plan a Joint Action Plan 2010–14.

The picture therefore shows rapidly deepening institutional involvement of China with the South, complementing and supporting growing Southern trade and investment links. These ties may well be poised to accelerate further in the next decade.

Concluding Remarks

This chapter assesses China's growing interactions through trade and FDI with the South and also provides an initial assessment of the impact of the financial crisis on China's trade. Based on Chinese source data, the picture that emerges shows rapidly growing trade and FDI links, which in recent years (precrisis) have been accelerating. At 2005–07 growth rates, we project that China's Southern trade will be around 50 percent of its total by 2015 and that trade with India will account for around 50 percent of China's trade by 2023 (such trade increased by 33 percent between 1997 and 2007). Initial data show this rapid relative growth in Southern engagement, if anything, has been accelerated further by the financial crisis, especially on the export side.

China is rapidly become the manufacturing center of the global economy, and with more rapid growth in Brazil, India, Indonesia, and other Southern countries than in the OECD, the prospect is for even more significant Southern investment by China. In FDI flows, this trend is seemingly accelerating even more rapidly, if from a lower base. The South may be poised to become the epicenter of trade in the global economy by 2030, with China at its hub.

Note

1. Ministry of Foreign Affairs, People's Republic of China. "China and Brazil Signed Joint Communique." http://www.chineseembassy.org/chn/gxh/zlb/smgg/t118446.htm.

Bibliography

Kowalski, P., and B. Shepherd. 2006. "South-South Trade in Goods." Trade Policy Working Paper 40, Organisation for Economic Co-operation and Development, Paris.

UNCTAD (United Nations Conference on Trade and Development). 2007. *World Investment Report 2007: Transnational Corporations, Extractive Industries and Development.* Geneva: United Nations Conference on Trade and Development. http://www.unctad.org/en/docs/wir2007_en.pdf.

———. 2008. *World Investment Report 2008: Transnational Corporations, and the Infrastructure Challenge.* Geneva: United Nations Conference on Trade and Development. http://www.unctad.org/en/docs/wir2008_en.pdf.

Zhang, Q. 2007. "China's Foreign Relations." *Foreign Affair Review* 94: 22–28.

11

VOLATILITY, EXPORT DIVERSIFICATION, AND POLICY

Mona Haddad, Jamus Lim, Laura Munro, Christian Saborowski, and Ben Shepherd

Although the global economic crisis erupted in the financial markets of the industrial world, developing countries have not escaped its effects. Many, including those without close financial ties to the developed world, were driven into recession, as global demand plummeted. The recent crisis has resulted in the largest drop in global trade volumes since the Second World War. Naturally, open economies heavily reliant on export revenues were among those hardest hit by the crisis. This observation has led to renewed questioning of the merits of export-led growth strategies for developing countries (Harrison and Rodriguez-Clare 2009; Rodrik 2009).

While the relationship between openness and growth has been investigated thoroughly, the link between openness and growth volatility is less well understood. Various studies have argued that trade openness increases macroeconomic volatility (Rodrik 1997); yet there is no clear consensus in the literature to date. Di Giovanni and Levchenko (2009) find that trade openness leads countries to become more specialized in their exports. This finding implies that a higher degree of openness not only exposes countries to a larger number of external shocks but that greater openness also makes them more vulnerable.[1] At a more aggregate level, Easterly and Kraay (2000) find that terms-of-trade volatility is an important driver of growth volatility, especially for smaller states. Yet, they argue that the high income volatility typically experienced by small economies is due mainly to their openness and that export concentration plays only a minor role.[2]

Raddatz (2007) shows that external shocks—such as those transmitted by prices, foreign growth, and real interest rates—have a substantial and significant impact on the volatility of real activity in low-income economies. External shocks are indisputably crucial in accounting for external sources of variation. However, they can explain only a small fraction of the long-run variation in real per capita gross domestic product (GDP) (Ahmed 2003; Becker and Mauro 2006). The underlying institutional and policy environment cannot be ignored (Easterly, Islam, and Stiglitz 2001).

In studying the mechanisms by which the trade channel affects growth volatility, this chapter considers three questions that have been neglected thus far. First, does the effect of trade openness on growth volatility vary with the degree of diversification of a country's export basket? Second, if a conditional relationship exists, is there a threshold—in a given measure of export concentration—above which the total effect of trade openness on growth volatility changes from negative to positive?[3] Third, what policies are available to governments to promote export diversification efficiently?

This chapter is based on the empirical work reported in technical detail in our working papers (Haddad, Lim, and Saborowski 2010; Shepherd 2010; and Dennis and Shepherd, 2011). We show that the effect of openness on volatility indeed depends on the degree to which a country's export basket is diversified. We then go on to demonstrate that policies such as trade facilitation—reducing the fixed and variable costs facing exporters and importers—can be effective in promoting diversification.

The rest of this chapter is organized as follows. The next section discusses the relationship among trade openness, growth volatility, and export diversification. The following section shows how most countries' export baskets meet the threshold of diversification and indeed benefit from trade openness. We then discuss the policies available to governments to promote export diversification and help manage openness, focusing on trade facilitation. The final section concludes with policy implications flowing from our findings.

The Effect of Increased Trade Openness on Vulnerability to Global Shocks

Due to the large number of variables included in the dataset, we limit our discussion here to the key dependent and independent variables. Full technical details are available in the working paper version of this chapter.[4] Our main dependent variable is volatility of output growth, measured as the standard deviation of GDP per capita across each five-year period.

The two main independent variables of interest are export diversification and trade openness. We include a variety of export diversification measures that capture the dimensions of product and geographical market concentration for any given country. These are fairly standard and include the top 5 and top 10 shares of products and markets as well as Herfindahl-Hirschman Indexes for products and markets. We supplement these direct diversification measures with summary ones that we construct using principal-components analysis. We extract the first principal component of the three product and three market diversification measures.[5]

Consistent with much of the literature, we compute trade openness as the ratio of the sum of exports and imports to GDP, while financial openness is measured with an index of restrictions on cross-border transactions taken from Chinn and Ito (2008).[6] Both these indicators provide measures of the actual exposure of a country to international markets. They reflect structural as well as policy-related characteristics of a country.

The Effect of Openness and Diversification on Volatility

One of the chief arguments against export-led growth strategies for developing countries is that economically open countries are more prone to external shocks. But are they necessarily more strongly affected by external shocks by way of higher volatility? The total effect of openness on volatility could in fact be positive, due to the enhanced possibility of international risk sharing through explicit and implicit insurance schemes. Examples include joint ventures, international lending, production diversification, and formal insurance contracts. Moreover, the disciplinary effect of international competition and the prevalence of formal international contracts could potentially limit the risk of domestic policy mistakes.

It is therefore unclear, ex ante, whether the effect of openness on growth volatility should be positive or negative. We find that the degree of diversification matters in the determination of this sign. The evidence suggests that the vulnerability of countries to some types of external shocks is reduced when these countries are better diversified in their exports.

Our empirical analysis also suggests that while trade openness, at least initially, may induce production specialization and concentration through comparative advantage, financial openness may result in *production* diversification, which reduces growth volatility. This argument is similar in spirit to the central message of our chapter, namely, that *export* diversification reduces growth volatility through a country's improved ability to weather economic storms. Better integration of a country into a broader range of global value chains and implicit or explicit insurance schemes also have this effect.

These findings are based on a panel of 77 developing and developed economies over the period 1976–2005. The main findings do not change much when high-income economies are excluded from the analysis.[7] By contrast, the relationship does not always hold when we exclude low-income economies from the analysis. This finding suggests that much of the action driving our results indeed lies with low- and middle-income economies, for which export diversification matters more in shielding their economies from the adverse effects of external shocks. A likely explanation is that developed economies have better access to other forms of insurance schemes, whereas developing countries depend more strongly on implicit insurance as represented by a more diversified export structure.

Does Product or Market Diversification Matter Most?

Product diversification clearly moderates the effect of trade openness on growth volatility. Market diversification measures yield more mixed results. Evidence in favor of a role for market alongside product diversification in shielding an economy from shocks is limited at best. Furthermore, thresholds (at which the total effect of openness on growth volatility changes sign) of the market diversification indicators cannot be established with confidence. In the product diversification regression, this is not the case, as the following section demonstrates.

Most Countries Benefit from Increased Openness

The second research question of this chapter concerns the existence and extent of a threshold at which export diversification is sufficient to ensure that openness does not have an overly large effect on volatility. Based on the econometric

Figure 11.1. Total Effect of Trade Openness on Growth Volatility

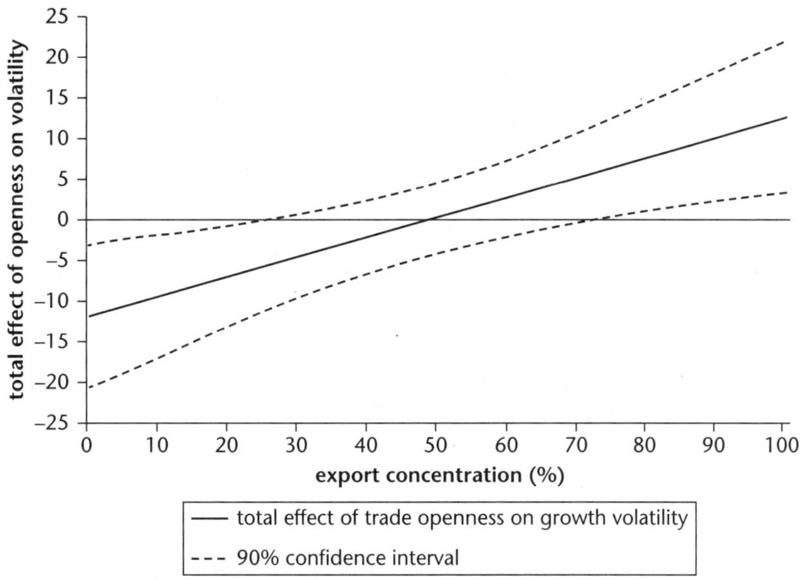

Source: Authors' calculations.

results reported in the working paper, we can identify positive thresholds in our product diversification indicators at which the effect of openness on volatility changes sign. On the basis of our preferred model,[8] this threshold occurs in the upper part of the distribution of the respective diversification indicators. The current degrees of diversification in the export baskets of the countries in our sample suggest that most countries benefit from increased openness.

This relationship is illustrated by the plot in figure 11.1, which uses the share of the five most important products in total exports as a measure of diversification. We can see that the impact of trade openness on volatility is significantly lower than zero, with 90 percent confidence, as long as a country scores lower than about 0.24 on the diversification variable. The effect gradually increases and changes sign at the threshold, which is at about 0.48. In contrast, above a value of about 0.71, the impact of trade openness on growth volatility is significantly positive. With indicators of geographic diversification, however, the results are not as telling.

It is important to put the threshold value of 0.48 in context. Based on figure 11.1, determining the share of countries in the sample whose value on the five-product indicator lies below the threshold and the share of those whose value lies above it is straightforward. Performing this exercise for a variety of measures of export diversification, we consistently find that the threshold value is located in the upper part of the respective indicator's distribution. A large share of the sample of countries benefits from trade openness in the sense that it reduces the volatility of income growth.

Table 11.1. Thresholds and Shares Based on Error Components and System GMM Regressions for Growth Volatility on Openness and Product Diversification

Indicator	Threshold	Share
Herfindahl	0.154	0.797
5-product	0.481	0.563
10-product	0.575	0.469
Principal component (product)	–0.516	0.672

Source: Authors' calculations.
Note: GMM = generalized method of moments.

The value of the five-product measure lies below the threshold of 0.48 for 56 percent of all countries (table 11.1). In the case of the 10-product indicator, we see a similar picture emerge. The total effect of trade openness on growth volatility is again highly significant, and the system generalized method of moments (GMM) estimator points to a threshold that lies at 0.58, which covers about 47 percent of countries. For the Herfindahl indicator, this share of countries is even higher, at 80 percent.

The threshold of diversification can also be understood relative to degrees of trade openness (figure 11.2, panel a) and income per capita (figure 11.2, panel b). When compared to trade openness, the distribution of countries below the diversification threshold appears to be relatively even. In contrast, countries above the threshold appear to be largely clustered around moderate levels of openness (with the exception of outliers, such as Zambia). This finding suggests that the countries that currently experience reduced volatility as a consequence of diversification are

Figure 11.2. Distribution of Countries by Product Diversification, Trade Openness, and Income per Capita

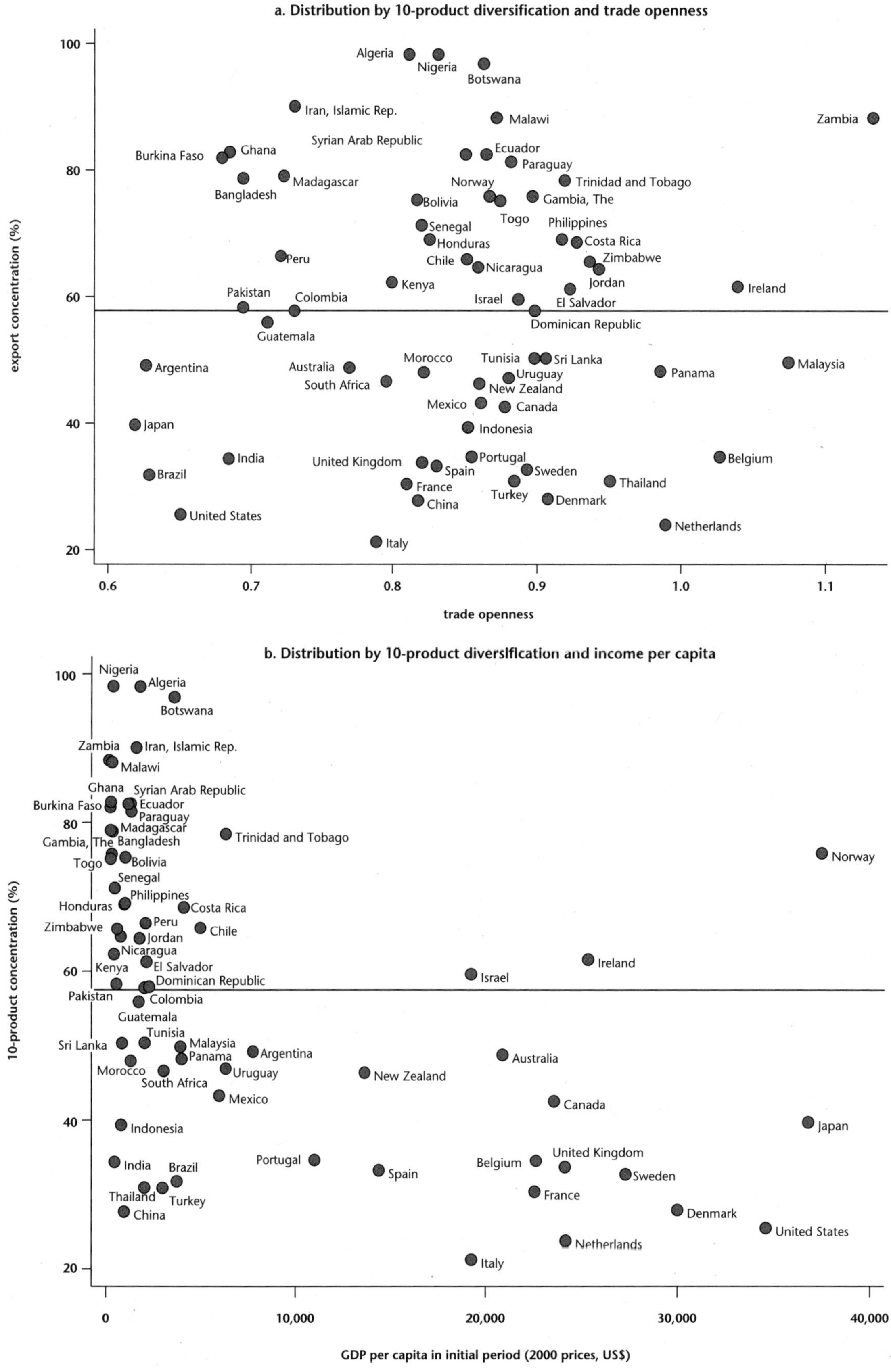

Source: Authors' calculations.

not limited to the most open economies. Conversely, the economies that do not benefit from the diversification effects of reduced volatility are not necessarily closed.

Naturally, countries in the lower-right quadrant of the plot are in a beneficial situation, given their very open and well-diversified economies. They should be well shielded against foreign shocks and benefit from less growth volatility. Countries in the upper-left quadrant of the plot, in contrast, are in a problematic situation. Botswana and Malawi, for instance, lie well above the threshold but have relatively open economies. Their relatively open economies may expose them to a large number of global shocks, and their highly concentrated export baskets may make them very vulnerable to those shocks.

The threshold of diversification can also be understood relative to income per capita. Figure 11.2, panel b, illustrates that, as expected, all high-income economies, with the exception of Norway and Ireland, have attained levels of diversification that lie substantially below the threshold value. Thus, they are likely to enjoy the benefits of trade openness while being well shielded from foreign shocks through the participation in a large number of global value chains. The vast majority of countries above the diversification threshold are low-income countries, although a large number of low-income economies also fall below the threshold. Whereas countries such as Botswana and Nigeria are troubled by extremely high export concentration, China has reached a level of diversification that falls well below the threshold. The question then arises: Can developing countries that choose to pursue a diversification path do so expediently, so that they quickly fall below the diversification threshold?

The answer is yes, as figure 11.3 clearly illustrates; it follows the path of six developing countries toward greater diversification over the sample period, using the five-product measure. Although countries such as Colombia, Kenya, and Nicaragua had very concentrated export baskets at the beginning of our sample period, they have successfully diversified to levels close to or below the threshold value we have identified. This example illustrates that diversification—as a means of deriving larger benefits from trade openness and at the same time shielding the economy against global shocks—is indeed a feasible and realistic policy goal.

Facilitating Export Diversification

Thus far, this chapter has highlighted the importance of export diversification in mediating the links between economic openness and volatility. In the remainder of the text, we look at the ways in which developing countries can promote export diversification. Indeed, they have enormous scope to do so: although diversification has been taking place in recent years, most countries still export only a relatively small number of products (figure 11.4) to a relatively narrow range of foreign markets (figure 11.5).

Dennis and Shepherd (2011) examine the policy determinants of export diversification using an econometric model. They focus in particular on trade facilitation, that is,

Figure 11.3. Diversification Trends among Selected Countries, 1981–2005

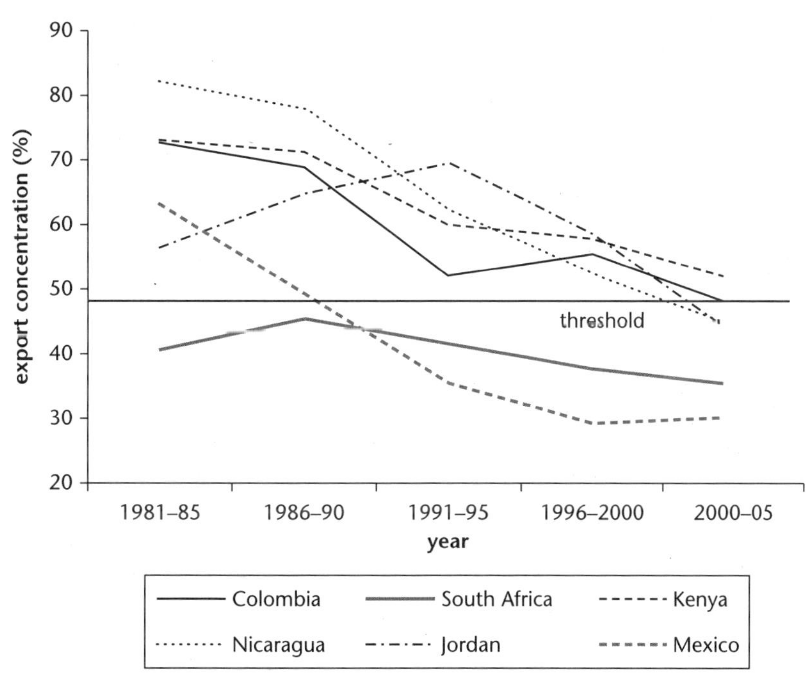

Source: Authors' calculations.

Figure 11.4. Histogram of the Number of 8-Digit Product Lines Exported to the EU by Each Partner Country

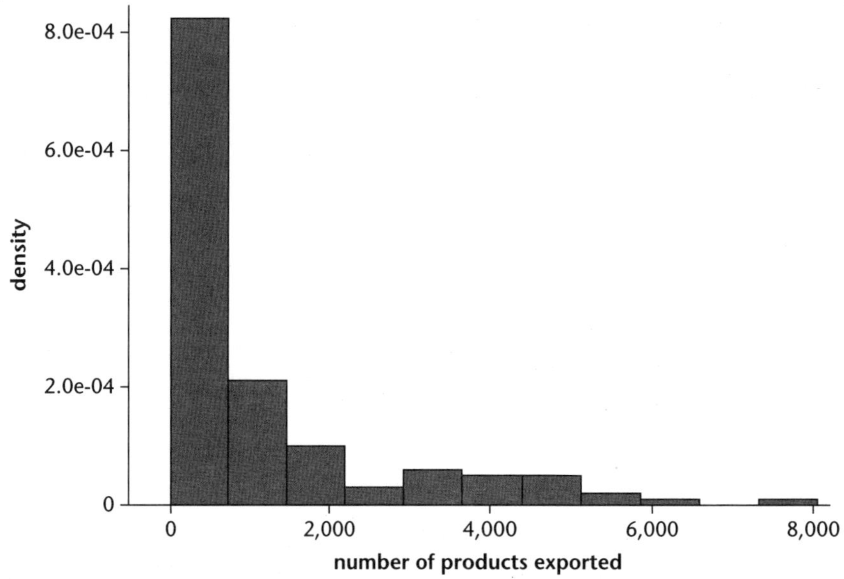

Source: COMEXT and authors' calculations.

Figure 11.5. Histogram of the Number of Export Destinations Served by Each Country

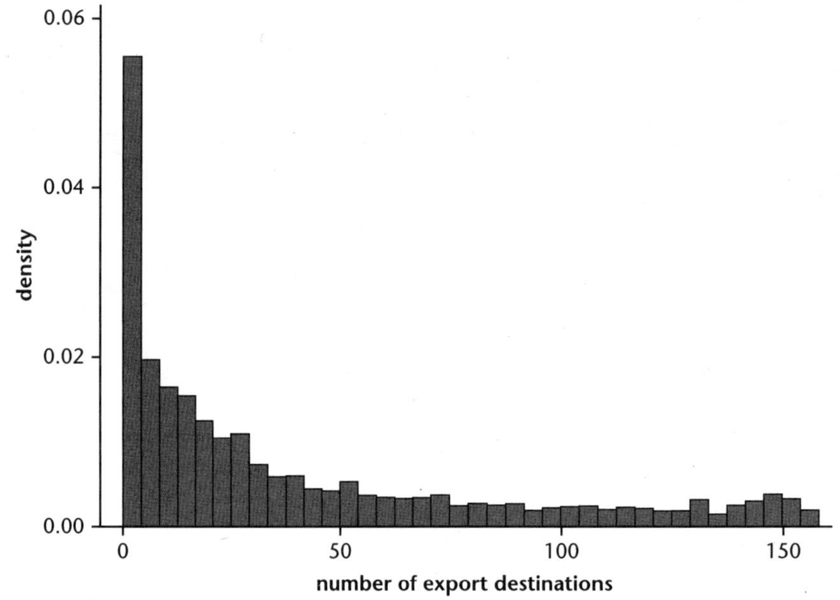

Source: COMTRADE and authors' calculations.

the range of policies that reduce the cost of exporting goods and the costs of market entry. Data on export costs are sourced from the World Bank's *Doing Business* project (Doing Business Indicators database, http://www.doingbusiness.org). They are defined as the total official costs for exporting a standardized cargo of goods, excluding ocean transit and trade policy measures such as tariffs. The four main components of the costs of exporting captured here are the costs related to the preparation of documents required for trading, such as a letter of credit, bill of lading, and the like; the costs related to the transportation of goods to the relevant seaport; the administrative costs related to customs clearance, technical controls, and inspections; and ports and terminal handling charges. The indicator thus provides a useful cross-section of information on a country's approach to trade facilitation. It covers elements of variable costs (transportation and handling charges) and fixed costs (standardized document preparation). These *Doing Business* data are collected from local freight forwarders, shipping lines, customs brokers, and port officials, based on a standard set of assumptions, including the traded cargo travels in a 20-foot full container load; the cargo is valued at US$20,000; and the goods do not require any special phytosanitary, environmental, or safety standards beyond what is required internationally. These export operations cost as little as US$300–US$400 in China, Israel, Singapore, Tonga, and the United Arab Emirates, whereas they run nearly 10 times that amount in Gabon and Tajikistan. On average, the cost is around US$1,278 per container, excluding countries in the Organisation for Economic Co-operation and Development and the European Union (EU).

Market-entry costs are also sourced from *Doing Business*. The data provide indicators on the costs, time, and number of procedures required for an entrepreneur to start up and formally operate a local limited liability company with general industrial or commercial activities. This process includes legal preregistration, registration, and postregistration requirements. Only official costs are considered, based on information gathered from the company law, commercial code, and specific regulation and fee schedules.

Dennis and Shepherd (2011) find that market-entry costs, export costs, distance, and foreign tariffs negatively affect product diversification. Market size, GDP per capita, and exporter country tariffs, however, are positively related to the degree of market diversification. These findings are based on new measures of export diversification constructed from EU data on imports from 118 developing countries. Although it is true that export diversification is thereby measured vis-à-vis the EU and not the world as a whole, these measures remain highly relevant, given that the EU is one of the most important outlets for developing-country exports.

These results are broadly consistent with previous work examining the diversification impacts of GDP, per capita income, and trade costs, such as that of Hummels and Klenow (2005), Debaere and Mostashari (2005), and Feenstra and Kee (2008). Moreover, the finding that lower market-entry costs are associated with greater export diversification is consistent with the results of Helpman, Melitz, and Rubinstein (2008).

In practice, trade facilitation can have a significant impact on the range of products that countries export (figure 11.6). Concretely, a 10 percent improvement in trade facilitation—as measured by the *Doing Business* data set's cost of exporting—is associated with product diversity gains on the order of 3–4 percent. Moreover, differentiated goods (such as manufactures) appear to have stronger diversification responses to trade facilitation than do homogeneous goods (such as agricultural products). When export costs are disaggregated into four components—customs costs, documentation costs, inland transport costs, and port costs—it appears that customs costs are the primary driver of the finding on trade facilitation.

Recent findings also suggest that geographical diversification—an expansion in the number of foreign markets served by a country's exports—can be an important mechanism

Figure 11.6. Number of Products Exported versus *Doing Business* Cost of Exporting

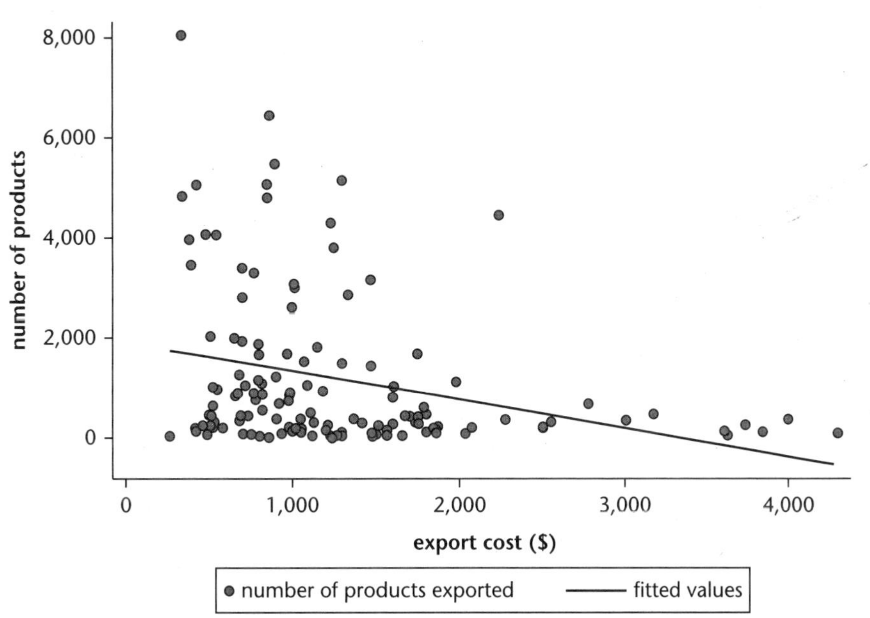

Source: Authors' calculations.

Figure 11.7. Number of Export Markets versus *Doing Business* Cost of Exporting

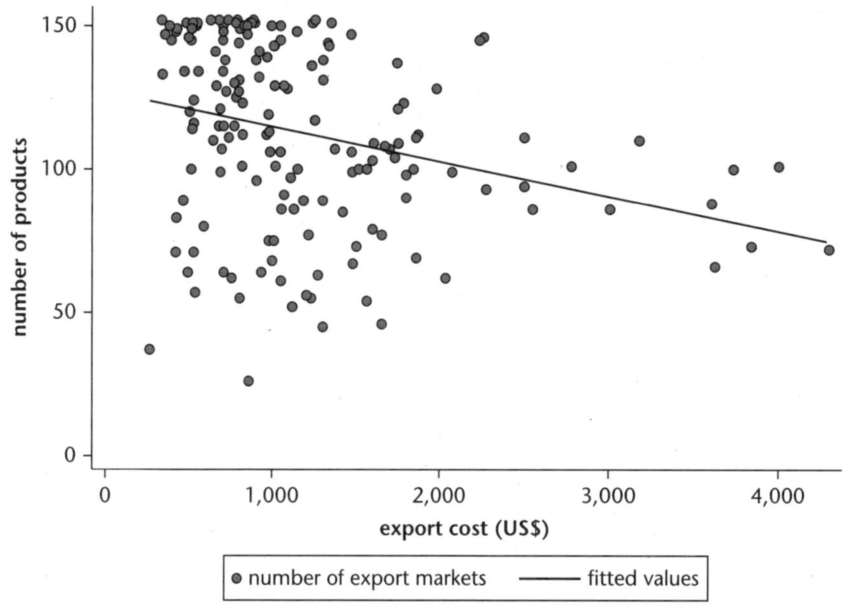

Source: Authors' calculations.

through which developing countries can become more integrated in the world trading system. Shepherd (2010) finds that increases in export costs (figure 11.7), distance as a proxy for transport costs, and tariffs are consistently associated with a decrease in geographical diversification of exports. However, as the size and development of the home economy increase, the number of export markets tends to grow. Moreover, improved trade facilitation—that is, lower export costs at home—has stronger potential for increasing geographical diversification than do comparable changes in market access abroad or international transport costs.

Concretely, 10 percent reductions in international transport costs and importer tariffs are associated with increases of 2 percent and 5 percent, respectively, in the number of export destinations. A 10 percent increase in the size of the domestic market is associated with increased geographical diversification of 3 percent. The elasticity of export destinations with respect to export costs is weaker than for distance or tariffs: a reduction of 10 percentage points in the ratio of export costs to per capita income is associated with a nearly 1.5 percent increase in the number of foreign markets served.

How important are trade costs for geographical diversification of exports in a quantitative sense? To examine this question, we consider one-standard-deviation decreases in each of the three factors of trade cost independently, that is, changing one variable but keeping all others constant. Evaluated at the sample mean, one-standard-deviation reductions in transport costs (distance) and in overseas tariffs increase the number of export markets by 4 percent and 3.5 percent, respectively. A similar reduction in export costs relative to per capita GDP increases geographical diversification by more than 12 percent. These results line up well with the trade facilitation literature, in which measures that reduce nontariff trade costs are usually found to have bigger trade impacts than tariff cuts (see, for example, Hertel and Keeney 2006).

Another way of looking at the impact of lower export costs is in terms of their absolute U.S. dollar level. With per capita income constant, reducing the U.S. dollar cost of exporting in Tajikistan (the highest-cost market, US$4,300) to the level of the median country (St. Lucia, US$1,053) would be associated with an increase of nearly 40 percent in the number of foreign markets entered.

Conclusion

It is widely believed that trade openness is, under suitable conditions, positively associated with growth. But does that growth come at the cost of more volatility due to greater vulnerability to global shocks? After all, an open economy may face a larger number of adverse shocks than a more closed economy.

This study explores the relationship among diversification, trade openness, volatility, and policy. We find strong evidence for the role of export diversification in reducing the vulnerability of countries to global shocks. Indeed, openness appears to reduce volatility in diversified economies and to have the opposite effect in poorly diversified economies. Our empirical findings suggest that product diversification in particular plays an important role in shielding an economy from the detrimental impact of foreign shocks. The evidence for market diversification is more mixed. There appears to be a threshold for product diversification at which the effect of openness on growth volatility switches sign. Most countries appear to experience less growth volatility as they pursue increased openness to trade.

These findings are of major relevance for policy makers in developing countries. One case against export-led growth strategies for developing countries is that economically open countries are more likely to be buffeted by external shocks. This observation could well be true, but the relevant question is whether the combined impact of these shocks is large and whether the effect of trade openness on volatility is indeed positive. For reasons discussed before, the theoretical case is indeterminate. This chapter has shown that the effect of openness on growth volatility is likely to be negative when a country possesses a sufficiently diversified export basket. These findings amount to a powerful argument in favor of making export diversification a first-order policy concern for developing countries as they consider exit strategies from the global financial crisis. At the same time, this research serves as an important counterargument against the recent rise in protectionist sentiment worldwide (Baldwin and Evenett 2009).

How can policy be used to enhance diversification? We show that reducing the costs facing exporters and potential exporters—particularly export costs and market-entry barriers—can be highly effective in promoting export diversification, both in the product and in the geographical dimensions. Of course, these policies not only affect export diversification but also have a range of other beneficial impacts on the economy. The overall cost-benefit balance of reform is likely to be strongly in their favor.

Furthermore, our findings suggest a more phased approach toward introducing trade reform. Countries should pursue an expanded production base and export diversification strategies before broad tariff removal. This sequencing of liberalization efforts—especially for countries that currently have a very concentrated export base—may be important for minimizing the disruptive effects that expanded trade could have on growth volatility.

This approach does not mean protecting domestic producers with "infant industry" tariffs—a classic inward-oriented strategy—but rather an outward-oriented one in which barriers to domestic market entry are removed to encourage innovation and development of new markets by companies at home. Strong evidence also suggests that better trade facilitation (through the reduction of fixed and variable costs of moving goods across borders) can be highly effective in promoting export diversification. Focusing on removal of red tape affecting exports and imports and promoting the development of trade-related infrastructure and services sectors can, therefore, make a major contribution to diversifying exports and helping manage outward orientation.

Notes

1. Finally, the authors illustrate that more open sectors also become increasingly detached from the overall economy in their growth processes, thus leading to less volatility in growth economy-wide. However, they do find that this latter effect is smaller in magnitude relative to the earlier two.

2. A number of papers—including Bevan, Collier and Gunning (1993), Dehn (2000), and Kose and Riezman (2001)—have documented important effects of commodity price shocks on growth volatility.

3. To our knowledge, these questions have not been addressed in the empirical literature. The closest study in spirit to ours is Jansen (2004). She uses a cross-section of countries to show, first, that export concentration determines terms of trade (ToT) volatility and, second, that ToT volatility drives income volatility. However, the paper does not directly test how the link between openness and income volatility is affected by different levels of diversification. It does not establish confidence-bound thresholds at which the total effect of openness on growth volatility changes sign. Last but not least, the author does not use market and product conceptions of diversification, as we do in this study.

4. In our preferred specification, we include the following control variables: inflation volatility, exchange-rate volatility, the volatility of capital flows to the region, and an indicator for the frequency of systemic banking crises, as well as the volatility of foreign shocks, such as foreign growth volatility and terms-of-trade volatility. The robustness checks in the working paper expand this set to include several additional controls that may also potentially affect volatility.

5. Both first-principal components capture more than 85 percent of the variation in the underlying variables, which makes it acceptable to rely on the first-principal component alone.

6. In addition to these measures, we have explored alternative measures of trade and financial openness, such as the import share of GDP and the ratio of foreign direct investment and portfolio liabilities to GDP, respectively. Our central results are not altered, although some of the control variables lost statistical significance (while maintaining their signs).

7. See the working paper version of this chapter (Haddad et al. 2010) for further information on robustness checks.

8. The preferred model is the system GMM estimator. See the working paper for full details.

Bibliography

Ahmed, S. 2003. "Sources of Economic Fluctuations in Latin America and Implications for Choice of Exchange Rate Regimes." *Journal of Development Economics* 72 (1): 181–202.

Baldwin, R. E., and S. J. Evenett, eds. 2009. *The Collapse of Global Trade, Murky Protectionism, and the Crisis: Recommendations for the G20.* London: Centre for Economic Policy Research/VoxEU.org.

Becker, T. I., and P. Mauro. 2006. "Output Drops and the Shocks that Matter." Working Paper 06/172, International Monetary Fund, Washington, DC.

Bevan, D. L., P. Collier, and J. W. Gunning. 1993. "Trade Shocks in Developing Countries: Consequences and Policy Responses." *European Economic Review* 37 (2-3): 557–65.

Chinn, M. D., and H. Ito. 2008. "A New Measure of Financial Openness." *Journal of Comparative Policy Analysis* 10 (3): 309–22.

Debaere, P., and S. Mostashari. 2005. "Do Tariffs Matter for the Extensive Margin of International Trade? An Empirical Analysis." Discussion Paper 5260, Centre for Economic Policy Research, London.

Dehn, J. 2000. "The Effects on Growth of Commodity Price Uncertainty and Shocks." Policy Research Working Paper 2455, World Bank, Washington, DC.

Dennis, A., and B. Shepherd. 2011. "Trade Facilitation and Export Diversification." *World Economy* 34 (1): 101–22.

Di Giovanni, J., and A. A. Levchenko. 2009. "Trade Openness and Volatility." *Review of Economics and Statistics* 91 (3): 558–85.

Easterly, W. R., R. Islam, and J. E. Stiglitz. 2001. "Shaken and Stirred: Explaining Growth Volatility." In *Annual World Bank Conference on Development Economics*, ed. B. Pleskovic and N. H. Stern, 191–211. Washington, DC: World Bank.

Easterly, W. R., and A. C. Kraay. 2000. "Small States, Small Problems? Income, Growth, and Volatility in Small States." *World Development* 28 (11): 2013–27.

Feenstra, R. C., and H. L. Kee. 2008. "Export Variety and Country Productivity: Estimating the Monopolistic Competition Model with Endogenous Productivity." *Journal of International Economics* 74 (2): 500–518.

Haddad, M., J. J. Lim, and C. Saborowski. 2010. "Trade Openness Reduces Growth Volatility When Countries Are Well Diversified." Policy Research Working Paper 5222, World Bank, Washington, DC.

Harrison, A. E., and A. Rodriguez-Clare. 2009. "Trade, Foreign Investment, and Industrial Policy for Developing Countries." Working Paper 15261, National Bureau of Economic Research, Cambridge, MA.

Helpman, E., M. Melitz, and Y. Rubinstein. 2008. "Estimating Trade Flows: Trading Partners and Trading Volumes." *Quarterly Journal of Economics* 123 (2): 441–87.

Hertel, T., and R. Keeney. 2006. "What Is at Stake? The Relative Importance of Import Barriers, Export Subsidies, and Domestic Support." In *Agricultural Trade Reform and the Doha Development Agenda*, ed. K. Anderson and W. Martin, 37–62. Washington, DC: World Bank.

Hummels, D., and P. Klenow. 2005. "The Variety and Quality of a Nation's Exports." *American Economic Review* 95 (3): 704–23.

Jansen, M. 2004. "Income Volatility in Small and Developing Economies: Export Concentration Matters." Discussion Paper 3, World Trade Organization, Geneva.

Kose, M.A., and R. Riezman. 2001. "Trade Shocks and Macroeconomic Fluctuations in Africa." *Journal of Development Economics* 65 (1): 55–80.

Raddatz, C. E. 2007. "Are External Shocks Responsible for the Instability of Output in Low-Income Countries?" *Journal of Development Economics* 84 (1): 155–87.

Rodrik, D. 1997. "Has Globalization Gone Too Far?" Washington, DC: Institute for International Economics. http://bookstore.piie.com/book-store/57.html.

———. 2009. "Growth after the Crisis." Discussion Paper 7480, Centre for Economic Policy Research, London.

Shepherd, B. 2010. "Geographical Diversification of Developing Country Exports." *World Development* 38 (9): 1217–28.

12

THE EFFECTS OF EXPORTS ON PRODUCTIVITY AND VOLATILITY: EVIDENCE FROM MALAYSIAN FIRM-LEVEL DATA

Mona Haddad, Deborah Winkler, and Albert Zeufack

The large and rapid slowdown in economic activity since 2007 has resulted in even larger and more rapid declines in international trade, with potentially devastating effects on economic growth, value added, and employment in export-oriented developing countries. The situation is particularly serious, because since the 1980s developing countries have experienced large increases in the ratio of exports to gross domestic product (GDP) (Milberg and Winkler 2010). That change has led to a renewed interest in the merits and costs of export-led growth strategies, particularly for developing countries (Rodrik 2009). Using the example of Malaysia, this chapter addresses the gains from exports in the form of higher productivity and the risk of outward orientation in the form of volatility in output growth.

Malaysia's experience is particularly useful for our study because government policy gradually shifted from import substitution in the 1960s to export-oriented industrialization from the 1970s onward. Export promotion was "the vehicle for achieving the twin objectives—alleviation of poverty and restructuring of employment and the ownership of assets—of the New Economic Policy" (Khalafalla and Webb 2001). Moreover, since the establishment of a free-trade zone in Penang in 1971, Malaysia has successfully attracted multinational firms, initially from Japan and the United Sates and later from Europe. Export-led industrialization has transformed Malaysia into Asia's third-most-open economy in trade terms (World Bank 2010).

As a result, Malaysia's combined exports of goods and services as a percentage of GDP more than doubled from 46 percent in 1974 to its peak of 121 percent in 1999 (see figure 12.1, panel a). In 2007, Malaysia was ranked the world's 18th largest goods exporter, compared to 23rd in 1990 and 30th 1980. It exceeded the export volumes of much larger countries, such as Brazil, India, and South Africa. While exports grew strongly, imports expanded even more quickly, resulting in a mostly negative contribution of net exports—that is, exports minus imports—to real GDP growth (see figure 12.1, panel b). This result reflects the country's assembly-type export sector, which is characterized by a large import content (World Bank 2010).

This chapter is structured as follows. In section two, we estimate the impact of exports on productivity at the plant level in Malaysia and also take plant-level characteristics into account. Section three focuses on the effect of sectoral exports on the volatility of output growth at the firm level and on the role of product and market diversification of exports. Section four concludes and makes some policy recommendations for Malaysia.

The Effect of Exports on Productivity

Motivation

Advocates of the export-led growth hypothesis generally refer to the success stories of the Asian Tigers—Hong Kong SAR, China; the Republic of Korea; Singapore; and Taiwan, China—that were characterized by high and continuous growth and rapid industrialization between the early 1960s and the 1990s. That success is attributed to their export-oriented free-market economies. Most developing countries that followed an inward-oriented import substitution

Figure 12.1. Malaysian Exports, 1971–2008, and Their Contribution to Real GDP Growth, 1988–2009

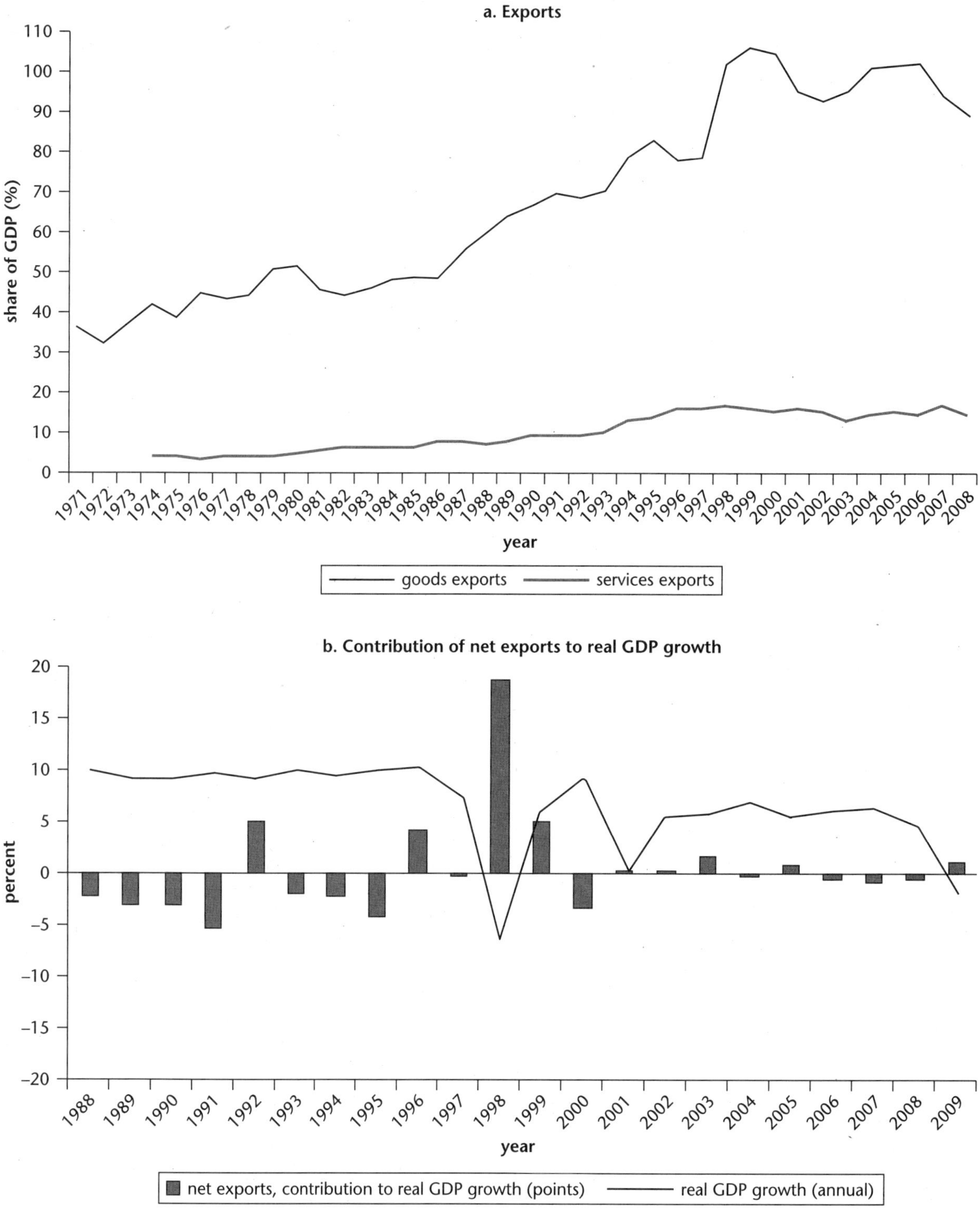

Sources: World Development Indicators (panel a) and EIU Country Data (panel b).

strategy (mostly in Latin America) experienced relatively poor economic achievements, which were taken as further evidence of the validity of the export-led growth model (Medina-Smith 2001; Furuoka 2007).

The channels through which export expansion enhances aggregate productivity and growth are well known. Exports allow for specialization according to a country's comparative advantage, which thereby raises growth. Export orientation also includes dynamic efficiency gains in the more productive export sector due to higher competition, greater economies of scale, better capacity utilization, the dissemination of knowledge and technological progress, and improved allocation of scarce resources throughout the economy. Moreover, higher exports are linked to productivity gains, which should lead to real wage increases and potentially to employment creation, thereby fostering domestic demand, growth, and consequently the economic well-being of a country. Finally, increased export earnings relax current account pressures by making it easier to import necessary intermediate and capital goods and to attract foreign investment. Such activity stimulates growth through capital accumulation (World Bank 1993; Medina-Smith 2001; Mahadevan 2007).

At the firm level, several determinants of total factor productivity (TFP) have been identified, of which knowledge (human capital), technology, and technology spillovers appear to be the most important. Besides a firm's own research and development (R&D) intensity, technology can be acquired by technology spillovers through economic integration into world markets, including exports and foreign direct investment but also through imported intermediates and trade liberalization (see, for example, Damijan et al. 2003; Fernandes 2008). Labor productivity (LP) at the firm level is affected mainly by capital intensity and TFP.

The hypothesis of the export-led growth model is far from being universally accepted, because of ambiguous results and econometric weaknesses of earlier studies. We put this hypothesis to the test by estimating the impact of exports on TFP and LP in the Malaysian manufacturing sector using plant-level data for 1999–2006. To our knowledge, no study at the firm level has yet focused on the impact of exports on productivity. Our analysis attempts to fill this gap by using plant-level data of Malaysian manufacturing firms. The data are retrieved from the "Productivity and Investment Climate Survey," which is a collaborative effort of the Malaysian government and the World Bank. Especially relevant to our study is the availability of plant-level data on exports. The presentation here is nontechnical and focuses on key results and interpretations. Full details of data, estimation techniques, and regression results are available in the working paper version of this chapter.

This section contributes to the vast export-led growth literature in several ways. First, no previous studies to our knowledge have directly measured the effect of export levels on productivity. Second, we use plant-level data for Malaysia, while most of the export-led growth literature focuses on either time-series data or cross-country regressions. Third, we interact exports with four plant characteristics—namely, export duration, the share of skilled labor, the share of private domestic ownership, and the share of private foreign ownership—to test whether the impact of exports on productivity is different taking these characteristics into account. Fourth, we apply modern estimation techniques including the dynamic system generalized method of moments (GMM) estimator. And fifth, our data allow us to test the export-led growth hypothesis for more recent years.

Key Findings

We estimate the impact of exports on both TFP and LP. At the firm level, several determinants of TFP have been identified. We capture knowledge by the share of high-skilled labor in a firm's total labor force. In general, technology is measured by a firm's R&D intensity. However, our dataset reports R&D expenses only for 2001 and 2006 and only for a few firms. We therefore use a firm's telecommunication costs as a proxy for telecommunication technology. Finally, we include several variables as proxies for technology spillovers; most important are exports, but we also include the share of imported material inputs in total material inputs (off-shoring) and sectoral trade liberalization. We include tariffs in the equation to account for the literature around the Melitz (2003) model that focuses on the effect of trade liberalization on productivity.

We hypothesize that a higher share of high-skilled labor and a larger use of telecommunication technology both increase TFP. Analogously, we expect exports to have a positive effect on TFP. The impact of materials off-shoring is not straightforward and depends on whether Malaysian manufacturing firms source high- or low-quality material inputs from abroad. We expect trade liberalization to increase TFP because of more competition among firms.

We estimate the impact of exports on TFP for the Malaysian manufacturing sector using plant-level data for the period 1999–2006. Our data cover two subperiods, 1999–2001 and 2004–06. In our baseline specification, we find that the share of high-skilled labor in total labor and spending on telecommunication technology both significantly increase TFP. Exports also have a significantly positive impact on TFP and show the biggest positive elasticity (figure 12.2). Materials off-shoring significantly lowers TFP, indicating that Malaysian manufacturing firms source low-quality inputs from abroad. As expected, higher tariffs at the sectoral level lower TFP.

The effect of exports on TFP might be influenced by individual firm-level characteristics such as export duration, the skill intensity of labor, the share of private domestic ownership, and the share of foreign ownership. In a second step, we interact exports with such characteristics. We expect that

Figure 12.2. Firm-Level Exports and Total Factor Productivity for the Malaysian Manufacturing Sector, 2006

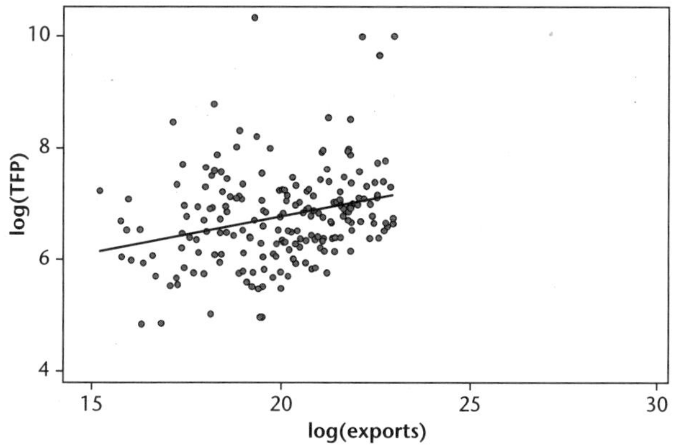

Source: Authors' calculations.

Figure 12.3. Firm-Level Exports and Labor Productivity in the Malaysian Manufacturing Sector, 2006

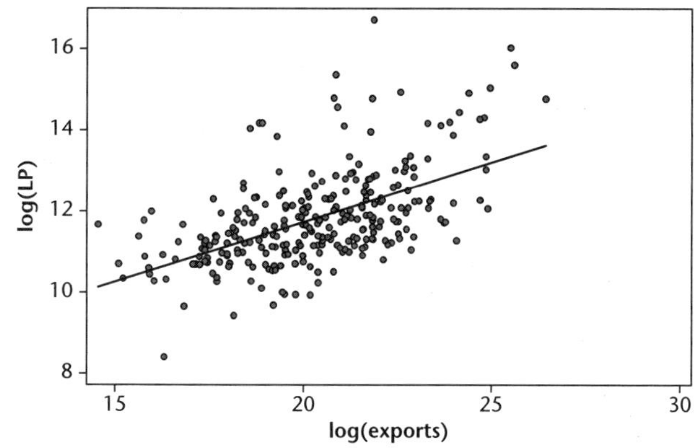

Source: Authors' calculations.

firms with a longer export duration might have knowledge and network advantages over younger firms; that is, the effect of exports on productivity should be positively correlated with export duration. Likewise, a higher share of skilled labor might translate into higher productivity gains from exports due to faster learning. However, this effect depends on the skill intensity of labor used in manufacturing operations in Malaysia. Finally, we expect that a higher share of private foreign ownership will increase the positive productivity effect of exports, while a higher share of private domestic ownership will reduce it, based on the assumption that foreign firms are more productive than domestic firms, a finding supported by several firm-level studies (see, for example, Temouri, Driffield, and Higón [2008] for a literature review focusing on industrial countries or Fernandes [2008] for Bangladesh).

When we interact exports with four plant characteristics—export duration, the share of skilled labor, the share of private domestic ownership, and the share of private foreign ownership—we find as follows. The interaction of exports with export duration and the share of high-skilled labor has no significant effect on TFP. As hypothesized, a larger share of private domestic ownership reduces the positive productivity effects from exports, whereas a larger share of private foreign ownership contributes positively to the overall effect of exports on productivity.

What do our results mean in quantitative terms? Using our baseline specification, we find that a 1 percent increase in real exports raised TFP in Malaysian manufacturing firms by on average 0.31 to 0.44 percent between 1999 and 2006. When we control for firm characteristics, we find that a larger share of private domestic ownership can cause the positive effect of exports to be lowered or even reversed. A larger share of private foreign ownership, in contrast, contributes positively to the overall effect of exports on TFP.

We also estimate the effect of exports on LP. As hypothesized, capital intensity and TFP have a significantly positive effect on LP in the baseline specification. Machinery and equipment intensity has a larger positive effect on LP than building intensity when capital intensity is subdivided into its subcomponents. Exports also show a significantly positive effect on LP (figure 12.3). Export duration has no significant impact on the productivity effects from exports. Surprisingly, the interaction of exports with the share of high-skilled labor significantly reduces the positive productivity effects from exports, which is not in line with our conjecture. We interpret this as a result of the fact that Malaysia's export-oriented manufacturing sector is dominated by low-skilled assembly-type operations, which create low value added. Although Malaysia has been successful in integrating its manufacturing sector into regional and global production networks, it nevertheless remains highly reliant on low- and semi-skill intensive assembly-type manufacturing (World Bank 2010). A larger share of private domestic ownership significantly reduces the positive productivity effects from exports, while a larger share of private foreign ownership significantly increases it, which is in line with our conjecture.

In quantitative terms, our results suggest that a 1 percent increase in real exports raised LP by on average 0.09 to 0.21 percent between 1999 and 2006. When we control for firm characteristics, we find that this positive effect of exports is lowered or even reversed, the larger the share of high-skilled labor and private domestic ownership is, while a larger share of foreign domestic ownership significantly increases the gains from exports.

The Effect of Exports on Output Growth Volatility

Motivation

The "great trade collapse," in particular the scale and velocity of the export decline during the recent economic crisis, has revealed an increased growth volatility in export-dependent countries and has led some to question the export-led strategy of development (Rodrik 2009). One of the main arguments against trade openness is the vulnerability of outward-oriented economies to external shocks such as changes in the terms of trade, the interest rate, capital inflows, and foreign demand.

What are the determinants of the volatility of output growth? Ahmed and Suardi (2009) provide a number of economic, noneconomic, and institutional factors that affect a country's aggregate volatility, including country size and the level of economic development, trade openness and export structure, development of a country's financial market, the role of institutions, natural disasters, and distortionary macroeconomic policies. Loayza et al. (2007) explain why developing countries face more aggregate volatility than developed countries and identify three sources: developing countries experience bigger exogenous shocks, suffer more domestic shocks, and have weaker "shock absorbers."

At the firm level, there has been little consensus on the causes of the volatility of output growth. The following factors, among others, have been shown to influence volatility at the firm level: firm size, R&D intensity, ownership status (publicly traded firms versus small private firms), inventory-sales ratio, access to external financing, deregulation of product markets, and greater international competition, exports, and export diversification (see, for example, Comin and Philippon 2005; Davis and Kahn 2008; Buch, Döpke, and Strotmann 2009; Buch, Doepke, and Stahn 2009; the chapter by Haddad et al. in this volume). Our focus is on how exports and export structure in the form of product and market diversification affect the volatility of output growth at the firm level.

Exports have an influence on this volatility through at least four channels. The first channel is the exposure of output to shocks in the form of volatility of aggregate shocks and the correlation of shocks across countries (Buch, Döpke, and Strotmann 2009). The second channel is the reaction of output to shocks in the form of the elasticity of factor demand and supply (Buch, Döpke, and Strotmann 2009). Both channels are likely affected by a firm's degree of openness (Rodrik 1997; Slaughter 2001). Exports are thus expected to increase the volatility of output growth through these two channels. The third channel refers to imperfect correlations between domestic and foreign shocks, which can have a stabilizing effect on volatility (Buch, Döpke, and Strotmann 2009). Fourth, exports can lead to changes in specialization patterns. If exports lead to a more diversified production structure, volatility is expected to be reduced and vice versa (Giovanni and Levchenko 2009). Because of these potentially conflicting effects, the net effect of exports on volatility is ambiguous. We explore the fourth channel in more detail when testing for the effect of exports on the volatility of output growth.

Firm-level volatility could be a concern for policy makers for the following reasons (see Buch, Döpke, and Strotmann 2009). First, changes in the volatility of output growth can affect economic welfare, which matters at the firm level rather than at the aggregate level for households and consumers, as they must find ways to protect their income and consumption against fluctuations of output. While access to financial markets could enable economic actors to insure against such volatility, many households hold few financial assets and would rely on public insurance mechanisms. Second, a higher exposure of households to risk could lead to resistance to open markets if this risk is associated with globalization. Third, changes in firm-level volatility can influence growth, but the empirical literature has remained ambiguous about this link.

In this second part of the chapter, we focus on the costs of trade openness by assessing the impact of sectoral exports on firm-level volatility of output growth in the Malaysian manufacturing sector for the period 1989–2007. Again, the presentation is nontechnical and focuses on key results and interpretation. For full details on data, estimation results, and methodology, readers are referred to the working paper version of this chapter.

This section thus adds to the small amount of empirical evidence on this subject, especially of studies using firm-level data. Second, we identify several variables that have a significant impact on volatility. Third, we interact sectoral exports with sectoral product and market diversification of exports to test whether the impact of exports on the volatility of output growth is different with diversification taken into account. And fourth, our data cover recent years, while other studies focus on older time series.

Key Findings

We define volatility as the standard deviation of output growth on a five-year moving average, an approach used in other studies measuring volatility (see, for example, Buch, Döpke, and Strotmann 2009 or Davis and Kahn 2008). While the Productivity and Investment Climate Survey has the advantage of reporting information on a plant's exports and imports, its disadvantage lies in the short period from 1999 to 2006, especially for measuring volatility. We therefore use firm-level data from Compustat, which covers the period 1989–2007.

At the firm level, there has been little consensus on the causes of the volatility of output growth. The following factors among others have been identified as increasing volatility at the firm level, at least for developed countries (see, for example, Comin and Philippon [2005] and Davis and Kahn [2008] for the United States and countries in the Organisation for Economic Co-operation and Development, and Buch, Döpke, and Strotmann [2009] and Buch, Doepke, and Stahn [2009] for Germany): R&D intensity, ownership status (publicly traded firms versus small private firms), access to external financing, deregulation of product markets and greater international competition, and exports. Firm size, however, has a stabilizing effect.

The impact of the inventory-sales ratio is ambiguous, depending on whether productivity or demand shocks dominate. While a higher inventory-to-sales ratio can smooth the impact of volatile production on sales (productivity shock), a lower inventory-to-sales ratio, reflecting improved inventory management, can help firms reduce their volatility of sales (demand shock). Buch, Doepke, and Stahn (2009) find for Germany that the first effect dominates. In addition, our chapter includes sectoral market and product diversification of exports, which have been identified as reducing the volatility-augmenting effects from exports but only at the national level (see Haddad et al. in this volume).

In our regression analysis, we include the number of employees and capital stock to capture firm size. R&D intensity is measured by calculating total R&D expenses over total sales. We obtained the ratio of inventory stock to sales analogously. The share of long-term debts over total sales as a measure for access to external financing is calculated following Comin and Philippon (2005). Since Compustat covers only publicly listed firms, we cannot control for the type of ownership. As in the previous section, we use sectoral import tariffs as an inverse measure for trade liberalization.

Since the Compustat database does not include firm-level trade data, we match these data with sectoral export data. This strategy follows the assumption that export activity at the sectoral level can influence firm-level output through spillover effects. Assume, for instance, that a domestic supplier B of automotive components purchases automotive parts from an upstream domestic supplier A before exporting the assembled components to a foreign automobile manufacturer C. Although supplier A does not export directly to C, its output will be indirectly affected by demand changes of C for assembled components from A.

In a first step, we estimate the impact of exports on the volatility of output growth, based on our baseline specification. Labor shows a negative coefficient sign, while capital shows a positive one, both being significant. What is the explanation for the differential impact of firm size on volatility? Labor has a stabilizing effect on volatility, because firms might not immediately adjust their required number of employees to demand changes. This delay might be because firms are not willing to lay off redundant workers immediately during an economic downturn, as search costs might be involved in identifying new workers once the business cycle picks up again. In addition, firms might be restricted in adjusting their amount of labor because of labor market rigidities. The required amount of capital, however, can be more easily adjusted to market needs and thus might favor volatility.

Firm-level R&D intensity shows no significant impact on the volatility of output growth. The firm's share of inventory stock significantly raises volatility, suggesting that demand shocks dominate productivity shocks in Malaysian firms, while the opposite has been confirmed for Germany (Buch, Doepke, and Stahn 2009). Thus, a lower ratio of inventory to sales, reflecting improved inventory management, helps firms reduce their volatility of sales.

Moreover, we find that a higher share of long-term debt in total sales significantly lowers volatility in Malaysia. Why would a higher share of long-term debt in total sales at the firm level lower volatility in Malaysia but increase it in Germany (Buch, Doepke, and Stahn 2009)? One explanation would be that a higher share of long-term debt is a good sign in developing countries, as it reflects a firm's creditworthiness (firms that are not creditworthy would simply not be given any credit). In developed countries, however, almost all firms are creditworthy, and a higher share might thus reflect unsustainability. As hypothesized, higher sectoral import tariffs (more regulation) reduce volatility, while larger sectoral exports significantly increase it (figure 12.4).

In the second step of our analysis, we evaluate whether this export-induced volatility can be reduced by higher product and market diversification of exports. We interact sectoral exports with measures of sectoral diversification. We measure product diversification using a modified version of the Hirschman-Herfindahl Index (HHI). The HHI is a measure of concentration and is defined as the sum of the squared world market shares of each exported product by sector j. The HHI can range between $1/n$ and 1, where n designates the total number of products being exported. The lower bound represents total diversification, that is, all

Figure 12.4. Average Annual Exports and Volatility Growth by One-Digit SITC Sector, 1992–2005

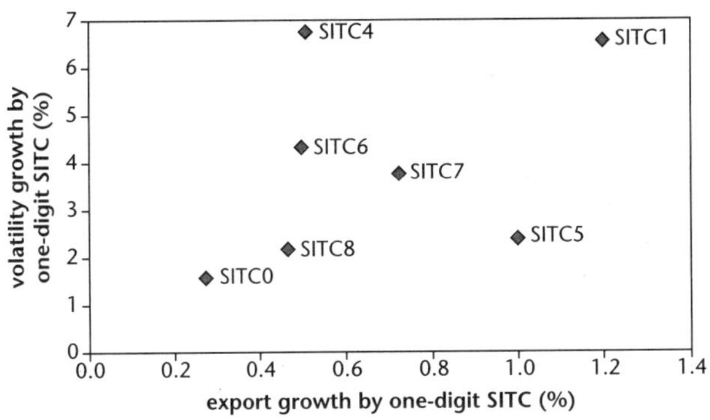

Source: Authors' calculations.
Note: Calculating volatility using five-year moving averages yields no volatility measures for 1989–91 and 2006–07. The x-axis shows the growth rate of exports in logarithms by SITC. In the y-axis, sectoral volatility is calculated using averages over available firms by SITC. The base year is 1997 for SITC4. SITC = Standard International Trade Classification.

products have an equal market share, while the upper bound reflects total concentration, that is, one product has the market share of 1. Analogously, we also focus on the number of export markets instead of products by each sector to measure market diversification. Since our focus in this study is on diversification and not concentration, we define $DIV = 1/HHI$.

Findings from this analysis are as follows. Market diversification of exports significantly reduces the positive impact of exports on the volatility of output growth. Such a stabilizing effect cannot be confirmed with product diversification of exports, however.

What could explain the insignificant effect of product diversification? Empirical observation shows a nonlinear relationship between product diversification and income. Thus, middle-income countries appear to be much more diversified than low-income countries, whereas rich countries have a much less diversified economic structure (World Bank 2010). Figure 12.5 shows the sectoral development of product and market diversification for the period 1989–2007 measured by the HHI. While this measure shows a clear trend of increasing market diversification (panel b), the same does not apply to product diversification (panel a). Many sectors show a trend toward more product diversification until the mid-1990s, followed by growing specialization. This finding could be an indication that Malaysia is in the process of growing from a middle- into a high-income country, and that would explain the insignificant effects of product diversification in the regressions.

To sum up, sectoral exports significantly raised firm-level volatility of output growth by between 0.065 and 0.252 percentage points in Malaysian manufacturing over the period 1989–2007. Controlling for export diversification, we find that market diversification significantly reduced this effect, while such a stabilizing effect could not be confirmed with product diversification of exports.

Conclusion

This chapter evaluated the gains from exports in the form of higher productivity and the risk of outward orientation in the form of volatility of output growth using recent data of Malaysian manufacturing firms. The hypothesis of the export-led growth model is far from being universally accepted, because of ambiguous results and econometric weaknesses of earlier studies. We put this hypothesis to the test by estimating the impact of exports on productivity in the Malaysian manufacturing sector using plant-level data for the period 1999–2006. Our estimation methodologies also addressed the endogeneity problem between exports and productivity. Our results confirm the positive effect of exports on productivity. Thus, exports significantly increased TFP and LP in Malaysian manufacturing firms over the period 1999–2006. Sectoral trade liberalization also has a positive impact on productivity.

Controlling for plant-level characteristics, we show that the positive impact of exports is lowered or even reversed the bigger its share of private domestic ownership. On the contrary, a bigger share of foreign domestic ownership contributes positively to the effect from exports. Surprisingly, we find that a higher skill intensity of labor reduces the effect of exports on labor productivity. We interpret this outcome as a result of the dominance of the export-oriented manufacturing sector by low-skilled assembly-type manufacturing in Malaysia, which creates low value added (World Bank 2010).

In a second step, we focused on the costs of trade openness by assessing the impact of sectoral exports on firm-level volatility of output growth in the Malaysian manufacturing sector for the period 1989–2007. Our results show that sectoral exports raise firm-level volatility, which we relate to a higher dependency on world markets. We also tested whether the export-induced volatility can be reduced by sectoral product and market diversification of exports. Market diversification of exports significantly reduces the volatility-augmenting effect of exports. Such a stabilizing effect cannot be confirmed for sectoral product diversification of exports. Finally, we find that a firm's number of employees, its share of long-term debt in total sales, and sectoral import tariffs lower volatility, while a firm's capital stock and its share of inventory stock in total sales increase it. Since our data source restricted us to

Figure 12.5. Product and Market Herfindahl-Hirschman Index by SITC1, 1989–2007

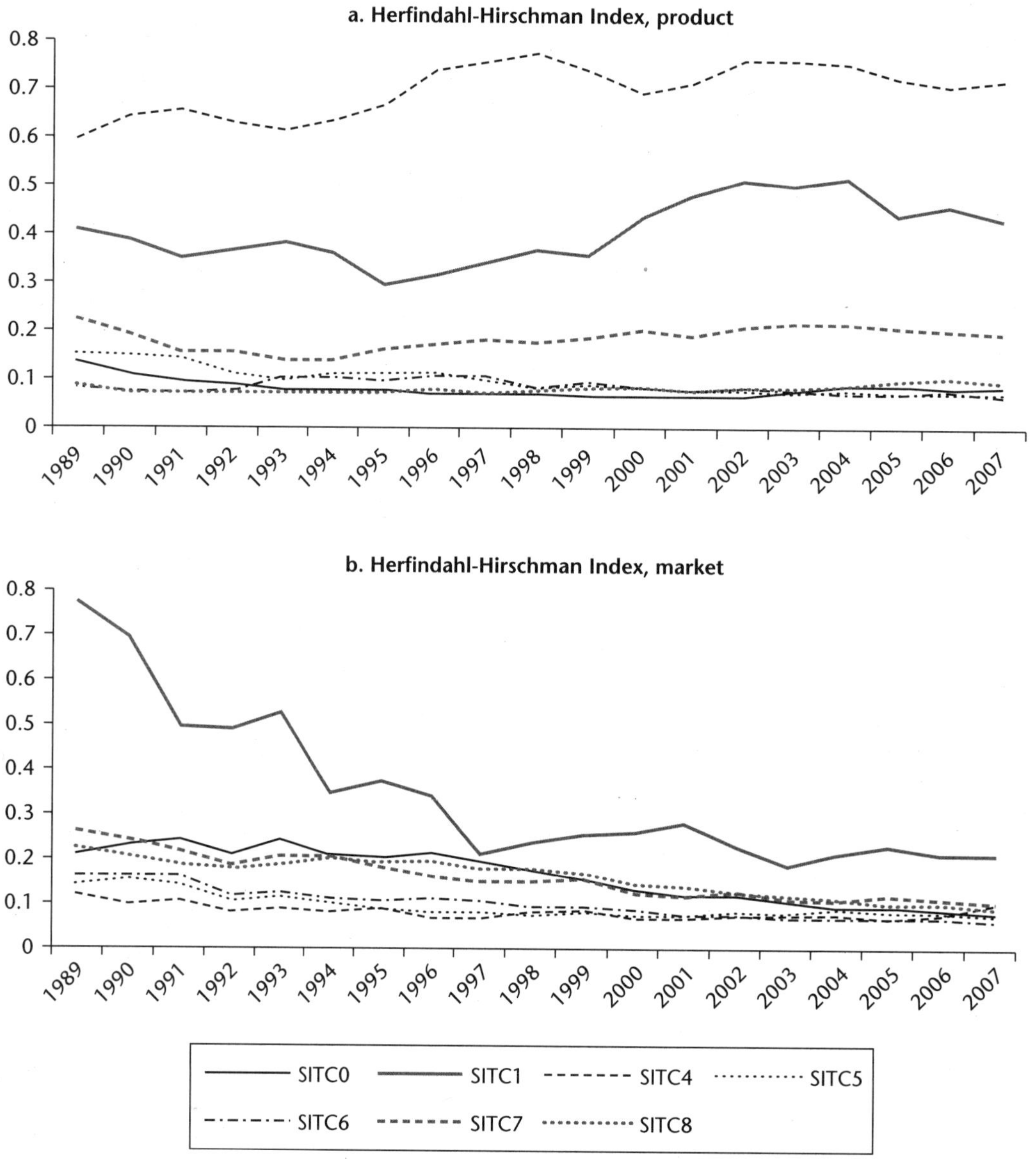

Source: Authors' calculations.
Note: A lower HHI reflects more diversification. SITC = Standard International Trade Classification.

sectoral export and diversification data, future research could estimate the effect of firm-level exports and diversification on firm-level volatility.

Our results imply that exports have counteracted the productivity slowdown Malaysia has experienced during the past decade. Average Malaysian LP grew at a rate of only 2.9 percent following the Asian crisis in 1997, compared to 5.5 percent in the decade preceding the crisis. The reasons for the productivity slowdown include a reduction in private investment since the Asian crisis, skills shortages, and lack of significant innovation. Average Malaysian TFP growth, however, remained stagnant over the two periods (World Bank 2010). Since exports had a positive effect on TFP and LP in the Malaysian manufacturing firms between 1999 and 2006, they seem to have prevented a more serious productivity slowdown in Malaysia.

Finally, countries need to assess which type of export-led growth model is appropriate given their stage of development. The growth process from middle- to high-income countries seems to be associated with greater specialization of production and a greater focus on higher-value-added products. Malaysia has been characterized by a greater sophistication of export mix over the past four decades—shifting from a reliance on the resource-based sector to a growing reliance on the electrical and electronics sectors—now showing one of the largest shares of high-tech exports in total exports in the world. However, the share of domestic value added in total output value stagnated or declined for most manufacturing sectors between 1981 and 2002, suggesting that Malaysia's exports still remain highly reliant on low- and semi-skill-intensive assembly-type manufacturing, which creates low value added (World Bank 2010). Specializing into higher-value-added activities seems to be the right way forward for Malaysia. Although this approach might increase the volatility of output growth due to a reduction in the product spectrum, a higher market diversification of exports could significantly counterbalance such effects.

Bibliography

Ahmed, A. and S. Suardi. 2009. "Macroeconomic Volatility, Trade and Financial Liberalization in Africa." *World Development* 37 (10): 1623–36.

Buch, C., J. Doepke, and K. Stahn. 2009. "Great Moderation at the Firm Level? Unconditional vs. Conditional Output Volatility." *B. E. Journal of Economic Analysis and Policy* 9 (1): Contributions, Article 20.

Buch, C., J. Döpke, and H. Strotmann. 2009. "Does Export Openness Increase Firm-Level Output Volatility?" *World Economy* 32 (4): 531–51.

Comin, D., and T. Philippon. 2005. "The Rise in Firm-Level Volatility: Causes and Consequences." Working Paper 11388, National Bureau of Economic Research, Cambridge, MA.

Damijan, J., M. Knell, B. Majcen, and M. Rojec. 2003. "The Role of FDI, R&D Accumulation and Trade in Transferring Technology to Transition Countries: Evidence from Firm Panel Data for Eight Transition Countries." *Economic Systems* 27 (2): 189–204.

Davis, S., and J. Kahn. 2008. "Interpreting the Great Moderation: Changes in the Volatility of Economic Activity at the Macro and Micro Levels." Working Paper 14048, National Bureau of Economic Research, Cambridge, MA.

di Giovanni, J., and A. Levchenko. 2009. "Trade Openness and Volatility." *Review of Economics and Statistics* 91 (3): 558–85.

Fernandes, A. 2008. "Firm Productivity in Bangladesh Manufacturing Industries." *World Development* 36 (10): 1725–44.

Furuoka, F. 2007. "Do Exports Act as 'Engine' of Growth? Evidence from Malaysia." *Economics Bulletin* 6 (37): 1–14.

Khalafalla, K., and A. Webb. 2001. "Export-Led Growth and Structural Change: Evidence from Malaysia." *Applied Economics* 33 (13): 1703–15.

Loayza, N., R. Rancière, L. Servén, and J. Ventura. 2007. "Macroeconomic Volatility and Welfare in Developing Countries: An Introduction." *World Bank Economic Review* 21 (3): 343–57.

Mahadevan, R. 2007. "New Evidence on the Export-Led Growth Nexus: A Case Study of Malaysia." *World Economy* 30 (7): 1069–83.

Medina-Smith, E. 2001. "Is the Export-Led Growth Hypothesis Valid for Developing Countries? A Case Study of Costa Rica." Policy Issues in International Trade and Commodities, Study Series 7, United Nations Conference on Trade and Development, Geneva, Switzerland.

Melitz, M. 2003. "The Impact of Trade on Intra-Industry Reallocations and Aggregate Industry Productivity." *Econometrica* 71 (6): 1695–1725.

Milberg, W., and D. Winkler. 2010. "Trade Crisis and Recovery: Restructuring of Global Value Chains." Policy Research Working Paper 5294, World Bank, Washington, DC.

Rodrik, D. 1997. *Has Globalization Gone Too Far?* Washington, DC: Institute for International Economics.

Rodrik, D. 2009. "Growth after the Crisis." Paper prepared for the Commission on Growth and Development, Kennedy School, Harvard University.

Slaughter, M. 2001. "International Trade and Labor-Demand Elasticities." *Journal of International Economics* 54 (1): 27–56.

Temouri, Y., N. Driffield, and D. Higón. 2008. "Analysis of Productivity Differences among Foreign and Domestic Firms: Evidence from Germany." *Review of World Economics* 144 (1): 32-54.

World Bank. 1993. *The East Asian Miracle: Economic Growth and Public Policy.* Oxford: Oxford University Press.

———. 2010. "Growth through Innovation." *Malaysia Economic Monitor.* April.

PART III

LESSONS IN MANAGING OPENNESS FROM COUNTRY AND REGIONAL EXPERIENCES

13

THE INTERNATIONAL CRISIS AND LATIN AMERICA: GROWTH EFFECTS AND DEVELOPMENT STRATEGIES

Vittorio Corbo and Klaus Schmidt-Hebbel

The international economy is recovering from the worst financial crisis since the 1930s. While the origin of the crisis was at the heart of the world's financial centers, it spread to other regions and countries through different transmission mechanisms. The financial crisis in major industrial economies was halted only by massive financial support and rescue programs, while the free fall of demand, output, and employment was reversed only by the combination of large-scale financial intervention and the most aggressive macroeconomic expansion recorded in history. All other economies where financial systems were not in crisis—industrial and developing alike—suffered from international contagion from the financial centers' crisis and the industrial world's recession through conventional financial and trade transmission channels.

This global financial crisis has raised concerns in developing economies about their macroeconomic policy frameworks and their development strategies. Among the questions raised by the crisis are, Which policies can best protect developing countries from world crises and shocks? What role does domestic demand play in shielding them from crises? And to what extent should they rely on a strategy of close trade and financial integration into a world economy punctuated by shocks and crises?

Latin America has been strongly affected by the international crisis and recession since late 2008. In comparison to previous crises, how has Latin America coped with the global crisis, what has been the role of different transmission mechanisms, and how have the region's structural conditions affected its sensitivity to foreign shocks?

This chapter addresses the latter issues by assessing the performance of growth in Latin America's seven major economies during 1990–2009. Results from an econometric model are used to decompose growth into long-term and cyclical determinants to explain the amplitude of the decline in gross domestic product (GDP) during the 1998–99 Asian crisis and the 2008–09 global crisis. This approach allows us to quantify and identify several factors: (a) the differences in unconditional and conditional effects of the global crisis on Latin America for both crises; (b) the role of structural and policy variables that have improved the region's resilience in the face of foreign shocks and crises; and (c) the main implications of the dominant development strategy adopted by the region since the 1990s. The presentation here is nontechnical and focuses on policy implications. For full details of the model and estimation results, readers are referred to the working paper version of this chapter (Corbo and Schmidt-Hebbel 2010).

The next section of the chapter describes the growth performance of Latin America during 1990–2009 and justifies the focus on the two regional recessions: the 1998–99 recession associated with the Asian crisis and the 2008–09 recession caused by the global financial crisis. The following section uses results from a growth regression model to decompose the amplitude of both recessions, comparing the very different roles of external and domestic growth factors in the downturns. The next section draws implications from the previous results for the choice of policy regimes and development strategies in support of the region's growth and resilience in the face of foreign shocks and crises. Final remarks close the chapter.

Latin America's Growth Performance

This study focuses on Latin America's seven largest economies—Argentina, Brazil, Chile, Colombia, Mexico, Peru, and the República Bolivariana de Venezuela—that account jointly for 91 percent of Latin America's 2008 GDP. The time sample spans the quarters from quarter one of 1990 through quarter four of 2009. The main variable of interest is the countries' annualized quarterly growth rate of seasonally adjusted real GDP.

Figures 13.1 and 13.2, panels a, b, and c, depict quarterly GDP growth rates for the region and the seven individual countries, respectively.[1] Figure 13.1 reflects four periods of at least two consecutive quarters of negative average growth in the seven countries that represent Latin America in our study: quarter three 1998–quarter two of 1992, quarter three of 2001–quarter one of 2002, quarter four of 2002–quarter one of 2003, and quarter four of 2008–quarter one of 2009. The first episode is linked to the 1997–98 Asian crisis and the last to the 2008–09 global financial crisis and world recession. The second and third episodes reflect two very deep but idiosyncratic recessions in Argentina and the República Bolivariana de Venezuela, more clearly visible in figure 13.2, panels a and c. The two episodes in Argentina and the República Bolivariana de Venezuela were not caused by international but by domestic factors (a deep and generalized crisis in Argentina and a temporary collapse of oil production in the República Bolivariana de Venezuela associated with a strike in the sector), with almost no consequences for other countries in the region. In contrast to those two country-specific episodes, five of the seven countries suffered a recession during the 1998–99 regional contraction, and all seven countries suffered a recession during the 2008–09 contraction. Hence, we focus in this study on the two latter recessions only.

Figure 13.1. Average GDP Growth in Latin America, 1990–2010

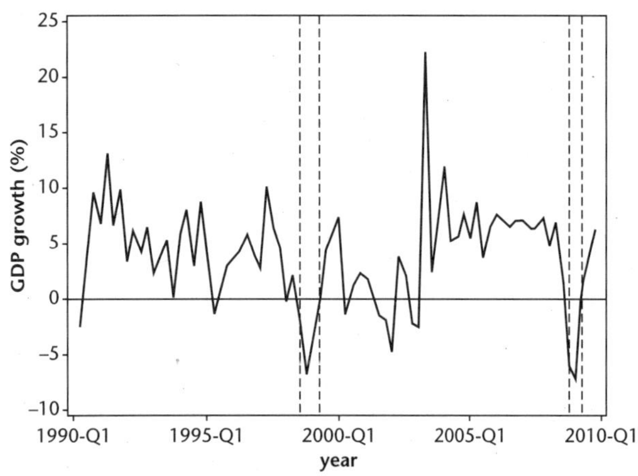

Source: Authors' calculations.
Note: Q = quarter.

We now turn to dating the precise extent of the recession. One possibility is to stick to the two windows of consecutive negative growth, depicted in figure 13.1. However, this aggregate regional growth behavior may mask significant country heterogeneity. Therefore, we exploit the full panel-data sample to test for recessions combining alternative recession windows for the 1998–99 recession with different windows for the 2008–09 recession, using panel-data estimations.[2] We find that the best results are those for the four-quarter window spanning quarter three of 1998–quarter two of 1999 (Asian crisis) and the two-quarter window from quarter four of 2008 to quarter one of 2009 (global financial crisis). The latter results are identical to the recession periods for aggregate Latin American GDP, depicted in figure 13.1.

However, for the purpose of the final choice of contraction periods relevant for our growth decomposition analysis performed below, we also consider the behavior of output gaps around recessions (figure 13.3).[3] The average output gap in Latin America during the first recession period declines precisely during the four-quarter window that was selected above, that is, from quarter three of 1998 through quarter two of 1999. The output gap starts to close in quarter three of 1999; that is, actual GDP growth exceeds estimated trend growth since the latter quarter. After the second recession period, however, the output gap continues to widen in quarters two and three of 2009, reflecting a weak growth recovery in the aftermath of the global financial crisis. This factor leads us to extend the contraction period relevant for our 1998–99 growth decomposition by one quarter to obtain a three-quarter recession period. Accordingly, we have identified quarter three of 1998—quarter two of 1999 (four quarters) and quarter four of 2008–quarter two of 2009 (three quarters) as the recession periods in this study.

Explaining the Amplitude of the 1998–99 and 2008–09 Recessions

The literature on long-term growth is very broad on both the theoretical and the empirical sides. While theoretical studies usually analyze the role of a key growth determinant

Figure 13.2. GDP Growth in Selected Latin American Countries, 1990–2010

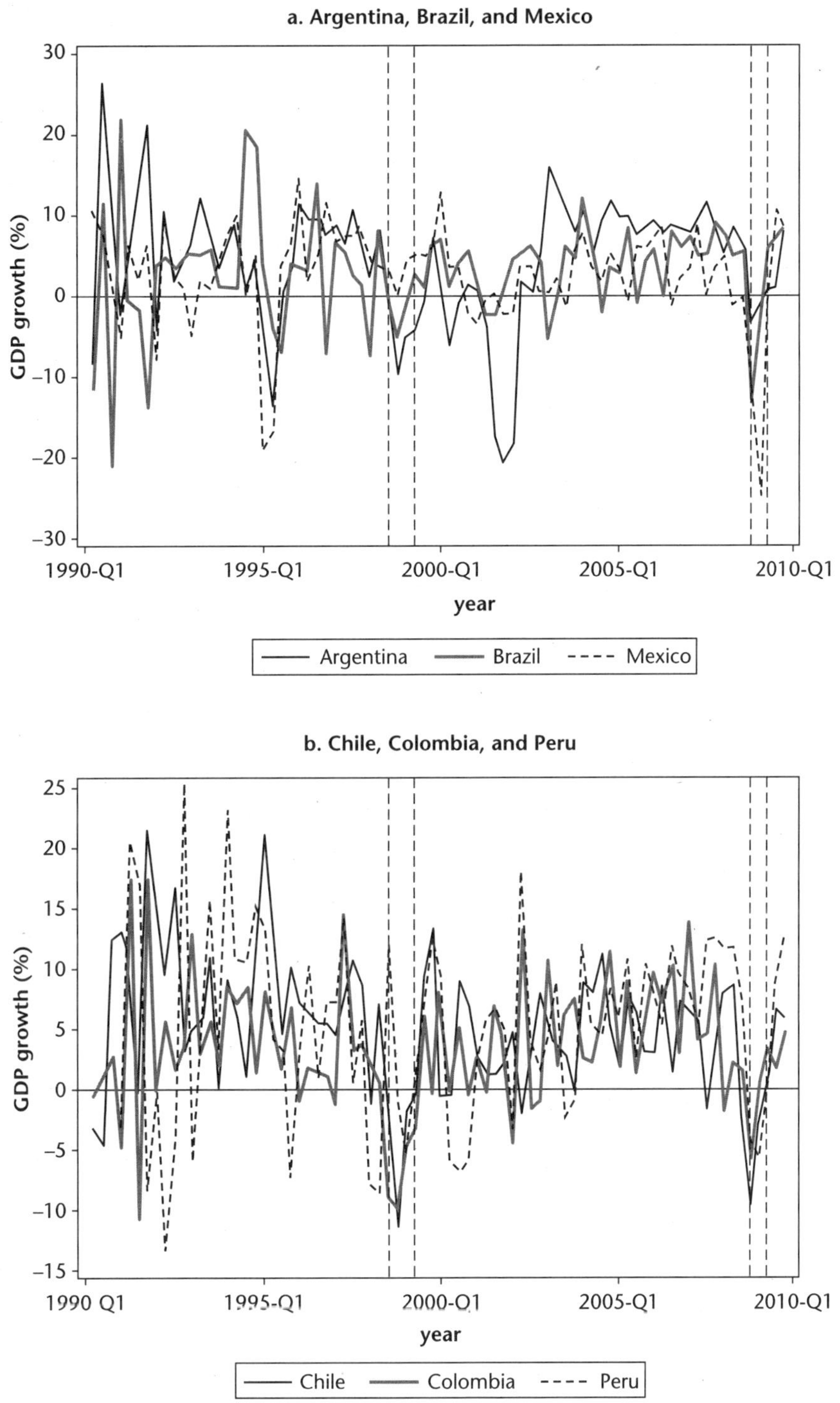

(continued)

Figure 13.2. *(continued)*

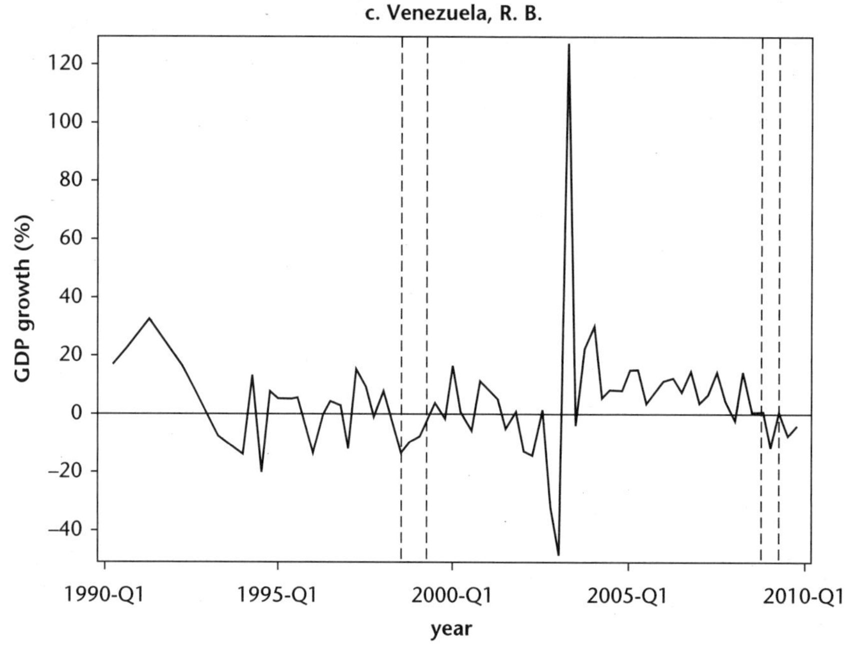

Source: Authors' calculations.
Note: Q = quarter.

Figure 13.3. Average Output Gap in Latin America, 1990–2010

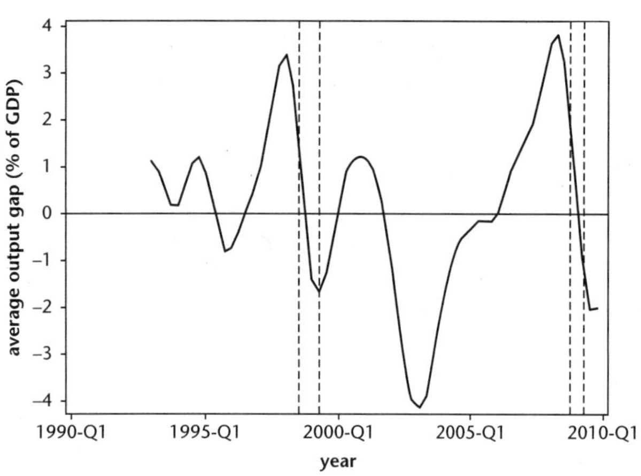

Source: Authors' calculations.
Note: Q = quarter.

in isolation, the empirical literature takes a wider view, considering several structural and policy growth factors. Our approach is to estimate a growth model encompassing the largest possible set of structural, institutional, policy, and cyclical determinants of short- and long-term growth, anchored in theory and international evidence. Our regression models, data sources, and estimation results are presented in full detail in the working paper version of this chapter.

We put our regression results to work by using them to explain the amplitude of Latin America's decline in GDP growth in the aftermath of both crises. To start, we compute the amplitude of the growth reduction in the seven sample countries during both recessions—that is, the cumulative GDP reduction (expressed in annualized terms) observed between the peak quarter before the recession (labeled in figure 13.4 as quarter 0) and the trough quarter of our selected recession periods (labeled in figure 13.4 as quarter 4 or quarter two of 1999 for the first recession and quarter 3 or quarter two of 2009 for the second recession). Table 13.1 reports the annualized recession amplitude for the seven individual countries and the region at large. The peak-to-trough cumulative GDP change ranges from a GDP loss of 8.5 percent in the República Bolivariana de Venezuela to a GDP gain of 3.4 percent in Mexico during the four-quarter 1998–99 recession. In contrast to the latter, the full country range is in negative terrain during the three-quarter 2008–09 recession, with cumulative GDP losses that range from 0.9 percent in Colombia to 11.1 percent in Mexico.

Simple (weighted) country averages of recession amplitudes for the region stand at –3.0 percent (–1.2 percent) for the first recession and –4.2 percent (–5.2 percent) for the second recession. By any of the weighted averages, it is clear that the second recession was much deeper than the first one. Our next task is to explain a significant part of the observed simple-average recession amplitude, making use

Figure 13.4. Average GDP Growth around the Asian Crisis, 1998–99, and the Global Financial Crisis, 2008–09

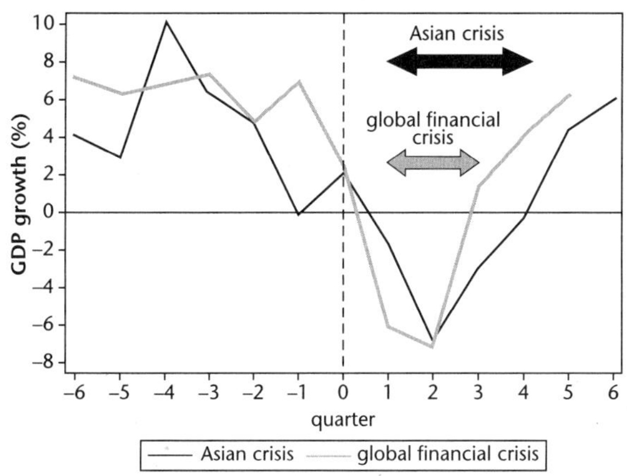

Source: Authors' calculations.

Table 13.1. Growth of GDP in Latin American Recessions, 1998–99 and 2008–09
percent

Countries	Asian crisis, Q3 1998–Q2 1999	Global financial crisis, Q4 2008–Q2 2009
Argentina	–5.20	–1.55
Brazil	–1.03	–3.99
Chile	–3.88	–4.40
Colombia	–6.82	–0.87
Mexico	3.37	–11.09
Peru	1.15	–3.64
Venezuela, R. B.	–8.51	–3.59
Simple average	–2.99	–4.16
Weighted average	–1.15	–5.24

Source: Authors' calculations.
Note: Cumulative GDP growth rates within the reference period. Series de-seasonalized using ARIMA X–11. Q = quarter.

of our coefficient estimates and the changes in independent variables (and in coefficient estimates, when applicable), according to our decomposition method, summarized in the working paper version of this chapter.

The results are reported in table 13.2, based on our most comprehensive regression results. There we report the recession amplitude decomposition for the Asian crisis (column 1) and for the global financial crisis (column 2). Column (2) is divided into three parts: the first is based on changes in explanatory variables only, the second is based on changes in estimated parameters only, and the third is the total contribution, the sum of the two previous parts.

The amplitude of the first recession is –3.0 percent (reported in the bottom line of table 13.2), of which we explain some 90 percent, that is, an annualized output decline of 2.7 percent. Of the much deeper second recession, with an amplitude of –4.2 percent, we explain some 95 percent, that is, an annualized output decline of 4.1 percent. What are the factors driving these results?

We start with foreign cyclical variables, which reflect the transmission mechanisms from international crises and recessions to the region. A striking difference emerges between Latin America's first and second recessions. On average (across countries and across the five foreign cyclical variables), international conditions improved during the first recession, contributing 0.5 percent to higher cumulative growth.[4] The opposite is observed during the recent recession, when international conditions deteriorated on average massively for Latin America, contributing –2.7 percent to (or more than half of) the recession's amplitude. In 1998–99, three out of five foreign variables improved for Latin America. However, in 2008–09 all five cyclical variables deteriorated, and the largest single external driver of the recession was the massive decline in trading partners' economic growth. Hence, the 1998–99 recession was largely homemade, while the global financial crisis and world recession were the main drivers of the 2008–09 downturn.

We now turn to long-term growth variables. They deteriorated significantly on average during the first recession, explaining a sizable –1.7 percent, which is more than half the 1998–99 recession's amplitude. In contrast, long-term variables improved on average during the second recession, contributing 0.8 percent to higher cumulative growth in 2008–09. Higher private credit flows (relative to GDP) and lower inflation contributed most to positive growth, while the deterioration in fiscal balances (relative to GDP) weakened growth. When we consider the reduced inflation coefficient observed since 2002, we find that the growth gain from lower inflation is much smaller in 2008–09. Therefore, when changes both in variables and in coefficients are combined, the contribution of long-term variables to the amplitude of the second recession is close to nil.

We come to similar conclusions on the very different role of changes in structural variables during both recessions: they deepen the recession in 1998–99 (by –0.6 percent), while they dampen the recession in 2008–09 (by 0.6 percent). While our ex post measures of financial and trade openness decline significantly during the most recent recession, the buildup of international reserves more than offsets the latter. Once we consider the large changes in coefficients after 2000 (smaller for financial openness, larger for trade openness, and smaller for international reserves), however, the overall contribution of structural variables to the amplitude of the 2008–09 recession—combining changes in their values and their estimated parameters—is very negative, equaling –1.7 percent.

Table 13.2. Decomposition of Latin America's Recessions, 1998–99 and 2008–09
percent

	Asian crisis, Q3 1998–Q2 1999	Global financial crisis, Q4 2008–Q2 2009		
Amplitude of GDP growth decline	**–2.99**	**–4.16**		
		Structural changes		
		No	Changes	Yes
Long-term variables	–1.68	0.77		0.05
Private credit	0.24	0.44		0.44
Inflation	0.65	0.97	–0.73	0.24
Secondary school enrollment	–0.14	0.15		0.15
Fiscal balance	–1.17	–0.73		–0.73
Political certainty	–1.26	–0.06	0.01	–0.05
Structural variables	–0.57	0.59		–1.70
Financial openness	0.73	–0.60	0.14	–0.46
Trade openness	–0.53	–1.32	–0.79	–2.11
Net external assets	–0.08	0.08		0.08
International reserves	–0.68	2.43	–1.64	0.79
Exchange rate regime	–0.01	0.00	0.00	0.00
Foreign cyclical variables	0.54	–2.60		–2.74
Terms of trade growth	0.02	–0.32		–0.32
Growth of trading partners	0.26	–1.36		–1.36
Growth of world exports	0.53	–0.05		–0.05
Capital inflows to Latin America	–0.05	–0.68		–0.68
Sovereign spreads	–0.22	–0.19	–0.14	–0.33
Domestic policy variables	–0.99	–0.14		0.99
Government consumption	0.69	1.12		1.12
Real interest rate	–1.68	–1.26	1.13	–0.13
Interactions	–0.02	–0.67		–0.67
Growth of trading partners * trade openness	0.00	–0.19		–0.19
Growth of trading partners * financial openness	0.10	–0.35		–0.35
Capital inflows to Latin America * financial openness	–0.09	–0.10		–0.10
Sovereign spreads * net external assets	–0.02	–0.03		–0.03
Structural changes post-2000		–2.02		
Explained variation	–2.72	–4.07		–4.07
Unexplained variation	–0.26	–0.09		–0.09
Total variation	–2.99	–4.16		–4.16

Source: Authors' calculations.
Note: Q = quarter.

Domestic macroeconomic policy played on average a contractionary role in 1998–99 and an expansionary role in 2008–09. Fiscal policy was expansionary in both recessions but much more so in the second experience, when it made a positive contribution of 1.1 percent to cumulative growth. As opposed to the latter, monetary policy was highly contractionary in both recessions (due to higher nominal interest rates in 1998–99 and negative inflation expectations in 2008–09), but much less so in the recent experience. Higher real interest rates deepened the 1998–99 recession by 1.0 percent, while higher real rates (combined with the decline in the absolute coefficient of the real interest rate) deepened the 2008–09 recession by just 0.1 percent.

Finally, the growth effects of interactions between structural conditions and foreign shocks were neutral for the first recession but deepened significantly the second recession, by 0.7 percent. This result is not surprising because the interaction terms largely reflect the amplifying effects of the deterioration in foreign conditions observed in 2008–09 but not in 1998–99.

Implications for Policies and Growth Strategies

The evidence presented in this chapter on Latin America's performance during its two last crises, 1998–99 and 2008–09, shows striking differences between the very different roles played by foreign and domestic growth factors. The first (less intense) recession was largely homemade, while the second (more intense) recession was due largely to a deteriorating world economy. The combined effect of foreign cyclical factors was positive for Latin America's growth during the first recession, while all foreign cyclical variables deteriorated sharply during the world financial crisis, explaining more than half the last recession. In contrast to foreign variables, all domestic variables explain more than 100 percent of the first recession and less than half the 2008–09 downturn.

The latter result is due to the large changes in development strategies and policy regimes that Latin America started in the 1990s and deepened in the 2000s. While populist policies have reemerged in some countries, the region's dominant development approach relies on market and private sector development, strong commitment to global integration, adoption of sustainable macroeconomic and financial regimes, and some progress on reforms to make governments more effective in their provision of public goods. Next, we derive the implications of our empirical findings for evaluating the region's development strategy in three key areas: macroeconomic regimes and policies, domestic financial development, and international integration of goods and financial markets.

Latin America began a major revamping of its macroeconomic policy frameworks in the 1990s, a drive that was consolidated in the 2000s. Fiscal policy had been unsustainable in many countries since the 1970s and through the early 1990s, leading to fiscal crises and hyperinflation. Fiscal orthodoxy replaced profligacy in the 1990s, a trend that intensified in the 2000s, when a significant part of commodity windfalls was saved. In turn, fiscal policy was used as a countercyclical stabilizing tool during the 2008–09 recession.

Trends in fiscal deficits were dramatically curtailed or turned into surpluses, and public debts were generally reduced to low and sustainable levels. Average public and publicly guaranteed debt fell from 30.1 percent of GDP in the early 1990s to 14.3 percent of GDP in the late 2000s (table 13.3). A final step toward further strengthening of fiscal frameworks in the region—adopting formal fiscal rules and fiscal councils—is still pending. Chile is the only country that has in put in place a fiscal rule since 2001.

Our results provide strong evidence on the growth impact of the shift in the region's fiscal policy. First, the fiscal balance makes a robust and economically large contribution to growth. Second, government consumption has a significant stabilizing effect on short-term growth. Our growth decomposition shows that the stabilizing role of government consumption was more heavily used during the 2008–09 contraction, when countries had more room for countercyclical fiscal policy.

The second regime change in macroeconomic policies was the shift from inflexible toward flexible exchange-rate regimes, largely implemented after the Asian crisis. Either forced by markets or prompted by policy makers' convictions, many countries replaced their crawling pegs or exchange-rate bands with floats, which occasionally are of the "clean" type (as in Mexico) and more frequently of the "dirty" type, that is, with high-frequency nonannounced interventions (as in Brazil or Peru) or low-frequency preannounced intervention periods (as in Chile). Latin America has reaped three benefits from flexible exchange rates: avoidance of recurring currency crises (that often lead to recessions), use of nominal (and, hence, real) exchange-rate adjustment as a buffer against adverse foreign shocks (therefore avoiding costly unemployment and output losses), and allowance of full conduct of an independent monetary policy.

Flexible exchange rates have not prevented countries from engaging in trend accumulation of international reserves to strengthen their foreign liquidity positions. Drawing lessons from recurring past experience with

Table 13.3. Public and Publicly Guaranteed External Debt in Latin America as a Percentage of GDP, 1990–2009
percent

	1990–94	1995–99	2000–04	2005–09
Argentina	23.59	23.92	56.35	25.84
Brazil	20.31	12.35	16.91	7.26
Chile	23.42	7.16	9.15	6.27
Colombia	28.04	17.05	22.71	14.10
Mexico	22.03	24.06	14.80	10.93
Peru	45.23	35.13	36.18	21.43
Venezuela, R. B.	48.10	34.11	24.51	14.41
Simple average	30.10	21.97	25.80	14.32
Weighted average	23.56	18.42	22.51	11.62

Source: World Development Indicators (database), World Bank, http://data.worldbank.org.

inflexible exchange-rate regimes and currency crises, Latin America has adopted an eclectic framework that combines exchange-rate flexibility with self-insurance in the form of holding significant levels of international reserves. Our empirical evidence shows that both a flexible exchange-rate regime and foreign exchange holdings contribute to growth in Latin America. Most revealing is our finding that while reserve holdings had a very large effect and the exchange-rate regime a nonsignificant effect on growth in the 1990s, the relative importance of both variables was reversed after the shift toward floats. Since 2000–2001, the flexible exchange-rate regime has had a significant and large effect on growth, while the effect of reserve holdings has declined in size albeit not in statistical significance. Moreover, during the 1998–99 recession, central banks sold reserves and therefore contributed to deepening the recession, while in 2008–09 they did the opposite, contributing to higher growth.

The third component of macroeconomic policy is the monetary regime. As noted above, a flexible exchange rate is a necessary condition for exercising an independent monetary policy. Fiscal sustainability and responsibility preclude fiscal dominance over monetary policy, which is a second condition of a macroeconomic regime for the exercise of an independent and credible monetary policy. Finally, de jure (or, at least, de facto) central bank independence strengthens the conduct of a monetary policy that is independent of direct interference by government or private sector interests. Adoption of inflation targeting, today's monetary regime of choice among many central banks in the world, requires the satisfaction of the three latter conditions. Therefore, it is no coincidence that several central banks adopted inflation targeting in Latin America after obtaining legal or de facto independence, after severing their links with government budgets, and during or after their transition toward floating exchange rates. With inflation targeting (and sometimes without it), central banks have made significant progress in adopting a framework of careful and responsible exercise of monetary policy. The success of monetary policy is reflected in lower inflation, declining in Latin America from an annual average of 34 percent in the early 1990s to 7 percent in the past five years (table 13.4). Our findings support the conclusion that lower inflation also contributes significantly to higher growth.

The gains in the credibility of monetary policy reaped from low inflation gradually allow central banks to adopt countercyclical monetary policies. While central banks were busy defending their inflexible exchange rates during the 1998–99 recession, they allowed their local currencies to depreciate in 2008–09 and exercised countercyclical monetary policy. Our evidence shows that central banks raised nominal (and, hence, real) interest rates in 1998–99, while they cut nominal interest rates in 2008–09. Although the latter cuts were not sufficient to compensate for a significant decline in inflation expectations, they helped avoid excessively high real interest rates. Our evidence shows that growth was significantly curtailed by contractionary monetary policy in 1998–99, as opposed to the 2008–09 experience.

The macroeconomic regime shifts that Latin America has implemented in the past decade have contributed to holding aggregate demand growth in check during the past decade, leading to healthy current account balances and significant reductions in public and private net external liabilities. Our findings confirm that the buildup of net external assets has had a significant positive effect on the region's growth performance, either directly or interacting with sovereign debt premiums. Moreover, when the global financial crisis and world recession of 2008–09 hit, Latin America's fiscal and external position was healthy, and policy regimes were strong, enabling the region to face very well the severe deterioration in international conditions (compared

Table 13.4. Inflation in Latin America, 1990–2009
percent

	1990–94	1995–99	2000–04	2005–09
Argentina	30.46	0.21	6.73	8.26
Brazil	85.91	8.56	7.79	4.54
Chile	13.66	5.26	2.68	3.69
Colombia	20.02	14.32	6.55	4.69
Mexico	12.32	19.01	5.40	4.04
Peru	47.09	7.08	2.19	2.54
Venezuela, R.B.	30.12	30.74	16.75	18.06
Simple average	34.23	12.17	6.87	6.55
Weighted average	51.68	11.16	7.11	5.45

Source: Authors' calculations.

to 1998–99 or 1981–82) and to adopt effective countercyclical policies for the first time in its recorded history.

The second area of significant progress in the region has been in the development of domestic financial and capital markets. During the past decade, Latin America's banking sector has developed both in size and in diversity of financial services, while improving its health and resilience in the face of domestic and external shocks. Domestic financial deepening (and financial integration) has been facilitated by macroeconomic stability, deregulation of domestic financial activities, privatization of banks, opening up to foreign ownership of banks, privatization of nonfinancial firms, and reduction of controls on foreign capital flows. Restrained from excessive risk taking by reformed financial regulation and supervision (showing that the right lessons were derived from previous financial crises), the region's banks have avoided exposure to U.S. toxic assets and have generally resisted well the recession of 2008–09. In fact, no financial crises were observed during 2008–09 in a region that had suffered recurring banking crises in the past when hit by severe foreign shocks and domestic recessions. In our findings, the ratio of private credit from commercial banks to GDP contributes significantly to the region's growth. Moreover, the increase in that ratio had a mild stabilizing effect during the 1998–99 recession and a larger expansionary influence during the 2008–09 recession.

Beyond banking, the region adopted reforms in capital markets that boosted the development of private debt and equity markets, insurance markets, and pension funds. Financial and capital market development is a major and robust growth determinant acting through several channels of transmission on saving and investment and, fundamentally, on productivity growth, as shown by a long literature (for example, Levine 2005). Deep pension reforms in many Latin American countries have replaced state-run pay-as-you-go pension systems with defined-contribution systems managed by private companies that invest pension funds both domestically and internationally. The latter systems contribute to financial deepening (and financial opening), improve domestic corporate governance, and raise aggregate efficiency. Hence, structural pension reform can contribute significantly to economic growth, as shown for the Chilean case (Corbo and Schmidt-Hebbel 2003).

The third key area of the region's development strategy is globalization. Latin America in general has deepened its trade and financial integration with the world economy. During the past two decades, the region has largely dismantled its massive historical barriers to trade in goods, services, and capital flows.

Latin American countries have made much progress in reducing import tariffs, eliminating most nontariff barriers, and putting in place a large number of multilateral and bilateral preferential trade agreements with major world trading partners. An open trade regime contributes to higher long-term growth by reaping the well-known benefits of improved resource allocation and helps to cushion the negative growth effects of adverse regional shocks (such as the 2008–09 recession in industrial countries) through a regionally more diversified trade pattern. The region's large progress in trade integration is reflected by an increase in its average total trade ratio to GDP from 32 percent in the early 1990s to 49 percent in the late 2000s (table 13.5). The countries that have progressed most in trade integration are Chile and Mexico—a result of their low general trade barriers and the fact that a dominant share of their foreign trade is conducted under preferential trade agreements. According to our findings, higher trade openness has a very significant and large effect on the region's growth performance. The drawback of this positive impact on long-term growth is that during recessions, when trade declines more than domestic output, shrinking trade ratios deepen domestic recessions; this pattern was observed moderately in 1998–99 and massively in 2008–09, according to our results.

Table 13.5. Trade Openness in Latin America, 1990–2009
Exports and imports as a percent of GDP

	1990–94	1995–99	2000–04	2005–09
Argentina	17.20	22.12	22.60	25.98
Brazil	15.45	20.44	22.36	27.40
Chile	49.72	60.85	68.41	83.56
Colombia	29.96	37.50	36.76	44.27
Mexico	27.26	40.47	53.32	60.89
Peru	26.00	32.74	35.43	40.56
Venezuela, R.B.	61.37	56.22	52.46	61.29
Simple average	32.42	38.62	41.62	49.14
Weighted average	22.64	29.53	33.74	39.77

Source: Authors' calculations.

Regarding financial integration, Latin America has complemented domestic financial liberalization with external financial opening: reducing restrictions on holdings, on inflows and outflows of short- and long-term foreign direct investment, on loans, and on portfolio and equity flows. Restrictions on short-term capital inflows—prevalent in some countries during the 1990s—have been abolished or not restarted in most countries. International financial integration leads to larger gross external asset and liability holdings, which contribute to more efficient resource allocation and better insurance against idiosyncratic national shocks and hence to higher growth and lower volatility in income and output. The region's progress in financial integration is reflected by a rise in the average total external asset and liability ratio to GDP from 88 percent in the early 1990s to 114 percent in the late 2000s (table 13.6). We have also found that higher financial openness has a very significant and large effect on the region's growth. However, while during the 1998–99 recession the GDP ratio of external asset and liability holdings increased, hence lessening the recession, the opposite occurred during 2008–09, when the significant decline of the latter ratio (reflecting in part the decline in capital inflows to the region) contributed to deepening the recession.

Despite considerable progress in applying a coherent and sustainable development strategy, Latin America still faces a large pending agenda of raising growth further and making faster progress in reducing poverty and improving income distribution. On growth, the region's main shortcoming is low productivity and slow productivity growth. The region has much room for improving the efficiency and competitiveness of domestic markets and for facilitating the process of creative destruction of firms. Labor markets are excessively regulated in the formal sector, leading to high structural unemployment and informal employment. Another area where the equity and efficiency costs of inadequate public policies are very high is in education, which is of very low quality. Although much progress has been made in school enrollment and educational attainment, Latin American countries still rank very low in international education achievement tests, even when controlling for per capita income. Public education suffers from low budgets, poor incentives, lack of accountability, and barriers to educational reforms aimed at improving teaching methods and raising teachers' productivity. Finally, regional growth is hampered by widespread government corruption and inefficient public administration. Government bureaucrats are selected largely on the basis of party affiliation instead of professional merit, resulting not only in the low quality of government bureaucracies but also in their short tenure, linked to government mandates. Notable exceptions are Brazil and Chile, which have introduced, at least partly, meritocratic hiring of government managers and staff. Hence, government reform at all levels—from municipalities to public enterprises and central governments—is also a major development challenge in the region's quest to attain higher growth and more equity.

Final Remarks

We conclude that Latin America changed significantly between the late 1990s and the 2000s. In this chapter's empirical results, we show that putting in place a better and stronger development strategy since the late 1990s has raised the region's growth rate. While there is still significant intraregional heterogeneity in economic regimes and policies, the predominant development strategy is based on the adoption of prudent and rule-based macroeconomic policies, deeper and healthier financial systems and capital markets, and strong integration into world goods and capital markets. Our results show that improvements in many specific variables associated with these three areas have led to higher average growth.

Table 13.6. Financial Openness in Latin America, 1990–2009
Total external assets and liabilities as a percent of GDP

	1990–94	1995–99	2000–04	2005–09
Argentina	78.47	103.80	176.51	147.57
Brazil	45.84	53.18	86.77	82.94
Chile	119.02	126.87	192.10	184.57
Colombia	51.70	61.62	87.07	78.97
Mexico	62.99	81.79	70.28	79.52
Peru	97.99	100.91	103.79	102.45
Venezuela, R.B.	156.85	131.10	145.50	122.00
Simple average	87.55	94.18	123.14	114.00
Weighted average	63.19	74.23	100.77	95.70

Source: Authors' calculations.

Moreover, adopting that development strategy has greatly improved Latin America's resilience in the face of adverse foreign shocks. According to our results, the last recessions suffered by the region were very different—in magnitude, in the role of foreign shocks, and in the contribution of domestic conditions and policies. The 1998–99 recession—of a smaller magnitude—was largely homemade, related to the weak macroeconomic and structural policy framework that Latin America had in place in the 1990s. In contrast, the second recession—much deeper and affecting all major Latin American economies—was largely due to deteriorating conditions in the world economy. The improved resilience of Latin America in the face of foreign shocks and world recessions is reflected in our results in four ways. First is the success in adopting macroeconomic policy regimes that better protect domestic economies against external shocks (like exchange-rate floats, lower foreign net liabilities, and higher gross international reserves) and strengthen adoption of countercyclical policies (like inflation targeting, contributing to lower inflation, and improved fiscal policy frameworks, reflected in lower public debts and deficits). Second is the success in building up deeper and healthier financial systems and capital markets. Third is the attainment of larger trade and financial integration. Finally are the indirect benefits of these improvements in reducing the sensitivity of growth to adverse conditions, reflected for example by the post-2000 reduction in the sensitivity of growth (that is, in growth coefficients) to inflation and political uncertainty and the increase in the sensitivity of growth to trade openness and exchange-rate floats.

Although much has changed in Latin America in the past two decades, many impediments to achieving higher and sustained growth and better opportunities for the poor still exist. An ambitious reform agenda for improving the region's business environment, labor market regulations, quality of education, and government efficiency has to be tackled to raise Latin America's efficiency and equity. Lack of progress in those areas could result in frustration with macroeconomic responsibility and structural achievements, creating conditions for further spreading of populist policies that have inflicted so much damage on the region in the past 50 years. To make significant progress requires significantly improving the quality and independence of the public sector, learning from the successful experience of countries like Australia, Canada, Finland, New Zealand, and Sweden.

Notes

1. Seasonally adjusted GDP data are from official national sources. The full database used in this chapter is available upon request.
2. Results are not reported here but are available on request.
3. Output gap series are built for each country using 2010–14 GDP projections from Consensus Forecast. Then we use the 1990–2014 quarterly country time series for past and projected future GDP levels to estimate trend GDP series based on the Baxter-King filtering method. The output gap is defined as the percentage deviation of actual (or projected future) GDP from trend GDP.
4. For simplicity, we use the term *percent change* instead of the more precise *percentage-point change* throughout this section.

Bibliography

Corbo, V., and K. Schmidt-Hebbel. 2003. "Macroeconomic Effects of Pension Reform in Chile." In *Pension Reforms: Results and Challenges.* Central Bank of Chile, Santiago.

———. 2010. "Is the Global Financial Crisis Different for Latin America?" Catholic University of Chile and Centro de Estudios Publicos, Santiago.

Levine, R. 2005. "Finance and Growth: Theory, Evidence and Mechanisms." In *Handbook of Economic Growth,* ed. P. Aghion and S. Durlauf. Amsterdam: North-Holland.

14

THE ECONOMIC CRISIS OF 2008–09 AND DEVELOPMENT STRATEGY: THE MEXICAN CASE

Jaime Ros

The international economic and financial crisis of 2008–09 has dramatically affected the Mexican economy. The contraction in economic activity and employment was considerable in late 2008 and early 2009. The fall in economic activity in 2009 was worse than the decline in gross domestic product (GDP) in 1983 in the wake of the 1982 debt crisis and was even greater than the drop in 1995 during the so-called Tequila crisis, which was the worst recession since the Great Depression of the 1930s. Mexico's contraction in output was by far the most severe in Latin America. In addition, the economic crisis of 2008–09 also caused a sharp increase in unemployment, underemployment, and poverty rates.

This chapter examines the economic crisis of the past two years in Mexico. The first section looks at the evolution of the main sectors of economic activity and the behavior of the components of aggregate demand, showing that the recession was largely an industrial recession led by the contraction in exports of manufactures. Comparing the economic performance of Mexico with that of the rest of Latin America puts in perspective the size of the external demand shock to Mexico's exports. The next section looks at the channels of transmission of the international crisis. The trade channel is certainly the most important but not the only one; the section also looks at the capital account shock caused by the "flight to quality" and the impact of the crisis on migration flows and remittances. The following section examines the fiscal, monetary, and exchange-rate policy response. It shows that while not quite procyclical (largely because the depreciation of the real exchange rate helped moderate the adverse effects of the external demand shock), the policy response could have done more to moderate the recession. The fiscal stimulus and the management of the interest rate were too cautious, given the size of the shock. Then the chapter brings together the conclusions of previous sections to explore why the crisis was so severe in the historical and international contexts, highlighting the role of the external shock and the domestic policy response. The next section looks ahead: the sharp output contraction was followed by a rather vigorous recovery in the third and fourth quarters of 2009. The section continues with a discussion of the changes in macroeconomic policy and development strategy that are necessary to sustain a faster pace of economic growth than that in the recent past. The final section offers some conclusions.

Dimensions of the Crisis

Mexico's economic expansion from 2002 onward came to an end in the first quarter of 2008, when the economy entered a recession that lasted over the following two quarters (table 14.1). Then, led by a precipitous decline in manufacturing production, overall economic activity contracted sharply in the fourth quarter of 2008 and the first quarter of 2009 (at annualized rates of 7.5 percent and 24.9 percent, respectively). Construction was also severely affected by the contraction of activity, while commerce and services largely mirrored the fall of total GDP. The turnaround began in the second quarter of 2009 and gained momentum in the third and fourth quarters, when total GDP grew at 2.5 percent and 2.0 percent over the previous quarter (at annualized rates of 10.4 percent and 8.2 percent, respectively). The recession thus appears to have been relatively brief but very

Table 14.1. GDP Growth in Mexico by Sector and Employment Indicators, 2008 and 2009
percent

Sector and employment indicator	2008 Q1	2008 Q2	2008 Q3	2008 Q4	2009 Q1	2009 Q2	2009 Q3	2009 Q4
Sectors								
Agriculture[a]	–0.5	2.8	0.1	0.4	–1.7	4.1	–1.3	0.9
Commerce and services	0.7	0.4	1.2	–2.5	–7.0	–1.5	4.9	1.0
Construction	2.9	–4.0	–0.1	–1.9	–4.0	–0.1	–1.2	–1.8
Electricity[b]	–2.5	–1.9	–2.5	0.6	1.3	0.5	1.5	–0.1
Manufacturing	1.0	–0.4	–1.3	–2.4	–11.9	1.0	4.4	5.9
Mining	0.8	–2.0	0.6	0.9	–0.5	0.2	1.8	–0.1
Whole economy	1.2	–0.4	–0.1	–1.9	–6.9	0.3	2.5	2.0
Employment indicators[c]								
Unemployment[d]	3.80	3.72	3.86	4.56	4.87	5.49	5.75	5.72
Underemployment[e]	6.75	6.55	6.86	7.25	8.38	10.16	8.99	8.93
Informal employment[e]	27.38	27.40	27.27	27.02	28.13	28.02	28.31	28.36

Source: Based on Instituto Nacional de Estadística y Geografía (INEGI), Banco de Información Económica, Indicadores de coyuntura (database), http://www.inegi.org.mx.
Note: GDP growth is seasonally adjusted. The percentages indicate changes over previous quarter. GDP levels are at 2003 prices. Q = quarter.
a. Includes livestock, forestry, and fishing,
b. Includes gas and water.
c. Quarterly average rates (seasonally adjusted).
d. Percentage of economically active population.
e. Percentages of employed population. Underemployment refers to the employed population that would work more hours than the current job allows.

deep, driven by the sharp contraction of industry and manufacturing in particular.

The recession led to a significant deterioration in employment indicators. The unemployment rate rose by about two percentage points between the second quarter of 2008 and the third quarter of 2009 (peaking at a rate of 5.75 percent) and started falling only in the fourth quarter of 2009.[1] The underemployment rate recorded a similar evolution, rising almost four percentage points and peaking at 10.16 percent in the second quarter of 2009. The share of unemployed and underemployed in the labor force thus reached a level of 15.65 percent in the second quarter of 2009. The share of the informal sector in the total labor force also rose and continued to climb in the fourth quarter of 2009.

Figure 14.1 shows the evolution of the main components of GDP. Clearly, exports were the component of aggregate demand that fell most sharply during the recession, collapsing at annualized rates of 50 percent and 21.9 percent during the fourth quarter of 2008 and the first quarter of 2009, respectively. From their peak in the second quarter of 2008 to the trough in the second quarter of 2009, exports fell 24.4 percent. Private investment was also severely affected and has yet to start a recovery, unlike exports, which began growing vigorously in the third quarter of 2009. Overall, public consumption and investment rose throughout the recession, despite small declines in public investment in the first quarter of 2009 and in public consumption in the second quarter of 2009. Taken together, the picture that emerges from table 14.1 and figure 14.1 on GDP by sector and the components of aggregate demand is one of a predominantly industrial recession driven by a collapse in exports.

Mexico's contraction in GDP has been by far the worst in Latin America (see table 14.2). The decline of GDP in Latin America and the Caribbean has been on the order of 1.8 percent, compared to a contraction of 6.7 percent in Mexico.[2] Mexico's output contraction was much greater than the contraction in world output (–0.8 percent) and greater than those in most regions in the world, comparable only, in fact, to that of the Commonwealth of Independent States (–7.5 percent) (see IMF 2010c). This severity is explained partly by the fact that, as noted, the recession in Mexico—driven by the collapse of exports and the shock to the volume of exports—was one of the worst in Latin America: a 14.3 percent decline compared to a fall of 9.6 percent for the region as a whole.

However, the size of the external shock may not explain why the recession in Mexico was the worst in Latin America. The difference in the size of the negative shock to export volumes in Latin America (an average of –9.6 percent) and Mexico (–14.3 percent) does not appear to justify the difference in the size of the decline of GDP (1.8 percent versus 6.7 percent), given that the degree of openness to trade is not much higher in Mexico than in Latin America as a whole (48.2 percent versus 58.9 percent). In addition, a few

Figure 14.1. Growth Rates of Components of Mexico's GDP, 2008–09

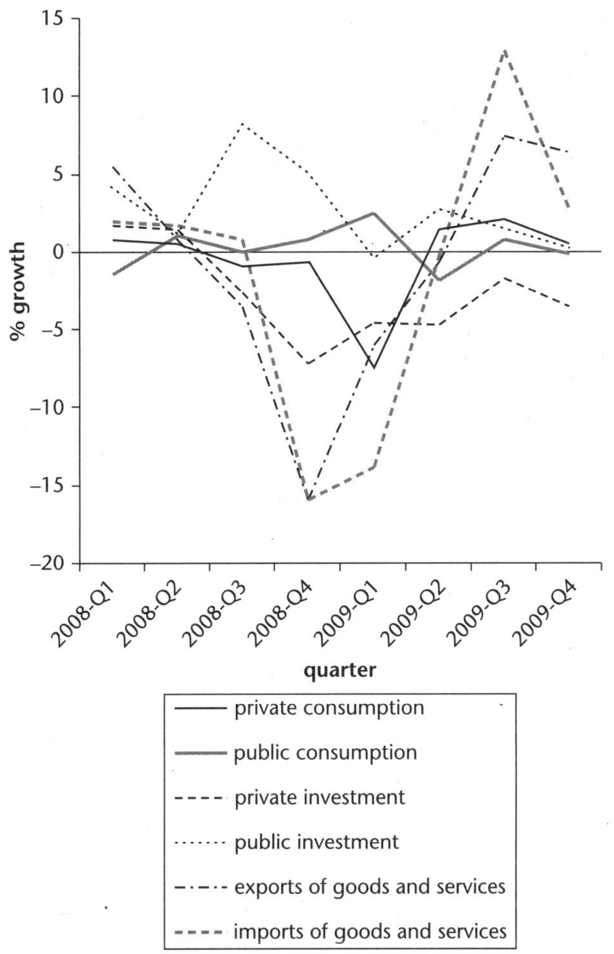

Source: Based on INEGI, Banco de Información Económica, Indicadores de coyuntura (database), http://www.inegi.org.mx.
Note: Data are seasonally adjusted. Percentage changes are over previous quarter. GDP levels are at 2003 prices. Q = quarter.

countries that experienced greater shocks to their export volumes than Mexico had more open economies but did not record the kind of output contraction that characterized the Mexican recession. The Dominican Republic (with an 18.1 percent decline in exports and an increase of 2.5 percent in GDP), for example, and Paraguay (with declines of 19.1 percent and 3.5 percent in exports and GDP, respectively) are two such cases. Nor did Bolivia and the República Bolivariana de Venezuela, with sharp contractions in export volumes, experience the size of the Mexican recession. Moreover, the shock to the *value* of Mexican exports is of the same order of magnitude as that for Latin America and the Caribbean as a whole and similar, or even smaller, than the shocks in several countries that recorded sharp declines in export prices (Brazil, Chile, Colombia, Ecuador, Peru, and the República Bolivariana de Venezuela). This puzzle will be addressed later, after we review the channels of transmission of the international crisis.

The Channels of Transmission

This section discusses the ways in which the crisis was transmitted to the Mexican economy. Consideration is given to both real and financial sector mechanisms.

The Trade Channel and the Collapse of Exports

Among the various mechanisms through which the international economic crisis has affected Mexico, the trade channel stands out, given that the United States, the epicenter of the world crisis, represents around 80 percent of Mexico's exports at a time when exports account for around 30 percent of Mexico's GDP (in 2008 at 2003 prices, INEGI database). The contraction in the value of total exports, coming largely from the fall in oil prices and manufacturing export volumes, proceeded at quarterly rates of nearly 20 percent in the fourth quarter of 2008 and nearly 14 percent in the first quarter of 2009. Indeed, the international recession brought about a sharp decline in the price of oil, one of Mexico's main export products, shown in a steep decline in the value of oil exports at quarterly rates of 50.3 percent in the fourth quarter of 2008 and 25.7 percent in the first quarter of 2009 (figure 14.2).[3] This fall affected not only the economy's terms of trade, but also government revenues and the fiscal deficit, given that Petróleos Mexicanos, (PEMEX), the state oil monopoly, is a major source of fiscal revenues (approximately 37 percent of the total in 2008).

Most important, the U.S. recession sharply affected export volumes, particularly manufacturing exports. The value of manufacturing exports (around 95 percent of non-oil exports and around 78 percent of total exports) fell at quarterly rates of over 13 percent in the fourth quarter of 2008 and the first quarter of 2009. Exports of the automobile industry, which make up around 22 percent of total exports (and 26 percent of non-oil exports), were particularly affected, with a contraction of nearly 38 percent in the first quarter of 2009 (compared to the previous quarter). The UN Economic Commission for Latin America and the Caribbean (CEPAL) has estimated that as many as 1.1 percentage points of the contraction of GDP in 2009 may be attributed solely to the *direct* effects (before considering multiplier effects) of the contraction in the automobile industry (around 35 percent), given the weight of this industry in total GDP (3.3 percent) (CEPAL 2009). Another important export-oriented sector that was severely affected was electrical and electronic products and equipment.

Table 14.2. Mexico's Balance of Payments, 2008 and 2009
US$, billions

	2008				2009			
	Q1	Q2	Q3	Q4	Q1	Q2	Q3	Q4
Current account deficit	2.9	2.0	4.3	6.7	1.2	–0.4	3.7	0.7
Capital account surplus	9.1	1.4	2.1	12.0	–2.7	–3.0	6.5	13.8
Foreign direct investment	6.4	7.2	3.5	6.1	4.0	5.1	1.6	0.7
Portfolio foreign investment	4.2	5.8	0.6	–5.8	–1.1	1.0	7.8	7.6
Assets in foreign banks	–4.2	–7.5	0.9	8.1	1.7	–7.1	–2.2	2.9
Other	2.7	–4.1	–2.9	3.6	–7.3	–2.0	–0.7	2.6
Errors and omissions	–0.2	2.3	–0.1	–3.2	–2.7	–2.0	–0.8	1.6
Change in reserves	6.1	1.6	–2.4	2.1	–6.6	–4.7	1.9	14.7

Source: INEGI, Banco de Información Económica, Balanza de pagos (database), INEGI, http://www.inegi.org.mx.
Note: Q = quarter.

Figure 14.2. Value of Mexico's Exports of Goods, 2008–09

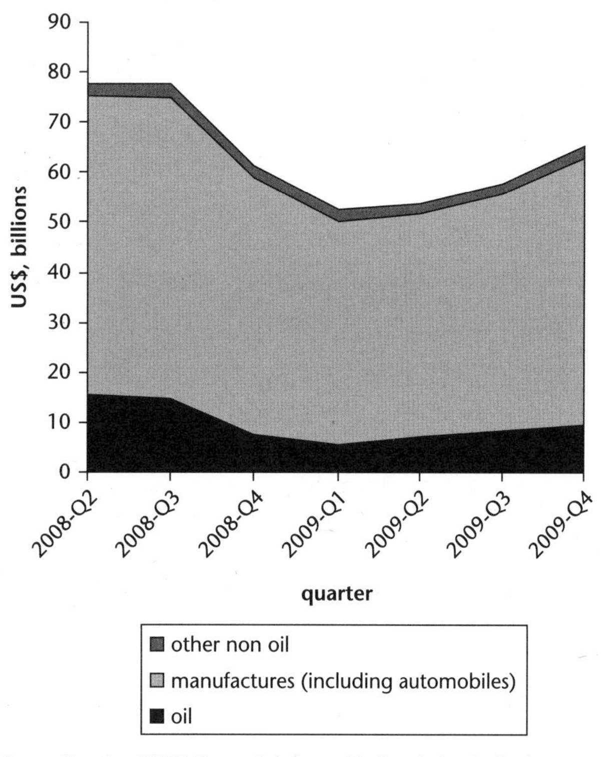

Source: Based on INEGI, Banco de Información Económica, Indicadores de coyuntura (database), INEGI, http://www.inegi.org.mx.
Note: Figures are seasonally adjusted. Current prices are provided. Q = quarter.

The Capital Account Shock and the Fall in Private Investment

In addition to the initial deterioration of the current account balance, the balance of payments was affected by the "flight to quality," the increased demand for safe foreign assets typical in situations of high uncertainty. As shown in table 14.2, portfolio foreign investment sharply declined starting in the third quarter of 2008 and only began to recover significantly in the third quarter of 2009. The fall in portfolio flows was especially deep in the fourth quarter of 2008, when the capital outflow reached almost US$6 billion. By contrast, foreign direct investment was much less volatile during the period of recession, and, adjusting with a relatively long lag to the output contraction, it declined significantly during the second half of 2009.

The flight to quality led to an increase in risk spreads that was wider than for many other emerging markets and to a significant depreciation of the Mexican peso. The risk premium reached a peak of nearly 600 points in October 2008 but fell afterward as a result of lesser risk aversion as well as a flexible credit line by the International Monetary Fund (IMF) (US$47 billion, March 2009), a swap line with the U.S. Federal Reserve (US$30 billion), and resources from multilateral development banks. Today, the risk spread has returned to precrisis levels.

In turn, the depreciation of the peso led to large unexpected losses on corporate derivative exposures, which caused financing difficulties for some large Mexican corporations from November 2008 to March 2009. These financing difficulties are likely to have contributed to the sharp decline in private investment, especially in the fourth quarter of 2008. Given the widespread ownership of the domestic banking system by global banks,[4] the negative direction of private investment may also have been affected by constraints on credit supply in the case of some global banks, derived from pressures on parent balance sheets.

Migration and Remittances

The crisis and recession in the United States have brought with them a sharp reduction in the net flow of migration out of Mexico, as the demand for migrant workers has fallen. Family remittances have also declined, to the extent that unemployment among migrants has increased with the U.S. recession. Indeed, the net migratory flow has sharply diminished. Mexico's National Survey of Employment and Occupation, which began in 2006, estimates that the net flow of migrants fell from 547,000 in the period February 2006 to February 2007 to 203,000 in the period February 2008 to February 2009, a 63 percent decline. This drop has been the result of a very sharp contraction in migration from Mexico in the face of a relatively stable migration to Mexico. It is worth noting that in the period November 2008 to February 2009 net migration even turned slightly negative (–1,000).

Since the reduction in migration flows took place during a severe recession in Mexico, the most likely factors behind the contraction come from the demand side (together with tighter border controls) rather than the supply side. The role of tighter border controls must also have been important, because the contraction in migration began before the recession.

More than 10 million Mexican immigrants are estimated to reside in the United States. They sent about US$26 billion back to Mexico in family remittances in 2007, the highest in the world after India. Although compared to other countries of outmigration (Central American countries, Portugal, and Turkey, for example), remittances as a percentage of GDP are relatively small at less than 3 percent of GDP, at their peak in 2007 they nevertheless amounted to around two-thirds of fuel exports and more than 100 percent of the net inflows of foreign direct investment (see World Development Indicators, http://data.worldbank.org). The contraction of migration flows and the recession in the United States have been accompanied by a decline in family remittances. They started falling in 2008 and sharply declined in 2009: a reduction of nearly US$4 billion, a 15.7 percent decline or around 0.4 percentage points of GDP.

All this means that the escape valve that migration has represented in the Mexican labor market—and its positive effects (along with those of remittances) on poverty alleviation—no longer has the important role that it has had in the recent past. As expected—given these conditions and the employment and income losses generated by the recession—unemployment, underemployment, and poverty have risen substantially in Mexico.

Other factors, of a domestic nature, further complicated the economic difficulties Mexico faced in 2009. One example was the case of the outbreak of influenza A (H1N1) in April and May of 2009, which paralyzed Mexico City (given the measures taken to address the epidemic) and had a significant adverse effect on tourism and the economic activities linked to it (hotels, restaurants, and commerce). CEPAL estimates the negative impact of the epidemic at 0.7 percent of GDP (CEPAL 2009) and the IMF at 0.5 percent (IMF 2010a).

The Policy Response

As discussed in the previous section, the crisis had both financial and real sector effects. This section examines the government response to them, focusing on fiscal policy, monetary policy, and the exchange rate.

Fiscal Policy

The impact of the global recession on Mexico's public finances was felt through a fall in oil revenues (2.1 percentage points of GDP), aggravated by a decline in domestic oil production and tax revenues (0.7 percentage points of GDP). According to the Ministry of Finance, the fall in government revenues was the worst in at least 30 years (SHCP 2010). Despite the balanced-budget rule, which severely constrained the use of a countercyclical fiscal policy in the face of this reduction in government revenues, the government managed to take a number of fiscal measures to respond to the impact of the global crisis. The program to boost growth and employment, initiated in October 2008, included a fiscal stimulus package aimed at increasing transportation and infrastructure investments.[5] The removal of long-term PEMEX investment schemes from the balanced-budget rule freed up some Mex$78.3 billion in the 2009 budget (or about US$5.5 billion), two-thirds of which was allocated to additional infrastructure investment[6] (see OECD 2009c; SHCP 2010). Overall, the fiscal stimulus for 2009 has been estimated at 1.5 percent of GDP by the IMF (see SHCP 2010) and at 1.4 percent of GDP by the Organisation for Economic Co-operation and Development (OECD) (OECD 2009c).[7]

The maintenance of a small budget deficit—or even a balanced budget when excluding PEMEX investment—in the face of a moderate increase in public spending as a percentage of GDP and a sharp fall in oil prices and tax revenues was made possible by a number of factors. First, the hedging of oil prices for 2009 at US$70 per barrel (twice the level at the end of 2008) generated savings of about Mex$118.4 billion (about US$8.5 billion). Second, as already noted, in 2008 the balanced-budget rule was amended to exclude the capital investments of PEMEX, an action that reduced budget expenditures and created a 13 percent increase within the budget for investment. Third, the depreciation of the peso increased the domestic currency value of revenues from oil exports. Finally, the government made use of nonrecurrent revenues in the oil stabilization fund and the operating surplus of the central bank for fiscal 2008 (SHCP 2010).

Monetary Policy

In industrial countries, a loosening of monetary policy generally began in the third quarter of 2008, and the same happened during the fourth quarter in some emerging-market economies. By contrast, in Mexico monetary policy was tightened at the beginning of the crisis in response to the capital account shock and the resulting exchange-rate pressures. The target interest rate of the Banco de México was increased by 25 basis points twice in June 2008 and again in July and August, remaining at 8.25 percent through January 2009. Then, as price pressures receded and the recession deepened, the policy rate was reduced in a series of steps starting in January 2009 (50 basis points) and continuing in February (25 basis points), March (75 basis points), April (75 basis points), May (75 basis points), June (50 basis points), and July (25 basis points), remaining thereafter constant at 4.50 percent. It is also worth noting the role of development banks in relaxing the credit constraints that resulted from the financial crisis by providing financing to the most affected sectors (Banco de Mexico 2010).

Exchange-Rate Policy

After a gradual appreciation of the peso that took it to around 10 pesos per U.S. dollar in July 2008, the foreign exchange pressures of the third quarter of 2008, derived from capital outflows and the shock to external demand, produced a rapid depreciation of the peso through February 2009, when the exchange rate reached a peak of around 15 pesos per U.S. dollar. The central bank then took a number of measures to reverse the depreciation and eventually stabilized the exchange rate at around 13 pesos per U.S. dollar. In March 2009, through an auction mechanism the bank started daily sales for US$100 million. These daily sales fell to US$50 million from the beginning of June to early September, when the announcement was made that the sales would continue until the end of September and then stop on October 1. In addition, daily auctions of US$250 million–US$400 million were undertaken at a minimum exchange rate 2 percent higher than the exchange rate the day before. Moreover, two measures to help bolster confidence during the global crisis were adopted: in October 2008 the establishment by the U.S. Federal Reserve of temporary liquidity swap facilities with the Banco de México of up to US$30 billion[8] (extended in February and again in June 2009); and the approval in April 2009 by the IMF of a flexible credit line arrangement, with no conditionalities, of approximately US$47 billion.

The real exchange rate followed closely, but with lesser amplitude, the evolution of the nominal exchange rate. Overall, the real depreciation of the peso was on the order of 20 percent between August 2008 and December 2009 and on the order of 11 percent between January 2008 and December 2009.

Why Was the Crisis So Severe?

To answer the question of why the crisis was so severe, one has to start by looking at the characteristics of Mexico's foreign trade. Since the early 1980s and later with the advent of the North American Free Trade Agreement (NAFTA), the processes of trade liberalization and international trade integration have gone hand in hand with an increasing importance of foreign trade in GDP, a rising share of manufactures in total exports, and a high concentration of exports in the U.S. market. The ratio of foreign trade to GDP rose from 27 percent in 1982–84 to 62.6 percent in 2004–06 (World Development Indicators, http://data.worldbank.org) as a result of a boom in imports as well as exports. This ratio is well above that of the other two largest Latin American economies (and in fact more than twice Brazil's ratio). The increase in exports was fundamentally a result of the boom in manufacturing exports. As a consequence, the share of manufactures in total merchandise exports rose to around 80 percent in 2008, compared to about 12 percent in 1980 (World Development Indicators, http://data.worldbank.org), when the export structure was dominated by oil (which then represented over two-thirds of total exports). Export concentration in the U.S. market increased significantly after NAFTA came into effect in 1994, jumping from 82.7 percent in 1993 to 88.7 percent in 2000. Since then, however, the export structure has diversified as all other regions increased their importance in Mexican exports, especially the rest of the Americas (which increased its share from 6 percent to 10 percent between 2000 and 2008). But dependence on the U.S. market continues to be very high, with the United States as the destination for more than 80 percent of Mexico's total exports of goods (figure 14.3).

New Vulnerabilities

These three features—a high degree of trade openness, a large concentration in manufacturing exports, and a high dependence on the U.S. market—have solved old problems: the excessively inward orientation of the economy before trade liberalization, the high dependence of foreign trade

Figure 14.3. Mexico's Exports to the World, 2008
% of total exports

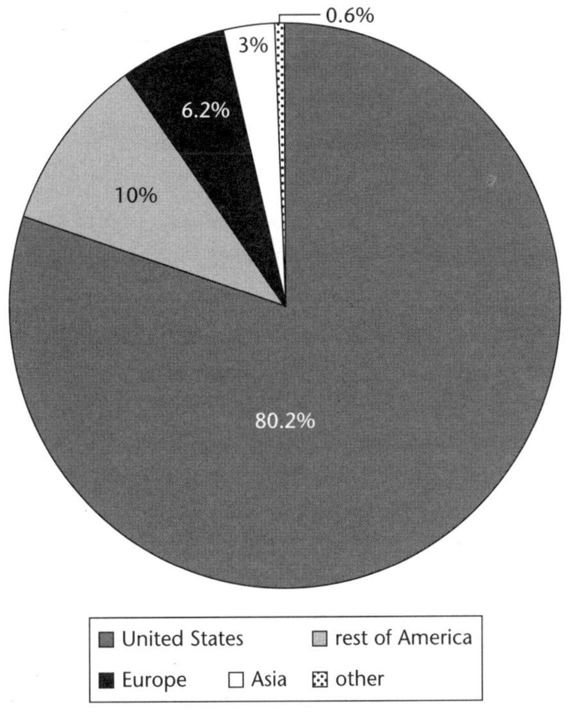

Sources: INEGI, *Estadísticas Históricas de México*, 2009; Banco de México, *Informe Anual*, 2008b.

on oil exports and high vulnerability of the economy to fluctuations in oil exports, and the failure to exploit the opportunities presented by proximity to the largest market in the world. But these features have at the same time created new vulnerabilities, which have exacerbated the negative effects of the external shock on the domestic economy. The high trade ratio enhances the impact on GDP of a fall in exports of a given product. Moreover, Mexico's exports are predominantly manufactures, in particular consumer durable and capital goods, and international trade in these products has been affected the most severely by the global crisis (SHCP 2010). In contrast, one consequence of the increased economic integration with the U.S. economy has been the synchronization of the economic cycles in the United States and Mexico (see Sosa 2008). The correlation between the GDP cycles in Mexico and the United States was above 0.8 in 1996–2008, while between 1985 and 1995 this correlation was practically nonexistent (SHCP 2010). The correlation between the cycles of industrial activity since 1997 is even greater (close to 0.99) (Esquivel 2009). Moreover, the industrial sector is more important in total GDP in Mexico than in the United States (30.3 percent versus 19.1 percent), so that for a similar fall in industrial output, the impact on Mexico's GDP is greater than that on U.S. GDP (SHCP 2010).

Table 14.3. Size of the Fiscal Stimulus as Percentage of GDP, 2008–10

Country	%	Country	%
United States	5.6	Netherlands	1.5
Korea, Rep.	4.9	United Kingdom	1.4
Australia	4.6	**Mexico**[a]	**1.3**
New Zealand	4.3	Austria	1.1
Canada	4.1	Slovak Republic	1.1
Luxemburg	3.6	Poland	1.0
Spain	3.5	Norway[a]	0.8
Finland	3.1	Portugal	0.8
Czech Republic	3.0	France	0.6
Germany	3.0	Switzerland	0.5
Sweden	2.8	Italy	0.0
Denmark	2.5	Hungary	–4.4
Japan	2.0	Ireland	–4.4
Belgium	1.6	Iceland	–9.4

Source: OECD 2009a.
a. Unavailable information for 2010.

The role of these new vulnerabilities should not, however, be exaggerated. First, these "vulnerabilities" become "strengths" in times of expansion of the U.S. economy. In particular, the composition of exports, strongly biased toward manufactures with a high income elasticity of demand, gives exports a very high dynamism when external demand grows. Second, because, as we show in the next section, Canada, where foreign trade has a similar importance and structure, suffered much less from the U.S. recession than Mexico, by reason of its different policy response to the crisis.

The Role of the Policy Response

The policy response also needs to be considered in explaining the severity of the crisis. Given the size of the external shock, Mexico's domestic policy response could have been more aggressive. The fiscal policy response, in particular, was timid. First, note that the size of the fiscal stimulus is one of the smallest among the OECD countries (table 14.3), while the size of the external demand shock was probably one of the largest. Second, the fiscal space available for a greater stimulus seemed to have been there. The central government debt as a percentage of GDP is on the order of 25 percent (2007), a very low value compared to other OECD countries. In a group of 20 OECD countries, only three (Australia, New Zealand, and Norway) had a ratio lower than Mexico, which in turn had less debt as a percentage of GDP than, for example, France, Germany, the United Kingdom, or the United States (OECD 2009c).[9] The balanced-budget rule and, probably too, fears that a larger fiscal deficit would have led to a deterioration in the country's credit rating prevented a greater mobilization of this fiscal space.

Monetary policy could also have been loosened earlier and more aggressively. The central bank's target interest rate was increased by 75 basis points in the second and third quarters of 2008, at a time when developed economies were well into the process of aggressively cutting interest rates (see, in particular, the case of Australia, Canada, and the Republic of Korea, countries with inflation-targeting regimes similar to Mexico's). Inflationary pressures, resulting largely from the increase in commodity prices in the first half of 2008, and fears that these pressures would lead to an upward revision of inflation expectations by economic agents were the main reason that the Banco de México increased the target interest rate (see Banco de México 2008a). Later, when in the first quarter of 2009 the central bank began reducing its target interest rate in the face of the sharp contraction of economic activity, it did so less aggressively than other developing countries with inflation-targeting regimes (such as Brazil, Colombia, and Peru).

The successful attempt to reverse the depreciation of the peso, after the exchange rate reached a peak of about 15 pesos per dollar in early 2009, is also questionable. With fiscal policy subject to a balanced-budget rule and monetary policy focused exclusively on price stability, the exchange rate is practically the only automatic stabilizer that the economy has when confronted by external shocks to aggregate demand.

A comparison between Canada and Mexico illustrates the overall role of the policy response in explaining the severity of the recession. As shown in table 14.4, both countries have nearly identical degrees of openness and concentration of their exports in the U.S. market. Yet, the recession was far more severe in Mexico than in Canada, where the fall of GDP (2.7 percent) was one of the mildest in the OECD area (where the overall decline in GDP was 3.5 percent). The difference probably has most to do with the more aggressive domestic policy response in Canada, where the fiscal stimulus package was far larger than in Mexico (4.1 versus 1.3 percent of GDP) and the reduction in the central bank's target interest rate more pronounced (table 14.4).

Table 14.4. A Comparison of Selected Economic Data on Canada and Mexico

	Canada	Mexico
Trade openness (%)	67.8	66.9
U.S. share of total exports (%)	77	80
2009 change in GDP (%)	–2.7	–6.5
Fiscal stimulus (% of GDP)	4.1	1.3
Reduction in interest rate in 2008 and 2009 (basis points)	450	300

Sources: Trade openness: Penn World table 6.3 (database), University of Pennsylvania, http://pwt.econ.upenn.edu; *U.S. share of exports:* Statistics Canada (database), Statistics Canada, http:// www.statcan.gc.ca; INEGI database, INEGI, http://www.inegi.org.mx; *GDP growth:* INEGI database, INEGI, http://www.inegi.org.mx; OECD Economic Outlook 86 database, OECD, http://www.oecd.org/document/18/0,3343,en_2649_34109_20347538_1_1_1_1,00.html; *fiscal stimulus:* table 14.3; *Interest rate reduction:* Banco de México, http://www.banxico.org.mx, and Bank of Canada, http://www.bankofcanada.ca.

Looking Ahead: The Crisis, Macroeconomic Policy, and Development Strategy

A vigorous recovery in the third and fourth quarters of 2009 followed the recession of 2008–09. The economy of Mexico, largely as a result of what has already happened, is expected to grow by about 4 percent in 2010. However, beyond the short-term recovery, Mexico faces the danger that without a number of policy reforms the economy could return to the lackluster growth performance that characterized the period 2000–2007, when GDP grew at 2.4 percent per year.

In the current strategy to put the Mexican economy on a path of high and sustained growth, the emphasis has been on microeconomic reforms in the labor market, the energy sector, competition policy, and other areas (see SHCP 2010, 6 and 7, for the government's reform agenda). In this strategy, macroeconomic policy reforms are hardly mentioned (with the exception of tax reform). It would appear that, according to this approach, all that macroeconomic policy can do to foster growth is to control inflation and thus that, even when inflation is low, inflation control must be its main, if not its only, objective. In effect, with macroeconomic stability (narrowly defined as low and stable inflation) having been achieved, macroeconomic policy can do little, if anything, to accelerate growth.

While microeconomic reforms in a number of areas are desirable in their own right, the disappointing growth performance in recent decades is probably not due to the lack of these reforms as often asserted (for a discussion of this point, see Ros 2008 and Moreno-Brid and Ros 2009, ch. 10). Thus, the currently dominant view fails to recognize that the lackluster growth performance of Mexico in recent decades has *macroeconomic* roots and that greater emphasis should be put on the need to reform macroeconomic policies to provide a more growth-oriented macroeconomic framework.

Growth, Public Investment, Procyclical Fiscal Policy, and Exchange-Rate Appreciation

A solid diagnostic of the lack of growth in the Mexican economy must start by recognizing that the slowdown in productivity growth that "explains," in a growth accounting sense, the growth slowdown of the Mexican economy in recent decades is largely an endogenous phenomenon, determined by the lack of growth itself and the resulting expansion of employment in the low-productivity sectors of the economy (see Ros 2008 and Moreno-Brid and Ros 2009, ch. 10). Rather than a deceleration in exogenous productivity growth, the proximate determinant of slow growth is the low rate of physical capital formation, which fell from 7.3 percent per year in 1960–81 to 4.0 percent in 1990–2008 and was only 3.4 percent for the period 1981–2008 as a whole.[10] The inability of capital formation to grow at a fast pace—after the years of decline during the debt crisis—has prevented the expansion of employment in high-productivity sectors and the modernization of productive capacity while at the same time constraining the growth of aggregate demand.

In turn, the proximate determinant of the reduction in the investment rate has been the contraction of public investment. While total fixed investment fell by almost 5 percentage points of GDP between 1979–81 and 2004–07, public investment fell even more (collapsing by 6.6 percentage points). Whether there are crowding-out or crowding-in effects of public investment on private investment is subject to controversy (see, for opposite views, Lachler and Aschauer 1998, who find a partial crowding-out effect, and Ramirez 2004, who finds an important crowding-in effect). There is, however, consensus on the view that, even if crowding-out effects exist, they are at worst partial; that is, an increase in public investment increases total investment rather than displacing fully an equal amount of private investment. It follows that the decline in public investment is partly responsible for the fall in the overall investment rate and may even have had an adverse effect on private investment (if crowding-in effects predominate).

The fall in public investment has partly to do with privatizations and partly also to do with the type of fiscal adjustment followed after the debt crisis. Mexico's macroeconomic adjustment was successful in correcting fiscal imbalances, in the sense of eliminating high and unsustainable public deficits. However, it relied excessively on the contraction of public investment and failed dramatically in the task of strengthening non-oil tax revenues. As shown by Giugale, Lafourcade, and Nguyen (2001), since 1980 fiscal deficit reductions have correlated closely with the fall in public investment (the correlation coefficient between the two turning out to be 0.82 between 1980 and 1997).

Infrastructure investment, which has the largest potential for affecting productivity growth and private investment, has suffered in this contraction. In the period 2001–06, Mexico was last, among the large Latin American economies for which information is available, in infrastructure investment as a fraction of GDP, in both public and private investment (figure 14.4). During that period, Mexico invested in infrastructure four percentage points of GDP less than Chile, the only country in figure 14.4 with an increase in infrastructure investment between 1981–86 and 2001–06. With the exception of Brazil, Mexico also stands out for having the largest contraction in infrastructure investment (50 percent). The fall in infrastructure investment took place in road construction, water provision, and electricity. Only in the case of telecommunications was there a recovery of investment in the 1990s. Even in this case, however, Mexico is today lagging behind other Latin American countries such as Brazil and Chile, which were behind Mexico in 1980 (Calderón and Servén 2004).

A second macroeconomic factor that constraints investment and growth is the tendency of fiscal policy to operate procyclically. This tendency has been amply illustrated by the available empirical studies. Pastor and Villagómez (2007) discuss the procyclical behavior of fiscal policy during the period 1990–2003, showing how the structural balance of the public sector increases in times of recession (1995, for example) and falls during expansions (1992–94 and 1999–2000). Other studies finding procyclical behavior in Mexico's fiscal policy are Talvi and Végh (2000), World Bank (2001), and Kaminsky, Reinhart, and Végh (2004).

The tendency of fiscal policy to be procyclical has its origin in the procyclical behavior of capital markets and in a very low tax burden, which implies that public finances continue to be very vulnerable to changes in volatile oil revenues. Moreover, the balanced-budget rule has further accentuated the procyclical character of fiscal policy. As is well known, maintaining a constant fiscal deficit through the business cycle exacerbates the economic cycle, because it ensures that the structural balance increases in recession years and falls during periods of expansion. Yet, this principle has inspired fiscal policy management during the past several administrations and was institutionalized in the legislation on fiscal responsibility approved in 2006.

The procyclical behavior of fiscal policy exacerbates the negative effects of shocks to economic activity and has adverse consequences on long-run growth. Indeed, a greater volatility in economic activity, with the corresponding increase in uncertainty, reduces the rate of investment and modifies the composition of investment in favor of short-term investments (with negative effects on productivity growth), while deeper recessions can have irreversible adverse effects on "learning by doing" and on workers' skills.

Figure 14.4. Infrastructure Investment by Selected Latin American Countries, 1981–86 and 2001–06

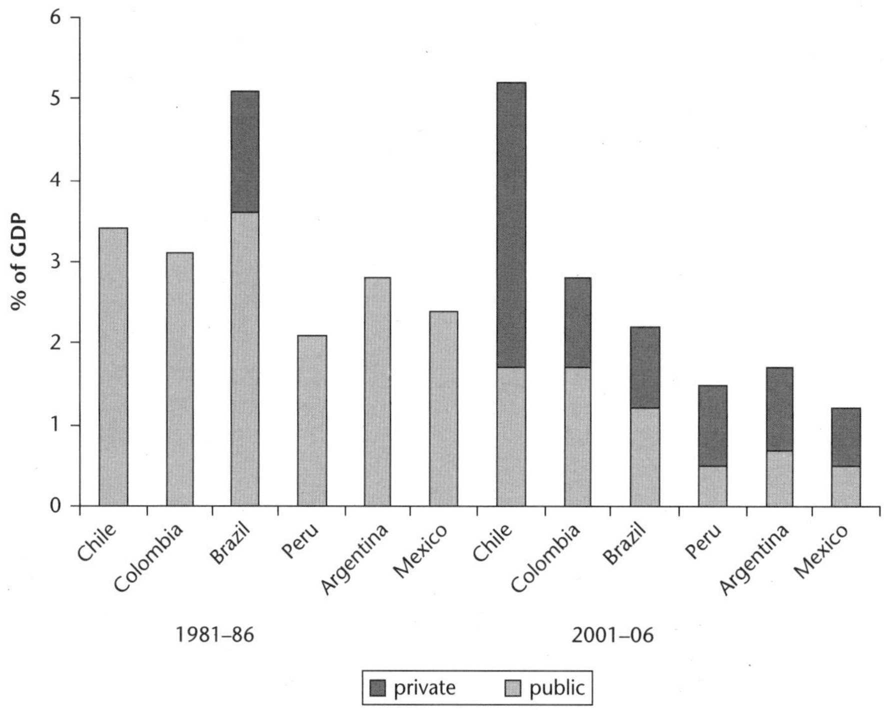

Source: Calderón and Servén (forthcoming).

The appreciation of the real exchange rate in 1988–94 and later in the period 2000–2007 further conspired against investment in manufacturing and more generally in tradable goods sectors. While real exchange-rate appreciation can encourage fixed investment in developing countries by lowering the relative prices of imported machinery and equipment, it also shifts relative prices in favor of nontradable goods sectors, reducing the profitability of the tradable goods sectors and inhibiting capital accumulation in these activities. Blecker (2009) estimates that the real appreciation of the peso between 1996–2000 and 2003–07 (a 9 percent appreciation) reduced Mexico's GDP growth rate by as much as 1.3 percentage points.[11] He also finds that an appreciated peso has had a more negative effect on growth since trade liberalization and especially since NAFTA took effect. Ibarra (2010) also finds a highly significant effect of the real exchange rate on investment even after controlling for industrial production and exports, suggesting, therefore, a very significant "profitability effect" of the real exchange rate.

The empirical evidence for other countries is also quite conclusive. Indeed, the relationship between the real exchange rate and growth has received much attention in recent years after the slow growth of many countries with overvalued real exchange rates and the extraordinarily high growth rates in countries that have deliberately undervalued their real exchange rate (as in China and, in the Latin American context and to a lesser extent, Argentina). As a result, today a large literature documents a positive relationship between a high real exchange rate and growth.

In this recent literature, the effect of the real exchange rate on investment profitability, already mentioned, is the main but not the only mechanism through which the real exchange rate affects growth. The impact of investment on growth is amplified by the greater productivity of invested capital, mainly in sectors subject to international competition (Polterovich and Popov 2002). Moreover, a high real exchange rate reallocates resources toward the tradable goods sectors, which present increasing returns to scale and whose expansion generates economies of specialization and technological externalities that are captured by the less dynamic sectors (Frenkel and Ros 2006; Rodrik 2008). Levy Yeyati and Sturzenegger (2007) highlight the increase in domestic saving that results from the redistribution of income in favor of profits derived from a high real exchange rate. In small and medium firms with limited access to external finance, the resulting increase in internal funds has a positive effect on investment. The increase in overall savings also tends to reduce the cost of capital for large firms that finance their investments in the capital market.

Although macroeconomic factors are not the only determinants of slow growth—broader diagnostics should also refer to the role of industrial policy and the lack of bank financing for productive activities (see, on the subject, Moreno-Brid and Ros 2009)—this analysis of the causes of slow growth in the Mexican economy suggests that a good deal of the economic policy agenda for growth should focus on the reform of macroeconomic policy.

The Reform of Monetary and Exchange-Rate Policy

Consider first monetary and exchange-rate policy. The empirical evidence seems to suggest that Mexico's central bank has adopted a strict inflation-targeting regime, focused exclusively on inflation targets, rather than a flexible framework that takes into account the output gap in the design of monetary policy (for a review of the evidence, see Esquivel 2009).[12] Some related evidence also shows that monetary policy reacts asymmetrically to exchange-rate shocks (tightening in the face of depreciations while not loosening enough in the face of appreciations) (Galindo and Ros 2008).

If one accepts that price stability is consistent with multiple configurations of real wages, interest rates, and exchange rate and that some of them are more favorable than others to economic growth, it follows that, without violating the constitutional mandate that requires the central bank to pursue price stability, monetary policy should seek such stability within the set of configurations favorable to growth.[13] Moreover, given that the configurations of relative prices that inhibit growth have often proved to be unsustainable, prudence dictates seeking price stability only within a context favorable to growth. There is thus a case for increasing the flexibility of the currently very strict inflation-targeting framework and its combination with some form of real exchange-rate targeting. Such a change would strengthen resistance to the temptation to use the exchange rate as a counterinflationary policy instrument, which is important for curbing the tendency toward real currency appreciation, and establish a competitive real exchange rate. This approach requires systematically avoiding exchange-rate overvaluation especially at times of recession: to avoid, that is, the implementation of a procyclical monetary policy such as the one followed in the early 2000s. More precisely, the central bank could promote a competitive exchange rate by establishing a sliding floor to prevent excessive appreciation (see Galindo and Ros 2008). This measure would imply managing interest rates or intervening in the foreign exchange market at times when the exchange rate hits the floor but allowing the exchange rate to float freely otherwise. Thus, under this alternative the central bank does not target a particular real exchange rate but only establishes a floor on it is value.

An objection to such a proposal is that by defending the floor the central bank loses control of the money supply and thus could fail to maintain the inflation target (for a fuller discussion, see Frenkel and Rapetti 2004). The problem arises at times of excess supply of foreign currency as a result, in particular, of massive capital inflows. It is worth noting, however, that speculative capital inflows will tend to be deterred to the extent that the central bank clearly signals that it will prevent the appreciation of the domestic currency, thus stabilizing exchange-rate expectations.[14]

Tax Reform and Public Investment

Relaxing the constraints on public investment leads directly to the issue of tax reform and the mobilization of the fiscal space given by low public debt. Despite recent attempts at tax reform by the Fox and Calderón administrations, non-oil tax revenues, at about 11–12 percent by the mid- to late-2000s, continue to be extremely low by international standards, well below those prevailing in OECD countries and even below those of Latin American countries with similar per capita incomes (see OECD 2007).

A priority area for investing the increased resources from a major tax reform is the development of the poor southern part of Mexico. A "new deal" that builds on the productive potential of the south and allows it to reach the level of development of the rest of the country would both generate further growth and reduce regional inequalities. This effort requires eliminating the regional bias that most public capital policies or development incentives have shown so far. Infrastructure investment in these regions and the introduction of positive discrimination in their favor in other policies would open up new areas of investment and new markets, thus liberating a growth potential that would contribute, for a considerable period, to a higher rate of growth of the economy as a whole (see, on the subject, Dávila, Kessel, and Levy 2002). Although there are no estimates for Mexico, the available estimates for Latin America suggest that the effects of such policies could be considerable. Indeed, using a cross-country regression framework, Calderón and Servén (forthcoming) estimate that growth in Latin America would rise by approximately two percentage points per year if the infrastructure development of each Latin American country were to rise to match the average among non–Latin American middle-income countries.

Toward a Countercyclical Fiscal Policy

Another aspect of the reform of fiscal policy refers thus to its procyclical behavior. The most frequently given justification for the adoption of a procyclical fiscal policy holds that governments characterized by their "fiscal excesses" in the past have credibility problems. As discussed in Casar and Ros (2004), in the case of Mexico this argument seems an exaggeration after four six-year administrations in which the principal banner of economic policy has been the achievement of "healthy public finances." Moreover, even if the diagnosis of a lack of credibility were true, the response should be to establish credibility rather than to continue with a practice that deepens recessions. One can think, for example, of institutional arrangements—such as a multiyear fiscal rule with a ceiling on public indebtedness as a proportion of GDP—that guarantee the stability of public finances over the medium term without eliminating the room for fiscal policy to maneuver in the short run (for a proposal in this direction based on the adoption of a structural balance, see Pastor and Villagómez 2007). The growth benefits of a countercyclical fiscal policy should not be underestimated, as suggested by recent research (Aghion, Barro, and Marinescu 2006; Aghion and Marinescu 2006) and its successful application in, for example, Chile.

It is worth noting that both the IMF and the OECD are advocating a reform of the balanced-budget rule. For example, in the most recent Article IV consultation the IMF staff report states:

> The balanced budget rule has been a key anchor, but there is a case for moving towards a structural rule over time. The current rule has built up the credibility of the fiscal framework. But moving to a structural rule would lower procyclicality and reduce the asymmetry inherent in the current framework. (IMF 2010b, 32)

Similarly, the OECD in the 2009 Economic Survey of Mexico states:

> Fiscal policy is highly dependent on volatile oil income. The balanced budget rule can create a bias for spending oil revenues as they are earned, especially as transfers to the stabilization funds are limited by caps at low levels. This can potentially lead to a pro-cyclical bias in fiscal policy . . . To better manage budget cycles and oil wealth, Mexico should establish a structural deficit fiscal rule. (OECD 2009b)

Is There Anything Wrong with Mexico's Insertion in the World Economy?

The emphasis on the low rate of investment in physical capital and the macroeconomic factors behind it as an explanation for Mexico's slow rate of economic growth in the postreform period suggests that other interpretations of Mexico's growth slowdown may be missing the point. The alleged incompleteness of microeconomic reforms is sometimes put forward as an explanation of Mexico's slow growth. This topic has been addressed elsewhere (see Ros 2008; Moreno-Brid and Ros 2009, ch. 10), where the argument is that the slow productivity growth rate, which is supposedly determined by the lack of microeconomic reforms, is in fact a consequence of the low rate of investment.

Mexico has integrated into the international economy as an exporter not only of oil but also of manufactures, both labor-intensive manufacturing (garment and assembly of electronic products) and medium- and high-technology intensity manufacturing (automobiles, metal, and mechanical industries). Thus, the share of manufactures in total exports climbed from below 20 percent in the early 1980s to nearly 80 percent today, at the expense of the share of oil exports, which fell from over two-thirds of the total in the early 1980s to less than 20 percent today. This transformation is remarkable in the international context. Today, the share of manufacturing exports in total exports is higher in Mexico than in several Latin American and East Asian countries.

Moreover, manufacturing exports have a high share of consumer durable and capital goods with a high income elasticity of demand. The technology intensity of Mexican exports has been increasing over time with the share of high-technology exports in total manufacturing exports reaching close to 20 percent by 2006. Although lower than that of China, Korea, Malaysia, and Thailand, this share is well above that of Argentina, Brazil, and Chile. A significant share of medium- and high-technology-intensive exports has also been found in other studies for the Mexican case (Moreno-Brid, Santamaría, and Rivas 2005).

It is also important to observe that among the major competitors in the U.S. market, Mexico is the only one that has not suffered a major decline in its share of U.S. imports in the face of the rapidly increasing participation of China. In fact, despite a slight decline throughout the 2000s, Mexico's share in U.S. imports was higher in 2001–08 than in 1994–2000. This position is in stark contrast with the decline of almost six percentage points in Japan's share or the fall on the order of two percentage points in Canada's share, the other major trading partners of the United States besides China and Mexico.

All this suggests that the pattern of integration with the world economy has not been a drag on Mexico's economic growth. In fact, the nature of Mexican exports should, if anything, have generated faster economic growth. Hausmann, Hwang, and Rodrik (2005) show that the level of technological sophistication of a country's exports relative to its per capita income is a good predictor of a country's subsequent growth, and it is clear from their findings that the level of sophistication of Mexico's export basket is relatively high, higher certainly than that of other Latin American economies with similar or even higher per capita income (Argentina and Chile, for example). In other words, Mexico has had poor growth performance in recent decades despite a rather favorable pattern of trade specialization.

Conclusions

The deep recession of 2008–09 in the Mexican economy confirms that shocks to U.S. industrial production constitute the largest foreign source of macroeconomic fluctuations in Mexico in the post-NAFTA period. The external demand shock caused a severe industrial recession led by manufacturing exports. It was further complicated by the collapse of private investment arising from the capital account shock and, less dramatically, by the fall in family remittances in 2008 and 2009. The recession was the most severe since the 1930s and the deepest in Latin America, a feature explained by the very close ties of the Mexican economy with the U.S. economy and also by the limited countercyclical response of economic policy, especially fiscal policy whose room for maneuver was constrained by the balanced-budget rule. By contrast, the depreciation of the exchange rate served as a cushion that made the collapse of exports less severe than otherwise and helps explain the early and vigorous recovery of exports and GDP since the second half of 2009.

A growth diagnostics exercise suggests that past development strategy has neglected the macroeconomic factors—such as low public investment, a procyclical fiscal policy, and a tendency toward the real appreciation of the peso—that are behind the lackluster growth of the economy in the 2000s. A redirection of development strategy should thus consider the reform of macroeconomic policies as a central ingredient of the reforms necessary to put Mexico on a path of fast and self-sustained growth. That goal implies the mobilization of the fiscal space, including tax reform, necessary to recover high rates of public investment, the establishment of a competitive and stable real exchange rate, and the move toward a structural budget rule that allows fiscal policy to act countercyclically.

Notes

1. The increase in unemployment is considerable, given that the unemployment rate is usually very low due to the definition of unemployment and the role of the informal sector as an employment shock absorber (see Frenkel and Ros 2004, for further discussion).

2. According to CEPAL estimates. The most recent Instituto Nacional de Estadística y Geografía figure for GDP in 2009 shows a decline of 6.5 percent.

3. The price of the Mexican oil export mix rose from an annual average of US$53.04 per barrel in 2006 to a peak of US$132.71 (July 14, 2008), falling thereafter to a minimum of US$26.23 on December 24, 2008 (SHCP 2010).

4. Foreign banks represent about 80 percent of the Mexican banking system (Sosa 2008).

5. The program also aims to ease credit to small and medium enterprises and a gradual reduction in tariffs applied to a wide range of goods between 2009 and 2013 (OECD 2009c).

6. Also worth noting is the national agreement in support of households and employment, announced in January 2009, although the main measures of this program, besides investments in infrastructure, are not fiscal policy actions but rather aim at improving the competitiveness of small and medium enterprises (OECD 2009c).

7. IMF (2010b) estimates the fiscal stimulus at 2.5 percent of GDP, but it is unclear if this is net of the budget cuts undertaken in the second half of 2009.

8. These new facilities also included the central banks of Brazil, the Republic of Korea, and Singapore.

9. In the nontraditional measure of the public debt—which includes the net debt of the federal government, nonfinancial public enterprises, development banks, official trust funds, liabilities related to banking sector restructuring, and PIDIREGAS—the ratio to GDP was 40 percent at the end of 2008 (OECD 2009c) and also quite low by OECD standards.

10. These amounts are based on estimates of the nonresidential net capital stock provided by André Hofman.

11. Other factors contributing to the fall in the growth rate (of about 2.1 percentage points between the two periods) were a slower growth of the U.S. economy and lower net financial inflows while a higher real oil price had a positive effect on the growth rate.

12. See, however, Villagómez and Orellana (2009) for an opposite view.

13. The mandate could of course also be changed to consider economic growth as an additional objective. The Mexican Senate is currently considering such reform.

14. When the increase in foreign currency is associated with massive inflows of family remittances or sharp improvements in the terms of trade, the challenge of avoiding a persistent real exchange-rate appreciation may be more complex but still manageable with appropriate interest rate management and intervention in the foreign exchange market.

Bibliography

Aghion, P., R. Barro, and I. Marinescu. 2006. "Cyclical Budgetary Policies: Their Determinants and Effects on Growth." Mimeo, Harvard University, Cambridge, MA.

Aghion, P., and I. Marinescu. 2006. "Cyclical Budgetary Policy and Economic Growth: What Do We Learn from OECD Panel Data?" Mimeo, Harvard University, Cambridge, MA.

Banco de Mexico. 2008a. "Informe sobre la inflación." Julio–Septiembre. http://www.banxico.org.mx.

———. 2008b. Informe Anual. Mexico: Banco de Mexico.

———. 2010. *Informe anual 2009*. www.banxico.org.mx.

Blecker, R. 2009. "External Shocks, Structural Change, and Economic Growth in Mexico, 1979–2000." *World Development* 37 (7): 1274–84.

Calderón, C., and L. Servén. 2004. "Trends in Infrastructure in Latin America, 1980–2001."Policy Research Working Paper 3401, World Bank, Washington, DC.

———. Forthcoming. "Infrastructure in Latin America." In *Oxford Handbook of Latin American Economics*, ed. J. A. Ocampo and J. Ros.

Casar, J., and J. Ros. 2004., "¿Porqué no crecemos?" *Nexos*. Octubre.

CEPAL (United Nations Economic Comission for Latin America and the Caribbean). 2009. *Balance preliminar de las economías de América Latina y el Caribe, 2009*. Santiago: CEPAL.

Dávila, E., G. Kessel, and S. Levy. 2002. "El Sur también existe: Un ensayo sobre el desarrollo regional de México." *Economía Mexicana* 11 (2): 205–60.

Esquivel, G. 2009. "De la inestabilidad macroeconómica al estancamiento estabilizador: El papel del diseño y conducción de la política económica en México." Mimeo.

Frenkel, R., and M. Rapetti. 2004. "Políticas macroeconómicas para el crecimiento y el empleo." Paper prepared for the International Labour Organization.

Frenkel, R., and J. Ros. 2004. "Desempleo, políticas macroeconómicas y flexibilidad del mercado laboral. Argentina y México en los noventa." *Desarrollo Económico* 173 (44): 33–56.

———. 2006. "Unemployment and the Real Exchange Rate in Latin America." *World Development* 34 (4): 631–46.

Galindo, L. M., and J. Ros. 2008. "Alternatives to Inflation Targeting." *International Review of Applied Economics* 22 (2): 201–14.

Giugale, M., O. Lafourcade, and V. H. Nguyen, eds. 2001. *Mexico: A Comprehensive Development Agenda for the New Era*. Washington, DC: World Bank.

Hausmann, R., J. Hwang, and D. Rodrik. 2005. "What you Export Matters". Working Paper 11905, National Bureau of Economic Research, Cambridge, MA.

Ibarra, C. 2010. "Capital Flows, Real Exchange Rate, and Growth Constraints in Mexico." Mimeo, Department of Economics, Universidad de las Américas.

IMF (International Monetary Fund). 2010a. "Mexico: Arrangement under the Flexible Credit Line and Cancellation of the Current Arrangement." Country Report 10/81. International Monetary Fund, Washington, DC.

———. 2010b. "Staff Report for the 2010 Article IV Consultation." IMF, Washington, DC.

———. 2010c. "World Economic Outlook Update: January 2010." IMF, Washington, DC.

INEGI (Instituto Nacional de Estadística y Geografía). 2009. Estadísticas Históricas de Mexico: INEGI.

Kaminsky, G., C. Reinhart, and C. Végh. 2004. "When It Rains, It Pours: Procyclical Capital Flows and Macroeconomic Policies." Working Paper 10780, National Bureau of Economic Research, Cambridge, MA.

Lachler U., and D. Aschauer. 1998. "Public Investment and Economic Growth in Mexico." Policy Research Working Paper 1964, World Bank, Washington, DC.

Levy Yeyati, E., and F. Sturzenegger. 2007. "Fear of Appreciation." Policy Research Working Paper 4387, World Bank, Washington, DC.

Moreno-Brid, J. C., and J. Ros. 2009. *Development and Growth in the Mexican Economy: A Historical Perspective.* New York: Oxford University Press.

Moreno-Brid, J. C., J. Santamaría, and J. C. Rivas. 2005. "Industrialization and Economic Growth in Mexico after NAFTA: The Road Traveled." *Development and Change* 36 (6): 1095–119.

OECD (Organisation for Economic Co-operation and Development). 2007. *Getting It Right: OECD Perspectives on Policy Challenges in Mexico.* Paris: OECD.

———. 2009a. *Economic Outlook: Interim Report March 2009.* Paris: OECD.

———. 2009b. *Economic Survey of Mexico 2009.* Paris: OECD.

———. 2009c. *OECD Review of Budgeting in Mexico 2009.* Supplement 1. Paris: OECD.

Pastor, J., and A. Villagómez. 2007. "The Structural Budget Balance: A Preliminary Estimation for Mexico." *Applied Economics* 39 (12): 1599–607.

Polterovich, V., and V. Popov. 2002. "Accumulation of Foreign Exchange Reserves and Long Term Growth." New Economic School, Moscow. http://mpra.ub.uni-muenchen.de/20069/1/ExchangeGrowth.pdf.

Ramirez, M. 2004. "Is Public Infrastructure Investment Productive in the Mexican case? A Vector Error Correction Analysis." *Journal of International Trade and Economic Development* 13 (2): 159–78.

Rodrik, D. 2008. "The Real Exchange Rate and Economic Growth." *Brookings Papers on Economic Activity* (Fall).

Ros, J. 2008. "La desaceleración del crecimiento económico en México desde 1982." *El Trimestre Económico* 299: 537–60.

SHCP (Secretaría de Hacienda y Crédito Público). 2010. *Weekly Report.* March 22– 26. Mexico City: SHCP.

Sosa, S. 2008. "External Shocks and Business Cycle Fluctuations in Mexico: How Important Are U.S. Factors?" Working Paper 08/100, International Monetary Fund, Washington, DC.

Talvi, E., and C. Végh. 2000. "Tax Base Variability and Procyclical Fiscal Policy." Working Paper 7499, National Bureau of Economic Research, Cambridge, MA.

Villagómez, A., and J. Orellana. 2009. "Monetary Policy Rules in a Small Open Economy: An Application to Mexico." Working Paper, Tecnológico de Monterrey, Monterrey.

World Bank. 2001. "Fiscal Policy, Business Cycles and Growth in Mexico: Fiscal Sustainability." Report 20236-ME, World Bank, Washington, DC.

15

THE INTERNATIONAL CRISIS AND DEVELOPMENT STRATEGIES: THE CASE OF CHILE

Roberto Zahler

During the past 25 years, the economic performance of Chile has been quite satisfactory. Although it is embedded in a relatively unstable region, far away from the great trade centers, this small country functions well, is open to goods and financial markets, and has a vibrant private sector.

Chilean Development Strategy

The allocation of resources in Chile takes place through decentralized markets. Most of the production of goods and services, as well as investment, functions within the private sector. As a productive agent, the state focuses on some specific lines of business, such as copper, petroleum, and railways, as well as other, less significant areas. Apart from its traditional roles, the state's action centers on regulating noncompetitive markets and on social areas for redistributive purposes.

The Chilean economy is very open to international trade and financial markets: the effective average tariff rate on imports is less than 2 percent, while goods exports and foreign direct investment (FDI) account for 31 percent and 9.9 percent of gross domestic product (GDP), respectively. Markets are able to operate with price freedom. However, the state intervenes in infrastructure industries that are subject to price regulations, such as electricity, telecommunications, and water, and also intervenes in oil prices through subsidies and indirect tax changes. Exchange rates, interest rates, and salaries are freely determined, with the sole exceptions of very sporadic interventions by the Central Bank of Chile in the foreign exchange market, the existence of a maximum conventional interest rate, and a minimum wage.

The state has contributed to increasing private sector participation in the economy through the privatization of public companies and the franchising of infrastructure works. This effort has enabled the private sector to build and operate highways, airports, prisons, and hospitals. The most important results for the past 25 years may be classified in the following categories: (a) macroeconomic strength; (b) commercial and financial integration into the world economy; (c) a sound financial sector; and (d) global competitiveness. In contrast, Chile's main constraints during this period have been the limited internal demand faced by domestic companies because of the size of the country, its per capita income, and its total factor productivity (TFP), which after having grown at very high rates until the mid-1990s, has experienced less dynamism and has stagnated during the past decade.

Macroeconomic Strength

During the past 25 years, the Chilean economy grew, in real terms, relatively quickly, with some variation in subperiods (table 15.1). In 1986–90 (the recovery period following the profound crisis suffered by the Chilean economy in the early 1980s), the annual average growth of GDP was 6.8 percent. Then, from 1991 to 1995 that rate accelerated

I would like to thank Hermann Gonzalez for his contribution to and comments on this chapter.

Table 15.1. Basic Macroeconomic Data for Chile, 1986–2009

	1986–90	1991–95	1996–2000	2001–05	2006–09
GDP growth (year-on-year, %)	6.8	8.7	4.2	4.2	2.7
Inflation rate (average, %)	19.4	14.0	5.2	2.6	4.5
Fiscal balance (% of GDP)	1.3	2.0	0.4	0.9	4.4
Investment rate (% of GDP)	15.4	19.2	21.5	21.1	26.3
International reserves (% of imports)	83.3	100.6	92.5	79.7	49.2
External debt (% of GDP)	77.2	39.1	40.1	51.8	38.3
Unemployment rate (%)	9.7	7.3	7.7	9.7	8.1

Source: Zahler & Co., based on data from the Central Bank of Chile and the Instituto Nacional de Estadísticas: Statistics Database, Central Bank of Chile, Santiago, http://www.bcentral.cl; and online database, Instituto Nacional de Estadísticas, Santiago, http://www.ine.cl.

to 8.7 percent. Subsequently, as a consequence of the Asian crisis and the domestic policy response to it, during the following two five-year periods the economy's economic growth fell to an annual average of 4.2 percent, and from 2006 to 2009 GDP growth fell further, to only 2.7 percent, a figure determined by the international financial crisis. GDP growth of 4.5–5.0 percent is expected for 2010, as a result of an improved external scenario, expansionary fiscal and monetary conditions, and the reestablishment of confidence among entrepreneurs and consumers.

Chilean inflation was, until the late 1980s, historically and chronically high and volatile. In 1990, the central bank became autonomous, and since then the 12-month inflation rate has fallen continuously from levels higher than 20 percent in the early 1990s to an annual average of 2.6 percent in 2001–05, well within the range the central bank established as the inflation target (2–4 percent). The years 2007 and 2008 were characterized by higher annual inflation—close to 10 percent in 2008—as a consequence of the various supply shocks affecting international food and fuel prices, with strong repercussions for domestic prices. But since late 2008 and throughout 2009, 12-month inflation dropped quite strongly, becoming negative for many months. It is expected that during the inflation target period set by the central bank (24 months), it will return to the target.

Management of public finances has been prudent, and, on average, during the past 25 years all five-year subperiods have recorded a surplus. In addition, in the past nine years the public sector has been able to play a countercyclical role without jeopardizing medium-term fiscal indicators. In 2001, Chile adopted a rule of targeting a structural budget surplus as a percentage of GDP. That surplus reflects the level of fiscal revenues and spending if GDP were at its potential level and the international price of copper were at its long-term trend. Chile took another important step forward in this direction in 2006 by approving the Fiscal Responsibility Law. This law allowed for setting up two sovereign wealth funds and establishing the basic institutional framework necessary for their management. The Pension Reserve Fund, created at the end of 2006, was established to finance minimum pensions; and the Economic and Social Stabilization Fund, launched in early 2007, was set up to finance other spending and public investment in the future.

Fiscal income, particularly that resulting from the high international price of copper, led to the accumulation of significant surpluses between 2004 and 2008—5.7 percent of average GDP—a trend that came to an abrupt stop in 2009. That year recorded a fiscal deficit of 4.5 percent of GDP as a consequence of the international crisis, which implied a significant drop in fiscal income and required an important increase in public spending to partially compensate for the fall of both external and internal private demand.

The economy's investment rate, measured in real terms, has increased significantly from the late 1980s, reaching over 20 percent of GDP during the past 25 years. Before the 2008–09 international crisis, the investment rate reached an important benchmark, coming close to 30 percent of GDP in 2008.

International reserves fluctuated in the range of US$14 billion–US$16 billion from 1994 to 2004, equivalent to just under a year of the country's goods imports. Subsequently, they vastly increased, surpassing US$25 billion in 2009. However, the strong rise in imports during the last five-year period implied a reduction in the ratio of reserves to imports, to half the average of the previous 20 years.

Chilean external debt dropped considerably from the early 1990s, when it was equivalent to 90 percent of GDP. By the end of 2009, it amounted to US$74 billion (47 percent of GDP). Only 3 percent corresponds to the public sector and is mainly a long-term obligation. The rest originated in the private sector, including 21 percent owed by banks. Seventy-six percent of Chile's total external debt corresponds to foreign commitments by nonbanking private enterprises.

On average, the unemployment rate has remained relatively high. Only during the most dynamic growth period, in the first half of the 1990s, did it drop to around 6 percent. However, the low GDP growth in the past three five-year periods contributed to the increase in the unemployment rate once more. In fact, immediately after the Asian crisis, Chile's unemployment rose to approximately 10 percent. Only from 2006 to 2008 did it fall again, averaging 7.6 percent. In 2009, as a consequence of the international crisis it increased again, reaching approximately 11 percent in some months.

Most of the literature that has analyzed this increase in Chile's unemployment highlights two considerations. The first is international and consists of successive external shocks that affected the Chilean economy after the Asian crisis, such as a fall in the country's terms of trade, the impact of the 9/11 attack on the United States, and the turbulence affecting Argentina and Brazil, among others. The second is a local consideration, associated with rigidities in the labor market that impede adjustment through a lowering of real wages.

The empirical evidence suggests that labor market rigidities in Chile are stronger than in Argentina and Mexico as well as in most East Asian countries. In Chile, wages respond little to an increase in unemployment and to negative external shocks. In the years following the Asian crisis, many workers, especially those with low education and qualifications and little labor experience, were affected by strong increases in the minimum wage. Furthermore, nominal wages in Chile are generally indexed to changes in the consumer price index so that inflationary (or deflationary) surprises have little impact on real wages. In addition, wage contracts tend to have a two-year duration, reducing their ability to react quickly to changes in economic conditions, thus further contributing to wage rigidity. Chile also has a relatively high minimum wage.

Figure 15.1. Effective Average Tariff on Chilean Imports, 1998–2009
percent

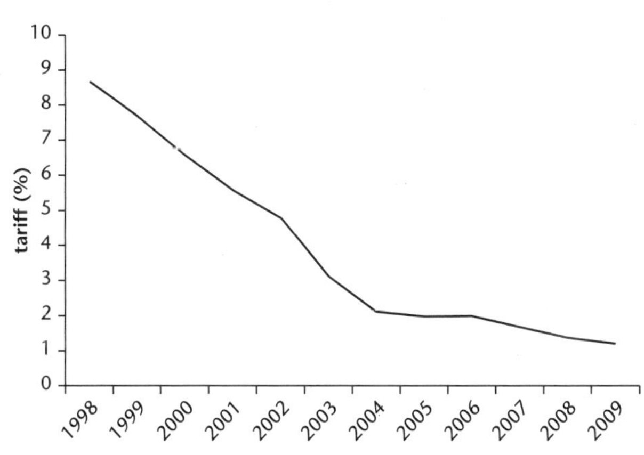

Source: Cámara de Comercio de Santiago, Santiago, http://www.ccs.cl/.

Integration into the World Economy

An important part of Chile's economic success is due to growth and diversification of its exports, especially with respect to their destinations. This result came about initially when Chile dismantled most quantitative import restrictions and began a process of continuously reducing import tariffs (figure 15.1). That process was reinforced later by an increasing number of free trade agreements, which include China, the European Union (EU), Mexico, and the United States, among others.

In fact, exports have been one of the main sources of growth in the Chilean economy. Figure 15.2 shows the ratio of the growth of exports of goods and services, in real terms, to the growth of GDP, also in real terms. In the period 1987–2009, excluding the crisis years of 1999 and 2009, on average the real rate of growth of exports exceeded by 1.4 times the average rate of growth of GDP. Too little evidence is available to analyze contraction periods, because the only year in which exports fell, in real terms, was 2009. During the recession of 1999, Chilean GDP fell by 0.7 percent, while exports increased by 7.3 percent. In 2009, both GDP and exports fell, by 1.5 percent and 5.6 percent, respectively.

Financial opening up to the international economy was initially executed gradually, selectively, and pragmatically. This approach partly explains why the major crises that took place in the 1990s—such as the Mexican ("tequila") crisis and the Russian crisis—had a minimal effect on the Chilean economy. Financial openness is reflected in the growing flows of capital to and from the country, bank financing, and other sources of funding and foreign investment. FDI is not discriminatory with respect to residents' investments. In the past 10 years, FDI averaged 6.6 percent of Chile's GDP, reaching a maximum of 9.9 percent in 2008. FDI is present in many sectors of economic activity, including mining, industry, finance (banks and insurance companies), energy, telecommunications, and highways.

Chilean companies began to invest directly abroad in the early 1990s, the annual peak coming in 2000, when it represented 5.3 percent of GDP; the average of the past 10 years was 2.7 percent of GDP. Most of Chilean FDI abroad is in Latin America—mainly Argentina, Brazil, Colombia, and Peru—and is concentrated in retail, energy, financing, and cellulose.

Figure 15.2. Growth in Exports of Chilean Goods and Services Relative to GDP, 1987–2009

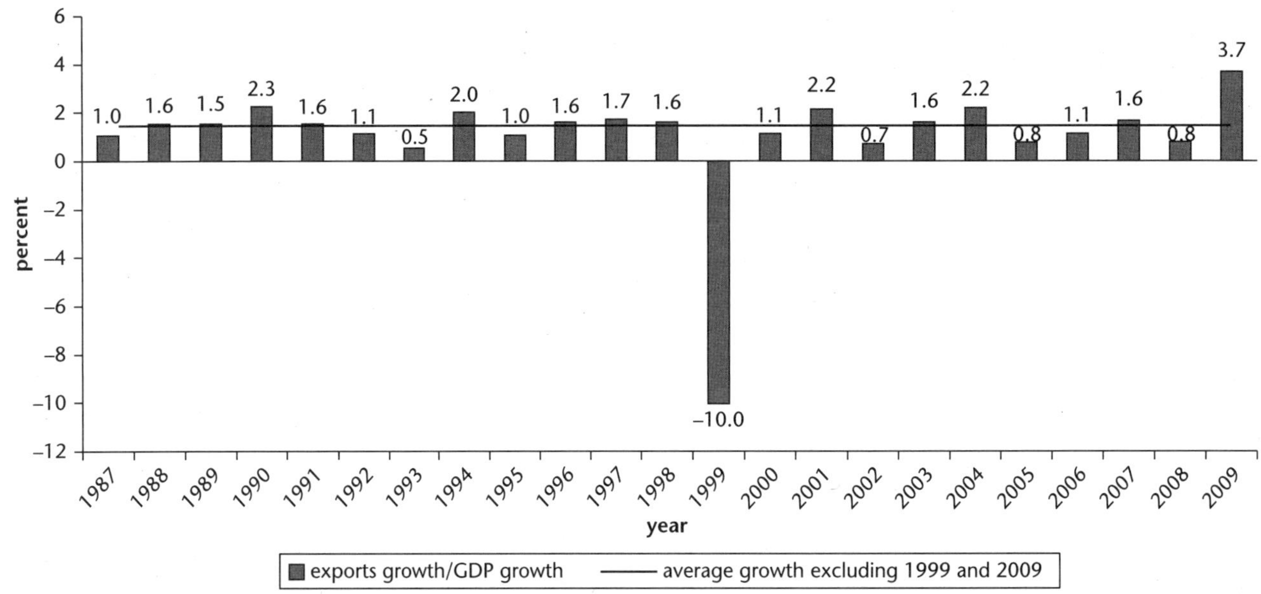

Source: Zahler & Co., based on data from the Central Bank of Chile: Statistics Database, Central Bank of Chile, Santiago, http://www.bcentral.cl.

In addition, the country's financial investment abroad is quite significant, through both the sovereign wealth funds and the private pension funds. Foreign investments in private pension funds are concentrated in stocks and bonds. By the end of 2009, they amounted to around US$52 billion, which represents 44 percent of total pension fund assets and 33 percent of Chile's GDP.

Sound Financial Sector

Following the deep economic crisis of 1982–83, regulation and supervision have been great strengths in the Chilean financial system. As the system has developed and become more professional, legislation and regulations have been adjusted and modernized.

One significant asset of the Chilean economy in the past 25 years is the dynamism and strength of its banking system. From 1995 to 2009, total bank loans grew at an annual real average rate of 9.3 percent. By the end of 2009, the proportion of total past due loans amounted to only 1.35 percent, and the system's average capitalization index (Basel Index) was 14.3 percent.

In the early 1980s, social security was reformed from a pay-as-you-go system to one of individual capitalization. This reform created institutional investors, which have since been a major source of demand for long-term financial instruments and have thus helped develop the domestic capital market. That market also benefited from the generalized use of price indexation in financial agreements (inflation-indexed financial contracts), the presence of institutional investors (mainly private pension funds and life insurance companies), and a housing finance circuit. All this has meant that much of the domestic financial savings invested in Chile becomes productive investment in the real sector of the Chilean economy.

Obstacles to Growth

Three main factors have limited Chile's economic growth. First, Latin America has been unstable economically and politically; that instability affects capital flows to the region and the demand for Chilean exports, of which 16 percent are shipped to the region.

Second, the size of the country (GDP of US$157 billion in 2009), together with its per capita income, limits internal markets and forces companies to sell abroad to exploit economies of scale and create efficiency gains. As a result, the local economy depends heavily on the health of the global economy.

A third element that has restricted economic growth, particularly in the past decade, is low growth in TFP. Although macroeconomic reforms and a policy framework based on sound and countercyclical fiscal policy, inflation targeting, and a free exchange rate have contributed to overall stability and to a reduction in the country's vulnerability to shocks, the slower rate of microeconomic reforms has limited growth.

World Economic Cycle and Chile's Growth

Its high degree of financial and commercial openness implies that Chile is very dependent on the world economy and especially on the country's main commercial partners. Therefore, a strong and widespread international recession, such as the one that took place in 2008–09, is almost sure to have a negative impact on Chile's economic growth.

In addition to being very open to world trade, Chile has been the biggest producer of copper in the world since 1982. Nearly 98 percent of Chilean copper output is exported, and copper has represented, depending on its price, from a third to a half of total Chilean exports. In the four major international crises of the past 40 years, the real copper price has dropped significantly (figure 15.3). In magnitude and speed of adjustment, the 2009 shock resembles that of the mid-1970s. In fact, in the mid-1970s, the real copper price fell 64 percent in nine months. Subsequently, in the early 1980s, the copper price fell 62 percent, but the drop was much smoother, lasting 28 months, from March 1980 to June 1982. During the Asian crisis, the real copper price fall was lower (47 percent) and took place over 21 months, from July 1997 to March 1999. In the latest crisis, the real price of copper fell 63 percent in only eight months.

Recent fiscal policy has reduced the impact of fluctuations in international copper prices on the Chilean economic cycle. In fact, Chilean fiscal policy—accompanied by coherent monetary and exchange-rate policies—has played a key stabilizing role in the Chilean economy since 2002. Therefore, it is not surprising that Chile's GDP growth rate in 2008–10 was lower than that registered in past episodes of high international copper prices (when the fiscal rule was nonexistent). The same stabilizing effect allowed the Chilean economy to grow, on average, more than 3 percent at the beginning of the current decade, when the real price of copper was the lowest since the Great Depression. In short, although Chile is very much affected by the international economy, it now depends much less on fluctuations in the international copper price.

Table 15.2 shows GDP growth rates in three recession episodes: 1982–83, the 1998–99 Asian crisis, and the most recent crisis of 2008–09. During 1982–83, world GDP grew 1.9 percent in purchasing power parity terms, and in 1982 world GDP growth was only 1.2 percent. In that crisis, only Latin American economies (where the crisis originated) suffered a drop in GDP. The 1998–99 crisis appears, by far, to have had the least severe effect on world GDP, which grew at an annual average of 3.1 percent. The 2008–09 recession is the most severe of these three episodes, resulting in an annual average world GDP growth of only 1.2 percent and a fall in GDP of 0.6 percent in 2009. In this recession, the unprecedented decline in GDP of developed countries and the 1.8 percent drop suffered by Latin American countries in 2009 also stand out, comparable only to the occurrence in 1983.

Figure 15.4 shows the annual rate of change of Chilean GDP, compared with that of the world and with selected economic regions. During the 1980s and 1990s, Chilean growth significantly differs—both in its level and its volatility—from the rest. It is clear that in the early 1980s

Figure 15.3. Nominal and Real Price of Copper in Chile, 1960–2010

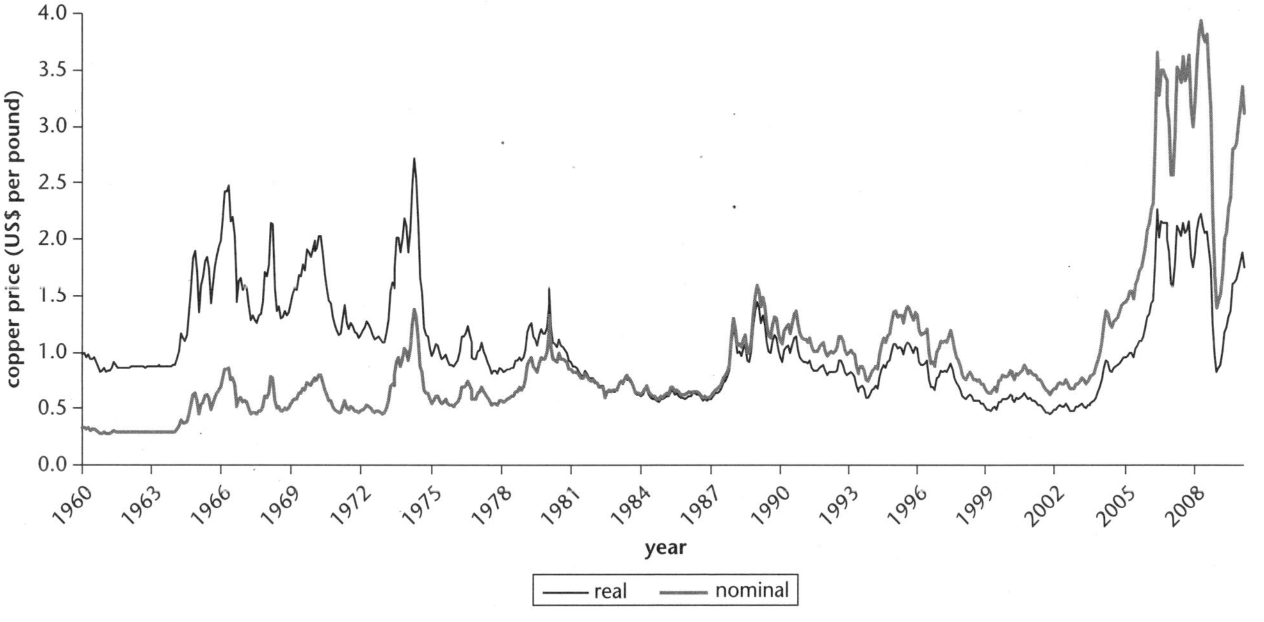

Source: Zahler & Co., based on data from the Central Bank of Chile: Statistics Database, Central Bank of Chile, Santiago, http://www.bcentral.cl.

Table 15.2. World GDP Growth in Recessions, 1982–83, 1998–99, and 2008–09

	1982	1983	1982–83 average	1998	1999	1998–99 average	2008	2009	2008–09 average
World	0.9	2.9	1.9	2.6	3.6	3.1	3.0	–0.6	1.2
Major advanced economies (G-7)	–0.1	3.2	1.6	2.7	3.3	3.0	0.2	–3.4	–1.6
Emerging and developing economies	2.2	2.7	2.4	2.5	3.5	3.0	6.1	2.4	4.3
Western Hemisphere	–0.6	–2.5	–1.6	2.3	0.4	1.4	4.3	–1.8	1.3

Source: Zahler & Co., based on purchasing-power parity data from the IMF: International Financial Statistics (database), IMF, Washington, DC, http://www.imfstatistics.org.
Note: G-7 = Group of Seven (Canada, France, Germany, Italy, Japan, the United Kingdom, and the United States).

Figure 15.4. Growth of GDP in Chile and Selected Country Groups, 1980–2009

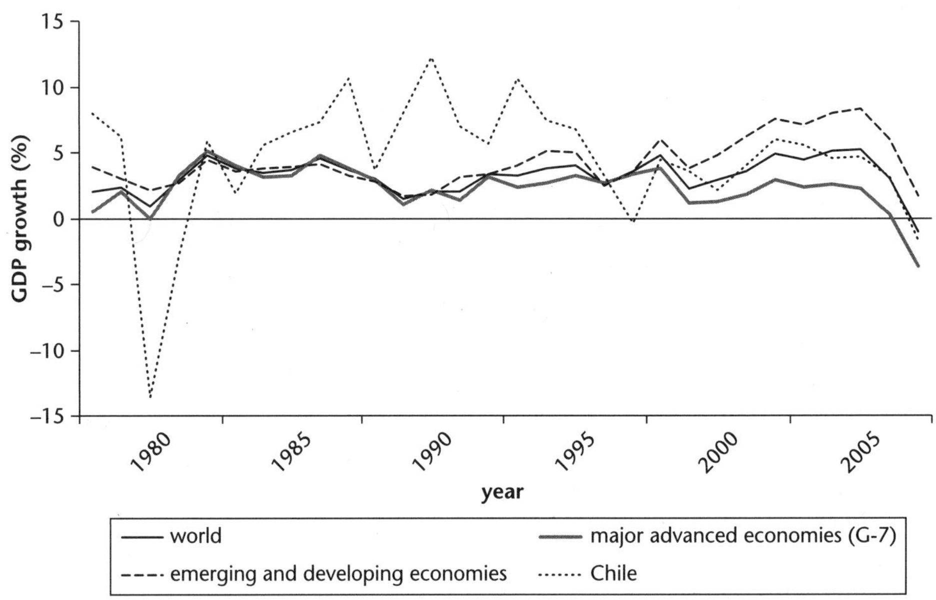

Source: Zahler & Co., based on International Monetary Fund (IMF) data: International Financial Statistics (database), IMF, http://www.imfstatistics.org.
Note: G-7 = Group of Seven (Canada, France, Germany, Italy, Japan, the United Kingdom, and the United States).

and late 1990s, the contraction of Chile's growth was greater than in all the regions considered. Particularly relevant is what happened in 1982, when Chile's GDP fell close to 14 percent, while world GDP grew by 0.9 percent and the Latin American region as a whole suffered a contraction of only 0.6 percent. However, Chile's recovery from that crisis was quite rapid, and during the rest of the 1980s it grew at a much higher rate than the rest of Latin America.

In the past 10 years, Chile's growth rate has been very similar to that of the world as a whole. In 2009, Chile's 1.5 percent fall compares to a decrease of 0.6 percent of world GDP and is clearly lower than the contraction suffered by developed countries, where the crisis originated. Even with the data from the 1960s, it is possible to observe that, with the greatest external crisis of the past 60 years and with the country's increasing financial and commercial integration into the international economy, Chile's performance in 2009 was much less negative than in the previous world recessions (figure 15.5). The 1.5 percent drop in Chile's GDP in 2009 compares with drops in its GDP of around 13 percent to 14 percent in both 1975 and 1982. Part of this improved performance is explained by the different macroeconomic policy frameworks prevailing in the three episodes and, especially, the capacity of the Chilean economy to apply countercyclical monetary and fiscal policies in the most recent crisis.

Despite the increasing commercial and financial integration of the Chilean economy, the volatility of its GDP has been falling since the mid-1980s (figure 15.6). During the 1998–99 crisis, GDP volatility temporarily increased, but its level was still less than half that experienced in the 1970s and 1980s. And volatility continued to fall in the recent crisis.

Figure 15.7 shows Chile's real seasonally adjusted GDP for 1998–2000 and 2008–09. With the quarter in which GDP reached its maximum precrisis level as a starting point (the second quarter of 1998 and the second quarter

Figure 15.5. World, Latin American, and Chilean Growth in GDP, 1961–2009

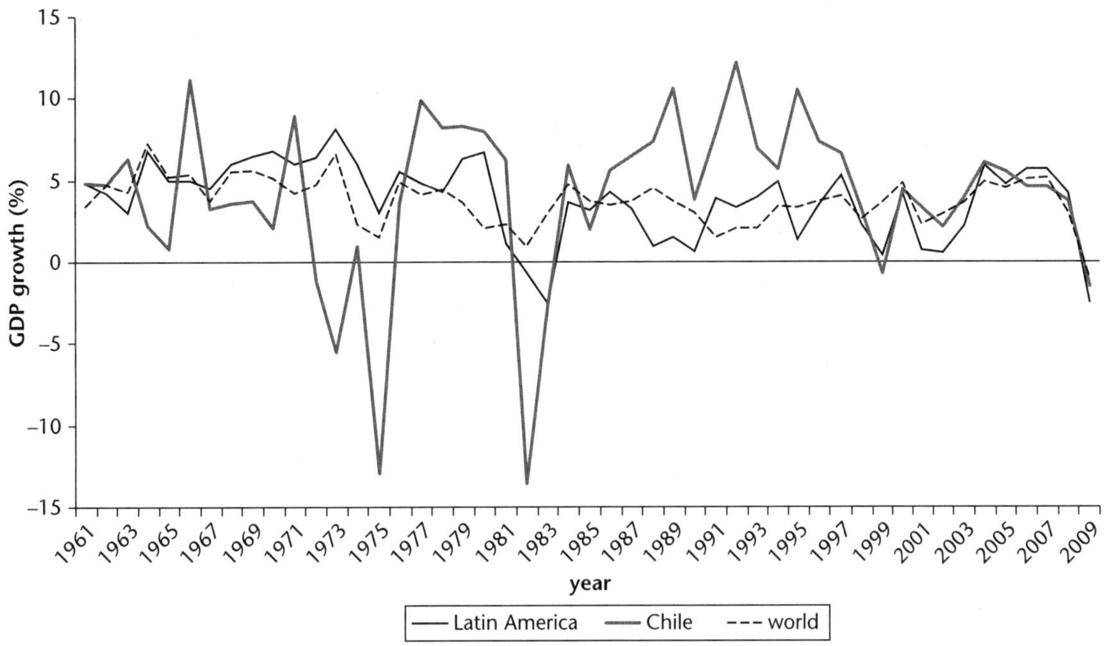

Source: Zahler & Co., based on data from the IMF, the Central Bank of Chile, and the OECD: International Financial Statistics (database), IMF, http://www.imfstatistics.org; Statistics Database, Central Bank of Chile, Santiago, http://www.bcentral.cl; and OECD Stat (database), OECD, http://stats.oecd.org.

Figure 15.6. Growth and Volatility of Chilean GDP, 1965–2009

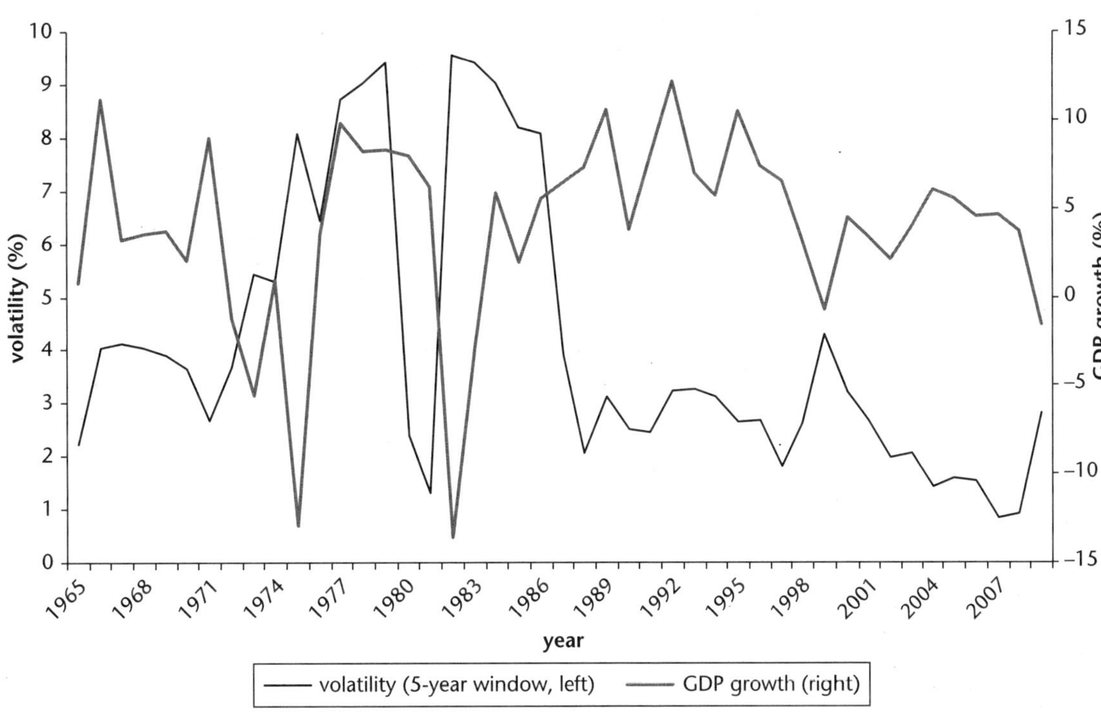

Source: Zahler & Co., based on data from the Central Bank of Chile: Statistics Database, Central Bank of Chile, Santiago, http://www.bcentral.cl.

of 2008), the impact of both crises on Chile's GDP is very similar as well as the time elapsed between peak and trough: four quarters. However, with the information up to the fourth quarter of 2009, the episodes differ in recovery speed. In the current crisis, recovery is taking place at a slower rhythm than during the Asian crisis and, after six semesters since activity began to diminish, GDP still has not recovered to its level before the beginning of the

Figure 15.7. Evolution of Chile's Real GDP in the Past Two Crises, 1998–2000 and 2008–09

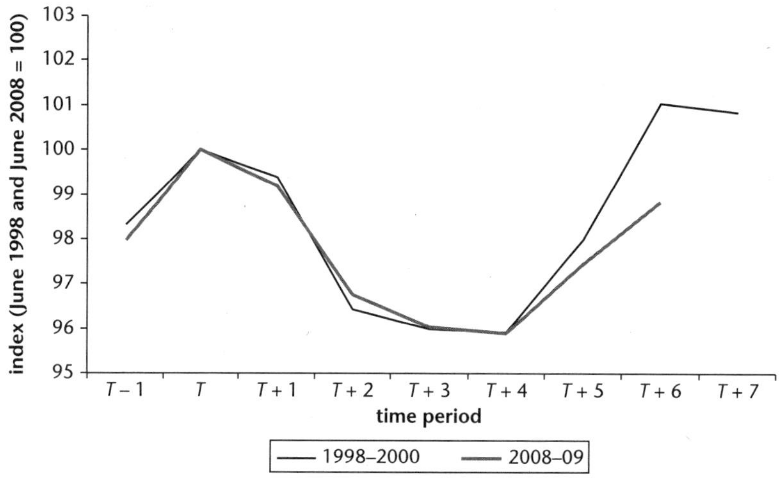

Source: Zahler & Co., based on data from the Central Bank of Chile: Statistics Database, Central Bank of Chile, Santiago, http://www.bcentral.cl.
Note: GDP is seasonally adjusted. *T* represents the period of maximum precrisis GDP.

contraction. During the Asian crisis, GDP had recovered its precrisis level in the fourth quarter of 1999, two quarters after having reached the minimum during the contractionary phase. One possible explanation for the slower speed of recovery is that, on average, in 1998–99 world GDP grew 3.1 percent, while in 2008–09 it grew by only 1.2 percent.

From a longer-term perspective, it is interesting to analyze Chile's GDP growth trend before and after the Asian crisis. During the 1990s, 1999 aside, the average growth rate of GDP was 7.1 percent, while from 2000 to 2008 it was 4.3 percent. In short, after the Asian crisis, Chile's growth was much lower than before that crisis. One of the main reasons for the high GDP growth from 1990 until the Asian crisis was TFP growth of around 4 percent, a situation that changed dramatically after 1997.

Evidence on the determinants of TFP suggests that in addition to cyclical factors, TFP growth reflects the effects of macroeconomic stability as well as of structural reforms. Given that Chile's macroeconomic environment has been stable for many years, the empirical evidence suggests that higher GDP growth depends, temporally, on improvements in the terms of trade, such as what Chile experienced in 2004, and, more permanently, on the implementation of additional structural reforms.

Transmission Mechanisms of the 2008–09 Economic Crisis

The 2008–09 crisis was transmitted to Chile through two main mechanisms. The first was an external demand shock, which is discussed in comparative perspective and specifically with regard to Chile. The final part of this section discusses the shock that came from global capital markets.

External Demand Shock: An International Comparison

The external demand shock experienced in 2008 and 2009 affected all countries in Latin America through two channels: lower demand for their exports and a fall in the price of exported goods and services. Table 15.3 shows an international comparison of the external demand shock experienced by several Latin American countries and other high-income exporters of raw materials.

The upper part of table 15.3 shows Latin American economies. Despite differences in the degree of openness and in the composition of exports, the fall in value of Chilean exports does not differ substantially from the average drop in the region, around 50 percent in six months. The greatest decline was in Ecuador—whose exports account for a high proportion of GDP—followed by Brazil, the economy with the lowest ratio of exports to GDP.

The recovery of exports shows greater homogeneity than the contractionary phase, essentially accounting for the speed of recovery in their prices. In Chile, export value increased by 60 percent between March and December 2009, after Peru, which had an 80 percent rise in the same period. Both economies are within the group of countries with greater commercial openness in the region, but they also have another element in common: the relevance of copper in their exports. Given the speedy recovery shown by the price of this metal, it is the main candidate for explaining the increased value of exports in both countries.

Table 15.3. Effect of the International Crisis on the Exports of Selected Countries, as of December 2009

	Fall (maximum-minimum)		Recovery to Dec. 2009		
	%	months	%	months	exports/GDP
Argentina	–49	5	30	11	22
Brazil	–53	7	51	10	13
Chile	**–51**	**11**	**60**	**10**	**39**
Colombia	–40	4	40	13	16
Ecuador	–59	9	50	9	34
Mexico	–45	6	51	11	27
Peru	–47	6	80	11	25
Uruguay	–45	6	33	11	19
Average excluding Chile	–48	6	48	11	22
Australia	–33	7	15	11	23
Canada	–45	9	24	8	23
Chile	–51	11	60	10	39
New Zealand	–46	9	43	11	24
Norway	–46	13	24	7	38
South Africa	–57	6	41	11	29
Average excluding Chile	–46	9	29	10	27

Source: Zahler & Co., based on data from Bloomberg (database): New York, http://www.bloomberg.com.

In contrast, Argentina, Colombia, and Uruguay—countries that did not see such a significant improvement in the price of their exported products during the second half of 2009—also experienced lower growth in the value of exports.

Figure 15.8 shows the relation in this wide sample of countries between the ratio of exports to GDP in 2008 and the GDP rate of change in 2009. There is a negative relation: that is, the higher the ratio of exports to GDP, the greater tends to be the fall in GDP. Given the linear adjustment, the drop in Chile's GDP in 2009 could have been around 2 percent because of its degree of commercial openness.

With the exception of Mexico, all other Latin American countries show a better relative performance than Chile, with GDP variations close to zero or even positive. Mexico, most likely because of its heavy ties to the U.S. economy, presents a significant GDP contraction, which goes further than what its degree of openness would suggest.

The higher-income commodity-exporting countries are generally positioned closer to the linear relation. It stands out that Norway, with an openness similar to Chile's, experienced a GDP contraction also similar to that of Chile. GDP changes in New Zealand and South Africa were consistent with their degree of commercial openness, while Australia did relatively better, and Canada, worse. It is possible that the close commercial and financial ties of Canada and Mexico to the United States may have had an influence, given that both economies performed more poorly than what their overall ratio of exports to GDP would explain.

External Demand Shock: Effects on Chile

Considering constant 2003 prices (the base year of the latest available national accounts), Chile's ratio of exports of goods and services to GDP practically doubled in 20 years, from 23 percent in the mid-1980s to nearly 40 percent in the mid-2000s (figure 15.9). Imports experienced an even larger jump, supported by the growth in national income and the continuous reduction in tariffs due to Chile's free trade agreements. In real terms, imports of goods and services went from representing 15 percent of GDP in the mid-1980s to over 50 percent in 2008. In 2009, real exports and imports both decreased as a percentage of GDP.

From 2005 on, in real terms, imports were higher than exports, a finding explained mostly by the differences in the evolution of export and import prices. Indeed, from 2005 to 2007, the increase in prices of imported goods was less than the increase in prices of exported goods. As from the third quarter of 2008, the price of imported goods decreased to levels similar to those that prevailed in 2005 and stabilized at that level, while the price of exports had a temporary drop but, by late 2009, had recovered considerably. In spite of everything, in current dollars, not only has the Chilean balance of trade maintained a surplus during the past five years, but also that surplus continued to increase until 2007.

The relevance of external demand to Chile's economic performance has grown significantly throughout the course of the past decades. The largest increase took place from 1970 to 1990, when exports of goods and services as a

Figure 15.8. Ratio of Exports to GDP in 2008 and GDP Growth in Selected Countries, 2009

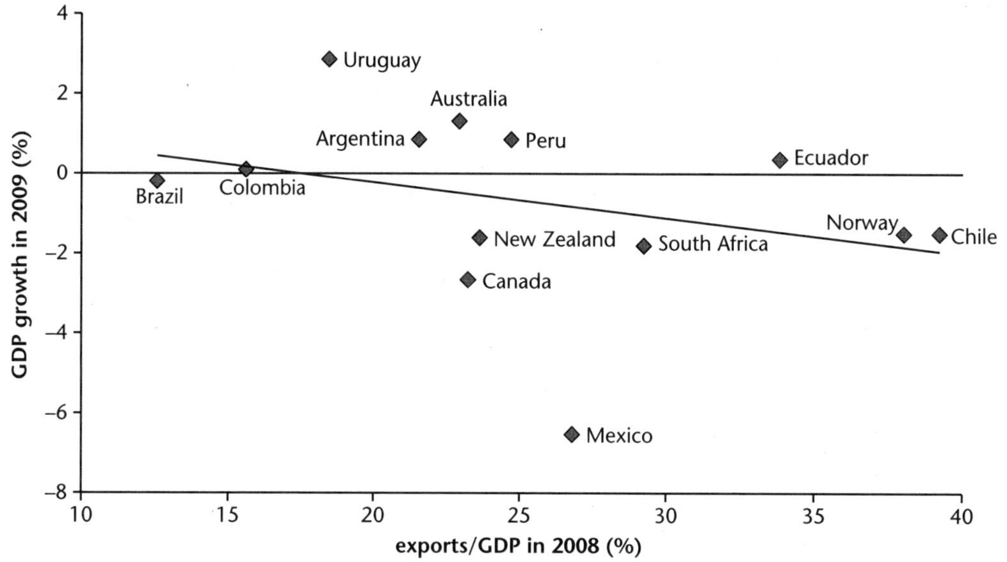

Source: Zahler & Co., based on data from Bloomberg and the IMF: Bloomberg (database), New York, http://www.bloomberg.com; and International Financial Statistics (database), IMF, http://www.imfstatistics.org.

Figure 15.9. Chile's Commercial Openness, 1986–2009

Source: Zahler & Co., based on data from the Central Bank of Chile: Statistics Database, Central Bank of Chile, Santiago, http://www.bcentral.cl.

proportion of GDP tripled, from 11 percent in 1970 to 33 percent in 1990. Subsequently, the increase in external demand became more gradual and at present represents slightly less than 40 percent of GDP (figure 15.10).

Chilean exports grew substantially from 2003 to 2007, with important increases in prices and quantities (figure 15.11). In 2008, prices and quantities stagnated, and in 2009, the Chilean economy suffered a negative shock. During the four quarters preceding the third quarter of 2009, export prices fell by 25 percent (year-on-year average), while quantities exported fell 4.6 percent. These events differ considerably from what happened during the 1998 Asian crisis, when prices fell by 15 percent but export quantities increased by 8 percent.

This difference in the evolution of export quantities during these two episodes may be explained, on the one hand, by the much greater magnitude of the 2008–09 shock relative to that of the late 1990s. On the other hand, Japan, Europe, and the United States, whose markets were most affected by the 2008–09 crisis, played an important part in Chile's decline in exports, notwithstanding the significant diversification of Chilean export destinations.

Diversification of Chilean exports has changed significantly since the beginning of the 1980s. Figure 15.12 shows that the relevance of Europe and Latin America as destinations of Chilean exports has decreased during the past 30 years, mainly in favor of Asia. U.S. participation in total exports, which increased from 12.6 percent in 1980 to around 17 percent in 1990 and 2000, had fallen to 11.3 percent in 2009. In 2007–09, Chilean exports to the United States were greatly affected (figure 15.13) by the subprime crisis and the lower U.S. demand for housing construction materials.

Figure 15.10. Chile's External and Internal Demand for Goods and Services, 1970–2009

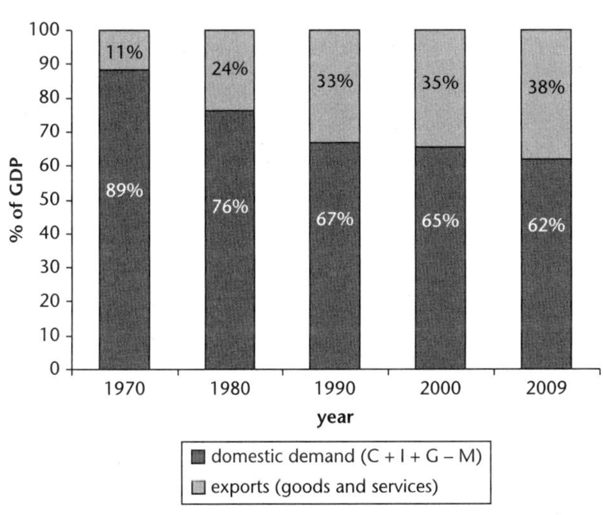

Source: Zahler & Co., based on data from the Central Bank of Chile: Statistics Database, Central Bank of Chile, Santiago, http://www.bcentral.cl.
Note: C = consumption; G = government spending; I = investment; M = imports.

Table 15.4 shows that in the early 1980s, U.S. participation increased from 22 percent to 28 percent, while Latin America's dropped from 19 percent to 12 percent, evidence that Latin America was one of the most affected regions during that crisis. During the Asian crisis, no major changes occurred in the relevant participation of the various economic zones. Also noticeable is the relatively low participation of China, which in 1999 represented only 3 percent of total Chilean exports. In the most recent crisis (2008–09), the principal change is the extreme increase in China's participation, reaching 23 percent of the total, more than double that of the United States.

However, most Chilean exports to China are mining products. In 2009, 85 percent of Chilean exports to China came from that sector, 14 percent were industrial shipments, and only 1 percent was agricultural exports. India is not a major destination for Chilean exports. In 2009, only 2 percent of Chilean exports (US$1.1 billion) were shipped to India. Of this amount, 93 percent were mining exports, 6 percent were industrial products, and 1 percent was agricultural products.

The global nature of the 2008–09 crisis reduced the effectiveness of the export diversification strategy as a mechanism to "shield" the Chilean economy from external shocks. According to estimates of the International Monetary Fund (IMF), 49 percent of the countries for which information was available experienced a fall in GDP during 2009. In 1999, the percentage of countries whose GDP fell was 19 percent, and in 1983 it reached 33 percent.

Furthermore, even with the high degree of export market diversification, more than 40 percent of Chilean shipments go to Europe, Japan, and the United States—the countries most affected in the recent crisis. Nearly 60 percent of Chilean exports go to the world's four largest economic zones or countries: China, Europe, Japan, and the United States. Until 2006, shipments to Europe, Japan, and the United States represented over 50 percent of the total, and China represented around 10 percent. The 2008–09 crisis, however, generated a significant change in the destination of Chilean exports. In fact, 40 percent of the shipments in 2009 went to Europe, Japan, and the United States, while 23 percent went to China, which has become the principal country destination for Chilean exports.

Chilean exports are much less diversified by product than by destination. They are still highly dependent on the situation of copper, the main export product. In 2009, mining exports represented close to 60 percent of total Chilean exports, and copper accounted for 90 percent of

Figure 15.11. Changes in Prices and Quantities of Chilean Exports, 1997–2009

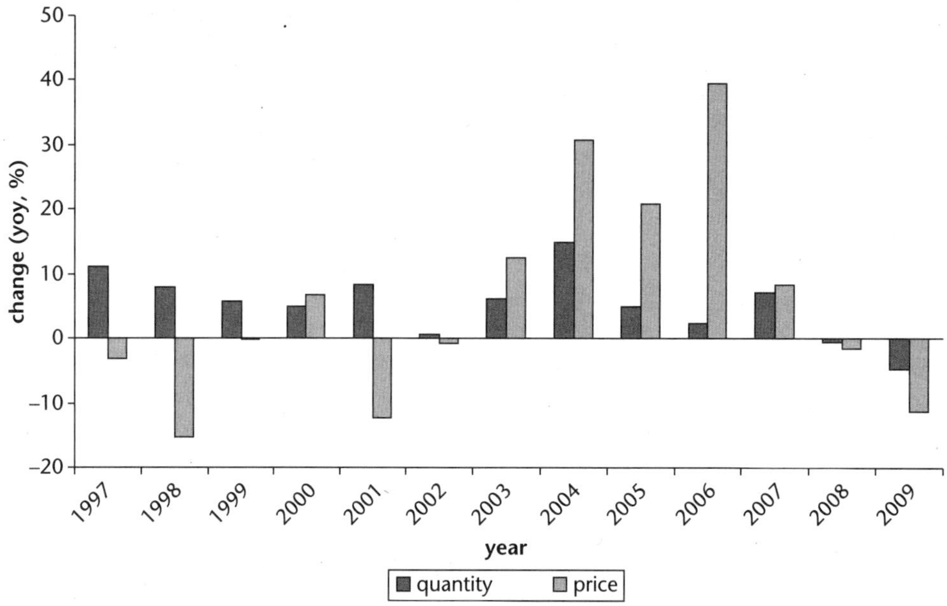

Source: Zahler & Co., based on data from the Central Bank of Chile: Statistics Database, Central Bank of Chile, Santiago, http://www.bcentral.cl.
Note: yoy = year over year.

Figure 15.12. Diversification of Chilean Exports by Destination, 1980–2009

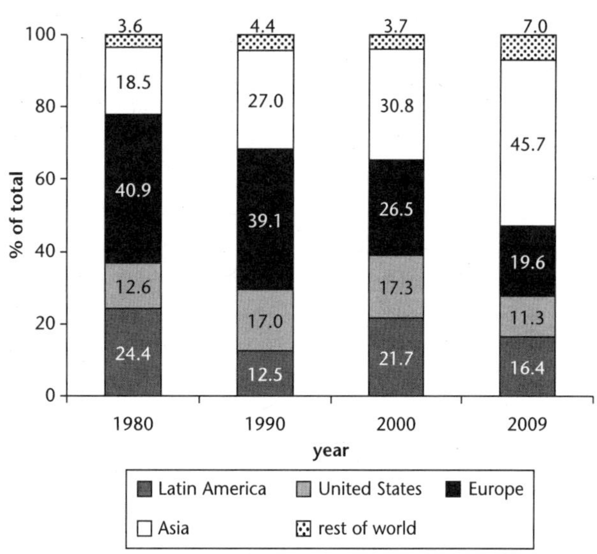

Source: Zahler & Co., based on data from the Central Bank of Chile: Statistics Database, Central Bank of Chile, Santiago, http://www.bcentral.cl.

Figure 15.13. Chile's Exports to the United States as a Percentage of Total Exports, 2003–09

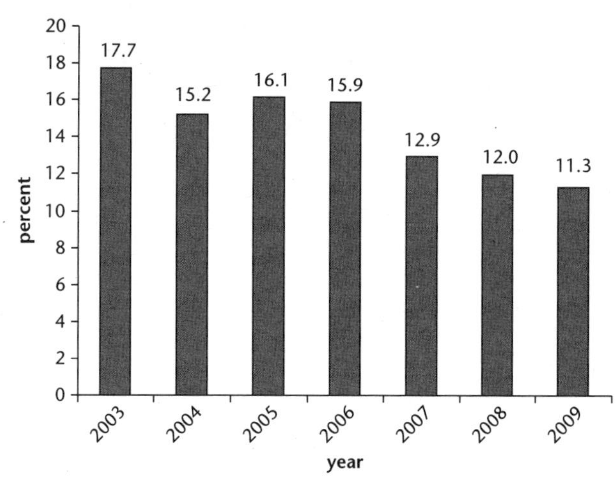

Source: Zahler & Co., based on data from the Central Bank of Chile: Statistics Database, Central Bank of Chile, Santiago, http://www.bcentral.cl.

mining sector exports (table 15.5). Asia remains the main buyer of copper, with 58 percent of the total, followed by Europe with 22 percent and the Americas (16 percent). Asia's demand is dominated by three countries: China (31 percent of the total), Japan (11 percent), and the Republic of Korea (8 percent). The United States is the fourth-largest buyer with 7 percent of the total and Brazil the fifth largest, with 6 percent.

Table 15.5 also shows that, at an aggregate level, the composition of exported goods has not significantly changed in the past 25 years. Although Chile's policies on exports were neutral during those years, on occasion government officials stated that their objective was to change Chile's export structure to one less dependent on natural resources; however, this shift has not occurred.

In a comparison of Chile's GDP per capita performance to that of Australia and New Zealand, Chile had a higher

Table 15.4. Chilean Export Diversification by Destination, 1982–2009
percent

	Asia total					
	1982	1983	1998	1999	2008	2009
United States	22	28	17	19	12	11
Europe	37	39	29	27	26	20
Asia total	18	17	27	29	36	45
Japan	12	9	15	14	10	9
China	2	2	4	3	14	23
Latin America	19	12	23	21	16	15
Other	3	4	3	3	9	8

Source: Zahler & Co., based on data from the Central Bank of Chile: Statistics Database, Central Bank of Chile. Santiago, Chile, http://www.bcentral.cl.

Table 15.5. Chile's Export Products, 1982–2009
percent

Product	1982	1983	1998	1999	2008	2009
Agriculture, fruit, livestock, forestry, and fish	10.1	8.5	11.4	10.8	6.2	6.9
Minerals	58.1	59.9	41.3	42.9	60.4	59.5
Copper	46.7	47.9	33.7	36.4	51.8	53.5
Industry	31.8	31.6	46.8	45.6	33.5	33.6
Other	0.0	0.0	0.5	0.6	0.0	0.0

Source: Zahler & Co., based on data from the Central Bank of Chile: Statistics Database, Central Bank of Chile, Santiago, Chile, http://www.bcentral.cl.

GDP growth rate than either Australia or New Zealand, after Latin America's lost decade of the 1980s. Although this outcome is the result of many factors, it may indicate that the Chilean development strategy of the past 25 years has been quite successful. Despite that success, however, the same strategy should not necessarily be pursued in the same manner in the future. In fact, Chile's GDP per capita in 2009 was similar to that of Australia in 1985 and of New Zealand in the mid-1990s; therefore, Chile should seriously consider development strategies followed by Australia and New Zealand, countries that have changed their export structure quite significantly. If implemented, such policies may lead to a change in Chile's productive structure, allowing more rapid growth of industrial goods production, services, and technology.

The recent international crisis caused a tremendous drop in the price of copper, as well as in the value of total exports. In effect, in April 2008 the price of copper reached a maximum of US$3.90 per pound, and in December of the same year, it fell to US$1.40 per pound, a deterioration of 65 percent. Sixty percent of this fall took place after September 2008, the month when Lehman Brothers went bankrupt. The greatest part of the fall in the value of mining exports during the first three quarters of 2009 was caused by a decrease in prices, because volumes did not experience significant changes (figure 15.14).

Industrial exports, which in 2008 and 2009 represented one-third of total shipments, are more diversified by product than mining exports, as may be seen in figure 15.15. The two most important products are salmon and trout, with 12 percent, and cellulose, with 11 percent. Despite this greater diversification, however, industrial exports also suffered a major fall during 2008–09. Figure 15.16 shows that, contrary to what happened with mining shipments, prices and quantities of industrial exports both suffered a significant drop as a result of the latest crisis.

Overall international goods prices faced by Chile (figure 15.17) indicate that its terms of trade in the recent world crisis began falling in the first quarter of 2008 and, after having dropped by close to 30 percent, they reached a minimum in the first quarter of 2009. Since then, the increase in the terms of trade was quite fast, by the end of 2009 recovering practically the entire fall experienced during the previous quarters.

Chile's exports of services and transport, including air and sea as well as freight and passengers, accounted for 58 percent of the total in 2003–09. Other important services exported by Chile were travel and tourism and business services; the former were 17 percent and the latter 16 percent of total export services in 2003–09. Chilean exports of services (in value terms) grew at a high rate (16.4 percent) in 2004–08, a trend that was abruptly interrupted in 2009, when they fell 21 percent as a consequence of the crisis (figure 15.18).

In recent years, growth in services trade in China, India, and the Russian Federation was at more than double the world average rate. Latin America's growth in services has been below the average, and therefore the region's participation in world trade in services has fallen in recent years. China and India and, to a certain extent, Brazil and Mexico can rely on an abundant and low-wage labor force, a resource not available in Chile, a country that faces other difficulties in substantially increasing its exports of services: the lack of knowledge of English and the scarce, although increasing, technically skilled labor force. Chile's macroeconomic and institutional stability, however, is an important asset that could favor the development of service exports.

International Capital Markets Shock: Effect on Chile

Chile's positioning as an attractive country for FDI is due to its relative openness to international capital flows, its political and economical stability, its high connectivity, its wide network of international agreements, and the legal certainty and stability it offers. These factors have given rise

Figure 15.14. Changes in Price and Quantity of Chilean Mining Exports, 1997–2009, as of Third Quarter 2009

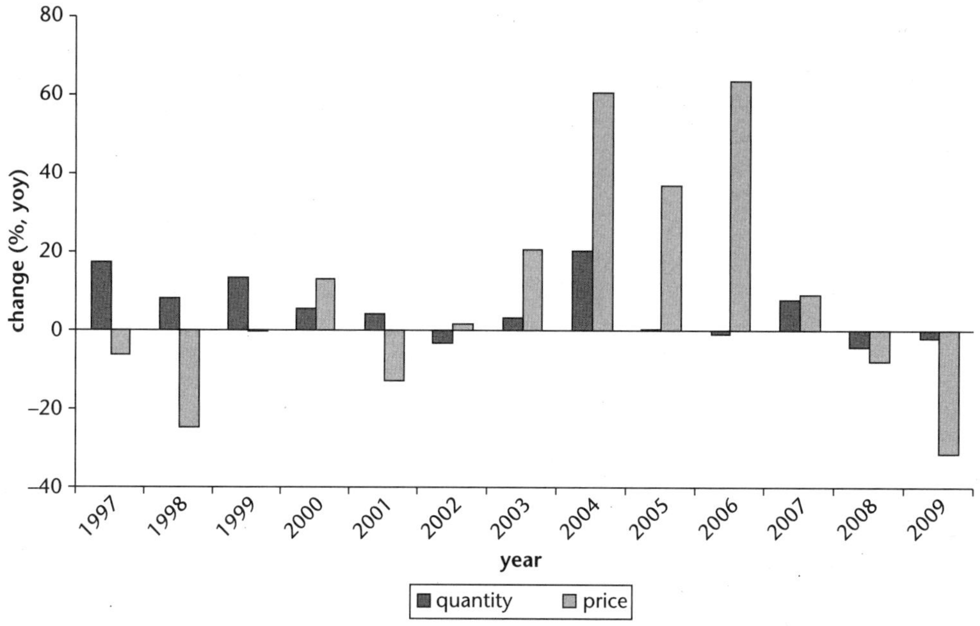

Source: Zahler & Co., based on data from the Central Bank of Chile: Statistics Database, Central Bank of Chile, Santiago, http://www.bcentral.cl.

Figure 15.15. Chilean Industrial Exports, 2009

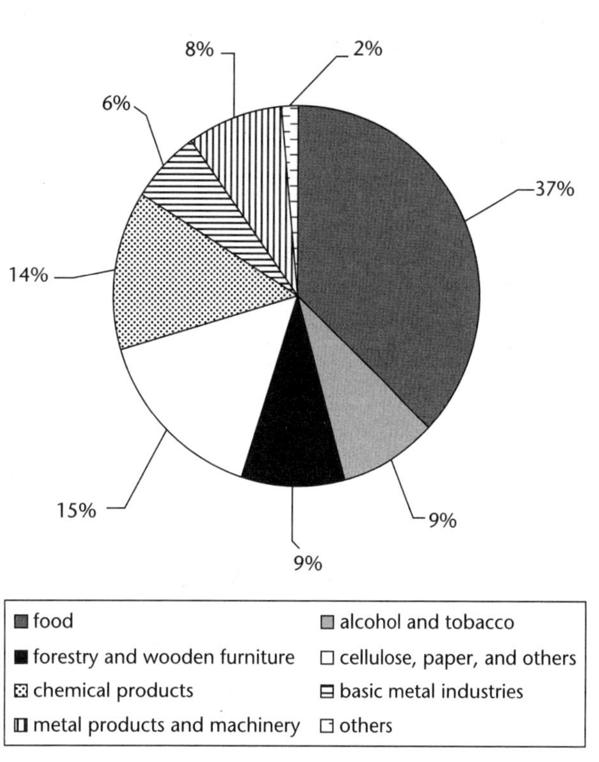

Source: Zahler & Co., based on data from the Central Bank of Chile: Statistics Database, Central Bank of Chile, Santiago, http://www.bcentral.cl.

to foreign companies' interest in investing in Chile, particularly during times of economic turbulence. Thus, during 1999 and 2008, FDI increased, perhaps the result of Chile's attractiveness as a shelter during times of greater regional uncertainty and volatility (see figure 15.19). In 2009, both FDI and portfolio investment fell; however, the magnitude of this reduction was not significant and appears secondary in comparison with the shock to export prices and quantities exported described above.

In 2009, FDI into Chile amounted to around US$12 billion, equivalent to 7.6 percent of GDP, lower than the previous year's figure of US$17 billion but much higher than the average of 1996–2007 (around US$6 billion annually). Portfolio investment exceeded US$2 billion, a lower figure than that for 2008 but much higher than the flows of 1996–2007 (annual average of US$1.2 billion).

Although FDI increased significantly in 2007–09, U.S. participation in those flows was relatively low. In fact, U.S. FDI in Chile has fallen systematically over time. In 1974–84, it reached 50 percent of total FDI in Chile. From 1985 to 1995, U.S. FDI fell to 36 percent, falling further to around 21 percent in 1996–2003. From 2004 to 2008, FDI originating in the United States represented, on average, around 9 percent of total FDI in Chile.

The major part (in absolute terms) of U.S. FDI took place from the mid-1990s to the early 2000s. Due to the high economic integration among the signatories to the North American Free Trade Agreement (NAFTA), any evaluation of a shock in the United States must also take into account the potential impact on investment flows originating in Canada and Mexico. FDI from Mexico into Chile is still minor; however, that from Canada has been quite steady since the early 1990s, totaling around US$2 billion in 2006 and 2008 (figure 15.20).

Figure 15.16. Change in Price and Quantity of Chilean Industrial Exports, 1997–2009

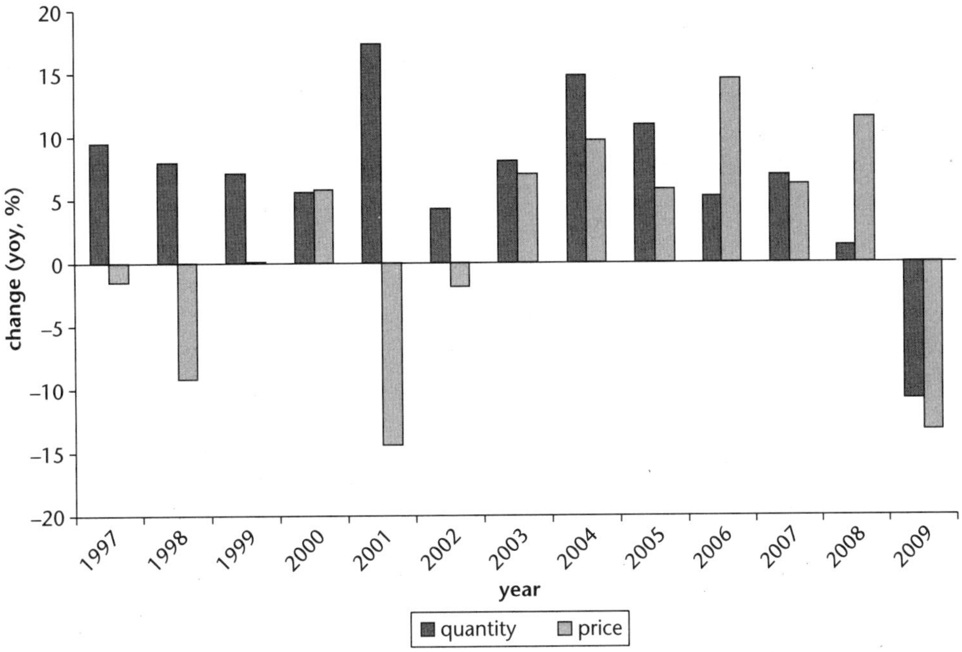

Source: Zahler & Co., based on data from the Central Bank of Chile: Statistics Database, Central Bank of Chile, Santiago, http://www.bcentral.cl.
Note: As of third quarter 2009. yoy = year over year.

Figure 15.17. Chile's Terms of Trade, 2003–09

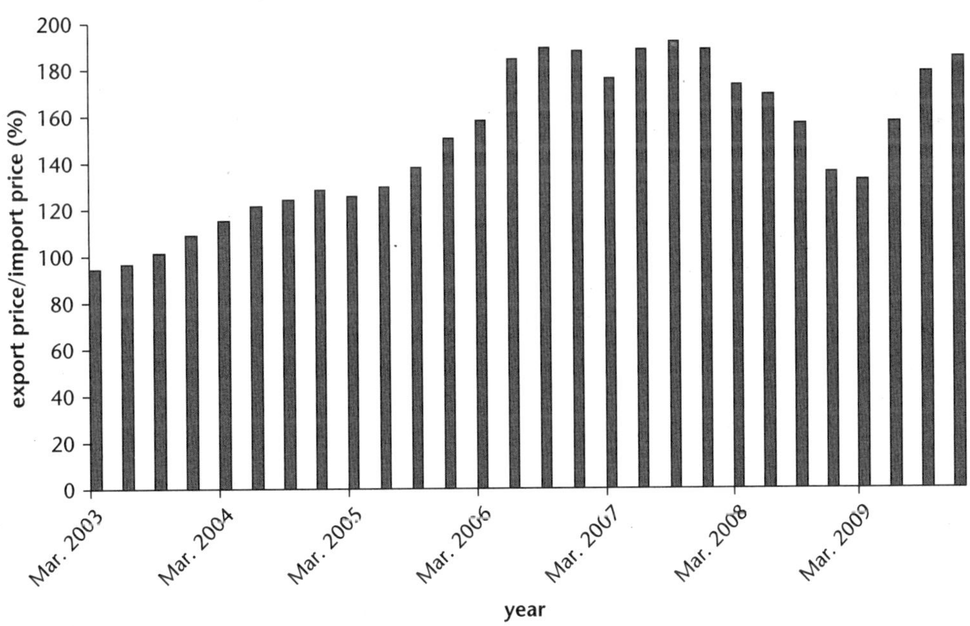

Source: Zahler & Co., based on data from the Central Bank of Chile: Statistics Database, Central Bank of Chile, Santiago, http://www.bcentral.cl.

China and India are not major sources of FDI into Chile. In 1974–2008, FDI from India amounted to only US$27 million, equivalent to 0.04 percent of Chile's total. Similarly, FDI from China from 1974 to 2008 totaled US$84 million, or 0.12 percent of the total.

As for portfolio investment, most of Chile's sovereign wealth fund investments are registered, for balance-of-payments purposes, as portfolio investments. During 2009, the balance-of-payments financial account recorded an income of US$7.95 billion from the central government,

Figure 15.18. Value of Chilean Exports of Services and Percentage Change, 2003–09
US$, millions

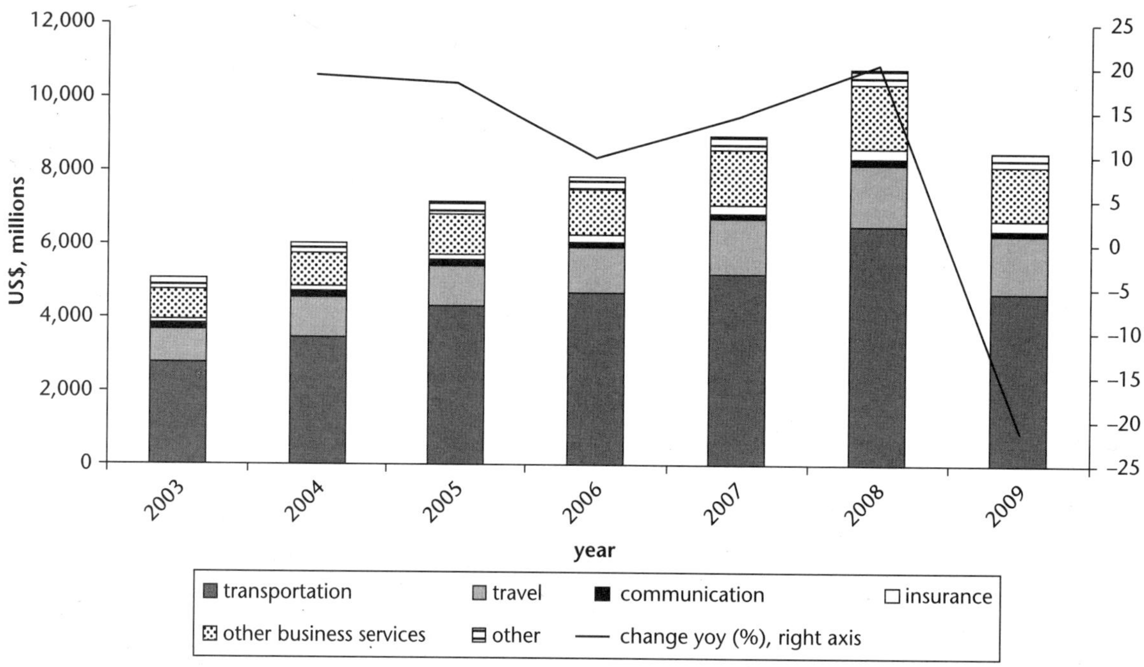

Source: Zahler & Co., based on data from the Central Bank of Chile: Statistics Database, Central Bank of Chile, Santiago, http://www.bcentral.cl.

Figure 15.19. Foreign Direct Investment and Portfolio Investment in Chile, 1996–2009

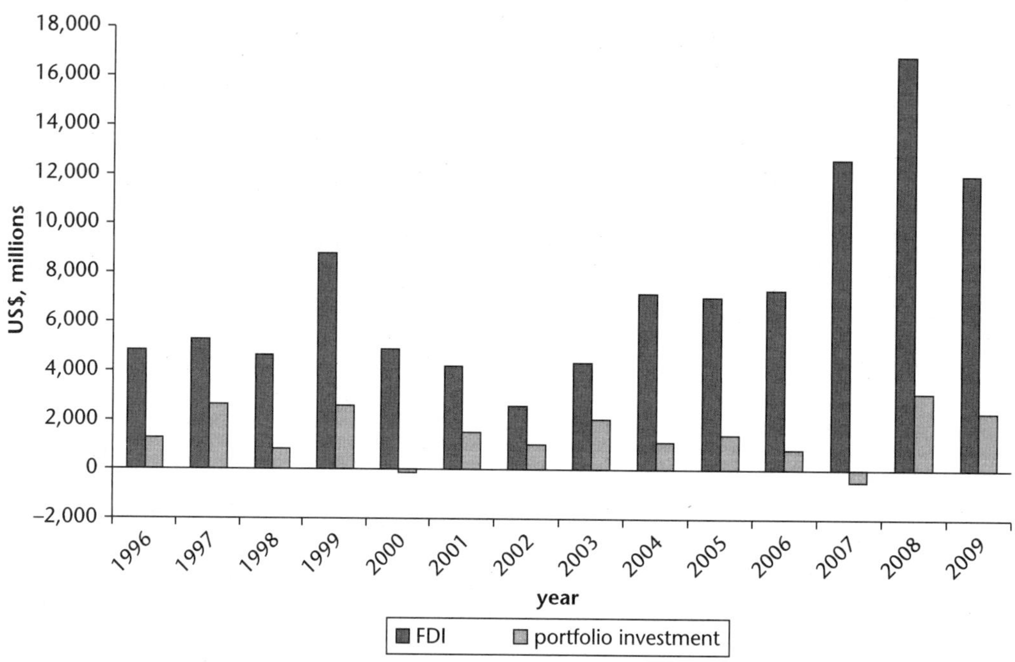

Source: Zahler & Co., based on data from the Central Bank of Chile: Statistics Database, Central Bank of Chile, Santiago, http://www.bcentral.cl.

as a result of the repatriation of foreign exchange to finance the countercyclical fiscal spending of that year. As for the other institutional players, in 2008 commercial banks repatriated US$6.3 billion from abroad, a figure that was reduced to less than half in 2009. In their turn, pension funds remitted abroad US$16.4 billion in 2009, a figure that is far above the average of the past six years (US$2.6 billion).

Figure 15.20. NAFTA Foreign Direct Investment in Chile, 1974–2008

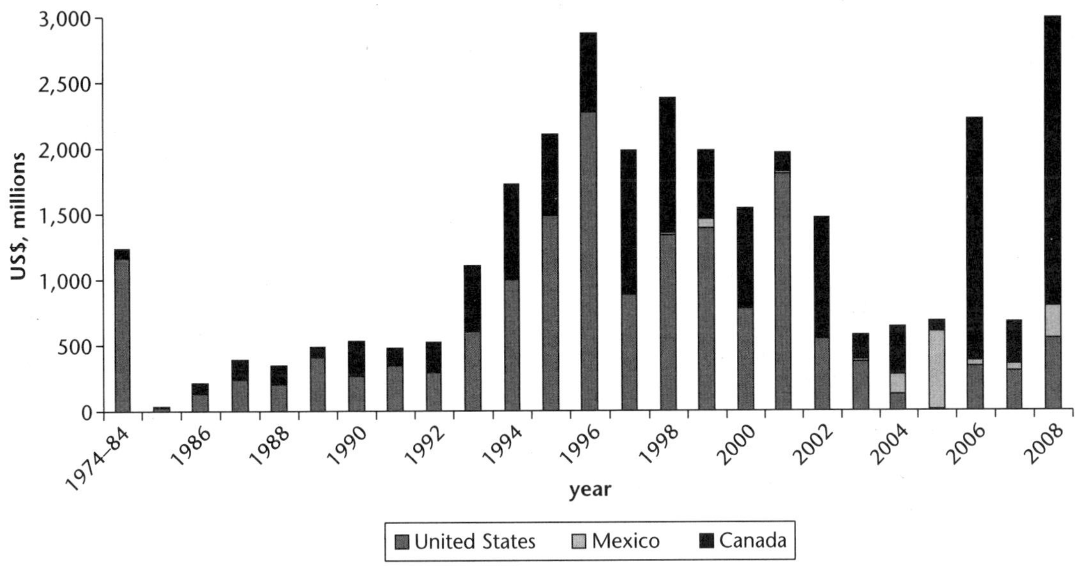

Source: Zahler & Co., based on data from Foreign Investment Committee: Government of Chile, Santiago, http://www.foreigninvestment.cl.

In brief, neither FDI nor portfolio flows into Chile were seriously affected during the 2008–09 crisis; in particular, the Chilean economy did not experience a reversal of capital flows. It did, however, face an increase in the cost of foreign financing (figure 15.21). The three-month LIBOR (London interbank offered rate) in U.S. dollars rose over 100 basis points from August to October 2008; in addition, there was a significant adjustment suffered by credit default swaps (CDS) for Chile's sovereign debt. If the two effects are added, the cost of a company's borrowing in international markets increased over 200 basis points in just a few weeks.

Overall Impact of the 2008–09 Economic Crisis on Chile

From 2003 to 2007, Chile's GDP grew at an average rate of 5 percent. This trend was interrupted by the 2008–09 international crisis. Chile grew 3.7 percent in 2008, but during the first three quarters GDP growth was 4.7 percent. In the fourth quarter of 2008, GDP grew only 0.7 percent and, in terms of quarter-on-quarter annualized change, GDP fell by 9.5 percent, the worst figure in 2008 and 2009 (table 15.6). GDP also contracted in 2009, but, as noted, the magnitude of the fall was considerably less than contractions in earlier episodes of world recession.

In mid-2008, figure 15.22 shows that market consensus expected the Chilean economy to grow by 4.5 percent in 2009, a projection that was corrected downward during the fourth quarter of 2008, when the impact of the international crisis on the terms of trade and the decrease in expected GDP growth of the country's principal commercial partners became clear. In April 2009, consensus was already considering the possibility of a fall in GDP, and by mid-year projections stabilized around the figure by which GDP finally fell: 1.5 percent.

The deterioration of credit terms, the loss of confidence felt by consumers and entrepreneurs, and the increase in unemployment had to be added to the external demand shock faced by the Chilean economy—all leading to a contraction in domestic demand. Firms lowered their inventories quickly and significantly, and families reduced their purchases of consumer goods, particularly durables (figure 15.23).

Banks began to restrict their loan offers as far back as 2007. According to a quarterly survey prepared by the Central Bank of Chile, credit supply conditions started to become more restrictive for consumer loans in the second quarter of 2007, while for companies they began to become more restrictive in the third quarter of 2007. The fall in credit demand came later, beginning in the first quarter of 2008 with respect to consumer credit and in the second quarter of 2008 in the case of companies. The global liquidity crisis, however, raised the cost of external financing significantly, although relatively briefly, as noted.

Consumer confidence began to deteriorate in early 2008, a pessimistic outlook that lasted until September 2009 (figure 15.24). Likewise, entrepreneurial confidence also fell in June 2008 and remained low until August

Figure 15.21. Three-Month LIBOR and Five-Year CDS for Chile, 2008–09

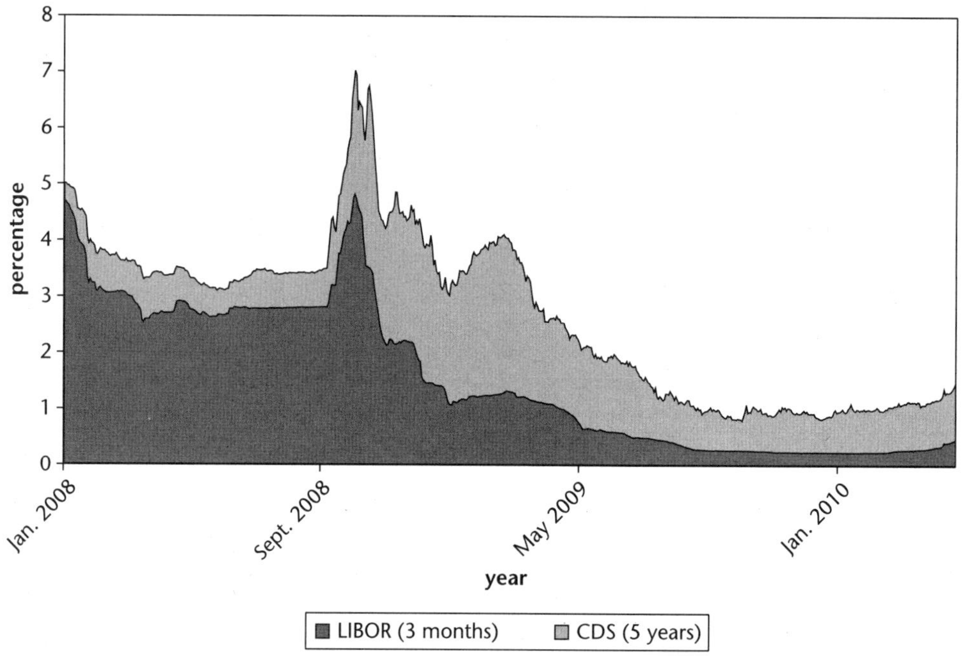

Source: Bloomberg (database): New York, http://www.bloomberg.com.
Note: CDS = credit default swaps, LIBOR = London interbank offered rate.

Table 15.6. Percentage Change in Chilean GDP, Year on Year, First Quarter 2008–Fourth Quarter 2009

	1Q 2008	2Q 2008	3Q 2008	4Q 2008	1Q 2009	2Q 2009	3Q 2009	4Q 2009
GDP (yoy)	3.7	5.1	5.2	0.7	−2.1	−4.5	−1.4	2.1
qoq SAAR	8.0	8.5	−3.2	−9.5	−3.0	−0.5	6.6	5.9
Internal demand	8.2	11.7	10.8	0.2	−6.6	−9.9	−8.1	1.4
Private consumption	5.5	6.2	5.7	1.3	−1.0	−2.0	0.8	5.5
Investment	13.9	22.7	29.0	9.8	−9.9	−19.4	−19.1	−11.9
Government consumption	2.1	−0.1	−0.3	0.5	7.2	7.8	5.8	6.4
Exports	2.3	0.0	7.2	3.4	−4.9	−7.2	−6.7	−3.7
Imports	12.8	16.1	19.4	1.5	−14.5	−18.9	−19.2	−4.0
Investment/GDP	26.4	29.1	31.1	30.1	24.3	24.6	25.5	26.0

Source: Zahler & Co., based on data from the Central Bank of Chile: Statistics Database, Central Bank of Chile, Santiago, http://www.bcentral.cl.
Note: Q = quarter, qoq SAAR = quarter-on-quarter seasonally adjusted annualized rate, yoy = year on year.

2009. The unemployment rate rose from 7.4 percent in September 2008 to 10.1 percent in August 2009; in the same period, the number of unemployed increased by 228,000.

The terms of trade fell 28 percent in the fourth quarter of 2008, and the drop in the price of exports between the maximum and minimum in 2009 was one of the highest in Latin America. In 2009, exports, in real terms, fell 5.6 percent and gross capital formation, which in 2008 had increased by 18.8 percent, fell by 15.3 percent in 2009. Economic authorities—monetary and fiscal—acted decisively and in coordination, implementing a set of measures that were among the largest in the world. In the first instance, these measures aimed at improving the availability of foreign currency (mainly U.S. dollars) liquidity and then counteracting the fall in foreign demand by means of greater public spending, a significant reduction in interest rates, state guarantees of access to credit, tax incentives, and incentives to hire workers, among others. These policy measures helped avoid a greater fall in GDP, which finally contracted 1.5 percent in 2009.

Chilean Policy Reaction to the 2008–09 Crisis

Chilean policy makers responded to the 2008–09 crisis on a number of levels. This section discusses the implications of the crisis for monetary policy, the exchange rate, and fiscal policy.

Figure 15.22. Forecasts of Chile's GDP Growth for 2009, June 2008–December 2009

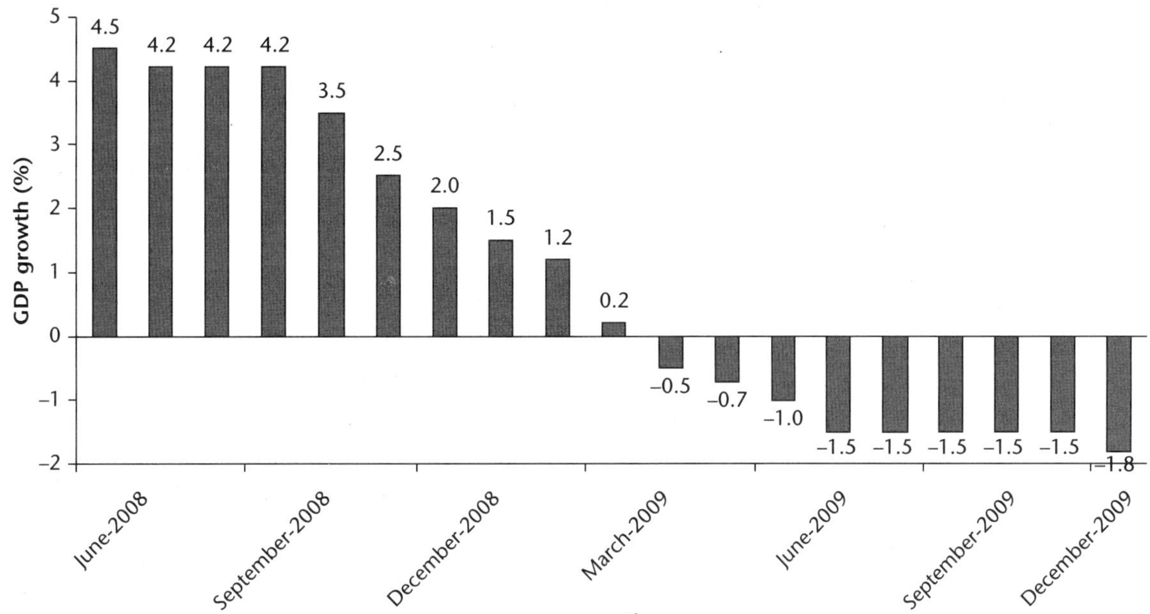

Source: Zahler & Co., based on data from the Central Bank of Chile: Statistics Database, Central Bank of Chile, Santiago, http://www.bcentral.cl.

Figure 15.23. Contribution of the Components of Aggregate Demand to Chile's GDP Growth, First Quarter 2008–Fourth Quarter 2009

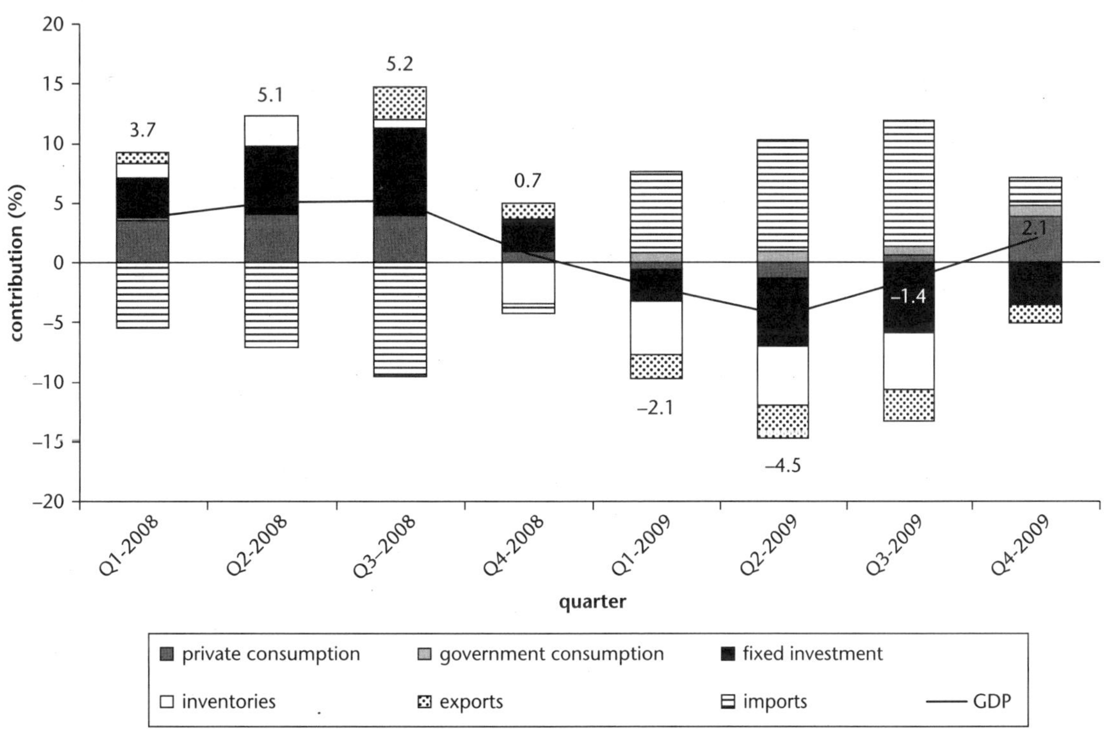

Source: Zahler & Co., based on data from the Central Bank of Chile: Statistics Database, Central Bank of Chile, Santiago, http://www.bcentral.cl.
Note: Q = quarter.

Figure 15.24. Index of Consumer Confidence in Chile, October 2008–December 2009

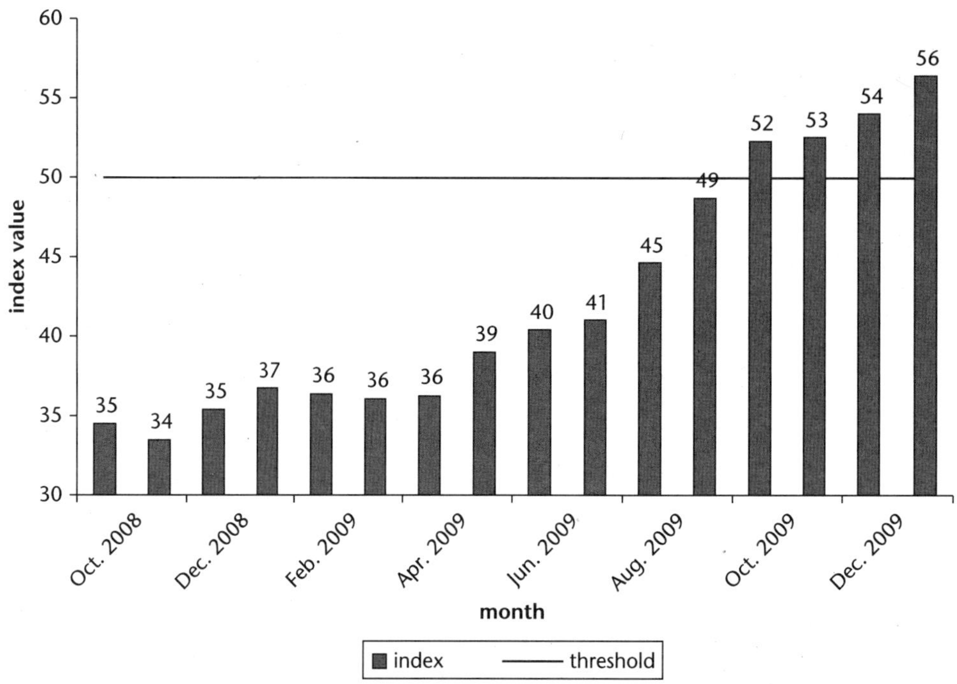

Source: Zahler & Co., based on data from Adimark, Santiago, http://www.adimark.cl.

Monetary Policy

Internal demand grew quite rapidly between 2004 and 2007. This growth was not entirely reflected in a higher GDP growth rate, because part of this demand went to the rest of the world through higher imports. During this period, internal demand grew an average of 8.1 percent annually, 2.9 percentage points higher than GDP growth. Private consumption grew by 7.2 percent annually, and investment grew 12.1 percent, more than doubling the GDP growth rate. This trend had to be slowed, a process initiated in 2007, by increasing the Central Bank of Chile's monetary policy interest rate. This policy continued during 2008.

In addition, during the first part of 2008 the Chilean peso experienced an unexpected and clearly excessive appreciation, at a moment when there were clear signs of a deteriorating international situation. In this context, the central bank decided to strengthen its international reserves by accumulating US$8 billion during an eight-month period. To preserve monetary policy independence from the exchange-rate policy, the central bank announced a predetermined and mechanical purchase of US$50 million per day. By mid-September 2008, liquidity tensions and constraints became severe worldwide, including in Chile. This development put an end to the policy, just when the central bank had accumulated nearly US$6 billion, putting it in a comfortable position for mitigating a possible sudden stop in net capital inflows into Chile.

In the fourth quarter of 2008, the impact of the international crisis was added to the decelerating phase of the domestic cycle. The Central Bank of Chile then reversed the monetary policy contraction. During the most critical stage of the crisis, the first policy reaction by the central bank was to establish extraordinary measures for liquidity provision, both in national currency and in U.S. dollars. This action ensured the normal operation of the financial system, notwithstanding the great increase in risk perception. In addition, motivated by local dollar liquidity restrictions and the shortage of foreign credit lines for banking institutions, the Treasury began to place resources in dollars in the local financial system—resources originating from one of the sovereign wealth funds—in the amount of US$1.05 billion—while the central bank started to provide liquidity in local currency and in dollars through repurchase (repo) and swap operations with banking institutions. Furthermore, the Treasury made a one-off increase in U.S. dollar deposits for US$700 million in the domestic banking system.

The first central bank policy measures to mitigate the impact of the crisis were taken in October 2008:

- Auctioned US$500 million for a term of 28 days, under the modality of foreign exchange swaps
- Extended the swap purchase of dollars from one to six months for a maximum amount of US$5 billion
- Opened the offer of cashier repo transactions for a term of 28 days
- Offered repo transactions at 60 and 90 days' term and broadened eligible collateral
- Temporarily relaxed the norms for requirements of bank reserves.

In January 2009, there was a clear assessment of reduced inflationary pressures: consumer price index inflation fell from 9.9 percent in October 2008 to 6.3 percent in January 2009, and inflation expectations for December 2009 fell in January 2009 to 3.5 percent from 4.9 percent in September 2008. Consequently, the central bank lowered the monetary policy interest rate by 100 basis points. Later, with evidence of further alleviated inflationary pressures and drastic increases in downward risks to growth and inflation, the central bank decided to cut the rate by 250 basis points at both its meetings in February and March. Thus, in the first quarter of 2008 the rate was cut by 600 basis points, from 8.25 percent to 2.25 percent. The monetary easing continued, bringing the rate down by 775 basis points in seven monthly meetings and lowering the monetary policy interest rate to 0.50 percent, the minimum deemed adequate for a normal functioning of money markets and the lowest of any Latin American economy (figure 15.25). The central bank stated that it would keep the rate constant for a prolonged period, at least until the second quarter of 2010.

To reinforce this decision and align financial asset prices with the path of monetary policy, the central bank implemented complementary monetary policy measures:

- It established a term liquidity facility (Facilidad de Liquidez a Plazo, or FLAP) for banking institutions, whereby it granted 90- and 180-day liquidity at the prevailing monetary policy interest rate.
- It adjusted its program of note issuance (Pagarés Descontables del Banco Central, or PDBC bonds) at maturities below one year.
- It suspended the issuance of debt instruments maturing in or after one year, corresponding to two-year central bank peso-denominated bonds (BCP-2) and one-year central bank notes (PDBC-360).

These monetary policy actions were decisive in reducing the interest rates faced by the financial system's clients. In addition, the government capitalized Banco Estado, a commercial 100 percent government-owned bank in the amount of US$500 million. Banco Estado played a very important de facto and nontraditional monetary policy role (the Chilean version of quantitative easing) by expanding its credit in very significant amounts while putting downward pressure on interest rates charged by the private banking system. In fact, Banco Estado's participation in total bank credit increased from 13.4 percent at the end of 2008 to 15.8 percent at the end of 2009.

In late 2009, the Central Bank of Chile announced the scheduled and gradual withdrawal of the complementary measures introduced earlier to strengthen monetary policy. Specifically, the liquidity facility would be reduced from 180 days to 150 days from December 2009. Subsequently, the term would continue to be reduced monthly by 30 days, bringing access to this facility to an end in May 2010.

Exchange-Rate Policy

Chile has a floating exchange regime, although the central bank reserves the right to intervene under exceptional circumstances, when it sees a significant misalignment in the real exchange rate. This exchange-rate policy—in combination with inflation targeting and a prudent and countercyclical fiscal policy—contributes to stability, allowing for changes in the real exchange rate, which, in the face of unexpected shocks, helps minimize effects on production and employment. All three crises in the past 35 years (1981–82, 1998–99, and 2008–09) have coincided with a previous appreciation of the Chilean peso until it reached a critical level (figure 15.26).

The crisis with the largest impact on Chile's GDP and unemployment rate (1981–82) coincided with the most significant peso appreciation, when the real exchange rate fell to an all-time low of 50 (base 1986 = 100; average real exchange rate from 1986 to 2010 = 96). Before the 1998–99 crisis, the real exchange rate also fell, although from a peak of 115 in the early 1990s to less than 80. In April 2008, as noted, the central bank began to accumulate international reserves, in part because of the appreciation of the Chilean peso (real exchange rate of 85 in March 2008).

Fiscal Policy

Chile's institutions of fiscal policy have constantly improved. Already noted, for example, were the adoption of a rule targeting a structural budget surplus as a percentage

Figure 15.25. Monetary Policy Interest Rates in Selected Latin American Countries, January 2007–March 2010

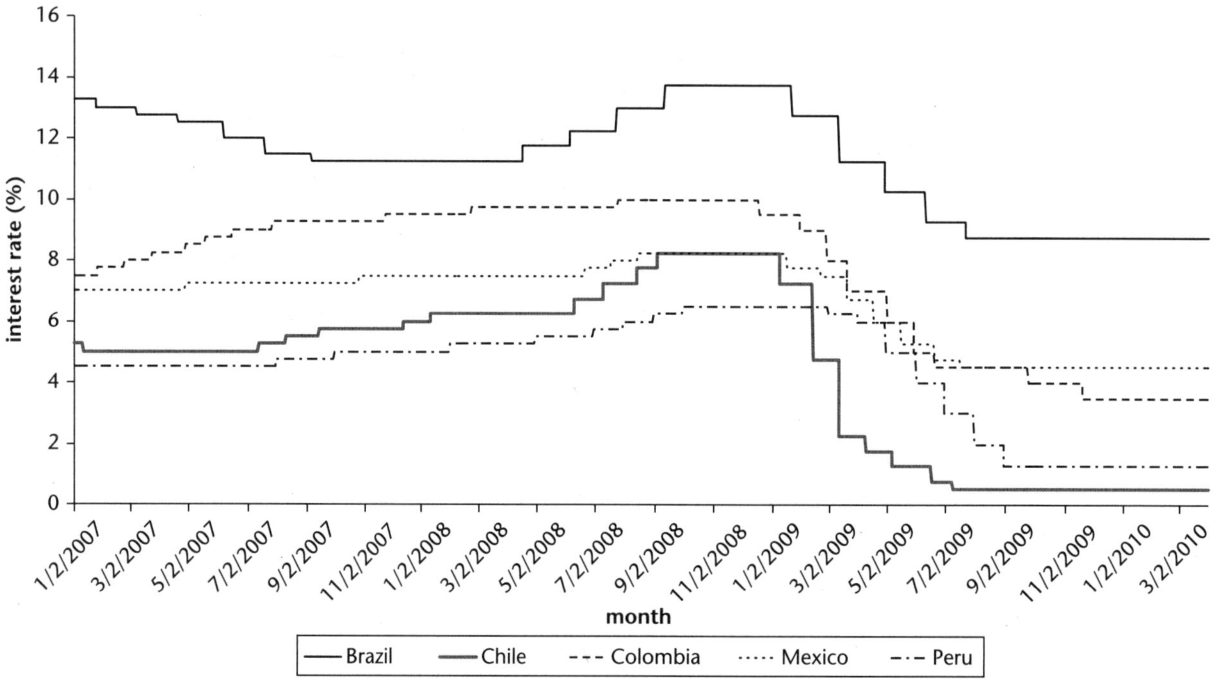

Source: Zahler & Co., based on Bloomberg data: Bloomberg (database), New York, http://www.bloomberg.com.

Figure 15.26. Chile's Real Exchange Rate Index, 1976–2008
1986 = 100

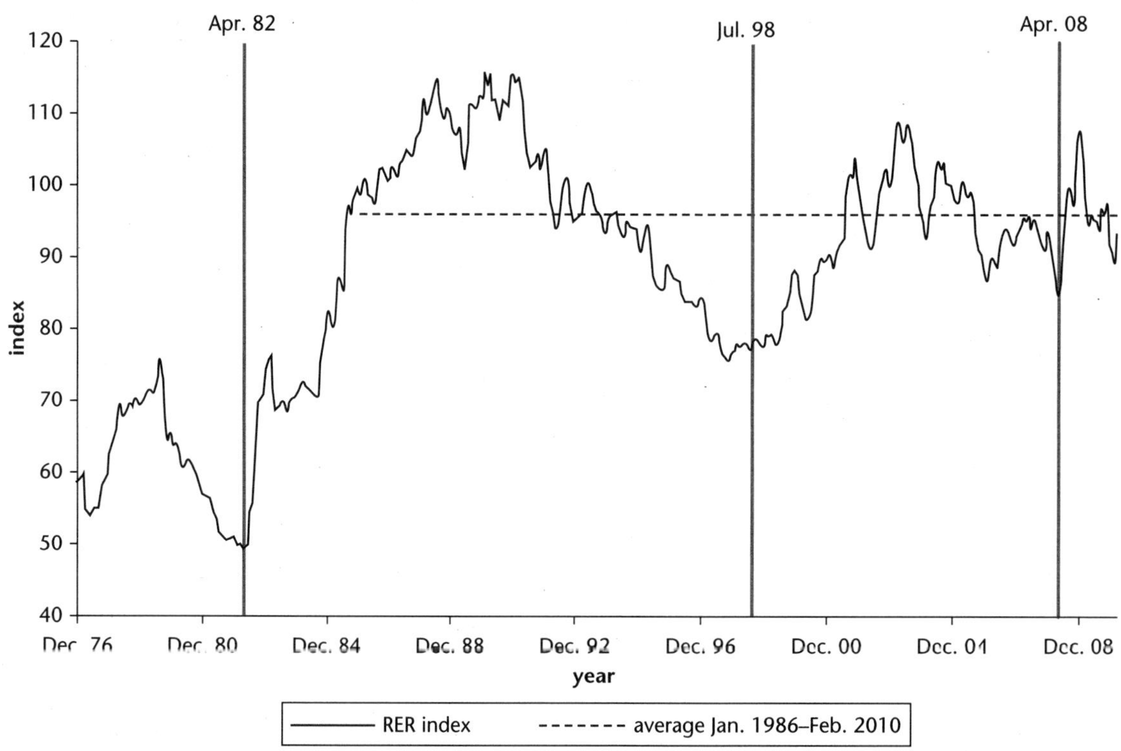

Source: Zahler & Co., based on data from the Central Bank of Chile: Statistics Database, Central Bank of Chile, Santiago, http://www.bcentral.cl.
Note: RER = real exchange rate.

of GDP (2002) and the mandate that the surplus be equivalent to 1 percent of GDP (which was reduced to 0.5 percent in the fiscal budget for 2008 and subsequently the ex ante target was reduced to 0 percent of GDP in 2009 because of the crisis). Such a budget surplus allows fiscal policy to be carried out in a countercyclical manner. This rule was formalized in the second semester of 2006, when the Fiscal Responsibility Law was enacted together with the creation of the Pension Reserve Fund and the Economic and Social Stabilization Fund.

The structural budget surplus rule was introduced to specify an annual level of fiscal spending in accordance with the structural (permanent) income of the central government. Therefore, the level of public spending rules out the cyclical fluctuations of economic activity, the copper price, and other factors that determine actual fiscal income. This policy implies saving during the up phase of the economic cycle and allows avoiding drastic adjustments of fiscal spending in the downturn of the economic cycle, such as the one that took place in late 2008 and part of 2009.

As a result of the very high prices of copper in the three-year period 2006–08, these funds accumulated more than US$22 billion. During 2009, the Economic and Social Stabilization Fund contributed to financing the incentive plans and the fiscal deficit, initiatives that allowed Chile to face the financial and economic world turbulence. The value of the Pension Reserve Fund as of December 31, 2009, was US$3.4 billion, while the value of the Economic and Social Stabilization Fund reached US$11.3 billion (figure 15.27).

To mitigate the huge fall in external demand and in internal demand for capital goods, as well as the expected fall in private consumption, the government launched a fiscal incentive plan in 2009 committing more than US$4 billion, equivalent to 2.8 percent of GDP. The fiscal incentive package contemplated providing support to individuals and families, boosting public investment, reducing taxes, giving other incentives to private investment, and strengthening the access to financing for small and medium enterprises, as well as measures to protect employment, among other initiatives.

The plan would increase public spending in 2009 by close to 1 percent of GDP (US$1.485 billion), and contemplated the temporary reduction of the structural surplus target of 0.5 percent to 0 percent of GDP in 2009. The plan also considered temporarily reducing fiscal income by US$1.455 billion, or the equivalent of 1 percent of GDP, which does not affect the fiscal structural income. It also included disbursements that do not constitute spending but rather the acquisition of financial assets, such as capital contributions to Corporación Nacional del Cobre (Codelco) and Corporación de Fomento de la Producción (Corfo).

The plan's financing originated from the resources of the Economic and Social Stabilization Fund and the issuance of bonds authorized by the 2009 Budget Law. Of the US$4 billion, it was announced that US$3 billion would be assigned to finance spending and investments in Chilean pesos, while the remaining US$1 billion would be used to finance spending and investments in dollars. In the case of the US$3 billion, the Treasury requested that the central bank, acting as fiscal agent, sell foreign exchange through a system of competitive bidding, consisting of daily sales of US$50 million.

As a result of the lower tax revenue triggered by the 2009 recession and the greater public spending to counteract the contraction in private demand, government spending in 2009 increased by 17.8 percent in real terms—three times the average increase registered from 2000 to 2008—and the fiscal deficit increased to 4.5 percent of GDP. This increase in spending implied a larger fiscal stimulus in Chile than in other Latin American countries (figure 15.28).

Conclusions

Chile's sound fundamentals and strong macroeconomic management provided a buffer against the global economic recession, which nevertheless hit the country through a sharp deterioration in its terms of trade and the fall in external demand for Chilean exports. There was room for significant macroeconomic stimulus, thanks to prudent fiscal policy during the boom years. This provision, together with the rebound in copper prices and the revival of global trade, contributed to a turnaround in - activity in 2010. Although the economy is coming out of recession, unemployment is projected to remain initially high, and inflation is likely to stay low.

From an *intertemporal perspective*, Chile was much more integrated into the world economy, both in trade and in finance, in 2008–09 than in the mid-1970s and in the early 1980s. However, when faced with the 2008–09 international crisis, Chile performed much better than in those previous crises. Indeed, in comparison with the very significant international crises of the mid-1970s and early 1980s (both much smaller than the 2008–09 crisis), the decline in Chilean GDP was significantly (10 times) lower; similarly, the highest unemployment rate registered in those two previous crises was 1.5 and 2 times bigger, respectively, than the 10 percent registered in 2009. And although in 2009 the decline in Chilean GDP (–1.5 percent) was bigger than the 0.7 percent drop in 1999 (Asian crisis), the size of the 2009 international shock was also much greater than in 1999.

Figure 15.27. Market Value of Chile's Sovereign Wealth Fund, 2006–09

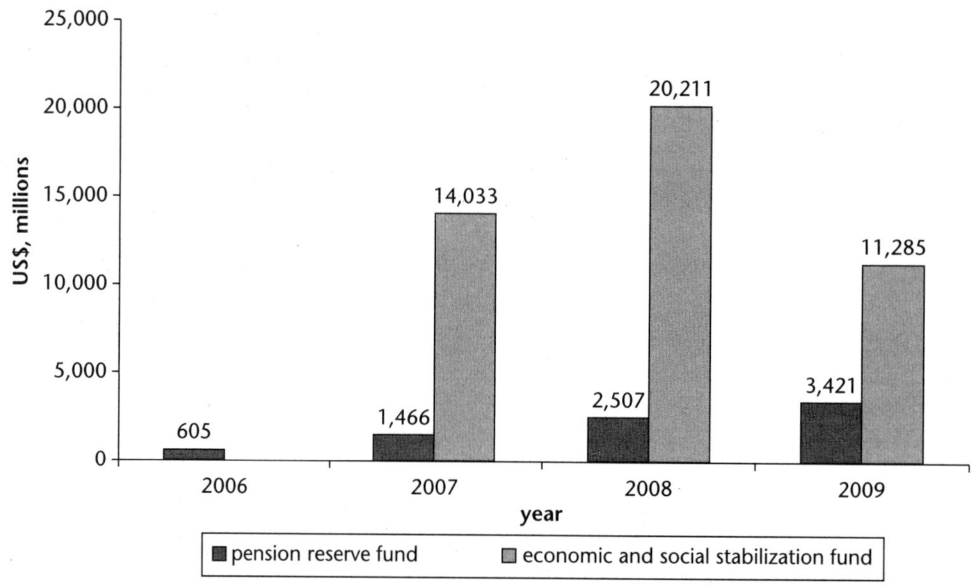

Source: Statistical Database, Ministry of Finance, Santiago, http://www.hacienda.cl/english/estadisticas/.

Figure 15.28. Chile's Fiscal Balance, 2003–09

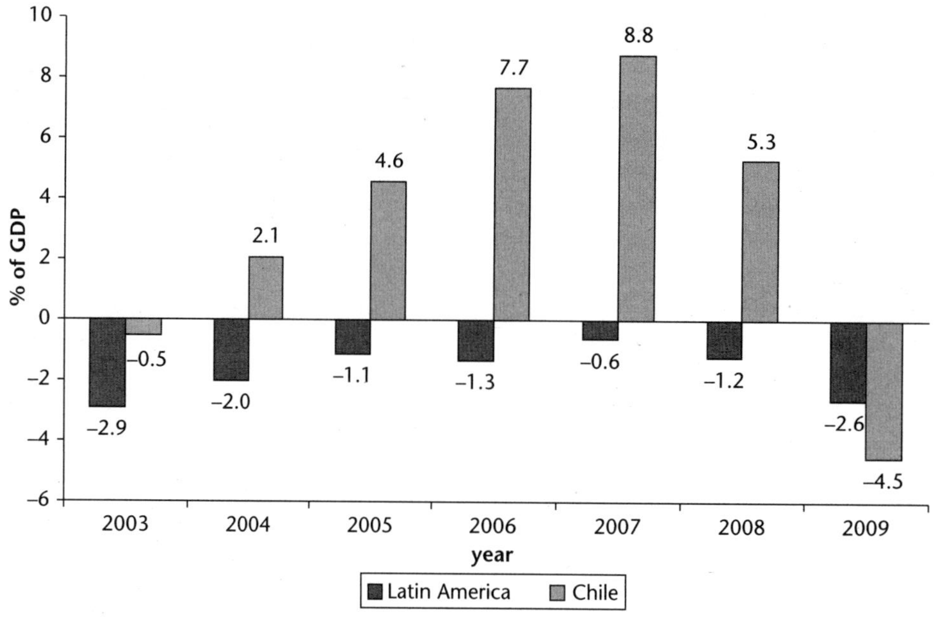

Source: Zahler & Co., based on data from the United Nations Economic Commission for Latin America and the Caribbean (ECLAC) and the Ministry of Finance: CEPALSTAT (database), ECLAC, Santiago, http://websie.eclac.cl/infest/ajax/cepalstat.asp?carpeta=estadisticas&idioma=i; and Statistical Database, Ministry of Finance, Santiago, http://www.hacienda.cl/english/estadisticas/.

A macroeconomic framework characterized by a prudent fiscal policy, a monetary policy of inflation targeting and a floating exchange rate, and a solvent and well-regulated financial system allowed the implementation of strong countercyclical fiscal and monetary policies in 2009. These policies contributed to substantially improving the performance of the Chilean economy in comparison with the mid-1970s and the early 1980s. More specifically, the accumulation of international reserves, both by the central bank and by the government, proved to be a good insurance policy against a major foreign shock. In fact, Chile's accumulation of significant fiscal surpluses during the boom years of the world economy and high copper prices (2003–07) allowed the country to engage in self-financed stimulus without jeopardizing the policies or the authorities' credibility. In short, the most recent world trade contraction hit Chilean external demand, but, thanks to countercyclical monetary and fiscal policies in 2009, internal demand turned out to be quite resilient, although not enough to lift global demand. This macroeconomic framework was not in place during the two prior crises, which required strong domestic adjustment through major fiscal contractions and increases in interest rates, together with abrupt and significant devaluations, all of which amplified the effects of those two previous world crises on the Chilean economy.

In contrast, from a *cross-section perspective*, the performance of the Chilean economy in 2008–09 was not better than that of several other Latin American countries, despite the magnitude of Chile's expansionary policies. In fact, the fall in Chile's GDP in 2009 was surpassed only by Mexico—a country with a high dependence on the U.S. economy—and the Républica Bolivariana de Venezuela. Other countries, such as Argentina, Brazil, Colombia, Ecuador, and Peru saw their economies growing marginally in 2009 or experiencing a smaller drop in GDP than the Chilean one. It is possible that, in this comparison, the Chilean economy was more affected because of its very high degree of trade and financial openness to the international economy.

However, when the crisis became acute, the conditions faced by Chile were quite different from the other countries considered. In 2008 and 2009, Chilean industrial activity suffered two major shocks not related to the crisis (methanol production and exports fell significantly because of lack of gas in the south of Chile); and salmon output and exports also fell drastically because of inadequate sanitary conditions and lack of appropriate sector regulation. Before the crisis erupted, Chile's GDP growth rate had been trending downward from 2004 (6 percent) to 2007 (3.7 percent), and the 2009 figure of 1.5 percent implies that, with the single exception of Colombia, Chile had, among the countries considered, the smallest drop in GDP growth rate between 2009 and 2008. In the same vein, Chile's average rate of inflation in 2008 (8.7 percent) was the highest, with the exception of the Républica Bolivariana de Venezuela, of all Latin American countries considered, requiring a stronger price stabilization policy (that is, higher interest rates), which inevitably had a negative effect on Chile's GDP growth rate in 2009. In fact, in 2009 Chile's average rate of inflation fell eight percentage points from 2008, by far the largest drop in the sample considered. Furthermore, Chile's current account improved by 3.7 percent of GDP in 2009 over 2008, the second-highest improvement in the sample considered and very similar to the 3.9 percent registered by Peru.

Although the medium-term *macroeconomic policy framework* has worked well and the Chilean economy benefited from its implementation by successive governments, there is room for further improvement. Chile could consider complementing its fiscal rule with a ceiling on growth in government spending. During booms, such ceilings help accumulate additional funds, which can then be used countercyclically in sharp downturns. The financial system is generally well regulated, but a consolidated approach to financial conglomerates and stronger supervision of nonbank financial institutions would be useful. Additional strengthening of the insurance element of the unemployment benefit system, in combination with lowering severance pay, would provide more effective protection for the unemployed and would contribute to greater flexibility in the labor market. Although the valued-added content of exports and product diversification are still lagging, this lag may be explained by Chile's development stage, in that it can still benefit from comparative advantages based on natural resource abundance and their "light" industrialization, while the country deals with—and perhaps solves—its major challenge: increasing the growth of total factor productivity.

Although Chile's per capita income on the basis of purchasing power parity has increased markedly over the past two decades, TFP has stagnated in the past decade. In addition, although poverty has been reduced quite significantly, income distribution remains extremely skewed, and many sectors of the population do not feel integrated into the country's development and modernization process. Income inequality, as measured by the Gini coefficient, has not declined much over the past 20 years and remains very high by standards of the Organisation for Economic Co-operation and Development (OECD). Sustained growth will need to be accompanied by the right social policies to reduce poverty further and improve income distribution. The OECD, Chilean think tanks, and academics generally agree that TFP growth should be dealt with by microeconomic policies and additional reforms, aimed at fostering competition, entrepreneurship, and innovation; improving the quality of education; and modernizing labor market practices and regulation.

Facilitating entrepreneurship could have beneficial effects on productivity and economic dynamism. For this purpose, the regulatory red tape that burdens start-ups should be reduced, and bankruptcy procedures could be further simplified. Until recently, the innovation policy framework focused on basic research in public institutes and universities. As a consequence, the private business sector's propensity to engage in technological (product or process) and nontechnological (marketing or organizational) innovation is still low. Several measures have been taken to improve industry-science relationships to make scientific research more market relevant. Efforts to strengthen links between companies and universities should be continued.

The quality and equity of primary and secondary education have to be improved. Notwithstanding impressive progress in school enrollment, much remains to be done if Chilean children are to reach OECD standards in learning outcomes. Better-qualified teachers and improved initial teacher education and training are key to this purpose.

As mentioned, rigidities in the labor market—relatively high minimum wages and wage indexation—tend to impede the response of wages to an increase in unemployment and to negative external shocks. In addition, severance pay rights are often several times higher than unemployment benefits, contributing to slower adjustment of the economy after adverse shocks. Unemployment benefits rest largely on individual savings accounts with small supplements from an insurance fund, the Fondo Solidario, which had very restrictive access until recently. Increasing replacement rates for all workers and extending duration, while simultaneously restricting severance pay, would provide more effective workers' protection and would allow for more efficient job search, thus maximizing workers' productivity. If these reforms could be put in place, Chile not only would likely be better prepared to face international shocks but also could enter another development stage, where exports have a higher degree of value added as well as greater diversification of goods and services.

Regarding *Chile's development strategy*, expected trends in the international economy tend to support the overall approach of the past 25 years. The most likely scenario after the 2008–09 crisis is that Asia will be the most dynamic region in the world economy. Asia has been steadily increasing its consumption of copper, as a share of total world consumption, in the past 10 years, from less than 40 percent in 1999 to nearly 55 percent in 2008, and this trend is likely to continue. The relative scarcity of natural resources, made more acute by rapid urbanization, has made Asia an important importer of commodities and copper. Furthermore, most of Asia and Chile have complementary roles in endowments, which are increasingly reflected in growing trade relations. Therefore, and in spite of high transport and communications costs, long delivery time, very different time zones, and no direct air links between Chile and Asia—given the high complementarity between China's and Chile's export structure and the number of free trade agreements signed with Asian countries—Chile's thus far rather neutral outward-oriented development strategy appears to be validated. However, given that Chile's 2009 per capita GDP was similar to that of Australia in 1985 and of New Zealand in the mid-1990s, Chile should seriously consider development strategies followed by those two countries, which changed their export structure quite significantly. Such policies could lead to a change in Chile's productive structure, allowing more rapid growth in production of industrial goods, services, and technology.

Chile will go on benefiting from Asia, especially from China's increasing demand for copper and cellulose and eventually for other Chilean exportable goods based on raw materials. This likely outcome should act as an incentive for further inward FDI in sectors related to raw materials. In this regard, China, which wants to ensure its access to raw materials and guarantee future supplies, could extend to Chile its recent policy of funding investment projects in other regions, because Chile is a country with a long-standing policy of openness and nondiscrimination against FDI. Chinese and Indian FDI into Chile is extremely small, and there is huge opportunity to increase it and help boost trade with Asia.

16

THE INTERNATIONAL CRISIS AND DEVELOPMENT STRATEGIES: THE CASE OF MALAYSIA

Mahani Zainal Abidin

Because it is a small and very open economy, where total trade is twice the size of its gross domestic product (GDP), Malaysia is very vulnerable to international economic events. All three crises that Malaysia has experienced in the past 25 years were triggered by external factors. The 1985 crisis, in which GDP contracted by 1 percent, was due to the collapse of commodity prices. The 1998 crisis, with a fall in GDP of 7.4 percent, was caused by regional contagion from massive short-term capital outflows. Finally, the 2009 crisis, in which GDP fell by 1.7 percent, was the result of an export slump.

Malaysia's economic growth has long been dependent on exports, starting with primary commodities (rubber and tin) in the 1950s and now including manufacturing exports (in particular electrical goods and electronics), palm oil, petroleum, and tourism. It is not surprising that international developments and global volatility are major concerns, because these factors can have a significant impact on Malaysia's short-term economic performance as well as on its medium- and long-term development strategies. The 2008–09 global crisis raises a fundamental question about Malaysia's development strategy, in particular, its dependence on manufacturing exports. This issue has led some to suggest a more balanced approach that would involve strengthening domestic demand as a counterbalance in case exports drop sharply in the future. This concern is based on the faltering economic recovery in the United States and the prospects of weak growth in the Euro Area, which may dampen global trade and economic development for some time to come.

This chapter will discuss the policy options available to Malaysia for producing sustained high growth based on its extensive global links and strong dependency on international trade and on financial and investment flows. It will focus on two issues in Malaysia's outward-oriented development strategy: first, its potential for producing sustained high growth and, second, its ability to cope with global volatility. The chapter begins by analyzing the state of the Malaysian economy before the 2008–09 crisis and the main differences between the present crisis and the other crises that Malaysia has faced in the past. The impact of the present crisis will then be discussed in the second part, followed by Malaysia's economic recovery. The chapter concludes with an analysis of options for Malaysia's outward-oriented development strategy.

State of the Malaysian Economy before the Global Crisis

The 1998 Asian financial crisis was a seminal experience for Malaysia. It provided the incentive for building up additional strength to mitigate the effects of future crises. One of the key reform measures undertaken was to strengthen the financial sector. The overcrowded banking sector (with 58 financial institutions) was consolidated into 10 banking groups with larger capital requirements. Improvements in the banking sector are reflected in the low level of nonperforming loans: the Malaysian banking sector's nonperforming loans as a share of financial assets were one of the lowest among Asian economies for 2008. Exposure to foreign loans was also kept to a minimum. Additional prudential measures were put in place, and corporate governance was strengthened. Malaysia took a more cautious approach to financial liberalization and set out guidelines and plans in the Financial Sector Masterplan and Capital Market Masterplan, both introduced in 2001. As a result, Malaysia was very cautious when approving the use of complex, innovative, yet risky financial instruments such as collateralized debt obligations.

Since 1998, Malaysia has produced continuous trade surpluses (for 151 months), which enabled the accumulation of large international reserves and a healthy balance-of-payments position. Manufactured exports continue to be the major component of exports, while palm oil and petroleum have increased their share, mainly thanks to high commodity prices. Table 16.1 gives the summary indicators of the health of the Malaysian economy in 2007, that is immediately before the current crisis.

Another good lesson that Malaysia learned from the 1998 Asian crisis was the importance of having sufficient international reserves. The possibility of large and volatile capital outflows through the loss of market confidence or activities of currency speculators made Malaysia more cautious in liberalizing its financial sector and capital markets. It began accumulating reserves to meet such eventualities.

Notwithstanding these sound macroeconomic fundamentals, Malaysia has a number of vulnerabilities. Since 1998, Malaysia has had a persistent fiscal deficit and has proved unable to revert to a surplus. This situation has constrained Malaysia's ability to stimulate the economy for a sustained period of time in the event of an export slowdown. Because of the rapid recovery from the 1998 crisis and Malaysia's unwillingness to undergo the structural adjustment programs imposed by the International Monetary Fund on other crisis-hit countries (Indonesia, the Republic of Korea, and Thailand, for example), the Malaysian economy, in particular the manufacturing sector, escaped deep restructuring. The exception was the financial sector, as mentioned earlier.

Table 16.1. Malaysia's Economic Conditions before the Global Crisis, 2007

Indicator	Malaysia
Current account balance (% of GDP)	15.5
Foreign exchange reserves	101.2
External debt (% of GDP)	32.2
Fiscal balance (% of GDP)	−3.2
Government debt (% of GDP)	38.5
Domestic credit (% change)	8.6
Nonperforming loans (% of total loans)	3.8
Interest rates (%)	3.54
Consumer price index (% change year on year)	2.0

Source: World Development Indicators database, World Bank, http://data.worldbank.org.

Impact of the 2008 Global Crisis

The global financial crisis of 2008–09 with its epicenter in the United States has had enormous ramifications for the world economy. It started as an asset bubble caused by an array of financial derivatives that, among other things, caused the subprime mortgage boom and bust. It then sent shock waves through banking and financial institutions with a subsequent effect on consumer demand. As consumer demand in the United States shrank, export-oriented Asian economies began to face an economic contraction in the real sector. Hence, although the Malaysian economy was insulated from the direct effects of financial exposure (partly because derivatives were not widely permitted) the crisis has affected the economy through a collapse in exports, a large capital outflow, and a slowdown in foreign direct investment (FDI). The Malaysian financial sector escaped unscathed from the global crisis because it was in a strong position as a result of the measures taken in the 1998 crisis and higher capital requirements.

As a consequence of the crisis, the Malaysian economy began to slow down in the fourth quarter of 2008, when GDP grew by only 0.1 percent (figure 16.1). The full impact of the global crisis was felt in the first three quarters of 2009, when GDP declined by 6.2 percent, 3.9 percent, and 1.2 percent, respectively. The indirect sources of contraction came from all sectors dependent on GDP growth—consumer and investment demand. Falling demand has already driven firms to retrench and lay off workers. Although retrenchments reported by government sources are few, it is believed that both underemployment (and with it the consequent contraction in incomes) and unemployment are really much higher.

During this global crisis, transmission of the impact to the Malaysian economy was different from that during the Asian crisis in 1998. This time, transmission was through the real sector, namely, exports, investment flows, and prices of exports, unlike the developed countries, where the primary channel was through the financial sector. While the impact on the real economy for the developed countries came later, for Malaysia the real sector was the first point of impact—the financial sector was almost unaffected.

Given Malaysia's high ratio of exports to GDP, contraction in external demand was the most serious factor burdening the economy. The direct sources of problems came from a contraction in export demand—particularly in manufacturing—as the developed markets (the European

Figure 16.1. Real GDP Growth in Malaysia, 2008–10

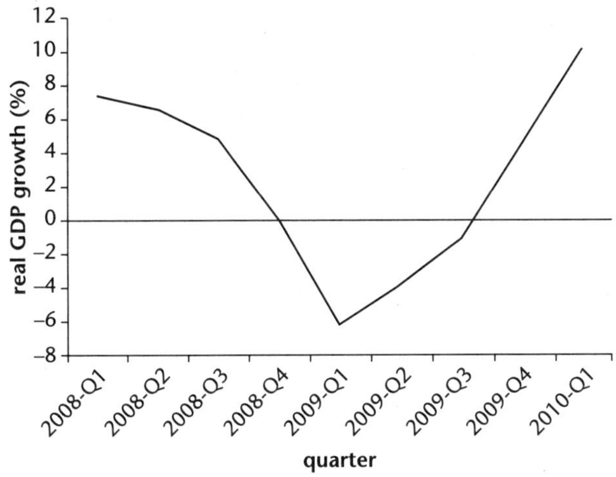

Source: East Asia Update database, World Bank, http://www.worldbank.org/eapupdate.

Figure 16.2. Merchandise Export Growth in Malaysia, Quarter 1, 2008–Quarter 1, 2010

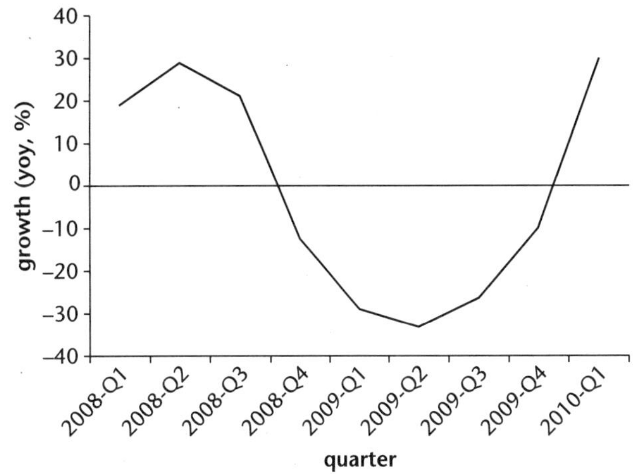

Source: External Trade Database, Department of Statistics, Malaysia, http://www.statistics.gov.my.
Note: yoy = year on year.

Union [EU] and the United States) were gripped by a recession. The slowdown through exports was also caused by East Asian trade and production links through intricate production networks and vertical specialization. As a result, demand for intermediate goods from Malaysia was affected when demand for final goods manufactured in regional production networks fell.

Malaysia has never before seen such steep drops in its manufactured exports, as shown by figure 16.2. In 2008, manufactured exports expanded by 13.4 percent, but in 2009, they fell by 21.1 percent. However, the drop in exports did not cause a deficit in the trade account, because imports fell even more sharply. The structure of its manufacturing sector provides a balancing mechanism that helps the balance of trade remain positive when exports decline. Imports are used mostly for producing export goods, while exports of resource-based industries use relatively few imported inputs. Consequently, the manufacturing sector was the worst hit among the economic sectors, with a contraction of 9.4 percent in 2009 as shown in table 16.2.

The second direct source is a contraction in inflows of FDI, particularly from the developed countries. Overall, FDI inflows into Malaysia started falling from the third quarter of 2008 until the second quarter of 2009.

Massive global risk aversion and greater demand for liquidity, coupled with pessimistic growth prospects, have resulted in sharp declines in equity prices. The decline was most pronounced in September 2008. Continuous and healthy trade surpluses had enabled Malaysia to accumulate a comparatively large stock of international reserves, which at its peak stood at about US$125 billion (as of June 2008), or nine months of retained imports. These reserves were able to meet the demand of the large capital outflows of US$8.7 billion in the second quarter and US$11 billion in the third quarter of 2008. Capital outflows gave rise to a small ringgit depreciation against the U.S. dollar.

The crisis also triggered a slump in commodity prices from their high in the first quarter of 2008. The collapse of commodity prices has affected the income of key sectors in the Malaysian economy, palm oil and petroleum. At the same time, though, it has removed the inflationary pressure experienced in the first half of 2008, when oil prices reached US$147 per barrel.

The deteriorating trade and production conditions and the large outflow of short-term capital did not significantly erode consumer confidence and business conditions. The consumer sentiment index survey conducted by the Malaysian Institute of Economic Research shows that consumer confidence is still relatively intact. Although consumer sentiment dipped slightly in the second quarter of 2008, it then rebounded in the third quarter. The institute's business conditions index showed that the private sector expected deteriorating prospects for business conditions in the middle of 2008.

Diminishing industrial production led to layoffs and higher unemployment. The number of laid-off workers due to the crisis was not very serious, however. According to the Ministry of Human Resources, total layoffs from October 1, 2008, to January 22, 2009, were 14,158, comprising largely local workers (10,636). The ministry tends to view the situation as manageable, because there were also 16,600 vacancies, that is, a number greater than the total number of layoffs.

Table 16.2. Malaysia's GDP by Sector, 2007–Quarter 1, 2010
annual % change

	2007	2008	2009	Q1 2009	Q2 2009	Q3 2009	Q4 2009	Q1 2010
Agriculture	1.4	4.3	0.4	–4.4	0.4	–0.4	5.9	6.8
Construction	4.7	4.2	5.8	1.2	4.5	7.9	9.3	8.7
Manufacturing	3.1	1.3	–9.4	–17.9	–14.5	–8.6	5.0	16.9
Mining	2.0	–2.4	–3.8	–5.2	–3.5	–3.6	–2.8	2.1
Services	9.6	7.4	2.6	–0.2	1.7	3.4	5.2	8.5

Source: Quarterly Malaysian Economy, various issues, Ministry of Finance, Malaysia, http://www.treasury.gov.my.

Recovery

Malaysia decided that domestic demand should play a bigger role in mitigating the economic recession and introduced fiscal stimulus programs to overcome the export contraction and maintain stability in the economy. The government implemented a monetary policy and fiscal injections to mitigate the negative impact of the global crisis. However, the fiscal injections were the more pronounced because they were quite big and covered many economic areas. The benefits of fiscal stimulus include, among others, raising output and incomes in the short run when the economy is operating below its potential. This approach is considerably different from the 1998 capital controls because the approach now retains a flexible exchange rate with minimum regulation from the central bank compared to the fixing of the ringgit against the dollar and the banning of ringgit transactions outside the country in September 1998. The stock market was also shielded in 1998, whereas it remains fairly liberal now.

The initial reaction of the government to the global crisis was to relax monetary policy. Expansionary monetary policy was implemented as early as December 2008. Bank Negara Malaysia (the Malaysian central bank) had maintained reasonably low interest rates before the global crisis, despite high inflation in early 2008 caused by the increase in world crude oil prices and the removal of petrol and diesel subsidies in the country. The liquidity ratio for the economy was reported to be satisfactory despite gloomy reports from export industries and increasing retrenchments in the manufacturing sector. Accordingly, the revision of the overnight policy rate and the statutory reserve requirement (SRR) led to a reduction in the base lending rate; in February, the overnight policy rate was reduced to 2 percent from 3.5 percent in 2007.

The government unveiled two economic stimulus packages (ESP) allocating RM 7 billion (US$1.9 billion) or 1.04 percent of GDP (ESP1) in November 2008, and RM 60 billion (US$16.2 billion) or 9 percent of GDP (ESP2) in March 2009. The ESP 1 was targeted to cover the first quarter of 2009. The ESP 2 covers two years, 2009 and 2010. The main purpose of the packages was to boost domestic aggregate demand.

Nearly 43 percent of the first package was intended for infrastructure, to upgrade, repair, and maintain public amenities, including schools, hospitals, roads, quarters for police and armed forces, and police stations, for example. It also covered the building of more low-cost houses, more public transportation, and the implementation of high-speed broadband. The package contained three main parts: ensuring citizens' well-being, developing quality human capital, and strengthening national resilience. While projects relating to these three main thrusts vary in nature, they focus primarily on construction and infrastructure, transport, the banking and finance sectors, and education.

Malaysia's second stimulus package was 8.5 times larger than the first and equivalent to 9 percent of its GDP. Nearly 48 percent went to assist the private sector through bank guarantees for small- and medium-size companies. Another 32 percent went to infrastructure. But of this sum, a substantial portion went to maintenance rather than to new spending on public facilities. Seventeen percent of the spending from the second stimulus was targeted to the vulnerable through food, toll, and fuel subsidies and for support of low-cost housing and laid-off workers. The remaining 3 percent went toward reducing unemployment and increasing job and training opportunities. Although a total sum of RM 60 billion was announced for this second stimulus, the actual spending in 2009 and 2010 was only RM 10 billion. Tax incentives amounted to RM 3 billion, and RM 10 billion is for strategic investment by the national sovereign wealth fund. With this large stimulus package relative to GDP, Malaysia's fiscal deficit rose from 4.8 percent in 2008 to 7.6 percent in 2009.

ESP 2 covers the period 2009 and 2010 and is focused on four main areas: reducing unemployment and increasing employment opportunities, easing the burden on citizens, assisting the private sector in facing the crisis, and building capacity for the future. Like other countries in the region, Malaysia recovered relatively quickly. After negative GDP growth in the third quarter of 2009, the fourth quarter registered growth of 4.5 percent. Growth in the first quarter of 2010 was very encouraging at 10.1 percent: Malaysia's growth was among the highest in East Asia. This commendable performance is attributed to the strong regional growth and revival of exports due to restocking by industries, although fiscal stimulus programs could have kept the economy buoyant during the export slowdown. The high growth rate in the first quarter 2010 is perhaps assisted by the low base (year-on-year).

Malaysia's Development Strategies Going Forward

The 2008–09 global crisis has sharpened the debate on the future of Malaysia's outward-oriented development strategy that began during the Asian crisis in 1998. This call for review of Malaysia's growth path is not unexpected, given the importance of the contribution of its external sector and its integration into the global economy. The contribution of the external sector comes in three ways: exports, financial flows, and FDI. Export industries have created employment, upgraded the skills of workers, acquired technology, and put Malaysia in regional production networks. Export surpluses have provided the liquidity to expand economic activities and buy imports. The financial flows and FDI are important sources of investment. Increasing global volatility has heightened concerns that the Malaysian growth strategy might be too dependent on external factors.

Although the two crises—the 1998 Asian and 2008–09 global—have had different impacts on the Malaysian economy, they both point to some very useful and pertinent lessons. On the one hand, in the 1998 crisis, the external shock had severe consequences for the Malaysian financial sector, whereas the export sector was only marginally affected and in fact led the recovery process. On the other hand, in the 2008–09 global crisis, the Malaysian financial sector escaped the spillover effects of the collapse of the developed countries' financial sector, especially major financial institutions. The unexpected outcome was the deep contraction of real sector exports. Likewise, the movement of the ringgit was very different in the two crises: in 1998, the ringgit depreciated by 45 percent causing massive damage to the economy, which prompted the imposition of capital controls and pegging of the ringgit. In contrast, the movement of the ringgit was mild in the 2008–09 crisis.

Lessons from the Two Crises

A number of lessons can be drawn from these two crises. First, the health of the real sector in the major markets for Malaysia (the developed markets) has an important and immediate impact on Malaysian exports. In this case, the issue of competitiveness and the state of Malaysian export industries are secondary, because the collapse in global demand automatically results in a fall in demand for Malaysian exports and leads to an economic slowdown or even a recession.

Second, because of Malaysia's heavy dependence on exports, the revival from the economic slowdown is very much dependent on external demand, be it regional or global. Recovery by expanding domestic demand may not be as quick because measures such as public sector infrastructure investment or tax deductions will take time to produce the required results. Recovery very much depended on exports in both the 1998 and the 2009 crises.

Third, for the financial sector, the state of the domestic sector is critical in determining its ability to withstand global shocks. When that sector is strong and well governed, the impact of external volatility will be manageable.

Fourth, building safeguards is important to assuring domestic and foreign constituencies that economic fundamentals are strong. In this regard, sufficiently large international reserves, low short-term external debt, and a realistic exchange rate are some of the fundamentals that maintain public and investor confidence.

Fifth, it is important to differentiate between external shocks that affect demand and those that affect the competitiveness and strength of the external sector—export industries, the financial sector, or the investment climate. It is difficult to be insulated from demand shocks, but recovery will be quick once demand is restored. However, if the external sector is uncompetitive, medium- and long-term growth will be jeopardized.

Is Malaysia's Outward-Oriented Strategy the Right Approach?

Why is Malaysia's external dependency and outward-oriented development strategy being questioned now? The seeds of doubt about its strategy were sown during the 1998 Asian crisis. Before that crisis, Malaysia was very positive about globalization and its close integration with the international economy. Moreover, the rapid recovery from crisis, partly based on the newly introduced measures, gave the impression that the crisis was a one-off event and that global volatility would be confined to short-term capital flows and currency speculators. In addition, expanding international trade was seen as a key reason for the recovery.

Unlike the 1998 crisis, this 2008–09 global crisis has called into question Malaysia's outward development strategies because of the gloomy prospects for trade growth as a result of the economic difficulties in its two major markets—the EU and the United States. This time the fundamental issue is weak demand for exports, and there is relatively little Malaysia can do about that. The massive export decline in 2009 has highlighted Malaysia's heavy reliance on global trade: cutting of costs, improvement of competitiveness, or currency depreciation will not revive demand for exports. The more cautious approach to financial liberalization and integration taken after the 1998 crisis was seen as having saved Malaysia from the potentially devastating damage that was suffered by the financial sectors in developed countries.

But the larger concern is the prospect of growth in Malaysia's largest export markets, the EU the United States. EU fiscal adjustments may see stringent government cutbacks that can reduce growth significantly, and the United States has to tackle its high unemployment if it is to have a sustainable recovery. With the developed countries likely to grow slower for some time, what are the prospects for demand for Malaysian exports? Although East Asia, China in particular, has stepped in to assist the global recovery, there are doubts about whether the region can create sustainable demand to replace that lost from the EU and the United States.

The call to review Malaysia's outward-oriented strategy was reinforced further with declining growth of manufacturing exports and FDI inflows. Before 1996, Malaysian manufacturing exports were growing at over 20 percent per year (for example, in 1994 the growth rate was 34 percent). However, the annual growth rate for 1996–99 was 13.2 percent, and for the period 2000–09, it was only 5 percent. Besides this performance, an added concern is the inability of manufacturing exports to move up the value chain: some industries continue making existing products by keeping costs low through the use of low-skilled, low-cost foreign workers. Smaller FDI flows are another concern because Malaysia's growth strategy has been premised on a high investment ratio. With the public sector cutting its investment to reduce the fiscal deficit, more efforts have been made to attract FDI, but with few results to show so far. Many incentives were offered for this purpose, which resulted in some parties' questioning the net benefit of FDI. The most obvious benefit is employment creation, but the net value added of multinational companies' exports, links to the domestic economy, and transfer of technology are generally small. Some have recommended promotion of domestic investment and technology development to deepen industrial integration.

In short, the calls for Malaysia to review its outward-oriented development strategies are prompted by the vulnerability caused by global shocks and potentially lower global demand, as well as Malaysia's own difficulties in sharpening its export competitiveness and attracting larger FDI volumes. But in the short and medium term, Malaysia is likely to continue depending on the international economy for its growth. Switching to domestic demand can be only a long-term strategy, because Malaysia has to increase its domestic market and purchasing power first before that strategy can be effective. Notwithstanding the importance of outward orientation, it is imperative for Malaysia to have a balanced growth strategy that expands domestic demand while at the same time improving its global competitiveness and links.

Malaysia realizes that it needs to continue the high-global-dependency approach; yet it is also aware that that approach will expose its economy to unpredictable swings with serious negative consequences. Continuing the present outward-oriented strategy, however, will also require frequent fine-tuning and refocusing. In the meantime, Malaysia still needs to mitigate possible negative impacts coming from future external shocks and volatility, since these are part and parcel of globalization. For this purpose, it is useful to give examples of how Malaysia has managed some past vulnerabilities.

Primary commodities are important export products for Malaysia in revenue contribution and participation in the global economy. For example, in 2008, exports of primary commodities—oil and gas, palm oil, sawn timber—contributed about 25 percent of total exports. Changes in commodity prices can negatively affect smallholders in the palm oil and rubber industries, whose incomes are already at low levels. Long cycles of commodity prices have produced surpluses that formed a substantial source of government revenues. These revenues were used to finance Malaysia's development program by building basic infrastructure such as schools and hospitals. In the case of oil, a significant proportion of these revenues were invested abroad to find new oil and gas reserves as well as in other business activities to diversify income sources. For the palm oil industry, a levy collected from large producers is used to fund development of the industry and to provide a buffer in case of a fall in prices.

The increasing global competition for FDI has prompted Malaysia to improve its investment climate. A number of measures have been introduced for this purpose, including a wide range of new incentives, reducing red tape for faster approval processes, liberalizing equity ownership rules (for example in 1998, full foreign ownership was allowed in the manufacturing sector), and establishing a more flexible policy on recruitment of skilled foreign workers.

Stronger governance, adherence to international standards, higher capital requirements, and consolidation of financial institutions are among the measures introduced for the financial sector. These enable such institutions to cope better with external shocks and deeper liberalization.

Proposals for Bringing Sustained High Growth to Malaysia

As noted earlier, Malaysia should continue with its outward-oriented development strategy, but it should refocus and improve that strategy. What sorts of policies can help Malaysia mitigate the impact of future global financial crises on trade? Can Malaysia minimize its exposure to the volatility that comes with globalization without moving away from an export-oriented growth strategy? The following are proposals for improving the outward-oriented strategy and bringing sustained high growth for Malaysia:

- *Have a balanced export structure.* At present, Malaysia's exports come from three major groups—manufacturing, mining, and primary commodities. In the past, this structure has produced a good counterbalance when one component suffered a slowdown; the other groups grew quite well because they had different consumers and demand cycles. Consequently, total exports did not experience a large decline. For example, when manufacturing exports fell, exports of primary commodities increased (sometimes because of either demand or price increases or both). Therefore, Malaysia should keep this balanced export structure. The structure of manufacturing exports, however, is too skewed toward the electrical and electronics industry. Expansion of other manufacturing exports is needed if Malaysia is to avoid any sharp drop in manufacturing exports as a result of a fall in global demand for electrical and electronics products.
- *Accelerate the expansion of services exports.* Malaysia has made good progress in promoting services exports: tourism is a major export earner, and the Multimedia Super Corridor is focusing on information technologies and business off-shoring services. Other services exports that have been identified are Islamic finance, health and education services, and air passenger transport services. Malaysia has strategic advantages in these areas, including its diverse cultural and ethnic society, good health and education services, and first-mover advantage in low-cost air transport services.
- *Upgrade existing exports.* Manufacturing and primary commodity exports should be upgraded to incorporate higher value added and innovation. This move will reduce the possibility of hollowing out the production of manufacturing exports to other low-cost producers. Technology acquisition and availability of skilled labor are essential for this transformation. Another important measure is to develop more exports that originate in Malaysia. Currently, a sizable portion of Malaysian manufacturing exports are produced as part of regional production networks (primarily in the electrical and electronics industry). Although this form of export is very important and has produced large benefits, Malaysia should also develop its own export capability separate from these production chains. For primary commodities, it is imperative to increase the proportion of downstream exports, especially with the emergence of more low-cost producers of upstream products.
- *Diversify markets.* East Asia has now become Malaysia's largest trading partner, although markets outside the region are the final destination of a large part of those exports. Notably, China's share in manufactured exports has increased from 1.7 percent in 1996 to 12 percent in 2009. The share of the Association of Southeast Asian Nations remains at about 27 percent. The share of traditional markets has declined, however: the United States to 13.2 percent in 2009 from 21.7 in 1996, the EU to 12.2 percent from 14.5 percent, and Japan to 7 percent from 11.1 percent for the same period. Diversification is important especially in view of the moderate growth prospects and consequent lower demand for imports from these traditional markets. If China and other Asian countries are able to generate their own domestic demand, then the prospects for Malaysia's exports will be bright.
- *Prepare the financial sector for more global competition.* Malaysia has already undertaken measures to prepare the financial sector for global competition, as discussed earlier. It should implement measures proposed in the Financial Sector Masterplan and Capital Market Masterplan as well as introducing additional steps to improve governance, enhance standards, and strengthen industry players.
- *Improve the investment climate to attract FDI.* Recently, Malaysia has restructured its main investment promotion agency (Malaysia Industrial Development Authority) as part of a larger initiative to attract both domestic and foreign investment. Another focus area is reducing unnecessary barriers in the investment approval process. Since Malaysia is already host to a large amount of FDI, more efforts should be made to encourage reinvestment because these investors are already operating locally and relationships have been formed.

Besides these specific proposals, the ability to withstand global volatility and to continue to be a destination of choice for businesses will depend on Malaysia's own initial conditions. Strong macroeconomic fundamentals such as low national and foreign debts, a sound fiscal position, low inflation and unemployment, a current account surplus, high international competitiveness, capacity for research and development and technological development, and availability of skilled workers are factors that provide confidence to the market and investors. In a way, the above recommendations are the insurance policy that Malaysia can establish to protect itself from global volatility, because markets and investors will be confident about the health of the domestic economy and of its ability to ride out the volatility.

The currency exchange rate also has a similar role in an outward-oriented development strategy as an important component of macroeconomic fundamentals and as an instrument for determining export competitiveness. An unsustainable exchange rate that does not reflect economic fundamentals can lead to speculative attacks and undermine market confidence. At the same time, if the exchange rate is kept at an unrealistically low level to ensure export competitiveness, there will be an upward pressure to reflect the true economic fundamentals. Thus, management of the exchange rate to balance export competitiveness against economic fundamentals is critical for stability in the outward-oriented development strategy.

Preferential trade agreements, economic integration, and regionalism are initiatives for ensuring a stable and predictable environment for external economic relationships. Liberalization is the major part of these initiatives wherein rules and regulations are set to ease market access and promote investment. For this purpose, Malaysia has embarked on a number of bilateral, regional, and multilateral trade agreements. They provide certainty in conducting trade, which is essential for increasing trade volume; trade agreements are, however, powerless to prevent global volatility. Nonetheless, such agreements are important for keeping trade channels open and preventing protectionism when economies face a slowdown. The 2008–09 crisis showed that.

In its present trade agreements, Malaysia has not made deep liberalization commitments because of political economy considerations. In the future, it should strive for higher-quality free trade agreements or economic integration pacts as part of its outward-oriented development strategy. Many beyond-the-border issues such as government procurement, opening up of sensitive sectors, ownership rules, and competition policy are liberalized in high-quality free trade agreements. Taking into account political economy sensitivities, Malaysia can still achieve high-quality agreements by selectively liberalizing the contentious areas and doing so progressively. Recently, the government has taken the bold step of removing equity restrictions in 27 services subsectors.

In summary, although Malaysia wants to minimize its exposure to global volatility, it would be difficult to find a substitute for the outward-oriented strategy to drive its growth. Turning to domestic demand as a source of growth is an option that must be considered seriously because it counterbalances sharp global swings. This effort will take time, however, because the government's fiscal position limits its ability to stimulate the economy. Also, household purchasing power needs to be increased through rising wages matched by productivity improvements and a better income distribution. A policy of ramping up demand when households have low savings or limited disposable income will only increase household debt.

Going forward, Malaysia should improve its outward-oriented development strategy as suggested above. This process should strengthen its competitiveness and make it more able to cope with both global volatility and structural changes in the international economy. Although the East Asia region and other emerging markets will be important to Malaysia, Malaysia does not seek to decouple itself from the EU and the United States. Finally, sharp global swings are likely to be increasingly common. Malaysia should get ready now, by buttressing its fundamentals. That approach will reassure domestic and international markets and give it the ability to take whatever measures are necessary to deal with short-term impacts.

17

SHOULD INDONESIA SAY GOODBYE TO ITS STRATEGY OF FACILITATING EXPORTS?

Muhammad Chatib Basri and Sjamsu Rahardja

Millions of Indonesians have witnessed their economy's relative resilience during the global financial crisis. The Indonesian economy continues to grow even though its export engine has been hit as badly as that in other Asian economies. Although Indonesia's share of exports in gross domestic product (GDP) is lower than that of its Asian neighbors, the collapse of global trade was powerful enough to lower GDP growth from 1.5 percent in the third quarter of 2008 to 0.2 percent in the fourth quarter of 2008 (quarter-to-quarter, seasonally adjusted). But domestic demand—that is, private and government consumption—expanded by 4.9 percent in 2009 and provided a cushion for Indonesian economic growth during the early period of the global crisis. It has also supported a quicker economic recovery than in other countries. Many believe that its relatively insulated economy is the reason that Indonesia has performed relatively better than other economies during the global financial crisis (Basri and Rahardja 2010). Given that what saved Indonesia from the dreadful effects of the global financial crisis was the domestic economy, the question arises whether an export-led growth strategy is still relevant. This question is not specific to Indonesia, because many other countries that are more supported by their domestic economies have performed better than export-dependent countries during the global financial crisis (Basri and Rahardja 2010).

The challenge for Indonesia is to manage its economic policy so that it can navigate through the global economic crisis. The crisis provides important lessons for Indonesia, including the need to strengthen domestic demand. However, this experience leads commentators, politicians, and some policy makers to embrace somewhat more nationalist or protectionist views for a new reason: many have argued that Indonesia should limit openness and integration with the global economy to prevent itself from being dragged into the global economic slump. This view adds to the existing notion that openness exposes Indonesian firms to unfair competition. Both views are popular. Political pressures against more openness sometimes influence policy makers to implement more inward-looking policies and rely less on exports. What, then, is the relevance of a strategy that facilitates exports and openness to economic growth?

The chapter examines the future of Indonesia's export-led growth strategy, focusing on questions such as, What reforms can help Indonesia benefit from continuing to open up to trade and investment? What kinds of policies best serve both domestic and global orientation? What was the impact of the global economic crisis on the Indonesian economy? Is the choice of an inward-looking strategy the right one? What role do composition and diversification of exports play in reducing vulnerability? What policies are needed to support export diversification?

The Impact of the Global Financial Crisis on Indonesia

On the financial side, the effects of the global crisis on the Indonesian economy appeared through several indicators, such as a depreciation of the exchange rate and a decline in the stock market.[1] The rupiah exchange rate had fallen by 30 percent by the end of 2008. The Indonesia Stock Market Index experienced a drop of 50 percent in 2008. Growth of banking credit also experienced a significant drop, from 32 percent to 10 percent (Basri and Siregar

2009). In addition, confidence among banks declined, as seen in the shrinking size of interbank borrowing and lending, which was down by 59.3 percent to Rp 83.8 trillion in December 2008 from Rp 206.0 trillion in December 2007 (Gunawan, Arman, and Hendranata 2009). The need to carry out the expansion of banks' funding bases, added to again by increases in interbank rates, had already created sharp competition between banks, which in turn had supported higher interest rates.

Weak global economic growth began reducing demand for Indonesian exports in the fourth quarter of 2008. In addition, the drop in global demand also resulted in weak demand for primary and mining exports, which led to a drop in the price of commodities and mining goods. The fall in global economic growth weakened demand for energy so much that the price of oil also declined. Papanek, Basri, and Schydlowsky (2010) point to an extremely sharp decline in exports in the first quarter of 2009 compared to the same period in the previous year (table 17.1), a decline driven more by price than volume. In fact, the demand for primary commodity exports, especially agriculture and mining, was relatively stable in quantity terms, as indicated by the relative stability of the export volume of agriculture and mining commodities, such as crude palm oil (CPO), coal, and copper (Basri and Rahardja 2010). With natural resources accounting for more than half of Indonesia's exports, they provided some life support for the Indonesian economy (figure 17.1). In addition, the depreciation of the rupiah that took place after September 2008 also compensated for the effects of the collapse in the demand for exports. However, the data show that the increase in demand due to the depreciation of the rupiah (substitution effect) was smaller than the fall in demand due to the decline in income (income effect). As a result, exports experienced an overall reduction.

With the export weakness that started in the fourth quarter of 2008, economic growth slowed to 5.2 percent year on year in the fourth quarter of 2009. Even so, Indonesia's overall economic growth was still 6.1 percent, the highest growth in Asia, after China and India.

Should We Say Goodbye to the Strategy of Facilitating Exports?

Indonesia was not the only country to experience a sharp decline in exports.[2] A similar decline was experienced by many countries, including China, Malaysia, Singapore, and Thailand. In fact, the large export contractions that occurred suggest that the force of the global economic crisis hitting the Indonesian economy was in fact very similar. Figure 17.1 shows how China, Indonesia, Malaysia, the Philippines, Singapore, and Thailand experienced a contraction in export growth of around 30 percent in the fourth quarter of 2008 and the third quarter of 2009.

Why did this sharp drop in exports have a limited effect on the Indonesian economy? We argue that this was because the contribution of exports within the Indonesian economy was relatively small compared with countries like Malaysia, Singapore, and Thailand. The total share of Indonesian exports in GDP was only as high as 29 percent. This percentage is far smaller than the share in other countries such as Singapore (234 percent); Taiwan, China (74); and the Republic of Korea (45).[3]

This phenomenon has led to lively discussions among commentators, politicians, and some policy makers about the importance of relying less on exports and focusing more on the domestic market. Often the conclusion of such discussions is advice to policy makers in Indonesia to pay less attention to "openness" to trade and investment and to concentrate more on protecting the domestic economy against external volatility. Given the close link between exports and openness to trade and investment, this issue leads to the question of whether Indonesia should leave behind its export-led growth strategy and adopt an inward-looking, more protectionist strategy.

Amid that debate, a study by Basri and Rahardja (2010) indicates that exports are in fact an important source of Indonesia's economic growth. Exports have a large supporting effect on economic growth, albeit a less stable effect than domestic demand (figures 17.2 and 17.3). Therefore, a strategy that safeguards a balance between the domestic economy and global orientation—such as joining production networks and promoting export-oriented growth—must be part of the development strategy of the national economy. Strengthening domestic demand can be done without resorting to protectionist policies.

The study by Basri and Rahardja (2010) also shows the strong link between exports and the strength of the domestic economy. Using quarterly data, they found that the relatively strong growth in consumption during the crisis period was a lagged effect from the relatively strong exports in the previous two to three quarters (table 17.2). Certainly, we are cautious in not interpreting this finding as a causal relationship. Given the scope of data covering the first quarter of 2001 until the last quarter of 2008, we are also taking the results as valid only for those time periods. Nevertheless, the exercise gives some idea of how much private consumption moves together with exports and government consumption. The comovement between private consumption and government consumption is somewhat expected. As a response to the global economic downturn, Indonesia implemented a fiscal stimulus targeted at infrastructure

Table 17.1. Exports at Current and Constant Prices, by Major Commodities, 1975 to Quarter 1, 2009

	Current prices (annual % change)						Constant prices (annual % change)						
							At 1980–2008 average prices						At 2008–09 prices
	1975–85	1985–90	1990–96	1996–08	2004–08	Q1 2008–Q1 2009	1975–85	1985–90	1990–96	1996–08	2004–08	Q1 2008–Q1 2009	Q1 2008–Q1 2009
Total exports	10.1	6.4	11.8	8.9	17.8	–31.8	0.7	7.3	9.1	5.1	5.4	–19.5	–16.2
Non-oil, gas total	12.6	19.4	17.6	9.2	18.0	–25.3	0.8	11.7	13.9	7.6	7.2	–20.5	–17.3
Labor-intensive manufactures[a]	61.8	44.6	17.1	3.2	7.1	–13.8	49.5	31.9	17.1	3.9	3.1	–13.6	–13.2
Commodity-based exports	9.6	2.6	7.5	9.9	21.7	–38.3	0.2	4.5	5.0	3.4	5.5	–22.8	–16.0

	Increase in US$ billions in current prices						Increase in US$ billions at constant prices = change in quantity weighted by price and unit value						
							At 1980–2008 average prices						At 2008–09 prices
	1975–85	1985–90	1990–96	1996–08	2004–08	Q1 2008 –Q1 2009	1975–85	1985–90	1990–96	1996–08	2004–08	Q1 2008–Q1 2009	Q1 2008–Q1 2009
Total exports	11.5	6.8	24.1	87.6	65.8	–10.7	1.6	9.7	22.4	45.4	19.1	–5.0	–5.0
Non-oil, gas total	4.1	8.4	23.4	70.2	52.3	–6.7	.7	7.3	20.5	52.7	21.8	–4.7	–4.4
Labor-intensive manufactures[a]	0.6	3.2	6.0	4.5	3.4	–0.5	.8	2.4	4.9	4.7	1.5	–.4	–.5
Commodity-based exports	10.6	2.4	10.9	64.8	52.2	–9.2	.5	5.3	9.3	9.3	10.4	–3.4	–3.4

Source: Papanek, Basri, and Schydlowsky 2010.
Note: Q = quarter.
a. Includes textiles, garments, footwear, and furniture.

Figure 17.1. Export Values in Selected Markets, Quarterly Growth, Seasonally Adjusted, 2008–09

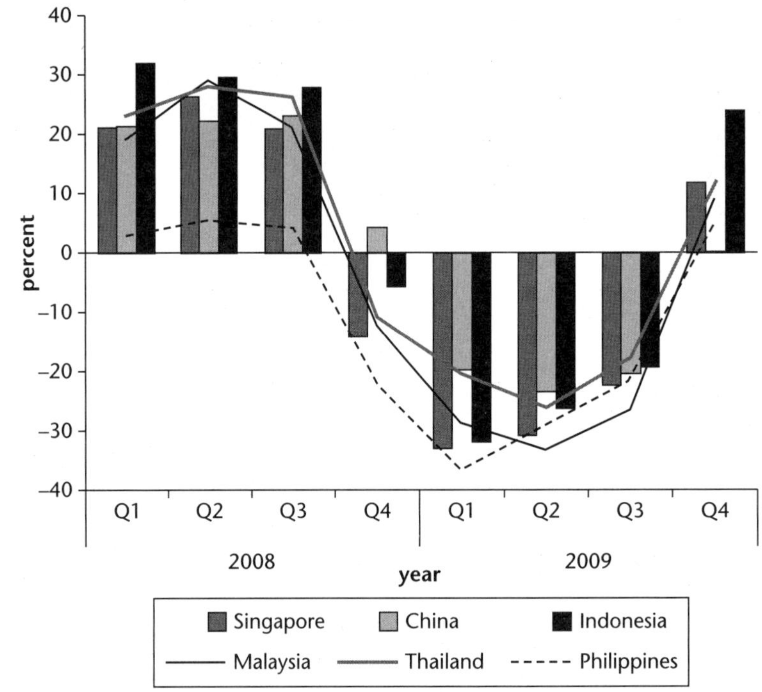

Source: Basri and Rahardja 2010.
Note: Q = quarter.

Figure 17.2. Impulse Response Function of GDP due to Export and Domestic Demand Shocks in Indonesia

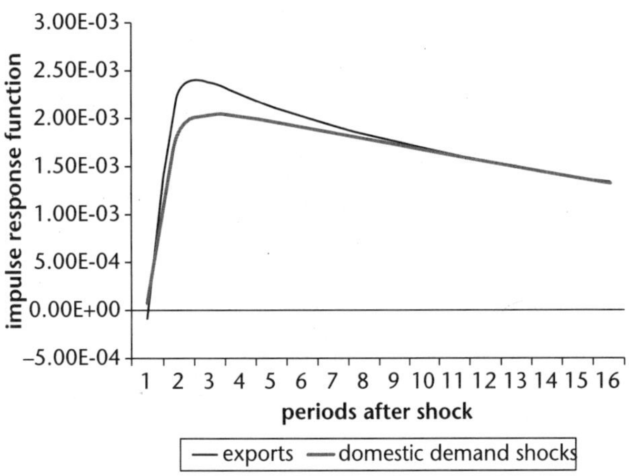

Source: Basri and Rahardja 2010.

Figure 17.3. Variance Decomposition of GDP due to Exports and Domestic Demand Shocks in Indonesia

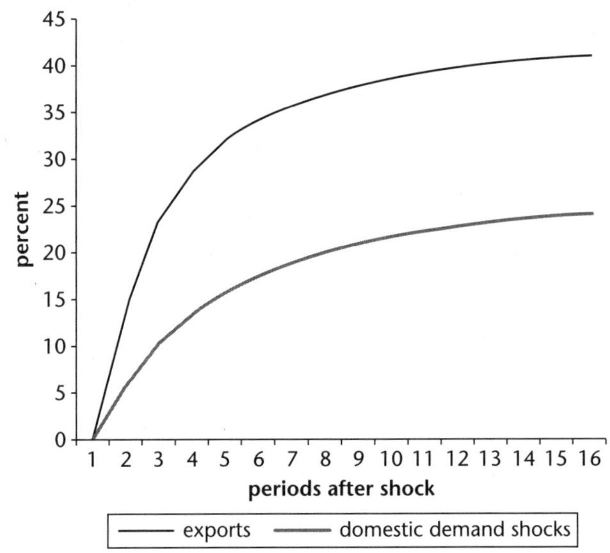

Source: Basri and Rahardja 2010.

spending. The fiscal stimulus has a rather poor disbursement record, however, and therefore one could argue that it was less effective than it should have been in stimulating the economy.

Because of the data period used, it is also likely that commodity exports played an important role in driving consumption. The effect of the commodity boom on economic activities is explained as follows. Economic activities outside Java increased as a result of the commodity boom that occurred several years before. This increase was reflected in relatively high credit growth outside Java

Table 17.2. Co-movements of Innovations in Private Consumption and Innovations of GDP Components, Quarter 1, 2000–Quarter 4, 2008

Lags (quarters)	Components of GDP		
	Government consumption	Gross fixed-capital formation	Exports
0	0.12	0.06	0.24
–1	–0.16	–0.04	–0.27
–2	–0.22	–0.01	–0.41
–3	0.26	–0.07	0.29
–4	0.20	–0.13	0.49

Source: Basri and Rahardja 2010.
Note: Comovements between innovations of each component derived from original data that span the first quarter of 2000 to the fourth quarter of 2008. Here growth is expressed as annual (year-to-year) growth.

several years ago (figure 17.4). The growth of third-party funds in commodity-producing regions also experienced a slow increase. These data strengthen the argument that the economy outside Java improved as a result of the commodity boom, and during the crisis period, residents outside Java were capable of making use of their accumulated savings to smooth their consumption during the global financial crisis. In addition, services exports played an important role because of surprisingly strong exports in tourism and creative designs, while workers' remittances are likely to have a direct link to private consumption.

Export Diversification: The Indonesian Experience

Chapter 11 of this volume shows a positive connection between export concentration and the total effect of economic openness on volatility. The more concentrated exports are, the higher the total effect of openness on volatility. By implication, export diversification would diminish the effect of growth volatility on an economy following an export-led growth strategy. This result provides a way for Indonesia to safeguard its export-led growth strategy so long as it diversifies its exports. Therefore, it is very important to look at the experience of export diversification in Indonesia.

Diversifying exports was not part of Indonesia's earlier development agenda. In addition to foreign aid and revenue from non-oil exports and gas, Indonesia had been relying on revenues from exporting rubber and crude oil in the late 1960s and early 1970s to finance its development. The quadrupling of the crude price in 1973 caused windfall gains for Indonesia, which, unfortunately, resulted in inflationary pressure.[4] After forceful anti-Japanese protests and riots, Indonesia embarked on a state-sponsored industrialization program to substitute imports. Trade and foreign investment policy also became relatively more restrictive in the 1970s to support a nationalist economic agenda through expansion of state-owned businesses (see Hill 1996).

The high crude price had a profound impact on discouraging diversification away from the oil sector. Aside from the inflationary pressure from swelling foreign exchange reserves, the high crude price provided incentives for state and private businesses to expand their activities around the business of Pertamina, the state-owned oil company. As inflationary pressure built up, the demand for protection also increased, and the government regulated business activities through multiple permits and prohibitions. Trade facilitation was poorly managed; for example, corruption in customs was costly for the private sector. Tariffs were raised, and nontariff barriers, such as import restrictions or trade through state trading enterprises, were put in place. With the inflationary pressure and incentive to expand oil-related businesses, Indonesia finally found that its industrialization program did not go far and that the oil sector still dominated the Indonesian economy.[5] As time passed, Indonesia found itself entrenched in a high-cost economy with low diversification.

However, the game totally changed when the crude price started falling. The government had to confront the reality that its main engine for economic growth, oil revenue, had fallen away and that it would have to jump-start a new engine. The fall of oil prices to US$14.30 per barrel in 1987 from an average of US$36.90 per barrel in 1980 was used by policy makers as the spur for a series of structural reforms to ensure the survival of Indonesia's development. Following a devaluation of the rupiah in 1983 and fiscal austerity measures, Indonesia finally started a sequence of deregulation to bring down the "high-cost" economy, that is, bureaucracy and red tape, to free up its non-oil sectors to private businesses. The government introduced often heavy-handed measures to slash licenses and procedures for opening businesses, impose market discipline on state-owned enterprises

Figure 17.4. Expansion outside Java because of the Commodity Boom, 2007–10

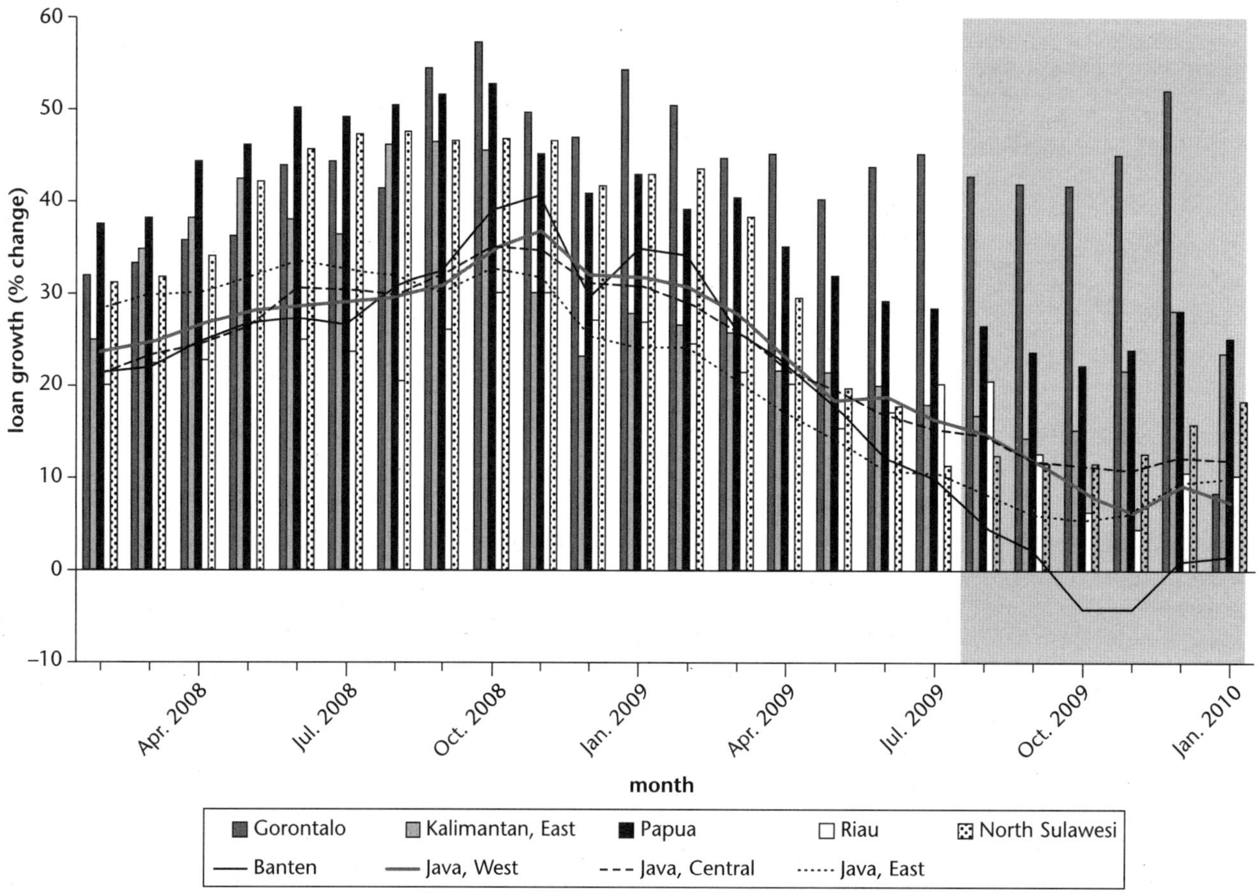

Source: Indonesia Financial Statistics, Bank Indonesia, http://www.bi.go.id/web/en/Statistik/Statistik+Ekonomi+dan+Keuangan+Indonesia/.

through privatization, increase competition from private businesses, and reform the tax system.

Aside from reducing bureaucracy and red tape, policy makers also introduced sweeping trade reforms. Starting in the mid-1980s, the government implemented a series of serious trade liberalizations. With respect to tariffs, the study by Fane and Condon (1996) showed that the weighted average rate of effective protection for manufacturing (excluding the special case of oil and gas processing) declined from 59 percent to 16 percent over the period 1987–95, while the dispersion (standard deviation) fell from 102 to 39. They also showed a sharp reduction in the coverage of nontariff barriers: the percentage of non-oil manufacturing value added affected by these barriers declined from 77 percent to 17 percent. The government also introduced a duty drawback system for exporters and reformed customs procedures. Starting from a point of high import tariffs, the duty drawback system on imports for export provided a fiscal incentive for businesses to enter export sectors, particularly activities with low domestic value added, such as garments.[6] Indonesia also took the unprecedented policy step of stripping customs of its mandate to perform inspections. Customs inspections were delegated to SGS, a Swiss-based company, which brought down corruption and sped up import clearances. Indonesia also replaced priority sectors for investment with a more relaxed negative list approach to attract foreign direct investment (FDI).

That deregulation in the 1980s was the main impetus for Indonesia's export diversification up to the Asian economic crisis. As a result of those policies, Indonesia's private sector had incentives to exploit the country's comparative advantages in non-oil industries. In 1985, Indonesia's non-oil exports took off, growing at an average rate of 17.8 percent between 1985 and 1996, higher than the average growth of total exports (9.3 percent). By 1996, Indonesia had successfully diversified its exports away from oil products, with non-oil exports accounting for 76.4 percent of total exports compared to only 28 percent in 1980 (figures 17.5 and 17.6).

Figure 17.5. Indonesian Oil and Non-oil Exports, 1970–96

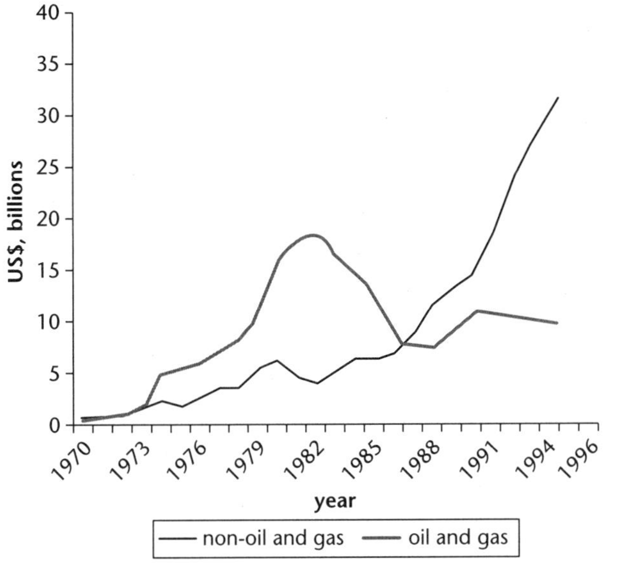

Source: Authors' calculations based on UN Comtrade (database), United Nations, http://comtrade.un.org.

Figure 17.6. Composition of Indonesia's Non-oil Exports, 1970–96

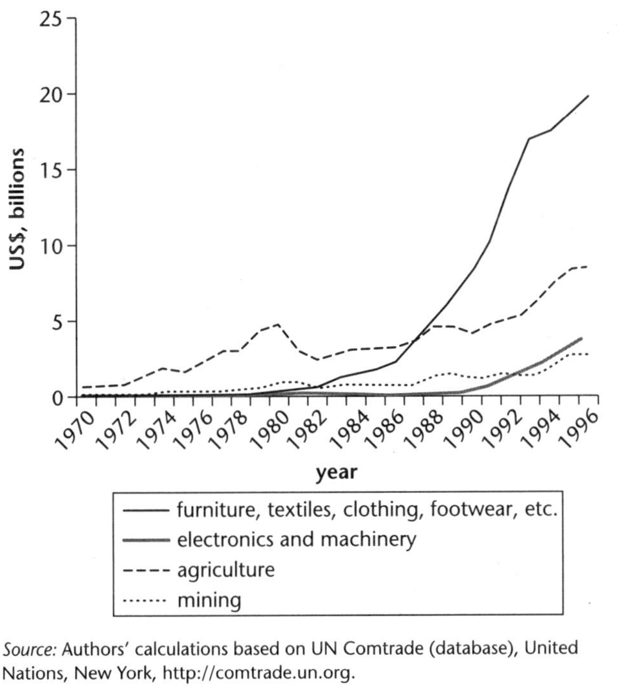

Source: Authors' calculations based on UN Comtrade (database), United Nations, New York, http://comtrade.un.org.

The reform package of the mid-1980s quickly reduced Indonesia's dependence on oil exports and significantly increased the share of manufactures in total exports. Before deregulation, private investment in the manufacturing sector was constrained by bureaucracy that created high costs. Those costs included business licenses, a complicated tax regime, and difficulties in obtaining inputs at world prices due to the powerful state enterprises that often influenced policy in favor of rent-seeking activities (Soesastro 1989). The deregulation packages helped transform the Indonesian manufacturing industry from inward looking to increasingly outward looking and internationally competitive (Hill 1996). Indonesian manufacturers were quick to exploit investment opportunities in footloose industries catering to the export market. Lower import tariffs, the duty drawback system, and improved trade facilitation enabled exporters to access materials and technology and combine them with low-cost labor to produce clothing, footwear, and furniture. By 1996, Indonesia managed to book US$20 billion worth of exports in textiles, clothing, footwear, and furniture, from less than US$2.5 billion in 1986.

Figure 17.7 indicates a dramatic increase in the diversification of export products following the reform package, as measured by a Herfindahl-Hirschman Index of Indonesia's export products from 1980 to 1995. It is apparent that product concentration fell dramatically after the government launched trade and investment reforms in 1985. By 1994, the concentration of Indonesia's export products was only 41 percent of its 1984 level. However, other important drivers were also behind the increase in export diversification in the late 1980s and early 1990s. First was the slump in commodity prices. Following the collapse of oil prices in 1986, exports of resource commodities were pushed back by the collapsing price of crude oil, which dropped to an average of US$14.35 per barrel in 1986 from US$36.80 per barrel in 1980. Second, the government imposed measures preventing exports of raw agricultural materials, such as logs and rattan, which made exporting raw materials less attractive and helped wood-based manufacturing activities.

However, the increase in market diversification was not as fast as the increase in product diversification. To see how concentrated Indonesia's exports were in certain markets for certain products, we construct the following bar charts with product and partner country pairs on the horizontal axis and share in total exports (percent) on the vertical axis. Between 1980 and 1984, there were only 4,569 product-country pairs, while in 1990 and 1994 the number expanded to 21,161 pairs. But the more interesting fact was Indonesia's complete dependence on one product and a few markets. Between 1980 and 1984, about 26 percent of Indonesia's exports were due to one product, petroleum exported to Japan (figure 17.8, panel a). But reform packages in the mid-1980s and the drop in the price of crude brought down the importance of oil in Indonesia's total exports. The importance of oil exports continued to drop as export growth in footloose and wood-based industries rose dramatically. The share of a single market and a single product

Figure 17.7. Concentration of Indonesia's Export Products, 1980–95

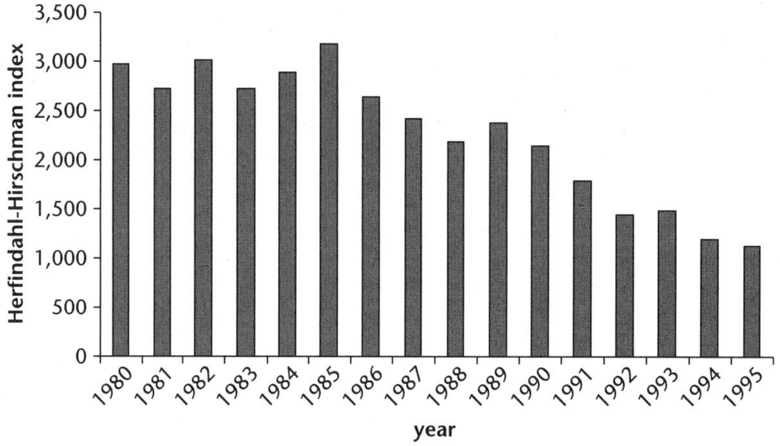

Source: Authors' calculations based on UN Comtrade (database), United Nations, http://comtrade.un.org.

Figure 17.8. Product and Country Concentration of Indonesia's Exports in the 1980s and 1990s

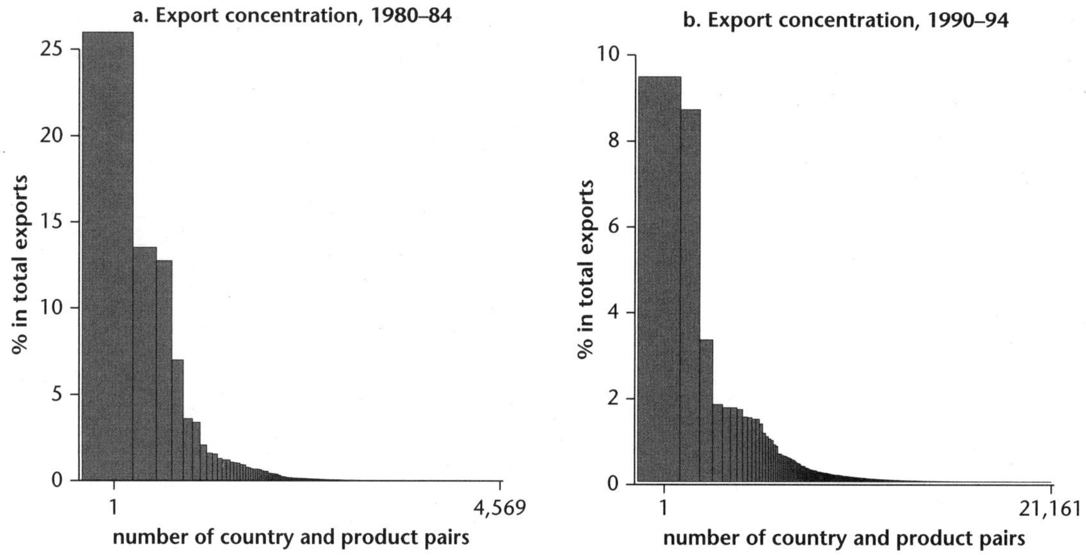

Source: Authors' calculations using UN Comtrade (database), United Nations, http://comtrade.un.org.
Note: Calculations are based on trade data up to the five-digit level of the Standard International Trade Classification (SITC).

in Indonesia's exports in 1990–94 dropped significantly compared to the share in 1980–84 (figure 17.8, panel b).

Ten years later, however, Indonesia's exports were still largely dependent on the Japanese market. One of the reasons was the emergence of liquefied natural gas (LNG), which quickly became the most important export commodity. About 9.4 percent of Indonesia's total exports in that period were accounted for by LNG exported to Japan. As for petroleum, 8.7 percent of Indonesia's total exports were due to exports of that product to Japan. Meanwhile, plywood products were already Indonesia's third-largest export commodity, and most of it went to the Japanese market.

After the Asian crisis, has Indonesia managed to produce more new products or to sell more to markets that it has not traditionally served? Unfortunately, casual observation using the same method as above does not produce a strong conclusion. Indeed, on the one hand, figure 17.9 suggests that Indonesia managed to double the number of country-product pairs, from 14,551 between 1990 and 1994 to 51,631 between 2004 and 2008. We could interpret this as a significant achievement in export diversification because more products are sold to more countries. China, India, and Malaysia are increasingly important markets for Indonesia's exports, taking over from the European and U.S. markets. The figure also indicates, however, that the

Figure 17.9. Pairs of Markets and Products in Indonesia's Exports, 2004–08

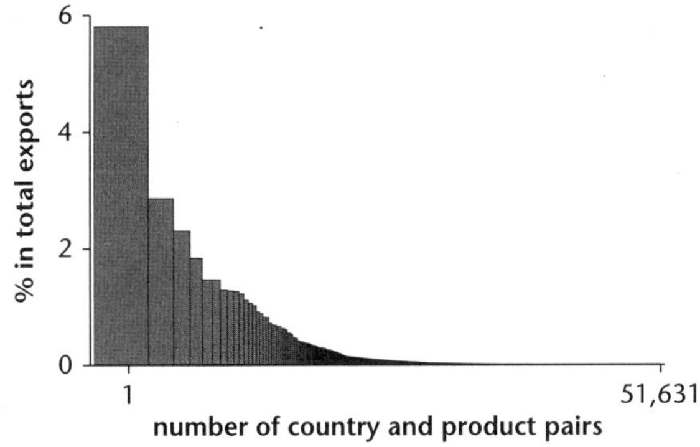

Source: Authors' calculations using UN Comtrade (database), United Nations, http://comtrade.un.org.
Note: Calculations are based on trade data up to the five-digit level of the Standard International Trade Classification (SITC).

Figure 17.10. Index of Export Product Concentration in Indonesia, 2001–08

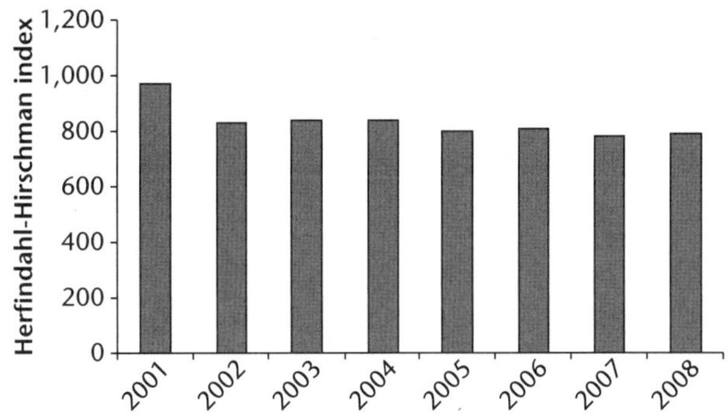

Source: Authors' calculations based on data from UN Comtrade, United Nations, http://comtrade.un.org.

role of a few markets and a handful of products remain important. About 14.2 percent of Indonesia's total exports in 2004 and 2008 were due to LNG, petroleum, and CPO sold to China, India, Japan, and Korea. In fact, 5.8 percent and 2.8 percent of Indonesian exports in 2004 through 2008 were due to LNG and petroleum exports, respectively, for the Japanese market. The period also marked the emergence of CPO as an important export commodity. CPO exports to India made up about 1.8 percent of Indonesia's total exports in that period.

The process of diversifying export products has been showing slow progress in recent years. Figure 17.10 presents a Herfindahl-Hirschman Index of product concentration of Indonesia's exports between 2000 and 2008. The figure suggests that concentration has not significantly declined since 2003. One possible explanation for the relatively flat concentration index is a lack of "discovery"—that is, new export products—in Indonesia's export portfolio. As we will show later, the data suggest that either not many new export products are coming out of Indonesia or that exports of new products have not been able to fully take off. The other possible explanation is that the rising exports of agriculture and resource commodities are offsetting the declining performance of Indonesia's "traditional" exports of labor-intensive manufactures, such as textiles, clothing, and footwear.

Nevertheless, the cause behind the declining performance of manufacturing exports in recent years is an interesting phenomenon that researchers have not fully explained. Popular reasons typically center on market access issues, as Indonesian firms are facing much tougher competition from products made in China and Vietnam, both at home and in third markets. For example, Indonesian firms can no longer use the provisions of the Multi-Fiber Arrangement to secure the value of their textile and clothing exports and have to compete head to head with Chinese products in the U.S. market. Meanwhile, local manufacturing firms have been concerned about the potential adverse impact of bilateral and regional free trade agreements, especially with large developing economies such as China.

Another possible explanation is that supply-side problems are affecting the competitiveness of Indonesia's manufacturing firms. Indonesian manufacturing firms may currently face greater global competition while equipped with worse physical and regulatory infrastructure compared to other middle-income economies. Indonesia's relatively rigid labor law could affect the ability of private businesses to set up larger manufacturing operations. Uncertainties in regulation could also reduce the expected return from investing in sectors with low economic rent. Indonesian manufacturing firms also contend with worse transportation infrastructure relative to those in other emerging economies.[7] Because discovering a new exportable product is a costly process, firms will not undertake such activity unless they are rewarded with adequate economic rents (Lederman and Klinger 2004; Rodrik 2004). In that context, Indonesia also lacks effective public institutions, such as an export credit agency, private equity or venture capital, and a public research and development (R&D) institute, all of which can provide manufacturing firms with the incentive to pursue discovery of new exportable products. Finally, coordinating coherent policy making is often difficult in a fully decentralized government system and in a noisy democracy.

Interestingly, the declining performance of Indonesia's manufacturing exports coincides with an appreciation in the real exchange rate and rising exports of resource-based commodities. Figure 17.11 indicates that the (one period lagged) real exchange rate is positively correlated with an increase in commodity exports and a decline in exports of manufactures. It is possible that all these coincidences are symptoms of a mild case of "Dutch disease." Because Indonesia is one of the largest exporters of minerals, rubber, and crude palm oil, it has some market power to influence the world price. Increases in the prices of commodities raise export revenues and increase pressure for a real appreciation of the rupiah. Meanwhile, an increase in the price of commodities could also increase factors of production intensively used in commodity sectors, either labor or capital, and squeeze the profitability of traditional manufacturing sectors that are facing competitive world prices and the strengthening of the rupiah.

Given the success in diversifying export products in the 1990s and the increase in new export markets in recent years, has Indonesia managed to rely on selling new products to new markets? Or is it that exports have largely depended on the same "old products" sold to "old markets"? To answer this question, we turn to an analysis of the intensive and extensive margins of Indonesia's exports (figure 17.12). The intensive margin is defined as exports going to the same set of products and markets. We use the approach introduced by Zahler (2007) to decompose the extensive margin into the following four components: (a) exports of old products to existing markets where those products have not been sold before; (b) exports of old products to new markets; (c) exports of new products (never produced before) to existing markets; and (d) exports of new products to new markets.

Decomposing export growth between 1990 and 2008 yields interesting results. About 71 percent of the increase in Indonesia's exports in the past 18 years was due to growth in the same set of products sold to the same markets. Given this finding along with the result of decomposing export growth in East Asia and the Pacific (Brenton and Newfarmer 2007), Indonesia may well be relatively less dependent on the intensive margin. Nevertheless, this finding stresses the importance of maintaining the export performance of existing products to existing markets for Indonesia.

The other interesting findings relate to the extensive margin. First is the significant role of "switching" pairs between existing markets and products in driving new exports. As Indonesia successfully exported certain products to certain markets, other markets that Indonesia already served started demanding those products. A simple example is the demand for footwear from China in 2008, as Indonesia already exported footwear to the United States and petroleum to China in 1990. These switching activities accounted for 26.5 percent of growth in Indonesia's exports. Meanwhile, the rapid increase in Indonesia's exports to new markets is apparently still relatively small compared to the intensive margin or switching between

Figure 17.11. Relationship of Indonesia's Commodity Exports, Manufacturing Exports, and Real Exchange Rate, 2000–08

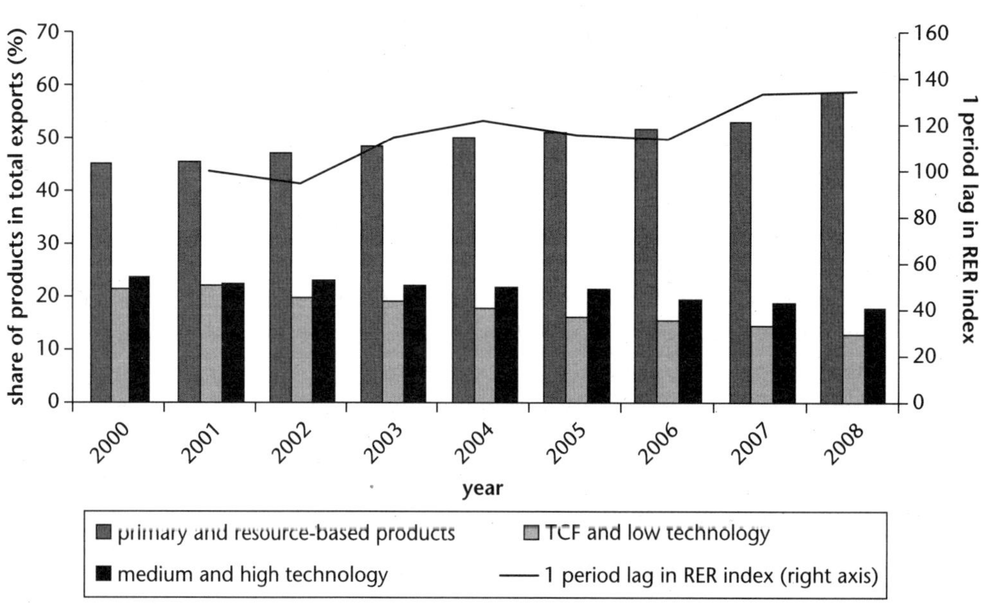

Source: Authors' calculations based on data from: Indonesia Financial Statistics, Bank Indonesia, http://www.bi.go.id/web/en/Statistik/Statistik+Ekonomi+dan+Keuangan+Indonesia/; and UN Comtrade, United Nations, http://comtrade.un.org.
Note: Classification is based on Lall (2000). RER = real exchange rate, TCF = textiles, clothing, and footwear.

Figure 17.12. Contribution of Intensive and Extensive Margins to Indonesian Export Growth, 1990–2008

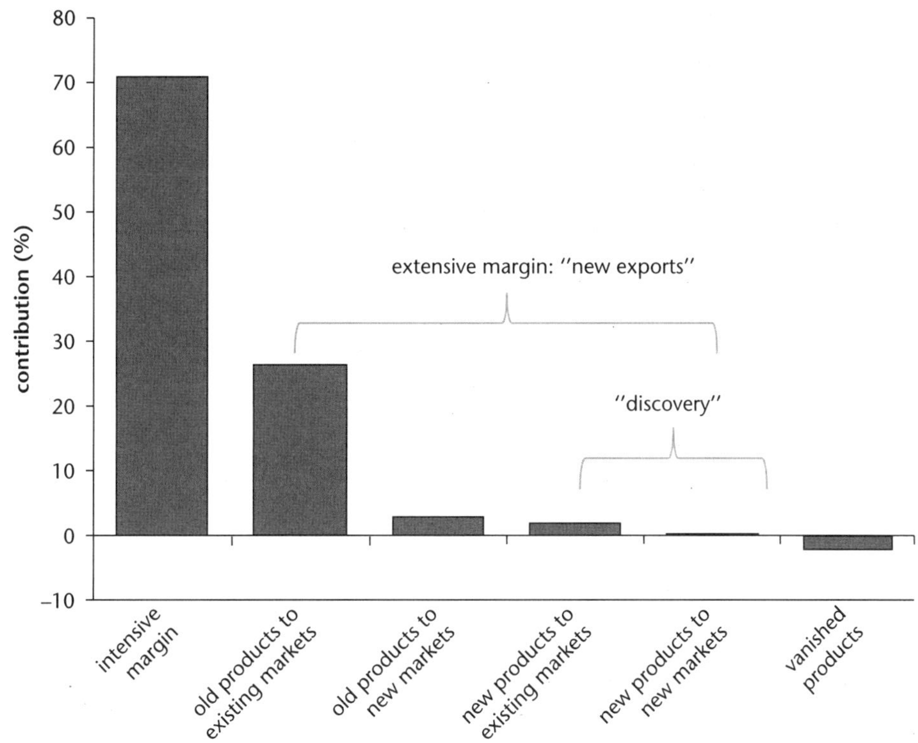

Source: Authors' calculations using UN Comtrade (database), United Nations, http://comtrade.un.org.

pairs of existing products and markets. Exports of existing products to new markets comprised only 2.9 percent of the increase in total exports between 1990 and 2008. Finally, "discovery" plays little part in Indonesia's exports. Exports of new products, either to existing or to new markets, contributed only 2 percent of the increase in total exports in that period.

How to Promote Export Diversification: The Role of Policy

Experiences in Indonesia and other countries suggest the important role that policy can play in supporting export diversification. Agosin, Alvarez, and Bravo-Ortega (2009) use a large data set for a 40-year period to show that export diversification is influenced by several factors such as trade openness, financial development, the real exchange rate, human capital accumulation, and trade costs determined by remoteness and terms of trade. In addition, Agosin, Alvarez, and Bravo-Ortega (2009) and di Giovanni and Levchenko, (2009) argue that openness will induce specialization and not necessarily a higher diversification of exports. As a result, as indicated by Haddad, Lim, Munro, Saborowski, and Shepherd in chapter 11 of this volume, openness must be accompanied by policies to support export diversification. This argument is extremely relevant for Indonesia, because the choice of an inward-looking strategy is not the choice that will provide the best results for the economy. We therefore argue that the trade reforms that Indonesia has carried out up to now and the choice of an export-led growth strategy have to be accompanied by policies to support export diversification. The government needs to implement several specific policies to minimize export volatility due to shocks such as the global financial crisis.

Development of the Financial Sector

Agosin, Alvarez, and Bravo-Ortega (2009) show a positive statistical relationship between financial sector development and export diversification. This finding is in fact consistent with the argument of Rodrik (2007) that there is an uncertainty problem in producing new products. Some upfront investments are needed to solve this problem, but those investments must be financed. Unfortunately, commercial banks cannot fully deal with this problem, and the corporate debt market, equity markets, and private venture capital funds are not likely to finance innovative investments (Rodrik 2007). Other sources of longer-term financing, such as development banks or venture funds, must be found. In Indonesia itself, financing still largely relies on banking sources. The Indonesian government must reform the financial sector so that insurance, the capital market, pension funds, venture funds, and development banks can finance new products to promote export diversification.

Better Connectivity to Reduce Trade Costs

Agosin, Alvarez, and Bravo-Ortega (2009) show that a reduction in trade costs will support new export production activities. Hausmann and Rodrik (2003) argue that entrepreneurs have to continue experimenting with new products and adapt foreign technology to local needs, a process referred to as self-discovery. However, there is a problem: if entrepreneurs fail in these experiments, they will absorb all losses, while if they succeed, other entrepreneurs will start to imitate and enter into these same activities. As a result, in practice no one is interested in self-discovery. Self-discovery means that there are rents to be provided to entrepreneurs, leaving insufficient incentive to carry out innovation in new products. Trade costs that arise because of logistics costs or high transaction costs will also be a disincentive for entrepreneurs to carry out diversification and develop new products, including those for export.

This problem is relevant for Indonesia, because in an archipelago nation transaction costs and especially logistics costs are relatively higher than in continental countries. Transport costs, inventory costs, and the need for interisland shipping are larger. A study by LPEM (2005) shows that logistics costs in Indonesia amount to 14 percent of total production costs, far higher than in Japan, for example, where they reach only 4.9 percent. Patunru, Nurridzki, and Rivayani (2007) show that inefficient harbors make transport more expensive, especially in export-oriented and import-based industries. Meanwhile, a study by LPEM-FEUI and Asia Foundation (2009) shows that the combination of complicated regulations and high domestic transport costs has already disrupted Indonesia's competitiveness. For several export commodities such as cocoa, rubber, and coffee, more than 40 percent of total logistics and transport costs are incurred before dispatch and in land transport, not yet including international dispatch costs (Carana 2004). With high logistics costs, only products with a high profit margin can be exported, and this factor is especially pronounced among primary products, in particular in a commodity boom. High logistics costs lower the profit margin and provide insufficient incentives for creating new products in the manufacturing sector or other sector where the profit margin is small because of extreme competition. As a result, Indonesia's effort to diversify its exports has been hampered.

In this sort of situation, logistics may be the key that will unlock the door to more export diversification for many regions in Indonesia. "Trade logistics"—the capacity for integrating domestic economies and connecting domestic economies with international markets through goods dispatch—is an extremely important factor in the potential for economic growth of a country. We therefore argue that Indonesia will obtain support for self-discovery and export diversification if logistics and infrastructure problems are dealt with. Although progress certainly has already begun in the logistics and infrastructure development system in Indonesia, it is still moving extremely slowly. Such delay is connected with land clearance problems, complicated bidding processes, and lack of coordination between government institutions in solving infrastructure problems.

Primary Products and Real Exchange-Rate Appreciation

Carrère, Strauss-Kahn, and Cadot (2007) show a relatively high export concentration in countries that export primary products. High concentration in the export of primary goods carries with it some risk of Dutch disease. We showed above that in the past Indonesia was extremely dependent on oil products and particular destination countries. At the end of the 1970s, for example, oil price increases and the dependence of the Indonesian economy on oil brought with them the Dutch disease (Pangestu 1986; Warr 1992).

It is interesting to see the changes that happened in Indonesia after the increase in commodity prices in 2000. The commodity boom that happened after that year had already raised credit growth in many provinces in Sumatra, Kalimatan, and Sulawesi (see figure 17.4). Symptoms of a mild case of Dutch disease were present: the boom in the mining and plantation sectors had already supported expansion, and then there was a spending effect outside of Java. In parallel was growth in the labor-intensive textile and leather products sectors, whose growth had declined over the previous several years. Consistent with these other developments, the real exchange-rate value continued to appreciate (Soesastro and Basri 2005; Athukorala 2006; Basri and Patunru 2006). As a result, competiveness in labor-intensive sectors seemed to decline. Consistent with that fall, the index of Indonesia's export concentration remained relatively flat, suggesting slow progress in diversifying export products. We therefore argue that to support export diversification, Indonesia must maintain its competitiveness in exchange rates. Of course, under a flexible exchange rate the nominal exchange rate cannot be depreciated; however, Indonesia can maintain its real exchange-rate competitiveness by curbing inflation. In addition, labor market reform is also extremely important for avoiding Dutch disease and for supporting export diversification.

The Role of R&D and Improvement of Product Quality

As discussed earlier, the diversification that occurred in Indonesian exports was driven more by the intensive margin than the extensive margin. The ability to create new products for new markets as well as for old markets was relatively small. Supporting new product lines requires R&D support. Rodrik (2007) states that technology cannot be obtained from advanced countries only. Therefore, the need for R&D financed by the public has to be identified and adapted with transfer of technology from developed countries. Woo and Hong (2010) believe that Indonesia should move toward a science-based economy. Indonesia needs R&D in agriculture, for example, new crop varieties (including agro-biotechnology), a new approach to the management of water and the environment, mechanization, improvements in superior seeds for agricultural products, infrastructure to support agriculture, and so forth. In the case of agriculture, the World Bank (2009) has shown that expenditure for agriculture has already increased significantly (in real terms) but that production is still low. Production in major crops has been stagnant since 1990 and is relatively low compared with other Asian countries.

World Bank (2009) also points out that the ratio of Indonesia's agricultural research intensity is relatively low.[8] In the future, to support diversification in exports and especially to increase the extensive margin, improvements in R&D are required. This R&D is also needed to improve product quality, so that better-quality products can satisfy the demands of the new export markets.

The Development of the Services Sector

As pointed out by Brenton, Newfarmer, and Walkenhorst (2007), the services sector is important for achieving export diversification. The services sector constitutes almost half the Indonesian economy. Links from the services sector are also very strong compared to other sectors (van Diermen, Basri, and Shan, forthcoming). Indonesia has several sectors that have great potential for the future, such as tourism and the movement of service providers (natural persons). Tourism is a sector with potential for growth and absorption of manpower. The cultural and geographical diversity of the Indonesian archipelago offers a range of trade in tourism opportunities. Particularly with increased stability, the potential exists for substantial growth in tourist numbers (van Diermen, Basri, and Shan, forthcoming).

In addition, the movement of natural persons (mode 4 in the General Agreement on Trade in Services, [GATS]) has great potential for Indonesia. By 2025, many of the countries in the Asia-Pacific region will be experiencing aging problems, while Indonesia will have a demographic dividend with a high proportion of residents of productive age. In this situation, the demand for working-age professionals will increase. If Indonesia increases the quality of its human resources, it will have the opportunity to become a supplier of skilled labor to the region. For this result, investment in human capital, such as education and health, becomes very important. Unfortunately, up to now, Indonesia has lagged behind in health and education (Woo and Hong 2010). The development of these services sectors will make Indonesian exports become more diversified. Up to now, attention paid to these services sectors in Indonesia has been small.

Promotion and Marketing

Rose (2007) shows a positive relationship between foreign missions (consulates and trade promotion agencies) and exports. Furthermore, the first foreign mission has a larger effect on the increase in exports than subsequent missions. Therefore, we see that promotion, marketing, and trade promotion organizations are important for supporting export diversification. LPEM-FEUI (2008) shows that the majority of world exports come from products manufactured for markets with the characteristic of monopolistic competition. In a monopolistically competitive market, the roles of nonprice variables such as advertising, promotion, and information are important. Until now, Indonesian exports have been supported by the results of the primary sectors (agriculture and mining). If Indonesia wants to penetrate monopolistically competitive markets, then exporters must be capable of competing not only on price but also on nonprice factors. One of the problems facing Indonesia is the asymmetric information between domestic producers and international consumers because of the lack of information about global demand, as well as the relative lack of promotion of Indonesian products. LPEM-FEUI (2008) showed that marketing and promotion problems were one of the main factors that delayed exports. Respondents supported the introduction of trade policies to overcome this problem. Some 70 percent of respondents stated that promotional agencies were important. LPEM-FEUI 2008 also indicated that trade, tourism, and FDI were sources of foreign reserve and should be connected naturally. Thus, to support export diversification, a promotion agency needs to be integrated with these three agencies.

Conclusion

The above discussion shows that the effects of the global crisis in 2008 on the Indonesian economy were relatively small, when compared with several other countries in Southeast Asia. The main reason for the relatively small effects on Indonesia's economic growth was the limited openness in the Indonesian economy. This result gives rise to the question whether Indonesia should give up its strategy of facilitating trade. Our answer to this is that the strategy of facilitating exports is still the right choice for Indonesia as long as it is accompanied with export diversification.

Our study shows that Indonesia can do much more to diversify its exports. It is true that the reforms in the 1980s dramatically increased Indonesia's export product diversification: that set of policies lowered barriers to entry, improved trade facilitation, and reduced bureaucratic inefficiencies, thus unlocking business opportunities in Indonesia's non-oil sectors. As a result, Indonesia became one of the platforms for footloose manufacturing industries. The process was also accompanied by a global quota arrangement on textiles and clothing, measures discouraging exports of raw agricultural commodities, and relatively low global commodity prices that made exporting manufactured products more attractive than exporting commodities. Our findings also suggest that Indonesia has increased exports of existing products to some new markets, part of the extensive margin. However, we also find that the discovery of new products and exports to new markets are still quite low.

Recent efforts to diversify exports, both markets and products, have become increasingly more challenging. Competitiveness issues are constraining Indonesian manufacturers and limiting their returns as they face an increasingly competitive global market. We also believe that the boom in commodity prices and the appreciation of the rupiah real exchange rate have increased the opportunity costs of investing outside commodity-related businesses and have lowered the margins for manufactures to compete globally. Meanwhile, insufficient capacity and lack of effective public institutions for facilitating R&D and new exports could limit the incentive for manufacturers to engage in new product discovery. As a consequence, Indonesia has depended more on exports of old products to existing markets as the main driver of export growth.

For these reasons, the relatively large decline in Indonesian exports—comparable with other countries in the Association of Southeast Asian Nations—did not translate into a major set of economic effects during the global financial crisis. Indonesia's experience in the past, when dependence on oil commodities was large, also highlights the risks for the Indonesian economy. In the future, therefore, Indonesia has to come up with policies to diversify exports. These policies include improving the financial sector, strengthening the logistics system or connectivity, reducing dependency on primary exports, safeguarding a competitive exchange rate (preventing Dutch disease), raising R&D and product quality, and increasing the role of the services sector as well as improvements in promotion and marketing. If these policies are implemented, then Indonesia can maintain an export-led growth strategy while still supporting domestic consumption.

Notes

1. For the details of the impact of the global financial crisis on the Indonesian economy, see Basri and Siregar (2009); Gunawan and Siregar (2009); Gunawan et al. (2009); Basri and Rahardja (2010); Papanek, Basri and Schydlowsky (2010).
2. This section is summarized and drawn from Basri and Rahardja (2010).
3. Total export of goods and services in national account as a percentage of GDP.
4. The Arab oil embargo caused the average price of crude oil to jump from US$2.80 per barrel in 1973 to US$11.00 per barrel in 1974 and finally to hit US$36.90 per barrel in 1980.
5. The government had to devalue the rupiah in 1978 to avoid a total loss of competitiveness.
6. However, there are reasons to be cautious in imposing the duty drawback system on exporters. Cadot, de Melo, and Olarreaga (2003) demonstrated that if the industry actively lobbies for the policy, the duty drawback can result in slower trade liberalization because exporters would have lower incentives to prevent high tariffs on their input. Another popular objection to the duty drawback system is the cost of administering the system, particularly the potential for redundancy if import tariffs are further lowered.
7. See Basri and Rahardja (2010) for comparisons.
8. This ratio is defined as the ratio of public agricultural R&D expenditures to agricultural output or agricultural gross domestic product.

Bibliography

Agosin, M. R., R. Alvarez, and C. Bravo-Ortega. 2009. "Determinants of Export Diversification around the World 1962–2000." Department of Economics Working Paper, University of Chile, Santiago.

Athukorala, P. 2006. "Post-Crisis Export Performance: The Indonesian Experience in Regional Perspective. *Bulletin of Indonesian Economic Studies* 42 (2): 177–211.

Basri, M. C., and A. A. Patunru. 2006. "Survey of Recent Developments." *Bulletin of Indonesian Economic Studies* 42 (3): 295–319.

Basri, M. C., and S. Rahardja. 2010. "The Indonesian Economy amidst the Global Crisis: Good Policy and Good Luck." *ASEAN Economic Bulletin* 27 (1): 77–98.

Basri, M. C., and R. Y. Siregar. 2009. "Navigating Policy Responses at the National Level in the Midst of the Global Financial Crisis: The Experience of Indonesia." *Asian Economic Papers* 8 (3): 1–35.

Brenton, P., and R. Newfarmer. 2007. "Watching More than the Discovery Channel: Export Cycles and Diversification in Development." Policy Research Working Paper 4302, World Bank, Washington, DC.

Brenton, P., R. Newfarmer, and P. Walkenhorst. 2007. "Export Diversification: A Portfolio Approach." Paper Presented at the Growth Commission Conference on Development, Yale University, September.

Cadot, O., J. de Melo, and M. Olarreaga. 2003. "The Protectionist Bias of Duty Drawbacks: Evidence from MERCOSUR." *Journal of International Economics* 59 (1): 161–82.

Carana Corporation. 2004. "Impact of Transport and Logistics on Indonesia's Trade Competitiveness." Paper for review by U.S. Agency for International Development, Jakarta.

Carrère, C., V. Strauss-Kahn, and O. Cadot. 2007. "Export Diversification: What's behind the Hump." Mimeo. http://r0.unctad.org/ditc/tab/events/emstrade/Speakers/Cadot_doc.pdf.

di Giovanni, J., and A. A. Levchenko. 2009. "Trade Openness and Volatility." *Review of Economics and Statistics* 91 (3): 558–85.

Fane, G., and T. Condon. 1996. "Trade Reform in Indonesia, 1987–1995." *Bulletin of Indonesian Economic Studies* 32 (3): 33–54.

Gunawan, A. H., H. Arman, and A. Hendranata. 2009. "Indonesia 2009 Economic Outlook: Slowing, Not Falling." *PT Bank Danamon Indonesia Tbk.* Jakarta, January 7.

Gunawan, A. H., and R. Y. Siregar. 2009. "Survey of Recent Developments." *Bulletin of Indonesian Economic Studies* 45 (1): 7–36.

Hausmann, R., and D. Rodrik. 2003. "Economic Development as Self-discovery." *Journal of Development Economics* 72: 603–33.

Hill, H. 1996. *The Indonesian Economy since 1966*. Cambridge, U.K.: Cambridge University Press.

Lall, S. 2000. "The Technological Structure and Performance of Developing Country Manufactured Exports, 1985–98." *Oxford Development Studies* 28 (3): 337–69.

Lederman, D., and B. Klinger. 2004. "Discovery and Development: An Empirical Exploration of New Products." Policy Research Working Paper 3450, World Bank, Washington, DC.

LPEM (Institute for Economic and Social Research). 2005. "Inefficiency in the Logistics of Export Industries: The Case of Indonesia." Report in collaboration with Japan Bank for International Cooperation, Jakarta.

LPEM-FEUI (Institute for Economic and Social Research–Faculty of Economics, University of Indonesia). 2008. "Studi Lanjutan Komisi Perdagangan Luar Negeri & Analisis Kelayakan Lembaga Promosi Indonesia" [Study on the Foreign Trade Commissioner and Indonesian Promotion Council]. Unpublished report to the Ministry of Trade, Jakarta.

LPEM-FEUI (Institute for Economic and Social Research–Faculty of Economics, University of Indonesia) and Asia Foundation. 2009. *The Cost of Moving Goods, Transportation, Regulations and Charges in Indonesia*. Jakarta: Asia Foundation.

Pangestu, M. E. 1986. "The Effects of an Oil Boom on a Small Oil Exporting Country: The Case of Indonesia." Ph.D. diss. University of California Davis.

Papanek, G., M. C. Basri, and D. Schydlowsky. 2010. "The Impact of the World Recession on Indonesia and an Appropriate Policy Response: Some Lesson for Asia." In *Poverty and Sustainable Development in Asia: Impacts and Responses to the Global Financial Crisis,* ed. Armin Bauer and Myo Thant, 13–50. Manila: Asian Development Bank.

Patunru, A. A., N. Nurridzki, and Rivayani. 2007. "Port Competition in Indonesia." Paper prepared for Asian Development Bank Institute. Forthcoming as "Port Competitiveness: A Case Study of Semarang and Surabaya, Indonesia." In *Infrastructure's Role in Lowering Asia's Trade Costs: Building for Trade*, ed. D. Brooks and D. Hummels. Cheltenham, U.K.: Edward Elgar.

Rodrik, D. 2004. "Industrial Policy for the Twenty First Century." Discussion Paper 4767, Centre for Economic Policy Research, London.

———. 2007. *One Economics, Many Recipes: Globalization, Institutions, and Economic Growth*. Princeton, NJ: Princeton University Press.

Rose, A. 2007. "The Foreign Service and Foreign Trade: Embassies as Export Promotion." *World Economy* 30 (1): 22–38.

Soesastro, H. M. 1989. "The Political Economy of Deregulation in India." *Asian Survey* 29 (9): 853–69.

Soesastro, H., and M. C. Basri. 2005. "The Political Economy of Trade Policy in Indonesia." *ASEAN Economic Bulletin* 22 (1): 161–78.

van Diermen, P., M. C. Basri, and E. Shan. Forthcoming. "Trade, Aid and Development: An Analytical Paper." Report prepared for Aus Aid, Indonesia Branch.

Warr, P. G. 1992. "Exchange Rate Policy, Petroleum Prices, and the Balance of Payments." In *The Oil Boom and After: Indonesian Economic Policy and Performance in the Soeharto Era,* ed. A. Booth, 132–56. Kuala Lumpur: Oxford University Press.

World Bank. 2009. "Revitalizing Agriculture in Indonesia." Policy Notes, World Bank, Washngton, DC.

Woo, W. T., and C. Hong. 2010. "Indonesia's Economic Performance in Comparative Perspective and a New Policy Framework 2049." *Bulletin of Indonesian Economic Studies* 46 (1): 33–64.

Zahler, A. 2007. "Decomposing World Export Growth and the Relevance of New Destinations." Working Paper 20, Center for International Development, Harvard University, Cambridge, MA.

18

INDIA: MANAGING OPENNESS FOR A RAPIDLY DEVELOPING DOMESTIC MARKET

Ulrich Bartsch and Abhijit Sen Gupta

India joined the elite group of fast-growing economies in the 2000s, when its gross domestic product (GDP) expanded by 9 percent per year during 2002–07 (figure 18.1). Since the early 1990s, India has been rapidly opening up to trade and capital flows, but because the opening started from a very low level, India's economy remains relatively closed, especially compared to East Asian countries. Indicators of economic openness increased along with those of overall economic growth, as promarket reforms, chipping away at the elaborate edifice of the "license raj," unshackled entrepreneurs after the 1991 balance-of-payments crisis.

The recent growth spurt seems to have taken only a short pause during the global financial crisis, when India's growth slowed down significantly but the economy avoided a recession. In the first half of 2010, signs emerged that India is returning to precrisis growth rates. India was affected by the shocks of 2008—first the commodity price boom and then the global financial crisis—along with most other countries in the world, but showed remarkable resilience. In fact, with Indian banks unaffected by the toxic asset crisis, India faced some limited capital outflows and a big decline in demand for its exports, but the main impact of the crisis was psychological: consumers and businesses took fright and postponed some decisions.

After the crisis, policy makers turned attention to the requirements of fast growth for the medium term. In the context of this book, we discuss two aspects: first, the prospects for fast growth in exports and their impact on factor productivity growth; and, second, the challenges of macroeconomic management with an ever more open capital account. The first section gives some background information on the Indian growth experience, which differed from other countries in that the services sector played a much larger role than in countries with comparable per capita incomes.

The second part is devoted to an analysis of the role of exports in India's economic growth by looking at factor intensities of exports overall and to specific country groups. This approach highlights the importance of the "old" countries of the Organisation for Economic Co-operation and Development (OECD)—Europe, Japan, and the United States—for exports of products that embody skills and technology and thereby provide impetus to factor productivity growth in India. Slow growth in the old OECD with the lingering effects of the global crisis could dampen the export demand crucial for economic growth. However, with India not easily fitting into the world of small open economies most often described by theorists, the domestic market seems to be no less demanding of sophisticated goods than the export market. Exports, therefore, can be expected to play a less prominent role in India than in some smaller emerging-market countries.

The third section analyzes challenges to macroeconomic management posed by volatile capital inflows. The section shows the loss of monetary policy independence in the face of massive capital inflows in 2006–07 and during earlier such episodes. It highlights the importance of a careful approach to capital account liberalization and policies that can limit the economy's vulnerability to the most volatile types of capital flows.

Figure 18.1. GDP Per Capita Growth in India, 1970–2009

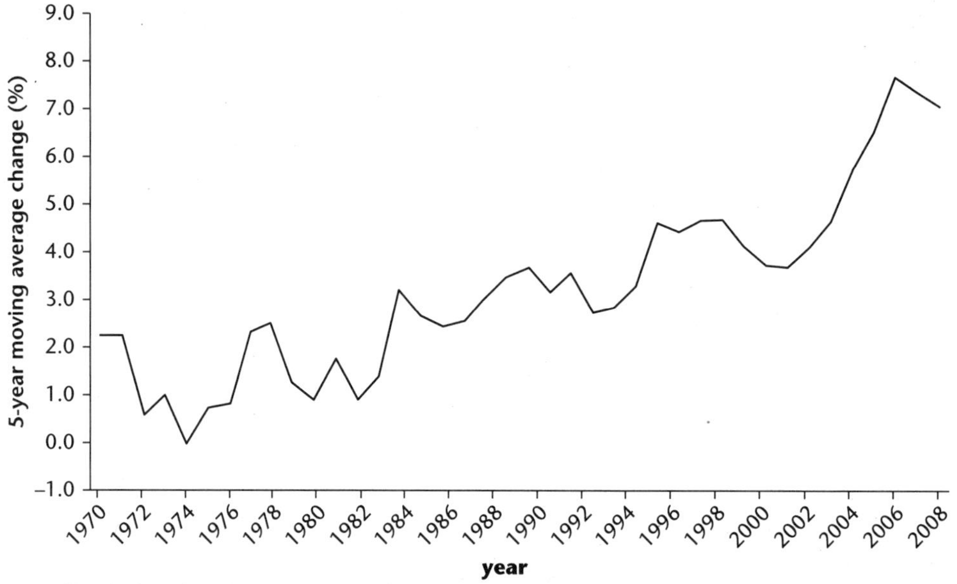

Source: Central Statistics Office database, http://www.mospi.gov.in/cso_test1.htm.

India's Recent Growth Experience

The recent growth spurt of the Indian economy is remarkable. Over three decades, India's anemic economic growth rate had gained notoriety as the "Hindu rate of growth." Changes began in the 1980s and accelerated after a balance-of-payments crisis in the early 1990s. Broad reforms aimed at dismantling the so-called license raj freed up the dynamism of India's entrepreneurs, and economic growth accelerated significantly. At the same time, the rise in per capita incomes was also helped by declining population growth. Per capita growth averaged only 0.7 percent between the early 1950s and the end of the 1970s. It accelerated to 3.3 percent in the 1980s and 1990s. However, in the five years 2002–07 average real GDP grew at almost 9 percent, and per capita growth at more than 7 percent. At this rate, India's economic growth was the second highest of any major economy in the world, behind only China's. A sustained performance at this rate would double real incomes every 10 years.

High growth was driven by a significant shift in domestic saving and investment, but the trade balance remained negative in almost all years. Private saving as a share of GDP languished below 20 percent until the beginning of the 1990s. From 24 percent in fiscal 1996–97, however, it increased steadily and reached 32 percent in fiscal 2009–10.[1] Private investment oscillated around 18 percent of GDP until fiscal 2004–05, when it jumped to 24 percent and continued climbing to nearly 28 percent in fiscal 2007–08. The share of exports and imports in GDP crossed into double digits in the mid-1990s and nearly doubled by fiscal 2004–05. Growth accounting, therefore, shows that accumulation of capital increased significantly starting in the late 1990s, but total factor productivity (TFP) also shifted into higher gear (see Bosworth, Collins, and Virmani 2007).

In contrast to fast-growing emerging economies in East Asia, India's manufacturing sector did not spearhead economic growth. As in other developing countries, the agriculture sector's share in production declined. The share of industry remained relatively stable, however, while the services sector showed the most dynamism (figure 18.2). From a share of 38 percent of GDP in 1965, the services sector produced 55 percent of GDP in fiscal 2009–10. During the same period, the share of agriculture declined from 41 percent to 17 percent of GDP. The industrial sector increased its share only from 21 percent to 28 percent of GDP. The high share of the services sector in GDP means that the structure of India's GDP resembles that of high-income countries more than that of countries at similar levels of per capita income.

India's Resilience during the Global Crisis

India was hit by the commodity price boom before the global financial crisis, which peaked in the summer of 2008. The terms-of-trade shock—mainly from rising oil prices—is estimated at 2.5 percent of GDP. Rising commodity prices led to higher inflation in India, although the government did not fully pass on higher oil prices to Indian consumers and increased fuel and fertilizer

Figure 18.2. Composition of GDP in India, 1965–2009

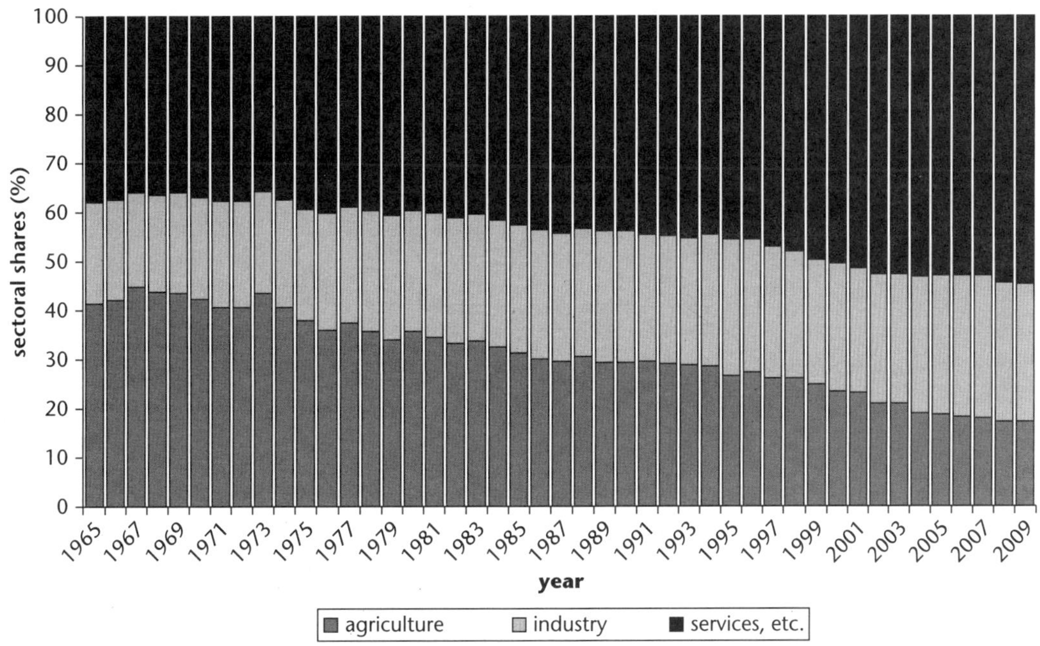

Source: Central Statistics Office database, http://www.mospi.gov.in/cso_test1.htm.

subsidies instead. Wholesale price inflation nevertheless peaked at nearly 13 percent in August 2008, an almost 10-percentage-point increase from the beginning of the year. Monetary policy reacted to higher inflation with higher interest rates and prudential requirements: the cash reserve requirement was raised by 150 basis points and the repurchase rate by 125 basis points between January and September 2008. With these actions, policy rates reached the highest level since the beginning of the decade, although the tightening obviously trailed inflation and was relatively modest.

At the time of the global financial crisis, India's economy suffered a significant slowdown in growth. However, India did not suffer a recession. In the fourth quarter of 2008, GDP growth was more than three percentage points lower than the five-year average before the crisis. But at its lowest point during the crisis, growth was still higher than in any major developed country during the boom period of the early 2000s. From a high of 10.1 percent in the second quarter of fiscal 2006–07, GDP growth (at factor cost) slumped to 5.8 percent in the fourth quarter of fiscal 2008–09, and the latest available data show a recovery to 8.6 percent in the last quarter of fiscal 2009–10. The downturn and recovery are much stronger in the growth rate of the monthly index of industrial production, which accelerated to a peak of 13 percent in January 2007, dropped to near zero in December 2009, and recovered to 17 percent in May 2010.

In the immediate aftermath of the Lehman Brothers collapse, financial sector liquidity dried up and caused a sharp spike in interbank lending rates. As in other countries, the Reserve Bank of India (RBI) scrambled to restore liquidity to the system. In a step-wise manner over a period of six months, it lowered prudential ratios and policy interest rates and directly injected liquidity through open market operations. According to its own estimates, the different liquidity operations injected rupees worth about 9 percent of GDP into the financial system. Interbank rates fell significantly and stabilized by November 2009. Expansionary fiscal policy, however, set in at the same time as the Lehman collapse, was eroding confidence because of India's electoral cycle: populist policies of farm debt waivers and higher civil servant salaries greatly supported private consumption demand in the last quarter of 2008, when the economy was hit by a significant slump in investment demand and destocking.[2] Three explicit stimulus packages added to government demand by lowering taxes and increasing spending, for example, on the National Rural Employment Guarantee Schemes. Overall, the general government fiscal deficit reached 8.8 percent of GDP in fiscal 2008–09, a widening by 3.8 percent of GDP over fiscal 2007–08.

At first sight, the global financial crisis should have had only a mild impact on India's economy because of the resilience of the country's banking system and relatively closed current and capital accounts. First, the banking system faced no exposure to the toxic assets that led to widespread financial distress in developed countries. Second, India's development model is not that of export-led growth, as in some other emerging-market countries, most notably in East Asia, although the importance of external transactions, both current and capital, has greatly expanded over the past two decades (see "India's Growth Model" below). The percentage of exports in GDP reached the mid-20s before the global crisis, compared with around 50 percent in many East Asian countries. Moreover, in the boom years before the global crisis and the severe recession in international trade, imports were growing faster than exports, and the net contribution of trade to GDP growth was therefore negative. Finally, India faced a sudden stop in capital flows but avoided large-scale capital flight. Portfolio flows rushed into India's equity market before the crisis and led to concerns about the competitiveness of domestic tradables. Nevertheless, some capital fled to safe havens, which the RBI managed by letting the exchange rate depreciate and intervening only marginally in the foreign exchange markets. The low level of short-term external borrowing, the relative resilience of foreign direct investment (FDI), and the confidence-inspiring level of RBI foreign reserves prevented a stronger upset.

The crisis nevertheless had a strong impact on business and consumer confidence. The main channel of transmission of the global financial crisis to India's real economy seems to have been psychological: uncertainty over the future caused consumers to postpone purchases of durable goods and businesses to postpone investment projects. This reaction led to the transmission of the global financial crisis to the real economy. However, it did not lead India into recession. Growth of industrial production slumped to zero in December 2009 but did not enter negative territory. Even fixed investment in the national accounts showed a near-zero growth rate, which means capacity continued to expand in the midst of the global crisis at the same level as before the crisis.

India's Growth Model: Greater Openness but Also a Rapidly Developing Domestic Market

During the past decade, India's economy has greatly opened up to the world. Since 2001, its exports and imports have grown by around 20 percent per year on average and amounted to 24 percent and 30 percent of GDP, respectively, in fiscal 2009–10. India has also emerged as the world's biggest recipient of worker remittances, which amounted to US$55 billion in fiscal 2009–10.[3] However, the net impact of trade on growth—in a national accounting sense—was negative over the five years before the global crisis, as imports grew faster than exports. India has diversified its trading partners, with China becoming increasingly more important (figure 18.3). While the shares of the European Union (EU) and the United States in total trade have declined over the past 20 years, China captured about 11 percent of India's exports and imports in fiscal 2009–10, as compared with negligible shares in fiscal 1987–88.

The global financial crisis and its lingering effects have led to concerns that increasing openness—that is, the share of trade and capital flows in the economy—cannot drive growth the way that it did in many countries before the global crisis (see, for example, World Bank 2010). According to this line of thought, emerging markets would derive smaller benefits than before from an export-led industrialization strategy because of the lingering recession in the OECD countries and higher risk aversion by foreign investors.

Economists have argued that trade can be a powerful driver of factor productivity growth. They point out that competing in the global marketplace through trade—and in particular exporting manufactured products—generally requires higher technology and skills than production for the domestic market. Because growth requires the accumulation of capital and skills and adoption of better technology to increase factor productivity, trade drives growth because it pushes domestic workers to acquire skills, entrepreneurs to innovate, and international investors to transfer technology through FDI. The corollary to this view is that production for the domestic market would employ less technology and human-capital-intensive processes because domestic consumers demand less sophisticated products than overseas markets. However, we point out below that the production of India's exports does not seem to employ higher technology and more human capital than the production for the domestic market. Exports, therefore, may not be as important for growth as they are in some other, smaller emerging markets.

This view of trade as an engine of growth and structural change stands in marked contrast to the earlier view that countries engage in trade in accordance with their comparative advantage. In the case of India, that process would mean a specialization in exports of goods that incorporate the country's relatively abundant natural resources and unskilled labor. While the type of trade based on comparative advantage increases demand for goods, it cannot explain the kind of total factor productivity growth and structural change observed in the fast-growing countries such as the Asian Tigers (Hong Kong SAR, China; the Republic of Korea; Singapore; and Taiwan, China). Their growth relied to a large extent on shifting production into more sophisticated products. Exports of natural resources

Figure 18.3. Direction of India's Trade, 1987–88 through 2007–08

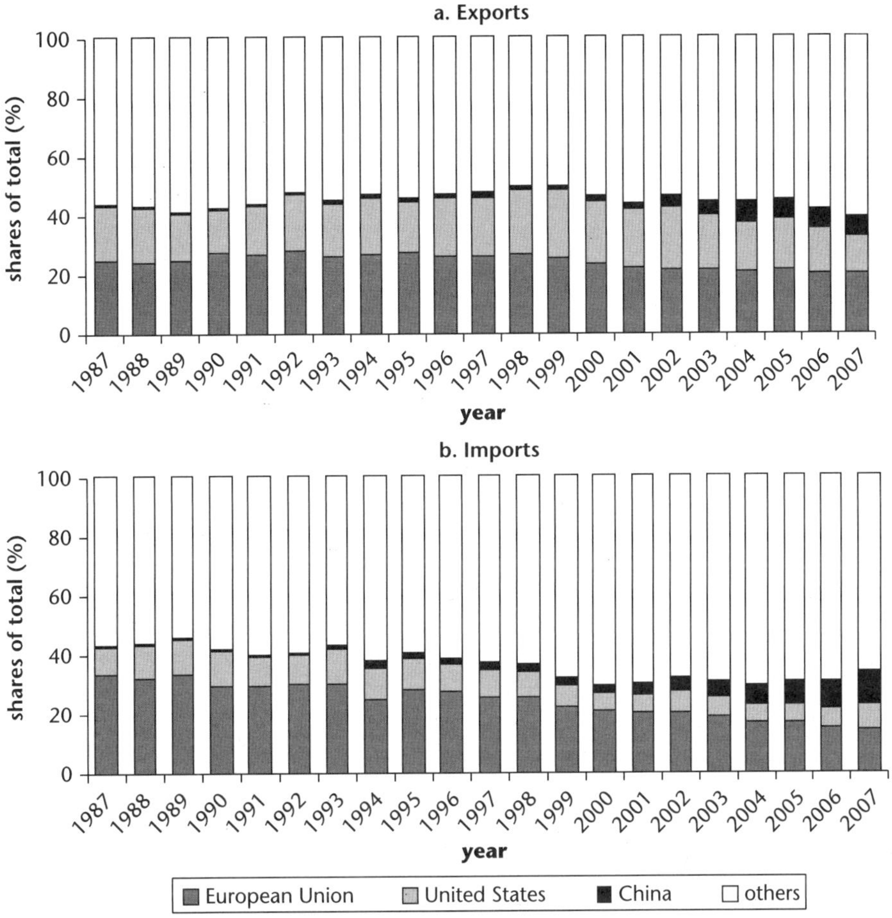

Source: Reserve Bank of India.

and unskilled labor–intensive goods would not have provided incentives for investment in technology and skills, while the domestic markets for sophisticated products in these countries were too small for production to benefit from economies of scale and scope. However, much of the literature discusses the experience of small, open economies, where domestic market size is limited and with it the opportunities for economies of scale and scope and where, therefore, international investors have little reason to set up manufacturing capacity if it is not meant to provide for exports. The question is whether there is evidence that this analysis also holds true for India.

Exports of human-capital-and-technology-intensive manufactures have grown fast in India since 1990. Until then, more than 80 percent of exports were based on natural resources and unskilled labor, arguably in line with India's endowments. However, by 2008 this share had declined to 63 percent (see table 18.1). The data in table 18.1 are derived from categorizing India's exports according to the relative intensity in their production of four factors: natural resources, unskilled labor, technology, and human capital (skills) using the three-digit Standard International Trade Classification (SITC) (see Pitigala 2010).[4]

While we can safely assume that the TFP spillover from "sophisticated" exports had some impact on domestic production, exports on the whole do not seem to employ more technology and skills than home market production. In fact, at first glance the data show the opposite. The share of such sophisticated processes was actually higher in home production than in exports, with 41 percent of domestic output coming from technology-and-skills-intensive industries compared with 37 percent of exports. However, this comparison rests on somewhat shaky ground. It compares data on trade with data from India's Annual Survey of Industry (ASI), although the two use different classifications.[5] More important, the total value of industrial production shown in the ASI is only about 40 percent of that in the national accounts (ASI data for 2008 show value added as Re 4.7 trillion as compared with

Table 18.1. Factor Intensities of Indian Exports and Domestic Production, Selected Years, 1962–2008
percentage of total

	Year	Natural resources	Unskilled labor	Technology intensive	Human capital intensive
All countries	2008	46.5	16.8	20.3	16.4
	2000	39.7	24.7	15.4	14.2
	1990	52.1	31.5	7.4	8.9
	1970	59.9	27.0	4.5	8.6
	1962	62.9	33.3	1.6	2.2
Domestic production	2008	49.6	9.0	25.3	16.0
	2004	47.1	9.8	25.9	17.2
Old OECD	2008	36.6	14.2	26.7	22.5
High-income East Asia	2008	64.1	8.7	17.7	9.4
China and Hong Kong SAR, China	2008	83.4	2.9	8.9	4.8

Sources: Authors' calculations based on UN Comtrade (database), United Nations, http://comtrade.un.org.

Re 12.7 trillion in the national accounts). At least part of the discrepancy would most likely be explained by problems in coverage: the ASI probably underrepresents small-scale industry in the informal sector. Because this sector accounts for 80 percent of nonfarm employment in India, the true share of unskilled labor–intensive production is probably much higher than shown in the ASI data. If the "missing" value added in the survey is added to unskilled labor–intensive industries, their share rises to 20 percent, and sophisticated processes now produce 38 percent of domestic output, equal to their share in exports.

Thus, from the limited data available, we cannot conclude that exports are more sophisticated goods than those produced for the home market. Possibly a finer classification of goods distinguishing between those produced for exports and those for the home market within categories under the three-digit SITC or International Standard Industrial Classification (ISIC) could have shown that televisions for sale in India, for example, are less sophisticated than televisions exported by domestic producers.

It has to be noted, though, that the composition of India's exports differs strongly between regions. India's exports to Europe, Japan, and the United States (the old OECD) are fairly diversified, but exports to China and Hong Kong SAR, China, are narrowly based on just two product categories. In its exports to higher-income East Asia (Indonesia; Korea; Singapore; Taiwan, China; and Thailand), India provides natural resource–based inputs to the manufacturing powerhouses, but it is also increasingly integrated into production networks for electrical goods, electronics, car parts, and machinery. A large share of India's exports to China and Hong Kong SAR, China (more than 60 percent), consists of mineral ores and woven fabrics using natural resources and unskilled labor–intensive production, respectively. Tobacco constitutes an impressive 43 percent of what high-income Asian countries buy from India, but technology and human capital–intensive goods make up 27 percent of the total. In contrast, nearly 50 percent of Indian exports to old OECD countries consist of products using relatively more technology and human capital.[6]

Growth in exports in the 1990s was predominantly in exports of technology and human capital–intensive production. They grew by around 17 percent per year as against 9 percent growth for all exports (see table 18.2). In contrast, export growth in the 2000s was much more balanced between sophisticated goods and goods more in line with India's static comparative advantage, natural resources and unskilled labor. In the 2000s, however, services exports with arguably much higher human-capital intensity took off with growth of 18 percent per year.

The sources of global trade growth provide no strong reasons for export pessimism. In recent years before the global crisis, high-income country imports have grown faster than GDP, driven by differentiation of goods and outsourcing of some elements of production. Developing-country exports, in contrast, have risen faster than global GDP because of continuing economic integration, fragmentation of production, and specialization in globalized production networks. The forces that drove these developments before the global crisis continue to operate. India stands to benefit from these developments, because its integration into East Asian production networks is still in its infancy and new opportunities arise as China moves up the value chain. The most hopeful recent development is the emergence of India as a hub for the production of cars and car components for export. Hyundai and Suzuki already export an important share

Table 18.2. Growth in Exports, Different Factor Intensities, 1990–2008

	US$, millions			Annual growth rates (%)		
	1990	2000	2008	1990–2008	1990–2000	2000–08
Export of goods	18,477	45,452	175,184	12.5	9.0	13.5
NR and UL	15,447	29,271	110,891	11.0	6.4	13.3
TN and HC	3,030	16,181	64,293	17.0	16.8	13.8
Export of services	4,551	16,268	101,224	17.2	12.7	19.3

Sources: CSO Balance of Payments, and UN Comtrade.
Note: NR = natural resources, UL = unskilled labor, TN = technology, HC = skills.

of their India-produced vehicles today, and Ford and Nissan will commence shortly.

Domestic market opportunities are growing fast. In fact, the domestic market was about three times the size of the export market during the high-growth years before the global crisis on average (US$458 billion as compared with US$150 billion for exports, table 18.3). And even though exports were growing fast, the additional domestic market demand was higher than additional demand from international markets in every year during the 2002–07 period. Over the five years on average, domestic demand increased by US$64 billion every year, as compared with US$35 billion for exports.

The Indian middle class—defined as people living in households with consumption patterns comparable to the middle class in the United States based on purchasing-power-parity exchange rates—was estimated as 5 percent of the population, or 50 million people in 2005 (see figure 18.4).[7] At the high rates of growth in per capita income observed before the global financial crisis, the middle class is projected to expand to 43 percent of the population or 500 million people by 2025. With 50 million consumers, the market size for many products is currently not big enough to allow for economies of scale and scope.[8] The outlook for the next 20 years, however, makes India an attractive market to invest in, and many international consumer goods companies do so. For now, however, many of them content themselves with sales outlets rather than production bases, because economies of scale allow them to produce cheaper elsewhere. This situation is expected to change, however, in particular because production costs in East Asia are rising with rising wages.

It would be risky for India to adopt policies that aim at replacing export growth with faster growth of the domestic market. Such a rebalancing is proposed for countries with current account surpluses such as China to reduce global imbalances, which are believed to be one of the factors that contributed to the global crisis. In India, however, with a small deficit in the current account over recent years, a strategy aimed at increasing domestic demand growth at the cost of savings—by encouraging higher consumer spending—would be risky because it would require India to rely to a greater degree on uncertain external financing of the massive investment needs of the country. Consequently, a balanced approach that builds on both domestic and external demand is needed to provide a solid foundation for medium-term growth.

India's Approach to Capital Account Liberalization

Alongside the opening and expansion of the current account, capital account flows also increased massively after the 1991 balance-of-payments crisis. The higher volatility of capital account flows relative to current account flows has posed challenges to macroeconomic management. India witnessed its first surge in capital inflows during 1993 and 1994, when net capital inflows increased to more than US$6.7 billion in 1993 and US$10.6 billion in 1994, from an average of US$3.7 billion during the previous two years. Capital flows declined in the second half of the 1990s for a variety of domestic and external reasons, including the contagion effects of different crises in Latin America and East Asia and sanctions after India's nuclear tests in May 1998. Net capital flows dropped from US$10.5 billion in 1994 to US$3.8 billion in 1995. There was some recovery in 1996 with net capital flows reaching US$12 billion, but subsequent years saw an average of US$9 billion between 1997 and the early 2000s. Net capital inflows picked up after 2002: they first touched US$12 billion with an improvement in global conditions, doubled by 2004, and rose quickly to US$37.7 billion in 2006 and US$95 billion in 2007. As a result of the onset of the subprime crisis in the United States and the associated "flight to safety," portfolio capital started flowing out of India in early 2008 and continued until early 2009, although FDI flows remained quite robust. Capital flows resumed again in early 2009, with India receiving net capital inflows of US$53 billion during fiscal 2009.

Table 18.3. Household Consumption and Exports, Level and Increment, 2002–08
US$, billions

	2002–03	2003–04	2004–05	2005–06	2006–07	2007–08	Average
Level							
Household consumption	324.1	379.2	416.7	466.1	516.4	643.7	457.7
Exports	73.5	88.7	126.6	160.8	203.1	249.0	150.3
Increment							
Household consumption	16.6	55.1	37.5	49.4	50.3	127.3	63.9
Exports	12.5	15.3	37.9	34.2	42.3	45.9	35.1

Source: Central Statistics Office National Account Statistics, Balance of Payments Statistics, RBI exchange rates, http://www.mospi.gov.in/cso_test1.htm.

Figure 18.4. Income Strata in India, 1985–2025

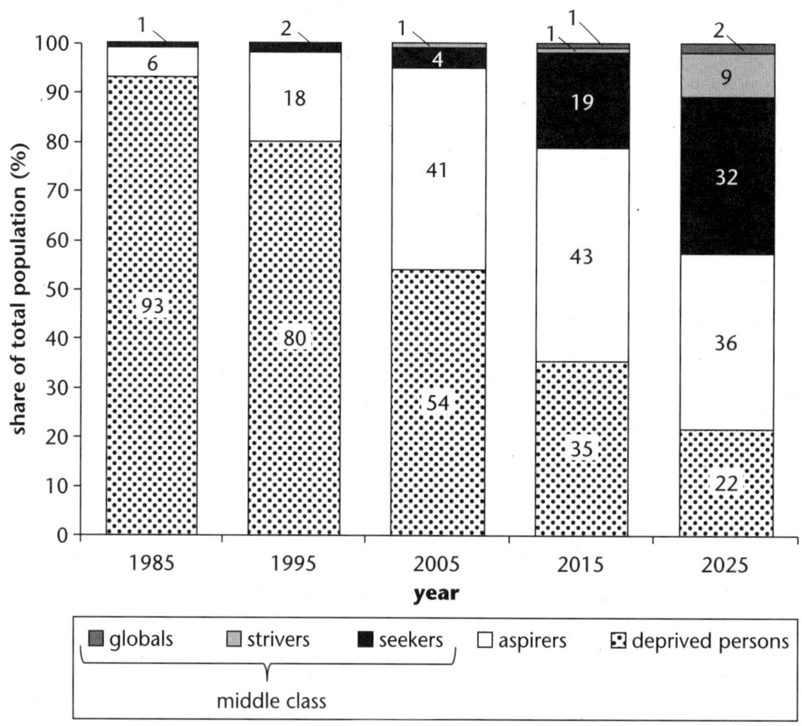

Source: Beinhocker, Farrell, and Zainulbhai 2007.

Despite the significant changes in the importance of external flows, India is still a relatively closed economy according to several benchmarks (figure 18.5). In fact, when evaluated on the basis of legal restrictions on cross-border capital flows, the openness of India's capital account has remained stagnant since the 1970s (Chinn and Ito 2008).[9] In contrast, a de facto measure of openness shows that India's international financial integration progressed significantly: the ratio of the sum of foreign assets and foreign liabilities to GDP increased from 17.8 percent in 1970 to 85.4 percent in 2007 (Lane and Milessi-Ferreti 2007). However, India has not kept pace with the liberalization of the capital account in other emerging markets. As a result, in a cross-country comparison India is placed at the restrictive end of the spectrum, for both de jure and de facto openness. It has been overtaken by several other countries like Brazil, Chile, China, and others, which lagged behind India in capital account openness during the 1980s.

Macroeconomic Management and Capital Flows

The increased volatility of international capital flows has rekindled the debate over capital account liberalization. Sharp changes in the direction of capital flows during the past two years have presented difficulties for macroeconomic

Figure 18.5. Cross-Country Comparison of Capital Account Openness, Selected Countries, 2000–07

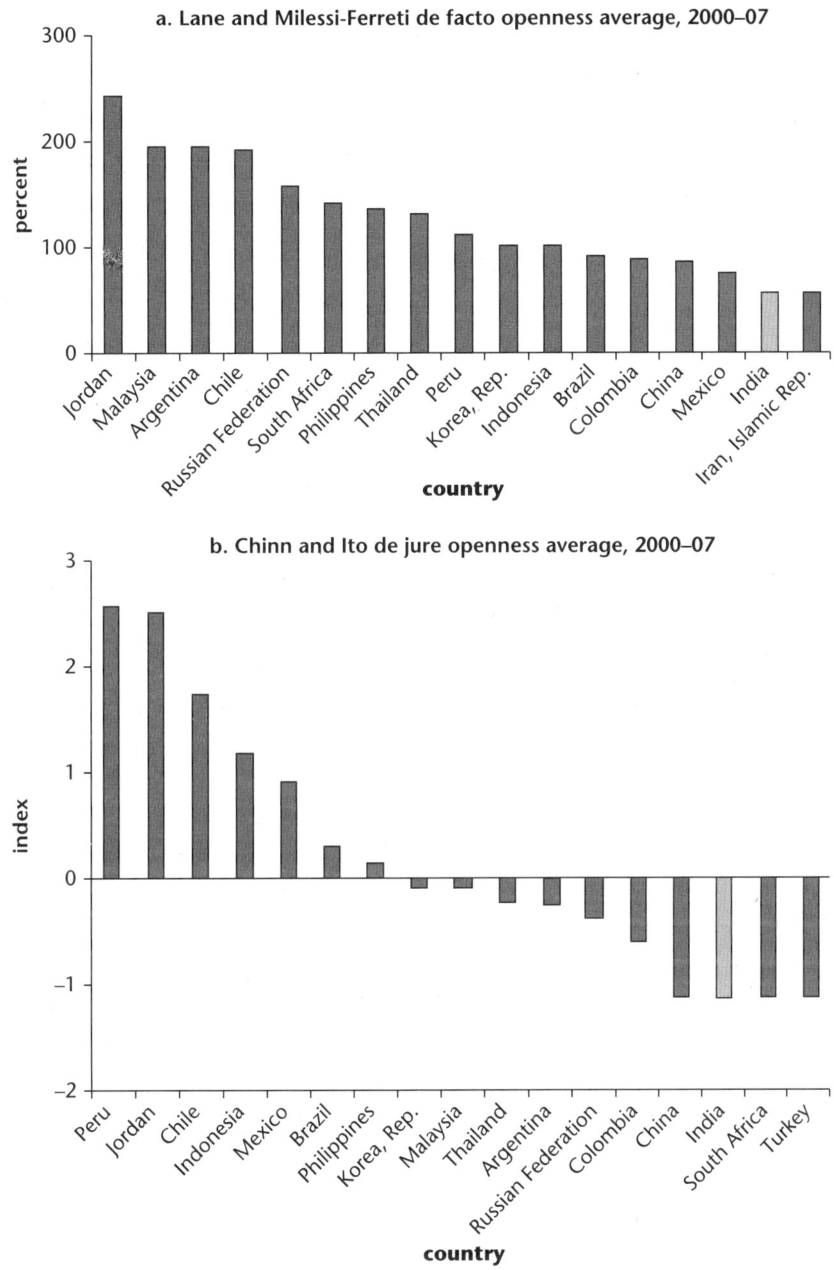

Sources: Lane and Milessi-Ferreti 2007; Chinn and Ito 2008.

management. Proponents of capital account liberalization have argued that it creates opportunities for diversifying portfolios, smoothing consumption, sharing risk, and addressing contracts and payments in trade. Furthermore, the threat of capital outflows in the face of opportunistic policies could have a disciplining effect on policy makers (see, for example, Fischer 1998 and Summers 2000). Conversely, critics point toward the East Asian crises at the end of the 1990s and maintain that speculative capital flows are extremely volatile for reasons outside the control of individual countries and that opening an economy to such capital results in financial crises. They argue, therefore, for the imposition of frictions to limit the short-term cross-border trade in financial assets (see, for example, Bhagwati 1998, Rodrik 1998, and Stiglitz 2000). In a recent paper, the International Monetary Fund—long-time champion of capital account opening—seems to concur with this view (Ostry et al. 2010). Furthermore, current thinking emphasizes the need for appropriate sequencing of capital account liberalization in the overall reform process and prioritizing liberalization of certain selected capital flows and taxing others (Rogoff 2002; Feldstein 2003). In particular, some are concerned that the low interest rates found in the high-income countries today could lead to a surge in capital flows to emerging markets through the carry trade, which could choke off the recovery in the receiving countries by affecting the competitiveness of domestic tradables production. Consequently, a number of countries have taken measures to deter inflows of short-term capital.

India has adopted a gradual, calibrated approach toward liberalizing its capital account, where certain flows and specific agents have been accorded priority. On one side of the spectrum, FDI has been significantly liberalized during the past few years. Currently, barring a few sectors, FDI is universally allowed.[10] Net FDI flows into India increased from just US$97 million in fiscal 1990–91 to nearly US$35 billion in fiscal 2008–09. India has been more cautious in liberalizing portfolio investment and has maintained separate investment caps on subaccounts of foreign institutional investors. Despite these caps, recent years have seen a sharp increase and reversals in net portfolio flows, which increased from less than US$2.0 billion in fiscal 2001–02 to US$29.5 billion in fiscal 2007–08.

Treatment of debt-creating flows has remained much more restrictive: both borrowers and lenders have to satisfy eligibility criteria with a limit of US$500 million per borrower per financial year and the Reserve Bank of India imposes minimum maturity and interest rate ceilings. However, attractive global interest rates have led to a sharp rise in the inflow of external commercial borrowing from US$2.7 billion in fiscal 2001–02 to over US$30.0 billion in fiscal 2007–08. Recent years have also witnessed a significant liberalization of outward FDI and portfolio investment, but upper limits still exist.

Macroeconomic management faces increasing challenges with rising integration in the global capital market. In fact, with free capital flows, policy makers cannot simultaneously aim to achieve a stable rate of capacity utilization, a low and stable rate of inflation, and a stable exchange rate, a problem known in the literature as the "impossible trinity." Capital account opening thus reduces policy makers' ability to run a monetary policy independently from policies of their trading partners. The panels in figure 18.6 illustrate India's macroeconomic management in a period of increasing integration with the global financial markets. They compare monetary independence (defined on the basis of the correlation between Indian and U.S. interest rates), exchange-rate stability, reserve accumulation as a share of GDP, and capital account openness (defined as the ratio of foreign assets and liabilities to GDP) over the period 1993–2007 (see Aizenman, Chin, and Ito 2010).[11] All indexes have been normalized between 0 and 1. The origin in the charts indicates a completely floating exchange rate, zero monetary independence, a completely closed capital account, and zero reserve accumulation. We distinguish six periods:

- *1993–96, exchange-rate peg.* During the first surge in capital inflows during 1993 and 1994, the RBI intervened heavily in the foreign exchange market to maintain the rupee peg to the U.S. dollar. As a result, India's reserve holdings more than doubled from US$12 billion in July 1993 to US$24 billion in October 1994. This intervention could not be sterilized because of a lack of instruments and an illiquid bond market. The intervention therefore contributed to reserve money growth of 23 percent in 1994 compared to 16.5 percent in 1992 and is reflected in low values on the monetary independence index.
- *1997–2000, low capital flows, moderate exchange-rate depreciation.* In the second half of the 1990s, capital flows dropped, and the rupee depreciated by around 8.5 percent against the U.S. dollar. The weaker peg is reflected in the drop in the index of exchange-rate stability in 1997 and 1998. In contrast, the drop in capital flows and increased flexibility of the exchange rate allowed a greater degree of monetary independence.
- *2001–05, increasing costs of sterilization, weakening exchange-rate peg.* Net capital inflows picked up after 2002, and the RBI intervened heavily. It purchased more than US$45 billion of foreign assets between January 2001 and December 2003. As a result, the RBI's stock of foreign assets increased by more than Re 2.6 trillion over this period, which is reflected in a jump in the reserve accumulation index and high values of exchange-rate stability. To limit the increase in the monetary base resulting from this intervention, the RBI reduced its holdings of government bonds by about half the increase in foreign assets. The policy trade-offs were becoming increasingly visible after 2003. Initially, the RBI continued to intervene heavily in the foreign exchange market. However, by late 2003, it started to run out of government bonds for sterilization, and in January 2004, a new instrument for sterilization—the market stabilization scheme (MSS) bond—was introduced. By August 2005, the amount of outstanding MSS bonds had increased to Re 0.71 trillion. However, with a rising number of outstanding MSS bonds, the quasi-fiscal costs of sterilization were also increasing. The RBI therefore gave up sterilization and reduced interven-

Figure 18.6. Configurations of the Impossible Trinity and Reserve Accumulation in India, 1993–2007

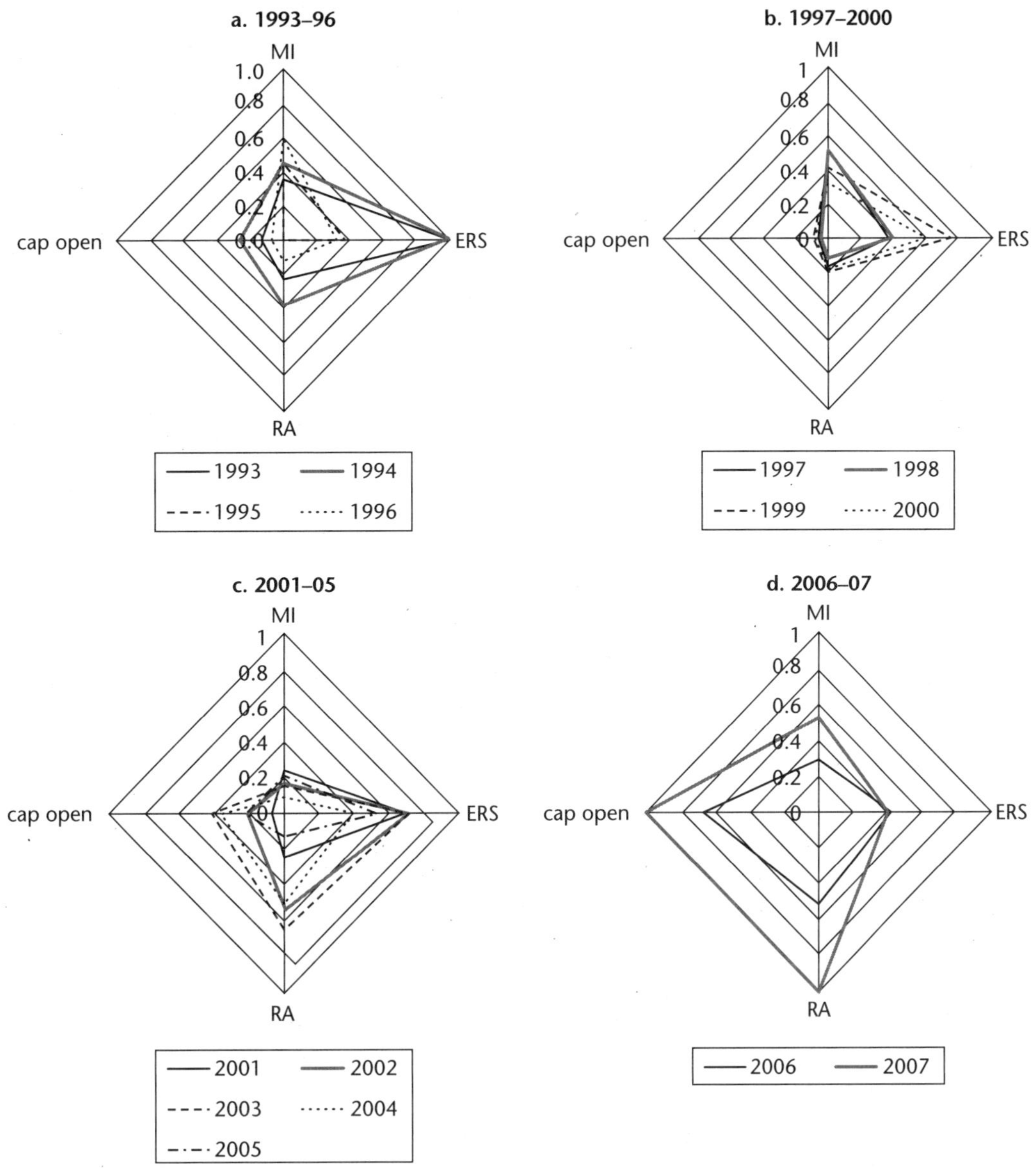

Source: Authors' calculations.
Note: MI = monetary independence; ERS = exchange-rate stability; RA = reserve accumulation; cap open = capital account openness.

tions.[12] Instead, the rupee appreciated from Re 46.3 to Re 43.5 per U.S. dollar between August 2004 and July 2005, reflected in a drop in the exchange-rate stabilization index in 2004 and 2005.

- *2006–07, surge in capital flows, appreciation of the exchange rate.* In 2006 and 2007, the RBI developed its "intermediate regime" in the face of a sharp increase in capital flows. The rupee was allowed to appreciate by 17 percent against the U.S. dollar between June 2006 and December 2007, as reflected in figure 18.6, panel d in a drop in the exchange-rate index. The RBI also resumed intervention in the foreign exchange market by purchasing more than US$95 billion between January 2006 and December 2007, resulting in the sharp increase in the reserve accumulation index in these years. To sterilize this intervention, the RBI issued additional MSS bonds, and the outstanding stock of MSS bonds increased by Re 1.5 trillion between April 2006 and November 2007. Liquidity was also absorbed with an increase in the cash reserve ratio by 200 basis points in 2007. However, this measure was still not enough to fully sterilize the market interventions, and the growth in reserve money jumped to 18 percent in 2006 and 26 percent in 2007. In addition, a number of measures were introduced in 2007 to curb capital inflows. These included restrictions on external commercial borrowing, curbs on the use of participatory notes, and restrictions on foreign institutional investors. The RBI also introduced measures to limit loans to both foreign and domestically held mutual funds operating in India. However, the effectiveness of these measures was limited, and capital continued to pour into the country.

- *2008–March 2009, portfolio capital outflow, loss of reserves, and weakening of the rupee.* As a result of the onset of the subprime crisis in the United States and the associated flight to safety, portfolio capital flowed out of India in early 2008, continuing until early 2009. In addition, in the worst crisis quarters between September 2008 and March 2009, banking assets were transferred abroad, and suppliers' credit was withdrawn. The capital outflow exacerbated a rise in the current account deficit because of high commodity prices and dwindling export receipts. The RBI reacted by selling foreign currency assets worth US$40 billion between June 2008 and March 2009.[13] In addition, the rupee was allowed to depreciate by more than 23 percent against the U.S. dollar in the same period. A number of monetary measures were also introduced to bolster liquidity, such as cuts in policy rates, opening up of refinance windows to allow easy access to credit for some of the troubled sectors, and reduction of prudential norms relating to provisioning and risk weights.
- *The present situation.* Capital flows resumed again in early 2009, with India receiving net capital inflows of US$53 billion during fiscal 2009. This resurgence prompted the RBI to re-introduce restrictions on capital inflows. The all-in-cost ceilings, which were withdrawn in January 2009 to encourage external commercial borrowing, were re-imposed in December 2009, with the re-imposed ceilings being higher than the precrisis levels. Foreign currency convertible buybacks were discontinued. The rupee was allowed to appreciate by nearly 17.5 percent between March 2009 and April 2010. Even the 36-currency nominal effective exchange rate appreciated by more than 9 percent.

Interestingly, the RBI has lately refrained from intervening in the foreign exchange market. While it actually sold more than US$6 billion of foreign currency between March and November 2009, it did not intervene at all in the foreign exchange market in the following five months. A number of reasons could be behind RBI's reluctance to intervene, including its preoccupation with managing record borrowing requirements of the government in fiscal 2009–10 and fiscal 2010–11. Sterilization of inflows could have resulted in higher interest rates, which the government wanted to avoid. At the same time, with inflation inching up and crossing 10 percent in March 2010, the RBI may have been more wary of increasing the money supply and exacerbating inflationary pressure. In addition, it may have welcomed an appreciation of the rupee to help to keep inflation in check by reducing the cost of imports. However, the RBI has left open the option for sterilization in the future by replenishing the MSS bonds to the extent of Re 500 billion (US$12 billion). This amount seems a paltry sum compared with the inflows of US$95 billion in the year before the global crisis.

In conclusion, India has resorted to multiple instruments to deal with capital flows with the aim of restricting those that are highly volatile and those that create debt. It had a moderately flexible exchange-rate regime with interventions to prevent excessive volatility, sterilization of these interventions through multiple instruments like MSS bonds and cash reserve requirements, and building up of reserves. This approach has suited India well, given that its economy has been able to maintain healthy growth, targeted monetary and credit growth, moderate inflation, and a sustainable current account deficit through most of the period.

Annex: Framework for Quantifying Policy Choices under the Impossible Trinity

We measure the extent of monetary independence as the inverse of the annual correlation of the monthly interest rates between India and the United States. The United States is taken as the base country following Aizenman, Chinn, and Ito (2010) and Shambaugh (2004), who argue that Indian monetary policy has been most closely linked to the United States. We use the money market rates for the interest rates. In India, the Reserve Bank of India uses several policy tools like the repurchase rate, reverse repurchase rate, and reserve ratio, among others, to conduct monetary policy. Any change in these policy tools is likely to have an impact on the money market rate. Following Aizenman, Chinn, and Ito (2010), the index for extent of monetary independence is given by

$$MI = 1 - \frac{corr(i, i^{*}) - (-1)}{1 - (-1)},$$

where i and i^{*} are the money market rates in India and United States. This index is bound between 0 and 1. By construction, a higher value implies greater monetary independence. Data on money market rates are taken from the International Financial Statistics database.

The index for exchange-rate stability (ERS) is calculated using the annual standard deviations of the monthly log change in the exchange rate between India and the United States,

$$ERS = \frac{0.01}{0.01 + \sigma(\Delta\varepsilon)}$$

where σ is the standard deviation, Δ is the first difference operator, and ε is log of the exchange rate between the Indian rupee and the U.S. dollar. The ERS index also lies between 0 and 1 with a higher number indicating greater exchange-rate rigidity. Aizenman, Chinn, and Ito (2010) argue that a simple application of this formula exaggerates the flexibility in cases where the exchange rate has followed a narrow band but has been devalued or revalued infrequently. To overcome this problem, they apply a threshold—and the regime is labeled *fixed* if the rate of monthly change in the exchange rate has stayed within ±0.33 percent bands—and assign a value of 1 for the ERS index. The data on exchange rate are also taken from the International Financial Statistics.

We deviate from Aizenman, Chinn, and Ito (2010) in construction of the index of capital account openness, who use the de jure measure of openness developed in Chinn and Ito (2008), for two main reasons. First, as discussed above, according to the Chinn-Ito measure, India's extent of openness remained virtually stagnant since the 1970s. Second, we think that it is the actual quantum of flows that create a conflict between retaining monetary independence and maintaining exchange-rate stability and not the regulations. A country with high de jure openness can have low inflow of foreign capital and not be worried about simultaneously stabilizing the exchange rate and exerting monetary autonomy. A country with low de jure openness, however, can experience a large volume of flows because of low enforcement of capital controls and face problems in ensuring monetary independence and exchange-rate stability. As a result, we use the de facto measure outlined in Lane and Milessi-Ferreti (2007), where capital account openness is described as the sum of foreign assets (FA) and liabilities (FL) as a share of GDP:

$$Cap_{Open} = \frac{FA + FL}{GDP}.$$

To make this measure comparable with monetary independence and exchange-rate stability, we also normalize it between 0 and 1.

Notes

1. India's fiscal year runs April 1 to March 31.
2. General elections were held in May 2010, which returned to power the incumbent United Progressive Alliance led by the Congress Party.
3. Biggest in absolute value. Of course, many countries received higher remittances when measured against their GDPs.
4. The methodology was first proposed by Krause (1987).
5. The United Nations' SITC classification for exports is not easily mapped into the classification used in the ASI by the Central Statistical Organization, which is based on the UN's International Standard Industrial Classification (ISIC).
6. Data are from the UN Comtrade database, factor intensity classification from Krause (1987). The three country groups account for more than 50 percent of India's exports, and the four product categories account for 92 percent of the total. See also Pitigala (2010).
7. The study by Beinhocker, Farrell, and Zainulbhai (2007) from the McKinsey Global Institute is based on household surveys by the National Council for Applied Economic Research. The study defines annual income brackets as follows: Globals = > Re 1,000,000, Strivers = Re 500,000–1,000,000, Seekers = Re 200,000–500,000, Aspirers = Re 90,000–200,000, Deprived = < Re 90,000. The middle class encompasses Globals, Strivers, and Seekers. They use Re 45.7/US$1 in real 2000 U.S. dollars, and Re 8.5/US$1 adjusted for purchasing power. Thus, the middle class is defined as people earning US$23,500–US$117,650 per year in 2000 international dollars.
8. For example, about 1.3 million cars were sold in India in fiscal 2009–10, a market hotly contested by three major players (Tata, Maruti-Suzuki, and Hyundai) and many others. By contrast, the top 15 global car companies sold more than that number of cars each during the year, and the top four sold more than 6 million each.
9. This measure is based on the International Monetary Fund's *Annual Report on Exchange Arrangements and Exchange Restrictions*, in which a score of 0 indicates presence of some restrictions on a particular transaction, while 1 indicates free movement of capital. Hence, even if capital transactions have been progressively liberalized, they would attract a score of 0 so long as there are some minimal restrictions. In India; while controls on capital flows have been eased over time, the presence of some minimal restrictions explains the low score.
10. Sectors where FDI is prohibited include atomic energy, certain agriculture and plantation activities etc. Some sectors which require an industrial license (alcoholic beverages, defense equipments etc.) or are reserved for the small units are constrained in getting FDI. Some sensitive sectors such as banking, insurance etc. are subject to caps.
11. The methodology is described in detail in the annex. The period coverage is limited by the availability of the measure for capital account openness. Presentation in calendar years.
12. In India, sterilization has an associated cost as the interest paid out on the sterilization bonds are higher than the interest earned on foreign currency assets.
13. Foreign reserves dropped by US$62 billion because of valuation effects.

Bibliography

Aizenman, J., M. D. Chinn, and H. Ito. 2010. "The Emerging Global Financial Architecture: Tracing and Evaluating the New Patterns of the Trilemma Configurations." *Journal of International Money and Finance* 29 (4): 615–41.

Beinhocker, E., D. Farrell, and A. S. Zainulbhai. 2007. "Tracking the Growth of India's Middle Class." *McKinsey Quarterly* 3: 51–61.

Bhagwati, J. 1998. "The Capital Myth: The Difference between Trade in Widgets and Dollars." *Foreign Affairs* 7 (3): 7–12.

Bosworth, B., S. Collins, and A. Virmani. 2007. "Sources of Growth in the Indian Economy. Working Paper 12901, National Bureau of Economic Research, Cambridge, MA.

Chinn, M. D., and H. Ito. 2008. "A New Measure of Financial Openness." *Journal of Comparative Policy Analysis* 10 (3): 307–20.

Feldstein, M. 2003. "Economic and Financial Crises in Emerging Market Economies: Overview of Prevention and Management." In

Economic and Financial Crises in Emerging Market Economies, ed. M. Feldstein, 1–20. Chicago: University of Chicago Press.

Fischer, S. 1998. "Capital Account Liberalization and the Role of the IMF." In *Should the IMF Pursue Capital-Account Convertibility?* ed. P. Kenen, 1–10. Vol. 207, Essays in International Finance. Department of Economics, Princeton University.

Krause, L. 1987. "The Structure of Trade in Manufactured Goods in the East and Southeast Asian Region." In *Trade and Structural Change in Pacific Asia* ed. C. Bradford and W. H. Branson. Chicago: University of Chicago Press.

Lane, P., and G.-M. Milessi-Ferreti. 2007. "The External Wealth of Nations Mark II: Revised and Extended Estimates of Foreign Assets and Liabilities: 1970–2004." *Journal of International Economics* 73 (2): 223–50.

Ostry, J., A. R. Ghosh, K. Habermeier, M. Chamon, M. S. Qureshi, and D. B. S. Reinhardt. 2010. "Capital Inflows: The Role of Controls." Staff Position Note SPN/10/4, International Monetary Fund, Washington, DC.

Pitigala, N. 2010. "Background Paper for South Asia Regional Economic Outlook." World Bank, Washington, DC.

Rodrik, D. 1998. "Who Needs Capital Account Convertibility?" In *Should the IMF Pursue Capital-Account Convertibility?* ed. P. Kenen, Vol 207, 55–65. Essays in International Finance, Department of Economics, Princeton University, Princeton, NJ.

Rogoff, K. 2002. "Rethinking Capital Controls: When Should We Keep an Open Mind?" *Finance and Development* 39 (4): 55–56.

Shambaugh, J. C. 2004. "The Effects of Fixed Exchange Rates on Monetary Policy." *Quarterly Journal of Economics* 119 (1): 301–52.

Stiglitz, J. 2000. "Capital Market Liberalization, Economic Growth, and Instability." *World Development* 28 (6): 1075–86.

Summers, L. H. 2000. "International Financial Crises: Causes, Prevention, and Cures." *American Economic Review* 90 (2): 1–16.

UN Comtrade (database), United Nations, http://comtrade.un.org.

World Bank. 2010. *Global Economic Prospects 2010.* Washington, DC: World Bank.

19

EXPORTS AND EXPORT DIVERSIFICATION IN SUB-SAHARAN AFRICA: A STRATEGY FOR POSTCRISIS GROWTH

Vera Songwe and Deborah Winkler

The past decade has been one of great volatility for Africa but also of substantial progress. Africa has become fully integrated into the world economy. At the turn of the decade, many in the developing world wondered if Africa would become "the doomed continent" (Quenum 2000), crippled by political and ethnic tensions (Easterly and Levine 1997), or if in fact Africa could claim the 21st century (Gelb 2000). In this environment, predictions that Sub-Saharan Africa as a continent was about to enter the fastest growth period of its young 50-year history would have seemed impossible. However, between 2002 and 2008 gross domestic product (GDP) grew by 6.5 percent annually in Sub-Saharan Africa. Commodity-exporting countries as well as non-commodity-exporting countries experienced high growth rates. In fact, some of the non-commodity countries such as Burkina Faso, Mali, and Rwanda grew faster.

The hitherto poor macroeconomic indicators that had become synonymous with Africa also changed. Inflation in most countries was brought down to single digits for the first time, debt ratios fell to sustainable levels, and deficits were reduced as countries moved to consolidate the size of government, rationalize spending, and obtain debt write-offs. In an overall favorable external economic environment, these reforms quickly began to produce results. Foreign exchange reserves, including gold, increased more than 300 percent from US$37 billion in 2001 to US$154 billion in 2008. Net flows of foreign direct investment (FDI) more than doubled from US$14 billion in 2001 to US$34 billion in 2008. Goods exports over the period 2000–08 grew by 18 percent per year, as the continent became increasingly more open and globally connected.

The channels through which export expansion enhances aggregate productivity and growth are well known. Exports allow for specialization in a country's comparative advantage and thereby raise growth. Ricardo, in the famed theory of comparative advantage, showed that countries benefit by specializing in the production of those goods with the lowest opportunity cost and trading the surplus of production over domestic demand, taking as given appropriate exchange-rate regimes. Under this model, a country should quickly specialize in sectors in which it has a comparative advantage. The new trade theory associated with Helpman and Krugman (1985) and generalized by Grossman and Helpman (1991), however, has shifted the focus of the trade debate from the static gains from trade to one in which increased investment, knowledge, and technology associated with increased productivity growth can transform trade patterns and accelerate overall economic growth. Under the new theory, specialization is a result of scale and concomitant efficiencies.

However, even as gross output increased in both commodity- and non-commodity-exporting countries, the debate over the quality of growth in Africa continued. This debate shifted from the need to support export-based growth to the quality of exports and its impact on growth—that is, what a country exports matters. The argument was as follows: a reliance on a less sophisticated export base is not sufficient to guarantee sustained long-term growth. Hausman, Hwang, and Rodrik (2006) developed an indicator that measures the productivity associated with a country's export basket. This research concluded that Africa needs to diversify its export base away from less sophisticated primary commodities into high-productivity sectors such as manufacturing to enjoy faster growth.

The Importance of Export Structure

This chapter argues that the export structure of Africa is one of the main reasons that Africa has been able to get a head start out of the recession. Africa has not missed the boat, as many predicted, because of a reliance on commodity exports; on the contrary, it has benefited from its export structure, which enabled it to rebound quickly after the crisis. Unlike the countries in East Asia, which followed a different export trajectory of diversification before specialization, Africa increased its export specialization first, and in some cases this strategy has served it well. In sum, while Africa's quick recovery from the crisis was mainly a result of sound precrisis macroeconomic fundamentals, the structural composition of its exports was the main reason for its quick rebound in economic activity.

We show that Africa's high export concentration in a few sectors helped improve productivity and build resilience. In addition, the chapter shows that the direction of exports matters just as much for resilience as it does for productivity. Exports to more sophisticated markets lead to higher productivity, while exports to less sophisticated markets do not. Finally, we argue that African countries, especially the resource-based economies, need to concentrate on improving productivity in areas where they have a comparative advantage and on moving up the value chain in those commodities. Oil-producing countries might, for example, move into pharmaceuticals, and agriculture-based economies might expand into agroprocessing and marketing.

In this chapter, we examine the effects of exports and export diversification on value added and labor productivity in 30 Sub-Saharan African countries. We find that exports are critical for increasing value added and improving labor productivity. These results confirm many studies, which have shown that increased trade may lead to growth and that a strong, outward-oriented trade regime facilitates the exchange and adoption of new technology and improves productivity. An extensive literature review on the relationship between trade openness and growth since the 1970s can be found in Harrison and Rodríguez-Clare (2009).

For 30 selected African countries, we find, first, that an increase in exports of 1 percent has a higher and more significant impact on value added than a 1 percent increase in capital stock. Second, we find that a 1 percent increase in exports has a higher impact on labor productivity than increases in capital intensity by the same percentage. These results are robust even if we exclude resource-intensive exporters from the country sample. Third, we find that product and market diversification increase value added and labor productivity. In addition and contrary to expectations, we find that the positive value-added and labor-productivity effects from exports are larger the more concentrated the countries in our sample are in export products and markets.

These results indicate that for Sub-Saharan African countries to develop product value chains as suggested by the new trade theory, they must continue to focus on exports of goods in which they have a revealed comparative advantage to help them move toward more value-added exports based on these commodities. For example, Nigeria and other oil-exporting countries could move into the pharmaceuticals industry, while Côte d'Ivoire and other cocoa-producing countries could move into the manufacturing of chocolate-based products such as biscuits and drinks. These results also indicate that while product and market diversification are important for growth, the effects may be nonlinear; that is, product specialization even at the commodity stage might be more beneficial for short-term growth than is product diversification over the medium term.

The remainder of the chapter is organized as follows. In the next section, we provide a brief overview of trends in exports and export diversification in Sub-Saharan Africa. In the following section, we estimate the effects of exports and export diversification on value added and labor productivity using regression analysis for 30 Sub-Saharan African countries over the period 1995–2008. We also examine whether product and market diversification, as measured by the Herfindahl-Hirschman Index, and the export share to China and the United States increase or lower the positive effects from exports on labor productivity and value added. We then analyze the impact of the economic crisis on exports from Sub-Saharan Africa. The final section points to the policy implications for postcrisis export strategies.

Trends in Exports and Export Diversification

We first examine trends in exports and export diversification for Sub-Saharan Africa. Figure 19.1, panel a plots Sub-Saharan African exports by broad category for the period 1976–2008. While exports have increased in all categories over this period, exports of fuels, manufactures, ores and metals, and, to some extent, commercial services have

Figure 19.1. Exports and Exports of Goods and Services in Sub-Saharan Africa

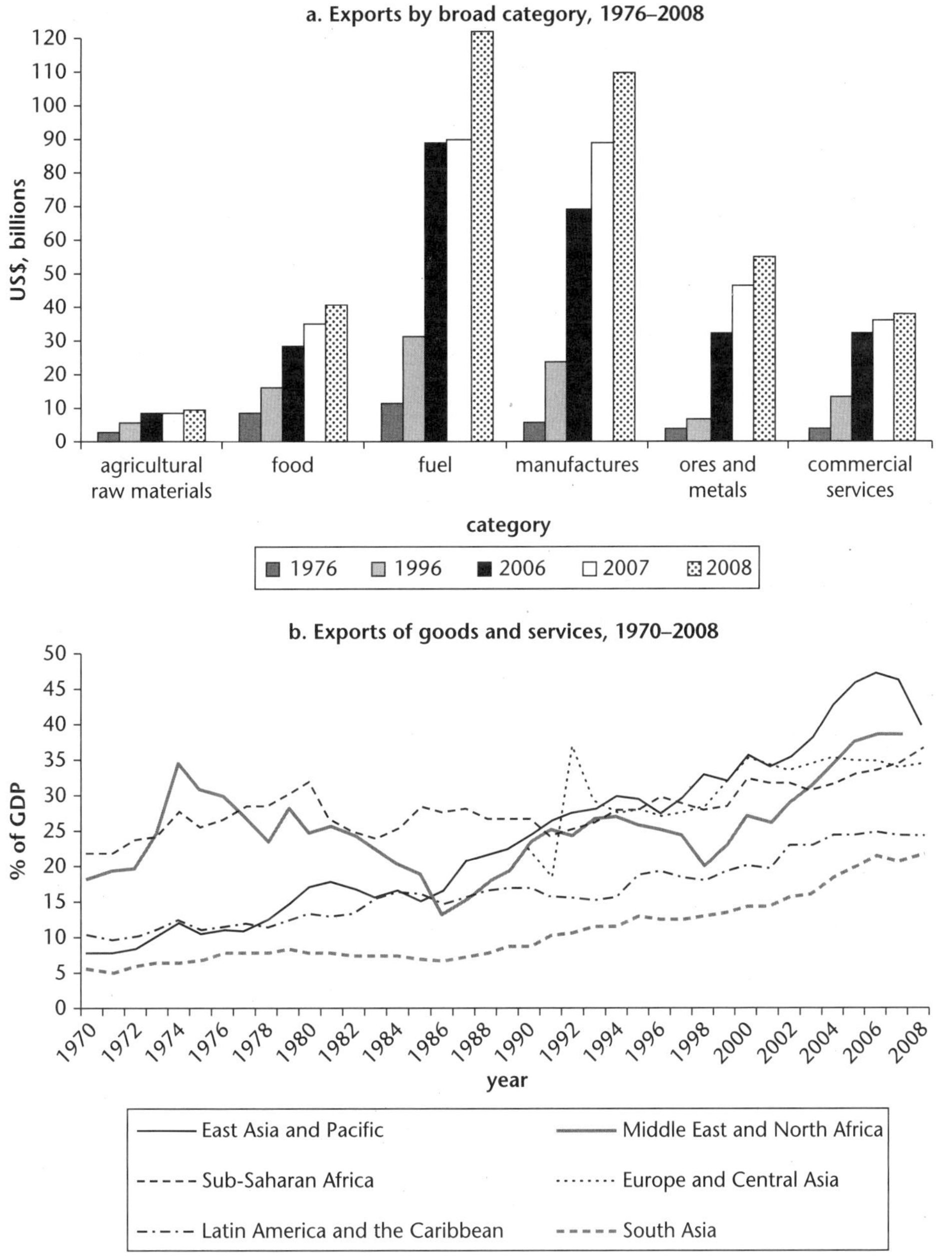

Source: Authors' calculations based on World Development Indicators (database), World Bank, http://data.worldbank.org.

grown more strongly since 1996. Moreover, while African exports are still dominated by fuel, exports of manufactures have expanded significantly over the past 20 years, growing at an average annualized rate of 14 percent between 1996 and 2008 compared to an average 12 percent in all merchandise exports. Only exports of ores and metals showed a higher annual growth rate of 19 percent, while exports of fuel (12 percent), commercial services (9 percent), food (8 percent), and agricultural raw materials (4 percent) all grew at lower rates over this period.

The share of goods and services exports in GDP in Sub-Saharan Africa increased by more than eight percentage points, from 27.7 percent in 1995 to 36.2 percent in 2008 (see figure 19.1, panel b). This expansion was driven mainly by goods exports, whose share in GDP rose from 23.4 percent to 34.4 percent over the same period. An international comparison reveals that in 2008 Sub-Saharan Africa showed the third-largest share of exports in GDP after East Asia and Pacific and the Middle East and North Africa. Moreover, while the export share over the 1980s through

2000—the so-called lost years—remained more or less constant in Sub-Saharan Africa, a clear upward trend took hold at the beginning of the 1990s. No other continent has experienced such a long period of export stagnation. The region that comes closest to Sub-Saharan Africa in this respect is Latin America and the Caribbean, which saw exports as a share of GDP plateau for a decade between 1984 and 1994 before growing again.

Which are the most important destination countries for export growth in Sub-Saharan Africa? Figure 19.2 plots average annual growth of Sub-Saharan African goods exports over the period 2000–08 by destination. Total goods exported from the region showed an impressive average growth of 18 percent per year over the period. Exports to low- and middle-income countries experienced higher growth than exports to high-income countries. Regional exports to high-income countries showed an annual average growth of 15.5 percent, while exports to low- and middle-income countries increased by 23 percent per year over the same period. Among high-income countries, Sub-Saharan African exports to the United States increased above average at 17 percent per year. Among low- and middle-income countries, annual export growth was highest for East Asia and Pacific and for South Asia, the result of strong demand from China and India. Sub-Saharan African exports to China alone grew at an annualized rate of 33 percent over the period. While developing countries played a bigger role in Sub-Saharan African export growth, high-income countries still absorb the major share of the region's exports, as we will show in the section on the effects of the economic crisis.

Next, we analyze the growth of Sub-Saharan African exports by product category for 2000–08. The region's annual average export growth was highest in electricity (30 percent), mining of metal ores (28 percent), tobacco (27 percent), and petroleum and natural gas (24 percent). Among manufactured products, export growth was highest in motor vehicles, trailers, and semitrailers (20 percent) and in machinery and equipment (17 percent). Export shares in 2008 reveal the strong dependency of Sub-Saharan African exports on commodities, especially of petroleum and natural gas (55 percent), or on manufacturing sectors that make use of commodities, especially basic metals (11 percent). The structure of export shares also indicates that the composition of Sub-Saharan African exports is shifting into second-generation exports, as witnessed by the increase in exports of motor vehicles and machinery.

The Effect of Exports and Export Diversification on Growth

In this section, we examine the impact of exports and export diversification on growth. We first analyze the effect of exports on value added and labor productivity. Second, we focus on the effect of export diversification of products and markets on value added and labor productivity for these countries. This chapter focuses only on the direct

Figure 19.2. Annual Average Growth of Export Goods by Destination, Sub-Saharan Africa, 2000–08

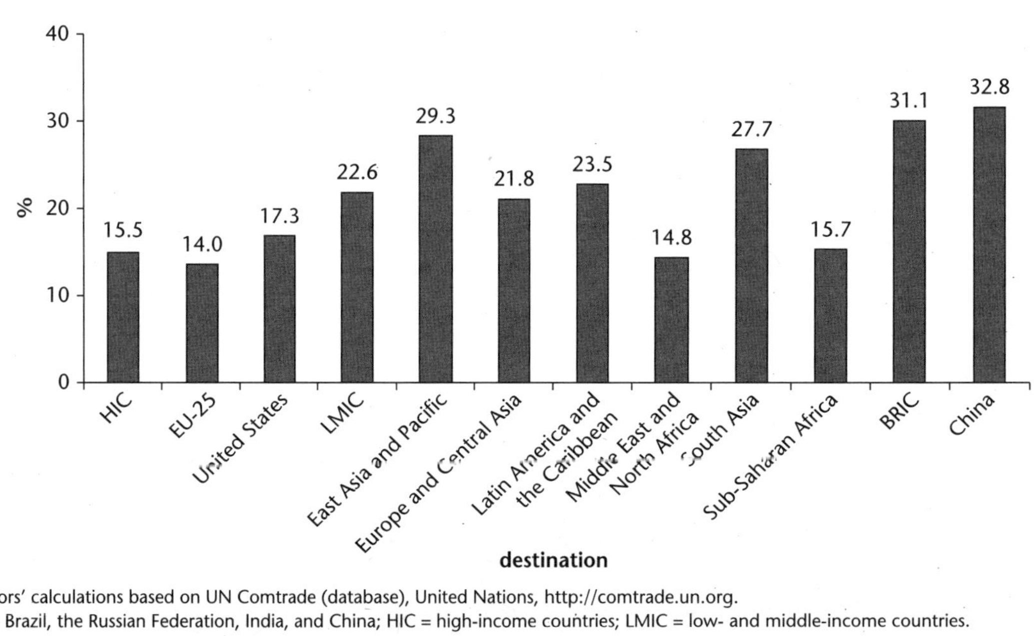

Source: Authors' calculations based on UN Comtrade (database), United Nations, http://comtrade.un.org.
Note: BRIC = Brazil, the Russian Federation, India, and China; HIC = high-income countries; LMIC = low- and middle-income countries.

effects of exports and export diversification on higher value added and labor productivity. Indirect effects of exports take a variety of forms and are basically induced by changes in prices and income. Indirect effects include a reduction of the foreign exchange gap—which makes imports of capital goods cheaper and, thus, facilitates technology spillovers—and also the effects of exports on employment and skills, among others.

Our empirical analysis covers 30 Sub-Saharan African countries for the period 1995–2008. The choice of countries was based on data availability only. Our sample of 30 Sub-Saharan African countries includes Botswana, Burkina Faso, Cameroon, the Central African Republic, Chad, Comoros, Côte d'Ivoire, Eritrea, Ethiopia, Ghana, Guinea, Guinea-Bissau, Kenya, Lesotho, Madagascar, Malawi, Mali, Mauritania, Mauritius, Mozambique, Namibia, Senegal, South Africa, Sudan, Swaziland, Tanzania, Togo, Uganda, Zambia, and Zimbabwe. For full details of our data set, see the working paper version of this chapter.

Figure 19.3. Annual Commodity Export versus Value-Added Growth in 30 Sub-Saharan African Countries, 1995–2008

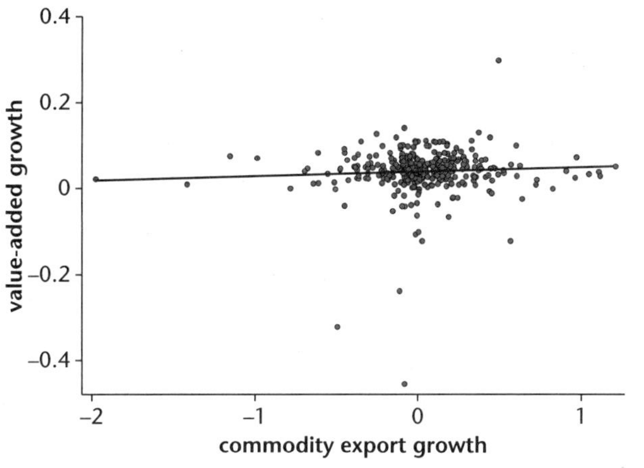

Source: Authors' calculations based on UN Comtrade (database), United Nations, http://comtrade.un.org.
Note: Annual export and value-added growth rates are based on values in logarithms.

Figure 19.4. Annual Manufacturing Export versus Value-Added Growth in 30 Sub-Saharan African Countries, 1995–2008

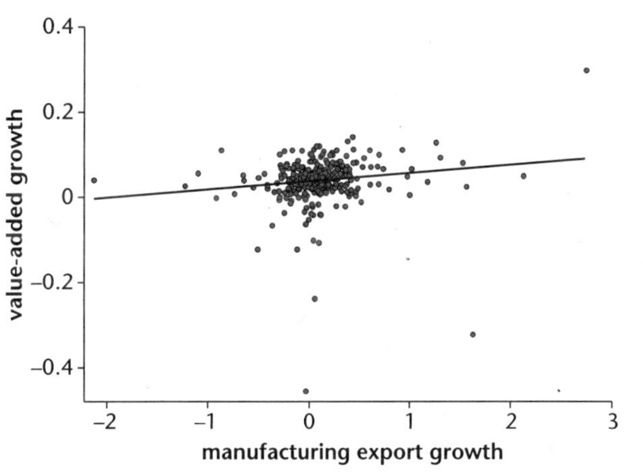

Source: Authors' calculations based on UN Comtrade (database), United Nations, http://comtrade.un.org.
Note: Annual export and value-added growth rates are based on values in logarithms.

The Effect of Exports on Value Added and Labor Productivity

We estimate an aggregate value-added production function in log-linear form in which capital, labor, and technology are the input factors (see the working paper version of this chapter for the empirical model). Value added is the difference between output and intermediate inputs. The technology shifter is a function of exports and tariffs. We also control for fixed-country effects and fixed-year effects. We hypothesize that capital, labor, and exports have a positive impact on value added, while tariffs—as an inverse measure of trade liberalization—should have a negative influence.

As a first indicator of the relationship between exports and growth, we plot annual export and value-added growth rates for our country sample for 1995–2008. Since there might be a differential effect on value-added growth depending on the type of exports, we split the product sample into commodities (figure 19.3) and manufactured goods (figure 19.4). The bivariate regression lines indicate a stronger positive relationship between annual export growth of manufactured goods and annual value-added growth than for commodity export growth. This finding confirms the result that growth is more responsive to exports of manufactured goods than it is to exports of commodities. Countries exporting goods with higher value added grow faster. While commodity exports interact positively with value added, the effects are less pronounced.

This result confirms the "law of development," according to which industrialization is the well-proven way to achieve rapid economic development in emerging markets. The East Asian successes, for instance, relied heavily on the manufacturing sector to achieve rapid economic growth. The East Asian Tigers (Hong Kong SAR, China; the Republic of Korea; Singapore; and Taiwan, China), Japan, and the second-generation successes (Indonesia, Malaysia, Thailand, and, recently, China) all have shares of manufacturing value added that exceed the global average (UNIDO 2009).

Full details of our regression results are contained in the working paper version of this chapter. Here, we focus on an intuitive presentation of the main results. As hypothesized, capital, labor, and exports have a significantly positive effect on value added. Remarkably, the elasticity of exports is larger than that of capital, while the labor elasticity is the highest. This finding reflects the labor-intensive production structure in these Sub-Saharan African countries. Tariffs have no influence on value added. Since we are concerned that the results above could be driven by natural resource–intensive countries, we drop four natural resource–intensive economies as identified by the International Monetary Fund (IMF), namely, Cameroon, Chad, Côte d'Ivoire, and Zambia, in the next regressions. The results above continue to hold.

In a second step, we formulate the value-added equation as a function of labor productivity. Labor productivity, defined as value added per worker, depends on capital intensity and the technology shifter, that is, exports and tariffs. Our study differs from studies that measure the effect on per capita GDP in a new growth theory model, which includes exports among other control variables such as the initial per capita GDP, human capital, population growth, terms of trade, and investment ratio (see, for example, Greenaway, Morgan, and Wright 1999). We hypothesize the same coefficient signs as for the value-added regressions.

Capital intensity and exports show a significantly positive effect on labor productivity, while tariffs have a significantly negative impact, which is line with our conjecture. Interestingly, the export elasticity is higher than that of capital intensity; that is, a 1 percent increase in exports results in larger productivity gains than a 1 percent increase in capital intensity. This finding reveals the potential of exports for increasing the region's competitiveness and growth. The results become more significant when we drop the four natural resource–intensive countries.

The Effect of Export Diversification on Value Added and Labor Productivity

In addition to export growth, export diversification has been shown to be strongly associated with economic growth (Lederman and Maloney 2007; Hesse 2009), particularly for developing countries. Diversity in exports can reduce income volatility for countries with large populations living in poverty and reduce vulnerability to sharp declines in the terms of trade. Diversification also increases the potential for generating spillovers, whereas reliance on only a few exports generally has greater negative consequences for growth (Lederman and Maloney 2007). This factor holds true especially for the countries in transition from low-income status to middle-income status.

Export diversification can take place in two ways, by exporting new products and by exporting to new markets. The first involves increasing the number of products exported to international markets. This effort requires discovering new products and moving up the value chain to produce products of higher value and sophistication. Much of the focus in the past has been on the process of discovering new exports. A second component of diversification relates to breaking into new geographical markets, that is, expanding market reach in products that have already proven competitive.

One of the primary challenges facing Africa's resource-rich economies is how to diversify production beyond the natural resource sector. Natural resource–based products have dominated exports for the past 50 years, but reliance on such products has not made African countries richer. Some economists refer to the "resource curse" as a reason that some African countries have not been able to use their wealth to drive economic growth. However, others believe that it is export concentration per se and not natural resources in particular that is negatively associated with growth (Lederman and Maloney 2007). In spite of the circumstances, resource-rich countries like Norway, Indonesia, and Malaysia have demonstrated that it is possible to use natural resource wealth to diversify and support economic growth.

As a first indication, we show the relationship between export diversification of both products (figure 19.5) and markets (figure 19.6) and value added for our 30 Sub-Saharan African countries over 1995–2008. We use the Herfindahl-Hirschman Index (HHI) of market and product concentration as an inverse measure of export diversification. The HHI of market concentration is defined as the sum over a country's squared market shares of export

Figure 19.5. Export Concentration of Products versus Value Added in 30 Sub-Saharan African Countries, 1995–2008

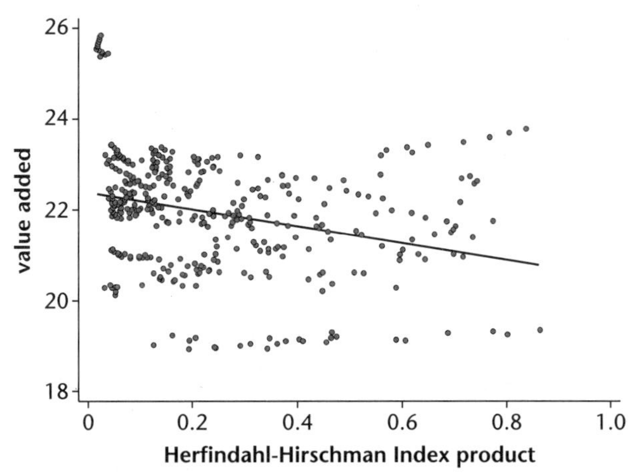

Source: Authors' calculations based on UN Comtrade (database), United Nations, http://comtrade.un.org.
Note: Value added is in logarithms.

Figure 19.6. Export Concentration of Markets versus Value Added in 30 Sub-Saharan Countries, 1995–2008

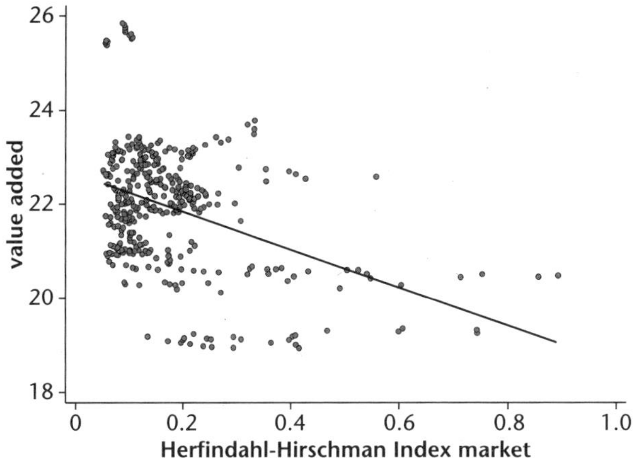

Source: Authors' calculations based on UN Comtrade (database), United Nations, http://comtrade.un.org.
Note: Value added is in logarithms.

destinations. If a country exports to only one destination, the HHI would be 1, while a lower HHI reflects a higher regional export diversification. Accordingly, the HHI of product concentration is defined as the sum over a country's squared market shares of different export products. Export concentration and value added are negatively correlated, or, analogously, export diversification and value added have a positive relationship. The steeper regression line in figure 19.6 suggests that the effect is stronger for export diversification of markets.

We then estimate the effects of export diversification and its interaction with exports on value added and labor productivity. We hypothesize that a higher HHI—that is, less export diversification—has a negative effect on value added. While these hypotheses are straightforward in value-added equations, we cannot unambiguously predict the effect of the interaction term with exports. The coefficient sign of the interaction variable depends on whether export growth is higher in countries with a higher export concentration or a higher export diversification.

The regression results using the full-country sample show that a higher HHI of product concentration of exports significantly lowers value added, which is in line with our conjecture, while a higher HHI of market concentration of exports has no significant effect. The negative effect of the HHI of market concentration on value added becomes significant when we drop the natural resource–intensive countries. We then interact exports with the two measures of export concentration. Interestingly, the interaction term of the HHI with exports yields a positive coefficient, which is significant in the full- and reduced-country samples. That is, the positive impact of exports on value added is higher the more concentrated exports are in different products and markets.

Finally, we interact exports with a country's export share to China, the EU-25 and the United States. In the full-country sample, a larger export share to China significantly increases value added, but the interaction with exports is negative. That is, the gains from exports are lowered the more dependent a country is on China. When we drop natural resource–intensive countries, a higher export share to the United States now significantly increases value added, but the positive value-added effects from exports are lowered for countries that depend more on the United States as an export destination. A higher market share to China, however, no longer shows significant effects on value added. The reason for these results might be that less natural resource–intensive countries have a greater dependence on the United States, while more natural resource–intensive countries have a greater dependence on China as a major export destination. A larger export share to the EU-25 has no influence on value added in both the full- and the reduced-country sample.

Next, we show the effects of export diversification and its interaction with exports on labor productivity. A higher HHI of market concentration of exports markedly lowers labor productivity, which is significant only when natural resource–intensive countries are excluded from the sample. The HHI of product concentration has no impact on labor productivity. When we interact the HHI with exports, a higher product concentration of exports significantly lowers labor productivity but significantly increases the positive productivity effects from exports. Analogously, a higher market concentration of exports has a strong negative effect on labor productivity but significantly increases the positive productivity effects from exports. This finding holds for both the full- and the reduced-country sample. Finally, higher market shares to China and the United States and their interaction with exports have no influence on labor productivity in the full-country sample. However, when we drop natural resource–intensive countries, a higher export share to the United States significantly increases labor productivity, but the positive productivity gains from exports are lowered for countries that depend more on the United States as an export destination. Again, a higher export share to the EU-25 has no effects on labor productivity in the full- and the reduced-country samples.

In sum, the results show that exports significantly increase value added and labor productivity. The export elasticity is larger than the elasticity of capital in the value-added regressions, while it is larger than the elasticity of capital intensity in the labor-productivity regressions. This finding reveals the potential of exports for increasing the region's competitiveness and growth. Moreover, the results imply that greater diversification of export products and markets has a positive impact on value added and labor productivity.

Surprisingly, the positive value-added and labor productivity effects from exports are larger the more concentrated the export markets are in our sample countries. In effect, export growth seems to be greater in countries with a higher concentration of exports. Finally, countries that are less natural resource–intensive depend more strongly on the United States, while natural resource–intensive countries depend more strongly on China as an export destination. Future research could include indirect effects of exports such as imports of capital goods and technology spillovers or the effects of exports on employment and skills in Sub-Saharan Africa.

The Economic Crisis in Sub-Saharan Africa

In 2008, the world economy was plunged into a deep and prolonged crisis—the worst recession since the Great Depression. Global GDP contracted for the first time on record. Africa's hard-won gains came under threat from the crisis. Between 2007 and 2008, Sub-Saharan Africa was hit by triple shocks—the food, fuel, and financial crises. Growth plunged from a 6.5 percent average between 2000 and 2007 to 1.6 percent in 2009 (see table 19.1).

The first hint of an impending crisis was the rapid rise in food prices caused by the high price volatility of oil markets, which was transferred to corn markets as oil prices rose above US$50 per barrel and use of corn-based ethanol increased. Second, many financial institutions, seeking safety and an exit from the more risky and less transparent derivatives market, diversified into commodity markets, putting further pressure on commodity prices (Songwe forthcoming). The standard literature on the food price crisis has attributed the rise in prices to increasing use of food crops for biofuels, and rapidly rising oil prices, as mentioned here, but also to increased food and meat consumption in emerging markets because of rising incomes and a growing world population. The rising commodity prices had a mixed impact on the continent: commodity-exporting countries such as Angola, the Democratic Republic of Congo, and Nigeria benefited from the steep increase in prices, while the non-commodity-exporting countries suffered from increases in food prices and a deterioration in their balance of payments. Third, the collapse of Lehman Brothers in September 2008 marked the beginning of the financial crisis. Asset values contracted, as stock markets hit historic lows. According to some estimates (Bollard and Gaitanos 2010), the amount of money lost in global stock markets totaled US$30 trillion dollars—a sum that could eradicate poverty in the developing world in 10 years.

The crisis reached Sub-Saharan Africa through three main channels of transmission: labor markets, capital markets, and export markets. The impact of the crisis on trade was devastating for Sub-Saharan Africa. Global trade growth dropped from 7.2 percent in 2007 to –12.3 percent in 2009, while Africa's exports of goods and services in 2009 dropped by about 16 percent compared to the 22.8 percent increase in 2008. Sub-Saharan Africa was the second-hardest-hit region on the trade front after the Middle East and North Africa (see figure 19.7). The trade collapse in Sub-Saharan Africa is also reflected in exports alone, which fell by more than 40 percent in January 2009 on a year-to-year basis (figure 19.8). It is no surprise that the collapse in commodity trade following the real sector collapse in the West affected Sub-Saharan Africa so severely, given that one-third of the world's resource-dependent countries are in the region.

During the second half of 2008, nonenergy commodity prices plunged 38 percent. In December, nonenergy prices fell 6.8 percent, down for the fifth consecutive month. Oil prices fell 69 percent between July and December 2008, reversing the oil price increases of the previous three and a half years. Oil exporters suffered a loss, but many of them such as Nigeria had built up a savings cushion during the boom years and were better able to withstand the crisis. By end 2009, however, oil prices

Table 19.1. Actual and Projected GDP Growth Rates, Selected Regions, 2007–11
percent

	Actual			Projected	
Growth	2007	2008	2009	2010	2011
World	5.2	3	–0.8	3.9	4.3
Advanced economies	2.7	0.5	–3.2	2.1	2.4
Sub-Saharan Africa	6.9	5.6	1.6	4.3	5.5
Central and Eastern Europe	5.4	3.1	–4.3	2	3.7
Middle East	6.4	5.3	2.2	4.5	4.8

Source: IMF 2009, 2010.

Figure 19.7. Trade Volume Decline from Peak to Trough, by Region, 2008–09

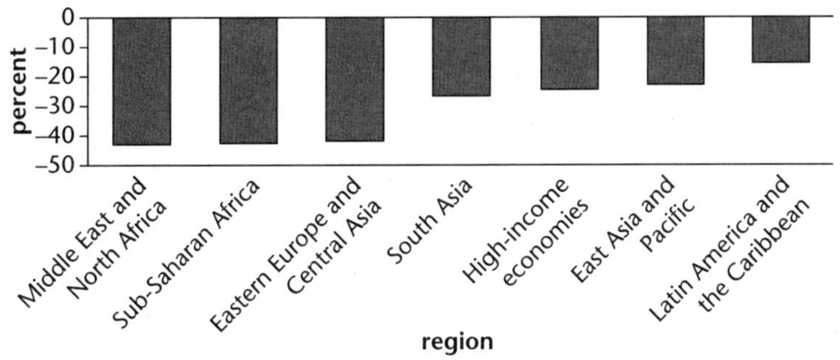

Source: Didier, Hevia, and Schmukler (2010).
Note: Percentage decline in trade from peak to trough is shown for each region.

Figure 19.8. Goods Exports for Six World Regions, Constant and Seasonally Adjusted, 2007–10

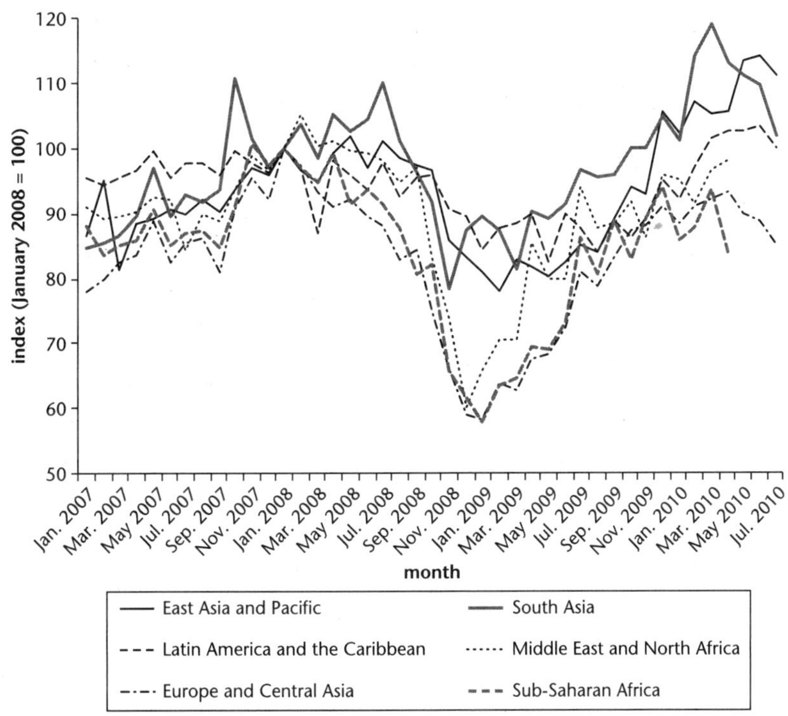

Source: Authors' calculations, based on Global Economic Monitor (database), World Bank, http://www.worldbank.org/gem.

had recovered from their low point of US$40 in December 2008 to about US$70. Some poorer countries suffered particularly large shocks. Many poor African countries experienced terms-of-trade losses of over 3 percent of 2008 GDP, with losses exceeding 5 percent in Chad, Guinea, Mozambique, and Zambia.

Has the crisis changed the pattern of export destinations for Sub-Saharan Africa? Figure 19.9 shows the share of goods exports by destination as a percentage of total goods exports from Sub-Saharan Africa pre- and postcrisis. The share of exports from Sub-Saharan Africa to high-income countries declined sharply from almost 70 percent of the total in 2000 to 60 percent in 2008 and fell further to 55 percent in 2009. This sharp drop was caused by a big decline in exports to the EU-25 countries, which fell from 35 percent in 2000 to 27 percent in 2008 and 22 percent in 2009. Exports to the United States, which absorbs almost a quarter of Sub-Saharan African exports, showed a weak decline during and after the crisis. In contrast, Sub-Saharan African exports to low- and middle-income countries as a

Figure 19.9. Shares of Sub-Saharan African Goods Exports, by Destination, 2000, 2008, and 2009

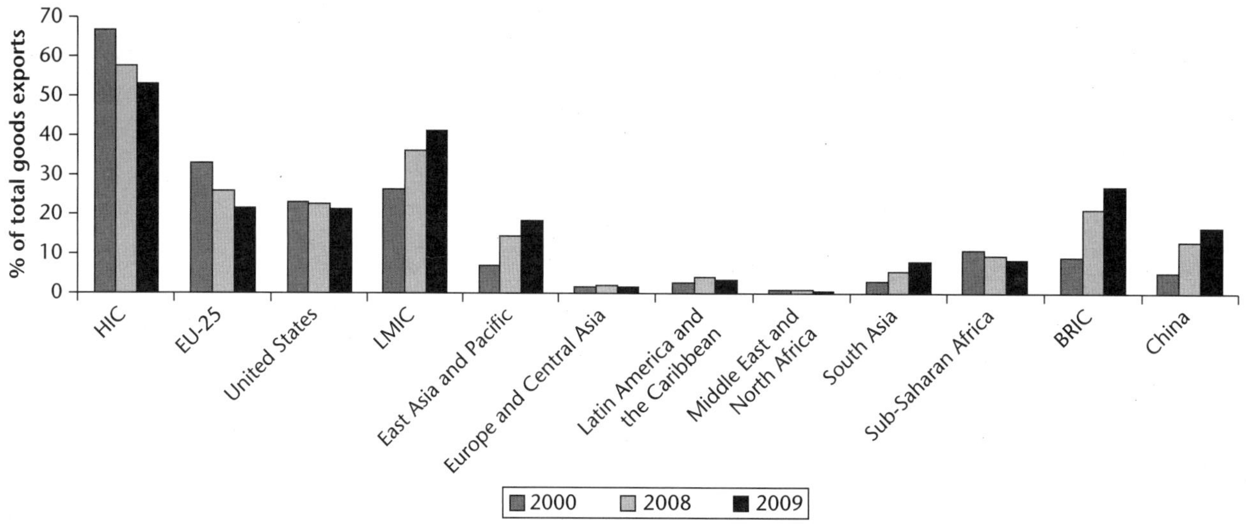

Source: Authors' calculations based on UN Comtrade (database), United Nations, http://comtrade.un.org.
Note: BRIC = Brazil, the Russian Federation, India, and China; HIC = high-income countries; LMIC = low- and middle-income countries.

percentage of total exports increased strongly from 27 percent in 2000 to 38 percent in 2008 and 43 percent in 2009. Among low- and middle-income countries, exports from Sub-Saharan Africa expanded in all regions except for the Middle East and North Africa and within Sub-Saharan Africa itself. The expansion of export share from Sub-Saharan Africa was strongest in East Asia and Pacific and grew from 7 percent in 2000 to 15 percent in 2008 and 19 percent in 2009. China was the main driver, whose export shares increased from 5 percent in 2000 to 14 percent in 2008 and 17 percent in 2009.

The share of exports to the EU-25 in all export categories dropped over the period 2000–08; however, this drop was compensated for by growth in intraregional trade and emerging markets' exports for some categories. The share of capital goods exports from Sub-Saharan Africa to high-income countries as a percentage of total capital goods exports fell from 49 percent to 44 percent between 2000 and 2008, with exports of capital goods falling especially sharply to the United States, while intraregional trade increased strongly from 37 percent to 42 percent over the same period. Sub-Saharan Africa's export share of consumption goods to high-income countries as a percentage of total consumption goods exports declined from 71 percent to 68 percent over the period 2000–08, a drop driven mainly by a drastic decline in EU-25 demand, which fell from 50 percent to 42 percent. Growing demand by the United States and the BRICs (Brazil, the Russian Federation, India, and China), however, counterbalanced this effect. The share of intermediate goods exports from Sub-Saharan Africa to high-income countries as a percentage of total intermediate goods exports dropped sharply from 71 percent to 60 percent between 2000 and 2008, a fall driven by declining demand in the EU-25. This drop was offset by increasing demand for intermediates from the BRICs. Intermediate goods exports from Sub-Saharan Africa to China alone rose from 6 percent to 15 percent over the period 2000–08. The crisis further accentuated the trends for capital and intermediate goods in 2009.

Intraregional trade continued to drop during the crisis. Africa trades more with itself than it does with Latin America and the Caribbean, Europe and Central Asia, and the Middle East and North Africa combined. And before the crisis, trade within Africa was higher than trade with South Asia, including India. However, the share of intraregional trade has been dropping, falling from 11.2 percent before the crisis in 2000 to 8.8 percent postcrisis. For Africa to realize its economic potential and achieve fast and sustained growth, it will have to increase intraregional trade.

Policy Implications for Postcrisis Export Strategies

Over the past decade, many developing countries embraced export-led strategies as an engine for growth and have increasingly diversified both export markets and products. The food, fuel, and financial crises were the first test of the resilience of this strategy to shocks. Our analysis shows that this strategy has served Africa well, helping facilitate its early recovery from the global crisis. Africa's GDP is projected to come out of the crisis faster than that of most other regions (see table 19.1). Africa's growth is projected to rebound to 5.5 percent in 2011, up from 1.6 percent in 2009. While this increase is still significantly below precrisis levels compared to other regions, Africa has bounced back faster than both Europe and Central Asia and the Middle East and North Africa. Africa has performed well but has also exhibited some structural weaknesses that must be addressed if it is to accelerate growth and reduce poverty.

The recent global economic downturn has highlighted the critical importance of trade as an engine for Africa's growth and, more important, as a way of smoothing out the crisis impact. In view of our regression results, we conclude that the export structure of Sub-Saharan Africa is one of the main reasons why it has been able to get a head start out of the recession. Africa has not missed the boat, as many predicted, because of its reliance on commodity exports; on the contrary, it has benefited from its export structure, particularly because of high demand from China. In sum, while Africa's rally was mainly the result of sound macroeconomic fundamentals in place before the crisis, the structural composition of Africa's exports also supported the region's economic resurgence.

While precrisis trade discussion on Africa focused on the need for increased *product* diversification, the crisis has demonstrated that increased *market* diversification is equally important. For resource-dependent exporting countries, especially those whose exports are highly concentrated in a few commodities, we conclude that market diversification is equally important for growth as product diversification. This important finding suggests that export concentration in a few products in which countries have a high comparative advantage yields more benefits than product diversification in goods in which they have less comparative advantage. In cases where countries have a comparative advantage in a few commodities, specialization should precede diversification. Product diversification must therefore be managed to safeguard market share of exports.

The analysis also suggests that the export landscape in the region is changing. Primary-commodity export countries are more dependent on emerging markets for exports, while as countries move up the value chain, they turn increasingly to the high-income countries as export destinations. If managed well, this pattern of diversification of export markets could help underpin the transition from market to product diversification on the continent, as more countries enter second-generation export phases.

Despite the strong rebound, the crisis has interrupted the growth acceleration experienced on the continent; growth averages have dropped. African countries will need to do more, better, and faster to catch up to pre-2008 growth levels. The first order of business should be to protect past gains in macroeconomic stability and continue structural reforms. Second, countries should put in place policies that exploit the increasing benefits of South-South trade, including improved intraregional trade. Growth in exports to low- and middle-income countries offers Africa a chance to diversify export markets further while it works to diversify its products.

Most important, Sub-Saharan African countries must pursue a dual strategy of diversifying both export markets and product markets to accelerate growth. African countries need to work to protect market share in existing commodity markets by retaining and increasing their competitiveness in the areas where they have a comparative advantage. The crisis has shown that this strategy allows countries to manage economic downturns better. The above analysis also shows that exports of manufactures contribute more to growth than exports of commodities.

Therefore, while acquiring new markets for commodities, countries also need to expand and diversify exports to high-value markets such as the EU and the United States. Our analysis shows that while export market share to the developed countries is dropping, a higher export share to the United States has positive growth effects in nonresource-intensive countries. Part of the strategy is to put in place policies that attract more foreign direct investment to facilitate more technology transfer. Countries therefore need to improve their business regulation, property rights legislation, and, most important, the governance environment for business.

Bibliography

Bollard, A., and S. Gaitanos. 2010. *Crisis: One Central Bank Governor and the Global Financial Collapse.* Auckland: Auckland University Press.

Didier, T., C. Hevia, and S. Schmukler. 2010. "How Resilient Have Developing Countries Been during the Global Crisis" Background Paper, World Bank, Washington, DC.

Easterly, W., and R. Levine. 1997. "Africa's Growth Tragedy: Policies and Ethnic Division." *Quarterly Journal of Economics* 112 (4): 1203–50.

Gelb, Alan H. 2000. *Can Africa Claim the 21st Century?* Washington, DC: World Bank.

Greenaway, D., W. Morgan, and P. Wright. 1999. "Exports, Export Composition and Growth." *Journal of International Trade and Economic Development* 8 (1): 41–51.

Grossman, G., and E. Helpman. 1991. *Innovation and Growth in the Global Economy.* Cambridge, MA: MIT Press.

Harrison, A., and A. Rodríguez-Clare. 2009. "Trade, Foreign Investment, and Industrial Policy for Developing Countries." Working Paper 15261, National Bureau of Economic Research, Cambridge, MA.

Hausman, R., J. Hwang, and D. Rodrik. 2006. "What You Export Matters." Working Paper, Center for International Development, Harvard University, Cambridge, MA.

Helpman, E., and P. Krugman. 1985. *Market Structure and Foreign Trade: Increasing Returns, Imperfect Competition, and the International Economy*. Cambridge, MA: MIT Press.

Hesse, H. 2009. "Export Diversification and Economic Growth." In *Breaking into New Markets: Emerging Lessons for Export Diversification*, ed. R. Newfarmer, W. Shaw, and P. Walkenhorst, 55–80. Washington, DC: World Bank.

IMF (International Monetary Fund). 2009. *World Economic Outlook: Crisis and Recovery.* Washington, DC: IMF.

———. 2010. *World Economic Outlook: Rebalancing Growth.* Washington, DC: IMF.

Lederman, D., and W. F. Maloney. 2007. "Trade Structure and Growth." In *Natural Resources: Neither Curse nor Destiny*, ed. D. Lederman and W. F. Maloney, 15–40. Palo Alto, CA: Stanford University Press.

Quenum, B. M. 2000. "Is Africa Doomed? The African Challenge." *Africa Business Magazine.* December.

Songwe, V. Forthcoming. "A Tale of Two Crises: Innovation and Diversification in Financial Markets and Impact on Africa." In *Food and Financial Crises Impacts on Sub-Saharan Africa*, ed. D. R. Lee and M. Ndulo. Wallingford, U.K.: CABI.

UNIDO (United Nations Industrial Development Organization). 2009. *Industrial Development Report 2009. Breaking In and Moving Up: New Industrial Challenges for the Bottom Billion and the Middle-Income Countries.* Vienna: UNIDO.

PART IV

EMERGING TRADE POLICY ISSUES IN THE POSTCRISIS ENVIRONMENT

20

STRUCTURAL CHANGES IN COMMODITY MARKETS: NEW OPPORTUNITIES AND POLICY CHALLENGES FOR COMMODITY EXPORTERS

Donald Mitchell and Enrique Aldaz-Carroll

The global financial crisis led to a sharp decline in merchandise trade. World trade volumes declined by an estimated 17.6 percent in 2009 from 2008 (World Bank 2010c). The decline in trade from peak to trough was even greater at 24–25 percent for both developed and developing countries. This sharp decline in merchandise trade exposed the vulnerability of countries heavily dependent on exports and has led to a reevaluation of the export-led growth model for developing countries.

Commodities trade, however, declined less than other merchandise trade and has rebounded more sharply since the global recession ended, largely because of strong growth in developing-country demand for imports (and demand for commodities, in particular). This relatively better performance of commodities suggests new opportunities as well as policy challenges for commodity exporters. Commodities account for roughly one quarter of the dollar value of global merchandise exports (table 20.1).[1] Although commodities have historically had slower growth than manufactures and declining relative prices, their share has been increasing in recent years.

Commodity exports accounted for only one quarter of global merchandise exports in 2007, but they accounted for more than half of export earnings for 57 countries (table 20.2). Twenty-two countries received at least 90 percent of their merchandise export earnings from commodities, and 37 countries received at least 80 percent of their merchandise export earnings from commodities.

Historically, countries that have relied on commodity exports have faced declining terms of trade and stagnant opportunities for export growth. Commodity price booms have often led to increased growth in commodity-dependent countries, but over the longer term these economies have had slower economic growth than those with more diversified export bundles, mainly because of the high price volatility that results from commodity booms and busts. Prices fluctuate because of the relatively low short-run supply response and low price elasticity of demand. Moreover, demand growth has been slower because of low income elasticities for most commodities and slowing population growth, particularly in developed countries.

However, the rapid economic growth of developing countries over the past two decades has begun to change these historical relationships. Growth in demand for commodities has increasingly shifted from developed to developing countries, where income elasticities and population and income growth rates are higher. Indeed, the share of global commodity imports going to low- and middle-income countries increased from 17 percent in 1990 to 27 percent in 2007 (World Bank 2009b). In China, for example, gross domestic product (GDP) grew more than 10 percent annually from 1990 to 2007, and the country now accounts for nearly 40 percent of global consumption of most metals (compared to 10–15 percent a decade ago). India, which had almost 7 percent annual GDP growth over this same period, has increased oil imports at 5 percent per year—twice the global average—albeit from a low base. Many other countries—including Chile, Malaysia, Mozambique, Uganda, and Vietnam—have had more than 5 percent annual GDP growth over the same

Table 20.1. Percentage Growth of Merchandise, Manufacturing, and Commodities Export Values and Shares of Merchandise Trade, 2005–08

	2005	2006	2007	2008
Merchandise	12.8	16.8	13.7	12.2
Manufacturing	10.6	13.5	14.4	8.8
Commodities	22.9	25.2	11.6	20.2
Share of merchandise trade				
Manufacturing	71.3	69.3	69.3	65.6
Commodities	23.7	25.4	24.9	26.7

Source: World Bank 2009b.

Table 20.2. Share of Commodities in Total Merchandise Exports for 57 Commodity-Dependent Countries, 2007

Share of commodities	Low-income countries	Lower-middle-income countries	Upper-middle income countries	High-income countries	Total countries
90–100	7	8	4	3	22
80–89	7	3	3	2	15
70–79	2	1	2	2	7
60–69	4	4	1	0	9
50–59	1	2	1	0	4
50–100	21	18	11	7	57

Source: World Bank 2009b.

period and are becoming larger consumers and importers of commodities.

While the prospects for commodity-dependent countries have brightened, vulnerability to price volatility and other risks still persists. Given that the majority of these countries are classified as low- and middle-income countries, the urgency of crafting policies to turn the current boom in commodity prices into sustainable economic growth is clear. This chapter discusses the structural changes in commodities markets over the past decade and the policy implications of these trends.

The rest of the chapter is structured as follows. The next section discusses recent structural changes in commodity markets. The following section considers the prospects for commodity markets in light of these changes. The subsequent section presents a historical account of the literature on commodity dependence. The next section discusses policy recommendations for resource-based economies. The final section concludes.

Structural Changes in Commodity Markets

Commodity prices have increased sharply in real terms since their cyclical lows at the turn of the 21st century. In fact, the increases from 2000–01 to 2008 were larger than any commodity boom of the 20th century: prices for crude oil, metals, and minerals nearly tripled, while agricultural prices nearly doubled (figure 20.1).

A combination of factors drove the rise in commodity prices. These factors include years of low investment in response to the low prices of the 1980s and 1990s, a surge in demand for commodities in developing countries, the declining value of the dollar relative to other major currencies, supply disruptions in major producing countries, policy changes, and temporary bans on exports of some commodities. Some of these factors were of short duration, and their impacts have already dissipated. However, others reflected structural changes that will have longer-lasting impacts and important consequences for the global economy and developing countries.

One of the main reasons that commodity prices rose so sharply during 2000–08 was underinvestment. During the 1980s and 1990s, investment in commodity production capacity fell (especially for crude oil, metals, and minerals) in response to a severe depression in commodity prices.[2] In particular, real spending by major U.S. multinational oil companies on exploration and development declined by half from 1981 to 1985 and stagnated at that depressed level for 15 years before rising in response to higher oil prices in the past decade (World Bank 2009a).

However, slow demand growth in the 1980s and 1990s largely offset underinvestment and allowed existing capacity to suffice. Global oil consumption increased by only 0.7 percent per year during the 1980s and 1.3 percent per year during the 1990s (BP 2009). Investment in agriculture also declined, but demand growth fell so rapidly that there

Figure 20.1. Real Commodity Prices, 1960–2009

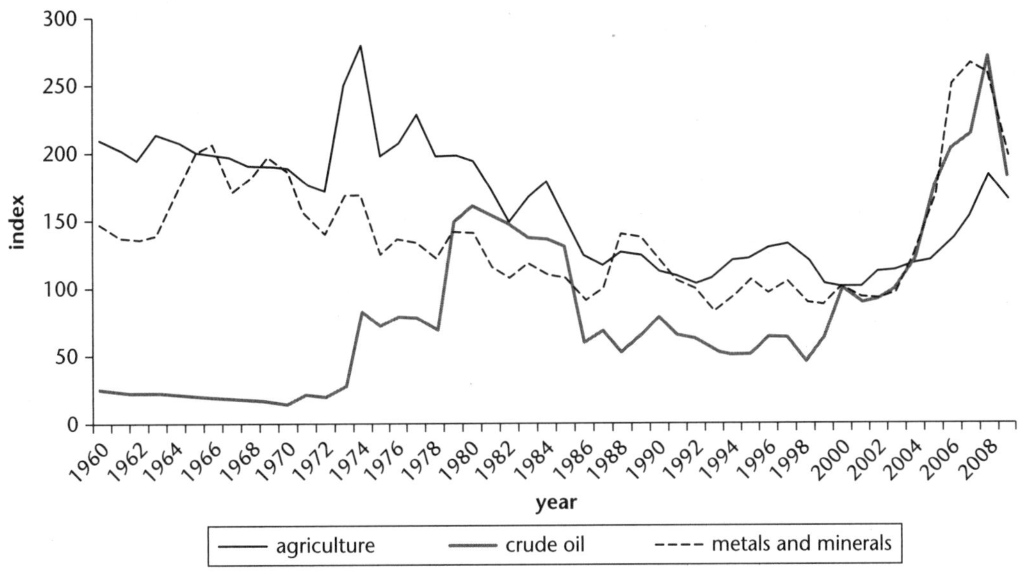

Source: World Bank 2010a.
Note: Prices are measured relative to the manufacturing unit value of the world exports index in constant 2000 U.S. dollars.

was little upward pressure on real prices of agricultural products. As a result of slower population growth and falling income elasticities as incomes rose, growth of global grain consumption fell from about 2.8 percent per year during the 1970s to 1.7 percent during the 1980s and 1.0 percent during the 1990s (Production, Supply, and Distribution database, U.S. Department of Agriculture, http://www.fas.usda.gov/psdonline). By the early 2000s, surplus capacity had waned, and demand had begun to increase, thus setting the stage for the rise in commodity prices.

A second reason for the rise in commodity prices was the rapid economic growth of developing countries. Eighteen low- and middle-income countries had real average GDP growth of at least 5 percent per year during 1990–2007.[3] These 18 countries have a combined population of nearly 3.0 billion people—nearly half the global population—and account for a large share of the increase in commodity demand.

Metals, Minerals, Crude Oil, and the Role of China

Demand growth in China was the dominant force behind the dramatic increase in the prices of metals, minerals, and crude oil from 2001 to 2008, during which period they nearly tripled. China's consumption of metals has risen significantly in the past decade (figure 20.2), and that country consumes between 30 and 45 percent of most metals produced.

Nearly all the growth in world oil consumption in the past decade has come from countries outside the Organisation for Economic Co-operation and Development (OECD), and about one-third of that growth has come from China (figure 20.3). China's share of world oil consumption increased from 3.5 percent in 1990 to 9.5 percent in 2008, while the share of other Asian developing countries increased from 17 percent to 21 percent over the same period. China and India are expected to account for just over half the increase in global demand for primary energy between 2006 and 2030, based on projections of continuing strong economic growth (IEA 2008).

Trends in the Agriculture Sector

Agricultural prices have also risen in the past decade but much less than the prices of oil and metal products. One of the main reasons for this slower rate of growth in prices was the rapid increase in per capita food production during the 1970s, 1980s, and 1990s (figure 20.4).[4] For instance, per capita calorie supplies in China rose by more than 50 percent from 1970 to 2000 and reached levels that rivaled consumption in high-income Asian countries such as Japan and the Republic of Korea (FAO 2010).[5] India, with its largely vegetarian diets, had lower per capita calorie supplies than China but still witnessed a 12 percent increase in per capita calorie supplies from 1970 to 2000 and a 29 percent increase in per capita food production.

Figure 20.2. China's Shares of Global Metals Consumption, 1996–2008

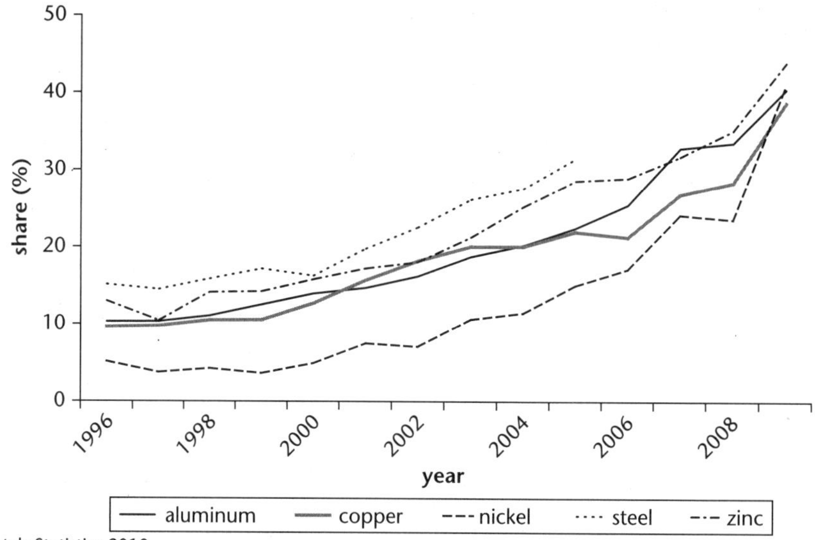

Source: World Bureau of Metals Statistics 2010.

Figure 20.3. Share of Growth of World Oil Consumption of OECD Countries, Non-OECD Countries, and China, 1988–2008

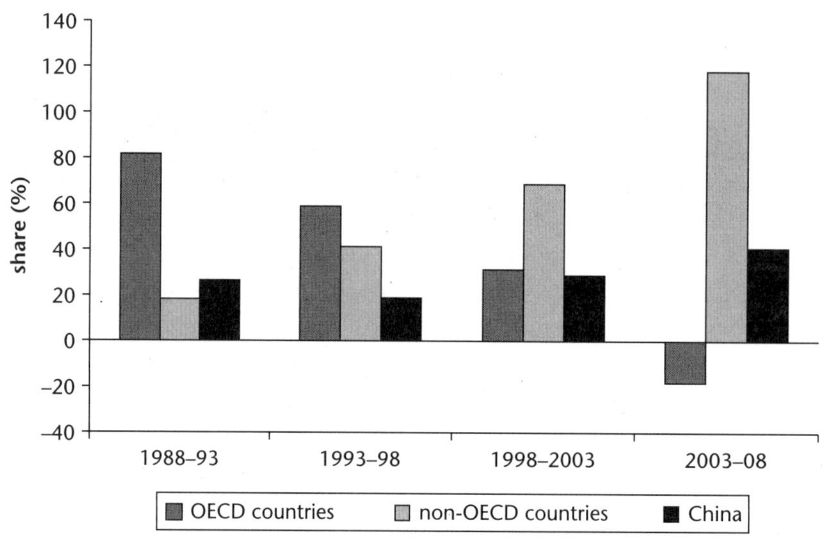

Source: BP 2009.

India also became an exporter of wheat and rice, its staple food grains, in the 1990s. The increase in per capita food production in South America was even greater than in Asia. South America emerged as a main exporter of grains and oilseeds during this period. In contrast, per capita food production in Sub-Saharan Africa remained relatively unchanged from 1970 to 2000, as modern inputs were not widely used and population growth rates remained high. Sub-Saharan Africa has become a large importer of grains and other food crops.

Although its role was much less significant than in fuels or metals, China has still contributed to the rising demand for agricultural imports, particularly nonfood imports. For instance, China has increased imports of natural rubber and cotton to support its tire and textile industries. China has also become the largest soybean importer in order to support its rapidly growing pork and poultry industries (World Bank 2010b).

While increased production has placed downward pressure on agricultural prices, the expansion of biofuel

Figure 20.4. Per Capita Food Production of World and Selected Regions, 1961–2007

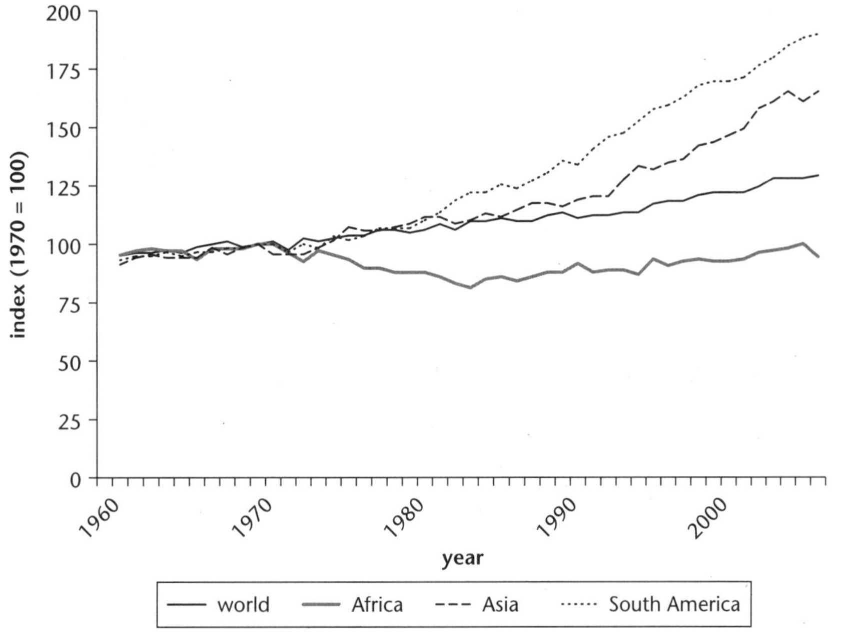

Source: FAO 2010.

production in recent years has encouraged a rise in agricultural prices. The price of food crops has steadily increased in recent years, culminating in a price spike in 2008 because the demand for food crops used to produce biofuels grew faster than the increase in supplies.

Brazil, the European Union (EU), and the United States account for 90 percent of current global biofuel production. The United States uses almost one-third of its maize production (13.2 percent of global production) for ethanol. Brazil currently uses approximately half its sugar cane crop (18 percent of global production) for ethanol. The European Union produces both ethanol from grains (wheat and maize) and biodiesel from vegetable oils (rapeseed and soybean and sunflower oils). In 2009, the EU-27 used an estimated 7.4 million tons of vegetable oils for biodiesel (5.4 percent of global production).

Prospects for Commodity Prices

The World Bank and many other organizations— the International Energy Agency, International Monetary Fund, Food and Agriculture Organization, OECD, U.S. Department of Agriculture, U.S. Department of Energy, Food and Agriculture Policy Research Institute, and International Food Policy Research Institute—forecast high commodity prices relative to historical levels for at least the next decade. As shown in figure 20.5, real commodity price indexes are projected to decline from their 2008 peaks but remain well above 1990–2000 levels (World Bank 2010c).

The Future of Oil

According to the World Bank (2010b), crude oil prices are expected to remain high (at more than double 2000 prices) until 2020. This projection is based on rapid demand growth in developing countries, declining production from mature fields, and higher costs for new production in remote areas and unstable regions.

Crude oil is expected to be more costly in the future because many of the most easily accessible and richest fields and deposits have already been developed. Countries that restrict access and plan to develop their resources slowly are where a significant proportion of remaining resources are located, a factor that will limit supplies and create upward pressure on prices. Still other resources are located in politically unstable regions such as the Niger Delta and are costly and dangerous to develop.

Restricted access to potentially rich oil fields has encouraged the development of offshore production. In fact, nearly all the increase in global oil production since 1970 has come from offshore fields (World Bank 2009a). However, as the oil spill in the Gulf of Mexico in April 2010 illustrates, such fields can pose severe environmental risks. Thus, future development of offshore fields will likely require more

Figure 20.5. Real Commodity Price Indexes, Historical and Projected, 1960–2020

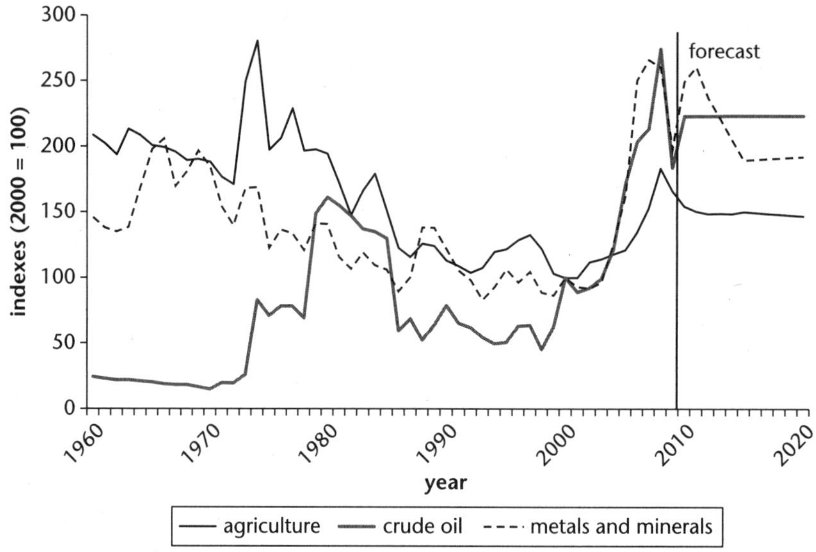

Source: World Bank 2010c.
Note: Prices are measured relative to the manufacturing unit value of the world exports index in constant 2000 U.S. dollars.

costly safety measures and location restrictions, which will limit supplies and increase costs.

Most experts seem to agree that while natural resources remain abundant, many are of lower quality than resources already developed. However, as prices rise, oil fields that were previously too small or too costly to develop will become profitable. For instance, the Bakken Formation oil field in the northern United States and southern Canada has pockets of oil dispersed throughout the formation that can now be tapped with newer, more expensive technology such as horizontal drilling and fracturing techniques (USGS 2008). By some estimates, this formation may have more recoverable oil than all other known U.S. reserves combined, but extraction will be more expensive than has been the case with discrete pools of oil in the past.

Indeed, the International Energy Agency recently declared that "the era of cheap oil is over" (IEA 2008). The agency projects that the price of crude oil will average US$100 per barrel over the 2008–20 period and will then rise to over US$120 per barrel in 2030 in constant 2007 dollars. This dramatic increase is based on the expectation that the output from mature fields will suffer a severe decline, developing countries will experience rapid demand growth, and investment in new capacity will fail to keep up with growth in demand (despite adequate global oil reserves). Assuming continued strong economic growth, China and India are expected to account for just over half the increase in global demand for primary energy between 2006 and 2030. However, the International Energy Agency also suggests that climate change and policies to mitigate emissions of greenhouse gases could push energy prices lower and carbon prices higher, to over US$100 per ton by 2030, resulting in greater demand for low-carbon biofuels (IEA 2008).

The U.S. Department of Energy also predicts a sharp rise in energy prices as a result of growing energy demand—particularly in China, India, and other developing countries—as well as efforts by many countries to limit access to their oil resources (2009). In the Department of Energy reference case, world oil prices are predicted to rise to US$130 per barrel in real dollars in 2030. However, they note significant uncertainty in their projections and forecast a range of oil prices from US$50 to US$200 per barrel in alternative scenarios. In the low-price scenario, many of the major oil-producing countries expand output more rapidly than in the reference case and increase their share of world production beyond current levels. In contrast, in the high-price scenario, major oil producers maintain tight control over access to their resources and develop them slowly. Other organizations generally share the view that energy prices will be higher in the future because of strong demand growth and dwindling supplies of easily accessible crude oil.

The Future of Agriculture

Rising energy prices are expected, in turn, to put upward pressure on agricultural prices. Energy is an important input to agricultural production as fuel and in the production of fertilizer. Moreover, as discussed in the previous section, growth of the biofuels industry has strengthened the connection between energy and agriculture by linking demand for food crops to energy prices. The energy market is so large relative to the volumes of biofuels that can be produced from food crops that energy prices will drive up food crop prices as long as policies encourage biofuel consumption and the use of food crops for biofuels is unrestricted.[6]

Efforts to mitigate greenhouse gas emissions may also contribute to the increase in biofuel production. Many countries appear committed to reducing dependence on fossil fuels and increasing reliance on renewable energy sources in the long term. Brazil, Canada, the EU, the United States, and other countries have mandated large increases in biofuel production, and other countries have set nonbinding targets (China, India, Japan, and others).[7] Consumption mandates in many countries, but especially in the EU and the United States, will require large increases in biofuels production through at least 2020.[8]

In the long term, second-generation biofuel technology may limit the upward pressure on prices by allowing agricultural waste to be used to produce biofuels. However, this technology has been slow to develop and may not be economically viable for a decade or more. Even when it becomes profitable, it will take many years to scale up production to significant levels. And until second-generation technology develops, the increased use of food crops for biofuels will divert resources from other food, feed, and fiber uses and raise all agricultural commodity prices (Mitchell forthcoming).

If crop prices remain high, agricultural production may increase. Argentina, Brazil, and other parts of Latin America (as well as Eastern Europe and Sub-Saharan Africa) have land that is suitable for crops and would likely come into production. Much of this land is already in pasture and could be used for crops if the necessary infrastructure were made available. Brazil, for example, has about 200 million hectares of pasture, and a portion of this land could be used for crop production without undue environmental stress. This area potentially rivals the 140 million hectares of cropland currently used for production of major field crops in the United States. Sub-Saharan Africa has more than 1 billion hectares of land with potential for rain-fed crop production, with less than one quarter of this land now being cropped, according to the Food and Agriculture Organization (FAO 2008). Marginal and abandoned lands may be even more abundant.

The Future of Metal and Minerals

The future of metal and mineral prices will depend mostly on demand from China. Currently, China's per capita consumption of metals is following historical trends of other rapidly growing developing countries at similar income levels (figure 20.6). However, China is such a large country, and its economic growth has been so rapid that following historical trends in per capita consumption has led to very large increases in metals consumption and a growing share of global imports. If historical increases in China's economic growth and exports continue, per capita metals consumption is expected to continue increasing for at least another decade. Indeed, China's share of global metals consumption is forecast to increase from 40 percent to 50 percent or more for many metals during this period (Mitchell, Tan, and Timmer 2007).

Once China moves through its period of rapid economic growth, its demand for metals will fall, and no other countries are expected to replace China's demand for metals and minerals. As a result, metals prices could be sharply lower in a decade or more. Although supplies of global metals and minerals deposits are abundant (USGS 2008),[9] many of these deposits will probably be costly to develop and under the best of conditions will take many years to begin producing.

In conclusion, while the boom in commodity prices may be long lasting, it is unlikely to be permanent because commodity demand will slow in rapidly growing developing countries as their economies mature and new resource supplies are developed. However, the period of high prices and strong demand growth may last for at least a decade and provide an opportunity for resource-rich countries to enjoy faster growth than in the past. How they manage such growth will largely determine whether it will be sustainable. Past efforts at managing commodity booms have not been very successful. For example, countries with abundant natural resources have experienced slowed economic growth because of overvalued exchange rates and volatile export earnings. However, countries that manage their policies well can avoid these problems.

A Historical Account of the Commodities Literature

Recent trends in commodity prices have revived discussion of the differing impact of commodity and manufactures production on economic growth. This debate has been emerging cyclically since the 1950s, starting with Raul Prebisch (1959) and Hans Singer (1950). Prebisch and Singer argued that natural-resource dependency leads to low growth because of the long-term deterioration of commodity prices relative to manufactures and the belief that opportunities for technical progress were limited relative to those in manufactures. Their analyses were further

Figure 20.6. China's Metals Consumption versus GDP as Compared to Selected Other Economies, Various Years

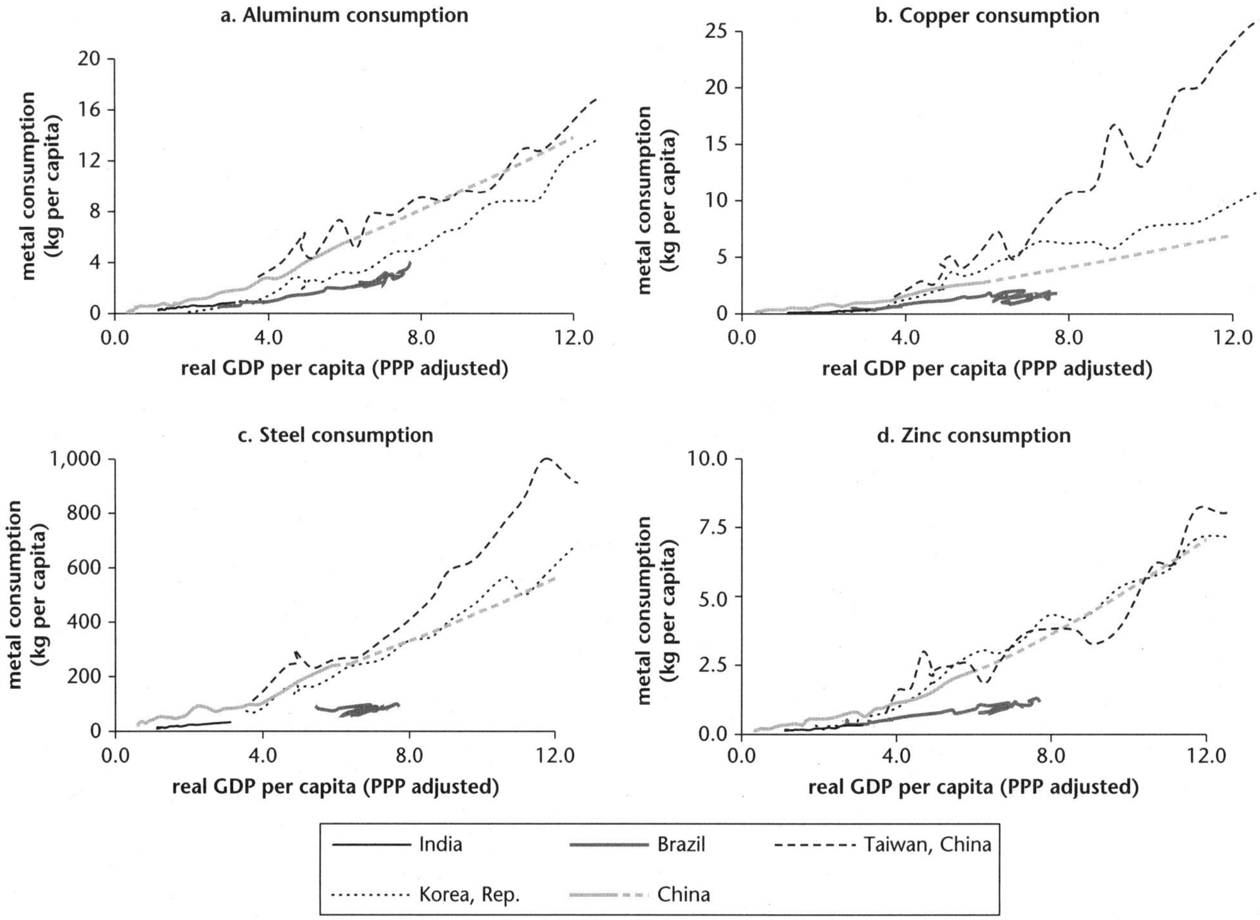

Source: Mitchell, Tan, and Timmer 2007.
Note: Data for all countries ends in 2005, and the beginning year for each country is shown in parenthesis: Brazil (1964); China (1962); EU-12 (1960); India (1975); Taiwan, China (1975); and the United States (1930). kg = kilogram, PPP = purchasing power parity.

supported by Kaldor's (1967) empirical observation of a link between industrial growth, productivity growth, and GDP.

In the 1970s, the so-called Dutch disease phenomenon linked the exploitation of natural resources and declines in the manufacturing sector. While a boom in production of natural resources increases wealth in the economy, it may also drive up the real exchange rate and draw away factors of production from the nonresource tradable sector to the resource tradable sector and the nontradable sector. These outcomes cause the nonresource tradable sector to lose competitiveness and shrink.

Dutch disease can cripple a country's long-term prosperity in four ways. First, if natural resources begin to run out or if there is a downturn in commodity prices, the (previously) competitive manufacturing industries will have difficulty recovering because they will have become technologically backward (Van Wijnbergen 1984). Second, a country's volatile real exchange rate—resulting from the inherent price volatility of natural resource exports—fuels uncertainty about future economic conditions and thus may reduce investment (Gylfason, Herbertsson, and Zoega 1999). Third, the greater income inequality associated with Dutch disease can make governance issues and internal conflicts more prevalent. Finally, Dutch disease can lead to corruption and protectionist policies for lagging industrial sectors, which, in turn, may increase inefficiencies.

However, recent research has shown that many of the shortcomings of commodities identified in the past are no longer relevant. For instance, a more recent analysis of the Prebisch-Singer hypothesis concludes that from the beginning of the 20th century to 1973 there was no trend in relative commodity prices (Cuddington, Ludema, and Jayasuriya 2007). The recent price increase and apparent structural break reinforce this view. Moreover, Martin and

Mitra (2001) show that total factor productivity (TFP) growth in agriculture from 1967 to 1992 was 50 percent faster than in manufactures, although the industrial countries experienced rates substantially above those of less developed countries. Lederman and Maloney (2007) draw on this work and find econometric evidence that natural-resource-based activities can spur long-term growth. Similarly, De Ferranti et al. (2002) argue that several of the natural resource success stories—Denmark and Sweden—continue to show the highest TFP growth rates in the agriculture sector.

De Ferranti et al. (2002) and Lederman and Maloney (2007) also question the view that manufacturing has something special in terms of backward and forward linkages, technological innovation, and other potential externalities. The most convincing evidence is offered by history: Australia, Canada, Finland, Sweden, and the United States developed and achieved technological progress based on their natural resources. The main driver of growth and industrialization was mining in Australia and the United States and forestry in Finland and Sweden. And even today, these countries remain exporters of natural-resource-based products, along with high-tech products (De Ferranti et al. 2002). The success of Chile over the past two decades has been almost fully led by exports of natural-resource-based products.

Moreover, the remaining shortcomings of commodities can be overcome with sound policy choices. The historical record is clear: when managed well and coupled with a strong institutional framework, natural resources can be vital for development. For instance, strong evidence now suggests that the U.S. industrial success resulted from a gradual transition to resource-intensive manufacturing industries and most recently in its development to more knowledge-intensive industries. Along these lines, the case of Canada inspired "staples theory"—where exports of primary goods drive development over an extended period of time through either demand or supply links. And although wool is Australia's most famous staple, success in mining (and the derivative industries of both) made that country one of the richest economies in the world by the early 20th century. Australia's discovery of new deposits and the generation and export of mining-related knowledge—in mineral detection, environmentally sound mining practices, and processing, all based on a massive educational and research infrastructure—may put it near the top of the list again.

In particular, natural resources seem to have furthered development in countries with strong organizational structures, knowledge networks, and aggressive human capital policies (which were developed to pursue resource processing but were transferable to high-tech industries) (De Ferranti et al. 2002). This phenomenon can be seen in the Scandinavian countries that built on their strengths in natural resources to produce aircraft, luxury cars, designer furniture, and, most recently, advanced telecommunications products. Sweden's Volvo and Saab emerged partially from backward linkages with the forestry industry. Similarly, Finland's Nokia, originally a wood-pulp producer, became a major player in the global cellular phone industry.

In light of these findings, the gap between the manufactures and commodity camps can be bridged by distinguishing between high-productivity and low-productivity activities, within both manufactures and commodities. Rodrik (2009) argues that the engine of growth since the end of the Second World War has been rapid structural change in the developing nations from low-productivity ("traditional") to high-productivity ("modern") activities. Although Rodrik is seen as a proponent of manufactures, he acknowledges that high-productivity activities are not exclusively in the manufacturing sector: they are also present in commodities (for example, horticulture) and services (for example, call centers). As De Ferranti et al. (2002) and Lederman and Maloney (2007) note, what is important is not *what* is produced but *how* it is produced—the ability to produce and commercialize knowledge. A key policy objective of countries with abundant natural resources should therefore be to embed knowledge into natural-resource production.

Policy Recommendations to Foster a Sectorally Balanced, Resource-Based Economy

High commodity prices offer countries with natural resources an opportunity to generate strong, broad-based growth. Indeed, commodities can generate needed revenue to improve competitiveness in the overall economy and promote development. However, the increase in export earnings can also result in Dutch disease. If the government does not implement policies to counter this possibility, the economy may become concentrated in the resource and nontradable sectors. Because the resource sector is not labor intensive, higher unemployment, increased exposure to costly boom-and-bust cycles, and unstable growth could result.

Appropriate policies can mitigate the inherent risks of a commodity-dependent economy. Interventions can mitigate the impact of price volatility, limit exchange-rate appreciation and increase competitiveness of the tradables sector, for example. The following section discusses how policy measures can foster sustainable growth in commodity-dependent countries.

Dealing with High and Volatile Commodity Prices

In addition to remaining high, commodity prices are also likely to experience considerable volatility over the next decade. High commodity prices will continue to create income opportunities for producers in resource-rich countries. However, price volatility will have negative macroeconomic and microeconomic effects. It can lead to higher inflation and unemployment and could cause variability in GDP, exchange rates, and public expenditures. The effect of such volatility on these variables will be greater in resource-rich economies, where the link between commodity prices and revenues is stronger.

As shown in table 20.3, historical experience suggests that some policy options are better than others at mitigating the impact of price volatility.[10] For instance, several short-run measures have proven effective at reducing the impact of volatility on the poor. These include transfers to target groups (for instance, cash transfers, feeding programs, and food for work), responses to macroeconomic problems provoked by rising food prices (balance of payment support, for example), and quick measures to expand supply and reduce prices (lifting of import restrictions, drawing down of food stocks, and reduction of tariffs and other taxes on key staples, for example). Four examples of targeted safety net measures that were successfully expanded during the past food crisis are Mexico's conditional cash transfer (Progresa, now called Oportunidades), which covered 5 million households in 2008 (one out of four Mexican families); Bangladesh's Public Food Distribution System, which covered 30.5 million people during fiscal 2007–08; Ethiopia's employment-based safety net program, with 8 million beneficiaries in 2008; and Indonesia's unconditional cash transfer for the poor, the largest cash transfer in the world, which covered 15.5 million households in 2008 (28 percent of the population) (FAO 2008).

Historical experience also highlights certain policies to be avoided. First, policy makers should steer clear of interventions that are expected to generate huge efficiency, equity, or fiscal costs over the medium term. Second, policies that are very costly to introduce and maintain should be avoided, because they may create disincentives on the supply side or promote black markets and inefficiencies. Third, it is important to consider whether policies are not well targeted or even biased against the poor. For instance, universal subsidies are poorly targeted and difficult to remove once introduced. Price controls are also biased against the poor, difficult to remove, and conducive to black market promotion.

Fourth, interventions should be avoided if they are politically difficult to scale back or remove down the line. For example, in 2007 and 2008, Indonesia's government spent almost two and a half times as much on energy subsidies as on social assistance. Although subsidy spending was finally scaled back in May 2008, about two-thirds of fuel subsidies still benefit the top 20 percent of the population, and the bottom 10 percent receive only 1 percent of the direct benefits (see figures 20.7 and 20.8).

Fifth and finally, food exporters should avoid applying "beggar-thy-neighbor" policies, which consist of restrictions or taxes on food exports. These policies push world

Table 20.3. Summary of Policy Options for Mitigating the Impact of Price Volatility

	Transfers to poor households	Public price stabilization	Transition toward market stabilization measures
Immediate responses	• Feeding programs • Food for work programs • Expansion of existing cash-transfer programs • Limited subsidies	• Lifting of import restrictions on food and quotas • Draw down of food stocks	• Reduction of red tape in transporting goods across regions • Limiting of intervention using variable tariff
Long-term responses	• Development of cash-transfer programs (where previously nonexistent) or improvement of targeting (where existent)	• Improvement of farm productivity • Improvement of village infrastructure • Improvement of food logistics network	• Encouragement of investments in private storage and warehouse receipt • Forward contracts • Domestic market efficiency • Future Market, Index-based weather insurance
Policies to avoid	• Universal subsidies • In-kind transfers	• Export bans • Price controls	• Import quota or import bans • Price controls

Source: Based on a World Bank note prepared by Cord et al. 2008.

Figure 20.7. Energy Subsidies in Indonesia, 2008

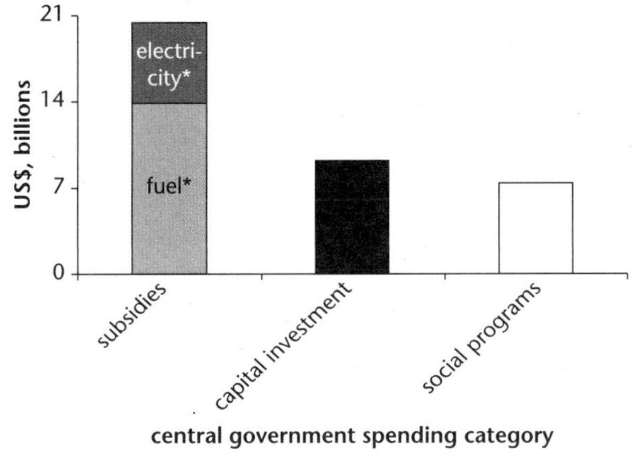

Source: World Bank staff calculations based on data from the Ministry of Finance of Indonesia.
* assumes ICP oil at US$95.

Figure 20.8. Benefits of Fuel Subsidies for the Rich and the Poor, 2007

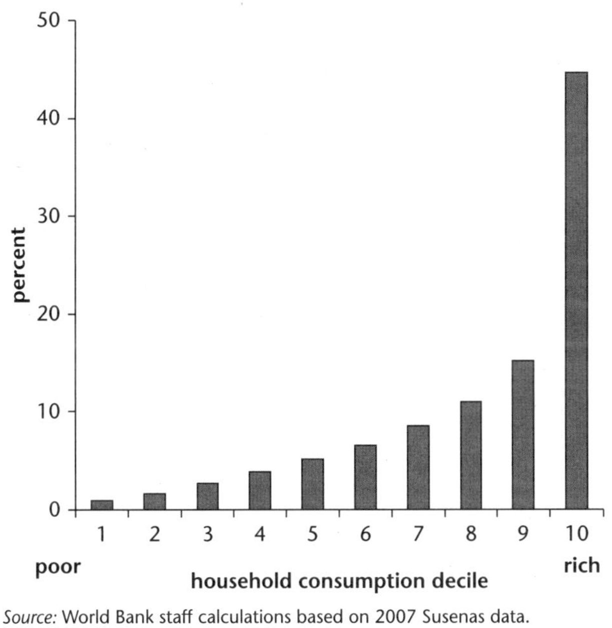

Source: World Bank staff calculations based on 2007 Susenas data.

prices even higher, as the rice price bubble in the first half of 2008 clearly illustrated (Aldaz-Carroll, Slayton, and Timmer 2010).

In the medium to long term, countries need to make their price stabilization policies more predictable, better targeted, less costly, and more effective. Above all, policy makers need to develop and publish well-defined stabilization strategies, moving from discretionary to rule-based interventions. For policy formulation to be transparent, consistent, and consultative, countries must ensure that standard operating procedures for price stabilization are in place. It is generally better to set a "tolerable" level of price variability than try to stabilize prices too much. Furthermore, the burden of proof for the need for stabilization should rest on the private sector (rather than on the government) to ensure that complaints are backed by data and decisions are based on cost-benefit analyses.

It is also advisable to use variable tariffs and targeted subsidies, because they are less costly and more effective than public marketing agencies. If the government chooses to intervene, it is preferable to rely more on the use of a small financial reserve for imports or domestic purchases of privately held stocks rather than relying mainly on governmental strategic commodity reserves. It is less costly for the government to tender public procurement, imports, and storage to the private sector. This approach will increase efficiency and develop storage capacity in the private sector. The government can be more effective at helping the poorest consumers deal with commodity price shocks by strengthening its social safety net program.

Strengthening market price stabilization (private storage and warehouse receipts, forward contracts, futures markets, and index-based weather insurance) would allow market-based instruments to help stabilize short-term price fluctuations. Moreover, strong intermediary institutions are needed to pool and repackage the risks facing small-scale producers, traders, and processors and then hedge the pooled risks using global futures, options, and insurance markets. Improved statistical capacity, technical support, and education are also needed to facilitate use of global futures and options markets by large domestic firms. Indeed, market stabilization mechanisms can help stabilize prices, thus minimizing the need for government stabilization and saving public funds.

At the same time, it is important to develop an environment that promotes a quick supply response that benefits producers and helps reduce a sudden price spike. A key step toward this objective is to expand the generally neglected agricultural extension services. It is also important to strengthen institutions that support rural finance markets and expand the availability of credit. Finally, regulations should be streamlined to ensure competitive behavior and reduce transport costs. As the national market becomes more integrated and subregional trade flows increase, price differences across regions and regional shocks will diminish.

Complementary Policies for Promoting Growth in Commodity-Dependent Countries

Humphreys, Sachs, and Stiglitz (2007, 323–26) identify several other policies that can help countries maximize the economic benefits of a natural-resource boom while minimizing governance issues and appreciation pressure on the exchange rate:

- Contracts on future prices, output, and other economic circumstances should be designed to avoid situations in which corporations receive an unconscionably high return and the government a marginal amount.
- Auctions should foster increased competition between corporations to reduce the risk of cronyism and increase returns to the country.
- Contracts should be made transparent, and domestic constituents should be involved in contract evaluation to reduce corruption and increase the bargaining power of domestic negotiators vis-à-vis corporations.
- Corporations should be required to post bonds in anticipation of future cleanups to protect the environment.
- National wealth should be calculated by taking into account not only earnings but also depletion of stocks and degradation of the environment. Doing so will avoid the temptation to spend too much of the depletable resource.
- Action should be taken to prevent inequities and potential social disturbance by ensuring a fair distribution of benefits within the country.[11]
- Expenditures should be stabilized to avoid costly boom-and-bust patterns. A sovereign wealth fund can be established to sterilize the boom revenues and spread expenditures across time, transforming a nonrenewable resource into a financial asset that will last forever.

In addition, governments should pursue a range of policies to increase the technological sophistication and dynamism of tradable sectors. First, they should *improve logistics.* Poor logistics reduce the competitiveness of products and can inhibit greater processing of commodities and the export of higher-value-added products. The high cost of transport leads to higher prices for products and inputs in remote areas and to producers' having poor access to domestic and international markets. Furthermore, in countries where the commodity-producing regions are poorly connected to industrial areas, commodities are more likely to be exported in raw form to be processed abroad rather than domestically. For instance, as a result of the high domestic logistics costs to Java-based processing facilities, some high-quality commodities with great potential, such as shrimp from eastern Indonesia, cannot be exported, and others, like pineapples, are canned abroad. A weak distribution and marketing network can also discourage a country from venturing into higher-value-added downstream activities. High cost and uncertainty in distribution channels can also prevent countries from integration into just-in-time production networks of higher-value-added products. High logistics costs can be caused by underdeveloped or poorly maintained infrastructure and a constraining business environment for logistics services.

Second, governments should also *foster foreign direct investment (FDI) flows and maintain an open economy to attract the skills and knowledge needed.* Greater opening to FDI is crucial for attracting needed technological and market knowledge that can lead to greater export diversification (within and outside natural-resource-based activities), higher intra-industry trade, innovation and skills promotion (De Ferranti et al. 2002). Establishing an enabling environment for FDI by improving the business regulatory environment, human capital, public infrastructure, and knowledge clusters is therefore crucial. Usual regulatory issues inhibiting FDI in commodity-abundant countries tend to be those surrounding land entitlement, labor laws, and conflicting regulations.

Third, government policies should *foster the development of knowledge industries* in natural-resource-based activities where the country has a comparative advantage. Natural-resource-based activities can become knowledge industries. That was the case, for instance, with mining in the United States, which led to the development of a strong technological system; forestry and forest products in Finland and Sweden, which are highly knowledge intensive; and fresh-fruit production and marketing in Chile, which have a high technology content. Developing a dynamic natural-resource-based sector is not incompatible with building new comparative advantages in footloose and high-tech manufacturing. Both sectors coexist not only in natural resource–rich developed economies but also in the already highly diversified export structures of Brazil and Mexico (De Ferranti et al. 2002). For success, natural resource wealth needs to be complemented with human capital, knowledge, and good institutions. For instance, a country can move from just extracting minerals to promoting the development of engineering services for mineral extraction and from just producing raw commodities to downstream higher value and knowledge derivatives.

Fourth, governments need to *build new endowments in human capital and knowledge.* As discussed in De Ferranti et al. (2002), a key lesson from the experience of other natural-resource-rich countries is that investing in knowledge and skills to build "new endowments" is crucial to promoting sustained and inclusive growth. Public policy has a large role to play by providing quality education in general and lifelong training to support product upgrading and innovation and by promoting research and development incentives and innovation systems to lead to knowledge and technological progress that raises productivity growth and promotes new comparative advantages. In addition, public policy should promote the establishment of knowledge clusters and networks, encompassing private firms, independent research institutions and universities and the public sector. This step is critically important not just for high-tech manufactures but also for many natural resource activities.

Fifth, governments should *develop better institutions*. To achieve productivity growth and develop comparative advantages in technologically sophisticated industries, governments need good institutions (rule of law, security, effective property rights, transparency, removal of excessive regulatory burdens, and efficiency of public service delivery). The experience of various Latin American countries with rich natural resources shows that the "curse" of natural resources appears to be driven not simply by the existence of rich endowments of natural resources per se but rather by multiple barriers to technology adoption usually associated with weak institutions, burdensome regulations, and artificially created monopolies (Lederman and Maloney 2007).

Finally, governments should *promote the development of the services sector*. Services have become a significant engine of growth in East Asia since the East Asian crisis, and they continue to have great potential for further development. Developing a competitive services sector will increase the competitiveness of other sectors and facilitate diversification into higher-value-added products, spurring dynamism in the economy. For instance, in Indonesia one-third of inputs used in the mining sector are services and around 15 percent in the case of agriculture, forestry, and fishing (Atje and Rahardja 2010). More specifically, greater efficiency of services would result in reduced service costs, greater variety of services, increased investments in related and supported sectors, enhanced goods and services exports, and higher economic growth. Improving access to competitive cyber-communication, design and marketing services, financial instruments, and tailored supply chain management, for example, would raise the efficiency of local producers in upgrading their products and finding new market niches, making them more competitive and increasing global market shares.

The development of information and communications technology can reduce coordination and marketing costs and enable firms to hook into international industrial clusters, expand resource-based tourism, and facilitate market access for nontraditional agricultural products and processed goods. For instance, setting up a website has allowed companies to serve the global market with little in the way of advertising costs and achieve significant growth in sales. Some services like export promotion are "public goods" that can be supported by the public sector. These export promotion services include image building, export support services, market research, and policy advocacy. Export promotion services have been shown to be potentially beneficial in terms of returns to invested public funds (see Lederman, Olarreaga, and Payton 2006) and could possibly help lower the costs of entering export markets and promote diversification (Iacovone and Javorcik 2008). But export promotion needs to be well targeted and appropriately designed.

Conclusions

The main conclusion of this chapter is that countries with abundant natural resources have new opportunities. To capitalize on these opportunities, the challenge for such economies is to improve the investment climate, build better institutions, and improve infrastructure, human capital, and knowledge while maintaining price stability.

Windfalls from commodity revenues should be invested to increase the technological sophistication of production across sectors. The competitiveness of the domestic and export sectors can be increased by relieving infrastructure bottlenecks, reducing regulatory uncertainty, and promoting the development of a knowledge economy. If these goals can be achieved, greater technology absorption and the development of knowledge industries in natural resources and other sectors will spur sustainable growth.

The government should also redistribute the resource windfall in a way that promotes social and political stability and mitigates the negative effects of volatile commodity prices on vulnerable households. Safety net approaches like cash transfers and food aid are more effective than price controls in ensuring food security. To lower domestic prices, the more effective options are to reduce tariffs and other taxes on key staples. Other policy actions that aim to lower domestic prices may be administratively easy to implement but often have unintended consequences. However, the government should not attempt to protect all consumers from price changes since that effort can lead to burdensome social programs that limit investment in areas that will foster sustained growth.

Notes

1. Commodities in this chapter refer to agricultural commodities, fuels, ores, and metals.

2. The depression of commodity prices in the 1980s and 1990s was caused by two main factors: overinvestment (in response to sharp price increases in crude oil in the 1970s) and surplus capacity (as a result of the collapse of demand for metals and minerals in the former Soviet Union).

3. These countries, ranked from highest to lowest based on GDP growth rates (percent), were China (10.5), Cambodia (8.5), Vietnam (7.9), Myanmar (8.1), Uganda (7.1), Mozambique (7.1), India (6.9), Lao People's Democratic Republic (6.6), Sudan (6.3), Malaysia (6.2), Botswana (5.7), Burkina Faso

(5.7), Jordan (5.7), Chile (5.6), the Dominican Republic (5.4), Costa Rica (5.4), Sri Lanka (5.3), and Bangladesh (5.3) (World Bank 2009b).

4 Production levels increased as a result of increased fertilizer use, expanded irrigation, improved seeds, and slowing population growth.

5. Calorie supplies measure calories available for consumption and are used as a proxy for calorie consumption since actual consumption is difficult to estimate and not available for most countries.

6. Current biofuels production accounts for only 1.5 percent of global transport fuels.

7. These mandates and targets are not tied directly to energy prices and should continue regardless of energy prices unless new legislation repeals existing laws.

8. The EU has mandated that 10 percent of transport fuels come from renewable sources by 2020, which will require almost tripling the approximately 15 billion liters of biofuels consumed in 2009. The United States has mandated that 36.0 billion gallons (136 billion liters) of biofuels be consumed by 2022, which requires more than tripling the 11.1 billion gallons (42 billion liters) of biofuels consumed in 2009.

9. The U.S. Geological Survey is a government body assigned to quantify and monitor such deposits.

10. Some of these recommendations come from a World Bank note prepared in 2008 by Louise Cord, Eduardo Ley, Hassan Zaman, Elena Ianchovichina, C. Hull, Emmanuel Skoufias, Mark Thomas, Brian Pinto, and Tahrat Shahid.

11. Humphreys, Sachs, and Stiglitz (2007) suggest that given the weaker capacity of subnational governments to manage extreme volatility of revenues and ensure oversight, it is better in most country cases to centralize revenue collection while allowing for decentralized expenditure to subnational governments. A redistribution of revenues between regions and the set-up of social protection to assist the poor will help make growth more inclusive and reduce potential political instability.

Bibliography

Aldaz-Carroll, E., T. Slayton, and P. Timmer. 2010. "Pricking the Price Bubble to Avert a World Rice Crisis." Background paper, World Bank, Washington, DC.

Atje, R., and S. Rahardja. 2010. "Indonesia's Services Industries: Questions Moving Forward." Presentation at workshop "Dialogue among Stakeholders: Growth and Efficiency in the Indonesian Services Sector," organized by the World Bank, Kadin, and the Center for International Studies, Jakarta, January 14.

BP (British Petroleum). 2009. Database on Energy Demand, Supply and Prices. British Petroleum, London.

Cuddington, J., R. Ludema, and S. Jayasuriya. 2007. "Prebisch-Singer Redux." In *Natural Resources: Neither Curse nor Destiny*, ed. Daniel Lederman and William Maloney, 103–40. Washington, DC: World Bank and Stanford University Press.

De Ferranti, D., G. Perry, D. Lederman, and W. Maloney. 2002. *From Natural Resources to the Knowledge Economy*. Washington, DC: World Bank.

FAO (Food and Agriculture Organization). 2008. *The State of Food and Agriculture 2008: Biofuels: Prospects, Risks and Opportunities.* Rome: Food and Agriculture Organization.

———. 2010. FAOSTAT (database). Food and Agriculture Organization, Rome. http://faostat.fao.org.

Gylfason, T., T. T. Herbertsson, and G. Zoega. 1999. "A Mixed Blessing." *Macroeconomic Dynamics* 3 (2): 204–25.

Humphreys, M., J. D. Sachs, and J. E. Stiglitz. 2007. "Future Directions for the Management of Natural Resources." In *Escaping the Resource Curse*, ed. M. Humphreys, J. D. Sachs, and J. E. Stiglitz, 233–36. New York: Columbia University Press.

Iacovone, L., and B. S. Javorcik. 2008. "Using Export Promotion to Stimulate Export Diversification in Indonesia." Mimeo, World Bank, Washington, DC.

IEA (International Energy Agency). 2008. *World Energy Outlook*. Paris: Organisation for Economic Co-operation and Development.

Kaldor, N. 1967. *Strategic Factors in Economic Development.* Ithaca, NY: New York State School of Industrial and Labor Relations, Cornell University.

Lederman, D., M. Olarreaga, and L. Payton. 2006. "Export Promotion Agencies: What Works and What Doesn't." Discussion Paper 5810, Centre for Economic Policy Research, London.

Lederman, D., and W. F. Maloney. 2007. "Trade Structure and Growth." In *Natural Resources: Neither Curse nor Destiny,* ed. D. Lederman and W. F. Maloney, 15–40. Palo Alto, CA: Stanford University Press.

Martin, W., and D. Mitra. 2001. "Productivity, Growth and Convergence in Agriculture and Manufacturing." *Economic Development and Cultural Change* 49 (2): 403–22.

Mitchell, D. 2008. "A Note of Rising Food Prices." Policy Research Working Paper 4682, World Bank, Washington, DC.

Mitchell, D. Forthcoming. *Biofuels in Africa: Prospects for Sustainable Development.* Washington, DC: World Bank.

Mitchell, D., S. Tan, and H. Timmer. 2007. "China's Demand for Primary Commodities and the Impacts on Global Markets." Unpublished manuscript, World Bank, Washington DC.

Mulat Demeke, M., G. Pangrazio, and M. Maetz. 2009. *Country Responses to the Food Security Crisis: Nature and Preliminary Implications of the Policies Pursued.* Rome: Food and Agriculture Organization.

Prebisch, R. 1959. "Commercial Policy in the Underdeveloped Countries." *American Economic Review: Papers and Proceedings* 49 (2): 251–73.

Rodrik, D. 2009. "Growth after the Crisis." Paper prepared for the Commission on Growth and Development. http://www.growthcommission.org/storage/cgdev/documents/financial_crisis/rodrikafterthecrisis.pdf.

Sachs, J. D., and A. Warner. 1995. "Natural Resource Abundance and Economic Growth." Working Paper 5398, National Bureau of Economic Research, Cambridge, MA. http://www.nber.org/papers/w5398.pdf

———. 2001. "The Curse of Natural Resources." *European Economic Review* 45 (4–6): 827–38.

Singer, H. W. 1950. "The Distribution of Gains between Investing and Borrowing Countries." *American Economic Review* 40 (2): 473–85.

USDA (U.S. Department of Agriculture). 2010. PSD Online (database). USDA, Washington, DC. http://www.fas.usda.gov/psdonline.

USDOE (U.S. Department of Energy). 2009. *Annual Energy Outlook 2009 with Projections to 2030.* Washington, DC: USDOE.

USGS (U.S. Geological Survey). 2008. "Assessment of Undiscovered Oil Resources in Devonian-Mississippian Bakken Formation Williston Basin Province, Montana and North Dakota, 2008." USGS, Reston, Virginia.

Van Wijnbergen, S. 1984. "The 'Dutch Disease': A Disease after All?" *Economic Journal* 94 (373): 41–55.

World Bank 2009a. *Global Economic Prospects: Commodities at the Crossroads 2009.* Washington, DC: World Bank.

———. 2009b. *World Development Indicators 2009.* Washington, DC: World Bank.

———. 2010a. *Commodity Price Data.* Washington, DC: World Bank. http://econ.worldbank.org/WBSITE/EXTERNAL/EXTDEC/EXTDECPROSPECTS/0,,contentMDK:21148472~menuPK:556802~pagePK:64165401~piPK:64165026~theSitePK:476883,00.html.

———. 2010b. *Global Commodity Markets: Review and Price Forecasts.* Washington, DC: World Bank.

———. 2010c. *Global Economic Prospects: Crisis, Finance, and Growth.* Washington, DC: World Bank.

World Bureau of Metals Statistics. 2010. London. http://www.world-bureau.com.

21

GLOBAL PRODUCTION NETWORKS IN THE POSTCRISIS ERA

Alyson Ma and Ari Van Assche

Vertical specialization has been one of the most notable trends in the international organization of production during the past few decades (Spencer 2005; Helpman 2006; Desai 2009). Thanks to reductions in communication costs, transportation costs, and other trade barriers, multinational firms have sliced up their supply chains and dispersed their production activities across multiple countries. As a result, each production step in the supply chain of a single final good is performed in the most advantageous location for that particular process.

A recent series of macroeconomic events, however, is threatening to reverse this trend of vertical specialization. First, the era of cheap and plentiful oil seems to be drawing to a close, thus leading to increases in transportation costs (Rubin and Tal 2008; Rubin 2009). Second, the global recession of 2008–09 has put pressure on many governments to raise trade and investment barriers that privilege domestic over foreign production. Because vertical specialization is considered especially sensitive to such changes in trade costs (Yi 2003), these trend reversals could cause firms to rethink their global production networks (GPNs) and abandon distant production sites for closer locations.

What will GPNs look like in the postcrisis era? To what extent will they become smaller if these macroeconomic events continue? To evaluate these questions, observers must understand and quantify the sensitivity of intra-GPN trade to trade costs. Yet, because of data limitations, empirical research on this topic is scant. A notable exception is Hanson, Mataloni, and Slaughter (2005), who have examined the role of trade costs in the decisions of U.S. multinationals to export intermediate goods to their foreign affiliates for processing.

In this chapter, we take advantage of a unique data set on China's processing trade regime from 1988 to 2008 to analyze the impact of trade costs on intra-GPN trade. Under this customs regime, firms are granted duty exemptions on imported raw materials and other inputs as long as they are used solely for export purposes. As a result, the data set provides information on trade among three sequential nodes of a vertically specialized global supply chain: the location of input production, the location of processing (in China), and the location of further consumption. This makes it possible to examine the role of both trade costs related to the import of inputs (*upstream trade costs*) and trade costs related to the export of final goods (*downstream trade costs*) on intra-GPN trade.

The rest of this chapter is organized as follows. In the next section, we discuss the key forces driving the vertical specialization process. In the following section, we analyze the role that both upstream and downstream trade costs play in China's processing trade. In the subsequent section, we investigate whether rising oil prices have rendered intra-GPN trade more sensitive to distance. The next section analyzes the role that GPNs played in the great export collapse that occurred during the recent global recession. The final section concludes.

Drivers in the Spread of GPNs

Reductions in trade costs are generally considered the key driving force behind the vertical specialization process. Three developments in the past few decades have been particularly important in decreasing trade costs within GPNs. First, the modularization of production in many industries has made it easier for firms to slice up their value chain into separable production stages, thus reducing transaction costs. Second, technological innovations in communication and transportation have improved the efficiency of coordinating geographically dispersed production stages. Third, liberalization policy reforms in home and host countries have considerably reduced barriers to trade and investment.

A minimum prerequisite for vertical specialization is the distinct separability of production stages. And in the past few decades, the modularization of products has significantly increased the separability of production (Sturgeon 2002; Gereffi, Humphrey, and Sturgeon 2005; Van Assche 2008). Modularity refers to a technological property of a product that describes how different components of a final good interact with one another. When a product is nonmodular, components need to be specifically adjusted to one another, and it is thus difficult to locate their production in different places. In contrast, modular products consist of loosely coupled components that interact with one another through well-defined and codified architectural standards. Advances in information technology in recent decades have enabled firms to standardize the interfaces between components more easily, thus allowing for production separability.

At the same time, technological advances have also driven vertical specialization through reduced communication and transportation costs. In the past few decades, significantly cheaper communication technologies have become available (for example, international telephone service, fax machines, and the Internet). These reductions in communication costs have made it easier for firms to coordinate, manage, and monitor production activities in different locations. Furthermore, global transportation costs for distance and time-sensitive goods have declined (Hummels 2007, 2009; Behar and Venables 2010), benefiting the international trade of goods produced in GPNs.

A final driver of vertical specialization has been the continued political efforts by governments to eliminate tariffs and nontariff barriers. Multilateral trade negotiations under the auspices of the General Agreement on Tariffs and Trade and the World Trade Organization have helped reduce average tariffs for manufacturing products to under 5 percent and have phased out quantitative restrictions.

Mapping Global Production Networks: China's Processing Trade Regime

While trade costs reductions are generally accepted as the main driver of vertical specialization, empirical evidence on the sensitivity of intra-GPN trade to trade costs remains remarkably scant.[1] We exploit a unique data set that allows us to overcome some of the shortcomings in the existing literature. Specifically, we use a data set collected by the General Administration of Customs of the People's Republic of China on China's processing trade regime for the period 1988–2008. Under this regime, firms are granted duty exemptions on imported raw materials and other inputs as long as they are used solely for export purposes. As a result, the data set provides a unique mapping of the source countries of processing imports and the destination countries of processed exports for each Chinese processing location. This information makes it possible to examine the role of both trade costs related to the import of inputs (upstream trade costs) and trade costs related to the export of final goods (downstream trade costs) on trade within GPNs. Such mapping of GPNs cannot be conducted with regular trade data, since imports are not necessarily used solely for export purposes but can also be consumed domestically.

China's processing trade regime was set up in the mid-1980s to attract foreign direct investment and promote exports. Largely ignored by many scholars, the regime reached farther than similar systems introduced in other East Asian countries. China's concessionary provisions applied to its entire territory, unlike in neighboring countries where concessions were geographically limited to export processing zones (Naughton 2006). As a result, China's processing trade regime has played an important role in its overall trade performance. Indeed, between 1988 and 2008, the share of processing exports (that is, exports conducted under the processing regime) in China's total exports rose from 30 percent to 51 percent, while the share of processing imports in total imports increased from 27 percent to 38 percent (figure 21.1). The rest of this section discusses three stylized facts that suggest that both upstream and downstream trade costs play an important role in China's processing trade.

Figure 21.1. Processing Trade in China as a Share of Total Trade, 1988–2008

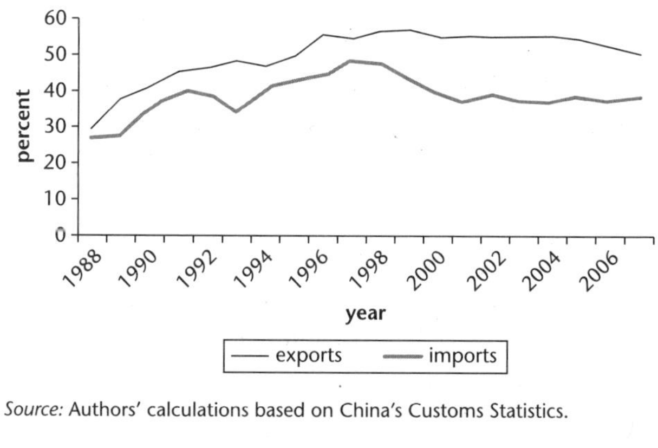

Source: Authors' calculations based on China's Customs Statistics.

Figure 21.2. Domestic and Foreign Content as a Share of China's Processing and Nonprocessing Exports, 2006

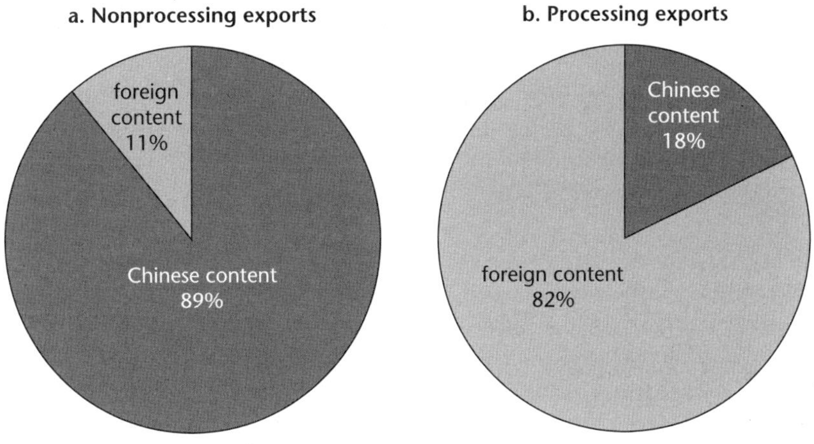

Source: Koopman, Wang, and Wei 2008.

First, China's processing exports rely heavily on foreign inputs, with a relatively low share of the value made in China. According to a recent estimate by Koopman, Wang, and Wei (2008), only 18 percent of the value of China's processing exports is produced in China, while the remaining 82 percent consists of the value of imported processing inputs (figure 21.2). In comparison, the domestic content share of China's nonprocessing exports is 88.7 percent, meaning that imported inputs represent only 11.3 percent of the export value.

Second, the average distance traveled by processing imports (import distance) is shorter than the average distance traveled by processing exports (export distance). As shown in figure 21.3, 75.1 percent of China's processing imports originated from within East Asia in 2008.[2] In contrast, Canada, the EU-19,[3] and the United States together accounted for less than 19 percent of processing imports in 2008. This asymmetric sourcing pattern of processing inputs has become more pronounced over time. Between 1988 and 2008, the share of processing imports originating from China's most important East Asian trading partners rose from 59.6 percent to 75.1 percent, while the share of processing imports originating from non-Asian countries in the Organisation for Economic Co-operation and Development (OECD) decreased from 37.7 percent to 18.7 percent.

Conversely, most processing exports were destined for non-Asian OECD countries from 1988 to 2008 (except for an interlude between 1992 and 1997). As shown in figure 21.4, the share of processing exports destined for non-Asian OECD countries rose from 54.7 percent in 1997 to 59.4 percent in 2008. In contrast, the share of processing exports destined for the East Asian region

Figure 21.3. Share of China's Processing Imports by Region of Origin, 1988–2008

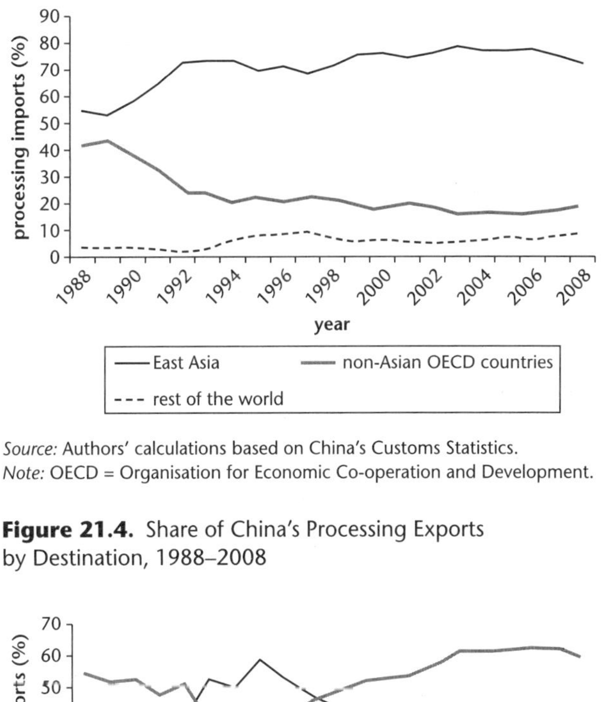

Source: Authors' calculations based on China's Customs Statistics.
Note: OECD = Organisation for Economic Co-operation and Development.

Figure 21.4. Share of China's Processing Exports by Destination, 1988–2008

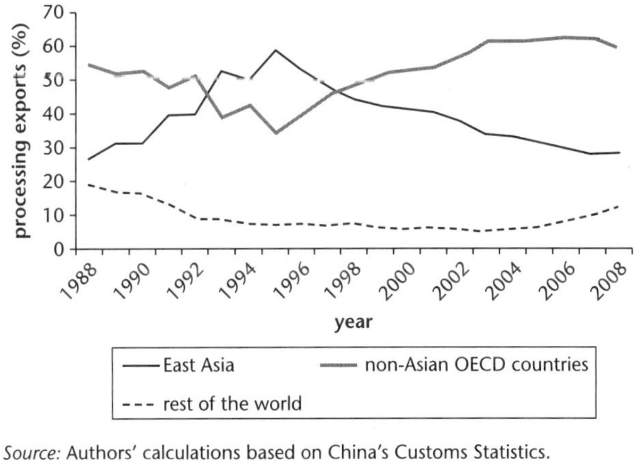

Source: Authors' calculations based on China's Customs Statistics.

declined from 36.0 percent to 28.3 percent during the same period.

This unbalanced processing trade pattern is generally attributed to the reorganization of GPNs in East Asia (Yoshida and Ito 2006; Gaulier, Lemoine, and Ünal-Kesenci 2007; Haddad 2007). With rising costs in Japan and the newly industrialized economies—Hong Kong SAR, China; the Republic of Korea; Singapore; and Taiwan, China—East Asian firms are increasingly using China as a lower-cost export platform. Instead of directly exporting their final goods to the Western markets, these firms now export high-value intermediate goods to their processing plants in China and then export them on to the West after assembly. As a result, a triangular trade pattern seems to have emerged in the GPNs in which China relies heavily on processing inputs from East Asia and sends processed goods predominantly to the West.

Moreover, the share of processing imports in China's total imports is greater for imports from East Asian countries than for imports from outside East Asia. Except for Indonesia and Vietnam, more than 35 percent of China's imports from its major East Asian trading partners were processing imports in 2007 (figure 21.5). Almost 40 percent of its imports from Japan and between 40 and 60 percent of its imports from the newly industrialized economies were aimed at supplying inputs for processing industries. This share is significantly higher than for Western countries. The share of processing imports in China's total imports from the EU-19, Canada, and the United States amounted to 15.4 percent, 17.6 percent, and 25.0 percent, respectively.

At the same time, processing exports represent a greater proportion of China's total exports to developed countries than to its East Asian neighbors. More than 50 percent of the exports that China sends to the EU-19, Japan, and the United States are processing exports (figure 21.6). The share of processing exports is significantly lower for most developing East Asian countries.

Third, this spatial pattern is not consistent across processing locations. In a cross-section of 29 Chinese provinces, the weighted average distance traveled by processing imports (import distance) has been negatively correlated to the weighted average distance traveled by processing exports (export distance) for most years between 1995 to 2008 (Ma, Van Assche, and Hong 2009). In other words, locations in China that import their processing inputs from nearby tend to export their processed goods far away and vice versa.

Our econometric analysis provides further empirical support that China's processing trade depends heavily on both upstream and downstream trade costs.[4] Specifically, we find that both import and export distance affect processing exports negatively. Furthermore, we show that processing exports to East Asian countries are more sensitive to export distance and less sensitive to import distance than processing exports to non-Asian OECD countries. As a result, for firms in advanced East Asian countries, the key distance factor that determines China's attractiveness as a processing location is its vicinity to Eastern input suppliers, that is, import distance. As import distance increases, China becomes less attractive as a location for processing activities, and therefore the volume of processed exports from China decreases. Conversely, for firms in Europe and North America, the critical determinant of China's attractiveness as a processing location is its proximity to the East Asian market, that is, export distance. As export distance increases, China becomes less attractive as a location for processing activities.

Figure 21.5. Processing Imports as a Share of China's Total Imports by Economy of Origin, 2007

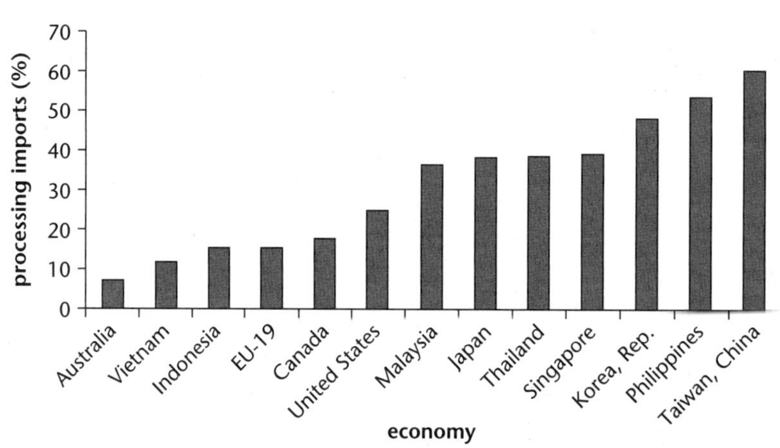

Source: Authors' calculations based on China's Customs Statistics.

Figure 21.6. Processing Exports as a Share of China's Total Exports by Destination Economy, 2007

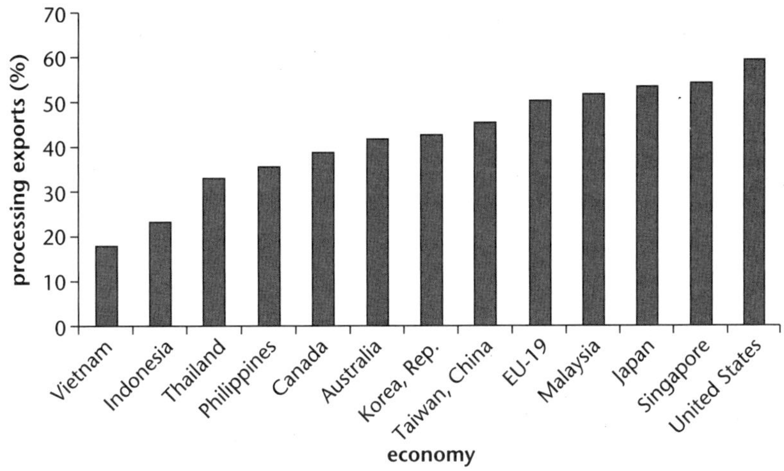

Source: Authors' calculations based on China's Customs Statistics.

Peak Oil and Intra-GPN Trade

Recent macroeconomic events may have reversed the declining trend in trade costs, thus threatening to undo some vertical specialization and making GPNs more local. Among them, the era of cheap and plentiful oil seems to be drawing to a close, thus leading to increases in transportation costs (Rubin and Tal 2008; Rubin 2009).

Just how vulnerable, then, are GPNs to such changes in trade costs? Will GPNs get smaller if oil prices continue to rise in the postcrisis era? In this section, we provide new insights into these questions by investigating whether rising oil prices have rendered China's processing trade more sensitive to distance.

As discussed in chapter 20 of this volume, oil prices have risen dramatically in the past decade. While crude oil prices were relatively stable and had even declined over the period 1980–99, they grew at an annualized rate of 20.6 percent over the period 1999–2008 (figure 21.7). Oil prices retreated during the global recession of 2008–09, but this decline is likely a temporary phenomenon. As the global economy comes out of the recession, oil prices are expected to return to and even exceed precrisis levels. Oil experts generally agree that peak oil will be reached before 2015 (De Almeida and Silva 2009).[5] When this moment occurs, the gap between oil production and demand is expected to increase. As a consequence, the price of oil is expected to rise significantly and become more volatile.

Rubin and Tal (2008) argue that rising oil prices are likely to lead to significant hikes in international transportation charges and thus reverse the trend of vertical specialization. They highlight the fact that, hand in hand with the oil price hikes, the cost of shipping a standard 40-foot container from Shanghai to the U.S. eastern seaboard has risen from US$3,000 in 2000 to US$8,000 in 2008. Other studies, however, have estimated that the sensitivity of shipping freight rates to oil prices remains relatively low, thus limiting the threat that rising oil prices will make GPNs significantly smaller. Hummels (2007) and UNCTAD (2010) estimate an elasticity of maritime cargo costs with respect to fuel prices of between 0.20 and 0.40. Mirza and Zitouna (2009) and OECD (forthcoming) estimate an even lower elasticity of freight rates to oil prices ranging from 0.02 to 0.15.

To determine if rising oil prices have made intra-GPN trade more sensitive to distance, we have taken advantage of the panel data structure of the Chinese processing trade

Figure 21.7. Average Prices for Crude Oil, 1980–2009

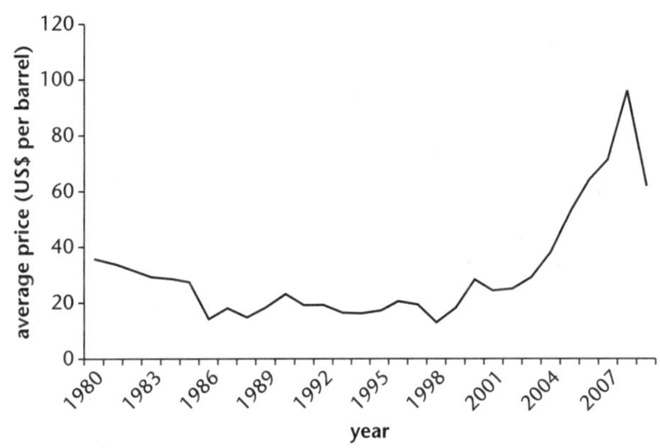

Source: International Financial Statistics (database), International Monetary Fund, http://www.imfstatistics.org.

data.[6] According to our results for 1988–2008, China's processing exports have become more sensitive to both import and export distance in times of rising oil prices but not more sensitive to internal distance (between a processing location and the nearest large seaport). We also find that processing exports are more sensitive to oil price movements than nonprocessing exports. Specifically, an increase in oil prices tends to reduce the share of processing exports in total exports, especially when destined for far away countries. These results are in line with Yi's (2003) prediction that intra-GPN trade is especially sensitive to changes in trade costs.

Intra-GPN Trade and the Global Recession

What has been the impact of the global recession on intra-GPN trade flows? This question has become particularly relevant in light of the collapse of trade during the crisis, which was significantly larger than the drop in world gross domestic product (GDP). A number of scholars have attributed the disproportionate trade collapse to vertical specialization. Barry Eichengreen, for example, has stated that "the most important factor is probably the growth of global supply chains, which has magnified the impact of declining final demand on trade" (International Economy 2009). Bems, Johnson, and Yi (2009) argue that "international supply chains are a leading contender for explaining why the great collapse was so great."

The channels through which vertical specialization exacerbated the trade collapse, however, have become the source of a heated debate. Using a simple Barbie doll example, O'Rourke (2009) demonstrated that vertical specialization does not automatically explain why the fall in world trade overshot the drop in world GDP. The fact that components of the Barbie doll cross borders multiple times to produce a final doll does not necessarily imply that a drop in Barbie sales should lead to a disproportionate drop in trade. To explain the role of vertical specialization in the trade collapse, scholars have therefore focused on three additional effects: a compositional effect, a trade cost effect, and a bullwhip effect. The rest of this section discusses evidence for the existence of these three channels in China's trade during the global recession.

The Compositional Effect

A number of studies have argued that vertical specialization worsened the trade collapse through a compositional effect (Francois and Woerz 2009; Levchenko, Lewis, and Tesar 2009; Eaton et al. 2010). Because vertical specialization has taken place primarily in the durable goods sectors,[7] trade and especially intra-GPN trade have become more intensive in durable goods than overall GDP. This compositional change has made trade more sensitive to fluctuations in business cycles.[8] In times of recession, households and companies tend to delay purchases of durable goods—not only because tightening budget constraints render high-ticket goods unaffordable for some but also because consumers and firms want to postpone their purchases until they know with more certainty whether and when the economic climate will improve. Just as an economic crisis leads to a disproportionate drop in the demand for durable goods, so the compositional effect can explain the lopsided collapse in trade compared to GDP.

We find evidence of a compositional effect in China's exports during the global recession. Specifically, the sectors that contributed most to the export collapse in China are those in which vertical specialization is more prevalent.[9] Figure 21.8 shows that vertical specialization in China is more common in the higher-technology categories than in the lower-technology categories.[10] In 2007, processing exports accounted for 84.9 percent of high-technology exports; 45.6 percent of medium-high-technology exports; 26.6 percent of medium-low-technology exports; and 29.8 percent of low-technology exports.

The higher-technology categories are also the industries that contributed most to the drop in China's exports during the global recession. High-technology exports contributed to 37.6 percent of the collapse in exports; medium-high-technology exports contributed to 25.4 percent; medium-low-technology exports contributed to 16.0 percent; low-technology exports contributed to 10.9 percent; and other nonmanufacturing exports contributed to 10.1 percent (table 21.1).

Figure 21.8. Processing Exports as a Share of China's Total Exports by Technology Level, 1992–2007

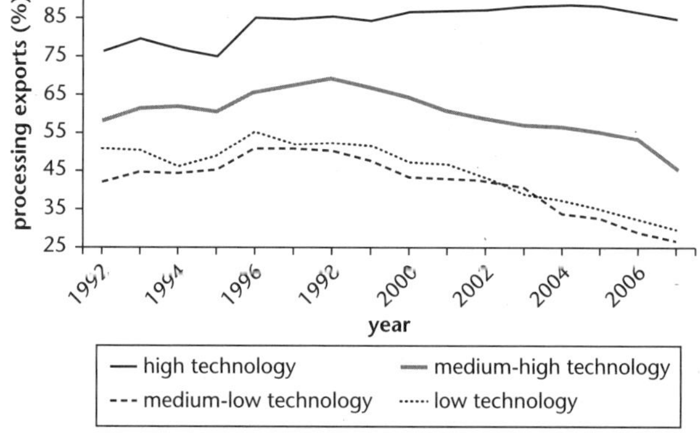

Source: Authors' calculations, based on China's Customs Statistics.

Table 21.1. Breakdown of China's Exports by Level of Technology, 2008–09

Category	Exports value (US$, billions) Q1 2008	Exports value (US$, billions) Q1 2009	Growth rate, Q1 2008–Q1 2009 (%)	Share of exports (%) Q1 2008	Share of exports (%) Q1 2009	Contribution to total export growth, Q1 2008–Q1 2009 (%)
High technology	94.6	71.8	–24.1	31.1	29.5	37.6
Medium-high technology	70.0	54.6	–22.0	23.0	22.5	25.4
Medium-low technology	44.9	35.2	–21.6	14.8	14.5	16.0
Low technology	73.8	67.2	–8.9	24.3	27.6	10.9
Other	20.5	14.4	–29.8	6.7	5.9	10.1
Total	303.8	243.2	–19.9	100.0	100.0	100.0

Source: Authors' calculations based on China's Customs Statistics Data.
Note: Q = quarter.

The Trade Cost Effect

A second set of studies argues that vertical specialization intensified the trade collapse through rising trade costs associated with evaporating credit, increasing nontariff barriers, and home bias in government stimulus plans (Jacks, Meissner, and Novy 2009; Yi 2009). Jacks, Meissner, and Novy (2009) estimate that trade costs increased by 11 percent on average between the second quarter of 2008 and the first quarter of 2009. As the previous section showed, intra-GPN trade is especially sensitive to changes in trade costs (Yi 2003), which can explain the greater fall in trade than in GDP.

Our analysis finds evidence of a trade cost effect in China's exports during the global recession. Controlling for compositional effects, we find that the share of China's processing exports in total exports at the eight-digit level of the Harmonized System (HS) significantly declined from the first quarter of 2008 to the first quarter of 2009 (table 21.2). This finding confirms that processing exports consistently dropped more than nonprocessing exports during the global recession. This result is in line with the trade cost effect and the findings of the previous section, given that intra-GPN trade should be more sensitive to trade costs than regular trade.

Table 21.2. China's Processing Exports as a Share of Total Exports, HS Eight-Digit Level, Quarter 1, 2008, and Quarter 1, 2009

Variables	Number of observations	Mean	Standard error
Share of processing exports in total exports, Q1 2008	4,760	0.31	0.004
Share of processing exports in total exports, Q1 2009	4,760	0.29	0.004
Difference	9,520	0.020***	0.003

Source: Authors' calculations based on China's Customs Statistics Data.
Note: Q = quarter.
* = significant at 10 percent; ** = significant at 5 percent;
*** = significant at 1 percent.

The Bullwhip Effect

A final explanation of how global supply chains intensified the trade collapse is the bullwhip effect (Escaith and Gonguet 2009; Escaith, Lindenberg, and Miroudot 2010; Ma and Van Assche 2010). The bullwhip effect is one of the most researched and documented symptoms in the field of supply chain management (Lee, Padmanabhan, and Wang 1997; Cachon, Randall, and Schmidt 2007). In the bullwhip effect, when a downstream firm is confronted with a drop in demand for its final products, its first reaction is to run down its inventories. Thus, a slump in downstream activities translates into a larger reduction in the demand for upstream inputs.[11] Because fluctuations in final demand become amplified as one moves upstream along the supply chain, this effect provides an alternative explanation of the magnified fall in trade compared to GDP.

Our analysis finds evidence of a bullwhip effect in intra-GPN trade during the global recession. The percentage drop in China's processing imports was larger than that of processing exports in the first quarter of 2009 compared to a year earlier.[12] China's processing exports dropped 23.7 percent, while processing imports declined 36.2 percent. Moreover, disaggregating the analysis at the industry level provides further evidence of a bullwhip effect: the percentage change in processing *imports* was more pronounced than the percentage change in processing *exports* in 15 out of 20 industries (table 21.3).

The existence of a bullwhip effect in China's processing trade helps at least partially to explain the resilience of its economy when faced with the great trade collapse (Ma and Van Assche 2009). When the crisis hit China in the second half of 2008, its economy was able to rapidly pass on the negative export demand shock to its input suppliers

Table 21.3. Changes in China's Processing Trade by Industry, Quarter 1, 2008–Quarter 1, 2009

	Processing exports (US$, billions)		Growth in processing exports, Q1 2008–Q1 2009 (%)	Processing imports (US$, billions)		Growth of processing imports, Q1 2008–Q1 2009 (%)	Bullwhip effect
	Q1 2008	Q1 2009		Q1 2008	Q1 2009		
High technology	78.32	57.23	–26.9	45.88	29.03	–36.6	Yes
Aircraft	0.21	0.23	8.6	0.11	0.09	–17.8	No
Pharmaceuticals	0.37	0.36	–3.3	0.08	0.09	24.0	No
Office and computing machinery	30.70	23.80	–22.4	3.59	2.43	–32.5	Yes
Radio, TV and communications equipment	38.50	27.80	–27.7	29.70	20.20	–31.9	Yes
Medical, precision, and optical instruments	8.54	5.05	–40.9	12.40	6.22	–49.8	Yes
Medium-high technology	34.01	24.90	–26.9	13.59	9.79	–27.9	Yes
Electrical machinery	10.50	7.43	–29.4	6.27	4.34	–30.7	Yes
Motor vehicles	3.37	1.37	–59.4	0.26	0.17	–35.0	No
Chemicals	2.47	2.01	–18.4	2.10	1.41	–32.9	Yes
Other transport equipment	0.87	0.79	–9.5	0.07	0.06	–13.1	Yes
Machinery and equipment	16.80	13.30	–21.0	4.89	3.81	–22.0	Yes
Medium-low technology	12.67	12.04	–5.1	10.12	5.69	–43.8	Yes
Shipbuilding and repairing	3.36	5.30	57.5	0.01	0.04	377.6	Yes
Rubber and plastic products	4.57	3.59	–21.5	1.59	1.09	–31.5	Yes
Petroleum products	0.05	0.04	–14.7	0.04	0.18	395.9	No
Nonmetallic mineral products	0.71	0.49	–31.1	0.66	0.37	–44.5	Yes
Metal products	3.98	2.62	–34.3	7.82	4.01	–48.7	Yes
Low technology	22.69	19.38	–14.6	6.57	4.69	–28.7	Yes
Manufacturing	8.17	6.79	–16.9	0.73	0.52	–27.7	Yes
Paper and paper products	1.38	0.98	–29.0	1.28	0.72	–44.0	Yes
Printing and publishing	0.32	0.32	–1.3	0.06	0.05	–13.3	Yes
Food, beverages, and tobacco	1.32	1.35	2.5	0.71	0.50	–29.5	No
Textiles, apparel, and leather	11.50	9.94	–13.5	3.80	2.90	–23.8	Yes
Other	4.55	2.63	–42.3	11.80	6.85	–41.8	No
Total	152.24	116.18	–23.7	87.95	56.06	–36.2	Yes

Source: Authors' calculations based on China's Customs Statistics.
Note: Q = quarter.

through a reduction in demand for processing inputs. Indeed, since the drop in imports was larger than the drop in exports in the first quarter of 2009 compared to a year earlier, China's net exports actually increased.

Those worst hit by the bullwhip effect in China's processing trade were its East Asian neighbors. As shown in figure 21.9, the global recession has affected most severely China's imports from countries that more intensively supply processing inputs to China (that is, its East Asian neighbors). With the exception of Indonesia and Vietnam, more than 40 percent of China's imports from its major East Asian trading partners in 2006 were processing imports, which is a

Figure 21.9. China's Processing Imports, 2008, versus China's Import Growth by Economy of Origin, Quarter 1, 2008–Quarter 1, 2009

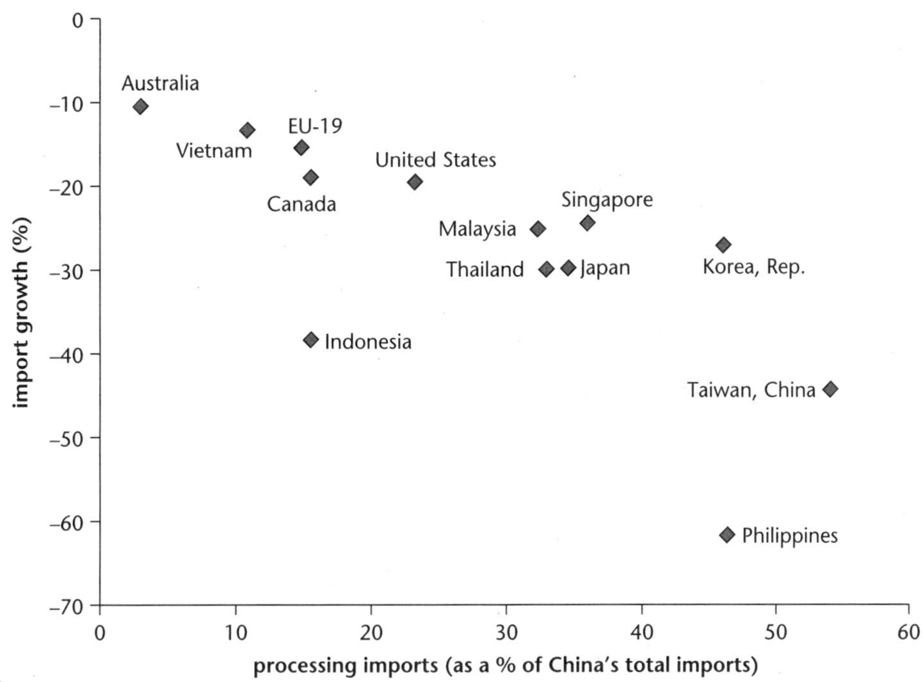

Source: Authors' calculations based on China's Customs Statistics.

significantly higher share than for countries outside of East Asia. During the recent global economic crisis, these East Asian countries witnessed a larger decline in imports than other countries. Compared to the previous year, China's imports from its major East Asian trading partners all declined between 25 percent and 61 percent in the first quarter of 2009. In contrast, China's imports from its major non-Asian trading partners fell less than 20 percent.

In sum, we find supporting evidence that intra-GPN trade has been especially vulnerable to the global recession. It has exacerbated the great trade collapse through three channels: a compositional effect, a trade cost effect, and a bullwhip effect. First, in line with the compositional effect, we find that the sectors that contributed most to the collapse of Chinese exports are those in which processing trade is more prevalent. Second, we show that, within industries, processing exports consistently dropped more than nonprocessing exports during the global recession. This finding is in line with the trade cost effect since intra-GPN trade should be more sensitive to trade costs than regular trade. Third, in line with the bullwhip effect, we show that in virtually all industries, the drop in demand for China's processing exports led to a bigger drop in processing imports.

The larger sensitivity of intra-GPN trade to business cycle movements of course also suggests that intra-GPN trade is likely to rebound rapidly as the global economy continues to gather strength. Full recovery of intra-GPN trade, however, will depend on the ability of policy makers to keep protectionism (and the related trade cost effect) in check.

Conclusion

In this chapter, we have relied on data from China's processing trade regime to analyze the impact of trade costs on intra-GPN trade. We found that intra-GPN trade differs from regular trade in that it depends not only on downstream trade costs but also on upstream trade costs and the interaction of both. Moreover, we showed that intra-GPN trade is more sensitive to changes in trade costs than regular trade. Specifically, intra-GPN trade is more sensitive to oil price movements, trade policy changes, and business cycle fluctuations than regular trade. These results suggest that the resilience of vertical specialization and GPNs in the postcrisis era will critically depend on our ability to keep trade costs in check.

Notes

1. See the background paper by Ma and Van Assche (2010) for further details.
2. The source and destination countries of Chinese processing trade are adjusted for Hong Kong re-exports. See Ma and Van Assche (2010) for further details on how we address this in the empirical analysis.

3. The EU-19 include all European Union countries prior to the accession of the 10 candidate countries on May 1, 2004, plus the four Eastern European member countries of the Organisation for Economic Co-operation and Development, namely, the Czech Republic, Hungary, Poland, and the Slovak Republic.

4. See Ma and Van Assche (2010) for full details.

5. Peak oil refers to the attainment of the maximum conventional oil output (that is, excluding heavy oil from tar sands, oil shale, and the like), expressed as millions of barrels of crude oil extracted per day (Deffeyes 2001).

6. See Ma and Van Assche (2010) for further details on hypotheses and construction of the model.

7. For example, consumer electronics, automobile and transport equipment, office equipment, and computers.

8. Engel and Wang (2008) found that U.S. durable goods imports are more sensitive to business cycles than nondurable goods imports.

9. In line with this result, Aziz and Li (2008) demonstrate that China's increasing specialization in electronics exports has led to an overall rise in the income elasticity of China's exports.

10. We use the OECD's technology classification (Hatzichronoglou 1997) to disaggregate China's exports into four categories: high-technology exports, medium-high-technology exports, medium-low-technology exports, and low-technology exports.

11. Mason-Jones and Towill (2000) provide the following explanation of a bullwhip effect: "If demand for products is transmitted along a series of inventories using stock control ordering, then the demand variation will increase with each transfer."

12. In the first and second quarter of 2009, China's GDP expanded at an annualized rate of 6.1 percent and 7.9 percent, respectively.

Bibliography

Aziz, J., and X. Li. 2008. "China's Changing Trade Elasticities." *China and the World Economy* 16 (3): 1–21.

Behar, A., and A. Venables. 2010. "Transport Costs and International Trade." In *Handbook of Transport Economics,* ed. A. de Palma, R. Lindsey, E. Quinet, and R. Vickerman. Cheltenham, U.K.: Edward Elgar.

Bems, R., R. Johnson, and K.-M. Yi. 2009. "The Role of Vertical Linkages in the Propagation of the Global Downturn of 2008." Unpublished. http://www.imf.org/external/np/res/seminars/2010/paris/pdf/keymu.pdf.

Cachon, G., T. Randall, and G. Schmidt. 2007. "In Search of the Bullwhip Effect." *Manufacturing and Service Operations Management* 9 (4): 457–79.

De Almeida, P., and P. Silva. 2009. "The Peak Oil Production: Timings and Market Recognition." *Energy Policy* 37: 1276–76.

Deffeyes, K. 2001. *Hubbert's Peak: The Impending World Oil Shortage.* Princeton, NJ: Princeton University Press.

Desai, M. 2009. "The Decentering of the Global Firm." *World Economy* 32 (9): 1271–90.

Eaton, J., S. Kortum, B. Neiman, and J. Romalis. 2010. "Trade and the Global Recession." Research Series 201010–196, National Bank of Belgium, Brussels.

Egger, P. 2008. "On the Role of Distance for Bilateral Trade." *World Economy* 31 (5): 653–62.

Ekholm, K., R. Forslid, and J. Markusen. 2007. "Export-platform Foreign Direct Investment." *Journal of the European Economic Association* 5 (4): 776–95.

Engel, C., and J. Wang. 2008. "International Trade in Durable Goods: Understanding Volatility, Cyclicality and Elasticities." Working Paper 13814, National Bureau of Economic Research, Cambridge, MA.

Escaith, H., and F. Gonguet. 2009. "International Trade and Real Transmission Channels of Financial Shocks in Globalized Production Networks." Staff Working Paper ERSD-2009-06, World Trade Organization, Geneva.

Escaith, H., N. Lindenberg, and S. Miroudot. 2010. "International Supply Chains and Trade Elasticity in Times of Global Crisis." Staff Working Paper ERSD-2010-08, World Trade Organization, Geneva.

Evans, C. and J. Harrigan. 2005. "Distance, Time, and Specialization: Lean retailing in General Equilibrium." *American Economic Review* 95 (1): 292–313.

Francois, J., and J. Woerz. 2009. "The Big Drop: Trade and the Great Recession." VoxEU.org. May 2. http://www.voxeu.org/index.php?q=node/3527.

Gaulier, G., F. Lemoine, and D. Ünal-Kesenci. 2007. "China's Integration in East Asia: Production Sharing, FDI and High-technology Trade." *Economic Change and Restructuring* 40: 27–63.

Gereffi, G., J. Humphrey, and T. Sturgeon. 2005. "The Governance of the Global Value Chains." *Review of International Political Economy* 12 (1): 78–104.

Grossman, G., E. Helpman, and A. Szeidl. 2006. "Optimal Integration Strategies for the Multinational Firm." *Journal of International Economics* 70: 216–38.

Haddad, M. 2007. "Trade Integration in East Asia: The Role of China and Production Networks." Policy Research Working Paper 4160, World Bank, Washington, DC.

Hanson, G., R. Mataloni, and M. Slaughter. 2005. "Vertical Production Networks in Multinational Firms." *Review of Economics and Statistics* 87 (4): 664–78.

Harrigan, J., and A. Venables. 2006. "Timeliness and Agglomeration." *Journal of Urban Economics* 59: 300–316.

Hatzichronoglou, T. 1997. "Revision of the High-Technology Sector and Product Classification." Science, Technology and Industry Working Papers 1997/2, Organisation for Economic Co-operation and Development, Paris.

Helpman, E. 2006. "Trade, FDI, and the Organization of Firms." *Journal of Economic Literature* 44 (3): 589–630.

Hummels, D. 2007. "Transportation Costs and International Trade in the Second Era of Globalization." *Journal of Economic Perspectives* 21 (3): 131–54.

———. 2009. Globalization and Freight Transport Costs in Maritime Shipping and Aviation. Paper 2009-3, International Transport Forum, Paris.

International Economy. 2009. "Collapse in World Trade: A Symposium of Views." *International Economy.* Spring: 28–38.

Jacks, D., C. Meissner, and D. Novy. 2009. "The Role of Trade Costs in the Great Trade Collapse." VoxEU.org. November 27. http://www.voxeu.org/index.php?q=node/4300.

Koopman, R., Z. Wang, and S.-J. Wei. 2008. "How Much of Chinese Exports Is Really Made in China? Assessing Domestic Value-added When Processing Trade Is Pervasive." Working Paper 14109, National Bureau of Economic Research, Cambridge, MA.

Lee, H., S. Padmanabhan, and S. Wang. 1997. "Information Distortion in a Supply Chain: The Bullwhip Effect." *Management Science* 43 (4): 546–58.

Levchenko, A., L. Lewis, and L. Tesar. 2009. "The Collapse of U.S. Trade: In Search of the Smoking Gun." VoxEU.org. November 27. http://www.voxeu.org/index.php?q=node/4280.

Ma, A., and A. Van Assche. 2009. "China's Trade in Crisis." *AIB Insights* 9 (2): 11–15.

———. 2010. "The Role of Trade Costs in Global Production Networks." Policy Research Working Paper 5490, World Bank, Washington, DC.

Ma, A., A. Van Assche, and C. Hong. 2009. "Global Production Networks and China's Processing Trade." *Journal of Asian Economics* 20 (6): 640–54.

Mason-Jones, R., and D. Towill. 2000. "Coping with Uncertainty: Reducing 'Bullwhip' Behavior in Global Supply Chains." *Supply Chain Forum* 1: 40–45.

Mirza, D., and H. Zitouna. 2009. "Oil Prices, Geography and Endogenous Regionalism: Too Much Ado about (Almost) Nothing." Working Paper 2009-26, Centre d'Etudes Prospectives et d'Informations Internationales (CEPII), Paris.

Naughton, B. 2006. "China's Emergence and Prospects as a Trading Nation." *Brookings Papers on Economic Activity* 2: 273–313.

OECD (Organisation for Economic Co-operation and Development). Forthcoming. "Determinants of Maritime Transport Costs." Mimeo.

O'Rourke, K. 2009. "Collapsing Trade in a Barbie World." *The Irish Economy* (blog). June 18. http://www.irisheconomy.ie/index.php/2009/06/18/collapsing-trade-in-a-barbie-world/.

Rubin, J. 2009. *Why Your World Is Going to Get a Whole Lot Smaller: Oil and the End of Globalization.* New York: Random House.

Rubin, J., and B. Tal. 2008. "Will Soaring Transport Costs Reverse Globalization?" *CIBC World Markets.* http://research.cibcwm.com/economic_public/download/smay08.pdf.

Spencer, B. 2005. "International Outsourcing and Incomplete Contracts." *Canadian Journal of Economics* 38: 1107–35.

Sturgeon, T. 2002. "Modular Production Networks: A New American Model of Industrial Organization." *Industrial and Corporate Change* 11 (3): 451–96.

UNCTAD (United Nations Conference on Trade and Development). 2010. "Oil Prices and Maritime Freight Rates: An Empirical Investigation." Geneva: United Nations Conference on Trade and Development.

Van Assche, A. 2008. "Modularity and the Organization of International Production." *Japan and the World Economy* 20: 353–68.

Yeaple, S. 2003. "The Complex Integration Strategies of Multinationals and Cross Country Dependencies in the Structure of Foreign Direct Investment." *Journal of International Economics* 60: 293–314.

Yi, K.-M. 2003. "Can Vertical Specialization Explain the Growth of World Trade?" *Journal of Political Economy* 111: 52–102.

———. 2009. "The Collapse of Global Trade: The Role of Vertical Specialization." In *The Collapse of Global Trade, Murky Protectionism, and the Crisis: Recommendations for the G20,* ed. R. Baldwin and S. Evenett. London: VoxEU.

Yoshida, Y., and H. Ito. 2006. "How Do the Asian Economies Compete with Japan in the U.S. Market? Is China Exceptional? A triangular Trade Approach." *Asia Pacific Business Review* 12 (3): 285–307.

22

THE 2008–09 RECESSION: IMPLICATIONS FOR INTERNATIONAL LABOR MIGRATION

Philip Martin

Demographic and economic inequalities between countries, combined with revolutions in communications, transportation, and rights, encourage and enable people to cross national borders in search of economic opportunity. In recent decades, these factors have contributed to a dramatic increase in international migration flows. Between 1985 and 2010, the global stock of migrants almost doubled, from 111 million to 214 million. The increase was concentrated in industrial countries, where the stock of migrants rose from 50 million to 128 million. Thus, the share of the world's migrants in industrial countries rose from 48 percent to 60 percent.[1]

The demand for migrant labor is expected to continue to expand in the coming decades. Most of this demand for migrants will come from the industrial countries, but some of the sharpest increases in the demand are expected to be in middle-income developing countries such as Brazil, Costa Rica, Libya, Malaysia, South Africa, and Thailand.

While migration flows are expected to increase, the 2008–09 global recession raises questions about future migrant patterns. Historical precedent suggests that the recent recession may alter international labor migration patterns. The recession that followed oil price hikes in 1973–74 stopped guest worker recruitment in Europe but opened new opportunities for migrant workers in the oil-exporting nations, especially in the member countries of the Gulf Cooperation Council. The 1981–82 recession accelerated labor-saving changes in industrial country manufacturing sectors, prompting European countries such as France and Germany to offer departure bonuses to jobless migrants. Moreover, the 1997–98 Asian financial crisis was followed by a relatively quick resumption of economic and job growth, with more migrant workers moving within Asia than before the crisis.

What, then, are the implications of increased migration from lower- to higher-wage countries for the global economy? The *Global Economic Prospects* report (World Bank 2005) estimated that increasing the number of developing-country migrant workers in industrial countries by 50 percent could increase global economic output by US$356 billion or 0.6 percent of global gross domestic product (GDP). This number is more than the estimated gains from reducing trade restrictions in the Doha round of negotiations.

While increased migration may benefit the economy as a whole, it is less clear to what extent foreign jobs and remittances can speed development in migrant countries of origin. Remittances to developing countries quadrupled in recent decades, from less than US$60 billion in 1990 to US$338 billion in 2008 (Ratha, Chami, and Fullenkamp 2009). Both remittances and migration increased, raising questions about the relationship between remittances and what might be called stay-at-home development, the type of development that ensures that the children of migrants do not have to follow their parents abroad.

The rest of this chapter discusses recent trends in international labor migration and the factors that will affect migrant flows in the coming decades. The next section discusses recent trends in population growth and migration. The following section analyzes projections of future migrant patterns and the factors that influence these flows. The subsequent section addresses the economic implications of international migration. The final section concludes.

Recent Trends in Population and Migration

This section provides an overview of recent dynamics in world population and migration patterns. Against that background, it then discusses the factors that influence migration flows in the global economy.

Population Trends

Between 1950 and 2000, the world's population rose by almost 150 percent, from 2.5 billion to 6.1 billion (table 22.1).[2] As of 2009, the world's population had reached 6.8 billion, including 1.2 billion residents in more-developed countries and 5.6 billion (or 82 percent) in less-developed countries (UN 2009a).

However, the rate of population growth varied by region and by country. Indeed, while Africa's share of the world's population rose from 9 percent to 13 percent, Europe's share declined from 22 percent to 12 percent. Moreover, the populations of major migrant-sending countries such as Mexico and the Philippines doubled or tripled during this period.

The global population is expected to continue growing until 2050, but at a slower rate and with significant variability. Fertility rates are projected to decline from an average 2.6 children per woman in 2005 to 2.05 by 2050.[3] Based on these estimations, the world's population is expected to reach 9.2 billion by 2050 (UN 2009a).[4] If fertility does not decline to below the replacement level of 2.1 as projected, the global population could approach 11 billion by 2050.

Moreover, significant variability is predicted in population growth across regions and income groups. A quarter of the world's countries are expected to have shrinking populations over the next decade, while another quarter are expected to grow at rates that will double their populations within a half-century (table 22.1). Almost all population growth is projected to occur in what are now considered less-developed countries. The share of global population of more-developed countries is expected to fall from 18 percent in 2009 to 13 percent by 2050. While the populations of Europe and Africa are currently similar in size, there are projected to be three Africans for every European in 2050.

Table 22.1. Percentage of World Population by Continent, 1800–2050

	1800	1950	2000	2050[a]
Africa	11	9	13	20
Asia	65	56	61	59
Europe	21	22	12	7
Latin America and the Caribbean	3	7	9	9
North America	1	7	5	4
Oceania		1	1	1
World (millions)	978	2,535	6,124	9,191

Source: UN 1999, 2009a.
a. Projected.

Recent Trends in International Migration

In 2010, the stock of international migrants was 214 million, meaning that 3 percent of the world's 6.9 billion people were living outside their country of birth.[5] One hundred twenty-eight million of these migrants were living in more-developed countries, making up 10 percent of their 1.2 billion population. The other 86 million were living in less-developed countries, making up less than 2 percent of their 5.7 billion population. The ratio of the share of migrants to the share of population in industrial countries was 3.3, reflecting the fact that industrial countries had 60 percent of the world's migrants and less than 20 percent of the world's people (table 22.2).

By region, immigrants were concentrated in Europe, Asia, and North America in 2010. Europe had the most migrants in absolute terms: Europe's 70 million migrants constituted almost 10 percent of the continent's population.[6] Asia followed with 61 million migrants, who made up 1.5 percent of the Asian population. Almost half of Asia's migrants were in western Asia, that is, the Persian Gulf countries and the Middle East. Last, North America had an immigrant population of 50 million in 2010, including 43 million in the United States and 7.2 million in Canada. One-seventh of North American residents were foreign born.

In contrast, Africa and Latin America had relatively few migrants in 2010 (about 19 million and 7 million, respectively). However, in both continents, a few countries had high shares of migrants in their population (for example, Costa Rica, Côte d'Ivoire, and Libya each had more than 10 percent migrants). Oceania also had a relatively lower number of immigrants in absolute terms (6 million), but it was the region with the highest share of migrants: 17 percent of the residents of Oceania were foreign born.

Six countries had 40 percent of the total migrant population: 43 million in the United States, 12 million in the Russian Federation, 11 million in Germany, and about 7 million each in Canada, France, and Saudi Arabia. Countries with the highest share of migrants in their populations were mostly Gulf oil exporters such as Qatar, where over 85 percent of residents were migrants, and Kuwait and the United Arab Emirates, where 70 percent of residents were migrants. The countries with the lowest shares of migrants in their population include China,

Table 22.2. Population and Migration, 2010

	Population (millions)	Migrants (millions)	Migrants as % of population	% of total population	% of migrants	Ratio of % of migrants to % of total population
World	6,909	214	3	100	100	1.0
More-developed countries	1,237	128	10	18	60	3.3
Less-developed countries	5,671	86	2	82	40	0.5
Africa	1,033	19	2	15	9	0.6
Asia	4,167	61	1	60	29	0.5
Europe	733	70	10	11	33	3.1
Latin America	589	7	1	9	3	0.4
North America	352	50	14	5	23	4.6
Oceania	36	6	17	1	3	5.4

Source: UN 2009b.

Cuba, Indonesia, Peru, and Vietnam, where less than 0.1 percent of residents were migrants.

Shifting patterns can also be seen in migrant destinations by income level. In particular, migration to middle-income developing countries has been on the rise in recent years. The cases of Malaysia and Thailand illustrate several common features of migration trends in fast-growing developing countries. These two countries attract significant numbers of migrants from poorer neighbors and have become increasingly dependent on migrant workers over time. While flows have increased because of the attraction of higher-wage jobs, the governments of both countries acknowledge significant gaps between the goals and the outcomes of their migrant labor policies. Malaysia and Thailand have been taking an ad hoc approach to employer requests for migrant workers and migrant worker policy, wavering between periods of openness and periods of restrictions. However, they are now making efforts to reduce irregular migration and employment in ways that avoid the settlement of immigrants. Indeed, in contrast to many European nations, most Asian nations do not have the goal of not becoming destinations for immigrants.

What Drives Migration?

Two key factors have contributed to the rise in migrant flows in recent decades. First, the revolution in communications, transportation, and rights, has made international migration easier. Cheaper communication has facilitated the growth of "migration infrastructure," a substantive network of private and public intermediaries that helps migrants cross national borders. Intermediaries include employers seeking migrants, public employment services that match local workers with foreign jobs, social networks such as friends and family who are or were abroad, and private recruiters. Recently, the role of direct employer recruitment and public employment services has been declining, as the role of networks and private agents has been increasing.

The transportation revolution has facilitated migration through the declining cost of travel. British migrants unable to pay one-way passage to North American colonies in the 18th century often indentured themselves, signing contracts that obliged them to work for three to six years for whoever met the ship and paid the captain. In contrast, transportation costs today are typically less than US$2,500 to travel anywhere in the world legally and US$1,000 to US$20,000 for unauthorized migration. Most studies suggest faster payback times for migrants today, so that even migrants who pay high recruitment or smuggling fees can usually repay them within two or three years.

The rights revolution has also facilitated migration by increasing the ability of migrants to stay abroad. After World War II, most industrial countries strengthened the constitutional and political rights of residents and granted social or economic rights to individuals in their evolving welfare states without distinguishing between citizens and migrants. As migration increased in the 1990s, policy makers began to roll back socioeconomic rights for migrants in an effort to manage migration.[7] Adjusting rights is widely acknowledged to be a blunt and often inefficient instrument for managing economically motivated migration.

A second factor that can explain the rise in international migration is the persistence of demographic and economic inequalities. Demographic differences between areas have historically driven large-scale migration in some parts of the world. For instance, in 1800, when 21 percent of the world's population was in Europe and 4 percent was in the Americas, millions of Europeans emigrated to the Americas in search of economic opportunity as well as religious and political freedom. Will history repeat itself? Africa is projected to have three times more residents than Europe by 2050. If Africa remains poorer than Europe, the diverging demographic trajectories of these two continents may propel increased migration flows.

Related to demographic differences, economic inequality has also been driving international migration. The 30 high-income countries account for a seventh of the world's people but over 70 percent of the world's economic output in 2008. Average gross national income per capita was US$40,000 a year in high-income countries, 14 times the US$2,800 average in the poorer 170 countries (World Bank 2009).[8] Such income differences encourage (especially, young) people to migrate over national borders.

Future Supply of Migrants

This section looks at the factors influencing the future supply of migrants. After examining baseline projections of the labor force and migration flows, it turns attention to issues that can have a major impact on migration, such as climate change.

Labor Force Projections

The world's economically active population (EAP)[9] is expected to gradually rise from 43 percent in 1980 and 47 percent in 2005 to 48 percent in 2020 (ILO 2008). And if the economically active share of the global population remains at 48 percent between 2020 and 2050, the world's labor force will increase from about 3 billion in 2005 to 4.4 billion in 2050 (table 22.3). However, the rate of labor force growth is projected to be only 4 percent in the decade of 2040–50, a dramatic decrease relative to labor force growth of over 20 percent in the 1980s and 1990s.[10]

In 2005, about 20 percent of the world's workers were in more-developed countries, and 80 percent were in less-developed countries. If the economically active population remains at 48 percent, the labor force in more-developed countries is expected to stay constant, largely because of the stable population size of industrial countries. The labor force of more-developed countries is projected to stop growing after 2020, but the labor force of less-developed countries is expected to continue rising and to converge with the 48 percent of more-developed countries after 2020 (table 22.4).

By continent, Africa is expected to have the fastest-growing labor force. The 357 million African workers in 2005 amounted to 15 percent of the total workforce in developing countries. By 2050, Africa's labor force is expected to be 930 million people. Thus, 40 percent of the 1.4 billion expected growth in developing-country labor forces will be in Africa. As the most rural continent,[11] Africa is likely to experience large-scale rural-urban migration, some of which may spill over national borders.

In contrast to the projections for Africa, the labor force in Europe is expected to shrink. For example, Bijak et al. (2007) have projected that the labor force of the EU-27 will fall from 233 million in 2002 to 210 million in 2052. Three policy levers could be used to offset projected declines in

Table 22.3. The World's Economically Active Population, 1980–2050
millions

	1980	1985	1990	1995	2000		
Total population	4,451	4,855	5,295	5,719	6,124		
World EAP	1,930	2,160	2,406	2,605	2,818		
% EAP	43	44	45	46	46		
	2005	**2010**	**2015**	**2020**	**2025**		
Total population	6,514	6,910	7,295	7,667	8,010		
World EAP	3,050	3,279	3,481	3,651	3,845		
% EAP	47	47	48	48	48		
	2030	**2035**	**2040**	**2045**	**2050**		
Total population	8,317	8,587	8,824	9,025	9,191		
World EAP	3,992	4,122	4,236	4,332	4,412		
% EAP	48	48	48	48	48		
	1980–90	**1990–2000**	**2000–10**	**2010–20**	**2020–30**	**2030–40**	**2040–50**
% change in world EAP	25	21	17	17	9	6	4

Source: LABORSTA (database), International Labour Organization (ILO), http://laborsta.ilo.org. Population data from UN 2009a, medium variant.

Table 22.4. Economically Active Population in More- and Less-Developed Countries, 1980–2020
millions

	1980	1985	1990	1995	2000		
More developed							
Population	1,083	1,115	1,149	1,175	1,194		
EAP	523	545	569	574	589		
% EAP	48	49	50	49	49		
Less developed							
Population	3,368	3,740	4,146	4,544	4,930		
EAP	1,407	1,616	1,837	2,031	2,229		
% EAP	42	43	44	45	45		
	2005	**2010**	**2015**	**2020**	**2025**		
More developed							
Population	1,216	1,232	1,245	1,254	1,259		
EAP	604	613	611	603	604		
% EAP	50	50	49	48	48		
Less developed							
Population	5,299	5,674	6,050	6,413	6,752		
EAP	2,446	2,666	2,870	3,048	3,241		
% EAP	46	47	47	48	48		
	2030	**2035**	**2040**	**2045**	**2050**		
More developed							
Population	1,261	1,260	1,257	1,252	1,245		
EAP	605	605	603	601	598		
% EAP	48	48	48	48	48		
Less developed							
Population	7,057	7,327	7,567	7,774	7,946		
EAP	3,387	3,517	3,632	3,732	3,814		
% EAP	48	48	48	48	48		
% Change in EAP	**1980–90**	**1990–2000**	**2000–10**	**2010–20**	**2020–30**	**2030–40**	**2040–50**
More-developed EAP	9	5	4	5	0	0	–1
Less-developed EAP	31	26	21	20	11	7	5

Source: LABORSTA (database), ILO, http://laborsta.ilo.org. Population data from UN 2009a, medium variant.

the number of workers: raising fertility, encouraging more residents to work longer, and admitting immigrants. Most European studies put more emphasis on the fertility and employment policy levers than migration.

Migrant Flow Projections

The Global Forum on Migration and Development and most academic literature expect international labor migration levels to continue to rise as a result of demographic and economic inequalities in a period of globalization (Pritchett 2006; Martin and Zuercher 2008; UNDP 2009). Indeed, migrant-receiving countries appear poised to accept more migrant workers over the next decade. Traditional immigration countries such as Australia, Canada, and the United States have sharply increased both guest worker and foreign student admissions. Governments navigating between employers requesting foreign workers and restrictionist public opinion are likely to continue to offer many of these so-called side door entrants a path to immigrant status or permanent residence if a local employer offers a job.

Moreover, the decline in labor migration in the 2008–09 recession is likely a temporary hiccup in the upward trajectory of international labor migration. While the recession prompted a reduction of migrant worker inflows into countries that had been receiving large numbers,[12] relatively few migrant workers were pushed out of host countries overall. What is more, the recruitment of migrant workers resumed with economic growth in many countries in 2010.

Factors Affecting Future Migrant Flows

In addition to the driving effect of inequalities and the facilitating effect of falling transportation and communication costs, three other factors are likely to affect migration flows in the coming decades. First, population aging is expected to increase demand for migrant workers. Second, climate change is predicted to drive a significant increase in rural-urban internal and international migration. And third, changes in international regulation are expected to affect future migrant patterns. The rest of this section discusses the implications of these factors for future migration.

The Age of Aging

Global population aging is unprecedented. While the world's population is growing by about 1.2 percent a year, the population of persons 60 and older is growing at least twice as fast. Moreover, population aging appears to be an enduring trend (UN 2002, 28).[13] The median age of all people on Earth, which was 24 in 1950 and 27 in 2000, is projected to be 38 in 2050.[14] About 20 percent of the population in developed countries is 60 and older, and that proportion is expected to rise to 33 percent by 2050. By contrast, the share of elderly among the residents of less-developed countries is expected to double from 10 percent today to 20 percent by 2050.

Many industrial countries will experience population aging amid population decline. These countries, including Italy, Japan, and the Russian Federation, have not yet developed migration responses that could include, for instance, admitting migrants to maintain their populations or the ratios between dependent and working-age populations.

While the aging trend poses challenges for growth of the global economy, economists highlight two "demographic dividends" that can speed economic and job growth to a certain extent. First, declining fertility will progressively reduce the number of youth to educate and thus could lead to an increase in the number of women who elect to work for wages (Bloom, Canning, and Sevilla 2003). Moreover, as families tend to invest more in each of their fewer children, the growing availability of well-educated young workers could fuel economic and job growth, as with the East Asian "economic miracle" economies (World Bank 1993).[15]

Second, as longevity prompts workers to increase their savings, the cost of capital will decline, thus promoting investment and raising productivity (Lee and Mason 2006). The life-cycle theory of consumption and savings assumes that households accumulate wealth during working years to maintain consumption in retirement. This pattern can result in a virtuous circle of low interest rates, more investment, and rising productivity and earnings. However, if governments provide the elderly with generous pensions and health care benefits that are financed from taxes paid by current workers, making it unnecessary for workers to save during their working lives for retirement, economic growth may slow because of rising taxes on a declining workforce.

Across industrial countries, the share of government resources devoted to the elderly is about the same as their share of the population (Papadimitriou 2007). With little prospect for an upsurge in fertility, many observers expect governments in countries experiencing both population aging and decline to reduce benefits for the elderly and to raise income taxes to support retirees. Alternatively, the United Nations (UN) estimated that raising the retirement age to 75 could maintain current support ratios[16] in most industrial countries (UN 2000, 5). One justification for more years of work is that older people are healthier than a generation ago; a French woman of 77 in 2000, in health and fitness, had the health equivalent to a 63-year old in 1900 (Bourdelais 1999).

Migration is also touted as at least a partial "solution" to the related issues of population aging and financing benefits of retirees. Working-age migrants can pay taxes that help sustain pay-as-you-go social security systems. However, unless immigration increases over time, migrants have a one-time effect on social security systems, since they also age and become eligible for government-provided benefits.

Moreover, immigration rates would have to increase quite substantially to compensate for population aging and decline. For instance, the UN estimated that for France, Germany, Italy, and the United Kingdom to maintain the 1995 ratio of workers to retirees,[17] immigration would have to increase 37-fold over 1995 levels, to almost 9 million a year (table 22.5). By contrast, the United States would have to increase immigration to almost 12 million to maintain the 1995 ratio of workers to retirees (UN 2000). As opinion polls suggest that neither Europeans nor Americans want to increase migrant flows, the feasibility of this solution to population aging is limited, at least in the short term.[18]

However, aging is likely to prompt some migration of the elderly to lower-cost areas and to increase migration of caregivers from lower- to higher-wage countries. The exact mix of responses is likely to vary across countries and depend on individual and policy decisions. Because aging is projected to increase the fastest in less-developed countries, the demand for caregivers for the elderly is likely to rise fastest there. It could also encourage some elderly to move to places with warmer weather and lower living costs for retirement, an idea that has prompted proposals for "retirement villages" in countries with low-cost care workers such as the Philippines.[19] Moreover,

Table 22.5. Replacement Migration in Europe and the United States, 1995
thousands

		Average annual number of migrants required, 2000–50					
	Actual immigration in 1995	To maintain 1995 population	Multiple of 1995 immigration	To maintain 1995 working-age population	Multiple of 1995 Immigration	To maintain population support ratio[a]	Multiple of 1995 immigration
EU-15[b]	270,000	949,000	4	1,588,000	6	13,480,000	50
EU-4[c]	237,000	677,000	3	1,093,000	5	8,884,000	37
France	7,000	29,000	4	109,000	16	1,792,000	256
Germany	204,000	344,000	2	487,000	2	3,630,000	18
Italy	6,000	251,000	42	372,000	62	2,268,000	378
United Kingdom	20,000	53,000	3	125,000	6	1,194,000	60
Other EU countries	33,000	272,000	8	495,000	15	4,596,000	139
United States	760,000	128,000	0	359,000	0	11,851,000	16

Source: UN 2000.
a. Migrants necessary to maintain 1995 population ratio of persons ages 15–64 to those age 65 or older.
b. EU-15: Austria, Belgium, Denmark, Finland, France, Germany, Greece, Ireland, Italy, Luxembourg, the Netherlands, Portugal, Spain, Sweden, and the United Kingdom.
c. EU-4: France, Germany, Italy, and the United Kingdom.

aging is likely to encourage the development of technologies that enable the elderly to care for themselves where they live. Japanese firms, for example, have pioneered a variety of technologies aimed at helping the elderly in their homes, such as robots that assist with daily chores and summoning help.[20]

Climate Change and Migration

A second factor that may affect international migration in the coming decades is climate change.[21] There are three major channels through which climate change could trigger new migrant patterns. First, climate change is expected to generate more severe storms, such as hurricanes, that destroy housing and erode land, thus encouraging migration, at least until recovery. Second, competition for scarce land and water could increase, especially in arid areas with rapidly growing populations, as in Sub-Saharan Africa. Competition for land and water can lead to conflict and migration, as when herders come into conflict with crop farmers. Third, rising and more variable temperatures are likely to make agriculture less productive in densely populated areas in developing countries. Since 40 percent of the world's workers obtain their income from farming,[22] climate change is expected to increase rural-urban internal and international migration. This increased migration will likely follow well-established migration networks, making it hard to isolate the extra migration due to climate change (World Bank 2009, 110).

Of course, the impacts of climate change are not uniform across regions, as global warming may open up farming opportunities in areas now too cold for crop production. Agricultural productivity is expected to decrease in Sub-Saharan Africa, South Asia, and parts of South America and may perhaps increase in colder areas such as Canada and the Russian Federation (Darwin et al. 1995; World Bank 2008, 16–17). However, new farming operations in sparsely populated regions that are now too cold for farming are not likely to be labor intensive. Thus, the net effect of these changes is likely to be more migration out of agriculture.

Observers generally agree that climate change will affect developing countries more adversely than industrial countries because less-developed countries have fewer resources to invest in prevention and adaptation. And within developing countries, the poorest residents are likely to suffer most. Because three-fourths of the poor in developing countries live in rural areas, climate changes that adversely affect agriculture are expected to increase out-migration from rural areas (World Bank 2008, 1).

The question is, What is the optimal policy response? Current government policies include helping rural-urban migrants integrate in urban areas by removing barriers to government services, as in China[23] and India, and creating nonfarm jobs in urban centers for migrants. Other policies to ease the transition of workers from rural to urban labor markets include extending labor exchanges to rural areas to expedite worker-employer job matching, providing accommodation for the often single youth who migrate, and ensuring that migrants who settle in urban areas have access to government services.

Alternatively, the World Bank (2008) made three policy recommendations to mitigate the pressure for developing-country farmers to migrate:

- First, additional investments should be made in agricultural research and development, including research on how to produce food and fiber despite climate change.
- Second, governments should implement policies to help small farmers and landless workers increase their incomes through reform of land, commodity, and water markets and create opportunities for rural people to supplement their incomes in rural nonfarm industries.
- Third, governments should change policies so that farmers and other rural residents have incentives to manage limited supplies of land, water, and other natural resources in sustainable ways.

However, assessments of these policy options should also consider that nonfarm industries often need subsidies to induce them to locate in rural areas that may have higher transportation costs and lack workers with needed skills.

Mass migrations due to climate changes that reduce the viability of farming will be much easier to identify but perhaps harder to deal with effectively. For example, storms that destroy shrimp farms, cover land with salt water, or erode top soil can displace large numbers of people quickly. The initial policy response is likely to be temporary support until the agricultural system can be repaired and those who were displaced can resume farming. Similarly, the response to flooding that covers low-lying land could be temporary shelter for the displaced followed by a return to farming. What is not clear is when or whether a mass movement as a result of a climate-related event will or should lead to permanent resettlement.

International Management of Labor Migration

Global politics will also affect future trends in international migration. At the extremes, two scenarios for the management of international labor migration are possible. In the first scenario, additional bilateral and regional free-movement regimes could emerge, such as that between Australia and New Zealand or among member states of the European Union. Eventually, this development could lead to the creation of a global World Migration Organization analogous to the World Trade Organization (WTO) to foster the migration of workers over national borders to, among other things, increase global economic efficiency.[24] The second extreme scenario is that current levels of migration will persist as national governments limit migrant admissions for reasons ranging from fears of crime and terrorism to the adverse effects of migrants on native workers and productivity.

The most likely scenario lies between these extremes, meaning that a variety of national and regional migration systems will probably prevail. Rentier societies such as Gulf oil exporters seem poised to continue relying on migrant workers in private labor markets. And more industrial countries are joining the four traditional immigration countries—Australia, Canada, New Zealand, and the United States—to select a certain number of immigrants each year and plan for their integration.

The great unknown is policy development in middle-income migrant-receiving countries such as Brazil, Malaysia, Mexico, Morocco, South Africa, and Thailand. Most migration literature predicts and endorses regional and global liberalization of labor migration (Ghosh 2000; Bhagwati 2003). But will migrant-receiving countries, some of which also send workers abroad, follow the lead of industrial countries and plan for immigration based on family, economic, or other criteria? Will they favor the return of descendants of previous emigrants, or will they follow the model of Singapore, welcoming professionals to settle with their families while aiming to rotate less skilled workers in and out of the labor force and country?

The answer to many of these questions depends on the nature of migration management at the global level. Currently, the global migration policy regime is primarily normative, with International Labour Organization (ILO) and UN conventions to ensure that migrant workers have the same wages and rights as national workers. International migration enables many people to earn higher wages and improve their standard of living, but it can also be associated with violations of fundamental rights and freedoms, unequal treatment and abuse, and sometimes trafficking and forced labor. Thus, the ILO's mission is to provide a framework to maximize the positive outcomes of migration and minimize negative outcomes. In particular, the ILO's Multilateral Framework on Labor Migration aims to protect migrant worker rights, but it does not spell out how many migrants should be admitted.

This normative or rights-based policy regime may be altered by Mode 4 of the General Agreement on Trade in Services (GATS) negotiations aimed at facilitating the movement of service providers over national borders.[25] While GATS is directly concerned with trade in services, not labor migration, GATS does apply to foreigners who provide services as self-employed independent contractors or as foreign employees of foreign firms. Foreign employee service providers covered by GATS are considered migrant workers under ILO Conventions.

Liberalizing trade in services to promote economic growth is one of the main goals of the current Doha development round of WTO negotiations.[26] The value of services is about 75 percent of the economy in high-income countries and half the economy in low-income countries. Trade liberalization occurs through requests and offers, and most developing countries want to liberalize Mode 4 movements of natural persons, reflecting their comparative advantage in lower wages (Mattoo and Olarreaga 2004). India has led other developing countries in the request for four major changes that would make it easier for service providers to cross borders:[27] eliminating the economic needs tests, expediting the issuance of visas and work permits, facilitating the recognition of credentials and the obtaining of needed licenses, and exempting foreign service providers from participating in work-related benefit programs and the payroll taxes that finance them. Ideally, liberalizers would like a "GATS visa" that would be uniform across WTO member countries (Chanda 2001, 648) and allow multiple visits within a given period of time, say, one to three years.[28]

However, developed countries are more concerned with liberalization of Mode 3 (commercial presence) and have given few signs of intentions to liberalize Mode 4. Except for some liberalization of intracompany transfers, few migrant-receiving countries have expanded existing channels or opened new ones for low-skilled migrant service providers. If developed countries make more commitments under GATS to facilitate the entry of foreigners to "provide services," developing-country governments could file trade complaints against the immigration and labor departments of WTO member countries that slow or block the entry and work of their service providers. The Doha round is thus unlikely to lead to significantly more movements of service providers, which has disappointed many developing-country negotiators.

Economic Implications of Migration

This section examines the economic impacts of migration. It considers the perspectives of both receiving and sending countries.

Economic Impact on Migrant-Receiving Countries

The World Bank estimated that adding 14 million migrant workers from developing countries to the 28 million already in industrial countries would generate global benefits of US$355 billion. This number is more than the estimated gains from reducing trade restrictions in the Doha round of negotiations (World Bank 2006).

The standard analysis of the economic impact of immigration assumes that the entry of foreign workers shifts the aggregate labor supply curve to the right along a fixed labor-demand curve, increasing employment and lowering wages (Borjas 1994). The major economic beneficiaries of immigration are the immigrants who earn higher wages in the destination area and employers who pay lower wages because migrants are available; the major losers are workers employed before the migrants arrived, whose wages are lowered by immigration.[29]

However, immigration also expands economic output. The presence of more workers can attract capital, which, in turn, expands employment. For instance, the availability of migrant farm workers can preserve jobs for local workers in packing and transportation industries. In this way, the unemployment rate can fall or remain unchanged in an area despite in-migration.

The Role of Temporary Worker Programs

In recent years, growth in the number of temporary migrant workers has been faster than growth in the number of permanent or long-term immigrants. This trend holds true both in countries that are newcomers to immigration, such as Ireland, Spain, and the United Kingdom, and traditional immigration countries such as Australia, Canada, and the United States. Rapid growth in temporary foreign workers raises several questions, including how to determine if foreign-born workers are "needed" and their effects on local workers in the short and long term.

Almost all countries that are richer than their neighbors have some type of temporary worker programs (TWPs), often called guest worker programs, to allow local employers to employ foreign workers. These programs aim to add foreign workers to the labor force but not necessarily settled residents to the population. TWPs can often be a solution for governments caught between competing interests, including employers requesting migrants, migrants eager for higher wages, and public constituencies that want migration reduced. However, the administrative elements of TWPs are often debated in migrant-receiving countries. For instance, What criteria must employers satisfy to receive permission to recruit and employ migrants? How is migrant employment monitored? How do governments ensure that migrant workers depart as scheduled? These issues may obscure an even more important issue—how are employer preferences, local workers' attitudes, and the operation of labor markets affected by the presence of migrants over time?

An evaluation of the economic impact of TWPs should also consider the potential for path dependence to emerge from short-term hiring of foreign workers. Employers hire migrants because they cannot find workers willing to fill jobs for the wages and benefits they offer. However, economic distortion or path dependence can increase the reliance of employers on migrant workers over time as they make investments based on the assumption that doors to migrants will remain open. The lower labor costs made possible by the availability of migrants are sometimes capitalized into asset values, giving asset owners an incentive to keep hiring migrants.

A similar path dependence can develop among migrants, as families, regions, and countries become dependent on earnings and remittances from a foreign labor market. If the money remitted by migrants is not invested to create jobs and generate stay-at-home development, incentives to migrate for employment may persist. In both Europe and the United States, decades of guest worker recruitment were followed, with lags, by asylum seeking from Turkey and unauthorized migration from Mexico (Martin 2009, chap. 2; Martin 2004).

Path dependence helps explain why temporary worker programs often get larger and last longer than expected. Many migrant worker programs were begun in wartime or at other "extraordinary" times, allowing employers to persuade governments to admit migrant workers to cope with "emergency" labor shortages. The anticipation that TWPs are short-lived minimizes serious discussion of alternatives to migrants and the trade-offs between migrant numbers and migrant rights (Ruhs and Martin 2008).[30]

Economic Impact on Migrant-Sending Countries

Migrant-sending nations also face difficult policy decisions. Recognizing the lack of decent work at home, many migrant-sending nations look to remittances to alleviate poverty and provide the investment needed to speed up development. In many developing countries, migrants generate more foreign exchange than foreign direct investment does. Moreover, migrants often send more money home after disasters and during recessions. In the wake of the recent financial crisis, remittances fell less than deployments of new migrant workers, reflecting the tendency of remittances to act as a countercyclical stabilizer as migrants resist returning and some remit more to family and friends in need.[31] In some countries, remittances rose even though migrant deployments fell. For example, the number of Bangladeshis deployed to foreign jobs fell from 875,000 in 2008 to 475,000 in 2009, but remittances rose 20 percent to US$10.7 billion in 2009.

Most studies show that remittances reduce poverty and increase spending on health and education in the families that receive them, but the effects of migration and remittances on development are more ambiguous (Adams 2004). Indeed, in many cases, remittances do not foster the type of development that ensures that the children of migrants do not have to follow their parents abroad.

However, international labor migration does have the potential to speed development in migrant-sending countries. Governments that have most successfully used migration to foster development often have more than just workers abroad. For instance, the government of the Republic of Korea supported Korean construction firms that employed Korean migrant workers in Gulf countries in the 1980s. China has had a similar strategy of providing both engineering services and migrant workers for foreign infrastructure projects. In contrast, countries that send mostly low-skilled workers abroad, from Bangladesh to Mexico to the Philippines, generate remittances that reduce poverty but do not necessarily set stay-at-home development in motion.

Given these opportunities and challenges, migrant-sending countries must decide whether to encourage, tolerate, or try to discourage the out-migration of their workers. What interventions are appropriate for migrant-sending governments? That is, should they aim to regulate private sector recruiters or develop government alternatives to them? If they choose the regulation approach, what is the optimal amount of regulation and predeparture orientation and training?

Conclusions and Recommendations

In spring 2010, unemployment rates remained high and international labor migration flows were smaller than in 2006–07, but developing and industrial countries alike appeared to be recovering from the worst recession in a half-century. Structural demographic and economic factors suggest that international labor migration will increase. The major destinations are likely to be the industrial countries that already have 60 percent of the world's migrants. Industrial countries with aging and shrinking populations, employers complaining of labor shortages, and large numbers of foreign students and others who can work at least part time are likely to expand current programs and experiment with new programs that admit migrant workers and allow some foreigners within their borders to become guest workers or immigrants. Migration to middle-income developing nations is also likely to increase, because the same demographic and economic inequalities that encourage migration to industrial countries also move migrants from poorer to richer developing countries.

The migration and development agenda is lengthy. As migrants tend to be concentrated in particular occupations and industries, migration policy has significant implications for labor demand, supply, and labor market operation in particular sectors of migrant-receiving countries. Migration policy may become one of the most important factors shaping the structure and functioning of labor markets (Martin, Abella, and Kuptsch 2006).

Richer countries need to deal with issues ranging from employers' requests for foreign workers to the options for sustaining the financing of pay-as-you-go social security systems in countries with shrinking and aging populations. Migrant workers are likely to be a key ingredient of the policies adopted to cope with demographic and economic change, but the fact that changes to immigration, social security, and health care policies are controversial makes it hard to debate policy options openly in some countries. Instead, governments often tolerate the irregular migration that fills jobs and provides some short-term help for social security systems.

Middle-income developing countries similarly avoid explicit discussions of the hard choices posed by migrant workers. Because most are avowedly not countries of immigration, governments periodically announce their intentions to "eventually" reduce or eliminate migrant workers. However, many governments are trying to achieve migrant worker reductions with rules that contradict the incentives of employers and migrants who want to prolong their employment relationship, resulting in irregular migration and thus uncertainties for both employers and migrants.

Some countries also actively seek to send more workers abroad to increase remittances, speed up development, and relieve some of the pressures resulting from displacements related to climate change. These countries have been among the most active in international forums, seeking to use the GATS Mode 4 negotiations, the Global Forum on Migration and Development, and climate-change forums to argue that richer countries should open their doors wider to workers from poorer countries. Thus far, however, these governmental efforts have not been successful.

Achieving international consensus to increase migrant numbers appears to be a very distant goal. The major goal of researchers and development institutions has been to highlight the economic benefits of more labor migration, emphasizing the cost of restrictions on the entry of more migrants. However, these economic arguments have so far not been persuasive in international forums. Many migrant-receiving countries feel free to raise barriers to migrants, especially in recession.

The experience with migrant workers during the 2008–09 recession prompts three major recommendations. First, the economic benefits of more migration need to be reevaluated. Politicians may be reluctant to embrace more migration for many reasons, including the fact that many of the studies estimating significant economic benefits to more migration are based in part on assumptions that may not square with the politicians' experience, such as the assumption that migrants get jobs without displacing local workers or depressing wages. What would happen to the estimated economic benefits of migrant workers if researchers allowed for some displacement and depression?

Second, we need to examine the longer-term impacts of more migration. Trade theory recognizes the possibility of different short- and long-term effects of freer trade, but migration theory, with some exceptions, rarely draws distinctions between short- and long-run effects. For example, what effects does easy access to migrants have on productivity trends, an issue recently being debated in Singapore?[32] If easy access to migrants leads to "underinvestment" in capital, what is the best corrective tool: quotas on migrants, taxes or levies on migrant employment that can be used to invest in labor-saving changes, or other tools?

And finally, further study of the link between migration, remittances, and development is needed. Many governments have embraced more labor migration in an effort to maximize remittances and accelerate development. As more governments adopt policies to promote foreign employment, a careful evaluation of what types of migration lead to the most rapid development is needed. In particular, are remittances a useful shorthand measure of the benefits of migration for development? Remittances clearly reduce poverty for families receiving them, and their spending has spillover effects that benefit nonmigrants, but it is less clear that remittances set stay-at-home development in motion (Ratha, Mohapatra, and Silwal 2009).

Notes

1. The stock of migrants in developing countries rose from 57 million to 86 million or 50 percent. The share of migrants in developing countries fell from 52 percent to 40 percent between 1985 and 2010.
2. This increase was driven by baby booms in both industrial and developing countries (Cohen 2003).
3. Fertility in the more-developed regions in 2005 was 1.6, versus 4.6 in less-developed regions. Fertility is expected to rise to 1.8 by 2050 in more-developed regions.
4. Keilman (1998, 15) finds that United Nations projections of population are most reliable for 10–15 years into the future.
5. See International Migration (database), United Nations, http://www.unmigration.org.
6. Europe is defined as 48 countries, including the Russian Federation.
7. For instance, European nations preserved the right to asylum but made it more difficult for asylum seekers to apply by designating some countries as generally safe, so that asylum seekers could be returned while their applications were pending. In the United States, Congress elected in 1996 to maintain the number of immigrants admitted but to reduce their access to welfare benefits. Some of these benefit reductions were reversed in the late 1990s (Migration News 1996).
8. The amount was not adjusted for purchasing power parity.
9. The International Labour Organization defines the share of persons who are in the "economically active population" as those who are employed or looking for work.

10. Growth in the 1980s and 1990s can be explained primarily by the baby boom of the 1960s and 1970s.

11. In 2008, 38 percent of Africa's population was urban, against a global average of 49 percent. See Population Reference Bureau, http://www.prb.org.

12. Those countries include, for instance, Ireland, Spain, the United Kingdom, and the United States. There were also a few well-publicized cases: (a) of migrants being blocked from entry, for example, 55,000 Bangladeshi migrants were prevented from entering Malaysia early in 2009; (b) some Filipinos lost jobs and were forced to depart before the end of their contracts when the Taiwanese factories that employed them closed; and (c) some migrant construction and service workers in Gulf Cooperation Council countries lost jobs and returned to their countries of origin.

13. In 2007, there were more people 65 and older than under age five, and this is unlikely to change in the future.

14. For more-developed countries, median ages were 29 in 1950, 37 in 2000, and 46 projected for 2050.

15. Real per capita GDP in East Asia rose almost 5 percent a year between 1960 and 2005. Credit is attributed to sound macroeconomic policies, infrastructure investment, and policies that favored exporters. The ensuing discussion focused on whether productivity growth or large increases in physical capital and labor were largely responsible for the rapid economic growth—that is, was the miracle due to innovation or perspiration.

16. The definition is the ratio of retired persons to those of working age.

17. Measurement is at prevailing fertility rates in 1995.

18. See Pew Research Center, "World Publics Welcome Global Trade—but Not Immigration," http://pewglobal.org/reports/display.php?ReportID=258; Polling Report, http://www.pollingreport.com/immigration.htm.

19. One proposal to attract elderly Japanese to the Philippines is at Japanese External Trade Organization, http://www3.jetro.go.jp/ttppoas/anken/0001051000/1051449_e.html.

20. Economist (2005) says that "although they are at ease with robots, many Japanese are not as comfortable around other people."

21. Climate change is defined as a significant change in temperature or precipitation that persists for several decades. Climate change can occur because of natural factors such as changes in the sun's intensity, natural processes such as changes in ocean currents, and human activities that change the atmosphere, such as burning fossil fuels or deforestation.

22. Climate change is not the only factor affecting agriculture. Other trends helping to transform agriculture include (a) a rapidly rising demand for meat in middle-income developing countries, which can accelerate deforestation and speed up global warming; (b) increased demand for biofuels that can push up food prices as crops are shifted from food to fuel production; and (c) a rising demand for seafood that encourages production in coastal areas in ways that can increase storm-related damage.

23. China is debating how to modify and perhaps eliminate the *hukou* or household registration system that limits access to public housing, education, medical, and other benefits to the place where a person is registered. The Organisation for Economic Co-ordination and Development's Economic Survey of China, released in February 2010, recommended that the *hukou* system be phased out and that the Chinese government develop national pension and health insurance systems to promote internal mobility. About 45 percent of China's 1.3 billion residents live in urban areas, but 104 million of the 612 million urban residents do not have urban *hukous*. In 2006, the government began allowing migrant children without local *hukous* to attend local public schools, and city governments started taking control of private schools for migrant children.

24. A World Trade Organization or World Migration Organization could also give national governments facing antimigrant publics "cover" to liberalize labor flows over national borders, as when they say they do not want to allow the entry of migrants but their international obligations require them to do so.

25. There are four major modes or ways to provide services over national borders: Mode 1 is cross-border supply; Mode 2 is consumption abroad; Mode 3 is commercial presence; and Mode 4 is temporary movement of natural persons. Thus, while "temporary" is not defined in the GATS, and GATS explicitly does not apply to permanent migration, Mode 4 refers to migration in broad terms.

26. GATS does not include all services: it excludes most air transport services as well as "services supplied in the exercise of governmental authority."

27. Chanda (2004, 634) calls these four categories restrictions on entry and stay, recognition of credentials, differential treatment, and regulations on commercial presence, a taxonomy that groups economic needs test and visa-work permit issuance.

28. The Coalition of Service Industries says that a "GATS visa" allowing multiple short-term visits would be limited to professionals and highly skilled individuals and proposed a model of how countries could implement a GATS visa regime. GATS visas would be given to employees of established foreign firms, which would post bonds on each GATS visa holder that would be forfeited if the visa holder did not obey the terms of the visa.

29. In a simple two-factor production function with homogeneous labor and constant returns to scale, adding immigrants to the workforce reduces wages in the short run (assuming full employment) but does not change the long-run return to capital and labor. If immigrant and native labor is not homogeneous, adding immigrants to the workforce has distributional consequences, helping complementary workers and hurting workers who are substitutes for the immigrants.

30. Migrant rights can cost employers money. With a negatively sloped demand for labor, ensuring full or equal rights can reduce the number of temporary foreign workers employed.

31. The World Bank in November 2009 projected that remittances to developing countries would fall from US$338 billion in 2008 to US$317 billion in 2009, a drop of 6 percent. World Bank, "Workers' Remittances Fall Less Than Expected, But 2010 Recovery Likely To Be Shallow," http://web.worldbank.org/WBSITE/EXTERNAL/NEWS/0,,contenMDK:22394180~pagePK:64257043~piPK:437376~theSitePK:4607,00.html.

32. Between 2005 and 2009, Singapore's population rose by an average 150,000 a year, mostly due to immigration. In 2010, a third of Singapore's 5 million residents were foreigners; in 1990, a seventh of 3 million residents were foreigners. Singapore has no unemployment insurance and a very thin social safety net. The open-door policy for low-skilled guest workers may have slowed productivity growth, which averaged only 1 percent a year between 1988 and 2008. The government-appointed Economic Strategies Committee (http://www.esc.gov.sg) in 2010 recommended an increase in the monthly employer levy to encourage employers to make the investments needed to raise productivity growth and train local workers.

Bibliography

Adams, R. 2004. "Remittances and Poverty in Guatemala." Policy Research Working Paper 3418, World Bank, Washington, DC.

Bhagwati, J. 2003. "Borders beyond Control." *Foreign Affairs* (January–February): 98–104.

Bijak, J., D. Kupiszewska, M. Kupiszewski, K. Saczuk, and A. Kicinger. 2007. "Population and Labor Force Projections for 27 European Countries, 2002–2052: Impact of International Migration on Population Ageing." *European Journal of Population* 23: 1–31.

Bloom, D., D. Canning, and J. Sevilla. 2003. *A New Perspective on the Economic Consequences of Population Change.* Santa Monica, CA: Rand.

Borjas, G. 1994. "The Economics of Immigration." *Journal of Economic Literature* 32 (4): 1667–717.

Bourdelais, P. 1999. "Demographic Aging: A Notion to Revisit." *History of the Family* 4 (1): 31–50.

Chanda, R. 2001. "Movement of Natural Persons and the GATS." *World Economy* 24 (5): 631–54.

———. 2004. "Movement and Presence of Natural Persons and Developing Countries: Issues and Proposals for the GATS Negotiations." Working Paper 19, South Centre, Geneva.

Cohen, J. 2003. "Human Population: The Next Half Century." *Science* 302 (5648): 1172–75.

Darwin, R., M. Tsigas, J. Lewandrowski, and A. Raneses. 1995. "World Agriculture and Climate Change: Economic Adaptations." Agricultural Economic Report 703, Natural Resources and Environment Division, Economic Research Service, U.S. Department of Agriculture, Washington, DC.

Economist. 2005. "Better than People," December 20. http://www.economist.com/world/asia/displaystory.cfm?story_id=5323427.

Ghosh, B., ed. 2000. *Managing Migration: Time for a New International Regime?* New York: Oxford University Press.

ILO (International Labour Organization). 2008. "Estimates and Projections of the Economically Active Population, 1980–2050." August. http://laborsta.ilo.org/applv8/data/EAPEP/EAPEP_methodology.pdf

Keilman, N. 1998. "How Accurate Are the United Nations' World Population Projections?" *Frontiers of Population Forecasting: Supplement to Population and Development Review* 24: 15–41.

Lee, R., and A. Mason. 2006. "What Is the Demographic Dividend?" *Finance and Development* 43 (3): 16–17.

Martin, P. 2004. "Germany: Managing Migration in the 21st Century." In *Controlling Immigration: A Global Perspective,* ed. W. A. Cornelius, T. Tsuda, P. L. Martin, and J. F. Hollifield, 221–52. Palo Alto, CA: Stanford University Press.

Martin, P. 2009. *Importing Poverty? Immigration and the Changing Face of Rural America.* New Haven, CT: Yale University Press.

Martin, P., M. Abella, and C. Kuptsch. 2006. *Managing Labor Migration in the Twenty-First Century.* New Haven, CT: Yale University Press.

Martin, P., and G. Zuercher. 2008. "Managing Migration: The Global Challenge." *Population Bulletin* 63 (1): 3–20.

Mattoo, A., and M. Olarreaga. 2004. "Reciprocity across Modes of Supply in the WTO: A Negotiating Formula." *International Trade Journal* 18 (1): 1–22.

Migration News. 1996. "Welfare Overhaul and Minimum Wage Changes." 3 (9). http://migration.ucdavis.edu/mn/more.php?id=1022_0_2_0.

Papadimitriou, D., ed. 2007. *Government Spending on the Elderly.* New York: Palgrave Macmillan.

Pritchett, L. 2006. *Let Their People Come: Breaking the Gridlock on Global Labor Mobility.* Washington, DC: Center for Global Development.

Ratha, D., R. Chami, and C. Fullenkamp. 2009. "Remittances in Development." *Finance and Development* 46 (4): 30.

Ratha, D., S. Mohapatra, and A. Silwal. 2009. "Migration and Remittance Trends 2009." Migration and Development Brief 11, World Bank, November 3. http://www.worldbank.org/prospects/migrationandremittances.

Ruhs, M., and P. Martin. 2008. "Numbers vs. Rights: Trade-Offs and Guest Worker Programs." *International Migration Review* 42 (1): 249–65.

UN (United Nations). 1999. *The World at Six Billion.* New York: UN.

———. 2000. *Replacement Migration: Is It a Solution to Declining and Aging Populations?* New York: UN.

———. 2002. World Population Aging: 1950–2050. New York: UN. Data available online at http://esa.un.org/unpp/index.asp?panel=1.

———. 2009a. *World Population Prospects: The 2008 Revision.* New York: UN. http://esa.un.org/unpp/.

———. 2009b. "International Migration 2009 Wallchart." http://www.un.org/esa/population/.

UNDP (United Nations Development Programme). 2009. *Overcoming Barriers: Human Mobility and Development.* New York: UNDP.

World Bank. 1993. *The East Asian Miracle: Economic Growth and Public Policy.* New York: Oxford University Press.

———. 2006. "The Economic Implications of Remittances and Migration." *Global Economic Prospects.* http://www.worldbank.org/prospects/gep2006.

———. 2008. *World Development Report 2008: Agriculture for Development.* Washington, DC: World Bank.

———. 2009. *World Development Report 2010: Development and Climate Change.* Washington, DC: World Bank.

23

TRADE AND CLIMATE POLICIES AFTER THE CRISIS

Jaime de Melo and Nicole A. Mathys

As the world begins to leave the financial crisis behind, sustained growth is expected to continue largely because the globalization of recent decades has unleashed technical progress that has spread increasingly rapidly across countries. That globalization is also expected to continue, because it is taken for granted that today's open world trading system will continue to function adequately. At the same time, the continuing difficulties at the climate change and Doha trade negotiations echo concerns that the equity challenges of growth recovery are not being met. The stalemates in these negotiations have the same losers: the least-developed countries and other vulnerable nations with weak institutional infrastructures. These countries have difficulties carrying out the policies needed for a sustained recovery, policies that include mitigation and adaptation measures to deal with climate change.

Several observers view the shift at the Copenhagen meeting in 2009 from a top-down approach with a collective target under the current Kyoto Protocol (KP1) to a bottom-up accord as a shift from an approach favoring environmental objectives to one favoring political feasibility. Under this approach, the world lacks an agreed standard for determining whether a country is doing its fair share to limit global warming. Because the United Nations Framework Convention on Climate Change works by consensus, a meaningful binding agreement with a mechanism for dispute settlement akin to the one in the World Trade Organization (WTO) does not appear likely at the next meetings. Some say that the global climate regime and the global trade policy regime represented by the WTO are on a collision course. Businesses fear that mitigation policies will affect their competitiveness, and environmentalists fear that international trade will undercut policies to reduce greenhouse gas (GHG) emissions. Both groups are appealing to the WTO for rescue.[1]

For a long time, trade and the environment have been odd bedfellows, as environmentalists have claimed that the interests of the trade community have trumped their concerns. In acknowledgment of this concern, the launch of the Doha round explicitly recognized that environmental concerns would be fully taken into account to address fears that the gains from growth and globalization could be undermined by their environmental side effects. First, globalization-induced increases in trade can magnify cross-border pollution. Second, improvements in technology make it increasingly easier to intensify the exploitation of natural resources, potentially exacerbating the depletion of natural capital.

As a consequence of globalization, national decisions have a growing impact on other countries. This changing landscape motivated the creation of the Global Task Force on Public Goods in 2003, and many policy publications have addressed the need to expand the provision of the global commons. Frequently mentioned areas include biodiversity and ecosystems; water resources; fisheries; and, now, mitigating climate change, the "ultimate" global public good. But the sheer magnitude of the climate problem justifies fears that trade and climate change objectives may be at odds.

This chapter takes stock of the challenges ahead, starting from the observation that trade and environmental

This is a shortened version of de Melo and Mathys (2010). We thank Jean-Marie Grether, Patrick Messerlin, Richard Newfarmer, Gisèle Schmid, and Ludivine Tamiotti for helpful comments on an earlier draft and the World Bank and the Swiss National Science Foundation (grant 100012-109926) for financial support. De Melo also thanks FERDI (Fondation pour les etudes et recherches sur le développement international) for support. All remaining errors are our sole responsibility.

negotiations both face the same problem: providing a "public good" whose supply requires widespread participation and compliance. Drawing on this analogy, we point out that the environmental negotiations can learn from the past evolution of the world trading system, first under the General Agreement on Tariffs and Trade (GATT) and then under the WTO. We recognize, though, that the compliance necessary to bring about collective action in the case of climate change policies is fundamentally different. As noted by Barrett (2010), trade is bilateral, so that trade agreements can more easily be enforced by a strategy of reciprocity. In contrast, climate change mitigation is a global public good in which reciprocity is a weak enforcement tool, because those who impose sanctions are hurt in the process. It is not surprising, then, that KP1 did not include trade sanctions as an enforcement mechanism.

Four aspects that complicate the design of appropriate trade policies for dealing with mitigation and its consequences are addressed. First, any serious attempt at mitigation will require a higher price, perhaps around US$100 per metric ton of CO_2e, that is, carbon dioxide equivalent. (Currently, the price in the over-the-counter market in the emission-trading system, or ETS, is around US$20 per metric ton.) The higher price will result in huge rents, whose contestability will lead to much resource waste that should be addressed in the architecture of the next climate agreements. Second, all forms of energy generation require irreversible investments in capital equipment. Very forward-looking decisions under uncertainty require a relatively predictable price of carbon, the predictability being enhanced by a multilateral framework outlining the contours of the path ahead, a requirement that cannot be achieved by unilateral action. (The life of an investment project is more than 50 years for electricity generators, for example, and 60–100 years for residential buildings.) Third, measuring the emission of GHGs in manufacturing and in agriculture is difficult, complicating the measurement of leakage. Furthermore, the carbon content of energy is not visible in a product, complicating the application of border measures to counter any leakage toward nonsignatories. Fourth, since the damages from GHGs are truly global, it is extremely difficult to achieve the necessary collective action, given that everyone shares the benefits while only the participants bear the costs. As a result, starting with unilateral actions to build confidence and reduce the gaps might be necessary.

The next section delineates desirable features for a multilateral agreement and the role of trade and trade policy in an evolving world trading system where climate change occupies a progressively larger role. The following section then examines the evidence of leakage effects from a carbon tax by examining first the evidence of ex post leakage in the case of SO_2, that is, sulfur dioxide, a pollutant prevalent in the same sectors as CO_2. We then report on the ex ante estimates for CO_2, questioning the likely accuracy of these estimates. We also discuss the consequences for developing countries of alternative border adjustment measures. The next section tackles the uncertain legality of border adjustment measures at the WTO and the recent stalled initiatives to reduce protection on environmental goods. The final section closes with some thoughts about lessons that the multilateral trading system could offer to the climate change negotiators.

The Contours of the Next Multilateral Climate Agreement

The challenge ahead is clear from figure 23.1, which shows the evolution of CO_2 emissions (outside of agriculture) over the past 40 years for a very large sample of countries. Even though it does not include all sources and sinks, the figure shows the emissions that are likely to be amenable to the trade policy levers, which are the concern of this chapter. For the world as a whole, emissions growth has not slowed down since concerns about climate change surfaced around 1990. Since GHGs stay in the atmosphere for over a century, the stock is increasing. Much of this growth is catch-up from Brazil, China, and India, shown in panels c and d. As with almost everything else on climate in which the only "certainty is uncertainty," orders of magnitude of the marginal damage are largely unknown. There is now broad consensus, however, that damage from emissions will increase at least until stabilization in the stock is achieved. Figure 23.1 also shows that per capita emissions have stabilized for the three high-income heavy per capita emitters (Australia, Canada, and the United States), in spite of growth in gross domestic product (GDP) and population, although still at about four times above safe levels. It is also evident from panels c and d that differences in per capita emissions are huge across country groupings and that Australia, Canada, and the United States have a long way to go to reduce their per capita emissions to that of the OECD-26 group. Finally, CO_2 emissions fell sharply during the two oil-price spikes in the 1970s, suggesting that a tax on the price of fossil fuels would lead to a fall in emissions.

Three arguments favor acting now on climate change. First, the uncertainty involved is not marginal, and the possibility of a tipping point lowers the discount rate and calls for early action. Intergenerational equity is another issue that has been debated in connection with the Stern report (Stern 2006). Second, because the hardest hit will be the poor, action needs to be taken now to reduce the adverse

Figure 23.1. Total and Per Capita Carbon Emissions for the World and Various Regions, 1960–2002

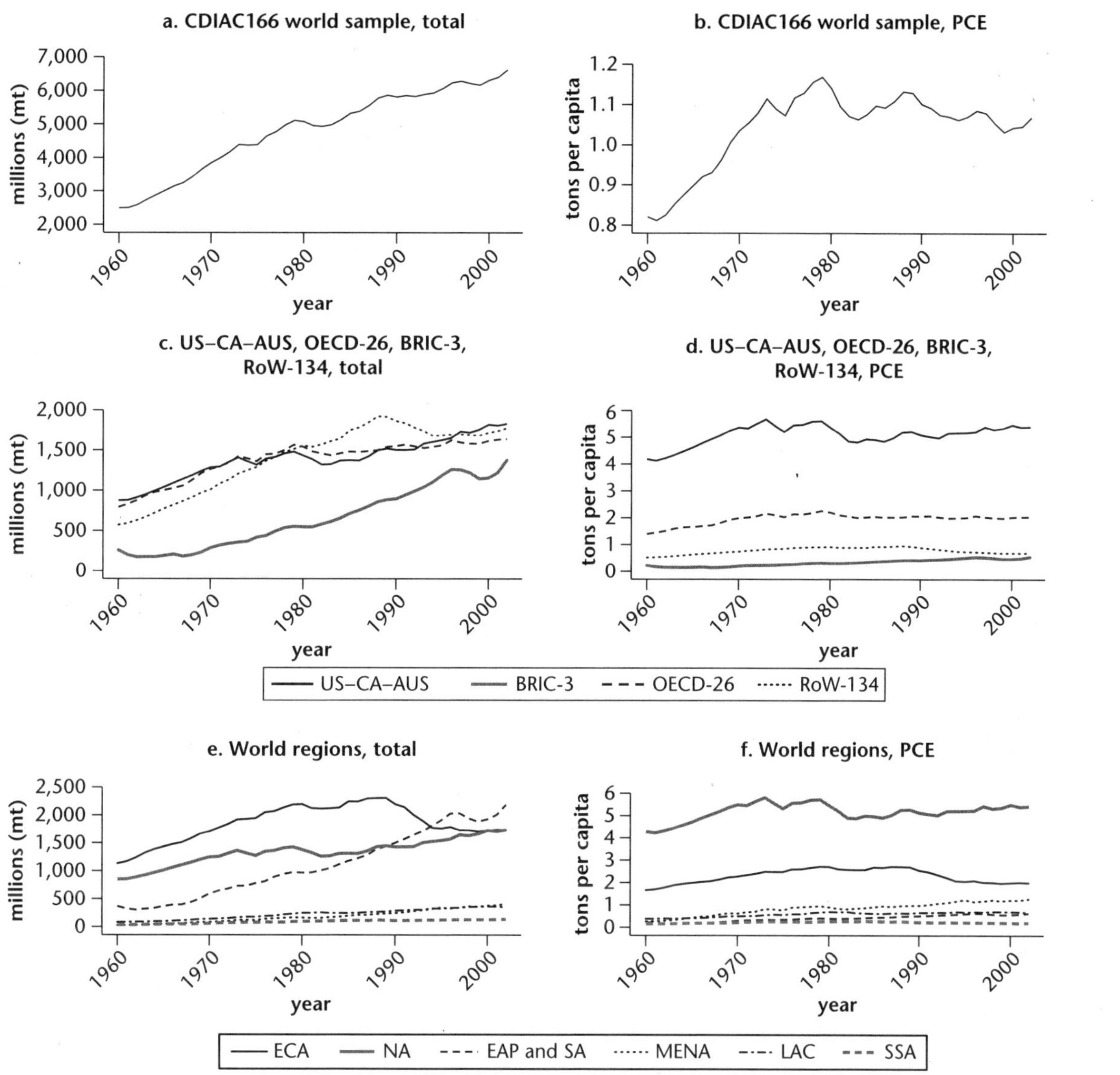

Source: Adapted from Ordás Criado and Grether forthcoming.

Note: BRIC-3 = Brazil, China, and India; USA–CA–AUS = United States, Canada, and Australia; OECD-26 = Organisation for Economic Co-operation and Development without Australia, Canada, and the United States; RoW-134 = the remaining countries, hence a total of 3 + 3 + 26 + 134 = 166 countries; ECA = Europe and Central Asia; EAP = East Asia and Pacific; SA = South Asia; MENA = Middle East and North Africa; LAC = Latin America and the Caribbean; SSA = Sub-Saharan Africa; PCE = per capita carbon emissions. Initial data are from the Carbon Dioxide Information Analsysis Center (CDIAC) and reflect anthropogenic emissions from fossil fuel consumption, cement manufacturing, and gas flaring, ignoring fuels supplied to ships and crafts. To convert carbon emissions into CO_2 emissions, apply a multiplicative factor of 3.67.

effects to which they will be subject. Third, the investments in green renewable energy called for are long term, and investment decisions are inherently dynamic. The longer action is delayed, the more investment will take place in emission-intensive activities because they will remain relatively more profitable than clean energies. However, the slow pace at which collective action is building indicates that acting rapidly will not happen.[2]

Because of the magnitude of the problem, mitigating climate change will require action on several fronts:

- Increasing spending on research and development (R&D), both public and private to develop green energies
- Combating deforestation, because it is an important source of GHG emissions
- Providing aid to support adaptation in the often-hostile environments in less-developed countries
- Establishing an effective emission-trading regime when countries choose to reduce emissions by issuing permits, a choice that could be adopted along with a tax and technical regulations in certain sectors.[3]

Addressing Equity Concerns

The United Nations Framework Convention on Climate Change calls for a common but differentiated responsibility in addressing climate change as well as long-term flexibility in implementation. In particular, any successful climate change regime will have to address burden sharing to take into account that since around 1990 (when global warming became a widespread public concern), high-income countries have been responsible for a larger share of the current stock of emissions. Taking into account intra- and intergenerational equity will also require that countries converge on some per capita measure. The two broad alternatives are "per capita comparability" and "carbon price equivalency." Because countries are reluctant to acquiesce to subsidiarity on tax matters, a top-down approach with an agreement calling on countries to converge on a carbon price subject to sanctions for deviation is unlikely ever to be agreed, despite its superiority on economic grounds.

As a result, any broadly supported agreement will have to rely on some convergence toward equal entitlements on a per capita basis, some arguing that it should be in terms of access to energy needs rather than emissions. Taking convergence in per capita emissions as an equitable target, Spence (2009) computes such emissions paths over a 50-year period. Per capita emissions would have to decline by 4 percent per year in Australia, Canada, and the United States and by 2.6 percent per year in the other high-income countries, mostly the OECD (Organisation for Economic Co-operation and Development)-26 in figure 23.1. All but the slow-growing developing countries, therefore, will have to accept an agreement that will call on emissions caps in the near future.

These trajectories suggest some building blocks for the next climate agreement. First, there should be broad participation in any future agreement and recognition that fast-growing developing countries should "graduate" soon from their current status under KP1. This graduation means being part of a cap on emissions. Second, because the uncertainty is great—a factor of 3 according to Schelling (2007)—regular negotiations are needed along the way (the specificities of each successive agreement taking place every five years). KP1, which covers the period 2008–12, has set up targets for renegotiation after a five-year period.

Trade and Trade Policy to Address the Kyoto Failure

KP1 is generally seen as largely ineffective because it lacks enforcement and participation has been low. This failure calls for a new architecture, and it is interesting that early on several commentators observed that its architecture—which was "deep and shallow" rather than "broad, then deep"—had received insufficient attention (see, for example, Schmalensee 1998). The lack of compliance mechanisms is particularly noteworthy, and a comparison with the hugely successful Montreal Protocol (MP) that addresses ozone depletion, another global public good, is instructive, even though ozone depletion and climate change are very different problems.

Barrett (2010) argues that trade policy played a significant compliance role in the MP. First, all countries complied with the MP through strong incentives against deviation (trade sanctions) and in favor of participation (financial payments from rich to poor nations). Also the MP minimized trade leakage by putting a cap on consumption (which is derived as production − exports + imports), whereas KP1 put a cap only on production. Finally, the MP's caps are permanent, thereby stimulating innovation. Interestingly, the MP is estimated to have been indirectly far more effective at mitigating hydrofluorocarbons (HFCs), a by-product of hydrochlorofluorocarbons (HCFCs), an ozone-depleting substance that is a GHG not covered by KP1. Had HFCs been addressed in a separate (that is, a sectoral) agreement, they could have been cut dramatically, and perhaps phased out. Interestingly, the MP was also strengthened over time with seven amendments (see Barrett 2010, appendix B); that is, its architecture was "broad, then deep," rather than "deep and shallow" as under KP1.

If participation and compliance were the missing elements in KP1 and trade was integral in achieving both compliance and participation under the MP, what potential role is there for trade policy under KP2 and its successors? Trade could come into play through four channels. First, an open trading system with high trade volumes is essential, including intellectual property rights that recognize that technology transfers will have to be encouraged at the same time that incentives for R&D are maintained. The reason is that much technology development and transfer take place through trade.

Second, it will be necessary to separate where abatement takes place from who bears the costs of abatement. Marginal costs of abatement differ widely with many "no-regrets" energy-saving opportunities in developing countries. Under those circumstances, a global carbon credit trading system building on an improved Clean Development Mechanism introduced under KP1 will be necessary. Implementing the mechanism involves not only trade in credits, but also trade through technology transfer.

Third, trade sanctions could enter as a participation mechanism, although how the role of sanctions would be rendered effective is difficult to assess. That role is likely to be more promising if the new architecture leans toward a system of treaties. Countries participate in an international treaty mostly to influence the participation of others and of nonsignatories rather than to tie their hands. Members of an international agreement can establish trade sanctions for nonparticipants who do not comply, as in the case of the MP. Although to be successful, this approach requires a high degree of participation, thereby obviating the need to use trade sanctions. This approach has the advantage that new principles could be drawn up for a climate change treaty rather than relying on the current complicated rules governing the use of border adjustment measures to address competitiveness effects (see the section on climate change and the WTO). For example, only a handful of high emitters of CO_2 would be covered under the new set of rules. Building such an agreement might be easiest with few participants but would come at a cost, because a substantial amount of trade might then take place among nonparticipants, making it costly (and, hence, not credible) for participants to apply the agreed-upon sanctions. It is necessary to be cautious, however, in transposing trade measures that worked under the MP to GHG agreements. The dimension of the problem is much larger in the latter case, and hence, any trade sanctions would have larger effects and might potentially be much more destructive.

Fourth is the issue of leakage and the pressure for border measures discussed in the section on climate change and the WTO. Non-CO_2 evidence suggests that leakage may not be as important as some might believe. Nonetheless, the pressure for countervailing action against countries (like the United States) that in effect subsidize their industries by not correcting the externality due to CO_2 emissions will be great. It has already surfaced under the mild cuts of KP1. It is hard to imagine that this pressure will not be strengthened in the successors to KP1, and trade wars are a real possibility as the parties involved are major players in international trade (China, the European Union, and the United States, for example). Dealing with the pressure for border adjustments will be an integral part of the current negotiations on climate change. As discussed in the section on climate change and the WTO, the WTO-legality of border measures is uncertain, and current rules appear inadequate to deal with the leakage issues raised by CO_2 emissions.

The Role of Trade in GHG Mitigation

Many sources of CO_2 emissions such as power (mainly electricity production) and buildings are nontradable activities, hence not directly subject to leakage. As for transport, which accounts for 13 percent of total emissions, much is national transport that does not involve trade. In sum, about 15 percent of emissions involve international trade. The issue then is how much trade really matters and what the potential is for leakage, a major source of concern in the climate negotiations.

Almost all the evidence on the environmental effects of trade has focused on local pollutants. The early evidence (for example, Grossman and Krueger 1993), identifies three effects through which trade liberalization may affect the environment:

- *A scale effect.* Increased economic activity from trade liberalization leads, ceteris paribus, to increased emissions.
- *A composition effect.* Trade liberalization may lead to changed specialization patterns across countries and sectors with different emission intensities, which can trigger changes in emissions.
- *A technique effect.* Through increased income and technology transfer, trade can lead to cleaner production technologies.

It is important, however, to know the origin of comparative advantage in polluting industries (is it energy subsidies, for example, or a lax environmental policy?) and whether those industries might migrate to "pollution havens" with less stringent environmental policies. In the case of the Kyoto Protocol, would caps among signatories lead to a migration of industries toward nonsignatories (or under KP1 to signatories that are not under a cap)? In an open-economy model incorporating trade and environmental policies, comparative advantage in polluting industries is shaped by two forces working in opposite directions:

- *A pollution haven effect.* Lax environmental regulation in low-income countries would give them a comparative advantage in emission-intensive industries.
- *A factor endowment effect.* Capital abundance in high-income countries would give them a comparative advantage in emission intensive sectors because they also happen to be capital intensive.

The first issue, then, is whether the possibility of trade results in more CO_2 emissions than if there were no trade. For example, is it the case that exporters of chemical products, an energy-intensive sector, emit more than countries that import chemical products? Next, is it likely that energy-intensive industries would migrate if the price of energy were to change differentially across countries as climate change policies are put in place? Finally, what level of emissions is embodied in international transport? We examine the evidence on all three issues below.

Emissions Embodied in Trade

If one takes into account indirect emissions through interindustry links, international trade and transport have made up roughly 23 percent of production-based emissions in recent years (see figure 23.2 and Davis and Caldeira 2010). Figure 23.2 also shows the emission content of imports and exports from which one can compute a country's balance of emissions embodied in trade, expressed as a percentage of production-based emissions. A positive (negative) balance means that the country is a net importer (exporter) of CO_2 emissions in its trade bundle. Developed countries are net importers (for example, –7 percent for the United States and –15 percent for Japan). Developing countries, in contrast, are net exporters of emissions, with China, Malaysia, South Africa, and Venezuela having positive balances above 15 percent. Other estimates indicate that China's net embodied emissions and energy content increased between 2001 and 2006 (Pan, Philips, and Cheng 2008). Although balances of emissions embodied in trade are not a measure of leakage (see later text), these patterns, especially those for China, suggest the possibility of carbon leakage.

Estimates of Carbon Leakage

Leakage[4] effects (known as the "pollution heaven" effect in the trade and environment literature) during reduction in GHG emissions come about through two channels. First, emission-intensive industries could simply relocate to countries where policies are less stringent (see, for example, Copeland and Taylor 2003). This effect can take place either through a reallocation of market shares or through increased investment in unconstrained industries. The second effect is indirect. By increasing the cost of emission-intensive goods through climate policy, the derived demand for carbon-intensive inputs (oil, for example) is reduced, potentially lowering the price of oil on world

Figure 23.2. Embodied CO_2 Emissions in Imports and Exports for Selected Countries, 2001

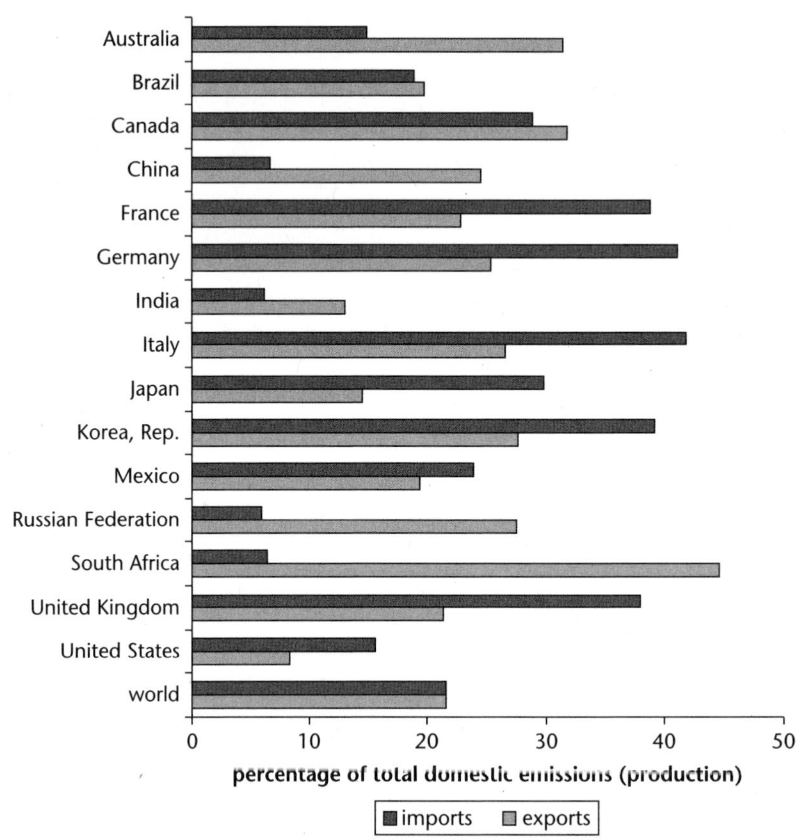

Source: Peters and Hertwich 2008.
Note: Originally based on data from the Global Trade Analysis Project (GTAP) version 6 database, GTAP v6 data for 87 countries in 2001 using domestic input-output data for bilateral trade flows.

markets. This indirect effect would also shift comparative advantage toward countries that are not implementing a climate policy. In both cases, the effectiveness of GHG mitigation would be reduced.

Instructive predictions about the likely effects of a rise in the price of carbon can be gleaned by looking at the case of SO_2. SO_2 is responsible for acid rain, a regional phenomenon. SO_2 and CO_2 (emission) intensities are in fact highly correlated across industries. Not surprisingly, the same six industries are the main emitters of both gases: petroleum products, pulp and paper, nonferrous metals, iron and steel, chemicals, and building material (cement). Therefore, it is worthwhile to review studies based on SO_2 and other energy-intensive industries to get a feeling for the potential leakage under likely policies mitigating climate change.

First, the more tradable among these sectors are largely weight-reducing industries. Smelting nonferrous metals (and the processing of paper from wood) usually takes place close to extraction sites to avoid transport costs. Grether and de Melo (2004) estimate a bilateral trade model for each of these dirty industries and an aggregate of "clean" industries and find a consistently higher absolute value of the distance coefficient for dirty industries (in the range –1.10 to –1.40 except for nonferrous metals estimated at –.95, while the average for clean industries is –0.82).[5] This finding, and the fact that extraction in natural resource–based industries cannot migrate, suggest that transport costs would deter relocation of much processing to countries with lower regulation standards.

Other work has also tried to detect pollution-haven effects in the case of SO_2, where national attempts at controlling acid rain could have led to leakage. Using concentration data, Antweiler, Copeland, and Taylor (2001), estimate that if an increase in trade openness generates a 1 percent increase in income and output, then pollution will fall by approximately 1 percent.[6] Drawing on an extensive database covering the same six sectors and a "clean" sector for 62 countries with emission coefficients for 1990 and 2000, Grether, Mathys, and de Melo (2009) decompose changes in SO_2 emissions. The scale effect accounted for a 10 percent increase in emissions, while the shift toward cleaner industries within (across) countries accounted for a decrease in emissions of 2 percent (3 percent) and the technique effect accounted for a decrease in emissions of 14 percent. As a result, while manufacturing growth was 8 percent over the decade, SO_2 emissions fell by 10 percent or 1 percent per year, about half the needed reduction in emissions for the OECD countries for a convergence in CO_2 emissions over a 50-year period.

On a sectoral level, only nonferrous metals had an increase in emissions per unit of output. Between-sector and between-country effects contributed to a reduction in emissions. Particularly noteworthy is the absence of leakage effects for the United States (the mandated reductions in SO_2 and the emission-trading system entered into effect in 1996). In sum, insofar as SO_2 is comparable to CO_2, SO_2 estimates suggest that leakage effects would be small. In addition, reduction in emissions came through the technique effect, pointing toward the (obvious) necessity of developing clean sources of energy in the struggle to mitigate CO_2 emissions.[7]

Most estimates, however, come from ex ante simulation models (multiregional general-equilibrium, or MR-GE, models). These models also provide estimates of the effects of border tax adjustments (BTA) to prevent carbon leakage (the legal aspects of the introduction of border measures are discussed later). MR-GE estimates suggest that a BTA will reduce leakage by half. The reason for the relative inefficiency of a BTA is that a tax on the CO_2 content of imports has a strong terms-of-trade effect in favor of the country that imposes the BTA, thereby leading it to increase its volume of imports.

These models also give estimates of the different BTAs that have been proposed in the political debate. One of the proposals circulated in the United States was to adjust the price of imports by applying the CO_2 tax in the United States to the total (direct and indirect) carbon content of imports, perhaps along with relief from paying the tax for exporters. Another proposal was to tax imports on the basis of their carbon content (U.S. legislation makes it possible to require importers to buy emission allowances equivalent to the carbon content of imports). Mattoo et al. (2009a, 2009b) estimate that if industrial countries reduce emissions by 17 percent without applying a BTA, manufacturing exports by developing countries remain unchanged but fall by about 2 percent under the first proposal and by 15 percent under the second proposal. Should developed countries try to impose across-the-board taxation on imports based on their carbon content, there would be a collision between developed and developing countries at the WTO.

While these model based estimates are transparent and are arguably the best game in town so far, they differ sharply from the few econometric and ex post studies. Drawing on data for 38 countries (26 of which have ratified Kyoto) and 12 sectors over the period 1995–2005, Aichele and Felbermayr (2010) estimate the impact of different GHG policies on trade flows and emissions. They estimate that carbon imports are on average 12 percent higher if the importer has ratified Kyoto but the exporter has not. Confirming previous work, the effect is most important in energy-intensive industries, where robust evidence for carbon leakage was found for seven sectors. Their findings suggest that, even though the volume of trade "caused" by Kyoto is rather small, on average about 40 percent of carbon savings due to the ratification of the Kyoto Protocol have been offset by increasing emissions in noncommitting countries.

We noted earlier that an open world economy is important in facilitating technological transfers. Di Maria and van den Werf (2008) and Acemoglu et al. (2009) argue that effective long-run carbon leakage might be smaller than the results from the previously mentioned studies, because induced technological change might have a positive effect. Using panel data in a gravity model, Costantini and Mazzanti (2010) analyze the effect of energy and environmental policy in the European Union (EU) on export dynamics of four sectors over 1996–2007. Including patent data, they find evidence that the overall effect of energy policy is not in conflict with export competitiveness. In general, these results support the Porter hypothesis (Porter and van der Linde 1995), which states that stricter environmental regulation can have a "halo" rather than a "pollution haven" effect by inducing efficiency and encouraging innovation.

The Environmental Consequences of Transport

Transport costs (national and international) account for approximately 13 percent of global CO_2 emissions (about two-thirds of the emissions related to manufacturing activity), with shipping-related emissions raising particularly strong concerns. How much, then, does international trade contribute to CO2 emissions?[8]

Two recent estimates provide orders of magnitude for a large number of countries. Hummels (2009) uses the Global Trade Analysis Project model to estimate that full trade liberalization would increase trade volumes by 5.8 percent. He then converts this growth into weight-distance profiles by modal usage (truck, air, and maritime) to which he applies GHG emission estimates. His results show a shift in trade away from close to distant partners and estimates that CO_2 emissions could increase by as much as 10 percent. Thus, insofar as trade liberalization is likely to involve growth at the extensive margin (new partners), it is not friendly to the environment. Hummels's estimates would thus suggest an elasticity of emission to trade growth of around 1.5.

Grether, Mathys, and de Melo (2010) carry out a similar exercise for worldwide SO_2 emissions over 1990–2000 during which manufacturing output grew by 8 percent. They first define an anti-monde in which countries produce what they actually consume in the trade equilibrium and find that international trade increases emissions by 10 percent in 1990 and by only 3.5 percent in 2000, largely a reflection of the all-around decline in emission intensity. Using a rough decomposition by mode of transport, they estimate that emissions related to international trade accounted for about 5–9 percent of total manufacturing emissions. Adding emissions related to trade and transport costs emissions, their estimates suggest that transport-related emissions rose from accounting for roughly one-third to accounting for three-fourths of total trade-related emissions over 1990–2000. To put it differently, if one adds emissions coming from trade-related composition effects to those coming from trade-related transport activities, the sum shows an increase in global manufacturing emissions through trade of 16 percent in 1990 and 13 percent in 2000.

Both sets of estimates are only rough orders of magnitude. Estimates of carbon footprints should factor in that favorable climatic conditions and the use of low energy-intensive production technologies in developing countries may lead to carbon efficiencies that outweigh additional emissions due to transport for products shipped to and consumed in developed countries.[9] Reducing trade-related GHG emissions would be best achieved by an agreement on transport that would impose low-emitting technologies (for example, hydrogen). Short of such an approach, raising transport costs by taxes on transport will reduce trade, which will in turn reduce GDP growth. If externalities were corrected where they occur (that is, in the GHG-emitting sectors rather than by raising taxes on trade), however, then world welfare would increase.

Climate Change and the WTO

Some fear that the gains from trade—which are huge—could easily be eroded by trade policies seeking to counteract spillover effects from mitigation measures. Many also agree that subsidies to energy and to substitutes for fossil fuels (biofuels, for example) should be removed. Here we focus on the interface of climate change and the WTO. First, are WTO rules and previous dispute settlement processes at the WTO adequate to deal with the pressures to apply border measures to counter leakage toward nonparticipants? Second, how much progress has taken place on liberalization of tariffs on environmental goods and services?[10]

Border Measures to Address Competitiveness and Leakage Concerns

By changing carbon prices across countries, climate policies will lead to demand for border adjustments to address competitiveness effects. Indeed, proposed U.S. legislation (the Warner-Lieberman and Waxman-Markey bills) included the possibility of border adjustments for energy-intensive industries that would lose competitiveness to countries without a similar policy. Such pressures have already appeared under KP1 against nonsignatories (for semifinished steel, clinker, aluminum, cement, and some basic chemicals).[11]

Ideally, a worldwide price on GHG emissions (through a tax or an emission-trading system) should be applied at the marginal social cost of the emissions. This approach would allow internalizing external costs, such as negative effects of emissions that are not taken into account by individuals, since property rights are badly defined when it comes to the world's climate.[12] However, as long as emitting activities (such as burning coal, oil, and gas) are not subject to a cost internalizing these negative effects in some countries (that is, the nonsignatories of KP1), energy-intensive industries are implicitly subsidized. Except in limited circumstances like agriculture, the WTO does not allow subsidies. Thus, nonsignatories of KP1 like the United States are in effect enjoying an unfair trade advantage that KP1 signatories could bring to the WTO. Given that a single worldwide price on GHG emissions is not politically achievable, many will call for border adjustments for the climate-induced change in competitiveness among WTO members.

Thus, much of the debate on the relation between trade and the environment revolves around a border adjustment to bring about a level playing field across countries in energy-intensive industries, following differential efforts at reducing emissions. Another motivation would be leverage, in the sense that the threat of border adjustment could be used to force countries to participate in climate negotiations. While the first motivation calls for trade controls, the second calls for trade sanctions. The focus here is on trade controls, applied to environmentally relevant sectors, as opposed to trade sanctions, where targeted products are unrelated to environmental discrepancies (Charnovitz 2003). In the case of KP1, no trade measures were included in the treaty, while in the MP, trade bans were included from the beginning as an instrument for achieving full participation in the treaty.[13]

From an economic point of view, if the externality in production were corrected through a tax on carbon, any tax imposed at the border would lead to inefficiencies. It would lead to trade diversion because countries without stringent climate policy would shift their exports to countries that do not apply any kind of adjustment at the border. For example, in the EU, where the tax on gasoline is about four times as high as in the United States, the externality is corrected. Then, a border tax on imports from, say, the United States would create an inefficiency.[14]

Hence, the thorniest issue for the functioning of the world trade system is how to resolve the conflicts from different carbon policies. Would trade intervention justified by differences in climate policy be allowed under WTO law?[15] So far, this territory is uncharted in spite of several environmental cases that have been settled by the dispute settlement process. The answer depends crucially on the specific design and implementation of the intervention. Generally, two types of trade measures could be imposed on imports to complement mitigation policies. Restrictions could be with respect to "locally emitted" GHGs or with respect to "foreign emitted" gases. In the first category, emissions take place when the imported goods are "consumed." Emission standards on cars, for instance, would fall in this group. Pauwelyn (2007) states that if such measures do not discriminate between imports and local products, they should generally be accepted under WTO law.

If, however, trade restrictions address GHGs of imports that are emitted in the exporting country (that is, embodied emissions in imported products), compliance with WTO law is more controversial.[16] An example would be imported aluminum produced with high CO_2-emitting Söderberg technology. Consider then the application of a BTA on imported aluminum.[17] Could it be defended under international trade law? Yes, if it were possible to convince the WTO panel that the imposed competitiveness provisions are only an extension of domestic climate policy applied on an equal footing to imports. We illustrate the difficulties in the case where one country (party B in figure 23.3) enacts a GHG tax and its trading partner (party A in figure 23.3) does not have an equivalent climate policy under the assumption that leakage has occurred, since losses of competitiveness by domestic firms will not be considered as a relevant argument. The idea is to apply at the border a charge equivalent to an internal tax, and conversely, one could rebate the same tax on domestic products that are exported (this was the practice under the application of the value added tax). Figure 23.3 shows the two main possibilities of how such a trade intervention could be justified under WTO law.

To be applied, a BTA must first be confirmed as covered by GATT articles II (tariff obligation, which requires members to fix tariff levels at bound rates) and III (national treatment, that is, not to apply internal taxes to protect domestic producers). Such BTA restrictions are not covered by GATT article II on tariffs but by GATT article III:2 on domestic taxes (imports can be subject to adjustable product taxes but not producer taxes). Article III.2 states that the instrument against which adjustment is requested must be an indirect product tax (value added tax or excise tax, for example) and

Figure 23.3. Justifying Border Measures under WTO Law in a Nutshell

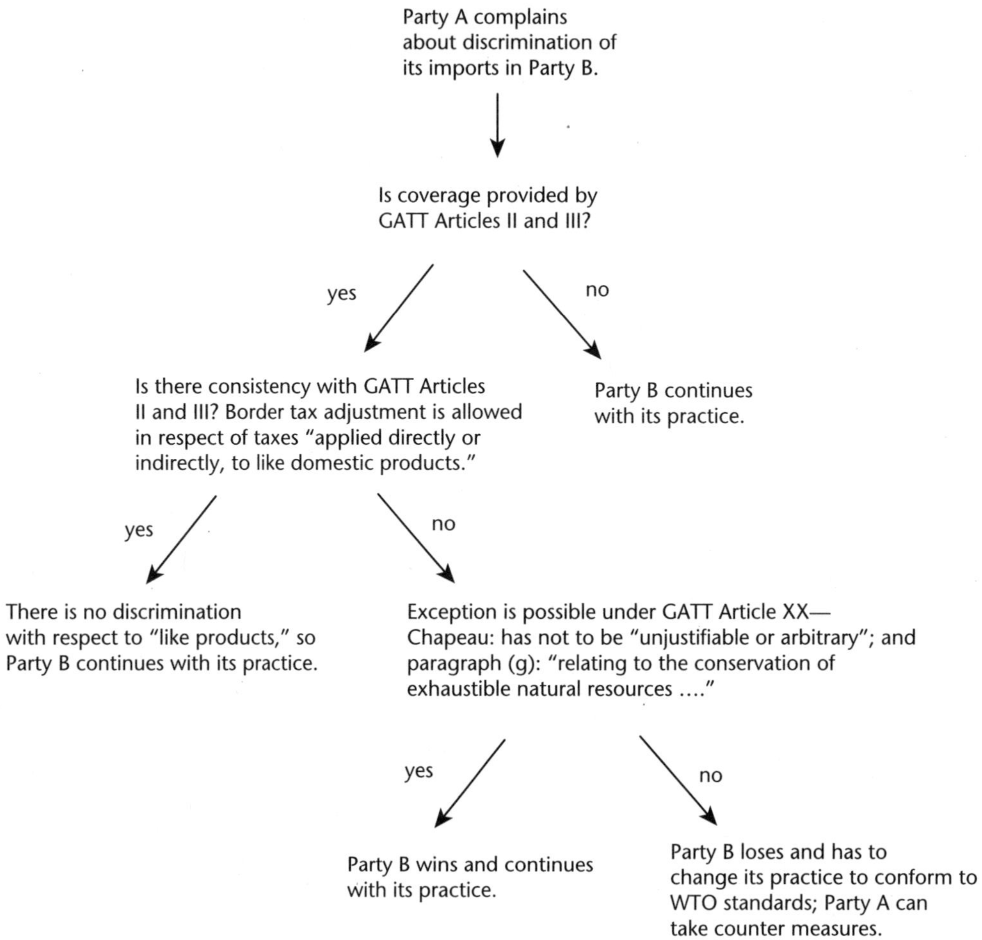

Source: Authors.

not a direct producer tax (payroll tax or income tax, for example) and that it must be nondiscriminatory (see later text). This distinction is based on the destination principle in which each product should be taxed only once, namely, in the country of consumption. As discussed in Demaret and Stewardson (1994), under GATT article III.2 border adjustment is allowed under taxes "applied directly or indirectly, to like domestic products." The crucial question then is whether this rule also applies to inputs that are physically not incorporated directly (such as GHG emissions released during production) in the final product. It has been argued that the GATT *Superfund* case[18] confirms that BTAs are possible for inputs that are not physically incorporated in the traded product. Under the presumption that the BTA can be justified under articles II and III, then the adjustment must meet the WTO principles of national treatment (article III) and most-favored-nation (article I).

If the previously mentioned justification for imposing trade restrictions were not allowed (left-arm in figure 23.3), violation of GATT articles II and III is still possible if environmental exceptions under article XX can be invoked. Paragraph (g) is the key article related to the environment,[19] and it asks for three cumulative conditions likely to be satisfied. First, it has to be shown that the planet's atmosphere is an exhaustible natural resource. Second, it has to be shown that the given climate change policy as a whole has a "substantial relationship" with the conservation of the atmosphere. And third, broadly similar conditions must be imposed on domestic producers. According to Pauwelyn (2007) and the latest scientific evidence, the first two conditions should be easily met, and a standard carbon tax should also meet the third.

However, to be WTO-law compatible, an adjustment at the border must also satisfy the conditions under the introductory (chapeau) phrase of article XX GATT. So far, whenever the Appellate Body has found that the article XX exception was not met, it has done so under the introductory phrase. Under this phrase, discrimination between different foreign countries (most-favored-nation type) and between foreign countries and the home country (national treatment type) are not allowed. Three specific elements are important. First, the legislation has to take into account local conditions in foreign countries. On the one hand, there are other ways to address climate change, and, on the other hand, developing countries may not be asked to carry the same burden of adjustment as industrial countries. Second, before imposing the unilateral trade restriction, the country must have previously engaged in serious across-the-board negotiations with the objective of concluding a bilateral or multilateral agreement. Finally, the implementation and administration of the imposed trade policy have to respect "basic fairness and due process." For example, concrete problems, like delayed imports related to border controls, should be avoided. Jurisprudence has highlighted the importance of flexibility in the design of the measure to take into account different situations in different countries.

In sum, the conditions related to the introductory phrase of article XX GATT are still highly controversial for leakage effects arising from cost differentials due to different energy and environment policies. Notwithstanding the recent environmental disputes that the WTO has adjudicated, it is easy to imagine that leakage concerns will be subject to extensive litigation.

In the case where an ETS is enacted instead of a carbon tax, concerns discussed earlier are also raised. In addition, it must be shown that the obligation to hold permits is equivalent to an internal tax since the ETS is also imposing a cost on firms if they have to be purchased. Moreover, if some permits are handed out for free, instead of being auctioned off, some kind of average market price would have to be used to determine the level of the effective cost and, hence, the tax. Ismer and Neuhoff (2007) investigate conformity and feasibility of a BTA for an ETS. They propose an adjustment level that does not exceed the upper bound of the amount payable for production in the country enacting the ETS using the best available technology.

Several other problems lurk on the horizon. To begin with, as others have pointed out (for example, Bhagwati and Mavroidis 2007), the implementation of such border adjustment with respect to embodied carbon would be very costly.[20] Indeed, Ismer and Neuhoff (2007) say that only an indirect scheme, using a measure highly correlated with effective embodied carbon emissions, would be implementable. They suggest using specific input mixes and multiplying these quantities by emission coefficients. A special case is electricity, where the mix varies considerably between countries and, therefore, contains very different levels of embodied emissions. Moreover, since exporting countries would be unlikely to truthfully cooperate in the computation of the carbon content of their products, Pauwelyn (2007) has suggested computing an implicit carbon content based on production techniques dominant in importing countries in this case. Ismer and Neuhoff (2007) propose a processed-material approach with the best available technology.

Still, implementing such a scheme would be a nightmare, even more so for developing countries, as ample experience with the less controversial tax rebate for tariffs on imported inputs in free trade zones has shown. Further, BTAs may open the door to capture by powerful domestic political interest groups and become the source of disguised protection. Finally, imposing carbon tariffs could be seen as leverage for inducing countries to participate in climate negotiations, but, more likely, it could undermine trust between trading partners and poison the hard-to-acquire trust in multilateral negotiations and endanger future agreements.

In sum, even if carefully constructed and implemented border measures could in theory pass WTO law, considerations of political economy suggest that it might not be a good instrument for leveling the playing field for energy-intensive industries. Pauwelyn (2007) puts forward several other instruments that might be used instead. As discussed earlier, a country that adopts an ETS can alleviate competition effects by adopting flexibility mechanisms (such as the Clean Development Mechanism under the Kyoto Protocol) that allow companies to trade emission permits and, hence, reduce abatement costs. Other possibilities are free distribution of all (or at least part of) emission permits or exclusion of industries that are most exposed to international competition from stringent emission-reduction programs. The problem with this measure is that it is in effect a subsidy that could be actionable under GATT law (that is, it does not follow the "polluter-pays" principle, and it might create windfall profits for highly polluting industries). Also, safety valves could be imposed, thereby assuring companies that permit prices would not exceed a maximum level.

Liberalization of Environmental Goods and Services

Under the 2001 Doha Ministerial Declaration, WTO members have been asked to negotiate on the reduction or, as appropriate, elimination of tariff and nontariff barriers on environmental goods and services.[21] The aim is to create a triple-win situation—for trade, the environment, and development. If negotiations are successful, trade will be facilitated through reduced or eliminated tariffs and nontariff barriers on environmental goods and services. Agreement on this measure would decrease the cost of environmental technologies, increase their use, and stimulate innovation and technology transfer.

Developing countries would benefit in two ways. First, producers of environmental goods and services would have better access to large markets in Europe, the United States, and high-income Asia, and, second, it would be easier for developing countries as a whole to obtain high-quality environmental goods on world markets. Such access should increase energy efficiency and improve the water and sanitation situation in developing countries. Increased trade in these products would lead to overall welfare gains and would help developing countries reduce emissions through technology transfer.

Even though liberalization in these particular product categories should be win-win, WTO members have been unable to agree on which goods should be liberalized. Three approaches have been proposed to identify these goods. In the *list approach,* WTO members would have to agree on a list of products (at the six-digit level of the Harmonized System, or HS) for which trade barriers should be reduced. So far, WTO members have been unable to agree on such a list. Developing countries argue that a number of products on the list are of export interest primarily to industrial countries. Also problematic is the issue of *dual use,* because many product categories proposed also include products that have nonenvironmental uses. It would be possible to select "ex-outs" (goods that are not separately identified at the 6-digit level of the HS and have to be identified in national tariff schedules at the 8- or 10-digit level), but this approach would be particularly costly and difficult for developing countries. In response to this issue, Argentina and India proposed a *define-by-doing* approach, in which national authorities would select projects. Environmental goods and services necessary for the selected projects would then temporarily benefit from enhanced market access. Categories of goods could be identified multilaterally in advance. Finally, Brazil suggested a *request-offer* approach. Under this approach, countries would request specific commitments on tariff cuts on products of interest and then extend those tariff cuts to all WTO members on the basis of the most-favored nation (MFN) clause. Such an approach might better take into account developing countries' specific interests.[22]

Including all HS-6 tariff lines that have so far been proposed in the lists officially submitted to the WTO,[23] environmental goods and services make up about 20 percent of total trade value. Developing countries account for about 40 percent of trade in environmental goods and services, with 40 percent of imports and 42 percent of exports. Concerning tariffs, however, there is a clear difference between countries of various income levels. Developed countries have MFN tariffs below 2 percent on average, whereas low-income developing countries and other developing countries have average MFN tariffs of 11 percent and 6 percent, respectively. Overall, the trade and protection pattern in the tariff lines submitted for negotiations over environmental goods and services seems to be very similar to the overall pattern.

The triple-win expectation from a liberalization of trade in environmental goods and services has been challenged. Consider a vertical industry in which the downstream good's production is polluting and the upstream industry that faces international competition is engaged in R&D to develop abatement technology that it can sell to the downstream firm. In this setting, Dijkstra and Mathew (2009) show that it might be best for developing countries to first liberalize trade in environmental goods with countries whose environmental technologies are not too much better than their own. This approach would stimulate R&D in the domestic eco-industry and put it in a better position to face competition from more advanced eco-firms later. They also show that when cleaner technologies become available, governments have an incentive to reduce the effective tax on polluting output to take the opportunity to increase welfare through the higher profits of the downstream firm and increased consumer surplus. Hence, they show that liberalization in environmental goods and services might lead to a situation in which consumer benefits come at the expense of the environment. Next, consider an environment in which the North innovates and its technologies diffuse to the South. In a stylized model, Di Maria and Smulders (2005) investigate the role of endogenous technology and technology spillovers. They conclude that endogeneous technological change is potentially but not necessarily a blessing. The lack of intellectual property rights in the South and innovation costs born asymmetrically by consumers in the North create distortions.

There is little evidence on the effects of liberalization of environmental goods and services. Using a partial equilibrium simulation model applying import elasticities to trade data for the 18 most important developing-country emitters of GHGs, the World Bank (2008) assessed the effect of trade liberalization (elimination of tariffs and nontariff barriers) for the following four technologies: clean coal technologies, wind energy, solar photovoltaic systems, and energy-efficient lighting. Eliminating trade barriers would increase import volumes by up to 13 percent. More generally, Dechezleprêtre, Glachant, and Ménière (2009) used patent data from 66 countries for the period 1990–2003 and investigated the forces that drive transfer of technologies mitigating climate change. Their regression results show that restrictions to international trade (treated as an exogenous variable) negatively influence the diffusion of patented knowledge. However, Managi and Kumar (2009) estimated exogeneous and trade-induced technological change for 76 countries over the period 1963–2000 and found that trade-induced technological change, which makes up roughly one-third of overall technological change, had a negative effect on GDP and increased pollution.

The lack of progress on negotiations on environmental goods and services could be attributed to traditional fears invoked by developing countries to protect sectors from international markets dominated by industrial countries. Infant industries would then deserve temporary protection. Also, if a first-mover advantage or lock-in effects exist, then developing countries may have incentives not to liberalize these markets too quickly. Finally, negotiations over environmental goods and services are only a secondary arena in the Doha negotiation round. Developing countries might well be using the possibility to block negotiations in environmental goods and services to better defend their interests in the agricultural negotiations, in which developing countries have greater interests at stake.

Final Reflections: Lessons from World Trade for Governing Climate Change

Reflecting on the outcome of the Earth Summit in Rio in 1992, as KP1 was under negotiation, Norwegian Prime Minister Brundtland said: "We knew the basic principles on which to build: cost effectiveness, equity, joint implementation and comprehensiveness. But not how to make them operational" (Schmalensee 1998). Fifteen years later, with KP1 nearing its end and negotiations for KP2 underway, what has been learned? Certainly, one would add that cost effectiveness has to go beyond flexibility mechanisms: it requires participation and compliance as shown by the success of the MP. Are there any lessons for the design of climate-related trade policies from the evolution of the world trading system, first under the GATT and then under the WTO?

An Umbrella Agreement with Leeway

In the early days of the GATT, participation was among a small group of countries where negotiation was easier than under the now unwieldy WTO where unanimity is required for all major decisions. The GATT thus made progress toward free trade with agreements that bound nations in ways that did not impinge on their national sovereignty. As proposed by Antholis (2009), taking their inspiration from the GATT, climate negotiators could set up a General Agreement to Reduce Emissions, avoiding moving too quickly into a full-blown organization like a world environment organization or a treaty under the UN process, which also requires unanimity.

It is noteworthy that under the GATT, sustained national tariff cuts took place without the appearance of the loss of sovereignty. Much tariff reduction occurred unilaterally. Adjudication and dispute settlement could evolve progressively as they did under the GATT and the WTO so that fears of loss of sovereignty would be alleviated (under the GATT, a panel decision against a member could be blocked by the member).

What should the principles for an umbrella climate code be? Commentators broadly agree:[24] carbon taxes should be encouraged, though not required; auctioning of permits should likewise be encouraged; trade-related GHG measures should be limited; like products should be defined at a broad enough level of aggregation (four-digit HS for Hufbauer, Charnovitz, and Kim 2009); and the modalities for border adjustments and the management of a Carbon Added Tax should be flexible. Countries that subscribe to this "green code" would benefit from a "peace clause" and, thus, avoid being subject to WTO disputes. It is likely, however, that this sensible approach would be difficult to establish, because all activities would want to qualify for "green space status" and the request for flexibility could easily lead to a made-to-measure rather than a transparent code.

This umbrella approach would give countries maximum leeway and create a more enabling environment for international negotiations, as countries would be more likely to commit. With well over two-thirds of CO_2 emissions coming from nontradable activities, and, hence, not subject to direct carbon leakage, countries with large energy subsidies would first enact energy legislation. For example, the United States could first pass an energy bill that would raise the price of carbon.[25]

Under the umbrella of a broad multilateral agreement, which would set the basic rules like MFN and national treatment under the GATT, much progress could still take place either in a small group, perhaps two or three countries, or even unilaterally, as it has so far in many instances. This route could be much easier than a treaty, at least for a country like the United States.[26] As mentioned earlier, unilateral reduction in tariffs was the way most progress was made in the early rounds of trade negotiations. Of course, unilateral action is certainly easier to envisage in the case of tariff reductions, where most gains are internalized, than under GHG emissions, where all gains are equally shared so that the need for collective action is much greater. Under this simpler architecture, in the initial steps forward, the UN process, which requires unanimity, would be bypassed. In the words of Antholis (2009), the new climate architecture would "gear up" domestic steps that nations are willing to take.

A Polycentric Approach

Drawing on the extensive experience with the provision of national and environmental public goods, Ostrom (2009) argues that, without denying the global nature of the problem, much progress on climate change can be achieved by actions at multiple scales (the household, the region, and the country). Ostrom argues that this approach is invaluable in building the trust necessary to achieve the collective action that is still so elusive for climate change. In fact, all progress is currently taking place at the local and national levels rather than at the multilateral level.[27] While this decentralized approach has the advantage of building confidence, the very different approaches across countries and states will require much effort later on at the national level to bring those measures into conformity with any future rules in the multilateral trading system. But the multilateral trading system has withstood several shocks successfully, including the rise of regionalism. Ideally, the confidence built by decentralized measures will pay off and will help build the needed commitment to achieve a binding General Agreement to Reduce Emissions.

Notes

1. Waters are further muddied by the disagreement in the scientific community and its impact on public opinion as well as differences about what needs to be done as reflected in the very different prognoses in Nordhaus (2008), Stern (2009), and McKibbin (2010). Frankel (2008), Hufbauer and Kim (2010), and others see a train wreck between climate change objectives and trade. One source of relative consensus is that damages will fall mostly on poor countries with little capacity to adapt. Recent estimates put up to 80 percent of the damage from climate change in low-latitude countries (Mendelsohn, Dinar, and Williams 2006).

2. Against acting rapidly is the concern that the marginal cost function for mitigation may be very steep, and for some because marginal damages rise as GHGs accumulate, the optimal policy is dynamic, growing stricter over time (see, for example, Nordhaus 2008).

3. All three approaches require measurement of carbon emitted. Trading schemes beyond hydrocarbon products will be severely limited by the costs and difficulty of measuring emissions—hence, the three levers for reducing emissions (Schmalensee 1998). Geo-engineering is also likely to be on the menu, but for most, it is considered a last-resort option with carbon capture and storage probably a more promising avenue (see Barrett 2008).

4. The carbon leakage rate = (increase in emissions due to climate policy *outside* enacting country/decrease in emissions due to climate policy *in* enacting country).

5. A distance coefficient estimate of –1.40 (–0.95) implies that if trade flows are normalized to 1 for a distance of 1,000 kilometers, a doubling of distance to 2,000 would reduce bilateral trade volume to 0.38 (0.52). On the basis of U.S, data, Ederington, Levison, and Minier (2005) also come to the same conclusion that these same polluting industries are not footloose.

6. Applied to CO_2 emissions, the Antweiler, Copeland, and Taylor (2001) framework suggests that trade is likely to increase emissions in the case of carbon dioxide (Cole and Elliott 2003). Managi and Kumar (2009) find that trade has a beneficial effect on emissions for OECD countries, but a detrimental effect for non-OECD countries.

7. Levinson (2009) also carries out retrospective calculations for the United States over 1972–2001 using U.S. emission data for 1997 and input-output data to capture the indirect SO_2-content for imports. Although his data do not allow him to capture the technical change in emissions or changes in emissions due to a within-sector shift toward producers with higher per unit emissions, he also finds a strong compositional effect away from the production of SO_2-intensive manufacturing activities coupled with a shift away from SO_2-intensive imports over this longer period of time.

8. International transport is only a fraction of transport. Cadarso et al. (2010) estimate that international trade accounts for 4 percent of transport embodied in Spanish consumption.

9. Brenton, Edwards-Jones, and Jensen (2009) survey results from carbon-accounting and carbon-labeling studies involving developing countries.

10. WTO and UNEP (2009) covers these issues in greater depth.

11. President Sarkozy of France proposed a BTA on U.S. exports to the EU because the United States did not participate in KP1, and it was a great cost in terms of concessions to industry (quasi-automatic access to free allowances) to obtain that BTAs would be left out of the EU proposal for KP2.

12. Allocative efficiency would be achieved when marginal abatement costs are equal to the marginal social costs of abatement. And if the same price applies everywhere, worldwide efficiency would be achieved. But it is very difficult to estimate with any confidence the social cost of carbon because it requires estimating the marginal damage from an extra unit of carbon, which depends on assumptions about the future path of the economy, the discount rate, science, and so forth.

13. See, for example, Frankel (2009). In fact, the variable of concern under the MP was consumption, defined as "production – exports + imports." Hence, trade flows were directly included.

14. As an example, since 2007 China has implemented export tariffs ranging from 5 to 25 percent on carbon-intensive products, including iron, steel, coke, and cement, so the United States would not seek to impose a BTA. See the comment by Hu Tao in Brainard and Sorkin (2009).

15. Relevant environmental WTO cases are *US-Gasoline*, *US-Shrimp*, and *Brazil-Retreaded Tyres*. In a first decision by the Appellate Body in the *Tuna-dolphin* case involving Mexico and the United States (under the GATT 1991), the United States lost the case when it argued that tuna could be imported only if it was not caught in purse-seine nets, jurisprudence that was overturned later in the shrimp-turtle decision, which in effect ruled that process and production methods could be invoked at the WTO for contingent protection. Technically, *Shrimp-turtle* did not explicitly approve that so-called nonproduct-related production and process methods, but it provided that they could in certain circumstances be justified under the GATT's article XX exception clauses.

16. Following Pauwelyn (2007), three measures in that category are most likely to violate international trade law. Import bans or punitive tariffs would violate article XI of the GATT, which imposes the elimination of quantitative restrictions, but also article I, which states that discrimination between imports from different countries must be avoided. The same holds for contingent measures that would also likely violate WTO law. Thus, antidumping duties against "environmental dumping" could be levied only if import prices are below the prices in the country of origin. This is not a measure adapted to address competitiveness concerns emanating from different climate policies. Countervailing duties to offset the de facto "subsidy" of imports in their country of origin are the third measure likely to violate WTO law. Several conditions are necessary to show that the government "fails to act"—that is, to impose a carbon policy

instrument—to be allowed to impose countervailing duties. Most important, not imposing a climate policy is not likely to be considered as either a specific subsidy (specific to a group of enterprises or industries) or an export subsidy.

17. Border measures could also take the form of mandatory allowance purchases by importers or embedded carbon product standards.

18. In the case of the GATT *Superfund* case, the dispute panel found that U.S. taxes on "chemicals used as materials in the manufacture or production of the imported substances" might be taken into account when imposing BTAs on imported like products.

19. The defendant party could also invoke paragraph (b) in article XX, which is more difficult to fulfill because it asks for a closer link between the policy and the environmental goal. It reads: "necessary to protect human, animal or plant life or health."

20. In Messerlin's (2010) words: one would need a gigantic database, generating astronomical transaction costs, and the risk of corruption would be huge.

21. Negotiations take place in the Special Session of the Committee on Trade and the Environment. The Doha negotiations also address the question of the relationship between the WTO and multilateral environmental agreements. For more on the link between the WTO and these environmental agreements, see WTO and UNEP (2009, 82–83).

22. One could also classify environmental goods and services along a different dimension. "Traditional" environmental goods are goods whose main purpose is to treat a specific environmental problem (for example, wastewater treatment equipment). A second, broader type of goods relates to the so-called environmentally preferable goods. For each of those, there exists a close substitute with a similar use but which is less environmentally friendly. An example of an environmentally preferable good is an energy-efficient washing machine. Another that is more doubtful is the use of biofuel to save on energy and reduce CO_2 emissions.

23. Four submissions have been made: a group of nine members (Canada; the EU; Japan; the Republic of Korea; New Zealand; Norway; Switzerland; Taiwan, China; and the United States), Saudi Arabia, Japan, and the Philippines.

24. Frankel (2008), Hufbauer et al. (2009), and Messerlin (2010) are the main recent commentators on a trade and climate code.

25. Following the demise of the Kerry-Lieberman bill, a new bipartisan bill (CLEAR [s.2877]) has been proposed by Senator Maria Cantwell (D-WA) and Senator Susan Collins (R-ME), in which no offsets would be allowed, all permits would be auctioned, and revenues from the tax would be distributed to U.S. residents. This unilateral approach would certainly put the United States in a better position to enter multilateral negotiations and may get support if American households believe that the political economy process will return to them a fair share of the revenues.

26. Such agreements would require a simple majority in the U.S. House rather the supermajority needed in the U.S. Senate for a treaty.

27. Wheeler and Shome (2010) estimate that India, which is seriously considering a goal of 15 percent renewable energy in its power mix by 2020, could effect the shift from coal-fired plants to renewables at a cost of US$50 billion. They note that India is contemplating this option despite the absence of any meaningful international pressure to cut emissions and no guarantees of compensatory financing and argue that the government has concluded that it should promote clean power anyway to develop an internationally competitive supplier industry, to bolster energy independence, and to help limit climate change because it poses dire threats to India itself.

Bibliography

Acemoglu D., P. Aghion, L. Bursztyn, and D. Hemous. 2009. "The Environment and Directed Technological Change." Working Paper 15451, National Bureau of Economic Research, Cambridge, MA.

Aichele, R., and G. Felbermayr. 2010. "Kyoto and the Carbon Content of Trade." Discussion Paper 10-2010, Center for Research on Innovation and Services, University of Hohenheim.

Antholis, W. 2009. "Five Gs: Lessons from World Trade for Governing Global Climate." Mimeo, Brookings Institution, Washington, DC. http://www.brookings.edu/articles/2009/0403_trade_climate_antholis.aspx.

Antweiler, W., B. Copeland, and S. Taylor. 2001. "Is Free Trade Good for the Environment?" *American Economic Review* 91 (4): 877–908.

Barrett, S. 2008. "A Portfolio System of Climate Treaties." Discussion Paper 08-13, Harvard Project on International Climate Agreements, Harvard Kennedy School, Cambridge, MA.

———. 2010. "Climate Change and International Trade: Lessons on Their Linkage from International Environment Agreements." Paper presented at TAIT (Thinking Ahead on International Trade) conference sponsored by the Graduate Institute Centre for Trade and Economic Integration, the World Bank, and the World Trade Organization, Geneva, June 16–18.

Bhagwati, J., and P. C. Mavroidis. 2007. "Is Action against U.S. Exports for Failure to Sign Kyoto Protocol WTO-legal?" *World Trade Review* 6 (2): 299–310.

Brainard, L., and I. Sorkin, eds. 2009. "Climate Change, Trade and Competitiveness: Is a Collision Inevitable?" *Brookings Trade Forum 2008/2009.* Washington, DC: Brookings Press.

Brenton P., G. Edwards-Jones, and M. F. Jensen. 2009. "Carbon Labelling and Low-income Country Exports: A Review of the Development Issues." *Development Policy Review* 27 (3): 243–67.

Cadarso, M.-A., L.-A. López, N. Gómez, and M.-A. Tobarra. 2010. "CO_2 Emissions of International Freight Transport and Offshoring: Measurement and Allocation." *Ecological Economics* 69 (8): 1682–94.

Charnovitz, S. 2003. "Trade and Climate: Potential Conflicts and Synergies." In *Beyond Kyoto: Advancing the International Effort against Climate Change,* 141–70. Arlington, VA: Pew Center on Global Climate Change.

Cole, M., and R. J. R. Elliott. 2003. "Determining the Trade–Environment Composition Effect: The Role of Capital, Labor and Environmental Regulations." *Journal of Environmental Economics and Management* 46 (3): 363–83.

Copeland, B., and S. Taylor. 2003. *Trade and the Environment: Theory and Evidence.* Princeton, N.J.: Princeton University Press.

Costantini, V., and M. Mazzanti. 2010. "On the Green Side of Trade Competitiveness?" Sustainable Development Papers, University of Minnesota, St. Paul.

Davis, S. J., and K. Caldeira. 2010. "Consumption-Based Accounting for CO_2 Emissions." *Proceedings of the National Academy of Sciences* (early edition). http://www.pnas.org/content/early/2010/02/23/0906974107.full.pdf+html.

Dechezleprêtre, A., M. Glachant, and Y. Ménière. 2009. "What Drives the International Transfer of Climate Change Mitigation Technologies? Empirical Evidence from Patent Data." Working Paper 14, Grantham Research Institute on Climate Change and the Environment, London.

Demaret, P., and R. Stewardson. 1994. "Border Tax Adjustments under GATT and EC Law: General Implications for Environmental Taxes." *Journal of World Trade* 28 (4): 5–66.

de Melo, J., and N. A. Mathys. 2010. "Trade and Climate Change: The Challenges Ahead." Discussion Paper 8032. Centre for Economic Policy Research, London.

Di Maria, C., and S. A. Smulders. 2005. "Trade Pessimists vs. Technology Optimists: Induced Technological Change and the Pollution Havens." *Advances in Economic Analysis and Policy* 4 (2): article 7.

Di Maria, C., and E. van den Werf. 2008. "Carbon Leakage Revisited: Unilateral Climate Policy with Directed Technical Change." *Environmental and Resource Economics* 39 (2): 9–15.

Dijkstra, B. R., and A. J. Mathew. 2009. "Liberalizing Trade in Environmental Goods." Working Paper, University of Nottingham, Nottingham, United Kingdom.

Ederington, J., A. Levison, and J. Minier. 2005. "Footloose and Pollution Free." *Review of Economics and Statistics* 87 (1): 92–99.

Frankel, J. 2008. "Global Environmental Policy and Global Trade Policy." Discussion Paper 08-14, Harvard Project on International Climate Agreements, Harvard Kennedy School, Cambridge, MA.

———. 2009. "Addressing the Leakage/Competitiveness Issue in Climate Change Policy Proposals." Trade Forum Working Paper, Brookings Institution, Washington, DC.

Grether J.-M., N. A. Mathys, and J. de Melo. 2009. "Scale, Technique and Composition Effects in Manufacturing SO_2 Emissions." *Environmental and Resource Economics* 43 (2): 257–74.

———. 2010. "Is Trade Bad for the Environment? Decomposing Worldwide SO_2 Emissions." *Review of World Economics* 145 (4): 713–29.

Grether, J.-M., and J. de Melo. 2004. "Globalization and Dirty Industries: Do Pollution Havens Matter?" In *Challenges to Globalization: Analyzing the Economics,* ed. R. E. Baldwin and A. Winters, 167–208. Chicago: University of Chicago Press.

Grossman, G. M., and A. B. Krueger. 1993. "Environmental Impacts of a North American Free Trade Agreement." In *The Mexico-US Free Trade Agreement*, ed. Peter M. Garber, 13–56. Cambridge, MA: MIT Press.

Hufbauer, G., S. Charnovitz, and J. Kim. 2009. *Global Warming and the World Trading System*. Washington, DC: Peterson Institute for International Economics.

Hufbauer, G., and J. Kim. 2010. "Climate Change and Trade: Searching for Ways to Avoid a Train Wreck." Paper presented at TAIT (Thinking Ahead on International Trade) conference sponsored by the Graduate Institute Centre for Trade and Economic Integration, the World Bank, and the World Trade Organization, Geneva, June 16–18.

Hummels, D. 2009. "How Further Trade Liberalization Would Change Greenhouse-Gas Emissions from International Freight Transport." Mimeo, Purdue University, West Lafayette, IN.

Ismer, R., and K. Neuhoff. 2007. "Border Tax Adjustment: A Feasible Way to Support Stringent Emission Trading." *European Journal of Law and Economics* 24 (2): 137–64.

Levinson, A. 2009. "Comment." In *Brookings Trade Forum 2008/2009,* ed. Brainard and Sorkin, 28–32. Washington, DC. Brookings Press.

Managi, S., and S. Kumar. 2009. "Trade-induced Technological Change: Analyzing Economic and Environmental Outcomes." *Economic Modelling* 26 (3): 721–32.

Mattoo, A., A. Subramanian, D. van der Mensbrugghe, and Jianwu He. 2009a. "Can Climate Change Mitigation De-Industrialize Developing Countries?" Mimeo, World Bank, Washington, DC.

———. 2009b. "Reconciling Climate Change and Trade Policy." Policy Research Working Paper 5123, World Bank, Washington, DC.

McKibben, Bill. 2010. *Earth: Making a Life on a Tough New Planet.* New York: Times Books.

Mendelsohn, R., A. Dinar, and L. Williams. 2006. "The Distributional Impact of Climate Change on Rich and Poor Countries." *Environment and Development* 11: 1–20.

Messerlin, P. 2010. "Climate Change and Trade: From Mutual Destruction to Mutual Support." Policy Research Working Paper 5378, World Bank, Washington, DC.

Nordhaus, W. 2008. *A Question of Balance.* New Haven, CT: Yale University Press.

Ordás Criado, C., and J.-M. Grether. Forthcoming. "Convergence in per Capita CO_2 Emissions: A Robust Distributional Approach." Resource and Energy Economics.

Ostrom, E. 2009. "A Polycentric Approach for Coping with Climate Change." Policy Research Working Paper 5095, World Bank, Washington, DC.

Pan, J., J. Philips, and Y. Cheng. 2008. "China's Balance of Emissions Embodied in Trade: Approaches to Measurement and Allocating International Responsibility." *Oxford Review of Economic Policy* 24 (2): 354–76.

Pauwelyn, J. 2007. "U.S. Federal Climate Policy and Competitiveness Concerns: The Limits and Options of International Trade Law." Working Paper 07-02, Duke University, Durham, NC.

Peters, G. P., and E. G. Hertwich. 2008. "CO_2 Embodied in International Trade with Implications for Global Climate Policy." *Environmental Science and Technology* 42 (5): 1401–07.

Porter, M. E., and C. vander Linde. 1995. "Toward a New Conception of the Environment-Competitiveness Relationship." *Journal of Economic Perspectives* 9 (4): 97–118.

Reinaud, J. 2008. "Ex Post Evaluation of the EU ETS: Impacts on the Aluminium Sector." Presentation at a Conference sponsored by Massachusetts Institute of Technology Center for Energy and Environmental Policy Research, Washington, DC, January 28.

Schelling, T. 2007. "Climate Change: The Uncertainties, the Certainties and What They Imply about Action." *Economist's Voice* 4 (3), article 3.

Schmalensee, R. 1998. "Greenhouse Policy Architectures and Institutions." In *Economics and Policy Issues in Climate Change*, ed. W. D. Nordhaus, 137–58. Washington, DC: Resources for the Future.

Spence, M. 2009. "Climate Change, Mitigation, and Developing Country Growth." Working Paper 64, Commission on Growth and Development, Washington, DC.

Stern, N. 2006. *Stern Review on the Economics of Climate Change.* London: Her Majesty's Treasury.

———. 2009. *The Global Deal: Climate Change and the Creation of a New Area of Progress and Prosperity.* New York: Public Affairs.

Wheeler, D., and S. Shome. 2010. "Less Smoke, More Mirrors: Where India Really Stands on Solar Power and Other Renewables." Working Paper 204, Center for Global Development, Washington, DC.

World Bank. 2008. *International Trade and Climate Change: Economic, Legal, and Institutional Experiences*. Washington, DC: World Bank.

WTO (World Trade Organization) and UNEP (United Nations Environment Programme). 2009. *Trade and Climate Change: A Report by UNEP and the WTO.* Geneva: World Trade Organization.

INDEX

Figures, notes, and tables are indicated with *f*, *n*, and *t* following the page number.

ECO-AUDIT
Environmental Benefits Statement

The World Bank is committed to preserving endangered forests and natural resources. The Office of the Publisher has chosen to print ***Managing Openness: Trade and Outward-Oriented Growth after the Crisis*** on recycled paper with 50 percent postconsumer fiber in accordance with the recommended standards for paper usage set by the Green Press Initiative, a nonprofit program supporting publishers in using fiber that is not sourced from endangered forests. For more information, visit www.greenpressinitiative.org.

Saved:
- 16 trees
- 5 million Btu of total energy
- 1,537 lb. of net greenhouse gases
- 7,404 gal. of waste water
- 450 lb. of solid waste

green press INITIATIVE